CONTENTS

INTRODUCTION

ILLUSTRATIONS

Plates

Tables

Full credit details are provided in the captions to the images in the text. The society and publisher are grateful to all the institutions and individuals for permission to reproduce the materials in which they hold copyright. Every effort has been made to trace the copyright holders; apologies are offered for any omission, and the publisher will be pleased to add any necessary acknowledgement in subsequent editions.

ACKNOWLEDGEMENTS

Above all I would like to thank Professor Huw Pryce, my principal PhD supervisor, whose idea it was to compile an edition of Bangor episcopal *acta*, and my medieval Latin tutor, Professor G. Rex Smith for giving me the ability to do so. This volume is largely the result of the research carried out for my PhD thesis, and I would like to thank all those at Bangor University who have provided me with advice and support especially Professor Peter Shapely, Dr Marc Collinson, Dr Shaun Evans, Dr Edwin Hustwit, Dr Nia Wyn Jones, Dr Euryn Roberts, and Dr David Stephenson. Thank you too to Professor Paul Russell, Professor Rosalind Love, Dr David Callander, Dr Ben Guy, Dr Alice Taylor-Griffiths, and Dr Rebecca Thomas in the Department of Anglo-Saxon, Norse & Celtic at Cambridge University. They are not the only ones to have given me invaluable counsel and guidance during my research and the preparation of this volume, and thanks go to Professor Philippa Hoskin, Professor Teresa Webber, and Dr Martin Brett also at Cambridge, Dr Paul Dryburgh at The National Archives, Professor Janet Burton at the University of Wales Trinity Saint David, Dr Elizabeth New and Dr Rhun Emlyn at Aberystwyth University, Professor Helen Nicholson at Cardiff University, Professor Julia Barrow, Professor David Crouch, Professor Marie Therese Flanagan, Professor Nicholas Vincent, Dr John Reuben Davies, Dr Felicity Hill, Dr Charles Insley, Dr Bryn Jones, Dr Nicholas Karn, Dr Alastair Lack, and Dr Steve Tibble as well as Canon Chancellor Edward Probert at Salisbury Cathedral. I am grateful to John Spearing for discussing all manner of matters with me, and to Dr Ian Bass for bringing two *acta* to my attention. Scott Lloyd at the Royal Commission on the Ancient and Historical Monuments of Wales brought his considerable knowledge of the commotes and cantrefs of medieval Wales to bear in the preparation of the map of the medieval diocese. Professor Janet Burton, Dr Nicholas Karn, and Dr Nigel Tringham kindly read drafts of this volume and provided incisive comments and suggestions.

I am grateful to Professor Barbara Bombi and Charles Fonge at The Canterbury and York Society, and Christy Beale, Laura Bennetts, Sarah Broadley and Daniela Elstone at Boydell and Brewer. Thank you also to all the archivists who have helped me, with particular thanks to Elen Wyn Simpson at Bangor University Archives and Special Collections, Cressida Williams at Canterbury Cathedral, Dr Rosemary Firman at Hereford Cathedral, and Emily Naish at Salisbury Cathedral.

Prior to this edition the most detailed work on the subject matter of this volume was carried out by James Conway Davies but, in large part, it was never published. Two volumes of his, commissioned by the Historical Society of the Church in Wales, providing English summaries of the *acta* of the bishops of Llandaff and St Davids, together with other documents relevant to those bishops, and their recorded *res gestae*, for the period 1066–1272, were published in 1946 and 1948 respectively.[1] Those volumes also contain an extensive introduction in which the author discussed the history of all four medieval Welsh bishoprics, and include detailed analysis of certain events that Davies believed warranted more consideration, such as the controversies concerning elections to the see of Bangor.[2] Had it been published, the third volume would have contained a calendar in English of the episcopal *acta* (and other documents, and recorded *res gestae*) for the bishoprics of Bangor and St Asaph, in the same format as that in volumes I and II, and for the same period.[3] I have been very fortunate in having access to a digital version of J. C. Davies' unpublished manuscript for volume III, which has proved invaluable for locating original *acta*, cartulary copies and much else besides for the bishops of Bangor up to 1272.

Canon Tracy Jones and the chapter of St Deiniol's Cathedral, Bangor, kindly gave me permission to use the magnificent image from the early fourteenth-century Bangor Pontifical that appears on the cover.

Dr Shaun McGuinness

---

[1]   *Episc. Acts Welsh Dioceses.*
[2]   *ibid.*, ii, pp. 415–37.
[3]   *Episc. Acts Welsh Dioceses Unpublished.*

MANUSCRIPT SOURCES CITED

Relevant Actum number shown in bold

ABERYSTWYTH

National Library of Wales

MS 7851D (Cartularium S. Petri De Salopesberia): **18**.
Peniarth MS 231B (*Llyfr Coch Asaph*): **51**, **52**, **55**.
Wynnstay Estate Records, Ystrad Marchell Charter GT16: **15**.

BANGOR

Prifysgol Bangor University Archives and Special Collections

Bangor Pontifical: **66**, **67**, **87**.

CAMBRIDGE

Cambridge University Library

MS EDR G3/28 (Ely 'Liber M', general cartulary of the cathedral priory): **1**.
Corpus Christi College, MS 16 (Matthew Paris, *Chronica Majora*, Part II): **38**, **42**.

CANTERBURY

Canterbury Cathedral Archives, Dean and Chapter

CCA-DCc/ChAnt/C/115: **3**, **7**, **13**, **16**, **24**, **36**, **56**.
CCA-DCc/ChAnt/C/167: **60**.

HEREFORD

Hereford Cathedral Library and Archives

1514: **30**.

LONDON

British Library

Additional Charter No. 22381: **19**.
Additional MS 4533: **34**.
Additional MS 30311 (Cartulary of Shrewsbury Abbey – Halston Library): **17**.
Cotton MS Cleopatra E i (fos. 17r–38r consist of a collection of copies of episcopal professions): **2**, **3**.
Cotton MS Domitian A iii (Leominster Priory Cartulary): **26**.
Cotton MS Nero D I (*Liber Additamentorum*): **47**, **48**.
Harley MSS 696 (Record of Caernarvon): **93**, **94**, **95**, **96**, **97**, **98**, **99**, **100**, **101**; 1708 (Chartulary of Reading Abbey): **6**, **27**, **28**; 1965 (Cartulary or Register of St Werburgh's Abbey, Chester): **12**; 4835 (Cartulary of Clare): **66**, **67**.

Royal MS 14 C VII (Matthew Paris, *Chronica Majora*, Part III): **47**, **48**.

Lambeth Palace Library

V/A/1Pecham (Register of John Pecham): **68**.

The London Archives

St Paul's Cathedral MS 25124/1: **40**; MS 25124/13: **41**.

The National Archives

Ancient Deeds, E 326/11297: **34**; E 326/12582: **35.**
C 53 (Charter Rolls), C 53/119 (6 Edward III): **44**.
C 54 (Close Rolls), C 54/45 (18 Henry III): **32**, C 54/63 (34 Henry III): **46**, C 54/82
    (49 Henry III): **54**, C 54/97 (8 Edward I): **69**.
C 66 (Patent Rolls), C66/74 (44 Henry III, Part 1): **49**, **50**.
C 77 (Welsh Rolls), C 77/5 (12 Edward I): **81**.
C 270/29/5: **82**.
E 36/274 (Miscellaneous Documents, Affairs of Wales, Henry III – Edward I,
    'Liber A'): **43**, **53**, **73**, **74**, **75**, **76**, **77**, **78**, **79**, **80**.
SC 1/15/6: **62**.
SC 1/22/101: **64**; 102: **65**; 103: **70**.
SC 8/276/13767: **89**.

OXFORD

Bodleian Library

MS Laud miscellaneous 647 (Liber Eliensis with substantial additions): **1**.
MS Tanner 342: **6**.

Exeter College

MS 158: **92**.

SALISBURY

Salisbury Cathedral Archives

Indulgences, BS/5/37: **88**.

SHREWSBURY

Shropshire Archives

MS 6001/6869 (Haughmond Cartulary): **4**, **5**, **8**, **9**, **10**, **11**, **14**, **25**, **45**, **58**.

VATICAN CITY

Archivio Segreto Vaticano
MS Vat. Lat. 4015: **92**, **102**.
Reg. Vat. 13: **31**, **33**.

WELLS

Wells Cathedral Archives

Dean and Chapter Muniments, Liber Albus I (Wells Cathedral Register): **20, 21, 22, 23**.

DETACHED SEAL

LONDON

Society of Antiquaries of London

SA. C 7 (Richard or Anian. Black gutta-percha. Privy seal).

PLASTER-CAST SEALS

LONDON

British Library

Seal LXXXII, 39 (Robert. White plaster cast. Main seal).
Seal LXXXII, 40 (Richard or Anian. White plaster cast. Privy seal).
Seal LXXXII, 41 (Cadwgan. White plaster cast. Privy seal).
Society of Antiquaries of London
SA. C 7 (Robert. White plaster cast. Main seal).

SEAL ATTACHED TO PAPAL DECREE

VATICAN CITY

Vatican Archive A. A. Arm. I–XVIII, 2190, no. 18 (Anian. Green wax. Main seal. 1274).

The Canterbury and York Socie

GENERAL EDITOR: BARBARA BOMBI

ISSN 0262-995X

CANTERBURY AND YORK SOC

Bangor Episcopal Acta,

1092–1306

EDITED BY

SHAUN McGUINNESS

The Canterbury and York Society

The Boydell Press
2025

First published 2025

A Canterbury and York Society publication
published by The Boydell Press
an imprint of Boydell & Brewer Ltd
PO Box 9, Woodbridge, Suffolk IP12 3DF, UK
and of Boydell & Brewer Inc.
668 Mt Hope Avenue, Rochester, NY 14620–2731, USA
website: www.boydellandbrewer.com

ISBN 978-0-907239-88-8

A CIP catalogue record for this book is available
from the British Library

Details of previous volumes are available from Boydell & Brewer Ltd

The publisher has no responsibility for the continued existence or accuracy of URLs for
external or third-party internet websites referred to in this book, and does not guarantee
that any content on such websites is, or will remain, accurate or appropriate

Printed and bound in Great Britain by
TJ Books, Padstow, Cornwall

For my mother and father

BIBLIOGRAPHY

(INCLUDING BIBLIOGRAPHICAL ABBREVIATIONS)

Abbreviations and short titles are used in the footnotes

PRINTED PRIMARY SOURCES

Unpublished

Annales Cambriae A-text – *Annales Cambriae, The A text from British Library, Harley MS 3859, ff. 190r–193r.*, ed. Henry W. Gough-Cooper (November 2015). Online: Welsh Chronicles Research Group, http://croniclau.bangor.ac.uk/editions.php.en, accessed 21 January 2024.

Annales Cambriae B-text – *Annales Cambriae, The B text from PRO MS. E164/1*, ed. H. W. Gough-Cooper (July 2014). Online: Welsh Chronicles Research Group, http://croniclau.bangor.ac.uk/editions.php.en, accessed 21 January 2024.

Annales Cambriae C-text – *Annales Cambriae C-text, with the intercalated annalistic notices. From British Library MS Cotton Domitian A.1, folios 138r–155r.*, ed. H. W. Gough-Cooper (February 2012). Online: Welsh Chronicles Research Group, http://croniclau.bangor.ac.uk/editions.php.en, accessed 21 January 2024.

Annales Cambriae D-text – *Annales Cambriae, The D text, from Exeter Cathedral Library MS 3514, pp. 523–8*, ed. H. W. Gough-Cooper (September 2015). Online: Welsh Chronicles Research Group, http://croniclau.bangor.ac.uk/editions.php.en, accessed 21 January 2024.

Annales Cambriae E-text – *Annales Cambriae, The E text, from Exeter Cathedral Library MS 3514, pp. 507–19*, ed. H. W. Gough-Cooper (February 2016). Online: Welsh Chronicles Research Group, http://croniclau.bangor.ac.uk/editions.php.en, accessed 21 January 2024.

Episc. Acts Welsh Dioceses Unpublished – *Episcopal Acts and Cognate Documents relating to Welsh Dioceses 1066–1272*. Volume III, ed. J. C. Davies.

Published

AC – *Annales Cambriae*, ed. J. Williams Ab Ithel (London, 1860).

Accounts of the Constables of Bristol Castle – *Accounts of the Constables of Bristol Castle in the Thirteenth and Early Fourteenth Centuries*, ed. M. Sharp, Bristol Record Society, 34 (Trowbridge, 1982).

Acta of Hugh of Wells, Bishop of Lincoln – *The Acta of Hugh of Wells, Bishop of Lincoln, 1209–1235*, ed. D. M. Smith, The Lincoln Record Society (London, 2000).

Acta Stephani Langton – *Acta Stephani Langton, Cantuariensis Archiepiscopi, A.D. 1207–1228*, ed. K. Major, The Canterbury and York Society, I (Oxford, 1950).

Annales Cestrienses – *Annales Cestrienses or Chronicle of the Abbey of S. Werburg at Chester*, ed. and trans. R. C. Christie, The Record Society for the Publication of Original Documents relating to Lancashire and Cheshire (London, 1887).

Annales de Theokesberia – 'Annales de Theokesberia', in *Annales Monastici*, 5 vols, ed. H. R. Luard, Rolls Series (London, 1864–9), vol. i, pp. 43–182.

Annales de Waverleia – 'Annales de Waverleia', in *Annales Monastici*, 5 vols, ed. H. R. Luard, Rolls Series (London, 1864–9), vol. ii, pp. 129–412.

Annales de Wigornia – 'Annales Prioratus de Wigornia', in *Annales Monastici*, 5 vols, ed. H. R. Luard, Rolls Series (London, 1864–9), vol. iv, pp. 353–564.

Annales Hirsaugensis – 'Annales Hirsaugensis', ed. J. Trithemius, 2 vols (n.p., 1690).

Annals of Roger de Hoveden – *The Annals of Roger de Hoveden, comprising the History of England, and other countries of Europe, from A.D. 732 to A.D. 1201*, ed. and trans. H. T. Riley, 2 vols (London, 1853).

Annals of Southwark and Merton – 'Annals of Southwark and Merton', ed. M. Tyson, *Surrey Archaeological Collections*, 36 (1925), 24–57.

Autobiography – *The Autobiography of Giraldus Cambrensis*, ed. and trans. H. E. Butler (London, 1937).

AWR – *The Acts of Welsh Rulers, 1120–1283*, ed. H. Pryce (repr. with corrections, Cardiff, 2010).

Bartrum, *Early Welsh Genealogical Tracts* – *Early Welsh Genealogical Tracts*, ed. P. C. Bartrum (Cardiff, 1966).

Becket Correspondence – *The Correspondence of Thomas Becket, Archbishop of Canterbury, 1162–1170*, ed. and trans. A. J. Duggan, 2 vols (Oxford, 2001).

Book of Fees – *Liber Feodorum. The Book of Fees, commonly called Testa de Nevill*, ed. H. C. M. Lyte, 2 vols (London, 1920–3).

Book of Llan Dâv – *The Text of the Book of Llan Dâv reproduced from the Gwysaney Manuscript*, ed. J. G. Evans and J. Rhys (Oxford, 1893; repr. Aberystwyth, 1979).

Brenhinedd y Saesson – *Brenhinedd y Saesson, or, The Kings of the Saxons. BM Cotton MS. Cleopatra B v and The Black Book of Basingwerk NLW MS. 7006*, ed. and trans. T. Jones (Cardiff, 1971).

Brut, Hergest – *Brut y Tywysogyon, or, The Chronicle of the Princes, Red Book of Hergest version*, ed. and trans. T. Jones (Cardiff, 1955).

Brut, Pen20 – *Brut y Tywysogion, Peniarth MS. 20*, ed. T. Jones (Cardiff, 1941).

Brut, Pen20Tr – *Brut y Tywysogyon, or, The Chronicle of the Princes, Peniarth MS. 20 version*, ed. and trans. T. Jones (Cardiff, 1952).

CAC – *Calendar of Ancient Correspondence Concerning Wales*, ed. J. G. Edwards, BCSHLS (Cardiff, 1935).

Cal. Pap. Reg. – *Calendar of Entries in the Papal Registers relating to Great Britain and Ireland. Papal letters, A.D. 1198–1304*, vol. I, ed. and trans. W. H. Bliss (London, 1893).

Calendar of Documents Preserved in France – *Calendar of Documents Preserved in France Illustrative of the History of Great Britain and Ireland, A.D. 918–1206*, vol. I, ed. J. H. Round (London, 1899).

Calendar of Documents Relating to Ireland – *Calendar of Documents Relating to Ireland, Preserved in Her Majesty's Public Record Office, London, 1171–1251*, ed. H. S. Sweetman (London, 1875).

Calendar of the Manuscripts of the Dean and Chapter of Wells – *Calendar of the Manuscripts of the Dean and Chapter of Wells*, 2 vols, Historical Manuscripts Commission (London, 1907).

Canterbury Professions – *Canterbury Professions*, ed. M. Richter, Canterbury and York Society, 67 (Torquay, 1973).

CAP – *Calendar of Ancient Petitions Relating to Wales (Thirteenth to Sixteenth Century), Public Record Office*, ed. W. Rees, BCSHLS (Cardiff, 1975).

Cartae Antiquae, Rolls 1–10 – *The Cartae Antiquae, Rolls 1–10*, ed. L. Landon, PRS, n.s., 17 (1939).

Cartae Antiquae, Rolls 11–20 – *The Cartae Antiquae, Rolls 11–20*, ed. J. C. Davies, PRS, n.s., 33 (1960).

Cartulaire général de l'ordre des Hospitaliers de Saint-Jean de Jérusalem – *Cartulaire général de l'ordre des Hospitaliers de Saint-Jean de Jérusalem (1100–1310)*, ed. J. Delaville le Roulx, 4 vols (Paris, 1894–1906).

Cartularies of St. Peter's Priory Bath – *Two Chartularies of the Priory of St. Peter at Bath*, ed. W. Hunt, Somerset Record Society (London, 1893).

Cartulary of Augustinian Friars of Clare – *The Cartulary of the Augustinian Friars of Clare*, ed. C. Harper-Bill (Bury St Edmunds, 1991).

Cartulary of Cirencester Abbey – *The Cartulary of Cirencester Abbey, Gloucestershire*, vol. 2, ed. C. D. Ross (London, 1964).

Cartulary of Haughmond Abbey – *The Cartulary of Haughmond Abbey*, ed. U. Rees (Cardiff, 1985).

Cartulary of the Knights of St. John of Jerusalem in England, Essex – *The Cartulary of the Knights of St. John of Jerusalem in England: Secunda Camera, Essex*, ed. M. Gervers, British Academy (Oxford, 1982).

Cartulary of Shrewsbury Abbey – *The Cartulary of Shrewsbury Abbey*, 2 vols, ed. U. Rees (Aberystwyth, 1975).

Cartulary of St. Werburgh's Abbey, Chester – *The Chartulary or Register of the Abbey of St. Werburgh, Chester*, ed. J. Tait, 2 vols (Manchester, 1920–3).

CChR – *Calendar of the Charter Rolls preserved in the Public Record Office*, 6 vols (London, 1903–27).

CCR – *Calendar of the Close Rolls preserved in the Public Record Office* (London 1900–).

CFR, 1272–1307 – *Calendar of the Fine Rolls preserved in the Public Record Office, Edward I, 1272–1307*, vol. I (London, 1911).

Charters of the Anglo-Norman Earls of Chester – *Charters of the Anglo-Norman Earls of Chester, c.1071–1237*, ed. G. Barraclough, Record Society of Lancashire and Cheshire, 126 (Chester, 1988).

Charters of Trefeglwys, Arch. Camb. – 'Charters of Trefeglwys', ed. R. Williams, *Arch. Camb.*, 3rd series, 6 (1860), 330–3.

Chronica Majora – *Matthaei Parisiensis, Monachi Sancti Albani, Chronica Majora*, ed. H. R. Luard, 7 vols, Rolls Series (London, 1872–83).

Chronicle of the Third Crusade – *Chronicle of the Third Crusade. A Translation of the Itinerarium Peregrinorum et Gesta Regis Ricardi*, trans. H. J. Nicholson (Aldershot, 2005).

Chronicles and Memorials of the Reign of Richard I – *Chronicles and Memorials of the Reign of Richard I*, ed. W. Stubbs, 2 vols (London, 1864–5. Digitally printed version, Cambridge, 2012).

CIM – *Calendar of Inquisitions Miscellaneous (Chancery) preserved in the Public Record Office*, 2 vols (London, 1916).

CLR – *Calendar of the Liberate Rolls preserved in the Public Record Office* (London, 1917–).

Concilia – *Concilia Magnae Britanniae et Hiberniae a Synodo Verolamiensi A.D. 446 ad Londinensem A.D. 1717; accedunt Constitutiones et alia ad Historiam Ecclesiae Anglicanae spectantia*, ed. D. Wilkins, 4 vols (London, 1737).

Conciliorum Oecumenicarum Decreta – *Conciliorum Oecumenicarum Decreta*, ed. J. Alberigo et al., 3rd edn (Bologna, 1973).

Coucher Book of Whalley Abbey – *Coucher Book or Chartulary of Whalley Abbey*, ed. W. A. Hulton, Chetham Society, 4 vols (Manchester, 1847–9).

Councils and Synods – *Councils and Synods, with Other Documents relating to the English Church*, ed. D. Whitelock, M. Brett, and C. N. L. Brooke, 2 vols (Oxford, 1981).

Court Rolls of the Lordship of Ruthin or Dyffryn-Clwydd – *The Court Rolls of the Lordship of Ruthin or Dyffryn-Clwydd of the Reign of King Edward the First, preserved in the Public Record Office, London*, ed. and trans. R. A. Roberts, Cymmrodorion Record Series, 2 (London, 1893).

CPR – *Calendar of the Patent Rolls preserved in the Public Record Office*, 52 vols (London, 1891–).

Cronica de Wallia – '"Cronica de Wallia" and Other Documents from Exeter Cathedral Library MS. 3514', ed. T. Jones, *BBCS*, 12 (1946), 27–44.

CVCR – *Calendar of Various Chancery Rolls, Supplementary Close Rolls, Welsh Rolls, Scutage Rolls, Preserved in the Public Record Office, A.D. 1277–1326* (London, 1912).

De Invectionibus – 'Giraldus Cambrensis, *De Invectionibus*', ed. W. S. Davies, *Y Cymmrodor*, 30 (1920).

Decrees of the Ecumenical Councils – *Decrees of the Ecumenical Councils*, ed. N. P. Tanner, 2 vols (London, 1990).

Documents Illustrating the History of St Paul's Cathedral – *Documents Illustrating the History of St Paul's Cathedral*, ed. W. Sparrow Simpson, Camden Society, n.s., 26 (1880).

Domesday, Cheshire – *Domesday Book, Vol. 26, Cheshire*, ed. P. Morgan (Phillimore, 1978).

Eadmeri Historia Novorum – *Eadmeri Historia Novorum in Anglia*, ed. M. Rule, Rolls Series (1884).

Eadmer's History – *Eadmer's History of Recent Events in England, Historia Novorum in Anglia*, ed. and trans. G. Bosanquet (London, 1964).

Earldom of Gloucester Charters – *Earldom of Gloucester Charters: the charters and scribes of the Earls and Countesses of Gloucester to A.D. 1217*, ed. R. B. Patterson (Oxford, 1973).

Early Charters of the Cathedral Church of St. Paul, London – *Early Charters of the Cathedral Church of St. Paul, London*, ed. M. Gibbs, Camden Society, 3rd series, 58 (1939).

EEA – *English Episcopal Acta Series*, 45 vols (British Academy, 1980–).

Ekkehardi Chronicon – *Ekkehardi Chronicon*, in *Monumenta Germaniae Historica, Scriptores VI*, ed. G. H. Pertz (1844).

English Austin Friars – *The English Austin Friars, 1249–1538*, ed. F. Roth, 2 vols (New York, 1961).

Episc. Acts Welsh Dioceses – *Episcopal Acts and Cognate Documents relating to Welsh Dioceses 1066–1272*, ed. J. C. Davies, 2 vols, Historical Society of the Church in Wales (1946–8).

Fifth Report of the Royal Commission on Historical Manuscripts – *Fifth Report of the Royal Commission on Historical Manuscripts* (London, 1876).

Five Strata Marcella Charters – 'Five Strata Marcella Charters', ed. N. G. Davies, E. D. Jones, and R. F. Roberts, *NLWJ*, 5 (1947), 50–4.

Flores Historiarum – *Flores Historiarum*, ed. H. R. Luard, 3 vols, Rolls Series (London, 1890).

Foedera – *Foedera, conventiones, litterae, et cujuscunque generis acta publica, inter reges Angliae et alios quosvis imperatores, reges, pontifices, principes, vel communitates*, etc., ed. T. Rymer and R. Sanderson, 20 vols (London, 1816–69).

Formulare Anglicanum – *Formulare Anglicanum or, a Collection of Ancient Charters and Instruments of Divers Kinds, taken from the Originals*, ed. T. Madox (London, 1702).

Gervase of Canterbury – *The Historical Works of Gervase of Canterbury*, ed. W. Stubbs, 2 vols (London, 1879–80).

Gesta Abbatum Monasterii Sancti Albani – *Gesta Abbatum Monasterii Sancti Albani a Thoma Walsingham*, ed. H. T. Riley (London, 1867).

Gesta Regis Henrici Secundi – *Gesta Regis Henrici Secundi Benedicti Abbatis. The Chronicle of the Reigns of Henry II. and Richard I. A.D. 1169–1192; known commonly under the name of Benedict of Peterborough*, ed. W. Stubbs, 2 vols (London, 1867).

Haddan and Stubbs – *Councils and Ecclesiastical Documents Relating to Great Britain and Ireland*, ed. A. W. Haddan and W. Stubbs, 3 vols (Oxford, 1869–78).

Handlist of the Acts of Native Welsh Rulers – *Handlist of the Acts of Native Welsh Rulers, 1132–1283*, ed. K. L. Maund (Cardiff, 1996).

Hargrave, F. (ed.), *A Complete Collection of State Trials and Proceedings for High Treason and Other Crimes and Misdemeanours*, 5th edn, vol. I (Dublin, 1793).

Henry of Huntingdon, Historia Anglorum – *Henry, Archdeacon of Huntingdon, Historia Anglorum, The History of the English People*, ed. and trans. D. Greenway (Oxford, 1996).

Historia et Cartularium Monasterii Sancti Petri Gloucestriæ – *Historia et Cartularium Monasterii Sancti Petri Gloucestriæ*, ed. W. H. Hart, 3 vols, Rolls Series (London, 1863–7).

Historia Gruffud vab Kenan – *Historia Gruffud vab Kenan*, ed. D. S. Evans (Cardiff, 1977).

History of Gruffudd ap Cynan – *The History of Gruffudd ap Cynan, The Welsh Text*, ed. and trans. A. Jones (Manchester, 1910).

Hugh the Chanter – *Hugh the Chanter: The History of the Church of York, 1066–1127*, ed. and trans. C. Johnson, revd M. Brett, C. N. L. Brooke, and M. Winterbottom (Oxford, 1990).

Itinerary of King Richard I – *Itinerary of King Richard I, with Studies on Certain Matters of Interest Connected with His Reign*, ed. L. Landon, PRS, n.s., 13 (1935).

John of Worcester – *The Chronicle of John of Worcester*, ed. and trans. P. McGurk, 3 vols (Oxford, 1998).

Jones, H. L., 'Arvona Mediaeva II: Beddgelert Priory', *Arch. Camb.*, 1st series, 2 (1847), 153–66.

Jones, O. W., '*O Oes Gwrtheyrn*: A Medieval Welsh Chronicle', in B. Guy, G. Henley, O. W. Jones, and R. Thomas (eds), *The Chronicles of Medieval Wales and the March: New Contexts, Studies, and Texts* (Turnhout, 2020), pp. 169–230.

Journey and Description – *The Journey Through Wales; and, The Description of Wales by Gerald of Wales*, trans. L. Thorpe (London, 1978).

Karn, N., 'The Foundation Narrative', in *Foundation Documents from St Mary's Abbey, York 1085–1137*, ed. Richard Sharpe, Surtees Society, 227 (2022), 379–407.

Law of Hywel Dda – *The Law of Hywel Dda: Law Texts from Medieval Wales*, ed. and trans. D. Jenkins (Llandysul, 1986; repr. Llandysul, 2000).

Le Liber Censuum – *Le Liber Censuum de l'Eglise Romaine*, vol. I, ed. L. Duchesne, P. Fabre, and G. Mollat (Paris, 1905–52).

Letters and Charters of Gilbert Foliot – *The Letters and Charters of Gilbert Foliot, Abbot of Gloucester (1139–48), Bishop of Hereford (1148–63) and London (1163–87)*, ed. C. N. L. Brooke, Z. N. Brooke, and D. A. Morey (Cambridge, 1967).

Letters of John of Salisbury – *The Letters of John of Salisbury, The Early Letters (1153–1161)*, vol. I, ed. W. J. Millor, S. J. and H. E. Butler, revd C. N. L. Brooke (London, 1986).

Liber Eliensis – *Liber Eliensis, A History of the Isle of Ely*, ed. and trans. J. Fairweather (Woodbridge, 2005).

Liber Eliensis, Blake – *Liber Eliensis*, ed. E. O. Blake, Camden Third Series, 92 (1962).

Liber Extra – Decretalium Gregorii papae IX compilatio, ed. E. Friedberg, *Corpus Iuris Canonici*, ii (Leipzig, 1881).

Life of Gruffudd ap Cynan – A mediaeval prince of Wales: the life of Gruffudd ap Cynan, ed. and trans. D. S. Evans (Llanerch, 1990).

Lives of the British Saints – Lives of the British Saints, ed. S. Baring-Gould and J. Fisher, 4 vols (London, 1907–13).

Llandaff Episcopal Acta – Llandaff Episcopal Acta 1140–1287, ed. D. Crouch (Cardiff, 1988).

Llyfr Iorwerth – Llyfr Iorwerth: A Critical Text of the Venedotian Code of Medieval Welsh Law mainly from BM. Cotton MS. Titus Dii, ed. A. R. Wiliam (Cardiff, 1960).

LW – Littere Wallie preserved in Liber A in the Public Record Office, ed. J. G. Edwards, BCSHLS (Cardiff, 1940).

Mabinogion – The Mabinogion, trans. S. Davies (Oxford, 2007).

Martyrology of Tallaght – The Martyrology of Tallaght, ed. R. I. Best and H. J. Lawlor, Henry Bradshaw Society, 68 (1931).

Matthew Paris's English History – Matthew Paris's English History, from the year 1235 to 1273, trans. J. A. Giles, 3 vols (London, 1852–4).

'Merionethshire', *Arch. Camb.*, 5th series, 2 (1885), 227–9.

Monasticon – Monasticon Anglicanum, a history of the abbies and other monasteries, hospitals, frieries, and cathedral and collegiate churches, with their dependencies, in England and Wales; also of all such Scotch, Irish, and French monasteries, as were in any manner connected with religious houses in England, ed. W. Dugdale, revd edn, ed. J. Caley et al., 6 vols in 8 (London, 1817–30).

Notes and Queries for Somerset and Dorset – Notes and Queries for Somerset and Dorset, ed. G. W. Saunders, C. H. Mayo, T. F. Palmer, and R. G. Bartelot (Sherborne, 1920).

Opera – Giraldi Cambrensis Opera, ed. J. S. Brewer, J. F. Dimock, G. F. Warner, 8 vols, Rolls Series (London, 1861–91).

Orderic Vitalis – The Ecclesiastical History of Orderic Vitalis, ed. M. M. Chibnall, 6 vols (Oxford, 1969–80).

Parliamentary Writs and Writs of Military Summons – Parliamentary Writs and Writs of Military Summons, ed. F. Palgrave, 2 vols in 4, Record Commission (1827–34).

Pat. Rolls, 1216–1225 – Patent Rolls of the Reign of Henry III preserved in the Public Record Office, 1216–1225 (London, 1901).

Patrologia Latina – Patrologiae Cursus Completus. Series Latina, ed. J. P. Migne, 221 vols (1841–55). Available online: http://patristica.net/latina/, accessed 10 June 2024.

Petri Blesensis Bathoniensis Archiadiaconi Opera – Petri Blesensis Bathoniensis Archiadiaconi Opera Omnia Nunc Primum in Anglia Ope Codicum Manuscriptorum, ed. J. A. Giles, 4 vols (Oxford, 1846–7).

Pipe Rolls, Henry II, 2,3,4 – The Great Rolls of the Pipe for the Second, Third, and Fourth Years of the Reign of King Henry the Second, A.D. 1155, 1156, 1157, 1158, ed. J. Hunter, Rolls Series (London, 1844).

Pipe Roll, John, Year 4 – The Great Roll of the Pipe for the Fourth Year of the Reign of King John, Michaelmas 1202 (Pipe Roll 48), ed. D. M. Stenton, PRS, n.s., 15 (1937).

Pipe Roll, Richard I, Year 7 – The Great Roll of the Pipe for the Seventh Year of the Reign of King Richard the First, Michaelmas 1195 (Pipe Roll 41), ed. D. M. Stenton, PRS, n.s., 6 (1929).

Pipe Roll, Richard I, Year 8 – The Chancellor's Roll for the Eighth Year of the Reign of King Richard the First, Michaelmas 1196 (Pipe Roll 41), ed. D. M. Stenton, PRS, n.s., 7 (1930).

Pleas before the King and his Justices, 1198–1212 – *Pleas before the King and his Justices, 1198–1212*, iii, ed. D. M. Stenton, Selden Society, lxxxiii (1966).

Prynne – *The first-[third] tome of an exact chronological vindication and historical demonstration of our British, Roman, Saxon, Danish, Norman, English kings supreme ecclesiastical jurisdiction from the original planting, embracing of Christian religion therein, and reign of Lucius, our first Christian king, till the death of King Richard the First, Anno Domini 1199*, ed. W. Prynne, 3 vols (London, 1665–8). Available online via Early English Books Online: https://quod.lib.umich.edu/e/eebo/A70867.0001.001, accessed 4 February 2024.

Radulfi de Diceto – *Radulfi de Diceto Decani Lundoniensis Opera Historica*, ed. W. Stubbs, 2 vols, Rolls Series, lxviii (1876).

RC – *Registrum Vulgariter Nuncupatum, "The Record of Caernarvon," E Codice MSt° Harleiano 696 Descriptum*, ed. H. Ellis, Record Commission (London, 1838).

Reading Abbey Cartularies – *Reading Abbey Cartularies, British Library Manuscripts: Egerton 3031, Harley 1708 and Cotton Vespasian E xxv*, ed. B. R. Kemp, 2 vols, Royal Historical Society, Camden Fourth Series, 31 (London, 1986–7).

Records of the Templars in England – *Records of the Templars in England in the Twelfth Century: The Inquest of 1185, with illustrative charters and documents*, ed. B. A. Lees, British Academy Records of the Social and Economic History of England and Wales, IX (London, 1935).

Reg. Innocenz' III – *Die Register Innocenz III*, ii, *Pontifikatsjahr 1199/1200*, ed. O. Hageneder, W. Maleczek, A. Strand (Rome, 1979).

Regesta Henrici Primi – *Regesta Regum Anglo-Normannorum, 1066–1154*, ii, *Regesta Henrici Primi*, ed. H. A. Cronne, and C. Johnson (Oxford, 1956).

Regesta Honorii Papae III – *Regesta Honorii Papae III, Iussu et Munificentia Leonis XIII Pontificis Maximi ex Vaticanis Archetypis Aliisque Fontibus*, ed. P. Pressutti, 2 vols (Rome, 1888–95).

Regesta Regis Stephani – *Regesta Regum Anglo-Normannorum, 1066–1154*, iii, *Regesta Regis Stephani ac Mathildis Imperatricis ac Gaufridi et Henrici Ducum Normannorum, 1135–1154*, ed. H. A. Cronne and R. H. C. Davis (Oxford, 1968).

Regesta Willelmi Conquestoris et Willelmi Rufi – *Regesta Regum Anglo-Normannorum, 1066–1154*, i, *Regesta Willelmi Conquestoris et Willelmi Rufi*, ed. H. W. C. Davis (Oxford, 1913).

Register of Godfrey Giffard – *Episcopal Registers, Diocese of Worcester, Register of Bishop Godfrey Giffard, September 23 1268 to August 15 1301*, ed. J. W. W. Bund, The Worcestershire Historical Society (Oxford, 1902).

Register of John Pecham – *The Register of John Pecham, Archbishop of Canterbury 1279–1292*, ed. F. N. Davis and D. Douie, 2 vols, The Canterbury and York Society, 64 and 65 (Torquay, 1968–9).

Register of Thomas De Cantilupe – *The Register of Thomas De Cantilupe, Bishop of Hereford A.D. 1275–1282*, ed. W. W. Capes and R. G. Griffiths (Hereford, 1906).

Registrum Epistolarum Peckham – *Registrum Epistolarum Fratris Johannis Peckham, Archiepiscopi Cantuariensis*, ed. C. T. Martin, 3 vols (London, 1882–5).

Report on Manuscripts in Various Collections – *Report on Manuscripts in Various Collections*, 8 vols, Historical Manuscripts Commission (London, 1901–13).

Roger de Hoveden – *Chronica Magistri Rogeri de Hovedene*, ed. W. Stubbs, 4 vols (London, 1868–71).

Rolls and Register of Bishop Oliver Sutton – *The Rolls and Register of Bishop Oliver Sutton, 1280–1299*, ed. R. M. T. Hill, 8 vols (Hereford, 1948–75).

Rot. Chart. – *Rotuli Chartarum, in Turri Londinensi asservati*, ed. T. D. Hardy, vol. I, part I, Record Commission (London, 1837).

Rot. Litt. Claus. – *Rotuli Litterarum Clausarum, in Turri Londinensi asservati*, ed. T. D. Hardy, 2 vols, Record Commission (London, 1833–44).

Rot. Litt. Pat. – *Rotuli Litterarum Patentium, in Turri Londinensi asservati*, ed. T. D. Hardy, vol. I, part I, Record Commission (London, 1835).

Sigilli Dell' Archivio Vaticano – *I Sigilli Dell' Archivio Vaticano*, ed. P. Sella and M. H. Laurent, i (Rome, 1937).

St. Anselm Letters – *The Letters of St. Anselm of Canterbury*, 3 vols, ed. and trans. W. Fröhlich, Cistercian Studies Series (Kalamazoo, 1990–4).

St Davids Episcopal Acta – *St Davids Episcopal Acta 1085–1280*, ed. J. Barrow (Cardiff, 1998).

Select Cases from the Ecclesiastical Courts – *Select Cases from the Ecclesiastical Courts of the Province of Canterbury c.1200–1301*, ed. N. Adams and C. Donahue (London, 1981).

Statuta Capitulorum Ordinis Cisterciensis – *Statuta Capitulorum Ordinis Cisterciensis*, ed. J. Canivez (Louvain, 1933).

Taxatio Database – *Taxatio* Database, University of Sheffield. https://www.dhi.ac.uk/taxatio/forms, accessed 12 August 2024.

Taxatio Ecclesiastica – *Taxatio Ecclesiastica Angliae et Walliae auctoritate P. Nicholai IV, circa 1291*, Record Commission (London, 1802).

Testamentary Records – *Testamentary Records of the English and Welsh Episcopate 1200–1413, Wills, Executors' Accounts and Inventories, and the Probate Process*, ed. C. M. Woolgar, The Canterbury and York Society, 102 (Woodbridge, 2011).

Thomas Becket Materials – *Materials for the History of Thomas Becket, Archbishop of Canterbury*, ed. J. C. Robertson and J. B. Sheppard, 7 vols, Rolls Series (London, 1875–85).

Valuation of Norwich – *The Valuation of Norwich*, ed. W. E. Lunt (Oxford, 1926).

Vita Griffini – *Vita Griffini Filii Conani, The Medieval Latin Life of Gruffudd ap Cynan*, ed. and trans. P. Russell (Cardiff, 2005).

'Vita Sancte Wenefrede (Robert of Shrewsbury; Laud)', ed. D. Callander – 'Vita Sancte Wenefrede (Robert of Shrewsbury; Laud)', ed. D. Callander, *Vitae Sanctorum Cambriae Project* (2023). Available online: https://saints.wales, accessed 19 May 2024.

Welsh Assize Roll – *The Welsh Assize Roll 1277–1284, Assize Roll no. 1147 (Public Record Office)*, ed. J. C. Davies, BCSHLS (Cardiff, 1940).

Welsh Chronicles Research Group, http://croniclau.bangor.ac.uk/index.php.en, accessed 20 June 2024.

Welsh Ecclesiastical Seals – D. H. Williams, 'Catalogue of Welsh Ecclesiastical Seals as known to 1600 A.D., Part II: Seals of Ecclesiastical Jurisdiction', *Arch. Camb.*, 134 (1985), 162–89.

Welsh Episcopal Seals – D. H. Williams, 'Catalogue of Welsh Ecclesiastical Seals as known to 1600 A.D., Part I: Episcopal Seals', *Arch. Camb.*, 133 (1984), 100–35.

Welsh History through Seals – D. H. Williams, *Welsh History through Seals* (Cardiff, 1982).

Welsh Law of Women – *The Welsh Law of Women*, ed. D. Jenkins and M. E. Owen (Cardiff 1980; repr. Cardiff, 2017).

William of Malmesbury, Gesta Pontificum Anglorum – *William of Malmesbury, Gesta Pontificum Anglorum, The History of the English Bishops*, ed. and trans. M. Winterbottom, 2 vols (Oxford, 2009).

William of Malmesbury, Gesta Regum Anglorum – William of Malmesbury, *Gesta Regum Anglorum, The History of the English Kings*, ed. and trans. R. A. B. Mynors, R. M. Thomson, and M. Winterbottom, 2 vols (Oxford, 2006).

Winchcombe Annals – 'Winchcombe Annals, 1049–1181', ed. R. R. Darlington, in *A Medieval Miscellany for Doris Mary Stenton*, ed. P. M. Barnes and C. F. Slade, PRS, n.s., 36 (1962), pp. 111–38.

Ystrad Marchell Charters – *The Charters of the Abbey of Ystrad Marchell*, ed. G. C. G. Thomas (Aberystwyth, 1997).

PRINTED SECONDARY SOURCES

Unpublished

Theses

Hill, F. G., 'Excommunication and Politics in Thirteenth-Century England', unpublished PhD thesis (University of East Anglia, 2016).

Huscroft, R. M., 'The political career and personal life of Robert Burnell, chancellor of Edward I', unpublished PhD thesis (King's College, University of London, 2001).

Jones, B., 'Welsh Contacts with the Papacy before the Edwardian Conquest, c.1283', unpublished PhD thesis (University of St Andrews, 2019).

Jones, O. E., 'Llyfr Coch Asaph: A Textual and Historical Study', 2 vols, unpublished MA thesis (University of Wales [Aberystwyth], 1968).

McGuinness, S., 'Arbitration and Dispute Resolution in Wales during the Age of the Princes c.1100–c.1283', unpublished MA thesis (Bangor University, 2012).

Runciman, D., 'Pastoral care according to the bishops of England and Wales (c.1170–1228)', unpublished PhD thesis (University of Cambridge, 2019).

Published

Anglia Sacra – *Anglia Sacra sive Collectio historiarum, partim antiquitus, partim recenter scriptarum, de archiepiscopis & episcopis Angliæ, a prima fidei christianæ susceptione ad annum MDXL, nunc primùm in lucem editarum*, ed. H. Wharton, 2 vols (London, 1691). Available online: https://archive.org/details/AngliaSacra/page/n7/mode/2up, accessed 25 June 2024.

Armstrong, L., 'A Misdated St Paul's Fabric Indulgence', *Notes and Queries*, 59/4 (December 2012).

Barbier, P., *The Age of Owain Gwynedd* (London, 1908).

Barlow, F., 'Corbeil, William de (d. 1136)', *ODNB*.

Barlow, F., *The English Church 1066–1154: A History of the Anglo-Norman Church* (London, 1979).

Barlow, F., *The Feudal Kingdom of England, 1042–1216* (London, 1983).

Barrow, J., 'The Canons and Citizens of Hereford c.1160–c.1240', *Midland History*, 24 (1999), 1–23.

Bass, I. L., 'Communities of Remembrance: Religious Orders and the Cult of Thomas de Cantilupe, Bishop of Hereford (1275–82)', *The Journal of Medieval Monastic Studies*, 7 (2018), 237–72.

Bass, I. L., 'Rebellion and Miracles on the Welsh March: Accounts in the Miracle Collection of St Thomas de Cantilupe', *WHR*, 29 (2019), 503–31.

Bolton, B. M., 'Ottobuono [Ottobuono or Ottobono Fieschi; afterwards Adrian] (*c*.1205–1276)', *ODNB*.

Brett, M., 'David (*d*. 1137x9)', *ODNB*.

Brett, M., 'The annals of Bermondsey, Southwark, and Merton', in *Church and City, 1000–1500: Essays in Honour of Christopher Brooke*, ed. D. Abulafia,M. Franklin, and M. Rubin (Cambridge, 1992), pp. 279–310.

Brett, M., *The English Church Under Henry I* (Oxford, 1975).

Brooke, C. N. L., 'English Episcopal *Acta* of the Twelfth and Thirteenth Centuries', in *Medieval Ecclesiastical Studies in Honour of Dorothy M. Owen*, ed. M. J. Franklin and C. Harper-Bill (Woodbridge, 1995), pp. 41–56.

Brooke, C. N. L., 'Gregorian Reform in Action: Clerical Marriage in England, 1050–1200', *The Cambridge Historical Journal*, 12 (1956), 1–21.

Brooke, C. N. L., *The Church and the Welsh Border in the Central Middle Ages* (Woodbridge, 1986).

Burger, M., 'Officiales and the Familiae of the Bishops of Lincoln, 1258–99', *Journal of Medieval History*, 16 (1990), 39–53.

Burton, J. and Kerr, J., *The Cistercians in the Middle Ages* (Woodbridge, 2011).

Burton, J. and Stöber, K., 'The Dominicans in Wales', in E. J. Giraud and J. C. Linde (eds), *A Companion to the English Dominican Province* (Leiden: Brill, 2021), pp. 138–79.

Camargo, M., *Ars Dictaminis, Ars Dictandi*, Typologie des sources du moyen âge occidental, 60 (Turnhout, 1991).

Cappelli, A., *The Elements of Abbreviation in Medieval Latin Paleography*, trans. D. Heimann and R. Kay (Kansas, 1982).

Carpenter, D., 'Dafydd ap Llywelyn's submission to King Henry III in October 1241: A new perspective', *WHR*, 23 (2007), 1–12.

Carr, A. D., 'A Debatable Land: Arwystli in the Middle Ages', *Montgomeryshire Collections*, 80 (1992), 39–54.

Carr, A. D., 'Jones Pierce Revisited: The Evidence of the Thirteenth- and Fourteenth-Century Extents', in *Wales and the Welsh in the Middle Ages, essays presented to J. Beverley Smith*, ed. R. A. Griffiths and P. R. Schofield (Cardiff, 2011), pp. 126–44.

Carr, A. D., 'Llywelyn ab Iorwerth, [called Llywelyn Fawr] (*c*.1173–1240)', *ODNB*.

Carr, A. D., *Medieval Anglesey* (Llangefni, 1982; 2nd edn, Llangefni, 2011).

Carr, A. D., 'The Black Death in Anglesey', *Transactions of the Anglesey Antiquarian Society* (2010).

Carr, A. D., 'The Last and Weakest of His Line: Dafydd ap Gruffydd, the last Prince of Wales', *WHR*, 19 (1998–9), 375–99.

Cazel, F. A. Jr., 'Ste Mère-Église, William de (*d*. 1224)', *ODNB*.

Chaplais, P., 'English Diplomatic Documents to the end of Edward III's Reign', in *The Study of Medieval Records: Essays in Honour of Kathleen Major*, ed. D. A. Bullough and R. L. Storey (Oxford, 1971), pp. 22–56.

Chaplais, P., *English Royal Documents: King John–Henry VI 1199–1461* (Oxford, 1971).

Chaplais, P., 'The seals and original charters of Henry I', in *Essays in Medieval Diplomacy and Administration* (London, 1981), pp. 260–75.

Charles-Edwards, T. M., 'Deiniol [St Deiniol, Daniel] (*d*. 584)', *ODNB*.

Cheney, C. R., 'Cardinal John of Ferentino, Papal Legate in England in 1206', *EHR*, 76 (1961), 654–60.

Cheney, C. R., *English Bishops' Chanceries: 1100–1250* (Manchester, 1950).

Cheney, C. R., *Handbook of Dates for Students of English History* (London, 1961).

Chew, H. M., 'The Priory of St John of Jerusalem, Clerkenwell', in *A History of the County of Middlesex*, i, *VCH*, ed. J. S. Cockburn, H. P. F. King, and K. G. T. McDonnell (London, 1969), pp. 193–199.

Clarke, P. D., *The Interdict in the Thirteenth Century: A Question of Collective Guilt* (Oxford, 2007).

Coflein website, RCAHMW. https://www.coflein.gov.uk, accessed 10 June 2024.

Cowley, F. G., *The Monastic Order in South Wales, 1066–1349* (Cardiff, 1977).

Cragoe, C. D., 'Fabric, Tombs and Precincts, 1087–1540', in *St Paul's: The Cathedral Church of London*, ed. D. Keene et al. (New Haven, 2004), pp. 127–42.

Cranage, D. H. S., *An Architectural Account of the Churches of Shropshire*, 10 parts (Wellington, 1894–1912).

Crouch, D., 'Robert, first earl of Gloucester (*b.* before 1100, *d.* 1147)', *ODNB*.

Crouch, D., 'Robert [Robert de Beaumont], second earl of Leicester (1104–1168)', *ODNB*.

Crouch, D., 'The Administration of the Norman Earldom', in *The Earldom of Chester and its Charters, A Tribute to Geoffrey Barraclough*, ed. A. T. Thacker, *Journal of the Chester Archaeological Society*, 71 (Chester, 1991), 69–96.

Crouch, D., 'Urban: first Bishop of Llandaff, 1107–34', The Journal of Welsh Ecclesiastical History, 6 (1989), 1–15.

Davies, H. R., *A Review of the Records of The Conway and The Menai Ferries*, BCSHLS (Cardiff, 1966).

Davies, J. C., 'A Grant by Llewelyn Ap Gruffydd', *NLWJ*, 3 (Summer 1944), 158–62.

Davies, J. C., 'Strata Marcella Documents', *Montgomeryshire Collections*, 51 (1949–50), 164–87.

Davies, J. R., 'Cathedrals and the Cult of Saints in Eleventh and Twelfth-Century Wales', in *Cathedrals, Communities and Conflict in the Anglo-Norman World*, ed. P. Dalton, C. Insley, and L. J. Wilkinson (Woodbridge, 2011), pp. 99–115.

Davies, J. R., 'The donor and the duty of warrandice: giving and granting in Scottish charters', in *The Reality Behind Charter Diplomatic in the Anglo-Norman Era*, ed. D. Broun (University of Glasgow, 2010), pp. 120–65. https://paradox.poms.ac.uk/ebook/index.html, accessed 17 May 2024.

Davies, R. R., *The Age of Conquest, Wales 1063–1415* (Oxford, 2000).

Davies, W., *Wales in the Early Middle Ages* (Leicester, 1982; repr. Leicester, 1996).

Davis, G. R. C., *Medieval Cartularies of Great Britain and Ireland*, ed. C. Breay, J. Harrison, and D. M. Smith, 2nd edn (London, 2010).

Davis, H. W. C., 'Some Documents of the Anarchy', in *Essays in History, presented to Reginald Lane Poole*, ed. H. W. C. Davis (Oxford, 1927), pp. 168–89.

Davis, R. H. C., 'Geoffrey Barraclough and the Lure of Charters', in *The Earldom of Chester and its Charters, A Tribute to Geoffrey Barraclough*, ed. A. T. Thacker, *Journal of the Chester Archaeological Society*, 71 (Chester, 1991), 23–36.

Denton, J. H., *English Royal Free Chapels, 1100–1300, A Constitutional Study* (Manchester, 1970).

Douie, D. L., *Archbishop Pecham* (Oxford, 1952).

Duffy, S., 'Ragnvald [Rögnvaldr, Reginald, Ragnall] (*d.* 1229)', *ODNB*.

Duggan, C., 'Richard [Richard of Dover] (*d.* 1184)', *ODNB*.

Evans, A. K. B. and R. H., 'Colleges: Wolverhampton, St Peter', in *A History of the County of Stafford*, iii, *VCH*, ed. M. W. Greenslade (London, 1970), pp. 321–31.

Evans, A. O., 'Three Old Foundations', *Y Cymmrodor*, 42 (1931), 69–109.

Evans, D. F., 'Welsh traitors in a Scottish chronicle: Dafydd ap Gruffudd, Penwyn and the transmission of national memory', *Studia Celtica*, 52 (2018), 137–55.

Eyton, R. W., *Antiquities of Shropshire*, 12 vols (London, 1854–60).

Fasti Bath and Wells – Fasti Ecclesiae Anglicanae 1066–1300, Volume 7, Bath and Wells, ed. D. E. Greenway (London, 2001).

Fasti Chichester – Fasti Ecclesiae Anglicanae 1066–1300: Volume 5, Chichester, ed. D. E. Greenway (London, 1996).

Fasti Ecclesiae Anglicanae Hardy – Fasti Ecclesiae Anglicanae, or a calendar of the principal ecclesiastical dignitaries in England and Wales, and of the chief officers in the Universities of Oxford and Cambridge, from the earliest time to year M.DCC.XV. Compiled by J. Le Neve, corrected and continued from M.DCC.XV. to the present time, by T. Duffus Hardy, ed. T. D. Hardy, 3 vols (Oxford, 1854).

Fasti Hereford – Fasti Ecclesiae Anglicanae 1066–1300: Volume 8, Hereford, ed. J. S. Barrow (London, 2002).

Fasti Lincoln – Fasti Ecclesiae Anglicanae 1066–1300, Volume 3, Lincoln, ed. D. E. Greenway (London, 1977).

Fasti London – Fasti Ecclesiae Anglicanae 1066–1300: Volume 1, St. Paul's, London, ed. D. E. Greenway (London, 1968).

Fasti Monastic Cathedrals – Fasti Ecclesiae Anglicanae, 1066–1300, Volume 2, Monastic Cathedrals (Northern and Southern Provinces), ed. D. E. Greenway (London, 1971).

Fasti Salisbury – Fasti Ecclesiae Anglicanae, 1066–1300, Volume 4, Salisbury, ed. D. E. Greenway (London, 1991).

Fasti Welsh Cathedrals – Fasti Ecclesiae Anglicanae, 1066–1300, Volume 9, The Welsh Cathedrals, ed. M. J. Pearson (London, 2003).

Fincham, H. W., *The Order of the Hospital of St John of Jerusalem and its Grand Priory of England* (London, 1915).

Finucane, R. C., 'Cantilupe, Thomas de [St Thomas of Hereford] *c*.1220–1282', *ODNB*.

Flanagan, M. T., *Irish Society, Anglo-Norman Settlers, Angevin Kingship: Interactions in Ireland in the Late Twelfth Century* (Oxford, 1990).

Franklin, M. J., 'Durdent, Walter (*d.* 1159)', *ODNB*.

Franklin, M. J., 'Pattishall [Pateshull], Hugh of (*d.* 1241)', *ODNB*.

Gardner, J., 'Some Cardinals' Seals of the Thirteenth Century', *Journal of the Warburg and Courtauld Institutes*, 38 (1975), 72–96.

Gaydon, A. T., 'Colleges of Secular Canons: Shrewsbury', in *A History of the County of Shropshire*, ii, *VCH*, ed. A. T. Gaydon and R. B. Pugh (London, 1973), pp. 114–23.

Gillingham, J., 'John (1167–1216)', *ODNB*.

Gillingham, J., 'Richard I (1157–1199)', *ODNB*.

Giry, A., *Manuel de Diplomatique*: diplômes et chartes, chronologie technique, éléments critiques et parties constitutives de la teneur des chartes, les chancelleries, les actes privés (1894).

Godwin, F., *A Catalogue of the Bishops of England, since the First Planting of Christian Religion in this Island together with a Briefe History of their Lives and Memorable Actions, so neere as can be gathered out of Antiquity. Whereunto is prefixed a Discourse concerning the first Conversion of our Britaine unto Christian Religion, by Francis Godwin, now Bishop of Llandaff* (London, 1615).

Goering, J. and Payer, P. J., 'The Summa Penitentie Fratrum Predicatorum: A Thirteenth-Century Confessional Formulary', *Mediaeval Studies*, 55 (1993), 1–50.

Goering, J. and Pryce, H., 'The *De Modo Confitendi* of Cadwgan, Bishop of Bangor', *Mediaeval Studies*, 62 (2000), 1–27.

Golding, B., 'Piety, Politics, and Plunder Across the Anglo-Welsh Frontier: Acquiring the Relics of Winifred and Beuno', in *Monasteries on the Borders of Medieval Europe: Conflict and Cultural Interaction*, ed. E. Jamroziak and K. Stöber (Turnhout, 2013), pp. 19–48.

Gooder, E. A., *Latin for Local History*, 2nd edn (London, 1978).

Gough, H., *Itinerary of King Edward the First, throughout his reign, A.D. 1272–1307*, 2 vols (London, 1900).

Graham, R., 'Letters of Cardinal Ottoboni, 1265–68', *EHR*, 15 (1900), 87–120.

Gransden, A., *Historical Writing in England c.550 to c.1307* (London, 1974).

Greenway, D., 'Ecclesiastical Chronology: Fasti 1066–1300', in *Materials, Sources and Methods*, ed. D. Baker, Studies in Church History, 11 (Oxford, 1975), pp. 53–60.

Gresham, C. A., *Eifionydd: A Study in Landownership from the Medieval Period to the Present Day* (Cardiff, 1973).

Gresham, C. A., 'Aberconwy Charter: further consideration', *BBCS*, 30 (1982–3).

Gruffydd, K. L., *Maritime Wales in the Middle Ages: 1039–1542*, ed. M. D. Matthews (Wrexham, 2016).

Guide to Bishops' Registers – *Guide to Bishops' Registers of England and Wales, A Survey from the Middle Ages to the Abolition of Episcopacy in 1646*, ed. D. M. Smith, Royal Historical Society (London, 1981).

Gwynedd Archaeological Trust, *The Bishop's Palace, Bangor. Archaeological Assessment and Evaluation Excavation. December 2003. GAT Project No. G1785, report no. 514* (January 2004).

Hamilton, J. S., 'Lacy, Henry de, fifth earl of Lincoln (1249–1311)', *ODNB*.

Handbook of British Chronology – *Handbook of British Chronology*, ed. E. B. Fryde, D. E. Greenway, S. Porter, and I. Roy, Royal Historical Society, 3rd edn (London, 1986).

Harding, A., 'Burnell, Robert (*d.* 1292)', *ODNB*.

Harding, A., 'Walerand, Robert (*d.* 1273)', *ODNB*.

Harper, S., 'The Bangor Pontifical', *Hanes Cerddoriaeth Cymru / Welsh Music History*, 2 (1997), 65–99.

Harrison, J., 'A Note on Gerald of Wales and *Annales Cambriae*', *WHR*, 17 (1994–5), 252–5.

Haseldine, J., 'Friendship and Rivalry: The Role of Amicitia in Twelfth-Century Monastic Relations', *Journal of Ecclesiastical History*, 44 (1993), 390–414.

Haseldine, J. (ed.), *Friendship in Medieval Europe* (Stroud, 1999).

Haseldine, J., 'Understanding the Language of Amicitia: The Friendship Circle of Peter of Celle (*c.*1115–1183)', *Journal of Medieval History*, 20 (1994), 237–60.

Hausmann, F., 'Reichskanzlei und Hofkapelle unter Heinrich V und Konrad III', *MGH Schriften*, 14 (Stuttgart, 1956), 122–34.

Hays, R. W., *The History of the Abbey of Aberconway, 1186–1537* (Cardiff, 1963).

Hays, R. W., 'Rotoland, subprior of Aberconway, and the Controversy over the See of Bangor 1199–1204', *Journal of the Historical Society of the Church in Wales*, 18 (1963), 9–19.

Heads of Religious Houses – Brooke, C. N. L., Knowles, D. and London, V. C. M. (eds), *The Heads of Religious Houses, England and Wales, 940–1216*, i, 2nd edn (Cambridge, 2001), and London, V. C. M. and Smith, D. M. (eds), *The Heads of Religious Houses, England and Wales, 1216–1377*, ii (Cambridge, 2001).

Hereford Cathedral Charters and Records – *Charters and Records of Hereford Cathedral*, ed. W. W. Capes (Hereford, 1908).

Holdsworth, C., 'Baldwin [Baldwin of Forde] (*c*.1125–1190)', *ODNB*.

Hoskin, P. M., 'Authors of bureaucracy: developing and creating administrative systems in English episcopal chanceries in the second half of the thirteenth century', in *Patrons and Professionals in the Middle Ages: Proceedings of the 2010 Harlaxton Symposium*, ed. E. A. New and P. Binski (Lincolnshire, 2012).

Hoskin, P. M., 'How to Travel with a Bishop: Thirteenth-Century Episcopal Itineraries', in *Princes of the Church: Bishops and their Palaces*, ed. D. Rollason (Abingdon, 2017).

Hoskin, P. M. and New, E. A., '"By the Impression of my Seal". Medieval Identity and Bureaucracy: A Case Study', *The Antiquaries Journal*, 100 (London, 2020), 190–212.

'Houses of Cistercian monks: The Abbey of Whalley' – 'Houses of Cistercian monks: The Abbey of Whalley', in *A History of the County of Lancaster*, ii, ed. W. Farrer and J. Brownbill (London, 1908), pp. 131–9.

Hudson, J., 'Nigel (*c*.1100–1169)', *ODNB*.

Huws, D., *A Repertory of Welsh Manuscripts and Scribes c.800–c.1800*, 3 vols (Aberystwyth, 2022).

Huws, D., 'Descriptions of the Welsh Manuscripts', in *The Welsh King and His Court*, ed. T. M. Charles-Edwards, M. E. Owen, and P. Russell (Cardiff, 2000), pp. 415–24.

Huws, D., 'Llyfrau Cymraeg 1250–1400', *NLWJ*, 28 (1993–4), 1–21.

Inventory of the Ancient Monuments in Caernarvonshire – *An Inventory of the Ancient Monuments in Caernarvonshire*, RCAHMW (1960).

Jenkins, D., 'A Lawyer Looks at Welsh Land Law', *Transactions of the Honourable Society of the Cymmrodorion* (1967), 220–46.

Johnstone, H., *Edward of Carnarvon, 1284–1307* (Manchester, 1946).

Jones, F., 'Welsh Bonds for Keeping the Peace 1283 and 1295', *BBCS*, 13 (1949), 142–4.

Jones, G., 'Maenol Bangor: an ancient estate on the north-west fringe of Wales', *Hommes et Terres du Nord* (1988), 56–60.

Jones, G. I. L., *Anglesey Churches* (2006).

Jones, G. R. J., 'Llys and Maerdref', in *The Welsh King and His Court*, ed. T. M. Charles-Edwards, M. E. Owen, and P. Russell (Cardiff, 2000), pp. 296–318.

Jones, H. L., 'Arvona Mediaeva: The Collegiate Church of Clynnog Fawr, Caernarvonshire', *Arch. Camb.*, 11 (1848), 247–57.

Julian-Jones, M., 'Sealing Episcopal Identity: The Bishops of England, 1200–1300', in *Episcopal Power and Local Society in Medieval Europe, 1000–1400*, ed. P. Coss, C. Dennis, M. Julian-Jones, and A. Silvestri (2017), pp. 239–57.

Karn, N., 'The Twelfth Century', in *Ely: Bishops and Diocese 1109–2009*, ed. P. Meadows (Woodbridge, 2010), pp. 1–25.

Kemp, B. R., 'Bingham, Robert (*d.* 1246)', *ODNB*.

Kemp, B. R., 'Corner, William de la (*d.* 1291)', *ODNB*.

Kennedy, B. H., *The Shorter Latin Primer* (London, 1902).

Kettle, A. J. and Baggs, A. P., 'Houses of Benedictine Monks: The Abbey of Chester', in *A History of the County of Chester*, iii, *VCH*, ed. B. E. Harris (London, 1980), pp. 132–45.

Kingsford, C. L., revd P. Dalton, 'Lacy, Roger de (*d.* 1211)', *ODNB*.

Latham, R. E., *Revised Medieval Latin Word-List, from British and Irish Sources* (London, 1983).

Lewis, C. P., 'Avranches, Hugh d', first earl of Chester (*d.* 1101)', *ODNB*.

Lewis, C. P., 'Gruffudd ap Cynan and the Normans', in *Gruffudd ap Cynan: A Collaborative Biography*, ed. K. L. Maund (Woodbridge, 1996), pp. 61–78.

Leyser, K., 'England and the Empire in the Early Twelfth Century', *TRHS*, 5th series, 10 (1960), 61–84.

List of Historic Place Names Website – Rhestr o Enwau Lleoedd Hanesyddol/List of Historic Place Names, RCAHMW. https://historicplacenames.rcahmw.gov.uk, accessed 10 June 2024.

Lloyd, J. E., *A History of Wales from the Earliest Times to the Edwardian Conquest*, 2 vols (London, 1912).

Luscombe, D., 'Salisbury, John of (late 1110s–1180)', *ODNB*.

Malden, A. R., 'The burial places of the bishops of Salisbury', *The Wiltshire Archaeological and Natural History Magazine*, 37 (1911–12), 339–52.

Marritt, S., 'Seffrid (I) [nicknamed Pelochin] (*d.* 1150)', *ODNB*.

Marshall, A., 'Wooden Monumental Effigies', *Transactions of the Woolhope Naturalists' Field Club* (1918–20), 189–97.

Mayr-Harting, H., 'Hugh of Lincoln [St Hugh of Lincoln, Hugh of Avalon] (1140?–1200)', *ODNB*.

McGuinness, S., 'Betrayal in the Belfry – The Bishop of Bangor and the demise of Llywelyn ap Gruffudd, Prince of Wales', *Journal of the Mortimer History Society* 6 (2023) 67–86.

McGuinness, S., 'The Medieval Bishops of Bangor, 1092–1283: Intrusion, Exile and Diplomacy', in *Episcopal Power and Patronage in Medieval Europe, 998–1503*, ed. E. A. Gatti and A. M. Silvestri (forthcoming).

McGuinness, S., 'The Medieval Bishops of Bangor and the Writing of Welsh History', in *Memory and Nation: Writing the History of Wales*, ed. R. Thomas, S. Jarrett, and K. Olson (forthcoming).

Miller, E., *The Abbey and Bishopric of Ely; the social history of an ecclesiastical estate from the tenth century to the early fourteenth century* (Cambridge, 1951).

Milman, H. H., *Annals of S. Paul's Cathedral*, 2nd edn (London, 1869).

Monastic Wales website, http://www.monasticwales.org, accessed 20 June 2024.

Moorman, J. R. H., *Church Life in England in the Thirteenth Century* (Cambridge, 1946).

Morant, P., *The History and Antiquities of the County of Essex* (London, 1768).

Morgan, P., 'Cheshire and Wales', in *Power and Identity in the Middle Ages, Essays in Memory of Rees Davies*, ed. H. Pryce and J. Watts (Oxford, 2007), pp. 195–210.

Morgan, R., 'The Territorial Divisions of Medieval Montgomeryshire [II]', *Montgomeryshire Collections*, 70 (1982), 11–39.

Morris, J. E., *The Welsh Wars of Edward I* (Oxford, 1901).

New, E, A., *Seals and Sealing Practices* (London, 2010).

Nicholson, H., *Medieval Warfare, Theory and Practice of War in Europe 300–1500* (Basingstoke, 2004).

Owen, D. M., 'Hervey (*d.* 1131)', *ODNB*.

Owen, M. E., 'Royal Propaganda; Stories from the Law-Texts', in *The Welsh King and His Court*, ed. T. M. Charles-Edwards, M. E. Owen, and P. Russell (Cardiff, 2000), pp. 224–54.

Oxford Dictionary of the Christian Church – The Oxford Dictionary of the Christian Church, ed. F. L. Cross and E. A. Livingstone, 3rd edn (Oxford, 2005).

Palmer, C. F. R., 'The Friar-Preachers, or Blackfriars of Bangor', *The Reliquary*, 24 (April 1884), 225–30.

Patterson, R. B., 'William, second earl of Gloucester (*d.* 1183)', *ODNB*.

Paxton, J., 'Textual Communities in the English Fenlands: A Lay Audience for Monastic Chronicles?', *Proceedings of the Battle Conference, Anglo-Norman Studies 26*, ed. J. Gillingham (2003), 123–38.

Pearson, M. J., 'The Creation and Development of the St. Asaph Cathedral Chapter', *Cambrian Medieval Celtic Studies*, 40 (2000), 35–56.

Pearson, M. J., 'The Creation of the Bangor Cathedral Chapter', *WHR*, 20 (2000–1), 167–81.

Pennington, K., *Pope and Bishops: The Papal Monarchy in the Twelfth and Thirteenth Centuries* (Philadelphia, 1984).

Perry, G. G., *The Life of St. Hugh of Avalon, Bishop of Lincoln* (London, 1879).

Phillips, T. and Hulbert, C., *The History and Antiquities of Shrewsbury, from its First Foundation to the Present Time*, 2 vols (Shrewsbury, 1837).

Powel, D., *The Historie of Cambria, now called Wales: A part of the most famous yland of Brytaine, written in the Brytish language aboue two hundreth yeares past: translated into English by H. Lhoyd Gentleman: corrected, augmented, and continued out of records and best approved authors* (London, 1584).

Powicke, M., *The Thirteenth Century, 1216–1307*, 2nd edn (Oxford, 1962).

Prestwich, M., *Edward I* (London, 1997).

Prestwich, M., 'Kirby, John (*d.* 1290)', *ODNB*.

Pryce, H., 'Anian [Einion] (*d.* 1305x7)', *ODNB*.

Pryce, H., 'Esgobaeth Bangor yn Oes y Tywysogion', in *Ysbryd Dealltwrus ac Enaid Anfarwol: Ysgrifau ar Hanes Crefydd yng Ngwynedd*, ed. W. P. Griffith (Bangor, 1999), pp. 37–57.

Pryce, H., 'Gruffudd ap Cynan (1054/5–1137)', *ODNB*.

Pryce, H., *Native Law and the Church in Medieval Wales* (Oxford, 1993).

Pryce, H., 'Negotiating Anglo-Welsh Relations: Llywelyn the Great and Henry III', in *England and Europe in the Reign of Henry III (1216–1272)*, ed. I. W. Rowlands and B. K. U. Weiler (London, 2002), pp. 13–29.

Pryce, H., 'Owain Gwynedd (*d.* 1170)', *ODNB*.

Pryce, H., 'The Church of Trefeglwys and the End of the "Celtic" Charter Tradition in Twelfth-Century Wales', *Cambridge Medieval Celtic Studies*, 25 (Summer 1993), 15–54.

Pryce, H., 'The Dynasty of Deheubarth and the Church of St Davids', in *St David of Wales, Cult, Church and Nation*, ed. J. W. Evans and J. M. Wooding (Woodbridge, 2007), pp. 305–16.

Pryce, H., 'The Household Priest (Offeiriad Teulu)', in *The Welsh King and His Court*, ed. T. Charles-Edwards, M. E. Owen, and P. Russell (Cardiff, 2000), pp. 82–93.

Pryce, H., *Writing Welsh History: from the Early Middle Ages to the Twenty-First Century* (Oxford, 2022).

Raban, S., 'Edward I's Other Inquiries', in M. Prestwich, R. Britnell, and R. Frame (eds), *Thirteenth Century England IX: Proceedings of the Durham Conference* (2001), pp. 43–58.

Radford, C. A. R., 'Bangor Cathedral in the Twelfth and Thirteenth Century: Recent Discoveries', *Arch. Camb.*, C, part 2 (1949), 256–61.

Ray, M., 'Three Alien Royal Stewards in Thirteenth-Century England: The Careers and Legacy of Mathias Bezill, Imbert Pugeys and Peter de Champvent', in M. Prestwich, R. Britnell, and R. Frame (eds), *Thirteenth Century England X: Proceedings of the Durham Conference* (2003), pp. 51–68.

Rees, W., *A History of the Order of St. John of Jerusalem in Wales, and on the Welsh Border: including an Account of the Templars* (Cardiff, 1947).

Registrum Sacrum Anglicanum – Registrum Sacrum Anglicanum, an Attempt to Exhibit the Course of Episcopal Succession in England, ed. W. Stubbs (Oxford, 1897).

Rhys, J., *Lectures on Welsh Philology* (London, 1877).

Richter, M., *Giraldus Cambrensis: The Growth of the Welsh Nation*, 2nd edn (Aberystwyth, 1976).

Ridgeway, H. W., 'Henry III (1207–1272)', *ODNB*.

Ridyard, S. J. and Ashbee, J. A., 'The Resuscitation of Roger of Conwy: a Cantilupe Miracle and the Society of Edwardian North Wales', in *Power, Identity and Miracles on a Medieval Frontier*, ed. C. A. M. Clarke (2019), pp. 61–76.

Ross, C., *Canons of Salisbury: A Record of the Dignitaries, Prebendaries and Office Holders and their Place in the Quire of Salisbury Cathedral* (Salisbury, 2000).

Round, J. H., 'Garnier de Nablous, Prior of the Hospital in England, and Grand Master of the Order of St. John of Jerusalem', *Archaeologia or Miscellaneous Tracts Relating to Antiquity, 1770–1992*, 58 (January 1903), 383–90.

Russell, P., 'Scribal (In)competence in Thirteenth-Century North Wales: The Orthography of the Black Book of Chirk (Peniarth MS 29)', *NLWJ*, 29 (1995), 129–76.

Russell Smith, T., 'Further Manuscripts of Matthew Paris' Flores Historiarum and Continuations', *Notes and Queries*, 67/1 (2020), 6–7.

Saltman, A., *Theobald, Archbishop of Canterbury* (London, 1956).

Sayles, G. O., *Functions of the Medieval Parliament of England* (London, 1987).

Seintiau website, https://saints.wales, accessed 19 May 2024.

Serjeantson, R. M. and Adkins, W. R. D. (eds), 'Hospitals: St David & the Holy Trinity, Kingsthorpe', in *A History of the County of Northampton*, ii, VCH (London, 1906), pp. 154–6.

Sharpe, R., *A Handlist of the Latin Writers of Great Britain and Ireland before 1540, with additions and corrections*, Publications of the Journal of Medieval Latin, I (Turnhout, 2001).

Sims-Williams, P., 'Beuno [St Beuno] (*d*. 653/9)', *ODNB*.

Sims-Williams, P., 'Edward VI's Confirmation Charter for Clynnog Fawr', in *Recognitions: Essays Presented to Edmund Fryde*, ed. C. Richmond and I. Harvey (Aberystwyth, 1996), pp. 229–41.

Smith, B., 'Fitzgerald, Maurice (*c*.1194–1257)', *ODNB*.

Smith, D. M., 'The Episcopate of Richard, Bishop of St. Asaph: A Problem of Twelfth-Century Chronology', *Journal of the Historical Society of the Church in Wales*, 29 (1974), 9–12.

Smith, D. M., 'The "Officialis" of the Bishop in Twelfth and Thirteenth-Century England: Problems in Terminology', in *Medieval Ecclesiastical Studies in Honour of Dorothy M. Owen*, ed. M. J. Franklin and C. Harper-Bill (Woodbridge, 1995), pp. 201–20.

Smith, G. R., 'The 1284 Extent of Anglesey Revisited: Some Facts and Figures', *Studia Celtica*, 45 (2011), 83–103.

Smith, J. B., 'The "Cronica de Wallia" and the Dynasty of *Dinefwr*', *BBCS*, 20 (1962–4), 261–82.

Smith, J. B., 'Crown and Community in the Principality of North Wales in the Reign of Henry Tudor', *WHR*, 3 (1966), 145–72.

Smith, J. B., 'Dafydd ap Llywelyn (*c*.1215–1246)', *ODNB*.

Smith, J. B., 'Gruffudd Llwyd, Sir [Gruffudd ap Rhys] (*d*. 1335)', *ODNB*.

Smith, J. B., 'Llywelyn ap Gruffudd (*d*. 1282)', *ODNB*.

Smith, J. B., *Llywelyn ap Gruffudd, Prince of Wales* (Cardiff, 2014).

Smith, J. B., 'Magna Carta and the Charters of the Welsh Princes', *EHR*, 99 (1984), 344–62.

Smith, J. B., 'Welsh Dominicans and the Crisis of 1277', *BBCS*, 22 (1966–8), 353–7.

Smith, L. B., 'The *Gravamina* of the Community of Gwynedd against Llywelyn ap Gruffudd', *BBCS*, 31 (1984), 158–76.

Smith, L. T. (ed.), *The Itinerary of John Leland in or about the years 1535–1543*, Parts IX, X and XI (London, 1910).

Stephenson, D., 'In Search of a Welsh Chronicler: The *Annales Cambriae* B-text for 1204–30', *Cambrian Medieval Celtic Studies*, 72 (2016), 73–85.

Stephenson, D., 'Madog ap Maredudd, *Rex Powissenium*', *WHR*, 24 (2008), 1–28.

Stephenson, D., *Medieval Powys. Kingdom, Principality and Lordships, 1132–1293* (Woodbridge, 2016).

Stephenson, D., *Medieval Wales c.1050–1332, Centuries of Ambiguity* (Cardiff, 2019).

Stephenson, D., 'St David's arm at Leominster', *Arch. Camb.*, 169 (2020), 209–12.

Stephenson, D., *The Governance of Gwynedd* (Cardiff, 1984).

Stöber, K. and Austin, D., 'Culdees to Canons: the Augustinian Houses of North Wales', in *Monastic Wales: New Approaches*, ed. J. Burton and K. Stöber (Cardiff, 2013), pp. 39–54.

Suppe, F., 'John (*d.* 1190)', *ODNB*.

Suppe, F. C., 'Roger of Powys: Henry II's Anglo-Welsh Middleman, and His Lineage', *WHR*, 21 (2002–3), 1–23.

Survey of English Place-Names, https://epns.nottingham.ac.uk, accessed 12 June 2024.

Swanson, R. N., *Indulgences in Late Medieval England. Passports to Paradise?* (Cambridge, 2007).

Talbot, C. H., 'Cadogan of Bangor', *Cîteaux in de Nederlanden*, 9 (1958), 18–40.

Thacker, A. T., 'The Earls and Their Earldom', in *The Earldom of Chester and its Charters, A Tribute to Geoffrey Barraclough*, ed. A. T. Thacker, *Journal of the Chester Archaeological Society*, 71 (Chester, 1991), 7–21.

Thurlby, M., *Romanesque Architecture and Sculpture in Wales* (Little Logaston, 2006).

Tonkin, J., 'After the Dissolution', in *A Definitive History of Dore Abbey*, ed. R. Shoesmith and R. Richardson (Little Logaston, 1997), pp. 153–4.

Tout, T. F., revd A. D. Carr, 'Gruffudd ap Gwenwynwyn (*d.* 1286)', *ODNB*.

Vale, M., 'St John, Sir John de (*d.* 1302)', *ODNB*.

Vaughan, R., *Matthew Paris* (Cambridge, 1958).

Vincent, N., 'Edmund of Almain, second earl of Cornwall (1249–1300)', *ODNB*.

Vincent, N., 'Jocelin of Wells: The Making of a Bishop in the Reign of King John', in *Jocelin of Wells, Bishop, Builder, Courtier*, ed. R. Dunning, Studies in the History of Medieval Religion, 36 (Woodbridge, 2010), pp. 9–33.

Vincent, N., 'Lacy, John de, third earl of Lincoln (*c.*1192–1240)', *ODNB*.

Vincent, N., *Peter des Roches: An Alien in English Politics, 1205–1238* (Cambridge, 2002).

Vincent, N., 'Richard, first earl of Cornwall and king of Germany (1209–1272)', *ODNB*.

Vincent, N., 'Some Pardoners' Tales: The Earliest English Indulgences', *TRHS*, 6th series, 12 (2002), 23–58.

Walker, D., 'Cadwgan (*d.* 1241)', *ODNB*.

Walker, R. F., 'Marshal, William, fifth earl of Pembroke (*c.*1190–1231)', *ODNB*.

Watkins, M. G., 'Antiquarian Discoveries at Abbey Dore', *Transactions of the Wool-hope Naturalists' Field Club* (1890–2), 146–7.

Webber, T., 'The Scribes and Handwriting of the Original Charters', in *The Earl-dom of Chester and its Charters: a tribute to Geoffrey Barraclough*, ed. A. T. Thacker, *Journal of the Chester Archaeological Society*, 71 (Chester, 1991), 137–51.

Whitaker, T. D., *A History of the Original Parish of Whalley, and Honor of Clitheroe, in the Counties of Lancaster and York, to which is subjoined an Account of the Parish of Cartmell*, 3rd edn (London, 1818).

White, G., 'Ranulf (II), fourth earl of Chester (*d.* 1153)', *ODNB*.

Whitehead, D., 'St Ethelbert's Hospital, Hereford', in *Hereford Cathedral, A History*, ed. G. Aylmer and J. Tiller (London, 2000), pp. 599–609.

Williams, D. H., 'The Abbey of Dore', in *A Definitive History of Dore Abbey*, ed. R. Shoesmith and R. Richardson (Little Logaston, 1997), pp. 15–36.

Williams, G. A., 'The Succession to Gwynedd, 1238–47', *BBCS*, 20 (1964), 393–413.

Willis, B., *A Survey of the Cathedral Church of Bangor and the Edifices belonging to it* (London, 1721).

Maps

Davies, R. R., *The Age of Conquest, Wales 1063–1415* (Oxford, 2000), p. 198, Map 4.

Rees, W., *An Historical Atlas of Wales from Early to Modern Times*, 2nd edn (London, 1972), Plate 33.

OTHER ABBREVIATIONS

Arch. Camb.	*Archaeologia Cambrensis.*
BBCS	*Bulletin of the Board of Celtic Studies/Bwletin y Bwrdd Gwybodau Celtaidd.*
BCSHLS	Board of Celtic Studies, History and Law Series.
BL	British Library, London.
cons.	consecrated.
CUL	Cambridge University Library.
DMLBS	*Dictionary of Medieval Latin from British Sources*, ed. R. E. Latham et al., 17 fascicules (Oxford, 1975–2013). Available online: http://clt.brepolis.net/dmlbs, and (in part) via https://logeion.uchicago.edu, accessed 20 June 2024.
ed.	edited by.
edn	edition.
eds	editors.
EHR	*The English Historical Review.*
fo(s)	folio(s).
Geiriadur Prifysgol Cymru	*Geiriadur Prifysgol Cymru*. Available online: http://geiriadur. ac.uk/gpc/gpc.html, accessed 12 June 2024.
m.	membrane.
MED	Middle English Dictionary, University of Michigan. Available online: https://quod.lib.umich.edu/m/middle-english-dictionary/dictionary, accessed 20 May 2024.
MS(S)	Manuscript(s).
n.s.	new series.
NLW	National Library of Wales/Llyfrgell Genedlaethol Cymru, Aberystwyth.
NLWJ	*National Library of Wales Journal/Cylchgrawn Llyfrgell Genedlaethol Cymru.*
ODNB	*Oxford Dictionary of National Biography*. Available online: https://www.oxforddnb.com, accessed 24 June 2024.
pd	printed.
PRS	Pipe Roll Society
RCAHMW	Royal Commission on the Ancient and Historical Monuments of Wales/ Comisiwn Brenhinol Henebion Cymru
repr.	reprinted.
revd	revised.

s. -ex.	late-century (see Editorial Method).
s. -in.	early-century (see Editorial Method).
s. -med.	middle-century (see Editorial Method).
TNA	The National Archives, London.
trans.	translated by.
TRHS	*Transactions of the Royal Historical Society.*
VCH	*The Victoria History of the Counties of England.*
WHR	*The Welsh History Review/Cylchgrawn Hanes Cymru.*
YBC	*Y Bywgraffiadur Cymreig/Dictionary of Welsh Biography*. Available online: https://biography.wales, accessed 4 February 2024.

MAP OF THE MEDIEVAL DIOCESE OF BANGOR

The areas shaded in green represent the approximate boundaries of the diocese of Bangor from 1141 to the end of the thirteenth century. See the section of the Introduction entitled 'Gwynedd Uwch Conwy, Arwystli and Dyffryn Clwyd' below. Map based upon the RCAHMW Cantref and Commote boundary dataset and licensed under the Open Government non-commercial License 2.0.

INTRODUCTION:

THE DIOCESE OF BANGOR

GWYNEDD UWCH CONWY, ARWYSTLI AND DYFFRYN CLWYD

Medieval Gwynedd was divided into Gwynedd Uwch Conwy, those districts to the west of the river Conwy, including the mountain ranges of Eryri, and Gwynedd Is Conwy, also known as Perfeddwlad (literally 'Middle Country'), or the Four Cantrefs, being those districts to the east of the river Conwy, between that river and the river Dee near Chester.

According to Domesday Book, 1086, lands of the bishopric, presumably Bangor, were excluded from the lands in north Wales held by Robert of Rhuddlan from the king.[1] As Matthew Pearson has pointed out, this illustrates that a bishopric with its own estates pre-dated the intrusion of the first Norman nominee into the see in 1092.[2] R. R. Davies said it was the revival (in 1141) of the old bishopric centred on the *clas* church of St Kentigern as the new territorial diocese of Llanelwy/ St Asaph which resulted in the see of Bangor, now confined to Gwynedd Uwch Conwy, being compensated with two major enclaves within the new bishopric, namely Arwystli and Dyffryn Clwyd.[3]

Thus from 1141 the medieval diocese of Bangor consisted of Gwynedd Uwch Conwy, comprising the cantrefs of Arllechwedd, Arfon, Llŷn, Ardudwy,[4] and Meirionnydd,[5] the commote of Eifionydd, and the island of Anglesey.[6] There were, in addition, two detached portions of the diocese, which were rural deaneries, firstly the cantref of Arwystli (in Powys), and secondly the cantref of Dyffryn Clwyd (in Gwynedd Is Conwy) to which was added the adjoining commote of Ceinmeirch.[7]

---

[1]   Robert is said to have held the whole of north Wales for £40 per annum: *Domesday, Cheshire*, p. 269b. Lloyd, *History of Wales*, ii, p. 387; Pearson, 'Bangor Cathedral Chapter', 170.

[2]   Pearson, 'Bangor Cathedral Chapter', 170, n. 20. That nominee was the Breton, Hervey.

[3]   Davies, *Age of Conquest*, p. 183. For the date of 1141: *Fasti Welsh Cathedrals*, p. 33; Smith, 'The Episcopate of Richard', 9–12.

[4]   Cf. *Actum* **75** and note to the same for the status of Ardudwy and Dunoding.

[5]   Minus the commote of Mawddwy, which along with the adjoining commote of Cyfeiliog, formed a deanery in the diocese of St Asaph: *Valuation of Norwich*, p. 471; Stephenson, *Medieval Powys*, p. 236, n. 99, and p. 256.

[6]   Anglesey was made up of three cantrefs, namely Aberffraw, Cemais and Rhosyr: Carr, *Medieval Anglesey*, 2nd edn, p. 272, and Map 1. The Welsh territorial term *cantref* (pl. *cantrefi*) has, for the sake of consistency in this volume, been treated as an English noun and rendered as cantref (pl. cantrefs) – this follows *AWR*, p. xvii.

[7]   That the rural deanery of Dyffryn Clwyd included the adjoining commote of Ceinmeirch was confirmed in the *Valuation of Norwich*, p. 194; see also Lloyd, *History of Wales*,

The 'Valuation of Norwich', of 1254, confirmed the status of Arwystli as a rural deanery of Bangor.[8] The first dean was recorded at the end of the twelfth century/beginning of the thirteenth century.[9] According to Domesday, the Norman Robert of Rhuddlan, he who held north Wales from the king, claimed Arwystli; it was also recorded that the Welsh themselves considered Arwystli to be part of north Wales.[10] This could be because the ruler of Arwystli, Trahaearn ap Caradog, had taken over the kingship of Gwynedd after the death of Bleddyn ap Cynfyn in 1075.[11] When Trahaearn was killed in 1081 his lands may have come under the rule of Gruffudd ap Cynan, king of Gwynedd (d. 1137), before he was imprisoned by the Normans.[12] This connection with Gwynedd may explain why Arwystli was considered part of the diocese of Bangor,[13] and was subsequently carved out of the bishopric of Llanelwy/St Asaph when it was revived in 1141.

The 'Valuation of Norwich' also confirmed the status of the cantref of Dyffryn Clwyd as a rural deanery of Bangor,[14] and in 1243, Bishop Richard of Bangor witnessed a grant there (at Llannerch where he had an estate).[15] The inclusion of Dyffryn Clwyd in the diocese may just be the compensation Rees Davies assumed it was, but there was also a connection with the ruling house of Gwynedd Uwch Conwy. Gruffudd ap Cynan had married Angharad, the daughter of Owain ab Edwin of Dyffryn Clwyd, and in 1125 their eldest son, Cadwallon, annexed the cantref; which, after his death in 1132, was to be constantly in the sights of his uterine brother, Owain ('Owain Gwynedd').[16] Indeed, he in c.1140 married the daughter of one of Angharad's brothers, Cristin or Christina ferch Gronw ab Owain ab Edwin.[17]

It was clearly thought that the time was right in 1141 to resurrect a bishopric in Gwynedd Is Conwy, indeed such a project had been considered as recently as 1125. A proposal had been put forward in the autumn of that year that Canterbury, in return for York's recognition of its primacy, should cede to the northern archbishop the bishoprics of Chester, Bangor and a third in the midst of the two (clearly Llanelwy/St Asaph) vacant of a bishop 'owing to the desolation of the

---

i, p. 241, and Smith, *Llywelyn*, p. 43, n. 23. Arwystli is described as a cantref by A. D. Carr, 'A Debatable Land', 39 and by R. R. Davies in *Age of Conquest*, p. 183. Dyffryn Clwyd is described as a cantref in *AWR*, pp. 21 and 840, and Davies, *Age of Conquest*, p. 183.

[8]   *Valuation of Norwich*, p. 191.

[9]   *AWR*, p. 753, no. 548; *Ystrad Marchell Charters*, p. 49. See also *Actum* **15** and note to the same.

[10]   *Domesday, Cheshire*, p. 269b; Carr, 'A Debatable Land', 39 and 44.

[11]   *AWR*, p. 2. See also Bartrum, *Early Welsh Genealogical Tracts*, p. 104, and Morgan, 'Territorial Divisions [II]', 28–32.

[12]   See discussion in Carr, 'A Debatable Land', 39 and 44. Trahaearn's son Llywarch was to prove to be an ally of Gwynedd: *ibid.*, 44. Gruffudd's imprisonment: *Vita Griffini*, pp. 70–3 and p. 149.

[13]   *AWR*, p. 2; Carr, 'A Debatable Land', 44; Pryce, 'Church of Trefeglwys', 17, and n. 7.

[14]   *Valuation of Norwich*, p. 194. As noted above, the adjoining commote of Ceinmeirch was included in the rural deanery: *ibid.*; Lloyd, *History of Wales*, i, p. 241; Smith, *Llywelyn*, p. 43, n. 23.

[15]   *AWR*, p. 491, no. 318. Estate: *RC*, pp. 113–15; Smith, *Llywelyn*, p. 43, and n. 23.

[16]   *Brut, Pen20Tr*, pp. 49–50; *Brut, Hergest*, pp. 108–11 and 112–13; Lloyd, *History of Wales*, ii, p. 467.

[17]   Pryce, 'Owain Gwynedd (d. 1170)', *ODNB*.

country and the rudeness of the inhabitants'.[18] Whilst the proposal came to nothing, the idea that the diocese might be resurrected was relatively fresh in the mind in 1141, and Canterbury may have seen an opportunity. As Michael Richter has noted, the consecration by the archbishop of Canterbury, Theobald of Bec, of the new bishop of Llanelwy the year (1141) after he had consecrated Meurig as bishop of Bangor, and Uhtred as bishop of Llandaff (1140), was an important step in establishing the subjection of the Welsh sees.[19]

David Stephenson points out that the creation of the new territorial diocese (of Llanelwy/St Asaph) was in the context of the political and military alliance of Ranulf (II) earl of Chester (d. 1153) and Madog ap Maredudd of Powys (d. 1160) and argues that because Madog's brother-in-law Cadwaladr ap Gruffudd (Owain Gwynedd's younger brother) was a party to that alliance, the interests of the see of Bangor, and indeed those of Owain Gwynedd, may have been taken into account.[20] There was, however, another member of this alliance who has gone largely unnoticed and that is the bishop of Bangor, Meurig, whom it appears Ranulf described as 'his' bishop.[21] Meurig, having been consecrated in 1140 by Theobald, may have been perfectly placed to influence the decision that Arwystli and Dyffryn Clwyd should remain part of his diocese of Bangor. Indeed, he seems to have found shelter for a time in the early 1140s with the earl of Chester and is known to have spent periods in exile with Theobald.[22]

A map of the medieval diocese of Bangor is provided at the start of this volume.[23]

---

[18] 'pro uastitate et barbarie episcopo uacantem': *Hugh the Chanter*, pp. 206–7. See also Barlow, *The English Church*, pp. 39 and 44; *EEA, V, York, 1070–1154*, p. xx; Stephenson, *Medieval Powys*, pp. 252–3, and n. 21; Brooke, *The Church and the Welsh Border*, p. 12.

[19] Richter, *Giraldus*, p. 47. The bishop consecrated by Theobald to the see of Llanelwy was Richard: *De Invectionibus*, pp. 139–41; *Gervase of Canterbury*, ii, p. 385; *Fasti Welsh Cathedrals*, p. 33; Pearson, 'The Creation and Development of the St. Asaph Cathedral Chapter', 36–9. Davies, 'Cathedrals and the Cult of Saints', pp. 109–10; Smith, 'The Episcopate of Richard', 9–12. Cf. Haddan and Stubbs, i, pp. 347–8.

[20] Stephenson, *Medieval Powys*, pp. 46–7, and ns. 49, 50 and 51, and p. 253, and ns. 22 and 23; Stephenson, 'Madog ap Maredudd, *Rex Powissenium*', 11–12; Carr, 'A Debatable Land', 44. Stephenson wonders if the earls of Chester had previously attempted to sustain a bishopric west of the river Dee; but the appointment of Daniel ap Sulien as archdeacon of Powys, probably *c*.1116 by Bishop Bernard of St Davids, he says, 'suggests a lacuna in ecclesiastical organisation that Bernard attempted to fill'. Stephenson, *Medieval Powys*, p. 252, and n. 20. J. E. Lloyd thought it probable that the re-establishment of Llanelwy as a bishopric was a pre-emptive move directed against the see of Bangor, which would necessarily increase in size following any military conquests of Owain Gwynedd in the Four Cantrefs: Lloyd, *History of Wales*, ii, p. 485. He dismissed another idea that the scheme was part of St Davids' metropolitan campaign and was designed to add a third Welsh suffragan bishop to the two existing ones in Bangor and Llandaff: *ibid*.

[21] 'episcopo suo Bangoriensi': in a notification of the earl's (*Charters of the Anglo-Norman Earls of Chester*, pp. 71–2, no. 59); the date of which may well have been 27 October 1140 (see Davis, 'Geoffrey Barraclough and the Lure of Charters', 33, and the section of this Introduction entitled 'Meurig'), so the year before the creation of the new territorial diocese of Llanelwy/St Asaph.

[22] See the section entitled 'Meurig' below and McGuinness, 'The Medieval Bishops of Bangor, 1092–1283: Intrusion, Exile and Diplomacy' (forthcoming), for the bishop's involvement with Ranulf, Cadwaladr, and Theobald.

[23] See p. xxxvi. Maps showing interpretations of the boundaries of the medieval diocese of Bangor have also been produced by William Rees in *An Historical Atlas of Wales*, at Plate

CREUDDYN/GOGARTH/LLANDUDNO

The commote of Creuddyn (to the north-east of Arllechwedd and across the river Conwy) may have become part of the diocese of Bangor towards the end of the thirteenth century.[24] The manor of '*Gogerch*'/'*Gogerth*' (Gogarth) was recorded as belonging to the bishop of Bangor both in 1291 and 1306.[25] On the latter occasion lands *de donis domini regis* ('by gifts of the lord king') were also recorded.[26] It is also noteworthy that the commote was included in the new county of Caernarfonshire when it was created in 1284.[27] Gruffudd ab Iorwerth, bishop of Bangor (1307–1309) wrote to King Edward II from *Cogerth* in 1309,[28] and Bishop Matthew de Englefeld (1328–1357) wrote to the Exchequer, in 1345, from *Gogerth*.[29]

CLAS AND *FAMILIA*

Following his consecration in 1092, Hervey, the first Norman nominee to be imposed on the Welsh, most probably encountered an ancient *clas* church on arrival in Bangor.[30] *Clas* is derived from the Latin word *classis*, meaning a group of people.[31] In an ecclesiastical context, it denoted a community associated with a church.[32] Gerald of Wales recorded that at St Davids, prior to Bishop Bernard's institution of a cathedral chapter in the early twelfth century, the clerics were called *glaswir* (i.e. *claswyr*).[33] The reference to '*clas Bangor*' in the treatise *Breintiau Arfon* ('Privileges of Arfon') extant in two mid-thirteenth century manuscripts of the Welsh laws confirms that there was, or had been, a *clas* at Bangor.[34]

   According to certain sources, the *clas* enjoyed rights in the church in conjunction with the leader of the community, often termed the 'abbot'.[35] In an arbitration

---

33, and by R. R. Davies in *Age of Conquest*, p. 198, Map 4. A description of the diocese is given in the *Guide to Bishops' Registers*, p. 25.

[24] A fourteenth-century patent roll entry (1376) recorded the church of Llandudno as being in the diocese of Bangor: *CPR, 1374–1377*, p. 369. According to *Taxatio Ecclesiastica*, p. 294, Llandudno was in the deanery of Arllechwedd, however, the transcription printed on p. 294 was taken from an additional text sewn on to the end of the relevant manuscript; the additional text has been described by the *Taxatio* Database as 'a later undated assessment' (i.e. later than 1291): *Taxatio* Database: https://www.dhi.ac.uk/taxatio/forms?context=diocese_bangor, accessed 9 August 2024. I am very grateful to both Professor Huw Pryce and Scott Lloyd for discussing Creuddyn with me, and to Scott for the patent roll reference in this footnote.

[25] *Taxatio Ecclesiastica*, p. 292; *RC*, p. 109; Carr, *Medieval Anglesey*, 2nd edn, p. 68.

[26] *RC*, p. 109.

[27] Davies, *Age of Conquest*, p. 363, and Map 9.

[28] *CAC*, p. 178.

[29] *ibid.*, pp. 221–2.

[30] Pearson, 'Bangor Cathedral Chapter', 168.

[31] Pryce, *Native Law*, p. 187.

[32] *ibid.*

[33] *Opera*, iii, p. 153; Pryce, *Native Law*, p. 187.

[34] 'Ac o byd a amheuo un o'r breynnyeu hynny clas Bangor a rey Beuno a'e keidv.'/'And if there be anyone who doubts these privileges the clas of Bangor and the people of Beuno shall preserve them.': Owen, 'Royal Propaganda', pp. 253–4. See 'Introduction of a Chapter' below.

[35] Pryce, *Native Law*, p. 187.

award, made at Aberdaron in 1252, to which the then bishop of Bangor, Richard, appended his seal, the *clastrefi* (townships pertaining to the *clas* of the church of Aberdaron, i.e. the portioners) were exempted from certain procurations.[36] Elsewhere, portions known as *claswriaethau* were held by the abbot and *claswyr*.[37] Furthermore, J. E. Lloyd pointed out that, according to certain Welsh law codes, the *clas* received half of all the payments made to the church,[38] and this may be reflected in the equal division of four vills between Bishop Anian of Bangor and the successors of the *claswyr*, the canons of his chapter (half of each vill to the bishop, half to the canons), recorded in the 1291 *Taxatio Ecclesiastica*,[39] as well as the fourteenth-century source which recorded that 'from time beyond memory' the dean and chapter of Bangor had a moiety of the rents belonging to the bishopric of Bangor in times of voidance.[40]

Pope Alexander III, in a letter of 1165 to the clergy of Bangor, stated that he had heard that the archdeaconry of Bangor descended by hereditary right from father to son, without the authority or consent of the archbishop of Canterbury. As such, he annulled the practice.[41] The suggestion seems to have been that the then archdeacon of Bangor, David, was the son of the previous archdeacon, Simeon of Clynnog (d. 1152).[42] In fact, Archbishop Thomas Becket commanded Archdeacon David to appear before him 'with his son'.[43] In other words it seems likely that the archbishop had been informed that David was lining up his own son to succeed him as archdeacon.

At the end of the twelfth century, Gerald of Wales was to comment on the 'pollution of God's sanctuary' due to the custom in the Welsh Church that when fathers died, their sons succeeded to their benefices, not by election, but as if by hereditary right.[44] The letters of Alexander III and Thomas Becket show how entrenched the *familia* was at Bangor in the mid-twelfth century. The *familia* has been described as 'a group of clerics, perhaps in the main related to each other and derived from the *claswyr*, forming an executive body'.[45] It is clear that certain bishops had close family members who were engaged on episcopal business, suggesting that they were members of the *familia*, and very likely indicating that the

---

[36] *AWR*, pp. 634–8, no. 440.

[37] Pryce, *Native Law*, p. 187.

[38] Lloyd, *History of Wales*, i, p. 205, and n. 47.

[39] *Taxatio Ecclesiastica*, p. 290.

[40] *CIM*, ii, p. 259, no. 1044, except rents arising from the city of Bangor, *ibid*

[41] 10 December 1165: Haddan and Stubbs, i, pp. 367–8; *Thomas Becket Materials*, v, pp. 225–6; *Episc. Acts Welsh Dioceses*, ii, p. 422.

[42] For Simeon, see the sections entitled 'David the Scot' and 'Meurig' below. For Archdeacon David, see 'Vacancy and Arthur de Chargan'.

[43] Together with three or four of the older and more prominent dignitaries of the church of Bangor. Letter addressed to the archdeacon and canons of Bangor, written mid- to late 1166: *Becket Correspondence*, i, pp. 553–5, no. 114; *Episc. Acts Welsh Dioceses*, ii, pp. 424–5.

[44] 'polluentes sanctuarium Dei': *Opera*, vi, p. 214; *Journey and Description*, p. 263. Furthermore, if a bishop dared to appoint and induct anyone else, the people would avenge this insult both on him and on the man he chose: *Journey and Description*, p. 263; *Opera*, vi, p. 214. In 1222, in the neighbouring diocese of St Asaph, Master Johannes Walensis complained to the pope about hereditary succession to benefices there: *Cal. Pap. Reg.*, i, p. 85; Pryce, *Native Law*, p. 76, and n. 19.

[45] Pearson, 'Bangor Cathedral Chapter', 172.

bishops themselves had been promoted to the bishopric from the *familia*. Meurig had three brothers, all of whom acted as witnesses.[46] As one of the most reform minded of all the bishops of Bangor it is noteworthy that he had no son (or at least none that is recorded). Gwion had three brothers and a son all of whom acted as witnesses.[47] Even as late as the middle of the thirteenth century, it is clear that Richard, a former archdeacon of Bangor, had a son. *Ph(ilippo) filio episcopi* was the second-named witness, after his father, to a grant by Llywelyn ap Gruffudd.[48] Philip's name appeared before lay men of standing, including men in the service of the prince. The fact that, like Gwion, Richard had sired a son was clearly no obstacle to high ecclesiastical office.[49] Moreover, the fact that Philip was explicitly described as the son of the bishop demonstrates that the same was not viewed as in any way detrimental. In fact, such a designation may have added to the gravitas of the witness, and therefore have been seen as beneficial. Not much seems to have changed since the time of the late eleventh-century bishops of Llandaff and St Davids, Herewald and Sulien, both of whom were married.[50] Meurig's brothers, as well as Gwion's brothers and son, also appeared as senior witnesses, and were also described by their familial relationship to the relevant bishop.[51]

It seems likely that the cathedral's clerical elite, whether *familia* or chapter, was, on occasion, divided. During Meurig's episcopate, the *familia* may have been split between those who supported Owain Gwynedd and Archdeacon Simeon, and those who supported the bishop (and possibly Cadwaladr ap Gruffudd ap Cynan). Meurig's own brothers may, themselves, have been divided in their loyalties.[52] Furthermore, in the late thirteenth century, Anian's description (**70**) of his adversaries as certain incestuous adulterers of his own chapter (*adversarios quosdam adulteros incestuosos de capitulo nostro*) could indicate that the clerical elite was split in the months leading up to the second Welsh war of 1282–1283.[53]

[46] *AWR*, pp. 145–7, nos. 2 and 3, and pp. 329–31, no. 197.

[47] *Acta* **8**, **9** and **10**; *AWR*, pp. 331–3, nos. 198 and 199.

[48] *AWR*, p. 491, no. 318.

[49] In England, according to Christopher Brooke, a large majority of the upper clergy known to have had children between 1050 and 1200, had had their families, at the latest, by about 1130. By the middle of the twelfth century there was a noticeable decline: Brooke, 'Gregorian Reform in Action: Clerical Marriage', 15. In the second half of the twelfth century, Pope Alexander III (1159–1181) laid down that while a wife lived, no married man might be promoted to the bishopric, unless his wife became a nun: *ibid.*, 4. If Gwion and Richard were married, and their wives were still living when they were consecrated, it is not known if they took the veil. Alexander had earlier decreed that the vow of chastity, which was necessary for the ordination of a married man, had to be taken by both parties: *ibid.* Of course, the son of Gwion and/or the son of Richard may have been illegitimate. Nigel, bishop of Ely (d. 1169) had at least two sons, including one who became bishop of London, and he, Richard fitz Nigel (fitz Neal), born *c*.1130, is thought to have been illegitimate: Hudson, 'Nigel (*c*.1100–1169)', *ODNB*.

[50] Davies, *Wales in the Early Middle Ages*, p. 157.

[51] *Acta* **8**, **9** and **10**; *AWR*, pp. 145–7, nos. 2 and 3, pp. 329–33, nos. 197, 198 and 199.

[52] See McGuinness, 'The Medieval Bishops of Bangor, 1092–1283: Intrusion, Exile and Diplomacy' (forthcoming).

[53] *Actum* **70**. See also McGuinness, 'Betrayal in the Belfry – The Bishop of Bangor and the demise of Llywelyn ap Gruffudd'.

INTRODUCTION OF A CHAPTER

By the time of Bishop Gwion's death, in 1191, it seems that a chapter was in place at Bangor, for according to Gerald of Wales (albeit writing in 1216) Rotoland, the sub-prior of Aberconwy, had been unanimously chosen as bishop (and, therefore, successor to Gwion) by the *toto capitulo* of Bangor.[54] As all the evidence until 1170 points to a *clas*-derived *familia* governing in Bangor, it seems probable that Gwion was responsible for introducing the cathedral chapter. Matthew Pearson points out that it is difficult to be absolutely certain and either of Gwion's successors, Alan or Robert, may have been the real reformer.[55] However, the fact that Gerald refers to a chapter, combined with the fact that Alexander Llywelyn ('*Cuelin, Walensis*') was archdeacon of Bangor during Gwion's episcopate, probably swings the weight of evidence in favour of Gwion – Alexander, who acted as interpreter for Archbishop Baldwin on his journey around Wales in 1188, had been Archbishop Thomas Becket's cross-bearer, friend and companion-in-exile.[56] He was a *magister*, an accomplished diplomat, had taken part in the Council of Northampton in 1164, and had undertaken many missions on behalf of Becket, including as envoy to the papal curia.[57] Gerald described him as a man witty and eloquent in speech (*vir sermone facetus et facundus*).[58] It is perhaps easy to see how such a character as Alexander, a cosmopolitan Welshman, could provide the impetus to transform Bangor's long-established, and deep-rooted, *familia* into a modern late twelfth-century chapter, or at least to begin that process. The other possibility is that the impetus for change came from Archbishop Baldwin when he visited Gwion in Bangor in April 1188.[59] Of course, it may have been the influence of both Alexander and Baldwin that led to change. Furthermore, it is worth noting that the Cistercian abbey of, what was to become known as, Aberconwy was founded on 24 July 1186.[60] As a reformed order in Latin Christendom the Cistercians, with their emphasis on uniformity of

---

[54] *De Invectionibus*, p. 95; *Autobiography*, p. 213; Pearson, 'Bangor Cathedral Chapter', 176.

[55] Pearson, 'Bangor Cathedral Chapter', 180.

[56] Interpreter: *Opera*, vi, pp. 55 and 126; *Journey and Description*, p. 114, and pp. 185–6. Biographical notes and references for Alexander are in Appendix I to *Becket Correspondence*, ii, pp. 1363–4. See also *Chronicles and Memorials of the Reign of Richard I*, ii, pp. 32–3; *Letters and Charters of Gilbert Foliot*, p. 283; and *Thomas Becket Materials*, iii, p. 528 (confirming Alexander as the later archdeacon of Bangor).

[57] *Becket Correspondence*, ii, pp. 1363–4; *Thomas Beckett Materials*, iii, pp. 359, 610 and 635. See also, *Opera*, vii, pp. 68–9; Pearson, 'Bangor Cathedral Chapter', 177. *The Letters and Charters of Gilbert Foliot*, pp. 283 and 287, suggest that it was perhaps Alexander who denounced Gilbert Foliot at the papal curia in Rome, and that he may have been the 'single Welshman' who Foliot mentioned to Cardinal William of Pavia, as having given evidence leading to Foliot's condemnation and excommunication.

[58] *Opera*, vii, pp. 68–9.

[59] *Opera*, vi, pp. 125 and 133; *Journey and Description*, pp. 35–6, and 185. See the section entitled 'Gwion'.

[60] *Brut, Pen20Tr*, p. 73; Hays, *Abbey of Aberconway*, p. 6; Lloyd, *History of Wales*, ii, p. 601; Pearson, 'Bangor Cathedral Chapter', 176. The original site was at Rhedenog-fel (Rhedynog Felen) south of Caernarfon, but the harsh conditions there necessitated relocation and by 1192 the monks had resettled near the mouth of the river Conwy: Monastic Wales website, accessed 20 June 2024.

practice, may have influenced nearby Bangor to finally conform with the structure and organisation of cathedrals widely accepted elsewhere.[61]

At this point the treatise *Breintiau Arfon* ('Privileges of Arfon') needs to be considered because, as already noted, it includes a reference to *clas Bangor*.[62] If we are to accept that a chapter was in existence by the end of the twelfth century, the reference to a *clas* at Bangor is problematic. Whilst the origins of *Breintiau Arfon* 'are traced to an alarmingly distant era of British history',[63] the redactor of the same was operating in the thirteenth century and probably in Gwynedd.[64] It may be that the chapter at Bangor was still, in the local vernacular, considered as a *clas*. In an ecclesiastical context, *clas* denoted a community associated with a church,[65] and the introduction of a chapter with its constituent canons did not change that. The term 'canons' could also lead to confusion. Initially anyway, as Huw Pryce has pointed out, the term probably referred to a church's hereditary community, and canons are evidenced in native churches, under abbots, at Llancarfan and Llanilltud Fawr in the late eleventh and twelfth centuries, and there were canons at Llanbadarn Fawr in 1216.[66]

DIOCESAN STRUCTURE, ADMINISTRATION AND PERSONNEL

It is not until the episcopate of Bishop Richard (1237–1267) that we have the first detailed evidence of how the diocese was structured, and who was responsible for its administration, partly due to the compilation in 1254 of the 'Valuation of Norwich'.[67] More details are provided during Anian's episcopate (1267–1305/6) thanks in part to the *Taxatio Ecclesiastica Angliae et Walliae* of 1291.[68]

---

[61] For the Cistercian desire for uniformity in observance, see Burton and Kerr, *The Cistercians in the Middle Ages*, pp. 30–1.

[62] Owen, 'Royal Propaganda', pp. 253–4.

[63] Smith, *Llywelyn*, p. 269.

[64] Date of MS: *ibid.*, and Huws, 'Llyfrau Cymraeg', 19. Paul Russell has suggested that the *A* manuscript (Black Book of Chirk, Peniarth MS 29) of *Breintiau Arfon* may have been produced at a law-school in north Wales, possibly Arfon: Russell, 'Scribal (In)competence', 171. Another point worth noting is that Patrick Sims-Williams expressed doubt as to whether the redactor considered that at this juncture there was a clas at Clynnog (i.e. Clynnog Fawr/ the church of St Beuno): see n. 37 above and Owen, 'Royal Propaganda', p. 239, and n. 92, and p. 245; Sims-Williams, 'Edward VI's Confirmation Charter', p. 229.

[65] Pryce, *Native Law*, p. 187.

[66] *ibid.*

[67] The diocese was valued at £160 4s. 7d.: *Valuation of Norwich*, pp. 118 and 196. The names of the assessors were given but only that of William (described as 'dec[…]' of the cathedral church of Bangor, presumably dean) is now distinguishable, the remaining assessors appear to have been canons of the church: *ibid.*, pp. 169 and 194.

[68] Or the 'Pope Nicholas IV Taxatio' which valued the diocese at £861 5s. 9.5d.: *Taxatio Ecclesiastica*, pp. 290–4. The bishops of Lincoln and Winchester, appointed to carry through the new papal tenths, deputed a Master Anian ('Anyanus') archdeacon and another unidentifiable master to carry out the assessment in the diocese of Bangor; and the form of a letter from the two masters to the bishops has survived: *Taxatio* Database: https://www. dhi.ac.uk/taxatio/forms?context=diocese_bangor, accessed 12 April 2024.

Bishop Richard had been archdeacon of Bangor when he was elected in 1236.[69] Master David (possibly 'Dafydd') was archdeacon of Bangor for part of Richard's episcopate.[70] An archdeaconry of Meirionnydd was recorded in 1254,[71] as was an archdeaconry of Anglesey,[72] the archdeacon himself being referred to in 1261 in an *actum* of Richard's (**52**).[73] In the late twelfth century two of the witnesses to a confirmation of Bishop Alan, 1195 x 1196, were archdeacons of unnamed archdeaconries (**14**), and it has been suggested that one may have been the archdeacon of Anglesey, and the other, the archdeacon of Meirionnydd.[74] There was no archdeaconry of Llŷn by the time of the 'Valuation of Norwich' in 1254, although there had been in the late twelfth century, as Cynddelw was named as the archdeacon of Llŷn in Bishop Alan's said confirmation (**14**).[75] No other archdeacon of Llŷn appears in the historical record, and by the early thirteenth century it appears that the ecclesiastical status of Llŷn had been demoted to that of a rural deanery.[76]

Richard's twelfth-century predecessors as archdeacon of Bangor were Simeon of Clynnog (d. 1152),[77] David (possibly 'Dafydd') *fl.* 1165–1169,[78] Master Alexander Llywelyn *fl.* 1188,[79] and Iorwerth ('Gervase') 1195 x 1196 (**14**).[80] The names of the early thirteenth-century archdeacons of Bangor, before Richard are not recorded.

[69]   *CPR, 1232–1247*, p. 152. We can perhaps assume that by this time the archdeaconry did not descend by hereditary right from father to son as Pope Alexander III had alleged in 1165 (see '*Clas* and *Familia*' and 'Vacancy and Arthur de Chargan').

[70]   He first appears in 1247/8 as a canon of Bangor as a witness to an *actum* of Richard's (**45**); and then as archdeacon in 1257 (*CPR, 1247–1258*, p. 573). See also *Actum* **52**, and notes to the same; *CPR, 1258–1266*, p. 83; *AWR*, pp. 529–33, no. 358, and pp. 792–4, no. 601; and *Fasti Welsh Cathedrals*, p. 6.

[71]   *Valuation of Norwich*, p. 196.

[72]   *Valuation of Norwich*, pp. 195–6.

[73]   *Actum* **52**. This may have been Anian, Richard's successor, who was archdeacon of Anglesey when he was elected to the bishopric six years later: *CPR, 1266–1272*, p. 173.

[74]   'Abraham <filio> Griffini archidiacono … Philippo filio episcopi archidiacono': *Actum* **14**; Pryce, 'Esgobaeth Bangor', p. 47; Pearson, 'Bangor Cathedral Chapter', 175. Also, *Fasti Welsh Cathedrals*, p. 8.

[75]   'Candelano archidiacono de Lein': *Actum* **14**. Cynddelw was also a witness to another charter 1195 x 1199, 'Candelau archidiacono': *AWR*, pp. 340–1, no. 208.

[76]   *AWR*, p. 341; Pearson, 'Bangor Cathedral Chapter', 174–5. See also, *Fasti Welsh Cathedrals*, p. 7. The slate matrix '… Ennii Decani De Lein' (of Ennius, the dean of Llŷn) is extant in the National Museum of Wales (Dic. 18) and has been dated by D. H. Williams to the early thirteenth century: *Welsh Ecclesiastical Seals*, 188, and *Welsh History through Seals*, p. 7. Furthermore, there is in the British Library an impression from the 'stone matrix of the seal of Ennius, rural dean of Lain or Lleyn, diocese of Bangor', this time dated to the twelfth century: BL Seal CXXXV.63.

[77]   See the sections entitled 'David the Scot' and 'Meurig' below; also see *Fasti Welsh Cathedrals*, p. 5. Browne Willis, in 1721, thought that Simeon had been preceded by a Maurice *c.*1132, who was to become Bishop Meurig (Willis, *Survey*, pp. 61 and 131), but J. E. Lloyd convincingly explained why he thought Willis was mistaken: Lloyd, *History of Wales*, ii, p. 483, n. 93.

[78]   See the sections entitled '*Clas* and *Familia*' and 'Vacancy and Arthur de Chargan'; also see *Fasti Welsh Cathedrals*, p. 5.

[79]   See the sections entitled 'Introduction of a Chapter' and 'Gwion'; also see *Fasti Welsh Cathedrals*, pp. 5–6.

[80]   *Actum* **14**.

The first dean of the church of Bangor named in contemporary records was Master Guy (possibly 'Gwion' in Welsh) who in 1236 was given royal letters directed to the canons of Bangor of licence to elect their next bishop – they elected Richard.[81] The dean of Bangor in 1254 was William.[82] Addaf was named as the dean of Ardudwy in 1263.[83] As noted above, both Arwystli and Dyffryn Clwyd were shown to be rural deaneries of the bishopric in 1254;[84] the first dean of Arwystli to be recorded was Iorwerth ('Gervase') at the end of the twelfth century/beginning of the thirteenth century;[85] probably Iorwerth ap Hywel (**15**).[86] The other rural deaneries were Arllechwedd and Llŷn on the mainland, and Cantref, Dindaethwy and Twrcelyn on Anglesey.[87] A rural dean for Arfon was not recorded until 1291,[88] although the 'Valuation of Norwich' manuscript does have a portion missing and it has been suggested that this recorded the deanery of Arfon.[89]

The first person to be named in the historical record as a 'canon of Bangor' was Master Matthew who was a witness, 1215 x 1235/6, to one of Bishop Cadwgan's *acta* (**25**).[90] In 1247/8, two canons, namely Master David (possibly the future archdeacon) and a Madog, witnessed an *actum* of Richard's (**45**).[91] In 1254, the 'Valuation of Norwich' referred to canons of the cathedral church of Bangor,[92] and a Master Iorwerth ('Gervase') was named as a canon of Bangor in the patent roll for 1267.[93]

---

[81]   *CPR, 1232–1247*, pp. 149 and 152. Arthur de Bardsey may have been dean in 1162. Browne Willis writing in 1712 stated that according to John Le Neve (in his *Fasti Ecclesiae Anglicanae* of 1716) Jago ab Eli or Heli was the first dean of the church of Bangor in 603, but that the names of all deans after him, until 1286, were lost. In compiling a list of deans Willis stated that he had, for the most part, followed Le Neve, 'making some improvements and additions as I go along, as finding mention made of 1. Arthur de Bardsey's presiding here as Dean, Anno 1162 …': Willis, *Survey*, pp. 120–1. Unfortunately, he does not cite his source, although elsewhere Willis refers to the 'Book of Bangor', which would now appear to be lost: Willis, *Survey*, p. 60.

[82]   *Valuation of Norwich*, pp. 169 and 194.

[83]   *AWR*, pp. 529–33, no. 358, and pp. 792–4, no. 601.

[84]   Arwystli comprised the commotes of Arwystli Is Coed and Arwystli Uwch Coed (Lloyd, *History of Wales*, i, p. 249; Stephenson, *Medieval Powys*, pp. 199 and 224). Dyffryn Clwyd comprised the commotes of Colion, Dogfeiling, and Llannerch, to which was added the adjoining commote of Ceinmeirch (*Valuation of Norwich*, p. 194; Lloyd, *History of Wales*, i, p. 241; *AWR*, p. 639; Smith, *Llywelyn*, p. 43, n. 23, and p. 225).

[85]   'Gervasio decano de Arwistili', 1197 x 1208 or 1210 x 1216 (*AWR*, p. 753, no. 548); *Ystrad Marchell Charters*, p. 49. See also note to Actum **15**.

[86]   'Ioreuerth decanus filius Howel', 16 April 1195 x 19 May 1196: *Actum* **15**.

[87]   Cantref comprised the commotes of Menai, Malltraeth, and Llifon; Dindaethwy and Twrcelyn included Talybolion, the north-western commote of the island (Carr, *Medieval Anglesey*, p. 266, and n. 2). Arllechwedd comprised the commotes of Arllechwedd Isaf, Arllechwedd Uchaf, and Nanconwy (Lloyd, *History of Wales*, i, pp. 235–6; *AWR*, p. 494; Smith, *Llywelyn*, pp. 233–4) and Llŷn comprised the commotes of Cafflogion, Cymydmaen and Dinllaen (Lloyd, *History of Wales*, i, pp. 236–7; *AWR*, pp. 613 and 633).

[88]   *Taxatio Ecclesiastica*, p. 290.

[89]   *Valuation of Norwich*, pp. 193–4.

[90]   'Magistro Matheo Canonico de Bang'': *Actum* **25**. See *Fasti Welsh Cathedrals*, pp. 8–11 for others who may have been canons of Bangor without being so called.

[91]   'canonicis nostris': *Actum* **45**.

[92]   *Valuation of Norwich*, p. 194.

[93]   *CPR, 1266–1272*, p. 165.

More evidence of the structure of diocesan administration is extant from the years of Anian's episcopate. The *Taxatio Ecclesiastica* of 1291 recorded not only the offices of dean of Bangor, dean of Arfon, and those of the archdeacons of Bangor, Anglesey and Meirionnydd,[94] it also named the canons of the cathedral church: Gregory, Madog Fychan ('*Parvus*'), Master David, Master Cadwgan, *Dominus* Elias ('Elie'), and *Dominus* Gruffudd ('Griffin').[95]

According to the *Taxatio Ecclesiastica* of 1291, the diocese consisted of:[96]

    (a)the Archdeaconry of Bangor:

which comprised the deaneries of Arfon,[97] Arllechwedd,[98] and Llŷn.[99]

    (b)the Archdeaconry of Anglesey:

comprised of the deaneries of Cantref,[100] Dindaethwy,[101] and Talybolion.[102]

    (c)the Archdeaconry of Meirionnydd:

comprised of the deaneries of Ardudwy,[103] and Meirionnydd.[104]

    (d)the Deanery of Arwystli,[105] and

    (e)the Deanery of Dyffryn Clwyd.[106]

The archdeacon of Bangor in 1284 was identified by the initial K, and in 1287 as Master K (see *Actum* **85**) possibly standing for 'K[yndelw]', i.e. Cynddelw.[107]

---

[94] *Taxatio Ecclesiastica*, p. 290; *Taxatio* Database: https://www.dhi.ac.uk/taxatio/search?form=deanery&deanery=BN.00.BC, accessed 14 May 2024.

[95] *Taxatio Ecclesiastica*, p. 290; *Taxatio* Database: https://www.dhi.ac.uk/taxatio/search?form=deanery&deanery=BN.00.BC, accessed 14 May 2024. Canon Gregory had, in 1284, acknowledged receipt of monies for losses in the war of 1282–1283 (*LW*, p. xxi and p. 66, no. 110; and see note to *Actum* **80**, and *Fasti Welsh Cathedrals*, pp. 9–10). Archbishop John Pecham had written to Bishop Anian regarding the purgation of one 'Madoc dictus Parvus' in 1284 (*Registrum Epistolarum Peckham*, iii, p. 781; see also Stephenson, *Governance*, pp. 36 and 225; Smith, *Llywelyn*, p. 554). Dominus Elias may be Elias whom Anian described as his chaplain in 1284 (**79**). Chaplain Elias is named a second time in 1284, this time in the company of the dean of Bangor (*LW*, p. 68, no. 119). Gruffudd may be 'Griffin Werwerth', see *Fasti Welsh Cathedrals*, p. 10.

[96] Taken from *Taxatio Ecclesiastica*, pp. 290–1, and *Taxatio* Database: https://www.dhi.ac.uk/taxatio/forms, accessed 14 May 2024. Churches that were 'minute benefices', that is those valued at 6 marks or less, were excluded from the *Taxatio* as untaxable. The 'Valuation of Norwich' had shown that, in 1254, there were a very large number of such minute benefices: *Taxatio* Database: https://www.dhi.ac.uk/taxatio/forms?context=diocese_bangor (referring to the *Valuation of Norwich*, pp. 190–6), accessed 14 May 2024.

[97] 'decanatus de Arvon': *Taxatio Ecclesiastica*, p. 291; *Taxatio* Database.

[98] 'decanatus de Arlechwed': *Taxatio Ecclesiastica*, p. 291; *Taxatio* Database.

[99] 'decanatus de Len': *Taxatio Ecclesiastica*, p. 291; *Taxatio* Database.

[100] 'decanatus de Cantrefs': *Taxatio Ecclesiastica*, p. 291; *Taxatio* Database.

[101] 'decanatus Wyndaethwy': *Taxatio Ecclesiastica*, p. 290; *Taxatio* Database.

[102] 'decanatus de Talebolyon': *Taxatio Ecclesiastica*, pp. 290–1; *Taxatio* Database.

[103] 'decanatus de Ardudwy': *Taxatio Ecclesiastica*, p. 291; *Taxatio* Database.

[104] 'decanatus de Meryonyd': *Taxatio Ecclesiastica*, p. 291; *Taxatio* Database.

[105] 'decanatus de Arostly': *Taxatio Ecclesiastica*, p. 291; *Taxatio* Database.

[106] 'decanatus de Dryffyn Cloyt': *Taxatio Ecclesiastica*, p. 291; *Taxatio* Database.

[107] *LW*, p. 82, no. 153. 1287: *Registrum Epistolarum Peckham*, iii, pp. 940–1, and see note to *Actum* **85**.

Master Anian ('Anyanus') may have been archdeacon of Bangor in 1291,[108] if so, he may have been the same Master Anian who held a portion of the church of Clynnog Fawr.[109] The archdeacon of Anglesey, occurring in 1283, 1284 (**79** and **81**), 1287 (**85**), 1297, 1301 and 1305, was Madog ap Cynwrig.[110] The archdeacon of Meirionnydd had a messuage in the vill of Bangor, presumably a residence where he could stay when he was on church business at the cathedral (the archdeacon of St Asaph also had a messuage in Bangor).[111]

The dean of Bangor, for part, at least, of Anian's episcopate was another Cynddelw, who (as *Candelau decanus Bangorensis*) confirmed grants in favour of Haughmond Abbey,[112] and was referred to as Master K, dean of Bangor, in a letter written by the archbishop of Canterbury, John Pecham.[113] Browne Willis stated that a William was dean of Bangor in 1291, connecting him to the *Taxatio Ecclesiastica* of that year.[114] Una Rees (relying on '*Le Neve*, i, 110') also stated that 'Wm. had become dean of Bangor' in 1291.[115] However, the dean of Bangor was not named in the *Taxatio* of 1291.[116]

David, or Dafydd, was the dean of Arllechwedd (*David decanus de Arllecweth*) in 1278 and 1284.[117]

Meirionnydd had two rural deans; one named Gruffudd ('Gryffyn'), and another or second (*alterius*) rural dean.[118]

---

[108] *Taxatio* Database: https://www.dhi.ac.uk/taxatio/forms?context=diocese_bangor, accessed 14 May 2024.

[109] 'portio magistri Anyany Luffy in ecclesia de Kelynnauvaur': *Taxatio Ecclesiastica*, p. 291.

[110] See Stephenson, *Governance*, p. 237; *Fasti Welsh Cathedrals*, p. 7; the section of this Introduction entitled 'Anian', as well as *Acta* **79**, **81** and **85** and notes to the same. 1283: Smith, *Llywelyn*, p. 554 and n. 154. 1284: *Acta* **79** and **81** and *CVCR*, p. 284. 1287: *Actum* **85** and *Registrum Epistolarum Peckham*, iii, pp. 940–1. 1297: *CVCR*, p. 35. 1301: *CPR, 1343–1345*, p. 228. 1305: *RC*, p. 206.

[111] *RC*, p. 92; and see the section entitled 'Extent of 1306/7 – Manors, Lands and Tenants of the Bishop of Bangor' below.

[112] Confirmation by the dean and the chapter of Bangor: Shrewsbury, Shropshire Archives, MS 6001/6869 (Haughmond Cartulary), fo. 151. *Cartulary of Haughmond Abbey*, p. 162, no. 799. As Robert Burnell, bishop of Bath and Wells, witnessed their confirmation, the *terminus a quo* is the date of his consecration as bishop, namely 7 April 1275, and the *terminus ante quem* the date of his death, 25 October 1292: *Fasti Bath and Wells*, p. 6; Harding, 'Burnell, Robert (d. 1292)', *ODNB*.

[113] February 1287. 'K[yndelw] decano Bangorensi': *Registrum Epistolarum Peckham*, iii, pp. 940–1.

[114] Willis, *Survey*, p. 121.

[115] *Cartulary of Haughmond Abbey*, p. 162, no. 799.

[116] A point also noted by *Fasti Welsh Cathedrals*, p. 5 and n. 11. The confusion may have arisen because there was a reference to William, 'dec[...]' of the church of Bangor, in the *Valuation of Norwich*, p. 194.

[117] July 1278: *AWR*, pp. 796–8, no. 603. 3 November 1284: *LW*, p. 82, no. 153.

[118] 'Beneficium Gryffyny decani'. The second dean was named as a portioner in the church of Tywyn – 'beneficium alterius decani in ecclesia de Tewyn': *Taxatio Ecclesiastica*, p. 291; *Taxatio* Database: https://www.dhi.ac.uk/taxatio/benkey?benkey=BN.ME.ME.02, accessed 14 May 2024.

EPISCOPAL AND ARCHIDIACONAL HOUSEHOLDS

During Richard's episcopate, members of the episcopal household were listed for the first time.[119] Before this, in the twelfth and early thirteenth centuries, the make-up of episcopal households is perhaps best gleaned from the witness lists to individual *acta*.[120] In 1259, Bishop Richard's household is said to have comprised Master David, the archdeacon of Bangor, Guy (possibly 'Gwion' in Welsh) the chaplain, David the clerk, Adam Hen, David Foel ('*Woel*'), Adam the chaplain, and Iorwerth ('Gervase') of Llanfair.[121] The archdeacon of Bangor, Master David (possibly 'Dafydd'), was recorded the following year with his own household.[122] During Anian's episcopate, Edward I made a grant to the bishops of Bangor and their household (*familiares*),[123] and his episcopate provides further evidence that bishops of Bangor had chaplains of their own,[124] for in 1284 Anian appointed Elias his chaplain to act on his behalf (**79**).[125]

In England, *magistri* had become steadily more numerous by the end of the twelfth century.[126] Bishop Robert of Shrewsbury (1197–1212) was a master, and David the Scot (1120–*c*.1139) had been a master at the cathedral school of Würzburg.[127] The earliest masters to appear in the historical record amongst the diocesan personnel of Bangor, including episcopal households, were Master Alexander Llywelyn, archdeacon of Bangor (*fl.* 1188),[128] and in the early thirteenth century Master Matthew, a canon of Bangor who was a witness, 1215 x 1235/6, to one of Bishop Cadwgan's *acta* (**25**), and Master Guy, dean of Bangor, in 1236,[129] but *magistri* only occur regularly in the surviving documentary sources from the beginning

---

[119]   October 1259 at Westminster: *CPR, 1258–1266*, p. 57. J. Barrow listed the handful of members of the *familia* of Bishop Anselm of St Davids (1231–1247) noting that the number was tiny in comparison to even a medium-ranking episcopal household in England: *St Davids Episcopal Acta*, p. 27, referring at n. 150 to *EEA, VI, Norwich, 1070–1214*, pp. xliii–xlix; and *EEA, VII, Hereford, 1079–1234*, pp. l–lxii.

[120]   See for example *Acta* **8**, **9**, **10**, **14** and **25**. Cf. Brooke, 'English Episcopal Acta of the Twelfth and Thirteenth Centuries', p. 46.

[121]   *CPR, 1258–1266*, p. 57. Iorwerth may have been the same person as Master Iorwerth ('Gervase'), canon of Bangor, mentioned above and recorded in 1267 (*CPR, 1266–1272*, p. 165) and may have been the clerk and vice-chancellor to Llywelyn ap Gruffudd who accompanied Anian on a peace mission to Edward I in January 1277: *AWR*, pp. 586–7, no. 400. See also *ibid.*, p. 587; Stephenson, *Governance*, pp. 36–7, and 224; and *Fasti Welsh Cathedrals*, p. 9.

[122]   *CPR, 1258–1266*, p. 83. For Master David see *Acta* **45** and **52**, and notes to the same. See also *AWR*, pp. 529–33, no. 358, and pp. 792–4, no. 601; and *Fasti Welsh Cathedrals*, p. 6.

[123]   *CChR, 1257–1300*, p. 279; Willis, *Survey*, pp. 190–1; Haddan and Stubbs, i, pp. 580–1.

[124]   In England, bishop's chaplains were often two or three in number: Cheney, *English Bishops' Chanceries*, p. 9. It is clear that Anian's predecessor, Richard, had at least two chaplains: *CPR, 1258–1266*, p. 57.

[125]   *Actum* **79**. As noted above, 'Dominus' Elias was recorded as one of the canons of Bangor in 1291: *Taxatio Ecclesiastica*, p. 290.

[126]   Cheney, *English Bishops' Chanceries*, p. 11.

[127]   See sections entitled 'David the Scot' and 'Robert of Shrewsbury'.

[128]   *Thomas Becket Materials*, iii, p. 528; *Opera*, vi, pp. 55 and 126; *Journey and Description*, p. 114, and pp. 185–6; *Becket Correspondence*, ii, pp. 1363–4.

[129]   *CPR, 1232–1247*, p. 149.

of the episcopate of Bishop Richard (1237–1267) who was himself a master as well as being a former archdeacon as was his successor Anian.[130]

OFFICIALES, BAILIFFS AND SENESCHALS

At the end of the thirteenth century, Anian petitioned Edward I complaining, *inter alia*, that his *officiales* were being impeded (**89**).[131] The title of *officialis* is found in England as early as the middle of the twelfth century, and after the early years of the thirteenth century, *officiales* are found in every English diocese.[132] An official of Dyffryn Clwyd (by the name of David ap William) was recorded in 1263, and the benefice was recorded again in 1291.[133] The benefice of the official of Arwystli was recorded in 1291.[134] C. R. Cheney described *officiales* as administrators and lawyers, often presiding over the bishop's court as his deputy.[135] David Smith has noted that the officials of English bishops 'were regularly performing extensive administrative duties (such as holding enquiries, supervising elections of monastic heads, instituting clergy to benefices, and even inducting them) over and above judicial activities'.[136]

The episcopate of Richard provides the first evidence that the bishop had not only a court, but a court bailiff too (**52**).[137] During Anian's tenure, there is the first mention of a court steward,[138] and his episcopate also provides the first evidence that the bishop possessed a prison.[139]

---

[130] In the neighbouring diocese of St Asaph, a Master Johannes Walensis complained to the pope in 1222 about hereditary succession to benefices, and it may well be that he was connected with that diocese: *Cal. Pap. Reg.*, i, p. 85; Pryce, *Native Law*, p. 76, and n. 19. The archdeacon of St Asaph, David, who first occurred in 1231 is later recorded as being a master: see Stephenson, *Governance*, p. 223; *Fasti Welsh Cathedrals*, p. 38. At St Davids, J. Barrow noted that there was only one master under Bishop Peter de Leia (1176–1198) and one under Bishop Iorwerth (1215–1229): *St Davids Episcopal Acta*, p. 27. At Llandaff, archdeacons who were masters appear in the early thirteenth century: see *Fasti Welsh Cathedrals*, p. 19, see also precentors, chancellors and treasurers at Llandaff: *ibid.*, pp. 20–1.

[131] *Actum* **89**.

[132] Cheney, *English Bishops' Chanceries*, p. 20.

[133] *AWR*, pp. 529–33, no. 358, and pp. 792–4, no. 601. Was David the son of the William who was dean of the church of Bangor, mentioned in the 1254 'Valuation of Norwich' (*Valuation of Norwich*, p. 169 and p. 194)? 1291: *Taxatio Ecclesiastica*, p. 291, and *Taxatio* Database: https://www.dhi.ac.uk/taxatio/benkey?benkey=BN.ME.DC.01, accessed 3 November 2023.

[134] *Taxatio Ecclesiastica*, p. 291, and *Taxatio* Database: https://www.dhi.ac.uk/taxatio/benkey?benkey=BN.ME.AW.02, accessed 3 November 2023.

[135] Cheney, *English Bishops' Chanceries*, p. 20.

[136] Based on evidence from thirteenth-century episcopal registers: Smith, 'The "Officialis" of the Bishop', p. 204. In considering the functions of those termed 'officialis' in late twelfth- and thirteenth-century England, Smith has urged caution, highlighting terminological confusion: *ibid.*, pp. 219–20.

[137] *Actum* **52**. During Anian's episcopate, the bailiffs of the bishopric ('ballivorum episcopatus') were referred to in a grant made by Edward I: *CChR, 1257–1300*, p. 279; Willis, *Survey*, pp. 190–1; Haddan and Stubbs, i, pp. 580–1.

[138] 'Official of the bishop of Bangor, who was also steward of the bishop's court': *Court Rolls of the Lordship of Ruthin or Dyffryn-Clwydd*, p. 45. The year is not clear, but the entry appears on m. 6 of the court roll, m. 5 recording entries from 1299: *ibid.*

[139] A fourteenth-century source stated that Anian was quit of the escape of prisoners from his prison both before the Edwardian conquest of 1282–1283 and afterwards: *CIM*, ii, p.

Two of Anian's petitions of 1305 to Edward of Caernarfon concerned the bishop's *senescalli* (seneschals) and requested that they should not be impeded from holding pleas, of a certain amount, in the bishop's court (**97** and **100**).[140] The *senescallus* may have had the same role as the steward above-mentioned or may have had a different function.[141]

EXTENT OF 1306/7 – MANORS, LANDS AND TENANTS OF THE BISHOP OF BANGOR

An extent of the lands of the bishops of Bangor was undertaken in 1306/7.[142] It began with the bishops' manor of Treffos (in Dindaethwy, Anglesey) on 25 September 1306.[143] Bangor itself was investigated on 7 October.[144] The extent was completed at Llanwnnog in Arwystli on 5 January 1307.[145]

The *extenta ville de Bangor* begins with what appears to be the bishop's residence in the town and his demesne lands (amounting to seventeen bovates or sixty-eight acres).[146] The residence was described as a *mesuagium cum gardino et curtilagio*, valued at xx *d.* per annum.[147] Fifty-three other messuages were listed, and details of the tenants were recorded, together with their rents and services. The tenants included the archdeacon of Meirionnydd and the archdeacon of St Asaph, as well as *Dominus* Gruffudd ap Rhys (Sir Gruffudd Llwyd), one physician (who was also a *magister*), five other masters (Adam Goch, 'Eynon Ochloyt', Goronwy, and two Madogs – probably clerics), a priest (Madog), and two chaplains (Ithel and Iorwerth).[148] The bishop enjoyed tolls of the vill, and of the markets (*nundinarum*) held in Bangor,[149] as well as the pleas and profits from the court.[150] *Maenol* Bangor, as revealed by the extent, has been mapped by G. Jones.[151] Whilst there were some free tenants, most of the tenants of the twelve dependent hamlets of *maenol* Bangor

---

239, no. 962. For the possible location of the bishop's prison: Willis, *Survey*, p. 46.

[140] *Actum* **97** and *Actum* **100**.

[141] Cf. the secular 'distain' or 'dapifer': *AWR*, pp. 165–6, no. 22, for example.

[142] *RC*, pp. 92–116. For the dating of the extent see Stephenson, *Governance*, pp. 236–7, and Carr, *Medieval Anglesey*, 2nd edn, p. 213, and n. 16.

[143] *RC*, p. 93 and p. 100; Carr, 'Jones Pierce Revisited', p. 135; Carr, *Medieval Anglesey*, pp. 99, 132 and 269.

[144] *RC*, pp. 92–3.

[145] *RC*, p. 115. Carr, 'Jones Pierce Revisited', p. 135.

[146] Carr, 'Jones Pierce Revisited', p. 135; *RC*, pp. 92–3.

[147] *RC*, p. 92. Gwynedd Archaeological Trust have carried out an archaeological assessment and evaluation excavation of the former bishop's palace in Bangor. The trust's report incorporates the findings of an excavation in 1996: Gwynedd Archaeological Trust, *The Bishop's Palace, Bangor. Archaeological Assessment and Evaluation Excavation. December 2003. GAT Project No. G1785, report no. 514* (January 2004).

[148] *RC*, p. 92. 'Gruffudd Llwyd' (d. 1335) was the great-grandson of Llywelyn ab Iorwerth's seneschal, Ednyfed Fychan. He was knighted by 1301 and served terms as sheriff of each of the counties of Anglesey, Caernarfon, and Meirionnydd: Smith, 'Gruffudd Llwyd, Sir [Gruffudd ap Rhys] (d. 1335)', *ODNB*; Stephenson, *Medieval Wales*, pp. 138–9.

[149] *RC*, p. 92.

[150] 'placita et perquisitiones curie': *ibid*.

[151] Jones, 'Maenol Bangor', 56–60, and fig. 1 on 58. For an explanation of the territorial and administrative unit 'maenol', see *Law of Hywel Dda*, p. 363; *Geiriadur Prifysgol Cymru*, accessed 16 January 2024.

were unfree.[152] All the tenants owed rents, food renders or services or a combination of the same. For example, in return for their land, the tenants of the hamlet of Tyllfaen ('*Ityllnaen*') owed service to the church of Bangor and looked after the cathedral's books, presumably the books of service.[153]

Some examples from the rest of the diocese, taken from the 1306/7 extent, will suffice to illustrate the bishops' extensive landholdings. In Dindaethwy, Anglesey, there were free and bond settlements dependent on a central court – Treffos was a *maenol* like Bangor.[154] The bishop had *unum mesuagium cum domibus superstantibus*, although everything was ruinous and in need of repair.[155] The manor consisted of two carucates of land (one hundred and twenty acres),[156] and the bishop had a water mill, a ferry (*passagium aque*) and once again enjoyed the pleas and profits from his court.[157] Whilst the lands of the bishop on Anglesey were concentrated in Dindaethwy (particularly along the Menai), in Twrcelyn and in the north-west, the bishops held townships elsewhere, holding some forty townships on the island in total.[158] At Edern in Llŷn, the bishop had a *mesuagium … cum curtilagio*; here too there was a water mill, and the bishop enjoyed the pleas and profits from his court.[159] At the manor of Gogarth ('*Gogerth*') there was one *mesuagium cum curtilagio et gardino*, and the bishop had a windmill (*molendinum ad vent'*) but it was broken.[160] At the bishops' manor at Llanrhaeadr-yng-Nghinmeirch in Dyffryn Clwyd, there was one messuage *cum curtilagio et gardino*, and the bishop enjoyed the pleas and profits from his court.[161]

---

[152] Carr, 'Jones Pierce Revisited', p. 135.

[153] 'debent deservire ecclesie de Bangor' et ibidem custodire libros ecclesie': *ibid.*; *RC*, p. 94.

[154] Carr, *Medieval Anglesey*, p. 213, and n. 14.

[155] 'omnes ruinose sunt et indigent magna reparatione': *RC*, p. 100.

[156] *RC*, p. 100; Carr, 'Jones Pierce Revisited', p. 136.

[157] *RC*, p. 100.

[158] Carr, *Medieval Anglesey*, p. 213.

[159] *RC*, p. 97.

[160] *RC*, p. 109.

[161] *RC*, p. 112. 'Llanreadur/Llanreadir' – different spellings on the same folio: *ibid*. The church of 'Lanrayadyr' was listed in the 1254 *Valuation of Norwich* (p. 194) in the deanery of Dyffryn Clwyd.

THE BISHOPS OF BANGOR

HERVEY (1092–OCTOBER 1109)

Hervey, or Hervé, a Breton,[1] was consecrated as bishop of Bangor in 1092 by the archbishop of York, Thomas I, during the *sede vacante* at Canterbury, although no profession of his is recorded.[2] That a bishopric, with its own estates, pre-dated Hervey's appointment was confirmed in 1086.[3] The vacancy he filled may have been caused by the death, resignation, or removal of Revedun.[4] Hervey probably encountered an ancient *clas* church on arrival in Bangor.[5]

He was the first Norman nominee imposed on the Welsh, at a time of rapid Norman advances into Wales.[6] Whether or not his appointment was instigated by William Rufus, the king would presumably have approved it. Hervey may have been a royal chaplain, but he does not occur as such in any contemporary record.[7] Robert of Rhuddlan (who held Gwynedd from the king) and his cousin, Hugh d'Avranches, earl of Chester (d. 1101), may have been the men most instru-

---

[1] 'Hervei Britonis': *Orderic Vitalis*, vi, pp. 186–7; Lloyd, *History of Wales*, ii, p. 448. He is known to have been a kinsman of the notable Breton theologian and canon lawyer, Gilbert the Universal, the future bishop of London: *Liber Eliensis*, p. 339; *EEA, XV, London, 1076–1187*, p. li. He may have had the cognomen or surname 'Cruste': *Anglia Sacra*, i, p. 615, n. (m); Willis, *Survey*, p. 58; *Fasti Ecclesiae Anglicanae Hardy*, i, p. 95, n. 4.

[2] Consecration by Thomas I: *Hugh the Chanter*, pp. 12–13; *Canterbury Professions*, p. lxxxvii, n. 3; Haddan and Stubbs, i, p. 299. Sede vacante at Canterbury: Archbishop Lanfranc died in 1089. Archbishop Anselm was consecrated in 1093. The professions of two other bishops (Herbert Losinga, bishop of Thetford, later Norwich, and Ralph Luffa, bishop of Chichester) who were also consecrated by Thomas (probably in January 1091) are recorded in the records of Canterbury, but no profession of Hervey's is to be found. The professions of Losinga and Luffa were made to Canterbury, in the presence of Thomas: *Canterbury Professions*, p. lxxxvii, n. 3, and p. 33. See also *Fasti Chichester*, p. 1 and *Fasti Monastic Cathedrals*, p. 55.

[3] The lands of the bishopric (presumably Bangor) were excluded from the lands in north Wales held by Robert of Rhuddlan, for an annual rent of £40, from William I: *Domesday, Cheshire*, p. 269b; Lloyd, *History of Wales*, ii, p. 387; Pearson, 'Bangor Cathedral Chapter', 170. See the section above entitled 'Gwynedd Uwch Conwy, Dyffryn Clwyd and Arwystli'.

[4] According to Gerald of Wales, Revedun was said, in a letter supposedly preserved in the archives of St Davids, to have been consecrated to the see of Bangor by Bishop Sulien of St Davids (1072/3–1078 and 1080–1085): *De Invectionibus*, pp. 139–41.

[5] Pearson, 'Bangor Cathedral Chapter', 168. The 'Breintiau Arfon' refer to the 'clas of Bangor': Owen, 'Royal Propaganda', p. 254. See the section above entitled '*Clas* and *Familia*'.

[6] Davies, *Age of Conquest*, p. 179; Owen, 'Hervey (d. 1131)', *ODNB*.

[7] Owen, 'Hervey (d. 1131)', *ODNB*; Lloyd, *History of Wales*, ii, p. 448; Haddan and Stubbs, i, p. 299. The long list of royal chaplains appended to a charter of William Rufus of January 1091 does not include any 'Herveus': *Regesta Willelmi Conquestoris et Willelmi Rufi*, pp. 81–2. *Fasti Welsh Cathedrals*, p. 1; *EEA, XXXI, Ely, 1109–1197*, p. lxviii.

mental in Hervey's promotion. Hugh had recently built castles in north Wales, including one at Bangor.[8] Robert was Hugh's lieutenant, whom Orderic Vitalis described as 'commander of his forces and governor of the whole province'.[9] It is hard to imagine Hervey being appointed without their support.[10] The year after his consecration he was a witness to charters of the earl of Chester granting, *inter alia*, manors in his diocese to St Werburgh's Abbey, which Hugh was in the process of re-founding and endowing with extensive possessions.[11]

Hervey attended William Rufus' Christmas court of 1093, held at Gloucester.[12] However, he may have been expelled from Gwynedd as early as 1094, when the Welsh rose against the invader, although 1095, 1098, and 1101 have all been put forward as possible years.[13] The *Liber Eliensis* tells the story of how the Bangor populace had no reverence for their new bishop, and he had to employ a large force of men but his brother and most of his kin were killed or wounded, and so he fled to England, and the protection of the king.[14] In Pope Paschal II's opinion, Hervey had been promoted among barbarous people in a barbarous and stupid way (*inter barbaros barbarice et stolide promotus est*).[15] However, William of Malmesbury accused Hervey of having abandoned Bangor using the excuse that he did not get on with his Welsh neighbours, in the hope of making a richer living elsewhere.[16] The Benedictine monk and historian repeated the charge referring to Hervey's lack of livelihood when in Bangor.[17]

In *c.*1097, Hervey was gifted '*Estona*', probably the manor of Aston Somerville, on the present Gloucestershire/Worcestershire border,[18] which may explain his

---

[8]   After 1081: *Vita Griffini*, pp. 72–3; *History of Gruffudd ap Cynan*, p. 133; Lloyd, *History of Wales*, ii, p. 392; Lewis, 'Gruffudd ap Cynan', pp. 69–70.

[9]   'princeps militia eius et tocius prouincie gubernator': *Orderic Vitalis*, iv, pp. 138–9; Thacker, 'The Earls and Their Earldom', 9–10; Crouch, 'The Administration of the Norman Earldom', 75. It has also been suggested that he became the first constable of Chester: *ibid.*, 74.

[10]   Indeed J. C. Davies thought Earl Hugh certainly had a hand in Hervey's appointment: *Episc. Acts Welsh Dioceses*, i, p. 92.

[11]   *Monasticon*, ii, pp. 385–7; *CChR, 1257–1300*, p. 316; Lewis, 'Avranches, Hugh d', first earl of Chester (*d.* 1101)', *ODNB*.

[12]   *Regesta Willelmi Conquestoris et Willelmi Rufi*, p. 88, no. 338; and recorded in the foundation narrative of St Mary's Abbey, York: Karn, 'The Foundation Narrative', pp. 402–3. I am grateful to Dr Nicholas Karn for providing me with his new edition and translation.

[13]   *Episc. Acts Welsh Dioceses*, i, p. 95; *Brut, Pen20Tr*, p. 19; *Brut, Hergest*, pp. 34–5; *John of Worcester*, iii, pp. 72–3; *Vita Griffini*, pp. 76–7; Lloyd, *History of Wales*, ii, p. 403. 1095: Owen, 'Hervey (*d.* 1131)', *ODNB*. 1098: *AWR*, pp. 22 and 321. 1101: *EEA, XXXI, Ely, 1109–1197*, p. lxxi.

[14]   *Liber Eliensis*, p. 297.

[15]   *Eadmeri Historia Novorum*, p. 139; *St. Anselm Letters*, ii, no. 282. Lloyd, *History of Wales*, ii, p. 448.

[16]   *William of Malmesbury, Gesta Pontificum Anglorum*, i, p. 493.

[17]   *William of Malmesbury, Gesta Regum Anglorum*, i, p. 797.

[18]   Estona had previously been owned by another Breton, Hascoit or Harscuid Musard, who was to follow Hervey to Ely: *Liber Eliensis*, p. 245 and p. 336, n. 121; Lewis, 'Gruffudd ap Cynan', p. 74; Paxton, 'Textual Communities in the English Fenlands', 131; *EEA, XXXI, Ely, 1109–1197*, p. lxix; https://opendomesday.org/place/SP0438/aston-somerville/, accessed 9 February 2024.

appearances in that part of the country in the first decade of the twelfth century; 1100 (Gloucester), 1101 x 1102 (Monmouth), 1106 (Bath).[19] During his exile, Hervey attended at least one archiepiscopal council, at Michaelmas 1102.[20] It has been noted that 'this is the first clear case of a Welsh bishop attending an English church council since the Conquest'.[21] In time he became Henry I's confessor,[22] and it is his relationship with the new king which seems to have enabled him to broker a peace settlement between Henry and Gruffudd ap Cynan, the king of Gwynedd (d. 1137) – according to the twelfth-century *Vita Griffini Filii Conani* it was due to the intervention of the bishop of Bangor that peace was achieved.[23]

In 1105, he was with the king at Romsey, and in 1107, he was with the king once again at the Council of London.[24] Henry I was sufficiently interested in Hervey's fortunes that he suggested to the archbishop of Canterbury, Anselm, in 1106, that the exiled bishop be translated to Lisieux. The archbishop responded by pointing out the canonical difficulties with that suggestion, and the translation did not proceed.[25] Moves had already been made to seek an alternative bishopric for the exiled Hervey.[26] He was eventually translated to Ely, becoming its first bishop in 1109.[27] At the direction of the king, he had been made administrator of Ely Abbey, after the death of Abbot Richard (d. 1107), until Henry 'had more fully made up his mind what to do with regard to him'.[28] It is from this time that we have Hervey's only known episcopal *actum* (**1**), prior to him becoming bishop of Ely.[29] He died on 30 August 1131 and was buried the next day in the church of Ely.[30]

---

[19]   Gloucester: *John of Worcester*, iii, pp. 92–3; *EEA, VII, Hereford, 1079–1234*, p. 258; *EEA, XXXIII, Worcester, 1062–1185*, pp. 19–20. Monmouth: *Calendar of Documents Preserved in France*, i, pp. 408–9; *Episc. Acts Welsh Dioceses*, i, p. 96; Cowley, *Monastic Order*, p. 14. Bath: *EEA, X, Bath and Wells, 1061–1205*, p. 3; *Episc. Acts Welsh Dioceses*, i, p. 96; *Cartularies of St. Peter's Priory Bath*, pp. 53–4.

[20]   *Eadmer's History*, p. 149; *John of Worcester*, iii, pp. 102–3; *Councils and Synods*, i, part ii, p. 673.

[21]   *Councils and Synods*, i, part ii, p. 673, n. 2.

[22]   *Radulfi de Diceto*, ii, pp. 201–2, states '… rex Henricus … Herveium Bangorensem cpiзcopum … cui curam de salute sua commiserat …'. *Anglia Sacra*, i, p. 615; Willis, *Survey*, p. 59; Haddan and Stubbs, i, p. 299; Owen, 'Hervey (*d.* 1131)', *ODNB*.

[23]   Hervey is not named as the bishop of Bangor in the Latin text (*Vita Griffini*, pp. 84–5 and 163) but is in the Welsh text ('Esfyn' *History of Gruffudd ap Cynan*, pp. 150–1; *Life of Gruffudd ap Cynan*, pp. 48 and 124). See also Lewis, 'Gruffudd ap Cynan', pp. 73–4; Pryce, 'Gruffudd ap Cynan (1054/5–1137)', *ODNB*. For the date of composition of the *Vita Griffini Filii Conani* (possibly 1137 x 1148) see *Vita Griffini*, pp. 46–7.

[24]   *Regesta Henrici Primi*, pp. 40 and 68–9.

[25]   *Orderic Vitalis*, v, p. 322, n. 4; Haddan and Stubbs, i, pp. 304–5.

[26]   See Pope Paschal II's letter to Archbishop Anselm of 12 December 1102: *St. Anselm Letters*, ii, no. 282.

[27]   *Monasticon*, i, p. 482; *Fasti Welsh Cathedrals*, p. 1; *Winchcombe Annals*, p. 123; Karn, 'The Twelfth Century', p. 5.

[28]   *Liber Eliensis*, p. 297; *EEA, XXXI, Ely, 1109–1197*, p. lxxi; Owen, 'Hervey (*d.* 1131)', *ODNB*; *Heads of Religious Houses*, i, p. 45.

[29]   *Actum* **1**.

[30]   Obit: *Liber Eliensis*, p. 340; *John of Worcester*, iii, pp. 196–7. *Fasti Welsh Cathedrals*, p. 1. Burial: *Liber Eliensis*, p. 340.

Interestingly, the antiquarian Browne Willis stated that Bishop Urban of Llandaff took the church of Bangor into his care, and presided over it from '1109 (or 1107, as in the Book of Bangor) until the year 1119, when having successfully engaged the assistance of the king and pope, in rebuilding his cathedral of Llandaff, he yielded up' the diocese of Bangor to David the Scot.[31] The 'Book of Bangor' would now appear to be lost, but the year given, namely 1107, is the same year that Hervey was made administrator of Ely Abbey.[32] This therefore has a ring of truth about it.[33]

DAVID THE SCOT (4 APRIL 1120–*c*.1139)

The next bishop of Bangor was David the Scot, whose cognomen has led to scholarly debate about his nationality.[34] He was consecrated at Westminster by the archbishop of Canterbury, Ralph d'Escures, on Sunday 4 April 1120. The archbishop was assisted by, amongst others, Urban, bishop of Llandaff.[35] David professed his obedience to Canterbury (**2**) the same day.[36] The records suggest that Urban had been the first bishop of a Welsh see who had professed canonical obedience to an archbishop of Canterbury.[37] He did so in 1107.[38] Bernard, consecrated to St Davids, did the same in 1115.[39]

According to the Canterbury monk and historian Eadmer, the consecration was made with the consent of Henry I.[40] Eadmer described how a certain clerk, by the name of David, elected by the prince, clergy, and people of Wales to the bishopric of the church of Bangor, had come to the archbishop carrying a letter from the Welsh.[41] The monk recorded the text of the letter, which was from Gruffudd ap Cynan, and all the clergy and people of Wales, addressed to Archbishop Ralph. In it the Welsh leader requested the consecration of their

---

[31]   Willis, *Survey*, p. 60, and n. (b). *Fasti Ecclesiae Anglicanae Hardy*, i, p. 96, n. 10, stated that Urban 'is said to have administered to the see of Bangor from 1109 to 1119'.

[32]   *Liber Eliensis*, p. 297. *EEA, XXXI, Ely, 1109–1197*, p. lxxi; Owen, 'Hervey (*d.* 1131)', *ODNB*.

[33]   There is other evidence that bishops were operating in Gwynedd Uwch Conwy after Hervey became bishop of Ely in 1109 and before David the Scot's consecration as the new bishop of Bangor in 1120: *Brut, Hergest*, pp. 84–5 ('bishops and elders'); *Brut, Pen20Tr*, p. 40 ('prelates').

[34]   'Irensis' was used by Orderic Vitalis (*Orderic Vitalis*, v, pp. 198–9), and it does seem most likely that David was Irish (see discussions in Brett, 'David (*d.* 1137x9)', *ODNB*, and Lewis, 'Gruffudd ap Cynan', p. 75). J. C. Davies' first preference was that he was a Welshman, who had gone to Ireland to continue his training, and from there he had set out for Germany; Davies' second preference was that David was Irish (*Episc. Acts Welsh Dioceses*, ii, pp. 551–2, and n. 514). Another possibility is that he may have been of mixed Welsh-Irish parentage or upbringing, like Gruffudd ap Cynan himself (Lewis, 'Gruffudd ap Cynan', p. 75).

[35]   *John of Worcester*, iii, pp. 146–7. Willis, *Survey*, p. 60; Haddan and Stubbs, i, p. 314; *Fasti Welsh Cathedrals*, p. 2; Brett, 'David (*d.* 1137x9)', *ODNB*.

[36]   *Actum* **2**. *Eadmeri Historia Novorum*, p. 260.

[37]   Davies, *Age of Conquest*, p. 179.

[38]   *Fasti Welsh Cathedrals*, p. 13.

[39]   *Fasti Welsh Cathedrals*, p. 46.

[40]   *Eadmeri Historia Novorum*, p. 259.

[41]   *Eadmeri Historia Novorum*, p. 259. John of Worcester described David as a 'clericum venerandum' ('respected clerk'): *John of Worcester*, iii, pp. 146–7.

bishop-elect, as swiftly as possible. They had lacked a pastor for many years and the archbishop was reminded that it was his duty to aid their church, as it was the daughter of his church. The letter ended with the warning that if they did not have a bishop from the archbishop, they would seek one in Ireland, or in some other barbarous region.[42]

According to Eadmer, Archbishop Ralph kept David honourably for several days before his consecration, while he instructed him in some matters of divine learning.[43] However, the monk gave no hint as to the bishop-elect's esteemed past.[44] He did not mention that David was a former master at the cathedral school of Würzburg; nor, as J. C. Davies noted, that after attracting the attention of the German king, Henry V (d. 1125), by his worthy manner and the breadth of his knowledge, David was appointed chaplain to Henry V.[45] Further still, Eadmer failed to mention that such were David's credentials he was commanded to write an account of Henry V's Italian expedition of 1110/11, undertaken during the 'Investiture Controversy', when the German king went to Rome to coerce Paschal II and be crowned emperor.[46] David produced, as Henry V's literary apologist, a panegyric in three books as part of the publicity and propaganda campaign which the emperor was preparing against the papacy. The work was written in an easy style, to make a popular appeal to the lay reader.[47] So easy that it differed little from common speech.[48] Unfortunately all three books are now lost but they are mentioned and utilised by the chroniclers Ekkehard of Aura, Orderic Vitalis, and perhaps, most notably, William of Malmesbury.[49] Orderic Vitalis was impressed by David's stylish narrative.[50] However, William of Malmesbury stated that the story, told by *David Scottus Bancornensis episcopus*, was told 'with more prejudice in favour of the king than is proper for an historian', giving examples of this 'prejudice'.[51] However, William stepped back a little from his condemnation when he wrote 'rather than seem to condemn a good man out of hand, I think one should be lenient with him, on the ground he was writing panegyric, not history'.[52] Elsewhere, the chronicler told his readers that he had 'copied word for word from David's

---

[42]   *AWR*, pp. 321–2, no. 191. See also Brett, *The English Church Under Henry I*, p. 30.

[43]   *Eadmeri Historia Novorum*, p. 260. Brett, 'David (*d.* 1137x9)', *ODNB*.

[44]   Eadmer's failure to mention David's background, and his reason for doing so, have been discussed by Karl Leyser; Leyser, 'England and the Empire', 77–8.

[45]   *Ekkehardi Chronicon*, p. 243; *Annales Hirsaugensis*, i, p. 349. *Episc. Acts Welsh Dioceses*, ii, p. 550; *Fasti Welsh Cathedrals*, p. 1; Brett, 'David (*d.* 1137x9)', *ODNB*. Further information about David's time in Germany is to be found in Hausmann, 'Reichskanzlei und Hofkapelle unter Heinrich V und Konrad III', 83 and 310.

[46]   *Fasti Welsh Cathedrals*, p. 1; Lewis, 'Gruffudd ap Cynan', p. 75.

[47]   *Episc. Acts Welsh Dioceses*, ii, pp. 550–1. *Ekkehardi Chronicon*, p. 243.

[48]   Brett, 'David (*d.* 1137x9)', *ODNB*.

[49]   Ekkehard stated 'Hic itaque iussus a rege totam huius expeditionis seriem rerumque in illa gestarum stilo tam facili …'. Described as 'Igitur iuxta prescripti testimonium hystoriographi …' or 'Igitur iuxta iam dicti relationem hystoriographi …': *Ekkehardi Chronicon*, p. 243. *Orderic Vitalis*, i, p. 61, and v, pp. 198–9, n. 3. *William of Malmesbury, Gesta Regum Anglorum*, i, pp. 770–1.

[50]   'Irensis quidam scolasticus …': *Orderic Vitalis*, v, pp. 198–9.

[51]   *William of Malmesbury, Gesta Regum Anglorum*, i, pp. 764–5.

[52]   *ibid.*

book' the privileges and consecration rites which were agreed between Henry V and Paschal II, or as William has it, 'extracted from the pope'.[53]

David's first recorded act as bishop was, according to *The Book of Llan Dâv*, giving his assent to the translation of the relics of St Dyfrig (or St Dubricius) as well as the teeth of Elgar the Hermit from Ynys Enlli (Bardsey Island) to Bishop Urban's new cathedral at Llandaff. The first part of the translation took place on 7 May 1120, a mere month or so after David's consecration.[54] David returned to Westminster in January 1121 (where he witnessed a notification by Henry I), and was at Lambeth in the autumn (for the consecration of Gregory as bishop of Dublin).[55] In the spring of 1125, he was at Lambeth once again (for the consecration of Seffrid as bishop of Chichester), in May he was at Canterbury and Worcester (for the consecration and subsequent enthronement of Simon as bishop of Worcester), and in September of that year he attended Giovanni da Crema's legatine council.[56] In 1127, he and the bishops of the two other Welsh sees, Bernard of St Davids and Urban of Llandaff, were all present at Westminster for the council summoned by William de Corbeil, archbishop of Canterbury and papal legate.[57] R. R. Davies said that nothing proclaimed the supremacy of Canterbury over the Welsh bishoprics more effectively than their attendance.[58] After the council, however, nothing is heard of David for the next ten years. His absence from Henry of Huntingdon's list of those present at the legatine council of 1129 has prompted the remark that, in comparison with the bishops of Llandaff and St Davids, the bishop of Bangor was rarely in England.[59] Towards the end of his episcopate, David was involved in another translation of a Welsh saint's relics, for it was with his support that the relics of St Gwenfrewi (Winifred) were translated from Gwytherin to Shrewsbury Abbey.[60]

In 1137, David was at the deathbed of Gruffudd ap Cynan.[61] According to the *Vita Griffini Filii Conani*, famous and wise men from the whole of Gruffudd's realm came to his deathbed – the first man to be named was *David episcopus Bangor*.[62]

[53]   *William of Malmesbury, Gesta Regum Anglorum*, i, pp. 764–5 and 770–1.

[54]   *Book of Llan Dâv*, p. 5., and pp. 84–5; Haddan and Stubbs, i, p. 315; Reuben Davies, 'Cathedrals and the Cult of Saints', 106; Crouch, 'Urban: first Bishop of Llandaff', 12.

[55]   Hereford Cathedral Archive 1820; *Hereford Cathedral Charters and Records*, p. 4; *Regesta Henrici Primi*, p. 153, no. 1243. *Eadmeri Historia Novorum*, p. 298; *John of Worcester*, iii, pp. 150–1; *Registrum Sacrum Anglicanum*, p. 43.

[56]   *John of Worcester*, iii, pp. 158–9 and 160–1; Barlow, *The English Church*, p. 143; Barlow, 'Corbeil, William de (d. 1136)', *ODNB*.

[57]   Hervey, formerly bishop of Bangor, now bishop of Ely, was also present: *John of Worcester*, iii, pp. 168–9; *Councils and Synods*, i, part ii, p. 745; Barlow, 'Corbeil, William de (d. 1136)', *ODNB*.

[58]   Davies, *Age of Conquest*, p. 180.

[59]   *Councils and Synods*, i, part ii, p. 754, n. 4, referring to *Henry of Huntingdon, Historia Anglorum*, pp. 250–1. This clashes with Barlow's summary that David played a 'full part in the life of the English church': Barlow, *The English Church*, p. 84.

[60]   Translation occurred in 1137 or 1138; David had given his support prior to the death of King Henry I in 1135 and assisted once again in *c*.1137: 'Vita Sancte Wenefrede (Robert of Shrewsbury; Laud)', ed. D. Callander, 2, 45 and 98; vita written 1137 x 1142: *ibid.*, 2. Translation and David's involvement discussed in Golding, 'Piety, Politics, and Plunder', especially pp. 30–1.

[61]   Lloyd, *History of Wales*, ii, p. 483, n. 90.

[62]   *Vita Griffini*, pp. 88–9. Also, *History of Gruffudd ap Cynan*, pp. 156–7; *Historia Gruffud vab Kenan*, p. 32.

Gruffudd was buried with a gleaming monument erected to the left of the high altar in David's church at Bangor – a church to which Gruffudd bequeathed a large sum of money, and which it has been suggested may have undergone building works during David's incumbency.[63]

David's own death is not recorded. However, his successor, Meurig, was presented to King Stephen as bishop-elect in December 1139.[64] On this evidence, it seems likely that David died sometime after Gruffudd ap Cynan's death in 1137, and before Meurig's election late in 1139. However, Abbot Johannes Trithemius of Würzburg, writing in the sixteenth century, stated that David had become a monk of St James at Würzburg where his kinsman Macarius had recently become the first abbot.[65] If this is correct, then it seems that David retired to Würzburg shortly after the death of Gruffudd.[66]

MEURIG (1140–12 AUGUST 1161)

On, or about, 3 December 1139, Meurig (or Maurice), the new bishop-elect of Bangor, described by John of Worcester as a clerk of great piety, was presented to King Stephen at Worcester castle.[67] The Welsh chronicles record him variously as 'Meuric', 'Meuryc', and 'Maredudd'.[68] According to John of Worcester, he had been chosen by the clergy and people of Bangor, and was accompanied by Robert, bishop of Hereford, and Seffrid, bishop of Chichester, who attested his canonical election and fitness for office.[69] The king confirmed the election, but when Meurig was urged by the two bishops to do homage to Stephen he refused, saying that he would in no way do this, and added 'There is among us a man of great piety, whom I look upon as my spiritual father, and who was archdeacon to my predecessor David, who forbade me to take this oath'.[70] However, he was eventually persuaded to swear fealty to the king.[71] The archdeacon to whom Meurig was referring was undoubtedly Simeon of Clynnog (d. 1152).[72] Meurig was consecrated

---

[63]   Burial, monument, bequest: *Vita Griffini*, pp. 88–91. Also, *History of Gruffudd ap Cynan*, pp. 154–7. For building works to Bangor cathedral, see for example: Thurlby, *Romanesque Architecture and Sculpture in Wales*, pp. 194–6.

[64]   *John of Worcester*, iii, pp. 278–9. *Fasti Welsh Cathedrals*, p. 2.

[65]   *Annales Hirsaugensis*, i, pp. 349 and 403; Brett, 'David (d. 1137x9)', *ODNB*.

[66]   *Annales Hirsaugensis*, i, pp. 349, and 403–4; Brett, 'David (d. 1137x9)', *ODNB*; *William of Malmesbury, Gesta Regum Anglorum*, ii, p. 385.

[67]   'quidam clericus uir eximie religionis, Mauricius nomine': *John of Worcester*, iii, pp. 278–9. *Fasti Welsh Cathedrals*, p. 2. *John of Worcester*, iii, pp. 278–9, has King Stephen leaving 'Little Hereford or Leominster', as 'the holy day of the Lord's Advent [3 December] was approaching … and the king went back to Worcester'.

[68]   'Meuric': *Brenhinedd y Saesson*, p. 162; 'Meuryc': *Brut, Hergest*, p. 142; and 'Maredudd': *Brut, Pen20Tr*, p. 62, which, *ibid.*, p. 182, states that 'al[ias] Meuryg' is written in the margin in a later hand and suggests that 'Maredudd' is probably due to a wrong extension of a contraction. He is called Maurice ('Maurici(us)/ Mauritius') in his profession and by English chroniclers and writers: *Actum* **3**; *John of Salisbury Letters*, no. 87; *John of Worcester*, iii, pp. 278–9; *Gervase of Canterbury*, ii, p. 385. *Fasti Welsh Cathedrals*, ix, p. 2.

[69]   *John of Worcester*, iii, pp. 278–9.

[70]   'Vir … magne religionis apud nos est quem pro spirituali patre teneo, et predecessoris mei David archidiaconus extitit, hoc iuramentum mihi facere inhibuit.': *ibid*.

[71]   *John of Worcester*, iii, pp. 278–9.

[72]   *Episc. Acts Welsh Dioceses*, ii, p. 416. Simeon was one of the famous and wise men, who along with Bishop David the Scot were present at the deathbed of the king of Gwynedd,

by the archbishop of Canterbury, Theobald of Bec, probably at Worcester, on or shortly after 31 January 1140.[73] Uhtred of Llandaff was consecrated at the same time.[74] Meurig's profession of canonical obedience to Theobald and Canterbury (**3**) is extant.[75]

It seems that his swearing of fealty to Stephen was not welcomed by the leaders of Gwynedd, Cadwaladr, and his elder brother, Owain ('Owain Gwynedd'), the surviving sons of Gruffudd ap Cynan (d. 1137). Most probably it was for this reason (and possibly Meurig's profession of obedience to Canterbury) that during 1140, in a letter addressed to Bishop Bernard of St Davids, and recorded by Gerald of Wales, the two brothers alleged that Meurig had entered the church of St Daniel (Deiniol) like a thief, without any invitation from them. Because of Meurig's unjust status they had decided to submit the matter to Bernard's counsel. The brothers went on to say that they did not wish to have such a pastor at all, but desired to supplant him totally as was just.[76] It has been suggested that it was Archdeacon Simeon who inspired Owain and Cadwaladr to write to Bernard in 1140.[77] Further allegations against Meurig were made by the chapter of St Davids who, in another letter recorded by Gerald which complained that Canterbury had unlawfully promoted three persons to Welsh bishoprics, stated that 'Maurice' who had been unlawfully promoted to the bishopric of Bangor had taken a pastoral staff and ring from the church.[78]

An indication of Meurig's early exile from Gwynedd Uwch Conwy is perhaps provided by a notification from Ranulf II, earl of Chester (d. 1153). Ranulf wrote to 'his' bishop of Bangor, and others, from Lincoln.[79] Ranulf's notification con-

---

Gruffudd ap Cynan, in 1137 (*Vita Griffini*, pp. 88–9). He has been described as 'the power behind the episcopal throne' (Lloyd, *History of Wales*, ii, p. 483), and 'the ecclesiastical power behind the princely house of Gwynedd' (*Episc. Acts Welsh Dioceses*, ii, p. 416).

[73]   In the sentence before the one detailing Meurig's consecration the chronicler states that the king returned to Worcester (before setting out for Oxford): *John of Worcester*, iii, pp. 284–5. See also the itinerary of King Stephen in *Regesta Regis Stephani*, pp. xli–xlii. For the date: *AWR*, p. 323. Cf. *Fasti Welsh Cathedrals*, p. 2, which states 'early 1140'. *Canterbury Professions*, p. 42, gives the date as 3 December 1140, but this is surely a mistake, probably explained by the conflation of the date when Meurig was presented to the king at Worcester late in 1139 with the actual year of his canonical profession. *Gervase of Canterbury*, ii, p. 385, includes 'Mauricium Bangornensem' in the list of those consecrated by Theobald, but gives no date.

[74]   *John of Worcester*, iii, pp. 284–5.

[75]   *Actum* **3**. Image at Plate VI (i).

[76]   February x October 1140: *AWR*, pp. 322–3, no. 192; *Episc. Acts Welsh Dioceses*, i, p. 260. As the letter is only preserved in Gerald of Wales' *De Invectionibus* (completed 1216) it has been suggested that it may have been doctored by Gerald to emphasise the brothers' submission to St Davids: *AWR*, p. 323. Further commentary in Pryce, 'Owain Gwynedd (*d.* 1170)', *ODNB*, and Lloyd, *History of Wales*, ii, pp. 483–4.

[77]   *Episc. Acts Welsh Dioceses*, ii, p. 416.

[78]   *De Invectionibus*, pp. 139–41; Haddan and Stubbs, i, pp. 348–50; *Episc. Acts Welsh Dioceses*, i, pp. 89 and 262–3. The two other bishops whom the St Davids' chapter alleged had been unlawfully promoted were Uhtred, consecrated as bishop of Llandaff in 1140, and Richard, consecrated as bishop of Llanelwy/St Asaph in 1141: *Episc. Acts Welsh Dioceses*, i, pp. 89; *Fasti Welsh Cathedrals*, pp. 14 and 33; Smith, 'The Episcopate of Richard', 9–12.

[79]   'episcopo suo Bangoriensi': *Charters of the Anglo-Norman Earls of Chester*, pp. 71–2, no. 59.

cerned Robert, earl of Gloucester (d. 1147), and was dated 27 October. No year was given, however, R. H. C. Davis argued persuasively that the year could well be 1140.[80] When the earl of Gloucester came to assist Ranulf at the battle of Lincoln (2 February 1141) he came with an army which included Welshmen.[81] As troops from north Wales were to fight alongside Ranulf it was perhaps important that Meurig was told that the two earls, who had previously been on opposite sides, were now on the same side.[82] It was Owain's brother, Cadwaladr, who led one of the Welsh contingents at Lincoln, and it is known that he had a long-lived alliance with Ranulf.[83] It is hard to imagine Owain being happy to further the aspirations of the earl of Chester, the Welsh leader's nearest English rival.[84] It is possible that Cadwaladr sided with Ranulf, and the Angevin cause, to strengthen his hand against Owain.[85] As such, very shortly after Cadwaladr had joined his brother in complaining about Meurig, it appears that he and the bishop of Bangor had become allies in support of Ranulf and the Angevin cause.[86] Certainly, Meurig witnessed, and separately confirmed (**4**), Cadwaladr's gift of the church at Nefyn in Llŷn to Haughmond Abbey, which may have occurred at this time, or shortly thereafter.[87] The Empress Matilda, Ranulf, and other Angevin supporters, were benefactors of the same house.[88] Meurig's three brothers, David, Moses, and Rhys, also witnessed Cadwaladr's gift.[89]

The possibility that Meurig found shelter for a time in the early 1140s with the earl of Chester has already been raised by Huw Pryce,[90] and if this was the case, Meurig's stay in Bangor, after his consecration, was brief indeed. Furthermore, sometime prior to 18 June 1142, Meurig was in Northampton with Alexander, the bishop of Lincoln.[91] Alexander is known to have been in the Empress Matilda's company in the spring and summer of 1141; he was at Reading, Winchester and

---

[80]   Davis, 'Geoffrey Barraclough and the Lure of Charters', 33.

[81]   Crouch, 'Robert, first earl of Gloucester', *ODNB*.

[82]   See discussion in Davis, 'Geoffrey Barraclough and the Lure of Charters', 33.

[83]   Cadwaladr at Lincoln: Lloyd, *History of Wales*, ii, p. 489 and n. 10; *AWR*, p. 330. Alliance: Morgan, 'Cheshire and Wales', p. 198; Pryce, 'Owain Gwynedd (*d.* 1170)', *ODNB*; White, 'Ranulf (II), fourth earl of Chester (*d.* 1153)', *ODNB*.

[84]   Lloyd, *History of Wales*, ii, p. 489.

[85]   Pryce, 'Owain Gwynedd (*d.* 1170)', *ODNB*.

[86]   See McGuinness, 'The Medieval Bishops of Bangor, 1092–1283: Intrusion, Exile and Diplomacy' (forthcoming).

[87]   *AWR*, pp. 329–31, no. 197; *Cartulary of Haughmond Abbey*, p. 159, no. 784. *Actum* **4**.

[88]   *Cartulary of Haughmond Abbey*, p. 8. Matilda's first grant can be dated to June x July 1141: *Cartulary of Haughmond Abbey*, p. 228, no. 1250.

[89]   Cadwaladr's wife, Aliz, was also a witness to her husband's gift: 'Aliz de Clara uxore mea': *AWR*, p. 329. Cadwaladr married a noble Anglo-Norman lady, Aliz (or perhaps Adeliza) de Clare, possibly the sister of Earl Ranulf, and the widow of Richard de Clare (d. 1136): *AWR*, p. 330. This marriage would have further strengthened Cadwaladr's ties with Ranulf. Alternatively, 'Aliz' was an otherwise unknown daughter of Richard de Clare: Lloyd, *History of Wales*, ii, p. 491.

[90]   Pryce, 'Church of Trefeglwys', 46, and Pryce, 'Esgobaeth Bangor', p. 44.

[91]   There he witnessed a notification made by Alexander: *Cartulary of Cirencester Abbey*, p. 566, and *EEA, I, Lincoln, 1067–1185*, p. 15, no. 20. Other witnesses included Adelelm, archdeacon of Dorset. The date range starts with Meurig's own consecration and ends on 18 June 1142; 'Adelelm, archdeacon of Dorset, succeeded Philip de Harcourt as dean of

Oxford.[92] If Meurig was with Alexander and/or Matilda (for some or all of this period) it may have been about this time that he granted an indulgence (**6**) of fifteen days for those going to Reading Abbey (which was, of course, founded by, and beloved of, Henry I, Matilda's father).[93]

Further involvement with the Augustinians of Haughmond followed for Meurig witnessed a gift of land to the abbey by Hywel ab Ieuaf, lord of Arwystli (d. 1185).[94] Meurig also confirmed Hywel's gift (**5**) in a charter witnessed by Cadell ap Gruffudd of Deheubarth, 1143 x 1151.[95] Meurig made it clear, in his confirmation, that he had been present at the actual donation by Hywel, which would most probably put him in Haughmond or Arwystli (the latter, as we have noted, forming a detached part of his diocese).[96] In 1157, the year that Henry II administered a military check to the ambitions of Owain Gwynedd, Meurig may once again have been in Shropshire and/or Arwystli in the company of those allied to the new Angevin king (and against Owain). For he witnessed another charter of Hywel ab Ieuaf, which granted land to St Michael's church, Trefeglwys in Arwystli and, *inter alia*, acknowledged the subjection of the church to Haughmond Abbey.[97] One of Meurig's three brothers, Rhys, also witnessed Hywel ab Ieuaf's two above-mentioned charters.[98] In 1156–1157, Hywel was in the pay of the king, as was Hywel's overlord, Madog ap Maredudd of Powys (d. 1160).[99]

In the later years of his episcopate, Meurig sought refuge with the archbishop of Canterbury, and whilst he was in exile in Theobald's house, the archbishop wrote to the pope appealing on the bishop of Bangor's behalf.[100] Theobald described, in great detail, the trials and tribulations of his suffragan bishop, including that

---

Lincoln on the latter's election as bishop of Bayeux (before 18 June 1142).': *EEA, I, Lincoln, 1067–1185*, p. 15.

[92] Reading; *EEA, I, Lincoln, 1067–1185*, p. 207, Saltman, *Theobald*, p. 17, Davis, 'Some Documents of the Anarchy', 182–4, and *Regesta Regis Stephani*, p. 258. Winchester; *EEA, I, Lincoln, 1067–1185*, p. 207, and Saltman, *Theobald*, p. 16. Oxford; he witnessed a charter of Matilda's, June x July 1141: *Cartulary of Haughmond Abbey*, p. 228, no. 1250, also *EEA, I, Lincoln, 1067–1185*, p. 208.

[93] The list of archiepiscopal and episcopal grants of indulgences in favour of the abbey contained in the *Reading Abbey Cartularies* records Maurice of 'Menevens'' but this is surely a scribal error: *ibid.*, i, p. 177. Cf. Bodleian, Tanner MS 342, fo. 272b.

[94] 1143 x 1151: *AWR*, p. 145, no 2. Cf. *Cartulary of Haughmond Abbey*, pp. 221–2, no. 1214, which gives an earlier date range.

[95] *Actum* **5**. Huw Pryce has suggested that Hywel obtained the confirmation of the grant by Meurig (backed by Cadell ap Gruffudd) as a counterweight to the ambitions of Madog ap Maredudd: *AWR*, p. 2.

[96] '… tunc ibidem presentes fuimus …': *Actum* **5**. For the possibility that Meurig found refuge in Arwystli see McGuinness, 'The Medieval Bishops of Bangor, 1092–1283: Intrusion, Exile and Diplomacy' (forthcoming).

[97] U. Rees gives the date as *c*.1157, saying 'In that year Henry II obtained the support of the lords of Powys against Owain of Gwynedd and a money payment was made to Hoel son of Joaf … This alliance may explain why Hywel did not use the title *Rex* which he had used previously: *Cartulary of Haughmond Abbey*, p. 221, no. 1213. H. Pryce gives a wider date range of 1143 x 12 August 1161: *AWR*, pp. 145–7 no. 3, and 'Church of Trefeglwys', 41–2.

[98] *AWR*, pp. 145–7, nos. 2 and 3.

[99] *Pipe Rolls, Henry II, 2,3,4*, p. 89. Madog had established lordship over Hywel by 1151: *AWR*, p. 37.

[100] *Letters of John of Salisbury*, pp. 135–6. Pryce, 'Owain Gwynedd (d. 1170)', *ODNB*.

Owain Gwynedd had despoiled Meurig of his possessions, and driven him from his see (*ab episcopatu*).[101] It has been mooted that the pope in question was the Englishman Adrian IV (4 December 1154–1 September 1159).[102] If Meurig did retreat, to the welcoming arms of the archbishop in the mid- to late 1150s, the timing is interesting.[103] Simeon had died in 1152.[104] With his predecessor's archdeacon out of the way, perhaps Meurig seized the opportunity to make a lasting impression, and sought to introduce ecclesiastical reforms. However, as Theobald's letter recorded by John of Salisbury attests, in so doing Meurig upset many of his own clergy, whom he excommunicated for contumacy.[105] Meurig also criticised Owain's marriage to his cousin, Cristin, or Christina, ferch Gronw ab Owain ab Edwin (a union which also attracted criticism from successive archbishops) on the grounds that they were related within the prohibited degrees of consanguinity.[106] In the end, Meurig's reforms and his criticism of Owain led to his expulsion.[107] It is not known whether he returned to Bangor before his death.[108] He died on 12 August 1161.[109]

---

[101] *Letters of John of Salisbury*, pp. 135–6.

[102] Pryce, 'Esgobaeth Bangor', p. 45. However, the letter could have been written earlier, and it is noteworthy that on 14 March 1148 Meurig assisted Archbishop Theobald in the consecration of the new bishop of Llandaff, Nicholas (as well as Walter, bishop of Rochester: *Canterbury Professions*, p. 44; *Fasti Welsh Cathedrals*, p. 14; *Handbook of British Chronology*, p. 267). John of Salisbury was certainly in Theobald's service from 1147/8 onwards: Luscombe, 'Salisbury, John of (late 1110s–1180)', *ODNB*, and *Letters of John of Salisbury*, p. liii. Whilst it is assumed that the first of the two collections of John's letters covers the years 1153–61: Luscombe, 'Salisbury, John of (late 1110s–1180)', *ODNB*, the editors of *Letters of John of Salisbury* do admit that some of the letters could be earlier than 1153, indeed '… a third of the letters cannot be dated more closely than the general limits of the collection, and a number more cannot be dated at all exactly'. The same editors have put Theobald's letter concerning Maurice, no. 87, into the list (contained in their first index) of those letters whose dates are uncertain: *ibid.*, pp. lii–liii, and p. 275.

[103] For a discussion of Meurig's possible exile *c.*1154 x 1157: *AWR*, p. 323; Pryce, 'Owain Gwynedd (*d.* 1170)', *ODNB*; Pryce, 'Esgobaeth Bangor', p. 45. It is noteworthy in this context that Meurig witnessed a charter made by William, second earl of Gloucester, 1155 x 1159 (*Earldom of Gloucester Charters*, pp. 71–2, no. 66); the other witnesses included Walter Durdent, bishop of Coventry, Robert de Chesney, bishop of Lincoln, Robert de Beaumont, earl of Leicester, and a young Hugh, fifth earl of Chester (his father, Ranulf II, having died in 1153). The Empress Matilda's son, Henry, having been crowned king in December 1154, Robert de Beaumont was soon appointed justiciar of England (Crouch, 'Robert [Robert de Beaumont], second earl of Leicester (1104–1168)', *ODNB*). William had been one of Henry's most honoured 'familiares', and the bishop of Coventry was described as Henry's 'household companion and dear friend' (Patterson, 'William, second earl of Gloucester (*d.* 1183)', *ODNB*; Franklin, 'Durdent, Walter (*d.* 1159)', *ODNB*).

[104] *Brut, Pen20Tr*, p. 58; *Brut, Hergest*, pp. 130–1; Lloyd, *History of Wales*, ii, p. 469, n. 25.

[105] *Letters of John of Salisbury*, pp. 135–6; Barlow, *The English Church*, p. 95, n. 180.

[106] *Letters of John of Salisbury*, p. 136, and n. 4. For archiepiscopal censure: Pryce, 'Owain Gwynedd (*d.* 1170)', *ODNB*; *Journey and Description*, p. 192. See also 'Vacancy and Arthur de Chargan'.

[107] *Letters of John of Salisbury*, pp. 135–6.

[108] *AWR*, p. 323.

[109] August 1161 was given by a lost calendar of Shrewsbury Abbey, cited in *Fasti Ecclesiae Anglicanae Hardy*, i, p. 96, n. 13: 'In Kalendario S. Petri Salop. MS. Cott. Vitel. A. viii. "I. Id.

One event of great significance that occurred during his episcopate was the revival, in 1141, of the bishopric of Llanelwy/St Asaph, and Meurig may have had a pivotal part to play in ensuring that two detached portions, namely the deaneries of Arwystli and Dyffryn Clwyd, were carved out of the new territorial diocese and remained part of his diocese of Bangor (see the section entitled 'Gwynedd Uwch Conwy, Dyffryn Clwyd and Arwystli' above).

VACANCY AND ARTHUR DE CHARGAN (13 AUGUST 1161–21 MAY 1177)

In a letter probably datable to September x October 1165, Owain Gwynedd, who was at the height of his powers following the defeat of Henry II on the Berwyn Mountains, wrote to Archbishop Thomas Becket, stating that the archbishop would have heard how much harm had come to the right of Owain's church following the death of Bishop Meurig.[110] He reminded the archbishop how much the king of England unjustly hated him, and dishonoured him in both ecclesiastical and secular matters. Owain asked Becket, who was at the time in exile, to give permission for his bishop to be ordained 'elsewhere' (which must mean outside the province of Canterbury) but stated that the new bishop would give obedience to Canterbury and the archbishop as if he had been consecrated by the latter.[111] However, subjection to Canterbury was given as a favour rather than as of right. Owain requested Becket's written instructions, but warned that he could not remain in this situation much longer.[112] Perhaps pre-empting Becket's dismissive reply (which was contained in a letter to Owain, *c.*October x November 1165), Owain's bishop-elect Arthur de Chargan was probably consecrated in Ireland.[113] The archbishop admonished Arthur and his 'associates' in a letter, delivered at the same time as his letter to Owain.[114] Becket had been told that Arthur had gone to Ireland, and had contrived that the clergy and bishops of Wales might receive orders and consecration in Ireland as if a new metropolitan had been set up for them there.[115] Furthermore, by mid- to late 1166, when Becket summoned the archdeacon of Bangor, David, to appear before him,[116] he must have become aware of the full extent of what had happened, and

---

Aug. obiit Mauricius Bangor. Episcopus'". See also *Fasti Welsh Cathedrals*, p. 2; *AWR*, p. 146; and Barbier, *The Age of Owain Gwynedd*, p. 123, n. 6. *Brut, Hergest*, pp. 142–3 and 293, and *Brut, Pen20Tr*, pp. 62 and 182, give the year 1161.

[110] *AWR*, pp. 325–7, no. 195; *Becket Correspondence*, i, pp. 234–6, no. 57.

[111] *AWR*, pp. 325–7, no. 195; *Becket Correspondence*, i, pp. 234–6, no. 57. Becket went into exile in November 1164: *AWR*, p. 328.

[112] *AWR*, pp. 325–7, no. 195; *Becket Correspondence*, i, pp. 234–6, no. 57; Pryce, 'Owain Gwynedd (*d.* 1170)', *ODNB*.

[113] Becket's letter to Owain Gwynedd: *Becket Correspondence*, i, pp. 238–40, no. 59. J. C. Davies was sure that Arthur was consecrated in Ireland and returned to Gwynedd to exercise the functions of his episcopal office: *Episc. Acts Welsh Dioceses*, ii, p. 433. See also Flanagan, *Irish Society, Anglo-Norman Settlers, Angevin Kingship*, p. 65. In one of Becket's letters, Arthur is referred to as 'Arturus de Chargan' (BL MS Cotton Claudius B ii, fo. 193r; *Becket Correspondence*, i, pp. 239–42, no. 60) and, in the rubric to another recorded letter, as 'de Kargan' (BL MS Cotton Claudius B ii, fo. 193r; *Becket Correspondence*, i, pp. 240–3, no. 61).

[114] *Becket Correspondence*, i, pp. 240–3, no. 61.

[115] *Becket Correspondence*, i, pp. 240–3, no. 61.

[116] Together with three or four of the older and more prominent dignitaries of the church of Bangor. Letter addressed to the archdeacon and canons of Bangor, written mid- to late

he blamed the canons, and in particular, David for not only giving his consent to the plots of Arthur and his associates, but also agreeing to the bishop of his church (*episcopus ecclesie sue*) – 'if indeed there was any true bishop there' (*si quis tamen ibi esset*) – going to Ireland and receiving the sacraments as if a metropolitan had been newly created for him.[117] If Arthur was indeed consecrated as bishop of Bangor, as seems likely, no *acta* of his have survived. It is not known when he died.

GWION (22 MAY 1177–1191)

On Sunday 22 May 1177, at Amesbury Abbey in Wiltshire, Gwion, in the presence of Henry II, was consecrated as bishop of Bangor by the archbishop of Canterbury, Richard of Dover.[118] He made his profession of canonical obedience (**7**) to Richard the same day.[119] As J. E. Lloyd noted, the consecration of Gwion ended the long conflict between the clerical elite of Bangor and the crown as to the filling of the see.[120] It also ended the long conflict with Canterbury.

Gwion undoubtedly met with the king's approval, and Huw Pryce has suggested that it is possible that Henry II hoped that Gwion would become established as bishop with the assistance of the king's favourite for the succession to Gwynedd, namely Dafydd ab Owain Gwynedd (who had married the king's half-sister, Emma of Anjou, in 1174).[121] Certainly Gwion witnessed a charter of Dafydd's by which the latter, styling himself *rex Norwallie*, ordered the parishioners of Nefyn to pay tithes to the abbot and convent of Haughmond Abbey,[122] and furthermore, the bishop himself ordered the parishioners to comply with the payment (**11**).[123] Another grant by Dafydd in favour of Haughmond, of land in the township of

---

1166: *Becket Correspondence*, i, pp. 553–5, no. 114; *Episc. Acts Welsh Dioceses*, ii, pp. 424–5.

[117] *Becket Correspondence*, i, pp. 553–5, no. 114.

[118] 'Gwido Pangorensis ecclesiae electus': *Gesta Regis Henrici Secundi*, i, pp. 165–6. A bishop of Bangor was recorded in London on two occasions in March 1177, and if this was Gwion, as seems likely, he would have attended in the capacity of bishop-elect only, not bishop: *Gesta Regis Henrici Secundi*, i, pp. 144–5 and 154; *Roger de Hoveden*, ii, pp. 121 and 131. Huw Pryce has recently confirmed him as a Welshman: Pryce, 'Esgobaeth Bangor', p. 46. J. E. Lloyd (*History of Wales*, ii, p. 563, n. 143) reached the same conclusion. In a charter granted by Dafydd ab Owain Gwynedd (*AWR*, pp. 332–3, no. 199), his name appears as 'Wian', which according to Pryce, is the Welsh form of the bishop's name which bears comparison with the Latinised form 'Guianus' used by Gerald of Wales (*AWR*, p. 333, *Opera*, vi, p. 125). 'Gwiawn' was used in *Brut y Tywysogyon* (*Brut, Hergest*, p. 172). 'Gwido' was used in the bishop's profession (*Actum* **7**), and 'Guido' and 'Wido' in his other *acta* (*Acta* **8**, **9**, **10**, **11** and **12**); with 'Guido', 'Gwido' and 'Vidon'/Guidon'' being used by English chroniclers (*AWR*, p. 333, *Gesta Regis Henrici Secundi*, i, pp. 165–6).

[119] *Actum* **7**. Image at Plate VI (ii). *Gesta Regis Henrici Secundi*, i, pp. 165–6.

[120] Lloyd, *History of Wales*, ii, p. 563, n. 143.

[121] Pryce, 'Esgobaeth Bangor', p. 46. See also *AWR*, p. 24. For dating of the marriage see: Lloyd, *History of Wales*, ii, p. 551, n. 78.

[122] Dafydd made it clear that the bishop of Bangor had, by his own 'charter', confirmed that the tithes were so payable and, indeed, ordered the parishioners to comply. Madog, one of Gwion's three brothers, also witnessed Dafydd's charter: *AWR*, pp. 332–3, no. 199; *Cartulary of Haughmond Abbey*, p. 159, no. 785.

[123] *Actum* **11**.

Nefyn, was not only witnessed by one of Gwion's three brothers,[124] it was effectively confirmed by Gwion in his own, more detailed, charter (**8**) which granted, *inter alia*, the church at Nefyn to the abbot and convent.[125]

As well as having three brothers, namely Iorwerth ('Gervase'), Madog and Philip, Gwion also had a son, Philip – all of whom, at some stage, witnessed his *acta*, or the *acta* of others he himself was to confirm.[126] The texts of Gwion's five known non-profession *acta* are preserved in copies only. Four are found in the late fifteenth-century cartulary of the Augustinian abbey of Haughmond, the fifth is in the early fourteenth-century cartulary, or register, of the Benedictine house of St Werburgh's Abbey, Chester.[127] Gwion's two other *acta* in favour of Haughmond were in respect of Trefeglwys (in Arwystli) and the church there.[128] The first confirmed Gwion's grant and gift (**9**) of the church of Trefeglwys to the abbey, and was witnessed by his brother Philip.[129] It is noteworthy that this is the first of the Trefeglwys charters to appear in the Haughmond Cartulary, suggesting that the canons considered Gwion's charter to be the title deed to the church.[130] The second confirmed (**10**) the *donatio* of lands made by Hywel ab Ieuaf, lord of Arwystli, to St Michael's Church, Trefeglwys and the canons of Haughmond.[131] Once again, Gwion's confirmation was witnessed by his brother Philip.[132] Gwion's grant (**12**) in favour of St Werburgh's Abbey, Chester, sought to address the theft of goods from the abbey's men and its lands.[133] A similar concession was obtained by the abbey from Bishop Reiner of St Asaph (1186–1224/5).[134] The abbey had lands in

---

[124] Namely Iorwerth ('Gervase'): *AWR*, pp. 331–2, no. 198; *Cartulary of Haughmond Abbey*, p. 160, no. 786.

[125] *Actum* **8**. Philip, the bishop's son, and one of his brothers, this time unnamed, witnessed the same. If Gwion's grant occurred at the same time as Dafydd's grant or shortly thereafter, it is reasonable to assume that the unnamed brother was once again Gervase/Iorwerth.

[126] *Acta* **8**, **9** and **10**; *AWR*, nos. 198 and 199.

[127] Shrewsbury, Shropshire Archives, MS 6001/6869 (Haughmond Cartulary): *Acta* **8**, **9**, **10** and **11**. London, BL MS Harley 1965 (Cartulary or Register of St Werburgh's Abbey, Chester): *Actum* **12**.

[128] For Arwystli as a rural deanery, and a detached portion of the diocese of Bangor, see the section of the Introduction entitled 'Gwynedd Uwch Conwy, Dyffryn Clwyd and Arwystli'.

[129] *Actum* **9**.

[130] Pryce, 'Church of Trefeglwys', 42. It is unclear exactly when Trefeglwys church was granted to Haughmond, although it seems it occurred before the end of Meurig's episcopate in 1161: Pryce, 'Church of Trefeglwys', 42; *Cartulary of Haughmond Abbey*, p. 221 (note to no. 1212). However, the fact that Gwion confirmed the church to the abbey in perpetuity, leads one to think that the abbey's title was not secure, a point made by Pryce, 'Church of Trefeglwys', 42. This could suggest that the confirmation was obtained from Gwion early in his episcopate.

[131] *Actum* **10**. As the description of the land defined is verbatim the wording used in Meurig's confirmation (*Actum* **5**) of Hywel's gift, it is clear that the relevant grant is that printed in *AWR*, p. 145, no. 2.

[132] *Actum* **10**. It is, therefore, probable that it was executed at the same time as the first confirmation in respect of Trefeglwys, and for the same reason, namely securing the abbey's title at the earliest possible opportunity.

[133] *Actum* **12**.

[134] *Cartulary of St. Werburgh's Abbey, Chester*, i, pp. 126–7, and ii, p. 278; *Fasti Welsh Cathedrals*, p. 34.

Tegeingl, as well as on Anglesey, and there is certainly evidence that St Werburgh's suffered losses in the second half of the twelfth century.[135]

The most memorable appearance of Gwion in the historical record is provided by Gerald of Wales. During their journey through Wales of 1188, preaching the cross in readiness for the Third Crusade, Gerald and Archbishop Baldwin of Forde were entertained by Gwion in Bangor, on the evening of Sunday 10 April.[136] In the morning, Baldwin said mass before the high altar in the cathedral, and according to Gerald, Gwion was hard pressed by the archbishop to take the cross, which he finally did causing great concern amongst the congregation for, we are told, both men and women present wept and wailed very loudly.[137] Later, after having crossed by boat to Anglesey, Gerald and Baldwin returned to Bangor and were shown the tombs of Owain Gwynedd, and his brother Cadwaladr.[138] Gwion was ordered to watch for an opportunity to remove Owain's body from the cathedral (and to do this as quickly as possible).[139]

The following year, on 3 September 1189, Gwion attended the coronation of King Richard I, at Westminster.[140] Despite taking the cross, Gwion never did go on crusade. He died in 1191, *Brut y Tywysogyon* describing him as 'a man of great piety and honour and dignity'.[141]

For discussion of the possible development of a cathedral chapter at Bangor during Gwion's episcopate see the section of the Introduction entitled 'Introduction of a Chapter'.

ALAN OF ST CROSS (16 APRIL 1195–19 MAY 1196)

According to Gerald of Wales, on Gwion's death the chapter of Bangor had, by a unanimous vote, elected a 'good man' (*bonus vir*) whom the archbishop of Canterbury refused to confirm, and consecrate, because he was Welsh.[142] The 'good man' was Rotoland, sub-prior of the Cistercian house of Aberconwy.[143] Instead, Gerald tells us, the archbishop thrust into his place without any election at all the English

---

[135] Lloyd, *History of Wales*, ii, p. 456, n. 238; Kettle, 'Houses of Benedictine Monks: The Abbey of Chester', in *VCH Cheshire*, iii, pp. 132–45; *Monasticon*, ii, pp. 385–6; *CChR, 1257–1300*, p. 316; *Cartulary of St. Werburgh's Abbey, Chester*, i, pp. 30, 45, 101, 108, 127, 212, and 215.

[136] *Journey and Description*, pp. 35 and 185; *Opera*, vi, p. 125.

[137] *Journey and Description*, pp. 35–6 and 185; *Opera*, vi, pp. 125–6

[138] *Journey and Description*, p. 192; *Opera*, vi, p. 133.

[139] *Journey and Description*, p. 192; *Opera*, vi, p. 133. Owain Gwynedd had been excommunicated for failing to give up his wife, his first cousin Cristin or Christina ferch Gronw ab Owain ab Edwin, and he had died excommunicated in 1170: *Becket Correspondence*, ii, pp. 840–1, and 874–7; *Journey and Description*, p. 192; Lloyd, *History of Wales*, ii, p. 522; *AWR*, p. 24; Pearson, 'Bangor Cathedral Chapter', 176.

[140] *Roger de Hoveden*, iii, p. 8; *Annals of Roger de Hoveden*, ii, pp. 116–17; *Itinerary of King Richard I*, p. 3; *Fasti Welsh Cathedrals*, p. 2.

[141] 'gwr mawr y greuyd a'e anryded a'e teilygdawt': *Brut, Hergest*, pp. 172–3. Also, *Brut, Pen20Tr*, p. 74, and *Annales Cambriae E-text*, p. 1.

[142] *De Invectionibus*, p. 95; *Autobiography*, p. 213.

[143] Rotoland's election and subsequent appeal to the papal curia are discussed in *Episc. Acts Welsh Dioceses*, i, pp. 3–4, and ii, pp. 415–37; Hays, 'Rotoland, subprior of Aberconway', 9–10; and Hays, *Abbey of Aberconway*, p. 26.

Hospitaller, Alan.[144] Thus it was that on 16 April 1195, Alan, prior of the Hospital of Jerusalem in England, was consecrated as bishop of Bangor by Archbishop Hubert Walter.[145] Alan's profession (**13**) of canonical obedience and subjection to Canterbury was given the same day.[146]

Alan had been (grand) prior of the order in England, the evidence suggesting that he succeeded Garnier de Nablûs (de Nablous/de Naplouse/de Neapolis) in the autumn, or early winter, of 1190.[147] Certainly, later lists of the order's (grand) priors of England have him succeeding in that year, and, in turn, being succeeded by Gilbert de Vere in 1195.[148] What is also certain is that before he became prior of the order in England, he was a brother at the hospital of St Cross near Winchester, hence his name.[149]

Much as happened to Hervey a century earlier, the new bishop found no peace in Bangor and according to Gerald fled to exile and banishment in England.[150] No doubt his intrusion was too much to bear for those in Bangor who had elected Rotoland. Gerald had a term for these exiled bishops, wandering about vagrant-like, seeking lodgings, and employ, wherever they could: *girovagi*.[151] Alan's tenure was short-lived as his obit is recorded on 19 May 1196.[152] However, the canons of Haughmond lost no time in ensuring that he confirmed (**14**) the charters of bishops Meurig and Gwion in favour of the abbey; and they took the opportunity to obtain from him, in the same document, a grant that they could appoint and remove chaplains of their churches in his diocese.[153]

The only other known *actum* of Alan, whilst bishop, is a confirmation (**15**) of a gift and sale made by Cadwaladr ap Hywel of Arwystli (*fl.* 1185–1196) in favour of the abbey of Strata Marcella.[154] The monks, for one assumes it was they who drafted the confirmation, left nothing to chance; at the end of the document there

---

[144] *Autobiography*, p. 213; *De Invectionibus*, p. 95.

[145] 'Alanus prior Hospitalis Jerusalem consecratus est in episcopum de Bangor': *Annales de Wigornia*, p. 388, which gives the year. *Flores Historiarum*, ii, p. 113, gives the date as 'xvi. kal. Maii.'; as do the Annals of Southwark, BL Cotton MS Faustina A viii, fo. 137r. Also, *Annales de Theokesberia*, p. 55, and *Chronica Majora*, ii, p. 411 for the year. *Gervase of Canterbury*, ii, p. 410 gives the list of bishops consecrated by Hubert Walter.

[146] *Actum* **13**. Image at Plate VI (iii).

[147] Round, 'Garnier de Nablous', 384–5, and 388; *Calendar of Documents Preserved in France*, i, p. 15, *EEA, VI, Norwich, 1070–1214*, pp. 197–8, no. 246; *EEA, Bath and Wells*, pp. 107–8, no. 145.

[148] Fincham, *The Order of the Hospital of St John of Jerusalem and its Grand Priory of England*, pp. 78 and 85; Round, 'Garnier de Nablous', 384–7; Chew, *VCH Middlesex*, i, p. 199; *Cartulaire général de l'ordre des Hospitaliers de Saint-Jean de Jérusalem*, i, p. 570.

[149] In three witness lists of 1189 he appears as 'fratre Alano de Sancta Cruce': Round, 'Garnier de Nablous', 388–9; see also *ibid.*, 384–5; *Early Charters of the Cathedral Church of St. Paul, London*, pp. 224–5, no. 283; *EEA, VIII, Winchester, 1070–1204*, pp. 146–8; Chew, *VCH Middlesex*, i, p. 199; *Cartulaire général de l'ordre des Hospitaliers de Saint-Jean de Jérusalem*, i, p. 570.

[150] *Autobiography*, p. 213; *De Invectionibus*, p. 95.

[151] *Opera*, i, p. 215; *Episc. Acts Welsh Dioceses*, ii, p. 438.

[152] *Brut, Pen20Tr*, p. 75, *Brut, Hergest*, pp. 176–7, and *Brenhinedd y Saesson*, pp. 190–1 provide the year. *Cartulary of the Knights of St. John of Jerusalem in England, Essex*, p. 570, gives 19 May.

[153] *Actum* **14**.

[154] *Actum* **15**. Image at Plate VII. Cadwaladr's charter has not survived but may have been issued after the death of his father, Hywel ab Ieuaf, in 1185: *AWR*, p. 149.

is a threat of anathema by episcopal authority, directed at anyone who might pre-
sume to annul or disturb the gift, sale and/or the confirmation itself. Presumably
the reason the bishop of Bangor confirmed Cadwaladr's charter was because this
was a gift, and sale, of land in Arwystli, made by an Arwystli family, albeit in favour
of a monastic house near Y Trallwng (Welshpool) in the diocese of St Asaph –
Bishop Reiner of St Asaph (1186–1224/5) may also have confirmed but, if so, his
confirmation has not come down to us. The bishop of Bangor's confirmation may
have been obtained by the monks of Strata Marcella during a visitation by Alan of
Arwystli, or if Gerald was correct, when Alan was in exile from Bangor.[155]

The identity of the first-named witness (to *Actum* **15**) is interesting, *Laurentius
hospitalarius*. It has been assumed that he was the 'guest-master' of the abbey.[156]
However, he is not mentioned in any of the other surviving charters in favour of
the abbey, and bearing in mind Alan's background, he could conceivably have
been a Hospitaller, that is a knight of the Order of St John of Jerusalem. It is
perhaps unlikely that a guest-master would rank first in a hierarchical witness
list such as this, containing an archdeacon, and a dean, whereas a knight of the
Order of St John of Jerusalem might rank first.[157] Furthermore, Gerald used the
identical term when describing Alan, i.e. *hospitalarius*.[158] If Lawrence was indeed
a Hospitaller, he may have been travelling with Alan, and if Gerald was correct
in asserting the bishop's exile, Alan may have sought residence, for a time at least,
with the Hospitallers. There is certainly evidence of his continued association with
that order. This is provided by two confirmations made by senior members of the
Hospitallers, Alan witnessing both as bishop of Bangor.[159]

The only other mention of Alan, when bishop, is a record of payment that he
received, by the king's writ, for the wages of twelve mounted sergeants, and for the
warnistura of the castle of 'Timbei', probably Denbigh in north-east Wales.[160] It
has been said that members of the Order of the Hospital of St John, taking on, as
they did, both monastic and knightly functions, proved very popular.[161] Both King

---

[155]   Arwystli might have provided a refuge for Alan, where he could continue his episcopal
duties, just as Meurig may have done in the same rural deanery, and Bishop Richard
was to do in Dyffryn Clwyd, the other detached portion of the diocese of Bangor: see
McGuinness, 'The Medieval Bishops of Bangor, 1092–1283: Intrusion, Exile and
Diplomacy' (forthcoming).

[156]   *Ystrad Marchell Charters*, p. 52.

[157]   See note to *Actum* **15**.

[158]   *De Invectionibus*, p. 193.

[159]   'Alano Bangorien' episcopo qui fuit prior domus nostre in Angl'', at 'Senegeia[m]':
Bodleian Library, Ashmole MS 833, p. 15 (thank you to Dr Nigel Tringham for bringing this
to my attention); and 'Alano dei gratia Bangor' episcopo': *Early Charters of the Cathedral Church
of St. Paul, London*, pp. 225–6 (no. 284); *Cartulaire général de l'ordre des Hospitaliers de Saint-Jean de
Jérusalem*, iv, p. 331.

[160]   Michaelmas 1195: *Pipe Roll, Richard I, Year 7*, pp. xxvii and 244. 'Warnistura/warnestura'
(supplies/provisions/garrisoning): *DMLBS*, xvii, pp. 3732 and 3733, and via https://logeion.
uchicago.edu/warnestura, accessed 20 May 2024; also Latham, *Revised Medieval Latin Word-
List*, p. 208. The Middle English 'warnestōren' meant to furnish or provision (a castle): *MED*,
https://quod.lib.umich.edu/m/middle-english-dictionary/dictionary?utf8=✓&search_
field=hnf&q=warnestoren, accessed 20 May 2024. Thank you to both Professor Janet
Burton and Dr Nicholas Karn for discussing the meaning of 'warnistura' with me.

[161]   *Chronicle of the Third Crusade*, p. 25, n. 4.

Richard I and Hubert Walter would have become well acquainted with the order, and with Garnier de Nablûs during their time on crusade; and they may have come to know of Alan through this association.[162] Furthermore, in 1194, Richard granted a charter to the English Hospitallers increasing their privileges, and transferring to their care hospitals at Hereford and Worcester.[163] It is hard to imagine the prior of the order in England at the time, namely Alan, not being consulted, or involved. Moreover, Richard is known to have visited Winchester in 1194.[164] These associations would certainly go some way to explain Alan's preferment to the vacant bishopric of Bangor, and his subsequent military appointment.

ROBERT OF SHREWSBURY (16 MARCH 1197–1212)

Robert of Shrewsbury was consecrated as bishop of Bangor on 16 March 1197 by the archbishop of Canterbury, Hubert Walter.[165] It is likely that his profession (**16**) of canonical subjection and obedience to Canterbury, and to Hubert himself, was given the same day.[166] According to Gerald of Wales, as soon as the Bangor chapter heard that Alan (of St Cross) was dead, with one voice, they once again elected Rotoland, however, once again the archbishop refused to confirm his election, and had a certain Englishman called Robert consecrated in his stead, but he too, like his predecessor, Gerald wrote, is now a 'wandering exile, a bishop without a city, who runs to and fro, begging at every abbey in England, and going mitre-horned hunts for vicar-ships of vacant sees'.[167]

Robert had been dean of St Mary's college of secular canons, Shrewsbury, from c.1186.[168] He appears in that capacity as a witness to charters which are recorded in the cartulary of the Benedictine abbey of Shrewsbury, and in other charters of that abbey as well as in charters associated with the Augustinian priory of Wom-

---

[162] For instances of Richard's, and Hubert Walter's, involvement with the Hospitallers, and Garnier, on crusade: Nicholson, *Medieval Warfare*, p. 127, and *Chronicle of the Third Crusade*, pp. 189, 251, 330, 336, and 337. Also, Gillingham, 'Richard I (1157–1199)', *ODNB*.

[163] *Monasticon*, vi, (2), p. 839; *Cartulaire général de l'ordre des Hospitaliers de Saint-Jean de Jérusalem*, ii, p. 604; Chew, *VCH Middlesex*, i, p. 195; Rees, *History of the Order of St. John of Jerusalem in Wales*, p. 22.

[164] April 1194: Gillingham, 'Richard I (1157–1199)', *ODNB*.

[165] '… Robertus de Salopesbire consecratus est in episcopum de Bangor': *Flores Historiarum*, ii, p. 117, which gives the year, as does *Chronica Majora*, ii, p. 440, and Annals of Southwark, BL Cotton MS Faustina A viii, fo. 137. Annals of Merton, Cambridge Corpus Christi College MS 59, fo. 168rb gives the date; see also *Fasti Welsh Cathedrals*, p. 3. *Gervase of Canterbury*, ii, p. 410 lists the bishops consecrated by Hubert Walter.

[166] *Actum* **16**. Image at Plate VI (iv).

[167] '… vagus et profugus, puta nullius civitatis episcopus, per abbatias Anglie mendicando, discurrens, et cornutus incidens sedium vacantium vicarias': *Autobiography*, p. 213; *De Invectionibus*, pp. 95–6. Gerald contended that Rotoland had the unanimous support of the native people, the clergy, and his prince: *De Invectionibus*, p. 96; *Autobiography*, p. 213. See also *Opera*, iii, p. 193. In a charter of Llywelyn ab Iorwerth, of uncertain date, Rotoland witnessed as lord elect of Bangor: 'dominus … Rawatlan(us) electus de Bangor' (*AWR*, pp. 346–7, no 216).

[168] Gaydon, 'Colleges of Secular Canons: Shrewsbury', p. 123, and n. 253; Eyton, *Antiquities of Shropshire*, ii, p. 112, n. 14.

bridge, he is described as *magister*.[169] It is not clear where he was educated, nor when he obtained his title of 'master'. Robert had strong local connections, owned property in Shrewsbury, and his brother, Richard, was archdeacon in the town.[170] As St Mary's was a royal free chapel (later a 'royal peculiar') deans were often king's clerks.[171] Robert was both a king's clerk and a royal justice.[172] Furthermore, by 1194 x 1195, he was keeper (*custos*) of the silver mine at Carreghofa castle (Powys), as well as the money-change at Shrewsbury, and warden of Shrewsbury mint.[173] It seems probable that Robert continued as dean of St Mary's until at least *c*.1200, for on 6 October 1200 Robert and the canons of St Mary's were a party to a suit that was pending at Westminster.[174] There is further evidence of Robert's pluralism. It appears he was reluctant to give up another office he held, for according to a letter written by Peter of Blois, *c*.1196 x 16 March 1197, Robert held the 'little prebend' of Wolverhampton.[175] Peter, who had been dean of Wolverhampton since at least 1191, urged the bishop-elect of Bangor to give up the prebend on his ordination.[176] Apparently Robert had protested the poverty of his church (presumably Bangor), but Peter argued this was no excuse.[177]

---

[169]   *Cartulary of Shrewsbury Abbey*, i, pp. 18–19, no. 16, p. 94, no. 106, p. 269, no. 283, and p. 280, no. 300; ii, pp. 271–2, no. 286, and pp. 316–7, no. 351; Eyton, *Antiquities of Shropshire*, ii, p. 133, n. 98, vii, p. 341, and ix, p. 79.

[170]   Local connections and property: ns. 327 and 328 above; Gaydon, 'Colleges of Secular Canons: Shrewsbury', p. 119 and n. 166, p. 122 and n. 222; Shropshire Archives, 322, no. 10. For his brother Richard: Eyton, *Antiquities of Shropshire*, ii, p. 133, n. 98. He may have been responsible for extensive additions which were made to St Mary's church, after *c*.1190: Gaydon, 'Colleges of Secular Canons: Shrewsbury', p. 119, and n. 166; Cranage, *Churches of Shropshire*, x, p. 949.

[171]   Royal free chapels were, and are, exempt from the jurisdiction of the diocesan bishop. In the late twelfth century, it is possible that the dean had powers and privileges comparable to a prelate: Gaydon, 'Colleges of Secular Canons: Shrewsbury', p. 121, and n. 194; Denton, *English Royal Free Chapels*, p. 134; and Phillips and Hulbert, *History and Antiquities of Shrewsbury*, i, p. 84.

[172]   For examples of him acting as a royal justice in 1189 and 1191 (in Shrewsbury) and in 1192 (in Gloucester): Eyton, *Antiquities of Shropshire*, vi, p. 368, and viii, pp. 106–7; Gaydon, 'Colleges of Secular Canons: Shrewsbury', p. 121, and n. 196; *Pleas before the King and his Justices, 1198–1212*, iii, pp. lxxvii and xciii; *Historia et Cartularium Monasterii Sancti Petri Gloucestriæ*, ii, pp. 7–8.

[173]   Eyton, *Antiquities of Shropshire*, x, pp. 358–9; Gaydon, 'Colleges of Secular Canons: Shrewsbury', p. 122, and n. 222.

[174]   Eyton, *Antiquities of Shropshire*, x, p. 150. One of Robert's successors (possibly his immediate successor) as dean, Henry of London, who was appointed in 1203, continued as dean when he was archbishop of Dublin (1213–1228), only resigning in 1226: *Rot. Litt. Claus.*, ii, p. 161. Also, Eyton, *Antiquities of Shropshire*, x, p. 150, n. 1; Gaydon, 'Colleges of Secular Canons: Shrewsbury', p. 123, and n. 255.

[175]   'praebendula': *Petri Blesensis Bathoniensis Archiadiaconi Opera*, ii, pp. 74–6, Epistola 147; *Patrologia Latina*, ccvii, cols. 434–6. *Fasti Welsh Cathedrals*, p. 3. *DMLBS*, via https://logeion. uchicago.edu/praebendula, accessed 20 February 2024.

[176]   Peter as dean of Wolverhampton: A. K. B. and R. H., Evans, 'Colleges: Wolverhampton, St Peter', in *VCH Staffordshire*, iii, 322, and n. 31.

[177]   *Petri Blesensis Bathoniensis Archiadiaconi Opera*, ii, pp. 74–6, Epistola 147; *Patrologia Latina*, ccvii, cols. 434–6; *Episc. Acts Welsh Dioceses Unpublished*, B98.

After his consecration in March 1197, Robert's early exile may possibly be indicated by his presence south of the Thames in October of the same year. There, on the last day of the month, he dedicated a new altar at Merton Priory, in Surrey.[178] By September 1198 he was with King Richard, at Château Gaillard, in Normandy, and in October and November he was a few miles away at Lyons-la-Forêt.[179] After Richard's death (1199), he was entrusted by King John with business at the Roman *curia*, re-joining the new king on his return to England, and travelling with the court.[180] He was with John, Archbishop Hubert Walter and Geoffrey fitz Peter, the justiciar, on 13 January 1201, at Lincoln; interestingly, it was on, or by that date, that King John decided to extend a truce with Llywelyn ab Iorwerth, prince of Gwynedd (d. 1240).[181] The truce led to an agreement which was formalised in July 1201, Llywelyn swearing fealty before Robert, Geoffrey and others (the king by then being in Normandy).[182]

Exactly seven years after his consecration, on 16 March 1204, Robert, amongst others, was tasked by the king to ensure safe conduct for Llywelyn.[183] This may mark the *terminus ante quem* of Robert's enforced exile from his see, or at least the beginning of the end of his exile. In the spring of the following year, Llywelyn was married to Joan, King John's illegitimate daughter.[184] Certainly by then, one must assume, the prince – realising that the ecclesiastical powers in England and on the continent had defeated Rotoland's claim – would have wanted to be seen to be fully embracing the English establishment's choice of bishop.[185]

Robert was, perhaps, already acquainted with Llywelyn's family, before getting on settled terms with the prince himself for Hubert Walter appointed Robert,

---

[178]   Brett, 'The annals of Bermondsey, Southwark, and Merton', p. 304. Thank you to Dr Martin Brett for bringing this to my attention.

[179]   *Cartae Antiquae, Rolls 11–20*, pp. 44–8; Gillingham, 'Richard I (1157–1199)', *ODNB*; *Itinerary of King Richard I*, pp. 134, 136, 137 and 140; *CChR, 1226–1257*, i, pp. 323–4; *CChR, 1341–1417*, v, pp. 194–5; *Calendar of Documents Preserved in France*, p. 91. See also *Records of the Templars in England*, pp. 140–2.

[180]   *Rot. Chart.*, 31a. Travelling with King John: *Ystrad Marchell Charters*, pp. 167–8, no. 25. *Rot. Chart.*, 44b and 80a; *Rot. Litt. Pat.*, 'Itinerary of King John'; Eyton, *Antiquities of Shropshire*, i, p. 265. Robert's continued exile from Bangor no doubt explains why when Pope Innocent III, on 24 November 1199, responded to Llywelyn ab Iorwerth's petition to be allowed to marry the daughter of Ragnvald (Rǫgnvaldr Guðrøðarson), King of Man and Isles, the papal response was addressed to the archdeacon of Bangor not the bishop. The other addressees were the bishop of Man and the prior of Ynys Lannog: *Reg. Innocenz' III*, ii, pp. 430–1, no. 224; *AWR*, p. 25.

[181]   Lincoln: *Rot. Chart.*, 84a–b; *Cartae Antiquae, Rolls 1–10*, p. 79, no. 154; *Rot. Litt. Pat.*, 'Itinerary of King John'. Extension of truce: *Rot. Chart.*, 100b; *AWR*, p. 373.

[182]   *AWR*, pp. 371–4, no. 221. According to Gerald of Wales, Robert, in 1201, had complained about him to Geoffrey fitz Peter saying that Gerald had sided with Robert's adversary (Rotoland): *Opera*, iii, p. 200; *Autobiography*, p. 225; *Episc. Acts Welsh Dioceses*, ii, p. 436; Hays, *Abbey of Aberconway*, p. 27.

[183]   *Rot. Litt. Pat.*, 39a.

[184]   *AWR*, p. 26.

[185]   A commission issued (1203) by Pope Innocent III to investigate Rotoland's claim came to nothing, and furthermore, Rotoland was expelled from the Cistercian order (1202): *Patrologia Latina*, ccxv, cols. 81–2; *Cal. Pap. Reg.*, i, p. 14; *Opera*, iii, pp. 193, 241 and 287; Hays, *Abbey of Aberconway*, pp. 27–9. See also *De Invectionibus*, p. 116; *Autobiography*, p. 271.

together with the abbots of Buildwas, Combermere, and Haughmond, to hear the cause between the 'noblewoman M(arared), mother of Llywelyn prince of north Wales', and 'W., son of Ione'. The report of Robert and the three abbots to the archbishop is extant (**17**).[186]

In 1206, following Hubert Walter's death, and during the *sede vacante* at Canterbury, Robert was a party to two certificates (**20** and **21**) concerning the canonical election of Jocelin of Wells, addressed to Pope Innocent III, and the papal legate in England, John of Ferentino, respectively.[187] Two further certificates (**22** and **23**), in the same matter, addressed to the same recipients, were his alone.[188] The election had followed the death of Savaric, bishop of Bath. King John had given his assent, and the certificates petitioned for papal confirmation of the election.[189] Robert was present when Jocelin was consecrated in Reading by the bishop of London, William de Ste Mère-Église, on Trinity Sunday, 28 May 1206.[190]

The texts of two more of Robert's *acta* have survived. The first provides further evidence of his connections with Shrewsbury, for it is a grant and gift to the church of SS Peter and Paul, Shrewsbury (**18**), and the abbot and monks there of, *inter alia*, all messuages which he had in Coleham.[191] Coleham lies to the south of Shrewsbury, just across the river Severn. The other *actum* is the grant of an indulgence (**19**), the original being preserved at the British Library. Robert's relaxation of 20 days enjoined penance was granted when he dedicated a chapel at Kingsthorpe Hospital, near Northampton, '*anno primo post obitum felicis memorie Hugonis quondam Lincol(niensis) episcopi octavo kalendas Junii* ' (25 May 1201).[192] As noted above, the bishop of Bangor had been in Lincoln on 13 January 1201, and it may be that the dedication was discussed with Robert in light of Hugh of Avalon's recent demise; the bishop of Lincoln having died on 16 November 1200.[193]

The dearth of evidence relating to Robert in surviving English records after 1206 strongly suggests that he was in his bishopric from, the very latest, that time. Given Robert's frequent presence at court in the last year of the reign of King Richard I, and in the early years of King John's, his next appearance in the historical record comes as something of a shock. Robert had been a loyal and trusted servant for many years. However, in the summer of 1211 this changed. In August of that year, King John successfully invaded Gwynedd Uwch Conwy, and three native chronicles record that Robert was captured by the king's men. According to *Brut y Tywysogyon*, after crossing the river Conwy towards Eryri, the king 'incited some of his host to burn Bangor. And there Rhobert, bishop of Bangor, was seized in

---

[186] *Actum* **17**. Image at Plate IX.

[187] *Acta* **20** and **21**.

[188] *Acta* **22** and **23**.

[189] See the note to *Actum* **20**.

[190] The bishops of Llandaff and St Asaph were also present: *Canterbury Professions*, p. 62.

[191] *Actum* **18**.

[192] *Actum* **19**. Image at Plate VIII.

[193] *Fasti Lincoln*, p. 2. Interestingly, an allowance was recorded in the account of the archdeacon of Lincoln at Michaelmas 1202 of ten pounds paid to the bishop of Bangor, by writ of Geoffrey fitz Peter. And ten pounds to the same by the writ of the same ('Et episcopo Bangornensi x li. per breue G. f. Petri. Et eidem x li. per breue eiusdem': *Pipe Roll, John, Year 4*, p. 278). Perhaps Robert had been given other tasks to perform in the large diocese of Lincoln.

his church, but he was afterwards ransomed for two hundred falcons'.[194] A second chronicle, *O Oes Gwrtheyrn*, compiled in Gwynedd, gives a more precise location for John's whereabouts, namely Aber (Abergwyngregyn) and adds that it was his Brabançon mercenaries whom the king ordered to burn Bangor, and when there they captured Robert and imprisoned him until the king released him.[195] A third Welsh chronicle, the Cottonian chronicle, stated that John ordered Robert to be seized because the bishop had refused to come to him (*quia ad eum uenire noluit*).[196] As Abergwyngregyn is a mere six miles or so from Robert's cathedral this could well explain John's anger at being snubbed. Furthermore, the Cottonian chronicle tells us that when Robert was taken, he was in front of the altar wearing his episcopal vestments (*episcopum … in ecclesia bangorensi ante altare episcopalibus indutum*).[197]

His savage treatment at the hands of the king's men in August 1211 might well have been too much for Robert, for he died the following year.[198] He was, in accordance with his wishes, buried at Shrewsbury.[199]

CADWGAN OF LLANDYFÁI (21 JUNE 1215–1235/1 MARCH 1236)

Cadwgan, abbot of the Cistercian house of Whitland, was consecrated by Archbishop Stephen Langton on 21 June 1215 at the church in Staines, Middlesex.[200] He professed obedience to the archbishop and the church of Canterbury (**24**).[201] Royal letters of protection had been issued on 27 December 1214 for the abbot of Whitland.[202] Licence to elect, witnessed by King John himself, was granted to

---

[194] 'Ac anoc rei o'e lu a oruc y losgi Bangor. Ac yno y delit Rotbert escob Bangor, yn y eglwys, ac y gwerthwyt wedy hyny yr deu cant hebawc': *Brut, Hergest*, pp. 190–1. See also, *Brut, Pen20Tr*, p. 85.

[195] Jones, '*O Oes Gwrtheyrn*: A Medieval Welsh Chronicle', pp. 169, 215, 221 and 227.

[196] *Annales Cambriae C-text*, p. 45. John had been excommunicated by Pope Innocent III in 1209 (Gillingham, 'John (1167–1216)', *ODNB*) and so this may explain why Robert refused to meet him. See also Lloyd, *History of Wales*, ii, p. 635.

[197] *Annales Cambriae C-text*, p. 45.

[198] *Brut, Hergest*, pp. 194–5; *Brut, Pen20Tr*, p. 86; *Annales de Theokesberia*, p. 60; *Annales de Wigornia*, p. 401; *Fasti Welsh Cathedrals*, p. 3.

[199] 'Obiit magister Robertus episcopus de Bangor, et sepultus est in medio foro apud Salopesbiriam, sicut desideravit in vita sua.': *Annales de Waverleia*, p. 273. An entry in the 1212 Book of Fees not only confirms his intimate ties with Shrewsbury, but also that, until the last, despite everything that had happened, he may have still retained a measure of royal support: 'Hii sunt qui tenent de domino rege de excaetis Gerardi de Thurnay … Episcopus Bangour' tenuit Kingesland' et reddit per annum xij. d.': *Book of Fees*, i, p. 147. Kingsland lies a short distance to the west of central Shrewsbury, across the river Severn. The lands of the Norman lord, Gerard de Tournai (or Tornai) were in the power of the king, having escheated to the monarch in the reign of Henry II. In the extant records the lands are often described as the 'Escheats of Gerard de Tornai': Eyton, *Antiquities of Shropshire*, viii, p. 127.

[200] '… consecratus est in episcopum de bangor apud stanes in ecclesia eiusdem ville … qui fuit abbas de alba londa xi kal. Iulii' (*Annals of Southwark and Merton*, 50); '… Chadwgawn Landifei, abat y Ty Gwynn, yn escop y Mangor' (*Brut, Hergest*, p. 204); '… abbas Blanch-Landiae' (*Annales de Wigornia*, p. 404, which gives a date of 'xvi. die Iunii'); *Fasti Welsh Cathedrals*, p. 3; *Heads of Religious Houses*, i, p. 147, pp. 274–5, and ii, p. 323.

[201] *Actum* **24**. Image at Plate VI (v).

[202] Witnessed by the king personally, abbot unnamed: *Rot. Litt. Pat.*, p. 125. *Fasti Welsh Cathedrals*, p. 3.

the chapter of Bangor on 13 March 1215, the king requesting that they elect the abbot as their pastor.[203] Once the canons had elected the abbot, which they did so unanimously, royal assent was given to the election on 13 April.[204]

On the same day as the archbishop consecrated Cadwgan to Bangor, he consecrated Iorwerth to St Davids.[205] The author of *Cronicon de Wallia* was delighted by the appointment of two Welshmen.[206] As abbot of the mother-house of all the Cistercian houses in *Pura Wallia*, and a native Welshman, Cadwgan was no doubt acceptable to Llywelyn ab Iorwerth, if not actively promoted by the prince to succeed to the vacant bishopric.[207] In fact, Gerald of Wales stated that Cadwgan (who he seemed reluctant to mention by name) had gone to great lengths to obtain the support of Llywelyn whilst the latter was on campaign in Cardigan in 1212; knowing that the see of Bangor was vacant, he invited the prince to Whitland, entertained him lavishly, and claimed to be his cousin – it was due to the prince's support that Cadwgan was elected.[208] That may be, but King John clearly supported his promotion as is evidenced by the issue of royal letters of protection, and the king's *congé d'élire* which requested that the Bangor chapter elect the abbot of Whitland.[209]

He is called Cadwgan of Llandyfái in *Brut y Tywysogyon*.[210] Llandyfái (or Lamphey), near Pembroke, was one of the episcopal estates of St Davids.[211] Gerald said that he was the son of a Welshwoman and an itinerant Irish priest.[212] His half-brother was a monk at the Cistercian abbey of Llantarnam, near Caerleon.[213] Before he became abbot of Whitland, Cadwgan had been a monk at the daughter-house of Strata Florida, and may have been abbot there for a short

---

[203] *Rot. Litt. Pat.*, p. 130; pd in Willis, *Survey*, pp. 185–6; Smith, 'Magna Carta', 358; *Fasti Welsh Cathedrals*, p. 3.

[204] *Rot. Litt. Pat.*, p. 132; pd in Willis, *Survey*, p. 186; Smith, 'Magna Carta', 358; *Fasti Welsh Cathedrals*, p. 3.

[205] *Annals of Southwark and Merton*, 50; *Brut, Hergest*, pp. 204–5; *Fasti Welsh Cathedrals*, p. 47.

[206] *Annales Cambriae E-text*, p. 12; 'Cronica de Wallia', 36; Pryce, 'The Dynasty of Deheubarth', pp. 308–9. For discussion of the timing of the two consecrations see Smith, 'Magna Carta', 357–9.

[207] The Welsh chroniclers referred to Cadwgan as 'Chadwgawn Landifei' (*Brut, Hergest*, p. 204), 'Chadwgon' (*Brenhinedd y Saesson*, p. 212), and 'Caduganus' in 'Cronicon de Wallia' (*Annales Cambriae E text*, p 12). Two English sources call him Martin: *Annales de Wigornia*, p. 404 and *Annales de Theokesberia*, p. 61, and it has been suggested that Martin was Cadwgan's monastic name (*Episc. Acts Welsh Dioceses*, ii, p. 553; *Fasti Welsh Cathedrals*, p. 3, n. 8). However, J. E. Lloyd (*History of Wales*, ii, p. 688, n. 201) suggested that the reference to Martin was 'probably a slip', pointing out that a later entry in *Annales de Theokesberia* (at p. 122) had the correct name ('Caducanus').

[208] *Opera*, iv, pp. 162–3; Cowley, *Monastic Order*, p. 122; Goering and Pryce, '*De Modo Confitendi*', 3, and n. 8, 4, and n. 16. J. E. Lloyd stated that the unnamed bishop who is pilloried by Gerald is, beyond doubt, Cadwgan: Lloyd, *History of Wales*, ii, p. 688, n. 201.

[209] *Rot. Litt. Pat.*, pp. 125 and 130; Smith, 'Magna Carta', 358.

[210] 'Chadwgawn Landifei': *Brut, Hergest*, pp. 204–5; Goering and Pryce, '*De Modo Confitendi*', 1.

[211] *Episc. Acts Welsh Dioceses*, ii, p. 554; *Fasti Welsh Cathedrals*, p. 3, n. 8.

[212] *Opera*, iv, p. 161. Cowley, *Monastic Order*, p. 122; Goering and Pryce, '*De Modo Confitendi*', 1–2; Lloyd, *History of Wales*, ii, p. 688; *Fasti Welsh Cathedrals*, p. 3.

[213] *Opera*, iv, p. 163; Cowley, *Monastic Order*, p. 48; Goering and Pryce, '*De Modo Confitendi*', 2; Walker, 'Cadwgan (d. 1241)', *ODNB*.

time.[214] According to Gerald, in 1202, Cadwgan persuaded the then abbot of Strata Florida that it was against their 'Book of Uses' to allow Gerald to pawn his library to the house, and thus he was forced to sell his books.[215] Cadwgan's father was said to have been a fervent and effective preacher in Welsh, and Cadwgan had inherited his father's gift of eloquence.[216] However, Gerald claimed that when he was bishop Cadwgan delivered sermons at various abbeys in England and Wales, more for show than the edification of the congregation – he having plagiarised the sermons, committing them, word for word, to memory.[217]

Gerald's great animosity towards Cadwgan cannot conceal the fact that the author of *Cronicon de Wallia* described him as '*vir mire facundie et sapientie*' (a man of wonderful eloquence and wisdom).[218] Whilst *Cronicon de Wallia* is probably a product of Whitland Abbey, and as such could be expected to be biased towards one of its own abbots, it is noteworthy that both it and Gerald describe Cadwgan as eloquent.[219] Further praise is to be found in the Peniarth MS 20 version of *Brut y Tywysogyon* which described Cadwgan as 'a man of great accomplishments and learning' (*gwr mawr ygeluydodeu ay ysgolhectot*).[220] These 'accomplishments and learning' may, in part, refer to the written works for which Cadwgan was responsible, and which are generally well-regarded by scholars.[221] It has also been postulated by David Stephenson that Cadwgan could have been the inspiration for the B-text entries of the *Annales Cambriae* (the Breviate chronicle) for *c.*1211/12–1219, in that

---

[214] *Heads of Religious Houses*, i, pp. 147 and 274–5; cf. Walker, 'Cadwgan (*d.* 1241)', *ODNB*. See also *Opera*, iii, p. 240, and iv, pp. 146–50, 162–3 and 166–7; *Autobiography*, p. 265; Goering and Pryce, '*De Modo Confitendi*', 2, and n. 6; Cowley, *Monastic Order*, pp. 122–3; *Episc. Acts Welsh Dioceses*, ii, pp. 554–6.

[215] *Opera*, iv, 153–5; *Autobiography*, pp. 250–1; Harrison, 'A Note on Gerald of Wales', 252–3; Goering and Pryce, '*De Modo Confitendi*', 2, and n. 5.

[216] *Opera*, iv, pp. 163–4; Cowley, *Monastic Order*, pp. 48 and 122–3; Goering and Pryce, '*De Modo Confitendi*', 2; Walker, 'Cadwgan (*d.* 1241)', *ODNB*.

[217] *Opera*, iv, p. 165; Cowley, *Monastic Order*, pp. 122–3; Goering and Pryce, '*De Modo Confitendi*', 2.

[218] *Annales Cambriae E-text*, p. 12; 'Cronica de Wallia', 36.

[219] Provenance of *Cronicon de Wallia*: Hughes, *Welsh Latin Chronicles*, p. 250 and n. 1; Smith, 'The "Cronica de Wallia" and the Dynasty of Dinefwr', 279–80.

[220] *Brut, Pen20Tr*, p. 104; *Brut, Pen20*, p. 196.

[221] They are preserved in two thirteenth-century manuscripts: firstly, Dulwich College, London, MS 22 (L.8), fos. 46r–49r., being a treatise on confession (printed in Goering and Pryce, '*De Modo Confitendi*', 16–27; Sharpe, *Handlist*, no. 176) which is an example of a confessional formulary designed to give clergy specific and practical advice on hearing confessions; the need for such advice having become all the more pressing following the requirement for an annual auricular confession decreed by the Fourth Lateran Council in 1215 (Goering and Pryce, '*De Modo Confitendi*', 1 and 11; Goering and Payer, 'Summa Penitentie', 1; Davies, *Age of Conquest*, p. 208), and secondly, Hereford Cathedral Archive o.VI.8, Cadwgan's works having been printed in Talbot, 'Cadogan of Bangor'; Sharpe, *Handlist*, no. 176, see also Goering and Pryce, '*De Modo Confitendi*', 8–11; cf. Runciman, 'Pastoral care according to the bishops of England and Wales', pp. 108–13. In the sixteenth century John Leland recorded other works by Cadwgan: Smith, *The Itinerary of John Leland*, p. 178; Tonkin, 'After the Dissolution', p. 153; see also Talbot, 'Cadogan of Bangor', 24–5, and McGuinness, 'The Medieval Bishops of Bangor and the Writing of Welsh History' (forthcoming).

there is a strong possibility that those entries were compiled at Whitland.[222] Furthermore, Daniel Huws has suggested that Cadwgan was a possible channel for the passage into the Gwynedd legal circles of Llywelyn ab Iorwerth of the now-lost Whitland Abbey *Llyfr y Tŷ Gwyn* ('The Book of the White House').[223]

In the year following his consecration, 'all the learned men of Gwynedd' were summoned by Llywelyn ab Iorwerth to Aberdyfi,[224] and presumably Cadwgan was amongst them. In the same year, he was presumably one of the bishops who was sent by Llywelyn to Gwenwynwyn ab Owain Cyfeiliog (d. 1216) of Powys to beseech him to return to the prince – Gwenwynwyn having recently sided with King John.[225] In November, after John's death, Cadwgan was present in Bristol at the court of the young Henry III, along with the bishops of the three other Welsh sees, Llandaff, St Asaph, and St Davids.[226] In June 1218, all four bishops were once again with the king, at the consecration of Worcester cathedral.[227] The following year, at the Temple in London, Cadwgan was witness to a letter from Ragnvald (Rǫgnvaldr Guðrøðarson) King of the Isles, to Pope Honorius III.[228]

Llywelyn ab Iorwerth's trust in Cadwgan is evidenced by the fact that in 1223 the bishop was appointed as one of the prince's representatives in an inquisition into lands held by Llywelyn's adherents.[229] A few years later, Cadwgan and the bishops of St Asaph and St Davids petitioned (**31**) Pope Honorius III as part of Llywelyn's drive to ensure that Dafydd, his son by King John's daughter Joan, was accepted as his rightful heir, in preference to his elder son Gruffudd.[230] Cadwgan's loyalty to Llywelyn may account for the fact that when, in 1231, the bishops of the province of Canterbury were summoned by Henry III to a conference to discuss the excommunication of Llywelyn after the renewal of hostilities that year, the bishop of Bangor was not summoned.[231] It may have been about this time that Cadwgan granted an indulgence (**26**) to all penitents giving gifts to the church of SS Peter and Paul, Leominster – there is evidence that the lands, possessions,

[222] Stephenson, 'In Search of a Welsh Chronicler', 79 and n. 33, and 81–3.

[223] Huws, 'Descriptions of the Welsh Manuscripts', p. 418; Huws, *Repertory of Welsh Manuscripts and Scribes*, i, p. 665. See also Pryce, *Native Law*, pp. 23–5.

[224] 'holl doethon Gwyned': *Brut, Hergest*, pp. 206–7. Also *Brut, Pen20Tr*, p. 92.

[225] *Brut, Pen20Tr*, p. 92. Also *Brut, Hergest*, pp. 206–9. Lloyd, *History of Wales*, ii, p. 649 and ns. 192 and 193.

[226] November 1216, Llandaff (Henry), St Asaph (Reiner), and St Davids (Iorwerth): Archives Nationales, MS J655 Angleterre sans date no. 11. Lloyd, *History of Wales*, ii, p. 651.

[227] June 1218: *Annales de Wigornia*, p. 409.

[228] September 1219: *Cal. Pap. Reg.*, i, pp. 69–70; *Le Liber Censuum*, i, 260b–261a. Duffy, 'Ragnvald [Rögnvaldr, Reginald, Ragnall] (d. 1229)', *ODNB*. For a discussion of Cadwgan's involvement: Jones, 'Welsh Contacts with the Papacy before the Edwardian Conquest', p. 87, n. 216.

[229] *Pat. Rolls, 1216–1225*, p. 481. One of Llywelyn's other representatives was Ednyfed Fychan (d. 1246) who was the prince's seneschal from as early as the year of Cadwgan's consecration, 1215: Stephenson, *Governance*, pp. 207–8. He and Cadwgan would have been well-known to each other. See also Lloyd, *History of Wales*, ii, pp. 661–3; *AWR*, pp. 416–17, no. 254; Walker, 'Marshal, William, fifth earl of Pembroke (c.1190–1231)', *ODNB*.

[230] Bishop Abraham of St Asaph and Bishop Iorwerth of St Davids: *Actum* **31**.

[231] Haddan and Stubbs, i, pp. 462–3. Stephenson, *Governance*, p. 169; Goering and Pryce, '*De Modo Confitendi*', 3 and n. 12.

and indeed monks themselves of the Benedictine priory of Leominster had been attacked by the Welsh.[232]

As regards Cadwgan's other known *acta*, he granted two indulgences (**27** and **28**) in favour of Reading Abbey.[233] He also granted an indulgence (**30**) to those contributing towards the construction of an alms-house, by the dean and chapter of Hereford, for the maintenance and residence of the poor.[234] To his old abbey of Strata Florida he granted, with the consent of his chapter, the church of Llangurig (**29**) in Arwystli.[235] The documentary evidence for the connection between the bishopric and Haughmond Abbey resumes after a hiatus during Robert of Shrewsbury's episcopate; the abbey's cartulary recording a notification by Cadwgan of the peaceful resolution of a dispute (**25**) concerning the church of Nefyn (Llŷn).[236] Three other *acta*, concerning his resignation from his see, and subsequent retirement to Dore Abbey, are discussed below.[237] There is evidence of one other probable *actum*, namely a request for the assistance of Henry III (**32**) in respect a certain ship which the bishop of Bangor had caused to be laden with corn in Ireland for the sustenance of the poor in Wales.[238]

According to *Brut y Tywysogyon*, in 1236, Pope Gregory IX relieved Cadwgan of his episcopal care, and he became a monk at Dore Abbey.[239] Gregory IX granted permission for Cadwgan to resign on or before 1 March 1236, for on that date, at Viterbo, the pope issued a mandate to the chapter of Bangor, the see being void by resignation (**33**), to elect a bishop, applying the goods of the late bishop, except books and clothes, to the payment of the debts of the church.[240]

Once at Dore, Cadwgan, '*dei gratia episcopus minister quondam Bangor(e)n(sis)*', made his profession (**34**) to Stephen of Worcester, abbot of Dore, renouncing all possessions, and gave to the monastery, for the salvation of his soul, all whatsoever he owned in books, horses, and everything, entirely, without any claim by anyone, in perpetuity.[241] Later, and describing himself in similar terms, he made a notification (**35**) concerning his nephew.[242]

In 1239, the General Chapter of the Cistercian Order heard charges against Cadwgan; he was accused of neglecting the observances and institutes of the Order and the Chapter, both in silence and in his way of living, and breeding serious lawlessness, dissension, and scandal. It was therefore ordered that unless

---

[232] *Actum* **26** and note to the same.
[233] *Actum* **27** and *Actum* **28**.
[234] *Actum* **30**. Image at Plate X.
[235] *Actum* **29**.
[236] *Actum* **25**.
[237] *Actum* **33**, *Actum* **34**, and *Actum* **35**.
[238] *Actum* **32**.
[239] *Brut, Pen20 Tr*, p. 104. Also, *Brut, Hergest*, pp. 234–5. For discussion of why Cadwgan may have chosen to resign and why he chose Dore for his retirement see: Talbot, 'Cadogan of Bangor', 19; Goering and Pryce, '*De Modo Confitendi*', 6–8, and ns. 34, 35, 36, 37, 41 and 42; and Lloyd, *History of Wales*, ii, p. 689.
[240] *Cal. Pap. Reg.*, i, p. 151. See also *Actum* **33**.
[241] *Actum* **34**. Image at Plate XI (i).
[242] *Actum* **35**. Image at Plate XI (ii).

he desisted he be expelled from the Order.[243] It seems that he was not expelled for he died at Dore on 11 April 1241 and was buried there.[244] In the sixteenth century, John Leland noted that Cadwgan was buried in the abbey, and an oak effigy was recorded early in the eighteenth century.[245]

RICHARD/RHIRID. 1237–1267 (BEFORE 8 NOVEMBER 1267)

On 7 June 1236, Master Guy (possibly 'Gwion' in Welsh) dean of the church of Bangor delivered letters from his chapter announcing the voidance of that church and was given letters directed to the canons of Bangor of licence to elect.[246] On 3 July, royal assent was given to the election of Master Richard, archdeacon of Bangor.[247] Richard was consecrated the following year by the archbishop of Canterbury, Edmund of Abingdon, and professed canonical obedience (**36**) to Canterbury, Edmund, and his successors.[248] Richard would doubtless have met with Llywelyn ab Iorwerth's approval when elected in 1236. He was named '*Ririt*' (i.e. the Welsh name 'Rhirid') when he appeared as a witness to a charter given by Llywelyn's son Dafydd.[249] It is not known where he was educated, nor when he obtained his title of '*magister*'.

Within a few years of his consecration, Richard was embroiled in an event which would set the tone for his episcopate. According to *Brut y Tywysogyon*, in 1239 Dafydd seized Gruffudd (his half-brother) and imprisoned him.[250] However, Matthew Paris, the monk and historian of St Albans, gave a slightly different account stating that this did not happen until after the death of their father Llywelyn ab Iorwerth.[251] Llywelyn died on 11 April 1240, whereupon Paris tells us war ensued between the brothers until around Michaelmas 1240 when Dafydd lured Gruffudd to a peace council, under the safe conduct of the bishop of Bangor and other great men. Dafydd ordered Gruffudd to be taken, and, despite the protests of the bishop and others, imprisoned.[252] Richard, incensed, excommunicated Dafydd and fled

---

[243] *Statuta Capitulorum Ordinis Cisterciensis*, ii, p. 206 (1239/20); Cowley, *Monastic Order*, p. 123; Williams, 'Abbey of Dore', p. 24, and n. 46; Goering and Pryce, '*De Modo Confitendi*', 8.

[244] *Annales de Theokesberia*, p. 122. See also *Brut, Hergest*, pp. 234–5.

[245] Smith, *The Itinerary of John Leland*, p. 178; Tonkin, 'After the Dissolution', pp. 153, 154, and n. 5 (referring to Watkins, 'Antiquarian Discoveries at Abbey Dore', 146–7); Williams, 'Abbey of Dore', pp. 24, 25 (drawing, Fig. 12), and n. 47, referring to *The Reliquary* (January 1903), Hereford City Libr., Hill MSS III, 228, and Marshall, 'Wooden Monumental Effigies', 189–97.

[246] Marwell: *CPR, 1232–1247*, p. 149.

[247] Gloucester: *CPR, 1232–1247*, p. 152.

[248] *Actum* **36**. Image at Plate VI (vi). *Fasti Welsh Cathedrals*, p. 4.

[249] 'domino Ririt Bangoren(si) episcopo', 19 October 1238 x 11 April 1240: *AWR*, pp. 456–7, no. 289; *Cartulary of Haughmond Abbey*, p. 222, no. 1217. For the date range see *AWR*, pp. 456–7.

[250] *Brut, Hergest*, pp. 235–7; *Brut, Pen20Tr*, p. 105. See also, *Annales Cambriae E-text*, p. 17; 'Cronica de Wallia', 38.

[251] *Chronica Majora*, iv, pp. 8 and 47–8; Lloyd, *History of Wales*, ii, p. 694, n. 2.

[252] *Chronica Majora*, iv, pp. 8, 47–8, and 148; *Matthew Paris's English History*, i, p. 290. Williams, 'Succession', 404; Lloyd, *History of Wales*, ii, p. 694, n. 2.

to England, where he begged Henry III to intervene.[253] According to Paris, the bishop laid two grave complaints (**38** and **39**) before the king concerning Dafydd's treachery and betrayal in incarcerating Gruffudd.[254] Gwyn A. Williams cautiously argued that Paris' dating was to be preferred to that of the Welsh chroniclers, *inter alia*, because Richard is known to have personally informed Paris of at least one event, and the bishop not only visited St Albans but resided there for a time.[255] Other scholars have also concluded that Richard probably passed details of political developments in Gwynedd to the St Albans historian.[256] Certainly the evidence points to Richard being in England in the final months of 1240 for a little over a month after Michaelmas, on 5 November, he was present at the dedication of Rochester cathedral,[257] and it seems that on 13 December he was at St Paul's in London, where he granted an indulgence (**40**) in favour of those contributing towards the construction of the soon-to-be dedicated church.[258] Richard may have stayed in England for a while longer, as he may have been present at the actual dedication of the 'new' St Paul's, on 13 January 1241 – a second indulgence (**41**) of his survives in favour of that church, and this grant refers to the day of dedication.[259]

It seems that Richard had returned to Wales by August 1241, and that on his return there was some sort of reconciliation with Dafydd ap Llywelyn for the latter sent the bishop (*c.*8 x 29 August 1241) to Henry III to negotiate peace.[260] The peace mission did not succeed and the king quickly defeated Dafydd.[261] On 29 August, Richard gave Henry III a charter (**42**) in which he agreed to carry out all sentences of excommunication or interdict pursuant to the peace agreement imposed on Dafydd at Gwerneigron the same day.[262] On 31 August Richard sealed two notifications made by Dafydd.[263] The first requirement of the agreement reached at Gwerneigron was that Dafydd had to hand over his half-brother, Gruffudd, and Gruffudd's first-born son (Owain) to the king.[264] Gruffudd was then incarcerated in the Tower of London – he was there by September 1241.[265] According to Matthew Paris, Richard went to the king and tried to have Gruffudd set free, but

---

[253] *Chronica Majora*, iv, pp. 148–9; Williams, 'Succession', 404. See also Stephenson, *Governance*, p. 169, n. 12.

[254] *Acta* **38** and **39**.

[255] Williams, 'Succession', pp. 403–8; see also McGuinness, 'The Medieval Bishops of Bangor and the Writing of Welsh History' (forthcoming).

[256] Pryce, *Writing Welsh History*, p. 36; *AWR*, p. 469; Smith, *Llywelyn*, p. 35, n. 118; Carpenter, 'Dafydd ap Llywelyn's Submission to King Henry III', 4.

[257] *Flores Historiarum*, ii, p. 243.

[258] *Actum* **40**. Image at Plate XII.

[259] *Actum* **41**. Image at Plate XIII.

[260] *AWR*, pp. 465–6, no. 299; *LW*, pp. 153–4, no. 271. Richard was accompanied by, amongst others, Master David, the prince's chancellor. For the significance of Richard's appointment see *AWR*, p. 466.

[261] Williams, 'Succession', 404. Stephenson, *Medieval Powys*, pp. 115–16.

[262] Hywel II, bishop of St Asaph, did the same: *Actum* **42**; *AWR*, pp. 466–70, no. 300.

[263] As did the bishop of St Asaph, Hywel II: *AWR*, pp. 472–4, nos. 302 and 303; *LW*, pp. 12–13, no. 6, and p. 22, no. 22; *CPR, 1232–1247*, p. 264.

[264] *AWR*, pp. 466–70, no. 300.

[265] *CCR, 1237–1242*, p. 328; *CLR, 1240–1245*, p. 70; Smith, *Llywelyn*, p. 35, n. 122.

he laboured in vain.[266] Further evidence of the bishop's support for Gruffudd is possibly provided by the fact that he (and his son, Philip) witnessed a grant by Gruffudd's second son, Llywelyn, at Llannerch in Dyffryn Clwyd, where the bishop had an estate.[267]

Gruffudd died in 1244 trying to escape from the Tower, and in alliance with other Welsh leaders, Dafydd rose against the English and the Marcher lords, but he died suddenly in February 1246. Llywelyn ap Gruffudd decided to continue the war that his uncle Dafydd had started.[268] Within two months Richard was at Windsor, where on 20 April, he promised Henry III fidelity (**43**) stating, *inter alia*, that he would do everything in his power to bring those enemies of the king back to fealty.[269]

Richard was at Haughmond Abbey, in Shropshire, on 1 January 1247 or 1248 and there he confirmed (**45**) his predecessors' gifts to the abbot and convent in respect of the churches of Nefyn (Llŷn) and Trefeglwys (Arwystli).[270] According to Matthew Paris, by 1248 Richard was at St Albans – the impoverished bishop coming to the abbey so that he and his clerks might stay with the abbot until his bishopric, which had been ruined by war, had been restored.[271] Richard was still in England in 1249, for he assisted the bishop of Worcester (Walter de Cantilupe) in consecrating the new bishop of St Asaph (Anian I).[272] At Westminster the following year, no doubt pursuant to a request (**46**) from Richard, Henry III ordered Alan de la Zouche (the new justice of Chester and the Four Cantrefs) to enquire whether the bishop of Bangor and his predecessors were accustomed to have certain rights and tithes,[273] and in 1251, again at Westminster, a grant was made to Richard pursuant to the inquiry.[274] When he returned to Gwynedd is not clear but in July 1252 Richard was at Aberdaron (Llŷn).[275] In the same year, Matthew Paris recorded that the bishop of Bangor, on coming to St Albans, reported on the submission of the Welsh.[276]

Richard's pattern of residence in St Albans with visits to Wales continued for the next five or six years. On Maundy Thursday 1254, Richard prepared the

---

[266] *Historia Anglorum*, ii, p. 453. Protection without term was granted to Richard at Westminster on 20 October: *CPR, 1232–1247*, p. 261.

[267] *AWR*, p. 491, no. 318; see also Davies, 'A Grant by Llewelyn Ap Gruffydd', 160; Stephenson, *Governance*, p. 229. The bishop's estate at Llannerch (par Llanfair Dyffryn Clwyd) is recorded in the extent of the lands of the bishop in 1306/7: *RC*, pp. 113–15; Smith, *Llywelyn*, p. 43, and n. 23; *AWR*, p. 491. Bishop Gwion also had a son (also called Philip) – see the section of the Introduction entitled '*Clas* and *Familia*'.

[268] Williams, 'Succession', 410.

[269] *Actum* **43**. On the same day letters patent of safe conduct until Midsummer were issued for Richard and his men returning to Wales: *CPR, 1232–1247*, p. 478.

[270] *Actum* **45**.

[271] *Chronica Majora*, v, p. 2. For the possibility that Richard chose St Albans because Matthew Paris resided there see McGuinness, 'The Medieval Bishops of Bangor and the Writing of Welsh History' (forthcoming).

[272] The bishop of Meath assisted as well: *Annales de Wigornia*, p. 439; *Fasti Welsh Cathedrals*, p. 35.

[273] *Actum* **46**. *CCR, 1247–1251*, p. 338.

[274] *CPR, 1247–1258*, p. 94.

[275] *AWR*, pp. 634–8, no. 440; *RC*, p. 252. Protection for Richard had been granted on 27 March 1252, at Westminster: *CPR, 1247–1258*, p. 133.

[276] *Chronica Majora*, v, p. 288.

chrism in the church of St Albans, and in the same year he dedicated the church of Hexton in Hertfordshire.[277] *Brut y Tywysogyon* records that the great bell at Strata Florida was raised on 24 August 1255 and consecrated by the bishop of Bangor, and so Richard was back in Wales at this point.[278] He spent Christmas 1256 at the English royal court, and was present on 26 December when the crown of Germany was offered to Henry III's brother Richard, earl of Cornwall.[279] It was the bishop of Bangor who reported events to Matthew Paris – the earl of Cornwall was advised by Henry and others to accept the crown, which he did, turning to the bishops, including Richard, to make his acceptance speech.[280] A week later, Richard was back in St Albans, where on 2 January 1257 after the discovery of the body of St Alban,[281] he dedicated a new altar, and granted two indulgences; one of thirty days (**47**) to all those worshipping at the newly-discovered tomb, and one of ten days (**48**) to all those attending the altar.[282]

By April 1258 there must have been a reconciliation between Llywelyn ap Gruffudd and the bishop of Bangor for Richard had returned to Wales where he sealed, as J. B. Smith noted, the earliest surviving example of a formal agreement between the prince and a Welsh leader who acknowledged Llywelyn's supremacy by doing homage.[283] In August, Richard's seal was sought to a notification that another Welsh leader had similarly done homage to Llywelyn.[284] In the autumn of the following year, Richard delivered Llywelyn's proposals for peace to the king.[285] At Westminster, letters patent of safe conduct were issued to Richard and members of his household who were named as: Master David, archdeacon of Bangor, Guy the chaplain, David the clerk, Adam Hen, David Foel, Adam the chaplain, and Iorwerth ('Gervase') of Llanfair.[286] This is the earliest record listing the members of an episcopal household for Bangor. In December, it was the archbishop of Canterbury's turn to seek Richard's assistance; the bishop was charged with coerc-

---

[277] *Chronica Majora*, v, p. 432; *Flores Historiarum*, ii, p. 396; *Gesta Abbatum Monasterii Sancti Albani*, i, p. 321.

[278] *Brut, Pen20Tr*, p. 110; *Brut, Hergest*, pp. 246–7.

[279] *Chronica Majora*, v, pp. 601–3; Vincent, 'Richard, first earl of Cornwall and king of Germany (1209–1272)', *ODNB*. The bishop of Bangor had been granted simple protection for so long as he was faithful to the king and Edward his son: 18 December 1256, at Guildford (*CPR, 1247–1258*, p. 534).

[280] '… Et addidit, versa facie ad episcopos, quorum unus Bangorensis Ricardus, qui haec huius paginae scriptori assertive enarravit, extiterat, …': *Chronica Majora*, v, pp. 601–3. *Matthew Paris's English History*, iii, pp. 207–9; Williams, 'Succession', 406; Haddan and Stubbs, i, p. 475.

[281] *Chronica Majora*, v, pp. 608–9; Pryce, 'Esgobaeth Bangor', p. 49.

[282] *Acta* **47** and **48**.

[283] Agreement between Llywelyn and Maredudd ap Rhys Gryg of Deheubarth: *AWR*, pp. 501–2, no. 329; Smith, *Llywelyn*, p. 107.

[284] Hywel ap Rhys Gryg of Deheubarth: *AWR*, p. 225, no. 85.

[285] *AWR*, pp. 506–7, no. 338; *CCR, 1259–1261*, pp. 4–5.

[286] October 1259: *CPR, 1258–1266*, p. 57. 'Foel' recorded as 'Woel': *ibid*. Llanfair ('Thanveyr') may have been Llanfair in Ardudwy: see *Fasti Welsh Cathedrals*, p. 9 and n. 16, and Stephenson, *Governance*, pp. 36–7, and 224. The safe conduct (to last until Easter) was specified to be for them coming to the king and returning to their own parts, provided that they did the king no harm. Richard swore before the council to that effect: *CPR, 1258–1266*, p. 57.

ing Llywelyn to observe the peace with the king.[287] The following year, Richard took Llywelyn's peace proposals to Henry III,[288] and it is clear he had authority to make arrangements for further talks on the prince's behalf.[289] When in early 1260 he returned to Westminster, the king's council recognised his endeavours in trying to secure peace.[290] In July the trust placed in Richard by the king and his council, combined no doubt with the bishop's careful mediation, paid dividends for a prorogation (**49**) of the truce agreed at Oxford (in 1258) was made; Richard swearing on the soul of Llywelyn to observe the same.[291] In a notification (**50**) issued the following day Richard confirmed, on behalf of Llywelyn, that he had sworn to observe the prorogation.[292] In August 1260, at Montgomery, the truce was extended to the summer of 1262, Richard being the prince's main representative once again.[293] Having successfully negotiated a lengthy extension to the truce with the king's representatives, Richard now turned his attention to certain matters that were in contention between himself and the prince. Perhaps the bishop expected a little goodwill from Llywelyn as a *quid pro quo* for his many weeks of travel and negotiation, often in difficult circumstances, on the prince's behalf. The matters, concerning boundaries as well as lay and ecclesiastical rights and jurisdiction, were addressed by arbitration (**51**, **52** and **53**).[294]

In 1261, Richard was present at Lambeth for the council held by the archbishop of Canterbury, Boniface of Savoy.[295] Two years later, in Meirionnydd, Richard was once again part of Llywelyn ap Gruffudd's programme of documenting his dominance over other Welsh princes; for in 1263, Gruffudd ap Gwenwynwyn of Powys did homage for himself and his heirs, and touching relics swore fealty to Llywelyn before Richard, Master David, archdeacon of Bangor, and others, and in return, Llywelyn granted the Powysian prince all his lands and possessions.[296] Richard, and others, were to ensure that the agreement was complied with, by ecclesiastical censure if need be.[297] However, despite acting for Llywelyn on several occasions, it appears that Richard's episcopate was even more troubled than his many years in exile suggest. In 1265 he placed an interdict (**54**) on Llywelyn's chapel (apparently

[287] *CCR, 1256–1259*, p. 466.

[288] *AWR*, pp. 506–7, no. 338.

[289] *CPR, 1258–1266*, p. 57.

[290] *CCR, 1259–1261*, pp. 30–1.

[291] *Actum* **49**. Truce agreed at Oxford on 17 June 1258: *AWR*, pp. 503–4, no. 331; *LW*, pp. 27–8, no. 33; Smith, *Llywelyn*, p. 120.

[292] *Actum* **50**.

[293] He was accompanied by the abbot of Aberconwy: *AWR*, pp. 508–12, no. 342.

[294] *Acta* **51**, **52** and **53**.

[295] Council held 8–13 May. Also present were the bishops of Llandaff (William) and St Davids (Richard): *Councils and Synods*, ii, part i, 1205–1265, pp. 668–9. Canterbury Cathedral Archives, CCA-DCc/ChAnt/L/138A.

[296] At Ystumanner, Meirionnydd. Addaf, the dean of Ardudwy, and David, son of William, official of Dyffryn Clwyd were also present: *AWR*, pp. 529–33, no. 358 and pp. 792–4, no. 601. J. B. Smith made the point that the agreement drawn up was emphatically the documenting of a lord and vassal relationship: Smith, *Llywelyn*, pp. 159 and 288.

[297] The others so tasked were the bishop of St Asaph (Anian I) and the abbots of Aberconwy and Strata Marcella: *AWR*, pp. 529–33, no. 358 and pp. 792–4, no. 601.

in another dispute concerning lay and ecclesiastical jurisdiction),[298] and in 1267, shortly before he died, he begged Pope Clement IV, via the papal legate Cardinal Ottobuono, to be allowed to resign (**55**) not only because of age, and ill-health, but also because he was disturbed by so many seditions and insolences.[299]

Richard died before 8 November 1267, for on that date at Winchester Master Iorwerth ('Gervase'), a canon of Bangor, delivered letters patent from his chapter announcing the death of their bishop.[300]

Richard's other *acta* were an indulgence (**37**) in favour of Reading Abbey, and a collation and confirmation (**44**), with the consent of his chapter, in favour of the abbot and convent of Aberconwy in respect of the chapel of Cemais (Llanbadrig, Anglesey).[301]

ANIAN. CONSECRATED IN 1267 (AFTER 12 DECEMBER). DIED 15 SEPTEMBER 1305 X 27 MARCH 1306.

On 8 November 1267, at Winchester, Master Iorwerth ('Gervase'), a canon of Bangor, having delivered letters patent from his chapter announcing the death of the bishop of Bangor (Richard) was given licence to elect.[302] On 12 December, at Clarendon, signification was given to the archbishop of Canterbury of the royal assent to the election of Master Anian, archdeacon of Anglesey, and a canon of the church of Bangor, to be bishop of that place.[303] On 5 January 1268, at Westminster, it was enrolled that Henry III had received letters from archbishop B(oniface of Savoy) confirming the election of Master Anian to be bishop, and the king, having accepted that confirmation, restored the temporalities of the bishopric to Anian 'as the custom is and commands Llewelin son of Griffin, prince of Wales, to let him have seisin thereof so far as pertains to the said Llewelin'.[304]

Anian professed (**56**) canonical obedience and subjection to Archbishop Boniface of Savoy, his successors, and the church of Canterbury.[305] The endorsement to his profession states that he was consecrated at Canterbury by Boniface, who was assisted by Hugh de Balsham, bishop of Ely, and William de Briouze, bishop of Llandaff, '*anno domino MCCLXVII*'.[306] The endorsement is in the same hand as the endorsement to the profession of John II, elect of St Asaph, who was consecrated at Canterbury in 1267.[307] Hugh de Balsham and William de Briouze also assisted at John's consecration.[308] So the evidence suggests that Anian was consecrated before the end of 1267.[309]

[298] *Actum* **54**.
[299] *Actum* **55**.
[300] *CPR, 1266–1277*, p. 165. There is no record of him leaving a will: *Testamentary Records*, p. 1.
[301] *Acta* **37** and **44**.
[302] *CPR, 1266–1272*, p. 165. Sealed petition from the dean and chapter, to Henry III, for licence to elect a pontiff and pastor: TNA, Chancery: Ecclesiastical Petitions, C 84/4/19.
[303] Clarendon near Salisbury: *CPR, 1266–1272*, p. 173.
[304] *ibid.*, p. 178.
[305] *Actum* **56**. Image at Plate VI (vii).
[306] Canterbury Cathedral Archives, CCA-DCc/ChAnt/C/115/136.
[307] *Canterbury Professions*, p. 79.
[308] *ibid.*, p. 78.
[309] However, it is odd that when Henry III restored the temporalities on 5 January 1268, the archbishop had only confirmed Anian's election, not sent news of his consecration: *CPR, 1266–1272*, p. 178.

It is not known where Anian was educated, nor when he obtained his title of '*magister*'. Huw Pryce has said that he was almost certainly a native of north Wales.[310] David Powel, in the sixteenth century, called him 'Anianus or Eneon'.[311] A fourteenth-century source refers to him as Anian ap Kenewrek[312] ('ap Cynwrig').[313]

Anian, no doubt, met with Llywelyn ap Gruffudd's approval. Llywelyn, who had been recognised as prince of Wales by Henry III at Montgomery only a few months before Anian's election and consecration, was at the height of his powers, and it seems unlikely that he did not have a say in who should be the next bishop of Bangor.[314] In the year following his consecration, Anian was named as one of the arbitrators appointed by Llywelyn to settle various disputes between the prince and the Marcher lord Gilbert de Clare, earl of Gloucester and earl of Hertford (d. 1295).[315] In 1269, just as his predecessor had done, Anian was called upon to add his episcopal clout to another agreement which recorded an act of fealty and homage by a senior member of the princely class to Llywelyn, for he and his namesake Anian (II), the new bishop of St Asaph, sealed a letter patent confirming a peace agreement between Llywelyn, prince of Wales, lord of Snowdon, and his brother, Dafydd, in which Dafydd gave his fealty, homage, and service, in return for the restoration of lands.[316] If any grievances should arise between Llywelyn and Dafydd these would be settled by the bishops, together with worthy men chosen with the consent of both sides.[317] In fact, the bishops were subsequently called upon to interpret certain articles of the agreement which were said to be obscure and in doubt, and in a letter (**59**) of 1274 they gave their interpretation and explanation of the articles.[318]

In March 1269 at Caernarfon, Anian gave his consent to an exchange of land between Llywelyn and the prior and convent of Beddgelert, in which the latter quitclaimed to the prince certain land in Gwynedd Uwch Conwy, and, as such, in the diocese of Bangor. Anian and the Bangor chapter added their seals to those of Llywelyn and the prior.[319] In April 1272, once again at Caernarfon, Anian attached his seal to a gift and quitclaim made by Rhodri ap Gruffudd to his brother Llywe-

---

[310]   Pryce, 'Anian [Einion] (*d.* 1305x7)', *ODNB*.

[311]   Powel, *The Historie of Cambria*, p. 383. Godwin, writing in 1615, also wrote 'Anianus or Eneon' (Godwin, *Catalogue*, p. 537). Browne Willis, in 1721, had 'Anian or Eyneaun' (Willis, *Survey*, p. 67). I can find no source during Anian's episcopate, or lifetime, which names him as 'Einion'.

[312]   *CIM*, ii, p. 239, no. 962.

[313]   Or perhaps 'ap Cynfrig': Smith, '*Gravamina*', 161, n. 8. Cf. 'Cynwrig' in *AWR*, for example at p. 838.

[314]   Treaty of Montgomery, September 1267: *AWR*, pp. 536–42, no. 363.

[315]   September 1268. The arbitrators were to begin their office on 10 January 1269 at 'Eadbryn' (unidentified) in Brecon. The other arbitrators for Llywelyn were Goronwy ab Ednyfed, Tudur ab Ednyfed and Dafydd ab Einion: *AWR*, pp. 543–5, no. 366; Smith, *Llywelyn*, p. 344, ns. 20, 21 and 22. See also *CPR, 1266–1272*, p. 205.

[316]   *AWR*, pp. 546–7, no. 368. In 1263, Anian's predecessor, Richard, had put his seal to an agreement made between Llywelyn and Gruffudd ap Gwenwynwyn of Powys: *AWR*, pp. 529–33, no. 358, and pp. 792–4, no. 601.

[317]   *ibid.*, pp. 546–7, no. 368.

[318]   *Actum* **59**.

[319]   March 1269: *AWR*, pp. 545–6, no. 367. For the location of the lands exchanged: Gresham, *Eifionydd*, pp. 4 (Map 4), 38, and 61–3.

lyn of all his hereditary right and claim to lands and possessions in north Wales or elsewhere in the principality of Wales.[320] Thus, within the first four and half years of his episcopate, Anian was used by Llywelyn to cement the prince's dominance over two of his three brothers, first Dafydd and then Rhodri. Llywelyn had imprisoned his eldest brother, Owain, in 1255.[321]

The canons of Haughmond took their time in obtaining the new bishop's *confirmatio*, for it was not until 1272/3 that Anian confirmed (**58**), at Haughmond itself, the grants and confirmations of his predecessors namely bishops Meurig, Gwion, Alan, Cadwgan, and Richard concerning the churches of Nefyn (Llŷn) and Trefeglwys (Arwystli).[322] In March 1272, Anian's powers of censure were once again included in an agreement between parties in dispute, but this time the parties were churchmen, it was the jurisdiction of the bishop of Bangor '*per censuram ecclesiasticam*' that was the sanction agreed upon.[323] In the autumn of 1273, Anian was with Llywelyn and his brother Dafydd (possibly at Llanfair Rhyd Gastell, a grange of Aberconwy Abbey) and it was on this occasion that the prince of Wales stated that the bishop was a member of his council.[324]

In 1274 Anian was to travel considerable distances in execution of his episcopal duties. He was also to become ever more intimately involved in the machinations that were being played out amongst the native princes. The first mention of the bishop that year was on 18 April, the day after the trial of Gruffudd ap Gwenwynwyn of Powys and his son Owain, for plotting against Llywelyn.[325] The bishop of Bangor was named together with the bishops of St Davids (Richard de Carew), Llandaff (William de Briouze), and St Asaph (Anian II) in letters patent issued by Gruffudd and Owain on 18 April. If father and son were convicted of transgressing the terms imposed on them they were to be placed under the sentences of the bishops, so that the bishops, acting jointly or separately, could pronounce sentence of excommunication against them.[326] It had, by now, become routine for Llywelyn to employ the bishops of Bangor, first Richard, and then Anian, to threaten this most severe of ecclesiastical sanctions in his dealings with the other Welsh princes.[327] However, Anian was to prove even more useful to the prince of Wales. Later in 1274, Owain, by then a hostage of Llywelyn (pursuant

---

[320]   April 1272: *AWR*, pp. 657–8, no. 458. Anian II, bishop of St Asaph, the abbots of Aberconwy, Basingwerk, and Enlli (Bardsey), together with the archdeacons of Bangor and St Asaph also affixed their seals.

[321]   *Brut, Hergest*, pp. 246–7.

[322]   *Actum* **58**.

[323]   March 1272, agreement sealed at 'Rustock', between Anian II of St Asaph, Walter de Hangmere, and Luke of Wenlock, abbot of St Peter's Shrewsbury, concerning presentation to the church of St Oswald at Oswestry: Jones, 'Llyfr Coch Asaph: A Textual and Historical Study', i, pp. 133–4, and ii, pp. 129–31.

[324]   September 1273: *AWR*, pp. 555–6, no. 378. For location of Llanfair Rhyd Gastell (between Ysbyty Ifan and Gwytherin): *AWR*, p. 556; Gresham, 'Aberconwy Charter: further consideration', 313, and 321–6; Smith, *Llywelyn*, p. 366, n. 96. See also *AWR*, pp. 558–60, no. 383, and pp. 577–9, no. 394.

[325]   Both having been summoned by the prince to his new castle of Dolforwyn, in Cedewain: *Brut, Pen20Tr*, p. 116; *Brut, Hergest*, pp. 260–1; *LW*, p. liii; *AWR*, p. 798. Trial: *LW*, pp. liii–iv, and 108–10, no. 203; *AWR*, pp. 796–8, no. 603.

[326]   *AWR*, pp. 798–9, no. 604; *LW*, pp. liii–iv, and pp. 98–9, no. 193.

[327]   For an example of Richard being similarly employed: *AWR*, pp. 529–33, no. 358 and pp. 792–4, no. 601.

to the terms imposed in April) confessed the full nature of the conspiracy against the prince, implicating not only himself, and his father, but also Dafydd, Llywelyn's brother – he did so '*in presencia domini episcopi Bangorensis*', as well as certain members of the Bangor chapter.[328] Owain stated that all the documents connected with the plot were in his mother's castle of Welshpool (Y Trallwng).[329] The confession and information provided by Owain were relayed to Llywelyn, who, on or about 30 November, sent envoys to the castle, and soon arrived there himself at the head of an army.[330] As J. G. Edwards noted 'certain things which had previously been divulged privately to the bishop were now made known openly' to the prince.[331]

Before the revelations of late November, however, Anian had travelled to France, where in the summer of 1274 he had attended the Second General Council of Lyon, called by Pope Gregory X. The Council was held between 7 May and 17 July and met in six sessions.[332] The bishops of St Davids (Richard de Carew) and Llandaff (William de Briouze) were present, as were the archbishops of Canterbury and York, and at least six bishops of English sees.[333] Anian's green-wax seal survives, attached by a red silk cord to a decree made at the council on 13 July.[334] On his return from Lyon, Anian stopped in Canterbury and preserved in the muniments of the dean and chapter is his grant of an indulgence (**60**), dated 23 September 1274, for those praying for the soul of Adam de Chillendenne, late prior of the Cathedral Priory.[335]

There was yet another matter with which he had to contend that year. Before leaving for Lyon, Anian had deliberated with Anian II of St Asaph concerning certain articles in the 1269 agreement made between Llywelyn and Dafydd over which the brothers found themselves in dispute, and which were dubious and obscure in some part.[336] As we have seen, the two bishops set out their interpretation and explanation of the said articles in a sealed letter (**59**) – which Llywelyn then sent (June x July 1274) to the pope petitioning Gregory X for his confirmation of the episcopal interpretation and explanation provided.[337] The pope wrote to Llywelyn, from Lyon, on 18 August 1274, confirming his agreement.[338] The bishops' interpretation and explanation were described as 'prudent and salutary'.[339] Towards the end of a busy year, Anian once again joined with Anian II of St Asaph

[328] Owain's confession, and the hearing in the presence of Anian, was recorded in a letter the dean and chapter of Bangor wrote to Robert Kilwardby, archbishop of Canterbury, some eighteen months later, on 18 April 1276: *LW*, p. lv, and pp. 136–8, no. 245; *Foedera*, i, part ii, p. 532; Lloyd, *History of Wales*, ii, p. 749; Smith, *Llywelyn*, pp. 369–70; Stephenson, *Medieval Powys*, p. 145.

[329] *LW*, p. lv, and p. 137.

[330] 'amgylch Gwyl Andras': *Brut, Hergest*, p. 260; 'about the feast of Andrew the Apostle': *Brut, Pen20Tr*, p. 116. See also *LW*, p. lv; Lloyd, *History of Wales*, ii, pp. 749–50.

[331] *LW*, p. xxxiv, and p. 137.

[332] *Councils and Synods*, ii, part ii, p. 810.

[333] *ibid.*, and n. 4.

[334] *Welsh Episcopal Seals*, iii (no. 7). Vatican Archive, A. A. Arm. I–XVIII, 2190 (no. 18); *Sigilli Dell' Archivio Vaticano*, i, 76. *Councils and Synods*, ii, part ii, p. 810, n. 4. See the section entitled 'Seals'.

[335] *Actum* **60**. Image at Plate XIV.

[336] 1269 agreement made at *Aberreu*: *AWR*, pp. 546–7, no. 368.

[337] *Actum* **59**.

[338] *AWR*, p. 558, no. 382; Haddan and Stubbs, i, pp. 501–2; Smith, *Llywelyn*, p. 380.

[339] *AWR*, p. 558.

to write to Llywelyn (**61**), this time to warn the prince that he should desist from inflicting disturbances and injuries upon Dafydd and Gruffudd ap Gwenwynwyn and give due satisfaction for these, and furthermore that he should observe all the articles of the agreement between him and them.[340] In reply, Llywelyn wrote to the bishops on 20 December 1274 setting out his side of the story.[341] It may have been Anian II of St Asaph who persuaded Anian of Bangor, in December 1274, to write to the prince of Wales in such strong terms, for this is the first indication of a rift between the bishop of Bangor and Llywelyn. Anian II was embroiled in his own dispute with Llywelyn, and matters had come to a head earlier that year.[342] Anian of St Asaph's complaints about the prince presaged those of Anian of Bangor a few years later.[343]

The bishop of Bangor is next mentioned in the period immediately leading up to the outbreak of war in 1277. Anian once again acted on behalf of Llywelyn, this time as an envoy, delivering the prince's proposals for peace to the king. By way of a letter dated 22 January 1277 Llywelyn asked the king to grant safe conduct to his messengers, and stated that he was sending Anian, and Master Gervase, his clerk and vice-chancellor.[344] He asked the king to believe what these messengers were to tell him and to reply by the same messengers.[345] It is clear that Anian and Gervase's mission was in vain. On 10 February, less than three weeks after Llywelyn's letter, a convocation at the New Temple excommunicated the prince.[346] A little over a month later, on Palm Sunday (21 March) 1277, finally obeying the instructions which the archbishop of Canterbury had issued on 10 February, Anian publicly excommunicated Llywelyn and fled to England. Like Richard before him, he took refuge at St Albans. There he wrote to Edward I stating that whilst it was true that he loved the prince of Wales and his own people, and was the prince's confessor, he was anxious to avoid offence to the king, and after excommunicating Llywelyn he had escaped and come to England for fear of death or at least arrest; he described himself as a most faithful chaplain to Edward (**62**).[347] In another extant letter, Anian reinforced his professed faithfulness to the crown, and in dramatic terms. After his very public excommunication of Llywelyn, matters had clearly

---

[340]   *Actum* **61**.

[341]   *AWR*, pp. 558–9, no. 383; and see note to *Actum* **61**.

[342]   For a discussion of the issues in dispute between Anian II of St Asaph and Llywelyn in 1274: Smith, *Llywelyn*, pp. 378–80. The abbots of seven Welsh Cistercian houses, including Aberconwy, came together, in March 1274, to defend Llywelyn against, what they saw as false, charges brought by Anian II of St Asaph: Haddan and Stubbs, i, pp. 498–9; Smith, *Llywelyn*, pp. 379–80.

[343]   See discussion on the following pages, and *Acta* **62**, **64**, **65**, **68** and **70**.

[344]   At Aberalwen (a township belonging to Corwen, Edeirnion): *AWR*, pp. 586–7, no. 400. It has been said that Master Gervase, Llywelyn's 'clerk and vice-chancellor', can probably be identified as Iorwerth, a canon of Bangor (*ibid.*, p. 587; Stephenson, *Governance*, pp. 36–7, and 224). This may well be the same Master Gervase who, in November 1267, delivered the news that Bishop Richard had died (*CPR, 1266–1272*, p. 165; Stephenson, *Governance*, p. 224) and possibly the same Gervase who was named as part of Richard's household in 1259 (*CPR, 1258–1266*, p. 57; Stephenson, *Governance*, p. 224).

[345]   *AWR*, pp. 586–7, no. 400.

[346]   Anian II of St Asaph was in attendance: *Councils and Synods*, ii, pp. 820–2; *AWR*, p. 583.

[347]   *Actum* **62**. Image at Plate XVII (i). For the date of the letter (probably 29 March or 5 April 1277) see note to *Actum* **62**.

deteriorated between bishop and prince. Anian, by now back in his diocese, wrote to Robert Burnell, bishop of Bath and Wells, and chancellor (**64**).[348] He stated that whilst he had been with the chancellor at (the English camp at) Rhuddlan he had lost his brother, his sister's son, his cousin, and kinsmen to the number of sixty, in the king's service, and that Llywelyn greatly rejoiced in his misfortune.[349] He asked Robert to explain all these things to the king.[350] On 18 January 1278 at Westminster, the grant of a wardship to the value of £20 yearly may have been the result of Anian's letter to Burnell.[351] It is just possible that Anian was present when the king made the grant, for he may have attended a council of the province of Canterbury in London on 14 January, and he was certainly in London on 1 February 1278.[352]

It may have been after the war of 1277 that Anian requested (**63**) a ship be restored to him.[353] In the lead up to the war, Llywelyn ap Gruffudd had been declared a rebel and disturber of the peace,[354] and an embargo 'by land and sea' had been placed on victuals, horses, arms and other things that might have been useful to the rebels.[355] One of the casualties of this embargo may have been the bishop of Bangor's ship.

In another extant letter addressed to Robert Burnell (**65**), this time from Bangor, Anian thanked the chancellor, whom he described as 'defender of the oppressed, protector of the poor' (*oppressorum defensori, pauperum patro[n]o*) for all the benefits which he had conferred on the Church.[356] Anian sent for his inspection certain articles in which Llywelyn ap Gruffudd had, allegedly, offended God and the Church, and prayed that they might be explained to the king, so that he might grant a remedy, defending the Church of Christ 'against the tyrannical prince and his malevolent and satanic ministers' (*contra tirannidem principem et suos ministros malivolos sathanicos*).[357] The year is not given but in 1278 Edward not only wrote to Llywelyn concerning the spiritual rights and the temporalities of the bishop of Bangor, and injury to the bishop's liberties and the rights of his church,[358] the

---

[348] From Treffos in Dindaethwy on Anglesey, where according to the extent made in 1306/7 the bishop had a manor: *RC*, p. 100; and see the section of the Introduction entitled 'Extent of 1306/7 – Manors, Lands and Tenants of the Bishop of Bangor'.

[349] *Actum* **64**. Image at Plate XVI (i).

[350] *Actum* **64**.

[351] *CVCR*, pp. 163 4. A point made by J. G. Edwards, *CAC*, p. 112. The wardship was in respect of the manor of Fernham (Oxfordshire): *CVCR*, pp. 163–4. See also *CFR, 1272–1307*, p. 88. On 4 January, the king had enlisted Anian to assist in a dispute that had arisen on Anglesey concerning the royal forces that were occupying the island: Haddan and Stubbs, i, pp. 524–5.

[352] For the meeting of the council: *Councils and Synods*, ii, part ii, p. 825. On 1 February 1278 Anian was with the archbishop of Canterbury, and amongst others, the bishops of the other three Welsh dioceses: *Concilia*, ii, p. 31; *Register of Godfrey Giffard*, ii, pp. 94–5.

[353] *Actum* **63**. Or Anian's request may possibly have been connected with the second Welsh war of 1282–1283: see notes to *Actum* **63**.

[354] November 1276: *CCR, 1272–1279*, pp. 359–61; Smith, *Llywelyn*, p. 406.

[355] *CCR, 1272–1279*, p. 361; Gruffydd, *Maritime Wales*, p. 16.

[356] *Actum* **65**. Image at Plate XVI (ii).

[357] *Actum* **65**. For the date of the letter see note to *Actum* **65**.

[358] See *AWR*, p. 599, no. 409; *Foedera*, i, part ii, pp. 559–60; *CVCR*, pp. 174–5; *Welsh Assize Roll*, pp. 47–8; and note to *Actum* **65**.

king also confirmed the rights, liberties, possessions and customs of the see of Bangor.[359]

In 1279, Anian was in far-away Suffolk where, on 24 April, he dedicated the cemetery at the Augustinian friary of Clare and granted an indulgence (**66**). On the following day, he granted another indulgence (**67**).[360] In the summer of that year, Anian attended a council of the province of Canterbury, called by the new archbishop, John Pecham, held in the chapterhouse of Reading Abbey.[361]

In the same year, Anian complained (**68**) to the archbishop about Llywelyn's actions in respect of the goods of those who died intestate.[362] On 20 October 1279, Pecham wrote to Llywelyn about the matter.[363] At about the same time as the archbishop's letter, Edward I ordered ten librates of land in the Marches of Wales to be assigned, *de gratia nostra speciali*, to Anian.[364] The two matters might be unrelated, but the timing is interesting. The following summer, Pecham visited Wales in the hope that an amicable arrangement could be reached between Anian and Llywelyn.[365] After his return, the archbishop was able to write to Llywelyn to say that he rejoiced that a composition with the bishop of Bangor was imminent.[366]

Five days later, on 15 July 1280, Anian was granted land and buildings in Shoe Lane, Holborn.[367] Later the same year, on 6 October, Anian was with both the archbishop and the king at Lincoln Cathedral for the translation of the body of St Hugh of Avalon.[368] The bishop of Lincoln, Oliver of Sutton, was also present and it might have been about this time that Anian granted an indulgence (**57**) in favour of Bringhurst church, Leicestershire, which was mentioned in a later *ratificatio* of Bishop Sutton.[369] On 26 October 1280, perhaps pursuant to a request (**69**) from

---

[359]   November 1278: *RC*, p. 254 and p. 255; Willis, *Survey*, pp. 212–13; Haddan and Stubbs, i, p. 526.

[360]   *Actum* **66** and *Actum* **67**.

[361]   July to 1 August. Royal MS 9 B. ii., states that the bishop of Bangor was present: *Council and Synods*, ii, part ii, pp. 828–9. See also *ibid.*, pp. 851–3 and Oxford, University Archives, I. 2.

[362]   *Actum* **68**.

[363]   From Lambeth: *Registrum Epistolarum Peckham*, i, pp. 77–8; Pryce, *Native Law*, pp. 113–14 and pp. 117–18; Smith, *Llywelyn*, pp. 211 and 258–9; Smith, 'Gravamina', 165, and n. 6.

[364]   On 17 and 26 October 1279, at Westminster: *CPR, 1278–1279*, p. 12. See BL Add MS 15664 (fo. 5. 7 Edw. I) for the bounds of the land assigned.

[365]   *Welsh Assize Roll*, p. 64.

[366]   July 1280: *Registrum Epistolarum Peckham*, i, pp. 125–6. David Stephenson points out that whilst it has been assumed that the settlement had already been reached, such an interpretation is not supported by the text: Stephenson, *Governance*, p. 180, n. 64.

[367]   Willis, *Survey*, pp. 68 and 189; Pryce, 'Anian [Einion] (*d.* 1305x7)', *ODNB*. A further grant of land followed on 10 November 1281: Willis, *Survey*, p. 189.

[368]   *Opera*, vii, pp. 219–21 (*Vita S. Remigii et Vita S. Hugonis* – Appendix F); Perry, *The Life of St. Hugh*, p. 329, n. 1. Also, *Annales Oseneia*, pp. 285–6; *Annales Dunstaplia*, p. 283; *Chronicle Abbatie de Parco Lude*, ed. E. Venables (1891), pp. 18–19; Mayr-Harting, 'Hugh of Lincoln [St Hugh of Lincoln, Hugh of Avalon] (1140?–1200)', *ODNB*. Thomas Bek was consecrated by Archbishop Pecham, as bishop of St Davids, the same day (*Fasti Welsh Cathedrals*, p. 49). It seems likely that a council of the province of Canterbury was held in Lincoln at about the same time: *Councils and Synods*, ii, part ii, p. 871, and n. 3.

[369]   *Rolls and Register of Bishop Oliver Sutton*, iv, p. 101; and see notes to *Actum* **57**.

Anian, the constable of Windsor castle was ordered to cause 'A. bishop of Bangor' to have six oaks fit for timber in the forest of Windsor, by the king's gift.[370]

Anian was back in Gwynedd Uwch Conwy by November 1281.[371] However, preserved in The National Archives is another extant, albeit badly damaged, letter (**70**) from Anian to Robert Burnell written within the months following his return.[372] The bishop of Bangor explained that he was not able to live peacefully in the land of the prince, as his 'adversaries, certain incestuous adulterers of his chapter' (*adversarios quosdam adulteros incestuosos de capitulo nostro*), were being encouraged to impugn him.[373] By July 1282 Anian was with the king, Burnell, and the royal forces at Rhuddlan once again.[374]

The entry for that year in the Peniarth MS 20 version of *Brut y Tywysogyon*, before mentioning Llywelyn ap Gruffudd's final departure from Gwynedd, includes the passage 'And then was effected the betrayal of Llywelyn in the belfry of Bangor by his own men'.[375] J. B. Smith has considered in detail who might have been in the belfry, and who might have given them instructions.[376] One person worth mentioning here is Madog ap Cynwrig, who, as Smith noted, was well-favoured following the demise of Llywelyn.[377] Madog was archdeacon of Anglesey.[378] As 'Madoc son of Kenewreyk', archdeacon of Anglesey, he was given the benefice of *offeiriad teulu* (household priest) by Edward I.[379] He was also engaged in making extents.[380] That he was favoured by Edward I may be relevant to discerning if Bishop Anian had a part to play in the 'betrayal' in the belfry, because, as already noted, a fourteenth-century source refers to the bishop of Bangor as Anian 'ap Kenewrek'.[381] In other words, Madog may have been a relative of Anian's, indeed, he may have been Anian's brother.[382]

Llywelyn was killed on 11 December 1282,[383] however, it is unclear exactly when Anian felt it was safe to return to Bangor.[384] In April 1283, at Aberconwy, royal

---

[370] Westminster, 26 October 1280: *CCR, 1279–1288*, p. 35: Actum **69**.

[371] November 1281 at Ystumgwern (south of Harlech in Dyffryn Ardudwy): *LW*, p. xvii, and pp. 45–6, no. 69.

[372] For dating of the letter see the notes to *Actum* **70**.

[373] *Actum* **70**. Image at Plate XVI (iii).

[374] *CCR, 1279–1288*, p. 173; *LW*, pp. 165–6, no. 290.

[375] *Brut, Pen20Tr*, p. 120. Smith, *Llywelyn*, pp. 552–3.

[376] Smith, *Llywelyn*, pp. 552–61.

[377] 'ap Cynfrig': *ibid.*, p. 554 and n. 154.

[378] He is referred to as 'Matheus' in Anian's letter of 27 October 1284: *Actum* **79**. See also Stephenson, *Governance*, p. 237.

[379] April 1284: *CVCR*, p. 284; Pryce, 'Offeiriad Teulu', p. 91.

[380] Smith, *Llywelyn*, p. 554 and n. 154; Stephenson, *Governance*, p. 237.

[381] *CIM*, ii, p. 239, no. 962; Smith, '*Gravamina*', 161, n. 8.

[382] For a discussion of Anian's possible involvement in the betrayal of the prince of Wales, Llywelyn ap Gruffudd, see McGuinness, 'Betrayal in the Belfry – The Bishop of Bangor and the demise of Llywelyn ap Gruffudd'.

[383] *Brut, Pen20Tr*, pp. 120–1. Llywelyn's brother, Dafydd, continued the fight but was confined, until his capture in June 1283, to ever decreasing areas of the mountains: Smith, *Llywelyn*, pp. 575–6 and 578.

[384] J. E. Lloyd stated that Anian returned to his diocese in the company of the king (*YBC*, https://biography.wales/article/s-ANIA-N00-1306, accessed 12 January 2024). Lloyd did

grants were made to the bishop on account of the losses he had suffered in the war (of 1282–1283).[385] It was John de Kirkby, vice-chancellor in all but name, who was instructed to ensure that the exchequer paid the monies due expeditiously.[386] Anian wrote to Kirkby (**72**), *inter alia*, praying that he would instruct the clerks and barons of the exchequer at Shrewsbury not to detain the money which was due to him.[387] Whilst he was at Aberconwy, Anian granted an indulgence (**71**) in favour of the Cistercian abbey of Stanlaw in Cheshire.[388]

On 9 July 1283, no doubt at the behest of the crown, bonds (**73, 74, 75, 76, 77** and **78**) were taken by Anian from the more upright, noble, and trustworthy members of the *communitates* of Arfon, Arllechwedd, Llŷn, Dunoding, Meirionnydd, and Penllyn who bound themselves in the sum of £2,000, under threat of sentence of excommunication, to ensure that the peace was maintained.[389] There followed an assembly, held in the presence of Anian, on 2 August '*post mortem Lewelini principis Wallie*', of bailiffs and representatives from each commote of Gwynedd.[390] The result was the compilation of a list of *gravamina* against the rule of Llywelyn presented by the 'community of Wales' to the king in the presence of the bishop of Bangor.[391] The prince was criticised, *inter alia*, for matters relating to military service of tenants, shipwreck, and intestacy of tenants, as well as the right to make a will; all matters that figured in the disputes that had arisen between the bishops of Bangor and St Asaph and Llywelyn.[392] From studying the *gravamina* listed, L. B. Smith's impression was of a 'highly interventionist prince'.[393] As such, Anian's complaint that he could not stir a foot except under the prince's power (**62**) rings true.[394]

Further royal grants followed in 1284,[395] and in a letter of November that year Anian acknowledged receipt (**80**) of £250 by way of compensation for

---

not cite a source, but Edward I was in Aberconwy by 14 March 1283, and after excursions to amongst other places Dolwyddelan, the king was at 'Aber in Snawdon' (Abergwyngregyn) by 9 July, arriving in Bangor by 11 July 1283: Gough, *Itinerary*, i, pp. 142–5.

[385] Grants made between 15 and 18 April 1283: *CAC*, pp. 43–4; *CCR, 1279–1288*, p. 205; *CPR, 1281–1292*, p. 61.

[386] *CAC*, pp. 43–4. For John de Kirkby, a member of the royal council, and a future bishop of Ely see Prestwich, *Edward I*, pp. 234–5; Prestwich, 'Kirby, John (*d.* 1290)', *ODNB*; *Fasti Monastic Cathedrals*, p. 46.

[387] *Actum* **72**. Image at Plate XVII (ii).

[388] *Actum* **71**.

[389] *Acta* **73–8**.

[390] The assembly was held at Nancall, a grange of the abbey of Aberconwy in Eifionydd: Smith, '*Gravamina*', 160, n. 1, and 173.

[391] The document ends with a list of the prince's policies which found favour with the community. The text is recorded in a late sixteenth- or early seventeenth-century transcript of a thirteenth-century record (BL Cotton Vitellius C x, fos. 166–9). It has been transcribed, and considered in detail, by L. B. Smith in '*Gravamina*', 158–76. The assembly met on the morrow of the feast of St Peter in Chains (2 August). The year has not been recorded but 1283 is Smith's persuasive conclusion: *ibid.*, 160.

[392] Smith, '*Gravamina*', 162–3 and 168–9, and see *Actum* **52** and *Actum* **68**.

[393] Smith, '*Gravamina*', 172.

[394] *Actum* **62**.

[395] October 1284, at Caernarfon, grants were made to 'ecclesie cathedrali sancti Danielis Bangoren(sis)' and Anian and his successors of, *inter alia*, the return of the king's writs within all lands of the bishopric, and that the bishops and their households were to be quit of toll

ecclesiastical damages in the last war.[396] The previous month he had appointed (**79**) attorneys and proctors (namely the archdeacon of Anglesey, and Elias, the bishop's chaplain) to receive compensation on his behalf from the commissioners appointed by Archbishop Pecham to inquire into ecclesiastical damages.[397] Also in November of that year, the king granted to Anian and to the *offeiriad teulu* ('*Effeyriat Teulu*') of Wales two townships[398] in recompense for grants (**81**) they had made, at the king's request, to the abbot and convent of Aberconwy, whose monastery the king had caused to be re-founded at Maenan.[399] As we have seen, the king had appointed the archdeacon of Anglesey, Madog ap Cynwrig, *offeiriad teulu*.[400]

There were two other events in 1284 which are worth noting. Firstly, Eleanor of Castile gave birth to a baby boy in the diocese of Bangor, at Caernarfon castle.[401] According to the antiquarian Browne Willis, it was Bishop Anian who christened the future Edward II, and was rewarded with manors and two ferries.[402] The second event was the visitation of all four Welsh cathedrals by John Pecham.[403] When in Bangor, the archbishop wrote to the bishop of St Asaph, *inter alia*, ordering the bishop to enforce the wearing of the usual clerical dress in his diocese, as well as the statutes against married priests, and to exhort the Welsh to unity with the English.[404] Shortly afterwards on his way to St Davids, he wrote to Anian of Bangor in similar form.[405] As R. R. Davies noted, the bishops of all four Welsh dioceses were,

---

throughout the king's dominion, both on land and sea, so far as their goods were concerned (*RC*, pp. 134 and 255; *CChR, 1257–1300*, p. 279; Willis, *Survey*, pp. 190–1; Haddan and Stubbs, i, pp. 580–1). Earlier, on 12 February, Anian had been granted a wardship in Mears Ashby, Northamptonshire (*CPR, 1281–1292*, p. 115).

[396] *Actum* **80**.

[397] *Actum* **79**. The archbishop had appointed commissioners on 25 June 1284: *LW*, pp. xix and 219, and p. 71, no. 127; *Foedera*, i, part ii, p. 644; Raban, 'Edward I's Other Inquiries', p. 55.

[398] November 1284 at Castell y Bere: *CVCR*, p. 292.

[399] *Actum* **81**; *CVCR*, p. 292.

[400] April 1284: *CVCR*, p. 284; Pryce, 'Offeiriad Teulu', p. 91.

[401] April 1284: Prestwich, *Edward I*, p. 226; Willis, *Survey*, p. 68.

[402] Willis, *Survey*, p. 68. Willis does not identify his source(s), and as has been pointed out the alleged baptism by Anian is not corroborated by contemporary records: Pryce, 'Anian [Einion] (*d.* 1305x7)', *ODNB*. However, it is true that some of the manors referred to by Willis were included in either the *Taxatio* of 1291, or the extent of the lands belonging to the bishop of Bangor undertaken in 1306/7, or both (*Taxatio Ecclesiastica*, pp. 290 and 292; *RC*, pp. 93, 100 and 111); and the two ferries were recorded in 1588 (Davies, *The Conway and The Menai Ferries*, pp. 59 and 149–51).

[403] *Annales Cambriae C-text*, p. 56; *Annales Cambriae D-text*, p. 12; Davies, *Age of Conquest*, p. 374. The archbishop was in Bangor, at the latest, by 25 June: *Registrum Epistolarum Peckham*, ii, pp. 727–36.

[404] June 1284: *Registrum Epistolarum Peckham*, ii, pp. 737–43. Clerical dress was unpopular, the Welsh ecclesiastics wore striped cloaks with bright tunics, had long hair and bare legs, and drunkenness was rife: *ibid.*, p. 738; Harper, 'The Bangor Pontifical', p. 80; Douie, *Archbishop Pecham*, p. 262 and n. 1. Improper attire amongst the secular clergy was not confined to north Wales; for examples from thirteenth-century England: Moorman, *Church Life in England*, p. 149, and ns. 4, 5 and 6.

[405] July 1284, from 'Tewyn' (Tywyn in Meirionnydd): *Registrum Epistolarum Peckham*, ii, p. 743. Pecham was in St Davids on 10 July: *ibid.*, iii, pp. 780–1; *Annales Cambriae C-text*, p. 56;

in subsequent years, to issue constitutions for their clergy (often based on Pecham's injunctions).[406] Anian issued constitutions (**87**) at a synod of all the clergy of the diocese of Bangor in 1291.[407]

After the royal grants of 1283 and 1284, in 1285 the king granted Anian licence to make a will,[408] and in 1286, an order was given to Reginald de Grey, justice of Chester, that the bishop of Bangor was to have a third of the tithes of the king's demesnes and mills of Englefield (Tegeingl) and a third of the tithes from the king's lead mine there.[409] In fact, the order was made pursuant to a claim made by Anian himself (**84**).[410] However, it seems that de Grey did not comply with the order, certainly as far as it pertained to the tithes from the lead mining, for Anian subsequently wrote to Edmund, earl of Cornwall (**86**), seeking justice and accusing de Grey of detaining the said tithes.[411]

As there were no longer any princes of Gwynedd to turn to, it was to Anian that the Augustinian prior and convent of Beddgelert looked in 1286 to confirm the charters which had been granted to them by the princes before the war of 1282–1283. As such the bishop of Bangor issued a letter patent (**82**) attesting that he had seen various charters of the princes in favour of the priory.[412] At the end of his letter, in which he described the house as the senior religious house of all Wales except for Bardsey (Ynys Enlli), Anian granted an indulgence to all those who should help the priory (which had been damaged in a fire) by pious alms or favours.[413]

In the same year, Pope Honorius IV confirmed Edward I's foundation and endowment of a Cistercian monastery on royal land at Maenan.[414] This was pursuant to the king's castle-building programme that included the construction of a castle with an associated walled town at Conwy, and the consequent need to relocate the abbot and convent of Aberconwy. Anian gave his consent (**83**) to the

---

Annales Cambriae D-text, p. 12. Pecham wrote to Anian three more times, on 3 July requesting him to forbid a tournament that was about to be held at Nefyn in Llŷn (*Registrum Epistolarum Peckham*, iii, pp. 775–6; see also Prestwich, *Edward I*, p. 120), on 10 July instructing him to receive the purgation of two clerks of the church of Llan-faes, Gregory and Iorwerth/Gervase (*Registrum Epistolarum Peckham*, iii, pp. 780–1; see also Carr, 'The Last and Weakest of His Line', 392; Evans, 'Welsh traitors in a Scottish chronicle', 142; Smith, *Llywelyn*, p. 578, and n. 231), and on the same day instructing him to receive the purgation of a canon of Bangor, by the name of 'Madoc dictus Parvus' (*Registrum Epistolarum Peckham*, iii, p. 781); a Madog Fychan, 'Madoc Parvus', was named as a canon of Bangor in 1291 (*Taxatio Ecclesiastica*, p. 290).

[406]   Davies, *Age of Conquest*, p. 376.
[407]   *Actum* **87**.
[408]   May 1285, at Westminster: BL Add MS 15664 (fo. 6. 13 Edw. I.); *Foedera*, i, part ii, p. 654; Haddan and Stubbs, i, p. 584; *CPR, 1281–1292*, p. 161; *Councils and Synods*, ii, part ii, p. 881, n. 1. Archbishop John Pecham in his letter to Llywelyn ap Gruffudd of 20 October 1279 had accused the prince of using the laws of Hywel Dda to prevent bishops from making wills: *Registrum Epistolarum Peckham*, i, pp. 77–8; cf. *Actum* **34**; see also *Testamentary Records*, pp. 1 and 52; Pryce, *Native Law*, pp. 124–5; *CAP*, pp. 33–4.
[409]   December 1286, at Westminster: *CFR, 1272–1307*, p. 232.
[410]   *Actum* **84**.
[411]   *Actum* **86**.
[412]   *Actum* **82**. Image at Plate XV.
[413]   *Actum* **82** and notes to the same.
[414]   April 1286, at Perugia: *Cal. Pap. Reg.*, i, p. 480.

same.[415] In another *actum*, *c*.early 1287, the bishop authorised and commissioned (**85**) the dean and archdeacon of Bangor, and the archdeacon of Anglesey, to investigate a matrimonial case.[416]

In 1294, for the first time, the Welsh clergy were required to contribute to a clerical tax raised by the king,[417] and in September that year Anian was summoned to a council of the clergy to be held before the king in person at Westminster.[418] In November 1295, Anian was in London again, having been summoned to attend a parliament fixed for the thirteenth of that month at Westminster.[419] Whilst he was in London he granted an indulgence (**88**) in favour of Salisbury Cathedral and William de la Corner, the late bishop of Salisbury (d. 1291).[420]

After the many royal grants of 1278 and 1283–1286, Anian felt his rights and liberties were being infringed or ignored, for he petitioned the king (**89**), possibly in 1298.[421] In February 1301 Edward I granted royal lands in Wales to his son, Edward of Caernarfon,[422] and in April that year at Conwy Anian swore fealty to him.[423] In 1305, Anian felt the need once again to petition the crown, and at Kennington the bishop made nine petitions to Edward of Caernarfon, now prince of Wales (**93**, **94**, **95**, **96**, **97**, **98**, **99**, **100** and **101**).[424]

Anian gave or assigned (**91**) an acre of land in Bangor to the prior and friar preachers of the Dominican friary in the town.[425] Licence for the alienation in mortmain by Anian, to the prior and friar preachers, was granted on 23 February 1301 following an application (**90**) by the bishop the previous year.[426]

During his episcopate, Anian is recorded as assisting other bishops, including the bishop of Exeter, Walter of Bronescombe (d. 1280)[427] and the bishop of Hereford, Thomas de Cantilupe (d. 1282).[428] Anian's connection with Cantilupe continued after the bishop of Hereford's death for in 1303 Anian, in a joint testimony (**92**), recorded the miraculous resuscitation of a boy who had fallen from a bridge at Conwy castle, lain overnight, and been found dead in the morning, only

---

[415] *Actum* **83**.

[416] *Actum* **85**.

[417] Davies, *Age of Conquest*, p. 375. See also Prestwich, *Edward I*, p. 401.

[418] September 1294: *Parliamentary Writs and Writs of Military Summons*, i, p. 443. Anian and the Bangor chapter were appointed to collect tenths 'in aid of the Holy Land' in the bishopric: *CPR, 1292–1301*, pp. 89 and 173; *Parliamentary Writs and Writs of Military Summons*, i, p. 443.

[419] Which was, in the end, prorogued until 27 November. *Parliamentary Writs and Writs of Military Summons*, i, p. 443.

[420] November 1295: *Actum* **88**. Image at Plate XVIII.

[421] *Actum* **89**. Image at Plate XIX.

[422] February 1301: Prestwich, *Edward I*, p. 226.

[423] April 1301: *CPR, 1343–1345*, p. 231; Johnstone, *Edward of Carnarvon*, p. 62. Llywelyn de Bromfield, the new bishop of St Asaph, had sworn fealty on 22 April at Flint castle: *CPR, 1343–1345*, p. 229; Johnstone, *Edward of Carnarvon*, p. 62, and n. 2.

[424] *Acta* **93**–**101**.

[425] *Actum* **91**. The Friar Preachers were established in Bangor by 1251: see note to *Actum* **90**.

[426] *Actum* **90** and *CPR, 1292–1301*, p. 576.

[427] *Prynne*, iii, p. 209.

[428] *Register of Thomas De Cantilupe*, pp. 97–8, 103–4 and 253; Bass, 'Rebellion and Miracles', 514–15; Finucane, 'Cantilupe, Thomas de [St Thomas of Hereford] *c*.1220–1282', *ODNB*.

to be revived when the name of Thomas de Cantilupe was invoked.[429] The boy was taken to Conwy church where Anian was celebrating a memorial mass for the knight, royal servant, and diplomat John of St John.[430] Two years later, towards the end of a very eventful episcopate, Anian in his last-known *actum* petitioned Pope Clement V for a canonisation inquiry to be set in motion in respect of Thomas de Cantilupe (**102**).[431]

The date of Anian's death is unknown, and the date range for his obit has sometimes been given as 1305 x 1307, but this can be narrowed. The bishop described himself as old and in poor health '*senex et valetudinarius*' (**89**) but that was possibly eight years before he died.[432] The last known *actum* of Anian (**102**), was dated at Bangor on 15 September 1305.[433] The next mention in the historical record of a bishop of Bangor is the *cautio* preserved in Canterbury Cathedral Archives and dated 27 March 1306. It is from 'Gruffydd ("*Griffinus*") ab Iorwerth, bishop-elect of Bangor'.[434] So, it seems that Anian died sometime between 15 September 1305 and 27 March 1306. It has been suggested that he was buried in the south wall of the presbytery of his cathedral, in an arch opening into a new chapel.[435]

[429] *Actum* **92**.

[430] *Actum* **92** and notes to the same. The story is told in detail in two recent articles: Ridyard and Ashbee, 'The Resuscitation of Roger of Conwy', and Bass, 'Communities of Remembrance'. I am extremely grateful to Dr Ian Bass for bringing both the articles and the miracle story to my attention.

[431] *Actum* **102**. Many other prelates and nobles did the same (Ridyard and Ashbee, 'The Resuscitation of Roger of Conwy', p. 313, and n. 22). Anian's testimony of the miraculous resuscitation of the boy Roger in 1303 no doubt had a part to play in his decision to petition the pope (see *Actum* **92**).

[432] *Actum* **89**.

[433] *Actum* **102**.

[434] Canterbury Cathedral Archives, CCA-DCc/ChAnt/C/140.

[435] *Inventory of the Ancient Monuments in Caernarvonshire*, ii, p. 1, referring at n. 6 to Radford, 'Bangor Cathedral in the Twelfth and Thirteenth Century', 261, who also assigns building work and reconstruction of parts of the cathedral to Anian I: *ibid.*

DIPLOMATIC ANALYSIS OF THE *ACTA*

EXTERNAL FEATURES

Types of Documents

As well as 8 professions of canonical obedience, the categories of document represented in the corpus of Bangor episcopal *acta*, 1092–1306, are: letters (34), charters
(18), indulgences (17), petitions (12), agreements (6), bonds (6), with one record of
the issue of diocesan constitutions. Of the 18 charters, 8 were grants and 10 were
confirmations.[1] See Table A.

Table A: Number and type of documents

	Charters	Letters	Indulgences	Agreements	Petitions	Bonds	Cons's	Prof'ns	Totals
Hervey	1								1
David								1	1
Meurig	2		1					1	4
Arthur									0
Gwion	4	1						1	6
Alan	2							1	3
Robert	1	5	1					1	8
Cadwgan	1	4	4	1	1			1	12
Richard	3	6	5	5				1	20
Anian	4	18	6		11	6	1	1	47
Totals	18	34	17	6	12	6	1	8	102

By way of comparison, the categories of document best represented in the collection of St Davids episcopal *acta*, 1085–1280, are: confirmations (32), grants (24)
and inspeximuses (14).[2] For Llandaff, 1140–1287, the largest categories are: confirmations (31), dispute settlements (21) and grants (11).[3] Significations of excom-

---

[1] Grants: *Acta* **1**, **8**, **12**, **18**, **34**, **42**, **81** and **91**. Confirmations: *Acta* **4**, **5**, **9**, **10**, **14**, **15**, **44**,
45, **58** and **82**.
[2] *St Davids Episcopal Acta*, p. 18.
[3] *ibid.*

munication survive for both St Davids (4) and Llandaff (6),[4] however, none have survived for the bishops of Bangor.[5]

The number of Bangor charters is low compared with both St Davids and Llandaff, but this may partly be a reflection of the differences in preservation of *acta*.[6] There is no cathedral 'Statute Book' as at St Davids, and no equivalent surviving monastic archive from north Wales to compare with that of Margam Abbey (the charters that are extant from the Powysian abbey of Strata Marcella yield only one Bangor *actum*).[7] The monastic houses of Gwynedd Uwch Conwy suffered damage during the two Welsh wars of 1277 and 1282–1283.[8] Manuscripts kept in Bangor Cathedral fared no better; if they survived the attack by King John's forces in August 1211, and the second Welsh war seventy years later,[9] they were probably burnt during the fire in the belfry – a petition of the dean and chapter, *c.*1307, described how muniments put in the belfry for safe keeping were destroyed in the conflagration.[10] Any manuscripts kept at the bishops' palaces may similarly have been lost by the beginning of the fourteenth century.[11] Add to this the lengthy exiles of six of the ten bishops, and it is not surprising that Bangor episcopal *acta* are, for the most part, to be found outside Wales, preserved in English monastic cartularies, English government records (the BL and TNA being the major current repositories), English cathedral archives, or at the Vatican.[12] There may be a few more *acta* I have yet to discover in the archives of cathedrals and monastic houses in northern France, and elsewhere.[13]

---

[4]   *ibid.*

[5]   For the period 1241–1306: TNA, C 85/167 (file of significations for Wales, 1241–1499). Thank you to Professor Philippa Hoskin for bringing this to my attention.

[6]   See *St Davids Episcopal Acta*, pp. 18–20 for the archival preservation of St Davids and Llandaff *acta*.

[7]   *Actum* **15**.

[8]   The damages paid pursuant to the commission set up in June 1284 (*LW*, p. xix, and p. 71, no. 127. *Foedera*, i, part ii, p. 644) to inquire into ecclesiastical damages bear witness to this: Aberconwy: *LW*, p. 95, no. 187; Bardsey: *ibid.*, p. 82, no. 155; Beddgelert: *ibid.*, p. 61, no. 91; Cymer: *ibid.*, p. 96, no. 190; Ynys Lannog: *ibid.*, p. 81, no. 152; Dolgynwal (Ysbyty Ifan): p. 83, no. 159. Furthermore, independent evidence suggests that the Augustinian priory of Beddgelert was damaged by fire: *Actum* **82**; Stöber and Austin, 'Culdees to Canons: Augustinian Houses of North Wales', pp. 45–6.

[9]   In 1284, the dean and chapter of Bangor received £60 sterling as compensation for damage to the church of Bangor in the war of 1282–1283 ('pro dampnis ecclesie Bangorensi in ultima gwerra illatis'): *LW*, p. 90, no. 180; Bishop Anian received £250 by way of compensation for ecclesiastical damages (see *Actum* **80**): *LW*, p. 90, no. 179, and other compensation was also paid: *LW*, p. 66, no. 110, and *ibid.*, p. 68, no. 119. Attack on Bangor, 1211: *Brut, Hergest*, pp. 190–1; *Brut, Pen20Tr*, p. 85.

[10]   TNA SC 8/326/E769.

[11]   For example, the bishop's palace at Treffos was, by September 1306, in a ruinous state: *RC*, p. 100.

[12]   The *acta* preserved in Wales are at the NLW: *Actum* **15** ('Ystrad Marchell Charters'), *Actum* **18** ('Cartularium S. Petri De Salopesberia'), and *Acta* **51**, **52** and **55** ('Llyfr Coch Asaph'); and Bangor University Archives: *Acta* **66**, **67** and **87** ('The Bangor Pontifical').

[13]   Anian travelled to and from Lyon in the summer of 1274. As he granted indulgences on his travels/stays in England (e.g. *Acta* **57**, **66** and **67**), he might well have done the same in France. Robert was in Normandy in 1198, and he might have made grants whilst there.

The 34 letters, all but one of which are products of the thirteenth century, concern a variety of subjects, and include 4 certificates written, or co-written, by Robert concerning the election of Master Jocelin, canon of Wells, to the bishopric of Bath in 1206.[14] Six *acta* were specifically described (in the relevant *actum* or by the recipient) as letters patent.[15] Of the 12 petitions, 11 were Anian's, the majority of which complained about the infringement of ecclesiastical and seignorial rights.[16] The other belonged (jointly) to Cadwgan namely a petition that Dafydd ap Llywelyn ab Iorwerth be taken under the pope's protection.[17] The bonds were all issued in the presence of Anian in the summer of 1283, taken from the communities of Gwynedd to keep the peace, after the defeat of Llywelyn and Dafydd ap Gruffudd.[18] Dispute settlements account for 4 of the 6 agreements.[19] The constitutions were issued at a diocesan synod held by Anian in 1291.[20] Anian's confirmation in favour of Beddgelert Priory included an indulgence also.[21]

If one counts the grant to Beddgelert, the number of indulgences in the corpus of *acta* is 18 (out of a total of 102) which is high. There are 9 indulgences included in the collection of St Davids *acta* (out of 153), and 11 for Llandaff (out of a total of 143 *acta*).[22] By comparison the bishops of Hereford, 1079–1234, granted only 7 indulgences (out of 373 recorded *acta*).[23]

As Julia Barrow has noted, bishops of English sees often granted indulgences to churches in their own dioceses or ones with which they had some personal connection, whereas Welsh bishops seem to have granted them to institutions and churches outside Wales perhaps as an attempt to compensate English houses for hospitality while they were on journeys in England.[24] Welsh bishops were expected to live up to the standards set by their English counterparts but they were in receipt of much lower incomes.[25] For much of the twelfth and thirteenth centuries, Bangor had the lowest income of any English or Welsh diocese; that, coupled with the fact that six of its ten bishops spent long periods in exile, must account for the high number of indulgences granted.

Both he (1199) and Hervey (1108) travelled to Rome and they might have made grants on their journeys there and back.

[14]   *Acta* **20**, **21**, **22** and **23**.

[15]   *Acta* **30**, **34**, **51**, **52**, **82** and **92**.

[16]   *Acta* **89**, **93**, **94**, **95**, **96**, **97**, **98**, **99**, **100**, **101** and **102**.

[17]   *Actum* **31**.

[18]   *Acta* **73**, **74**, **75**, **76**, **77** and **78**.

[19]   *Actum* **25** (dispute between Cadwgan and Haughmond Abbey) and *Acta* **51**, **52** and **53** (disputes between Richard and Llywelyn ap Gruffudd).

[20]   *Actum* **87**.

[21]   *Actum* **82**. In fact, Anian initially described his *actum* as a letter (in the *inscriptio*), and later a charter (in the sealing clause).

[22]   *St Davids Episcopal Acta*, p. 17.

[23]   *EEA, VII, Hereford, 1079–1234*.

[24]   *St Davids Episcopal Acta*, p. 17. Although there are instances of English bishops granting indulgences to Dover Priory when they were travelling to and from the continent: Hoskin, 'Authors of Bureaucracy', pp. 63–4, n. 13; Hoskin, 'How to Travel with a Bishop', p. 173, ns. 44 and 45; *EEA, II, Canterbury, 1162–1190*, no. 124; *EEA, XXII, Chichester, 1215–1253*, no. 140.

[25]   *St Davids Episcopal Acta*, p. 17.

The number of original Bangor documents which are extant is 24. For St Davids the number is 28, and for Llandaff, 55.[26] There are 34 Bangor *acta* recorded in full, or in part, in cartularies, or other similar records, and there are 44 which we only know about because they are mentioned in other documents.[27] See Table B.

Table B: Originals, Copies, Mention only

	Charters	Letters	Indulgences	Agreements	Petitions	Bonds	Cons's	Prof'ns	Totals
Originals	2	8	6		1			7	24
Copies	10	10	3	3	1	6		1	34
Mention only	6	16	8	3	10		1		44

Beneficiaries and Addressees

The grants, confirmations and indulgences of the bishops of Bangor were in respect of religious houses in England and Wales (particularly the former) and cathedrals in England.

Haughmond Abbey in Shropshire was the greatest beneficiary (10), followed by Reading Abbey (4), and then Clare Friary, St Albans and St Paul's (with 2 each). Bringhurst Church, Leicestershire, Canterbury Cathedral Priory, Dore Abbey, Hereford Cathedral, Leominster Priory, Salisbury Cathedral, Shrewsbury Abbey, Stanlaw Abbey, the priory of St Andrew's, Northampton, and St Werburgh's Abbey, Chester, all have 1 grant each.

Welsh houses which benefitted were Aberconwy Abbey, Bangor Friary, Beddgelert Priory, Strata Florida Abbey and Strata Marcella Abbey (1 each).

Other *acta* which bestowed a benefit on an ecclesiastical institution, office, or person were the 8 professions of canonical obedience to archbishops of Canterbury, and Robert's 4 certificates concerning the bishop-elect of Bath. See Table C. For the sake of completeness, lay and ecclesiastical recipients of letters and petitions are given in Table D.

---

[26] *ibid.*, p. 19.
[27] Highlighted by way of an * in this edition (see 'Editorial Method').

Table C: Ecclesiastical Beneficiaries

	Hervey	David	Meurig	Gwion	Alan	Robert	Cadwgan	Richard	Anian	Total
Aberconwy Abbey								1		1
Bangor Friary									1	1
Bath and Wells, Bishop of						4				4
Beddgelert Priory									1	1
Bringhurst Church, Leics									1	1
Canterbury, Archbishop of		1	1	1		1	1	1	3	10
Canterbury Cath' Priory									1	1
Chester, St Werburgh's				1						1
Clare Friary									2	2
Dore Abbey							1			1
Haughmond Abbey			2	4	1		1	1	1	10
Hereford, Dean & Chapter							1			1
Kingsthorpe Hospital, N'thampton						1				1
Leominster Priory							1			1
Stanlaw Abbey									1	1
Reading Abbey			1				2	1		4
Salisbury Cathedral									1	1
Shrewsbury Abbey						1				1
St Albans								2		2
St Paul's, London								2		2
Strata Florida							1			1
Strata Marcella					1					1

Table D: Lay and Ecclesiastical addressees

	Hervey	David	Meurig	Gwion	Alan	Robert	Cadwgan	Richard	Anian	Total
Burnell, Robert, Chancellor									4	4
Canterbury, Archbishop of						1				1
Edmund, Earl of Cornwall									1	1
Edward of Caernarfon									9	9
Kirkby, John, Counsellor of the King									1	1
King Edward I									6	6
King Henry III							1	6		7
Llywelyn ap Gruffudd								5	2	7
Papal Legate						2				2
Parishioners of Nefyn				1						1
Pope						2	1	1	1	5

Products of the Beneficiary

Cadwgan's indulgence (**30**) in favour of St Ethelbert's Alms-House, Hereford, was one of a number of indulgences granted by bishops of Welsh, as well as English, sees, in favour of the project.[28] Whilst not in the same hand the wording of his grant is, *mutatis mutandis*, identical to the indulgence made *c.*1225 x 27 January 1229 by Bishop Iorwerth of St Davids,[29] and strikingly similar to the grants made on 18 October 1226 at Westminster, by Bishop Walter Mauclerk of Carlisle, and the Bishop of London, Eustace of Fauconberg.[30] This perhaps suggests that a precedent/pro forma of Hereford provenance was utilised.[31]

Cadwgan's grant may have been written by a scribe in his household or by one from Hereford, but whoever wrote it, it appears they followed the wording laid down by the canons of Hereford. There are perhaps other instances when *acta* were either written by the beneficiary on behalf of the bishop or written by a Bangor scribe following the pro forma of the benefitting house or cathedral (see *Acta* **15**, **58**, **60** and **82** for possible examples). Furthermore, the arenga, or pious preamble, used by Alan in his confirmation (**14**) of the charters of Meurig and Gwion in favour of Haughmond Abbey, 1195 x 1196, had earlier been used verbatim in a confirmation of possessions in favour of the same house by the bishop of Coventry, 1160 x 1182,[32] and was to be repeated in Anian's confirmation, 1272/3, of his predecessors' charters in favour of Haughmond (**58**). In fact, much of the wording of Anian's *actum* is identical to that of Alan's charter (see notes to *Actum* **58**).

Palaeography

Apart from professions of obedience (images of surviving originals are shown in Plate VI) the first original *actum* extant is Alan's confirmation, 1195 x 1196, in favour of the Welsh Cistercian abbey of Strata Marcella (**15**).[33] This displays the smaller, more controlled current hand which Teresa Webber has noted was becoming widespread from the end of the twelfth century.[34] The same is also apparent in Robert of Shrewsbury's grant of an indulgence, 25 May 1201, at his dedication of a chapel in Kingsthorpe Hospital, Northampton (**19**, Plate VIII).[35] There are the beginnings of a loop on the 'd' (e.g. *dedicasse*, line 4). Written about the same time, 1197 x 1205, was the report from Robert, and the abbots of Buildwas, Combermere, and Haughmond, to Archbishop Hubert Walter, in the matrimonial cause between the noblewoman M(arared), mother of Llywelyn prince of north Wales, and W., son of Ione (**17**, Plate IX). Once again, there are the beginnings of a loop on the 'd' (e.g. *audituris*, line 4), and 'long-s' (*accessisset*, line 6) is very similar to the

---

28   See the notes to *Actum* **30**.
29   Hereford Cathedral Archive 1517; *St Davids Episcopal Acta*, p. 102, no. 80.
30   *EEA, XXX, Carlisle, 1133–1292*, pp. 69–70, no. 85, and *EEA, XXVI, London, 1189–1228*, p. 188, no. 220.
31   See the notes to *Actum* **30**.
32   *EEA, XVI, Coventry and Lichfield, 1160–1182*, pp. 34–5, no. 38.
33   *Actum* **15**. Image at Plate VII.
34   Webber, 'Scribes and Handwriting', Plate II (depicting a charter 1198 x 1203) and note.
35   Cf. *ibid*.

'long-s' in Robert's Northampton indulgence (see *transeuntibus*, Plate VIII, line 5, for example).[36]

Faint ruled lines can be seen under each line of the text of Cadwgan's letters patent granting an indulgence in favour of St Ethelbert's Alms-House (**30**, Plate X).[37] There are the beginnings of a loop on the 'd', but the scribe does not use a 'long-s'. In fact, in many respects this *actum* is more similar to Alan's confirmation, 1195 x 1196, in favour of Strata Marcella, than Robert's *acta*, or the *acta* of Richard or Anian. The scribe has used a single-compartment 'a' and a single-compartment 'g', however, the Tironian *nota* for *et* is barred.

Richard's two indulgences in favour of St Paul's are strikingly different. His first indulgence, dated 13 December 1240 (**40**, Plate XII), was written by a scribe responsible for three other precisely datable indulgences in the same collection, all of them awarded in London between 1237 and 1241.[38] They are all in an elaborate chancery script that lacks the increasingly popular cursive traits of contemporary scripts.[39] In *Actum* **40**, the majuscules 'B', 'D', 'N', 'O', and 'Q' are written with doubled horizontal or vertical strokes, in the case of 'O', both. The ascender of 'a' often extends far above the headline as 'f' and 'long-s', 'g' has a long, horizontal tail to the left (e.g. *gratia*, line 1), and the Tironian *nota* for *et* is barred. Undoubtedly the most distinctive features of the script consist, firstly, in the horizontal flourishes, three or four strokes, with which the scribe decorates the top of the ascenders of 'f' and 'long-s' (*fidelibus*, line 1 and *spem*, line 4 for example); and secondly, the wave-like vertical abbreviation marks employed for, *inter alia*, 'er', 'm', 'n', and 'us' (e.g. *stabimus*, line 2, and *universitatem*, line 7). Richard's second St Paul's indulgence (**41**, Plate XIII) is much more in keeping with contemporary cursive script. The scribe has used the two-compartment 'g' (but not the two-compartment 'a'), together with hairline loops on the ascenders of 'b', 'd', and 'l'.[40] In fact, it is clear that the scribe responsible for Richard's second indulgence was also responsible for Robert, bishop of Salisbury's indulgence to St Paul's, as the hand is identical.[41]

Anian's 1274 indulgence in favour of Canterbury Cathedral Priory (**60**, Plate XIV), which based solely on the ample spacing of the text indicates it was a product of the beneficiary, displays an advanced stage in the evolution of cursive script. The scribe has used the two-compartment 'a' and two-compartment 'g', together with hairline loops on the ascenders of 'b', 'd', and 'l'.[42] It is noticeable too that the shaft of 'd' is executed with a much heavier stroke than the hairline loop.[43]

---

[36]   Cf. *ibid.*

[37]   *Actum* **30**.

[38]   The first, The London Archives, St Paul's Cathedral MS 25124/10, by Christian, bishop of Emly in Ireland (1236 × 1237–1249), is dated 28 October 1237; the second, 25124/12, by Richard Wendene, bishop of Rochester (1238–1250), 25 January 1240; and the third, 25124/15, by Hugh Pattishall, bishop of Coventry and Lichfield (1240–1241), 9 November 1241: Armstrong, 'A Misdated St Paul's Fabric Indulgence', 483–7.

[39]   *ibid.*, 486. A similar script can be seen used in a Hereford episcopal *actum* of 1196 x 1198: *EEA, Hereford, VII, 1079–1234*, Plate II, no. 180. For other similar *acta*: Armstrong, 'A Misdated St Paul's Fabric Indulgence', 486, n. 16.

[40]   Cf. Webber, 'Scribes and Handwriting', Plate VI and note.

[41]   The London Archives, St Paul's Cathedral MS 25124/14. See note to *Actum* **41**.

[42]   Cf. Webber, 'Scribes and Handwriting', Plate VI and note.

[43]   Cf. Webber, 'Scribes and Handwriting', Plate VI and note.

Anian's 1286 confirmation and indulgence in favour of Beddgelert Priory (**82**, Plate XV) displays a hand nothing like his Canterbury indulgence of 1274 (**60**, Plate XIV). It is much more compressed and gone are the two-compartment 'a' and two-compartment 'g', and hairline loops on the ascenders of 'b', 'd', and 'l'. There is the beginning of a loop on the 'd' (e.g. *audituris*, line 1), 'g' has a long, horizontal tail to the left (e.g. *Bangor'*, line 1), and the 'long-s' is not very long at all. The 'a' is a modern looking single compartment letter; the 'l', 'o', and 'u' all look very modern too. Anian's indulgence in favour of Salisbury Cathedral, given in London on 16 November 1295, is in a different hand again (**88**, Plate XVIII).

As regards, Anian's extant letters, two of his letters to Robert Burnell (**64** and **70**, Plates XVI (i) and (iii)) appear to be in a similar, if not the same, hand. Majuscule 'B' (*Bathon'*, line 1 in both *acta*) is almost identical, and the looped miniscules 'd' and 'l' (e.g. *dolens*, line 2, *Actum* **64**, and *adulteros*, line 5, *Actum* **70**) are very similar. Otherwise, his other letters (**62**, **65** and **72**, Plates XVI (ii), XVII (i) and XVII (ii)) and his extant petition (**89**, Plate XIX) are in different hands.

Household Scribes

Unlike certain volumes in the *EEA* series, it is not easy to identify one or more scribes who wrote two or more Bangor episcopal *acta*.[44] Julia Barrow also struggled to identify scribes for St Davids.[45]

The episcopate with the greatest number of *acta* is Anian's. Of his forty-seven *acta*, nine non-profession originals are extant.[46] Whilst one would not be surprised to find that indulgences were the product of the beneficiary, I had hoped to find the same hand (from the episcopal household) responsible for two or more of Anian's five surviving letters, written during the period 1277–1283.[47] As mentioned above, two of his letters to Robert Burnell (**64** and **70**, Plates XVI (i) and (iii)) may be in the same hand, but otherwise there is no evidence of a scribe being responsible for more than one *actum* in the corpus of Bangor *acta*.

Autograph

The last six bishops (from and including Gwion, cons. 1177) added crosses to their professions of obedience to Canterbury.[48] In the first half of the twelfth century it seems that bishops were not required to confirm their profession with an autograph cross. However, the custom was revived in 1148.[49]

Furthermore, two of the bishops, namely Cadwgan and Richard, signed their professions as follows:

Cadwgan signed his profession to Stephen Langton:

+ *et propria manu subscribo.* +

(**24**, Plate VI (v))

---

[44]   See for example *EEA, VII, Hereford, 1079–1234*, pp. ciii–cx.

[45]   *St Davids Episcopal Acta*, p. 26.

[46]   *Acta* **60**, **62**, **64**, **65**, **70**, **72**, **82**, **88** and **89**.

[47]   Anian's extant indulgences: *Acta* **60**, **82** and **88**. Anian's extant letters, 1277–1283: *Acta* **62**, **64**, **65**, **70** and **72**.

[48]   *Acta* **7** (Gwion), **13** (Alan), **16** (Robert), **24** (Cadwgan), **36** (Richard), and **56** (Anian).

[49]   *EEA, XXXIII, Worcester, 1062–1185*, p. 32.

The profession itself is written in a different hand, presumably by a Canterbury scribe (note that the loop from the single-compartment of Cadwgan's 'a' is much more abrupt than the scribe's, cf. *Bangorensis* and *propria manu*; furthermore Cadwgan's 'long-s' has a slight tail to the left, see *subscribo* and cf. *successoribus*; and also his Tironian *nota* for *et* is not barred, unlike the scribe's).

The final words of Richard's profession to Edmund of Abingdon were:

et subscribo. + + +

(**36**, Plate VI (vi))

The words, plus the crosses, are written in darker ink and seem to be in a different hand (note the lack of a loop on either 'b' of *subscribo*, cf. the 'b' in *obedientiam* and *subiectionem*) suggesting that the final two words as well as the three crosses were autograph.

Of even greater interest is Robert's profession to Hubert Walter (**16**, Plate VI (iv)). It is bookended by crosses, perhaps suggesting that the whole profession was autograph.

By comparing the hands of those who have signed (or written) their professions to Canterbury with their other extant *acta* it may be possible to ascertain if any of the bishops wrote, for example, their own letters.

I have, therefore, compared the handwriting of the signatures of Cadwgan's and Richard's Canterbury professions, as well as the handwriting of Robert's profession, with the respective extant *acta* for those three bishops.

Unless Cadwgan's handwriting changed over the twenty years of his episcopate, there would appear to be no correlation between his profession signature of 1215 and either the hand of his profession to the abbot of Dore, *c.*1236 (**34**, Plate XI (i)) or the hand of his notification to the same house *c.*1236 (**35**, Plate XI (ii)). Similarly, I can find no correlation between Richard's signature of 1237 and his two indulgences in favour of St Paul's (**40**, Plate XII and **41**, Plate XIII), the first of which was granted in 1240, nor between the handwriting of Robert's profession of 1197 and his 1201 indulgence in favour of Kingsthorpe Hospital, Northampton (**19**, Plate VIII). However, there are similarities between Robert's profession and his joint 1197 x 1205 report to Hubert Walter (**17**, Plate IX). For example, the two-compartment 'g' (cf. *Ego* and *Bangoriensis* in his profession and *gratia, Bangor(um)* and *Hageman* in the report) and majuscule 'H' (cf. *Huberte* in his profession and *H(uberto)* and *Hageman* in the report). There are also differences, 'long-s' extends below the line in the report only, and the Tironian *nota* for *et* differs. So, in conclusion, relying on the handwriting of professions alone, there is no evidence that the bishops were writing their own non-profession *acta*.

Seals

Seals attached to Bangor episcopal *acta*

Six seals remain attached to extant original *acta* of the bishops of Bangor. This survival rate compares well with St Davids, where J. Barrow noted that 'hardly any seals survive'.[50] C. R. Cheney stated that English episcopal seals were 'mostly,

---

[50] *St Davids Episcopal Acta*, p. 20: 'evidently because twelve of the surviving originals were sealed on the tongue, a method which is not kind to the survival of seals': *ibid*.

if not all, of a pointed oval shape', and of various colours.[51] However, David Williams noted that green wax was a favourite of 'the great laymen of "Welsh" Wales' and that, therefore, it is no coincidence that green wax predominated for episcopal seals in these areas.[52] In comparison, Llandaff episcopal seals display 'a considerable variety of colours'.[53] All the attached Bangor seals are oval or vesical (pointed-oval) in shape, and as can be seen from Table E, green is the predominant colour. Anian's seal attached to his 1274 indulgence in favour of Canterbury Cathedral Priory (**60**, Plate III (ii)) is in red wax, and this is about the time when red starts to become the preferred colour of episcopal seals.[54] One seal attached to a Bangor *actum* retains its silk-cloth seal bag (**19**, see Plate VIII).

Four of the seals attached to Bangor *acta* are main seals or seals of dignity, and two are privy or secret seals. Two of the seals have been countersealed – that is they bear impressions of a 'subsidiary' or 'secondary' seal matrix on the reverse of the wax.[55]

The best-preserved impression is that on Cadwgan's main seal, attached to his indulgence in favour of St Ethelbert's Alms-House, Hereford (**30**, see Plate I).[56] In relief, on the obverse side, is the figure of a robed and mitred bishop, standing on a corbel, holding in his left hand a crosier/pastoral staff (which reaches his eye level in height, and is turned inwards). His right hand is raised in blessing (rolled up, with one finger pointing skywards). The remaining legend, around the rim of the seal, reads '...... CADVCAN[I?] ..PISCOPI BANGOREN..'. The image conforms with the image most commonly found on twelfth- and thirteenth-century English and Welsh episcopal seals.[57] Furthermore, the mitre is worn with the peaks at the front and back of the head, rather than at the side, as was customary earlier in the period.[58] The legend is written in Lombardic capitals, another indication that this is a thirteenth century seal; Lombardic replacing Roman capitals in the late twelfth and early thirteenth centuries.[59] Interestingly, there are fingerprints preserved on the reverse of the wax.[60]

Cadwgan's privy or secret seal is also extant (**34**, Plate III (i)).[61] The image, on the obverse side, is very similar to his main seal. The remaining legend reads: 'S'

[51]   Cheney, *English Bishops' Chanceries*, p. 50.

[52]   *Welsh Episcopal Seals*, 106. See for example: *AWR*, no. 588 (seal of Gruffudd ap Gwenwynwyn), and nos. 226, 231 and 260 (seals of Llywelyn ab Iorwerth).

[53]   *Welsh Episcopal Seals*, 106.

[54]   *ibid.*, 108, chart.

[55]   Alan's confirmation in favour of Strata Marcella (*Actum* **15**), and Richard's first indulgence in favour of St Paul's (*Actum* **40**).

[56]   *Actum* **30**.

[57]   See for example: the seals of Henry (1193–1218) and William II (1219–1230) bishops of Llandaff (*Welsh Episcopal Seals*, 117–18, nos. 31, 32 and 35, Plate XXII), and Iorwerth (1215–1229) and Richard de Carew (1256–1280) bishops of St Davids (*ibid.*, 128–9, nos. 79 and 82, Plate XXX). Also, *EEA, XXXI, Ely, 1109–1197*, p. cxlvi and Plate IV (no. 154), and *EEA, VII, Hereford, 1079–1234*, Plate IV, no. 340.

[58]   *EEA, XXXI, Ely, 1109–1197*, p. cxlvi.

[59]   *Welsh Episcopal Seals*, 106. Alan's seal of 1195 x 1196 (*Actum* **15**) uses Roman capitals.

[60]   Fingerprints and palm prints impressed on wax seals relating to St Ethelbert's, and preserved at Hereford Cathedral, have been the subject of a recent study (Hoskin and New, 'By the Impression of my Seal') although no specific mention is made of the seal attached to Cadwgan's indulgence (Hereford Cathedral Archive 1514).

[61]   *Actum* **34**.

SECRETUM CADUCANI EPI'. As early as the middle of the twelfth century Archbishop Theobald had a smaller second seal known as the *signum secretum*.[62] Cadwgan's contemporary Llywelyn ab Iorwerth possessed a secret seal, with the legend 'SIGILLVM SECRETVM LEWELINI'.[63] Perhaps the prince of north Wales was influenced by Cadwgan.[64]

A different image, to that on Cadwgan's secret seal, appears on the privy seal (28 mm x 47 mm) attached to Anian's indulgence in favour of Canterbury Cathedral Priory, September 1274 (**60**, Plate III (ii)).[65] This shows a figure kneeling in prayer beneath the Virgin (crowned) and Child. In the thirteenth century, similar images were used on seals of certain members of the papal household, and also on the seals of English bishops.[66] On Anian's seal the person (presumably the bishop himself) is kneeling beneath an acute arch. The legend, as decipherable, reads, in Lombardic capitals, '..PVAT ...... EPISCOPI BNGOREN'.

<h3 style="text-align:center">Seal attached to papal decree</h3>

Another seal of Anian's is extant. It is attached to a decree made at the Second Council of Lyon on 13 July 1274.[67] It is pointed-oval in shape and given its dimensions (40 mm x 70 mm) this is his main seal.[68] The colour of the wax is green, and it is attached by a red silk cord. A bishop, in pontificals, standing on a corbel is depicted on the obverse side.[69] He holds a pastoral staff, turned inwards, in his left hand, and his right hand is raised in blessing. To his right is a six-rayed star, and to his left, what has been interpreted as a crescent moon, both on a diapered field strewn with flowers.[70] The remaining legend, in Lombardic capitals, reads: '..... IGILLU' ANNIANI DEI GRACIA B............ EPISC...'.[71] Rather than leave the area around the image of the bishop plain, increasingly in the thirteenth century there is evidence of the artistic choice to fill the background, hence the diapered field of Anian's seal.[72]

[62]   Cheney, *English Bishops' Chanceries*, p. 50.
[63]   Attached to an agreement of 1222: *Welsh History through Seals*, p. 19, no. 38; *AWR*, pp. 412–14, no. 252.
[64]   A suggestion made by Huw Pryce: *AWR*, p. 87. For a discussion about Llywelyn's use of his 'secret seal', and other possible influences (baronial and royal): *ibid*. See also, New, *Seals and Sealing Practices*, p. 46.
[65]   *Actum* **60**.
[66]   Papal household: Gardner, 'Some Cardinals' Seals', 74 and plate on 9. For an example of the use of the image by the bishop of an English see: *EEA, XXX, Carlisle, 1133–1292*, p. lix, and p. 153, no. 191 (bishop of Carlisle, Ralph de Ireton (1280–1292)).
[67]   Vatican Archive A. A. Arm. I–XVIII, 2190 (no. 18). *Sigilli Dell' Archivio Vaticano*, i, 76.
[68]   So Anian used his main seal in July 1274 in Lyon but his privy seal in September (*Actum* **60**) on his return to England.
[69]   *Welsh Episcopal Seals*, 111, and Plate XVII (7).
[70]   *ibid*.
[71]   *ibid. Sigilli Dell' Archivio Vaticano*, i, 76 records '..IGILLV.' at the beginning where the V is topped with a straight line contraction mark in superscript.
[72]   Bishop Richard Poore (1228–1237) at Durham did the same: Julian-Jones, 'Sealing Episcopal Identity', p. 252 (referring to *EEA, XXV, Durham, 1196–1237*, pp. lxix–lxx, and Plate VII). Poore also added a numeral 'II' to indicate that he was the second bishop called Richard at Durham (after Richard Marsh): *ibid*. It will be interesting to see if Anian II of Bangor (1309–1328) differentiated himself from Anian I on his seals.

Table E: Attached seals (with *actum* number in parentheses where relevant)

	Main Seal or Seal of Dignity	Privy or Secret Seal	Countersealed
Hervey			
David			
Meurig			
Arthur			
Gwion			
Alan	Off-white wax (**15**)		Yes (**15**)
Robert	Black or dark-green wax (**19**)		
Cadwgan	Green wax (**30**)	Green wax (**34**)	
Richard	Green wax (**40**)		Yes (**40**)
Anian	Green wax (papal decree)	Red wax (**60**)	

Detached Seal

A detached, and mounted, privy seal survives for a bishop of Bangor in the collections of the Society of Antiquaries of London (Society of Antiquaries, SA. C 7). See Plate V. It is listed by D. H. Williams.[73] It is also noted in the *Proceedings of the Society of Antiquaries of London*.[74] Both Williams and the Society of Antiquaries of London believe it could be Richard's.

Williams describes it as follows:

(?) Richard (1237–1267)

L; SA. C 7.

(Privy Seal)

Black, gutta-percha, p.o., 50 x 33 mm..

The Blessed Virgin crowned, with the child, under a canopy, above is perhaps the cathedral roof, a turret on either side; below – under an acute arch, the bishop mitred, kneeling in prayer.

S'PVAT ... (R) ... I. EPISCOPI . BNGOREN (Lom.)[75]

When published in 1887, the *Proceedings of the Society of Antiquaries of London*, recorded the remaining legend as:

S' PVAT[VM RICAR]DI. EPISCOPI . BĀGOREN[76]

---

[73]   *Welsh Episcopal Seals*, 111.
[74]   *Proceedings of the Society of Antiquaries of London*, 1885–1887, second series, vol. xi (London), pp. 295–6.
[75]   *Welsh Episcopal Seals*, 111. '*L*' stands for 'location', 'p.o.' stands for 'pointed oval', and 'Lom.' stands for 'Lombardic Capitals'.
[76]   *Proceedings of the Society of Antiquaries of London*, 1885–1887, second series, vol. xi (London), pp. 295–6.

It must be said that on inspection, in October 2018, there was no 'D' apparent where one would expect to find the bishop's name in the legend. Indeed the privy seal could equally be that of Bishop Anian as the image depicted is strikingly similar to that found on the seal attached to Anian's indulgence, dated 23 September 1274, in favour of Canterbury Cathedral Priory (**60**, Plate III (ii)).[77] However, as the *Proceedings of the Society of Antiquaries of London* recorded 'DI' as being extant in the legend in 1887, we must accept that such was faithfully recorded, and must conclude that the seal does indeed belong to Richard.

Countersealing

Countersealing was common before the end of the twelfth century.[78] Cheney used the term 'counterseal' to describe the impression of a matrix on the back of the wax when the front bears the impression of a seal of dignity. Modern scholarship prefers the use of the term subsidiary (or secondary) seal to describe the impression made on the back of the wax.[79]

The obverse of the seal (*c.*35 mm x *c.*55 mm) attached to Alan's confirmation, 1195 x 1196, in favour of the abbey of Strata Marcella (**15**) depicts a bishop vested (his head and the legend are missing).[80] The impression on the reverse (*c.*27 mm x *c.*42 mm) depicts a bishop vested, pastoral staff in his left hand, with his right hand raised in blessing (once again the head is missing), the remaining legend reads: '… GILLVM … BANGORIE' in Roman capitals.[81]

The only other Bangor seal that definitely bears the impression of a seal matrix on the back of the wax is that attached to Richard's grant of an indulgence to St Paul's in December 1240 (**40**, Plates II and IV (ii)).[82] The image on the reverse of the wax is of a figure holding up a large roundel with the Lamb of God facing right, the lamb's head turning back to look at the staff and banner. The human figure could be John the Baptist, but as the figure may be wearing ecclesiastical dress, it could represent Bishop Richard himself.[83] The subsidiary seals used by Richard's contemporaries to counterseal their grants to St Paul's display images such as St Andrew (used by the bishop of Rochester) and the Virgin and Child (employed by the bishop of Salisbury).[84]

Countersealing, including the possible increased cost of the added validation it afforded, whether certain types of documents warranted a subsidiary seal in addi-

---

[77] *Actum* **60**.

[78] Cheney, *English Bishops' Chanceries*, p. 50; New, *Seals and Sealing Practices*, p. 63.

[79] See for example, New, *Seals and Sealing Practices*, pp. 63–4. Thank you to Professor Philippa Hoskin and Dr Elizabeth New for bringing this to my attention.

[80] *Actum* **15**. Image at Plate VII.

[81] Image at Plate IV (i). Described in *Welsh Episcopal Seals*, 110 (and Plate XVI (2)). Image also available online at the NLW: http://hdl.handle.net/10107/5637244, accessed 12 May 2024. Given the respective dimensions and images, it may be that Alan used his privy seal as a subsidiary to his main seal, and this follows a practice established in England from at least the middle of the twelfth century. Robert Chesney, bishop of Lincoln (1148–1166), frequently did so: *EEA, I, Lincoln, 1067–1185*, p. lx; Cheney, *English Bishops' Chanceries*, p. 50.

[82] *Actum* **40**.

[83] Thank you to Dr Elizabeth New for her assistance in interpreting the impression created by the subsidiary matrix.

[84] The London Archives, St Paul's Cathedral MS 25124/12 and MS 25124/14 respectively. For a discussion of the images found on subsidiary seals: New, *Seals and Sealing Practices*, p. 64.

tion to the bishop's official seal, and whether its absence indicates that the bishop was not present, has been discussed in the *EEA* series.[85]

Plaster-cast seal impressions

Preserved by The Society of Antiquaries of London, and the BL, are plaster-cast seal impressions, as follows:

Robert – two plaster-cast main seals attributed to Robert. Firstly, BL Seal LXXXII, 39 (white plaster cast) listed by D. H. Williams.[86] The remaining legend, in Roman capitals, reads: '….TI DEI GRACIA: B…..RIENSIS ECLESIE EPISCOPI …'.[87] Secondly, the impression of a pointed-oval seal, in white plaster cast, is kept in the collections of the Society of Antiquaries of London (Society of Antiquaries, SA. C 7). It is not listed by Williams. The image is of the torso and head of a robed bishop, who is standing. The dimensions of the plaster cast are 50 mm at its widest point and 73 mm in height, suggesting this was a main seal. No legend is visible. The Society ascribe the seal impression to Robert of Shrewsbury.

Cadwgan – in the BL is a white plaster cast of a privy seal, 33 mm x 44 mm, depicting a bishop standing in eucharistic vestments, holding in his left hand a pastoral staff (turned inwards), with his right hand raised in blessing. The remaining legend, in Lombardic capitals, reads: '+ S' SECRETVM . CADVCANI . EPI'.[88] The dimensions indicate that Cadwgan had at least two privy seals, this one and the one attached to *Actum* **34** (Plate III (i)) which is 25 mm at its widest point x 39 mm in height.

Richard (or possibly Anian) – white plaster cast of a seal (BL Seal LXXXII, 40). This has been thought to be an impression of the detached privy seal, Society of Antiquaries, SA. C 7 (see Plate V).[89]

Sealing Arrangements

The following methods of sealing were used by the bishops of Bangor:

Sealed on a tongue (*simple queue*)[90]

Robert's indulgence, of 1201, concerning Kingsthorpe Hospital, Northampton (**19**, Plate VIII) was sealed on a tongue of parchment which was cut from the lower left-hand side of the document (the tongue passing through the middle and reappearing at the bottom of seal). The seal was kept in a red cloth bag which survives. No wrapping-tic.

The means of sealing for Cadwgan's indulgence, *c.*1225 x 1235/6, concerning St Ethelbert's Alms-House, Hereford (**30**, Plate X) was as follows: two strips of

---

[85]   See for example: *EEA, XXIX, Durham, 1241–1283*, p. lxvii. See also, New, *Seals and Sealing Practices*, p. 63.

[86]   *Welsh Episcopal Seals*, 110.

[87]   *ibid*. Williams assigns this legend to the seal attached to BL Additional Charter No. 22381 (i.e. *Actum* **19**), however, no legend remains on the fragmented seal attached to BL Additional Charter No. 22381.

[88]   BL Seal LXXXII, 41. Recorded in *Welsh Episcopal Seals*, 110, with a black and white photograph at *ibid.*, Plate XVI (5). An illustration of the same is to be found at Cardiff Central Library, MS 4.335.

[89]   *Welsh Episcopal Seals*, 111.

[90]   See Giry, *Manuel de Diplomatique*, p. 628, and fig. 29. P. Chaplais refers to the tongue as 'simplex cauda': Chaplais, 'The seals and original charters', p. 268.

parchment cut from the lower left-hand side of the document, namely a wrapping-tie below the tongue, and the tongue itself, to which was attached a pointed-oval-shaped seal in green wax (with the tongue passing through the middle and reappearing at the bottom of seal).[91]

Sealed on a tag (*sur double queue*)[92]

Alan's confirmation, 1195 x 1196, in favour of Strata Marcella (**15**) was sealed on a parchment tag, which passed through horizontal slits in the turn-up (plica) at the foot of the document. The tag and off-white-wax seal survive (Plate VII).

Two of Richard's *acta* were sealed in the same way, namely his two indulgences in favour of St Paul's (**40** and **41**). The first, dated 1240, retains its green-wax seal, albeit badly damaged, on a parchment tag (Plate XII). The slit in the turn-up at the foot of the second indulgence, 1241 x 1267, is clear to see, however, the tag and seal are missing (Plate XIII).

Two of Anian's *acta* were sealed using this method also, namely his 1274 Canterbury indulgence (**60**, Plate XIV) with red-wax seal, and his 1286 confirmation and indulgence in favour of Beddgelert Priory (**82**, Plate XV), which has a turn-up at the foot of the parchment with horizontal slits clearly visible; the tag and seal are, however, missing.

---

[91] For an explanation of the purpose of a wrapping-tie see Chaplais, *English Royal Documents*, p. 6.

[92] See Giry, *Manuel de Diplomatique*, p. 627, and fig. 28. Chaplais refers to sealing on a tag as 'duplex cauda': Chaplais, 'The seals and original charters', p. 268.

Plate I Cadwgan's main seal attached to *Actum* **30** [*c*.1225 x 1235/1 March 1236]. Dimensions: 41 mm at widest point x 66 mm in height. Hereford Cathedral Archive 1514. By permission of Hereford Cathedral.

Plate II Richard's main seal attached to *Actum* **40**. Obverse side. 13 December 1240. Dimensions: approx. *c*.33 mm wide x ? mm in height. The London Archives, St Paul's Cathedral MS 25124/1. Copyright The Chapter of St Paul's Cathedral/The London Archives.

Plate III (i)   Cadwgan's 'secret' seal attached to *Actum* **34** [*c.*1236]. Dimensions: 25 mm at widest point x 39 mm in height. The National Archives, ref. E 326/11297.

Plate III (ii)   Anian's privy seal attached to *Actum* **60**. 23 September 1274. Dimensions: 28 mm at widest point x 47 mm in height. Canterbury Cathedral Archives, CCA-DCc-ChAnt/C/167. Reproduced with permission from the Chapter of Canterbury Cathedral.

Plate IV (i)   Subsidiary seal on the reverse of Alan's main seal attached to *Actum* **15** [16 April 1195 x 19 May 1196]. Dimensions: *c.*27 mm at widest point x *c.*42 mm in height. Aberystwyth, NLW, Wynnstay Estate Records – Ystrad Marchell charter GT16. By permission of Llyfrgell Genedlaethol Cymru/The National Library of Wales.

Plate IV (ii) Subsidiary seal on the reverse of Richard's main seal attached to *Actum* **40**. 13 December 1240. Dimensions: approx. *c*.30 mm wide x ? mm in height. The London Archives, St Paul's Cathedral MS 25124/1. Copyright The Chapter of St Paul's Cathedral/The London Archives.

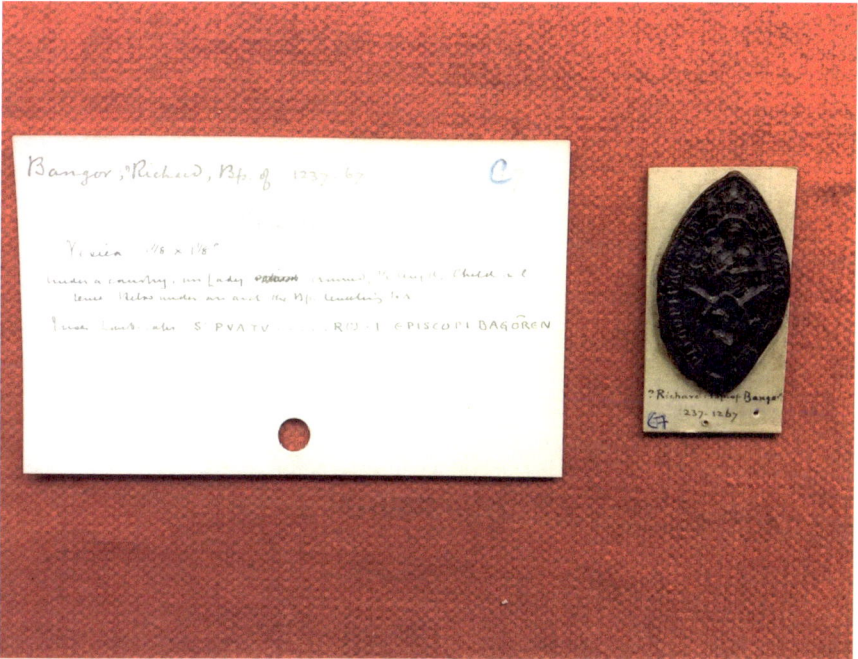

Plate V Detached seal – Richard's? privy seal (or Anian's?). Dimensions: 33 mm at widest point x 50 mm in height. Society of Antiquaries of London, SA. C 7. Reproduced with the permission of the Society of Antiquaries of London.

INTERNAL FEATURES

Language of the Bishops' Acta

The language of the bishops' *acta* was always Latin, and *acta* addressed to the bishops were always written in Latin.[93]

Welsh terms appear in the corpus of *acta* for the first time during the episcopate of Alan (1195–1196). Two of the lay witnesses to Alan's confirmation in favour of the abbey of Strata Marcella (**15**) were *Gurgeneu preco* ('Gwrgenau the rhingyll') and *Henir vates* ('Ynyr the poet').[94] The *preco* or *rhingyll* was the local serjeant.[95] The terms *keywannedd* and *halaucty* were used in the arbitration award (**52**) of April 1261 which settled disputes concerning seignorial rights between Bishop Richard and Llywelyn ap Gruffudd.[96] *Halaucty*, a 'polluted house', i.e. a house in which stolen goods were discovered, is confined to lawbooks compiled in thirteenth-century Gwynedd.[97] *Keywannedd* meant 'principal residence'.[98] Five of the six bonds (**73**, **74**, **75**, **76**, and **77**) to keep the peace, of July 1283, refer to *cantred* (the Welsh territorial unit cantref); and one bond (**75**) states that the *cantred* concerned is divided into *commotas* (commotes).[99] In 1286, Anian used *vab*, the Welsh for 'son (of)', twice in his confirmation (**82**) in favour of Beddgelert Priory.[100] In the same confirmation, he also used *yr efeyntt* (rendered as *yr efeyrat* by Edward I when reciting the charters in favour of Beddgelert that Anian had listed), meaning 'the priest'.[101] In 1305, he used *raglot* (i.e. *'rhaglaw'*) and the Latinised version of *'amobr'*, i.e. *ammobragium*, when petitioning Edward of Caernarfon (**95**, **96**, and **101**).[102] The *rhaglaw*, who, by the thirteenth century, was the Welsh princes' main local representative, and the chief resident officer of a commote, had replaced the *maer* and *cynghellor*.[103] *Amobr* was a payment due under Welsh law to a woman's lord in respect of a sexual relationship, both marital and extra-marital, that continued to be levied after the Edwardian conquest.[104]

Intitulatio

The earliest *actum* is a charter, 16 June 1107 x October 1109, granted by Hervey, whilst still bishop of Bangor, but given in his capacity as administrator of Ely

---

[93]   On 3 July 1284, John Peckham wrote to Anian twice, both times in Latin, but on the following day the archbishop preferred French in a letter to the king: *Registrum Epistolarum Peckham*, ii, p. 743, and iii, pp. 775–7. French was used by the burgesses of Beaumaris when they petitioned the king that, *inter alia*, he command the bishop of Bangor to dedicate the chapel which they had built in Beaumaris, because the parish church was over two miles away; and they could not go there in bad weather (1305 or 1314/15): *CAP*, pp. 471–2.

[94]   'Vates'/poet: *AWR*, p. 888.

[95]   Charles-Edwards, et al., *Welsh King and His Court*, pp. 573 and 599; *AWR*, p. 862.

[96]   *Actum* **52**.

[97]   *AWR*, p. 517; Pryce, *Native Law*, pp. 229–30.

[98]   *ibid.*

[99]   'Cantred': *Acta* **73**–**7**. 'Commota': *Actum* **75**.

[100]   '… Tegwaret vab Gueyr … Jorberd vab yr efeyntt …': when listing two charters of Dafydd (ap Gruffudd, d. 1283): *Actum* **82**.

[101]   i.e. 'yr effeiriad'/'yr offeiriad': *Geiriadur Prifysgol Cymru*, accessed 29 May 2024. See also *AWR*, p. 634, no. 439, and the notes to *Actum* **82**.

[102]   *Acta* **95**, **96** and **101**.

[103]   Stephenson, *Governance*, pp. 41–4; Jones, 'Llys and Maerdref', p. 304; Charles-Edwards, et al., *Welsh King and His Court*, p. 572, and *Geiriadur Prifysgol Cymru*, accessed 10 March 2024.

[104]   *AWR*, p. 723. See also: *RC*, p. xvi; Carr, *Medieval Anglesey*, p. xv.

abbey (**1**). He described himself as *Herveus dei gratia episcopus* without any reference to Bangor.[105] Meurig used (**5**) the style *dei gratia Bangor' episcopus*,[106] and this was the most common style used by the bishops of Bangor. Robert, at the end of the twelfth/beginning of the thirteenth century preferred *permissione divina* to *dei gratia*,[107] and this proved popular with Cadwgan and Anian. From as early as 1241, *miseratione divina* was on occasion used in place of *permissione divina*.[108] Sometimes *minister humilis* was preferred to *episcopus*, the earliest such use being by Gwion (**9**), who may have been following the style adopted by Archbishop Thomas Becket (not an unreasonable suggestion given that Gwion's archdeacon was Alexander Llywelyn, Becket's former friend and companion).[109] See Table F.

Table F: Intitulatio

	dei gratia Bangorensis episcopus	*dei gratia Bangorensis ecclesie minister humilis*	*permissione divina Bangorensis episcopus*	*permissione divina Bangorensis ecclesie minister humilis*	*miseratione divina Bangorensis ecclesie episcopus*	*suus Bangorensis/suus modicus etc*
Hervey	1 minus *Bangorensis*					
David						
Meurig	1					
Arthur						
Gwion	3 plus 1 minus *dei gratia*	1				
Alan	2					
Robert			5			
Cadwgan	1	2 minus *humilis*	2			
Richard	3 plus 3 minus *dei gratia*				1 replacing *episcopus* with *minister humilis*	
Anian	2 plus 11 minus *dei gratia*	1 plus 1 minus *dei gratia*[110]	4	5	8	3

[105] *Actum* **1**.
[106] *Actum* **5**.
[107] *Acta* **17**, **18**, **19**, **22** and **23**.
[108] See Richard's second indulgence in favour of St Paul's (*Actum* **41**) for the earliest use of 'miseratione divina'. Anian's six bonds of 1283 employed this style: *Acta* **73**, **74**, **75**, **76**, **77** and **78**.
[109] *Actum* **9**. For the new title adopted by Archbishop Becket, see Cheney, *English Bishops' Chanceries*, p. 64 and n. 6. For Alexander Llywelyn see the section of the Introduction entitled 'Introduction of a Chapter'.
[110] But edge of parchment torn away (*Actum* **62**).

Anian used *suus Bangorensis* twice (on both occasions without mentioning his own name) in letters to Robert Burnell and John de Kirkby respectively, in the latter case he added '*minimus*'.[111] He used *suus modicus capellanus* (as well as *minister humilis*) in his letter to Edward I shortly after he had publicly excommunicated Llywelyn ap Gruffudd in 1277 and fled to St Albans (**62**).[112] Interestingly, Llywelyn ap Gruffudd referred to himself as *suus devotus, suus devotus vasallus*, and other similar terms in letters to Edward I from 1275 onwards.[113]

Only twice was a bishop of Bangor referred to as *antistes*, and then only in professions of obedience to Canterbury.[114]

The genitive of Bangor (as in the bishop of Bangor) was most commonly written as *Bangorensis*,[115] but also as *Bangoriensis*,[116] *Bangornensis*,[117] *Pangorensis*,[118] *Bagoren*',[119] *Bangor*',[120] *Bangorr*',[121] *Bango*',[122] *Bang*',[123] and *Bagor*'.[124] It is interesting to note that in every one of Robert of Shrewsbury's non-profession *acta* the abbreviation mark for '*rum*'[125] was used at the end of *Bango*' or *Bangor*',[126] and *Bangorum* was written out in full in the rubric to one of his recorded *acta*.[127]

Inscriptio

The address for confirmations, grants, indulgences and the like varied from *universis Cristi fidelibus* in Meurig's confirmation in favour of Haughmond Abbey (**5**),[128] to *omnibus fidelibus* in Gwion's charter to the same house (**9**),[129] and from *omnibus sancte matris ecclesie filiis* (Alan's Strata Marcella charter, **15**),[130] to *universis sancte*

---

[111] *Acta* **70** (14 November 1281 x 11 December 1282) and **72** (about 18 April 1283).

[112] *Actum* **62**. An episcopal contemporary of Anian's used 'modicus' also; Thomas de Wouldham, bishop of Rochester (1291–1317): 'Thomas dei permissione modicus sacerdos Roffensis': *DMLBS*, via https://logeion.uchicago.edu/modicus, accessed 3 May 2024.

[113] According to Huw Pryce as a way of emphasising his subordination to the king: *AWR*, pp. 70–1, and n. 553.

[114] Meurig's profession to Archbishop Theobald, 1140: *Actum* **3**; and Anian's profession to Archbishop Boniface, 1267: *Actum* **56**.

[115] *Acta* **8**, **9**, **10**, **11**, **13**, **15**, **24**, **71** and see *Acta* **12**, **34**, **40**, **43**, **45**, **52**, **55**, **60**, **64**, **66**, **67**, **70**, **72**, **74**, **76**, **78**, **86**, **88**, **89**, **92** and **102**.

[116] *Acta* **7** and **16**.

[117] *Acta* **3**, **36** and **56**.

[118] *Actum* **2**.

[119] *Actum* **30**. See also *Actum* **26** and notes to *Actum* **32**.

[120] *Acta* **5**, **14**, **17**, **18**, **19**, **25**, **35**, **41**, **58**, **62**, **65** and **82**.

[121] *Actum* **73** and **77**.

[122] *Acta* **20**, **21**, **22**, **23** and **75**.

[123] *Acta* **53**, **79** and **80**.

[124] *Actum* **26**. See also *Actum* **30** and notes to *Actum* **32**.

[125] See Cappelli, *The Elements of Abbreviation*, p. 13.

[126] *Acta* **17**, **18**, **19**, **20**, **21**, **22** and **23**. Only twice in the remaining corpus of 102 *acta* is this abbreviation mark used in conjunction with Bango': **26** (Cadwgan, but not in the intitulatio) and **75** (Anian).

[127] *Actum* **22**.

[128] *Actum* **5**.

[129] *Actum* **9**.

[130] *Actum* **15**.

matris ecclesie filiis (in Cadwgan's indulgence in favour of St Ethelbert's, Hereford, **30**).[131] *Omnibus Cristi fidelibus* was employed by both Richard and Anian as an alternative to *universis Cristi fidelibus*, which they also used.[132] Those addressed were usually, but not always, further defined by the addition of wording such as *presens scriptum inspecturis*,[133] *tam presentibus quam futuris*,[134] *ad quos presens scriptum pervenerit*,[135] *ad quos presentes littere pervenerint*,[136] *presentes litteras visuris vel audituris*,[137] or *has litteras visuris vel audituris*.[138]

Huw Pryce, in *The Acts of Welsh Rulers*, commented that the address in Llywelyn ab Iorwerth's three letters patent at Worcester in 1218 ('*Universis tam presentibus quam futuris ad quos presens scriptum pervenerit*') resembled some contemporary episcopal acts rather than the general addresses of royal letters patent.[139] Unfortunately, said Pryce, surviving episcopal acts from Bangor were few, but pointed to an act of Bishop Cadwgan ('*omnibus Cristi fidelibus ad quos presens scriptum pervenerit*').[140] We can now add that Alan, 1195 x 1196, used *tam presentibus quam futuris*;[141] Robert of Shrewsbury, Llywelyn's first bishop, used *ad quos presens scriptum pervenerit* twice;[142] and Cadwgan, himself, used *ad quos presentes littere pervenerint*.[143]

Until the very end of the twelfth century, the bishop's title would usually precede the general address.[144] Alan was still using this sequence in 1195 x 1196.[145] The sequence was then transposed (see Robert's *Acta* **18** and **19**) in line with developments in most English dioceses.[146] However, there were still occasions in the thirteenth century when the bishops of Bangor used the title-before-address formula.[147]

When writing to the pope, the archbishop of Canterbury, the king and certain other dignitaries, the *inscriptio* would always precede the bishop's title and would always be very deferential, in line with the emphasis in the *ars dictaminis* on acknowledging distinctions of rank.[148] For example, Robert's report to Archbishop Hubert Walter began '*Reverentissimo patri et domino*';[149] Richard began his supplica-

---

[131] *Actum* **30**.

[132] Richard: *Acta* **40**, **41**, **43** and **45**. Anian: *Acta* **60**, **66**, **67**, **82** and **88**.

[133] *Actum* **5**.

[134] *Actum* **15**.

[135] *Acta* **18** and **19**.

[136] *Actum* **30**.

[137] *Actum* **60**.

[138] *Acta* **43**, **45**, **66** and **67**.

[139] *AWR*, pp. 61–2.

[140] This is *Actum* **25**.

[141] *Actum* **15**.

[142] *Acta* **18** and **19**.

[143] *Actum* **30**.

[144] See for example Gwion's *acta*: *Acta*, **8**, **9**, **10**, **11** and **12**.

[145] *Acta* **14** and **15**.

[146] See Cheney, *English Bishops' Chanceries*, p. 69.

[147] See for example Cadwgan's indulgence in favour of SS Peter and Paul, Leominster (*Actum* **26**).

[148] Camargo, *Ars Dictaminis*, pp. 22–3; Chaplais, 'English Diplomatic Documents', pp. 46–7. The rulers of Gwynedd followed the same conventions: *AWR*, p. 70.

[149] *Actum* **17**.

tion to Pope Clement IV '*Sanctissimo patri et domino*';[150] and Anian, in his letter to the king of 1277, began '*Illustri domino ac serenissimo Edwardo*' shortly followed by '*suus modicus capellanus Anianus Bangor(ensis) ecclesie minister hum[ilis] …*'.[151]

Salutatio

Salutem in domino was the most common greeting used in their *acta* by the bishops of Bangor;[152] sometimes *perpetuam in domino salutem*,[153] or *salutem eternam in domino*,[154] or *salutem in domino sempiternam* (a favourite of Anian's),[155] was preferred. Reflecting papal influence, *salutem et benedictionem*,[156] and *salutem et dei benedictionem*,[157] were also, on occasion, employed.

Notificatio

In notifications, forms of *noscere* were used by the bishops, not *scire* (the verb normally used in English royal charters, and in baronial charters),[158] usually followed by the accusative and infinitive construction. The use of *scire* was rare too in English episcopal *acta*;[159] and in the *acta* of the bishops of St Davids.[160]

Only in Gwion's *actum*, in which he ordered the parishioners of Nefyn to pay the canons of Haughmond tithes of fish caught at sea and tithes of the produce of the land (**11**), was the verb *scire* ('*sciatis*') used, and then only in the sanction.[161]

Noverit universitas vestra was common.[162] When addressing the papal legate, Robert used *noverit paternitas vestra*.[163] *Noveritis nos*, followed by the perfect infinitive, was popular with Anian.[164] Alternatives were *notum sit* used by Hervey and Cadwgan;[165] *ad omnium notitiam pervenire volumus* used by Gwion,[166] and *ad universitatis vestre notitiam volumus pervenire*, in Richard's letter to Henry III.[167]

Arenga

Cadwgan, in his indulgence in favour of SS Peter and Paul, Leominster (**26**), largely followed the wording (based on 2 Corinthians) suggested by Canon 62 of the Fourth Lateran Council, 1215, when he wrote *Quoniam, ut ait apostolus, omnes*

---

[150] *Actum* **55**.
[151] *Actum* **62**.
[152] e.g. *Actum* **5**.
[153] *Actum* **9**.
[154] e.g. *Actum* **45**.
[155] e.g. *Actum* **58**.
[156] *Actum* **11**.
[157] *Actum* **8**.
[158] *AWR*, p. 60; *St Davids Episcopal Acta*, p. 25.
[159] See for example *EEA, VII, Hereford, 1079–1234*, pp. xc–xci.
[160] *St Davids Episcopal Acta*, p. 25.
[161] *Actum* **11**.
[162] See for example *Acta* **18**, **19** and **45**.
[163] *Acta* **21** and **22**.
[164] *Acta* **79**, **80** and **82**.
[165] *Actum* **1** and *Actum* **34**.
[166] *Actum* **9**.
[167] *Actum* **43**.

stabimus ante tribunal Cristi, recepturi prout in corpore gessimus, sive bonum sive malum, oportet nos diem messionis extreme misericordie operibus prevenire, ac eternorum intuitu seminare in terris quod reddente domino cum multiplicato fructu recolligere debeamus in celis, firmam spem fiduciamque tenentes quoniam qui parce seminat parce et metet.[168]

However, whilst Archbishop Stephen Langton utilised the Canon 62 wording in his indulgence in favour of the alms-house (St Ethelbert's) being constructed by the dean and chapter of Hereford,[169] Cadwgan, at the beginning of the exhortation in his indulgence in favour of the same project (**30**), preferred: *Quoniam inter opera caritatis ea valde meritoria reputantur que ad sustentationem pauperum Cristi pia conferuntur largitione* ….[170] Bishop Iorwerth of St Davids used the same wording.[171]

It has been noted in the *EEA* series that if an arenga (the harangue or pious preamble) was employed it often stressed the necessity of good works for salvation or the responsibilities of the bishop's office.[172] As the thirteenth century progressed, pious preambles in episcopal *acta* became less common.[173] Although, Anian's 1272/3 confirmation of the charters of his predecessors in favour of Haughmond Abbey (**58**) stated that *cum sit opus pietatis locis religiosis providere et eadem in libertatibus sibi misericorditer indultis conservare nos ex pastoralis sollicitudinis officio nobis divinitus collato* ….[174] However, this was exactly the same wording used in Alan's *confirmatio*, 1195 x 1196, which had confirmed the charters of Meurig and Gwion in favour of Haughmond (**14**).[175] It appears, therefore, that whoever wrote Anian's confirmation merely copied the relevant text from seventy-six or so years earlier.[176]

As late as 1286 the arenga still had its place in the *acta* of the bishops of Bangor for Anian began his grant of an indulgence in favour of Beddgelert Priory (**82**), which had been damaged by fire, with the words *Et quia pium est oppressis et afflictis subvenire* ….[177]

---

[168] *Actum* **26**. The text from '*Quoniam*' to '*metet*' inclusive replicates the first sentence of the wording suggested by Canon 62, save that '*fuerit*' is omitted after '*sive bonum sive malum*', and '*et qui seminat in benedictionibus, de benedictionibus et metet in vitam aeternam*' is omitted at the end. The arenga employed by Richard in his first indulgence (1240) in favour of St Paul's (**40**) was more faithful to the first sentence of the wording suggested by Canon 62, with only '*operibus*' missing. The wording suggested by Canon 62 (*Conciliorum Oecumenicarum Decreta*, pp. 263–4) was later incorporated into Pope Gregory IX's decretal collection: *Liber Extra*, V, 38. 14 (cols. 888–9).

[169] August 1226: *Acta Stephani Langton*, p. 109, no. 90; Cheney, *English Bishops' Chanceries*, pp. 76–7.

[170] *Actum* **30**.

[171] c.1225 x 29 January 1229: Hereford Cathedral Archive 1517; *St Davids Episcopal Acta*, p. 102, no. 80. See the section entitled 'Products of the Beneficiary'.

[172] See for example *EEA, VII, Hereford, 1079–1234*, pp. lxxxviii–lxxxix, and *EEA, I, Lincoln, 1067–1185*, p. lv.

[173] *EEA, XLIII, Coventry and Lichfield, 1215–1256*, p. lxxxiv. Also, *EEA, IX, Winchester, 1205–1238*, p. lxvii; *EEA, XIII, Worcester, 1218–1268*, p. xlv.

[174] *Actum* **58**.

[175] *Actum* **14**.

[176] In fact, the arenga in Alan's confirmation (**14**) had itself been used verbatim in an earlier confirmation of possessions in favour of the same house by the bishop of Coventry, 1160 x 1182: *EEA, XVI, Coventry and Lichfield, 1160–1182*, pp. 34–5, no. 38. See 'Products of the Beneficiary'.

[177] *Actum* **82**.

Dispositio

Only once did a 'dispositive' clause begin with *Inde est quod* (and then only in a warning to pay tithes, **11**),[178] and never with 'the characteristically papal' *Eapropter*, the two most common openings in English episcopal *acta*.[179]

In grants, other than indulgences, the bishops used verbs such as *concedo/concedere* and *do/dare*;[180] thus, Hervey used the perfect active infinitives *concessisse et dedisse* (in an accusative and infinitive construction) in his only known *actum* while bishop of Bangor (**1**), as did Gwion in two of his grants in favour of Haughmond Abbey (**8** and **10**), and Robert in his grant to SS Peter and Paul, Shrewsbury (**18**).[181] The present active indicative *concedimus* appears less often (**14** and **26**).[182] For confirmations, not surprisingly, the verb usually used was *confirmo/confirmare*; and here the present active indicative *confirmamus* proved more popular[183] than the perfect active infinitive *confirmasse*.[184] Although the latter was used, with the ablative of instrument construction, when the bishop wanted to make it clear that his charter was to confirm the grant or confirmation, for example *hac presenti carta nostra confirmasse*.[185]

Anian used the verb *video/videre* ('*nos vidisse*', and later '*vidimus*') in his *actum* of 1286, in favour of the Augustinian priory of Beddgelert (**82**), to confirm that he had seen various charters of the Welsh princes in favour of the priory.[186] C. R. Cheney pointed out that it was only in the later part of the thirteenth century that the inspeximus predominated in episcopal chanceries.[187] However, older forms of confirmation-charters still survived.[188] It is noteworthy that there is no inspeximus in the corpus of Bangor episcopal *acta*.[189]

On two occasions, a saving clause was included in confirmations of predecessors' charters, and both were confirmations in favour of Haughmond Abbey.

---

[178] Gwion's order to the parishioners of Nefyn: *Actum* **11**.

[179] Cheney, *English Bishops' Chanceries*, p. 72 ('characteristically papal' is Cheney's description, *ibid.*, p. 73). See also, *EEA, VII, Hereford, 1079–1234*, p. lxxxix.

[180] J. R. Davies has discussed the use of, and difference between, 'dare' and 'concedere', and the work of Richard Sharpe in this regard: J. R. Davies, 'The donor and the duty of warrandice: giving and granting in Scottish charters', especially pp. 122–3. Thank you to Dr Nigel Tringham for bringing this to my attention.

[181] Hervey: *Actum* **1**. Gwion: *Acta* **8** and **10**. Robert: *Actum* **18**.

[182] *Actum* **14** and *Actum* **26**.

[183] *Acta* **5**, **8**, **14**, **15** and **58**.

[184] *Actum* **10**.

[185] *Actum* **45**. See also *Actum* **9**.

[186] *Actum* **82**.

[187] Cheney, *English Bishops' Chanceries*, p. 96.

[188] *ibid*.

[189] The defining feature of an inspeximus, according to C. R. Cheney and J. Barrow, is the verbatim quotation of one charter in another (*English Bishops' Chanceries*, p. 96 and *EEA, VII, Hereford, 1079–1234*, p. xcv). Alan's confirmation (*Actum* **14**) of the charters of bishops Meurig and Gwion, in favour of Haughmond, 1195 x 1196, was a confirmation-charter of the type described by Cheney; interestingly, it delineated the lands with which it was concerned in greater detail than did Anian's *actum* in favour of Beddgelert, ninety years later.

Richard used *salvo in omnibus iure episcopali* (**45**);[190] and Anian used *salvo iure nostro et aliorum in omnibus et per omnia* (**58**).[191] Saving clauses were frequently included in bishops' confirmatory *acta* elsewhere.[192]

As has been noted in England, bishops occasionally obtained the consent of their cathedral chapter to a grant.[193] Cadwgan's grant of the church of Llangurig to the abbey of Strata Florida (**29**), was made with the consent of his chapter.[194] Furthermore, Richard's collation and confirmation to Aberconwy Abbey of two parts of the chapel of Cemais (**44**) was made with the consent of his chapter.[195] During the same episcopate, it is noteworthy that the arbitration awards of April and August 1261 made it clear that they were in respect of disputes between Llywelyn ap Gruffudd on one side, and both Richard and his chapter on the other (**52** and **53**).[196]

It should be noted that charters, other than indulgences, were mostly records of transactions (*Beweisurkunden*) rather than having dispositive force themselves (*Geschäftsurkunden*).[197] Anian's gift or assignment of an acre of land in Bangor to the prior and friar preachers of Bangor Friary (**91**) may well have been an example of *Geschäftsurkunden*.[198]

First person singular and first person plural

Pierre Chaplais noted that from 1066 to 1189 English kings used the first person singular to refer to themselves in virtually all documents. However, from Richard I's coronation (in 1189) onwards, the royal chancery used the plural of majesty in all documents.[199] This, said Chaplais, referring to C. R. Cheney, followed the 'practice which had been current for some time in other royal European chanceries and in English episcopal chanceries'.[200] Cheney noted that before *c.*1140, in the majority of English episcopal *acta*, the bishop spoke of himself in the singular, whereas after *c.*1180 every bishop used the first person plural;[201] and that the English bishops in adopting the plural were following the lead of the pope and his cardinals.[202] In the case of the bishops of Bangor, Hervey in his grant of 1107 x 1109 used the first person singular (**1**).[203] However, by 1143 x 1151 Meurig was using the first person plural (**5**), and that was to be the norm (except for professions of canonical obedience) from then on.[204] The twelfth-century rulers of Gwynedd

---

[190] *Actum* **45**.
[191] *Actum* **58**.
[192] *EEA, I, Lincoln, 1067–1185*, p. xlviii.
[193] *ibid.*
[194] *Actum* **29**. Hervey's grant (*Actum* **1**) was made with the consent of the convent of Ely.
[195] *Actum* **44**.
[196] *Acta* **52** and **53**.
[197] As J. Barrow also noted at Hereford: *EEA, VII, Hereford, 1079–1234*, p. lxxvi.
[198] *Actum* **91**.
[199] Chaplais, *English Royal Documents*, p. 13.
[200] *ibid.*, referring to Cheney, *English Bishops' Chanceries*, pp. 58–9.
[201] Cheney, *English Bishops' Chanceries*, p. 58.
[202] *ibid.*, p. 59.
[203] 'me concessisse et dedisse … meo': *Actum* **1**.
[204] Meurig's confirmation of the gift of land by Hywel ab Ieuaf of Arwystli: *Actum* **5**.

did, on occasion, use the first person plural in their letters, but only with Llywelyn ab Iorwerth (d. 1240) was it used consistently.[205] Dafydd ap Llywelyn (d. 1246) and Llywelyn ap Gruffudd (d. 1282) continued the practice.[206]

There were occasions in the thirteenth century when the first person singular was used by the bishops of Bangor, and save for professions of canonical obedience, and Robert's letter to Pope Innocent III, of 1206, certifying the canonical election and fitness of Master Jocelin (**23**) whom he knew well, these were times of personal stress.[207] Shortly before he died, Richard used the first person singular in his heartfelt supplication to Pope Clement IV (**55**).[208] Anian used it in his letter to the chancellor, Robert Burnell, at the end of the first Welsh war of 1277, recounting how he had lost his brother, his sister's son, his cousin, and sixty of his kinsmen in the service of the king (**64**).[209]

At this point it is worth noting that Anian often used the formula *rogamus et requirimus* when asking for help during times of crisis; during one of the two Welsh wars, or when he was concerned that his rights were being infringed.[210] Francis Hargrave said that this formula was used when the thing required was a matter of good-will, and not of right, in which case it would have been a *mandamus* or *precipimus*; furthermore *rogamus* signified a commandment as a prayer.[211]

Interestingly, Cadwgan in his profession (**34**) to Stephen of Worcester, abbot of Dore, *c.*1236 used both the first person singular (in the main text of the profession) and the first person plural (in the sealing clause).

One final point that should be made here is that, in his petition to Edward I (**89**), Anian used the third person singular.[212]

Indulgences

In grants of indulgence the bishops always used *relaxamus*. The first text of such a grant to have survived is Robert's original indulgence of 25 May 1201 in favour of Kingsthorpe Hospital, Northampton (**19**).[213] The operative wording was ... *vere penitentibus et confessis de iniuncta sibi penitentia ... viginti dies relaxamus*, and this varied little throughout the thirteenth century. The relaxation was always of enjoined penance, and usually in favour of those of the diocese of Bangor (sometimes defined as the *parochiani*), and of others whose diocesan bishops had ratified the grant; who had confessed and were truly penitent or truly contrite.[214] The noun *indulgencia* was not used until Richard's first grant to St Paul's (**40**) in December 1240.[215] The prolifera-

---

[205] From 1220 at the latest: *AWR*, p. 71.

[206] *AWR*, p. 71.

[207] Robert's certificate to Innocent III: *Actum* **23**.

[208] *Actum* **55**.

[209] *Actum* **64**.

[210] *Acta* **65** and **70** addressed to Robert Burnell, *Actum* **72** addressed to John de Kirkby, and *Actum* **86** addressed to Edmund, earl of Cornwall.

[211] Hargrave was, albeit, commenting on legal proceedings some centuries later, but Anian did seem to use literary devices to further his case. Hargrave, *A Complete Collection of State Trials*, p. 714.

[212] *Actum* **89**.

[213] *Actum* **19**.

[214] See for example: *Acta* **26** and **30** (Cadwgan); *Acta* **40** and **41** (Richard); *Acta* **60**, **66**, **67**, **71**, **82** and **88** (Anian).

[215] *Actum* **40**. Richard repeated the word in his second grant in favour of St Paul's: *Actum* **41**. Anian used it in *Acta* **60**, **66**, **67**, **71** and **88**.

tion of pardons was already a problem when the Fourth Lateran Council decreed (in 1215) that bishops and archbishops could normally offer a maximum of forty days remission (even if several acted together).[216] At Bangor, the number of days relaxation of enjoined penance varied from ten to forty. Multiples of five were usual, and so Cadwgan's grant of thirteen days in favour of Leominster Priory (**26**) stands out; it may be that this was part of a combined grant.[217] Indulgences required some specific action, other than confession and contrition, on the part of the parishioner; and as such, they were granted for (i) those visiting named churches, (ii) visiting and/or giving alms, (iii) visiting and saying specified prayers for certain people, or (iv) visiting and a combination of prayers, alms-giving, and/or other actions; see Table G.

Table G: Indulgences – Number of days relaxation of enjoined penance and ecclesiastical beneficiary

	Visiting a named church	Visiting a named church and giving alms	Visiting a named church and saying prayers for a certain person	Combination of visiting a named church, listening to preaching, giving alms, and/or saying prayers
Hervey				
David				
Meurig	15 – Reading			
Arthur				
Gwion				
Alan				
Robert		20 – Northampton		
Cadwgan	20 – Reading 20 – Reading	15 – Hereford 13 – Leominster		
Richard	10 – Reading 10 – St Albans 30 – St Albans	40 – St Paul's (just give alms – church under construction) 30 – St Paul's (visit or give alms)		
Anian		40 – Beddgelert	10 – Clare 40 – Salisbury Unknown – Bringhurst Church (Leicestershire)	20 – Canterbury 20 – Clare 30 – Stanlaw

---

[216] Or a year at the consecration of a church: Swanson, *Indulgences in Late Medieval England*, p. 11, referring in n. 14 to Tanner, *Decrees of the Ecumenical Councils*, i, p. 264. Also, Vincent, 'Some Pardoners' Tales', 53.

[217] *Actum* **26**.

References to St Deiniol

St Daniel (or Deiniol, d. 584, the first bishop of Bangor and its patron saint)[218] was invoked only three times in the corpus of *acta*, and on each occasion it was in an indulgence granted by Anian.

After Hervey was styled '*Herveus sancti Danihelis episcopus*' at the Christmas court of William Rufus in 1093,[219] there are only two mentions of Deiniol in the documentary record until the episcopate of Anian. Firstly, Gerald of Wales confirmed (in 1191) that Deiniol was the patron saint of Bangor, and stated that his body was buried on Ynys Enlli (Bardsey).[220] The other mention was in a letter (written *c*.February x October 1140) preserved in Gerald's *De Invectionibus* (completed in 1216). According to Gerald, the letter was written by Owain Gwynedd, and his brother Cadwaladr, to Bishop Bernard of St Davids complaining that Bishop Meurig had entered the church of St Deiniol ('*Sancti Daniel ecclesiam*') like a thief, without any invitation from them.[221]

Anian's resurrection of St Deiniol in the last quarter of the thirteenth century may have been a conscious recalling of the venerable nature of his church at a time of uncertainty after the war of 1277, the resulting Treaty of Aberconwy, and the eventual fall of the house of Gwynedd in 1282/3.

His first use of the saint was in 1279, in two indulgences in favour of Clare Friary (**66** and **67**).[222] Then in 1284, at Caernarfon, a grant by Edward I, undoubtedly made at Anian's behest, was stated to be to God, the blessed Mary, Anian and *ecclesie cathedrali sancti Danielis Bangoren(sis)*.[223] Anian once again invoked the saint in 1295, in his indulgence in favour of Salisbury Cathedral (**88**).[224] Deiniol was described as bishop and confessor (*beati Daniel(is) episcopi et confessoris*) in all three of Anian's said *acta*, but the *actum* of 1295 added 'our patron' (*patroni nostri*) or perhaps, 'our protector'. Anian II of Bangor was also to refer to Deiniol in one of his early grants, another indulgence in favour of Salisbury in 1310.[225]

---

[218] For Deiniol see *Annales Cambriae A-text*, p. 6; *Annales Cambriae B-text*, p. 25; *Annales Cambriae C-text*, p. 10; *AC*, p. 5; *Martyrology of Tallaght*, p. 70; *Book of Llan Dâv*, pp. 3 and 71; *Opera*, vi, p. 124; *Journey and Description*, p. 184; Davies, *Wales in the Early Middle Ages*, p. 88; Charles-Edwards, 'Deiniol [St Deiniol, Daniel] (*d*. 584)', *ODNB*.

[219] Recorded in the foundation narrative of St Mary's Abbey, York: Karn, 'The Foundation Narrative', pp. 402–3. 'Danielis' is found in Cambridge, Corpus Christi College MS 139, and 'Daniel'' in Bodleian MS Bodley 39 (SC 1892): *ibid.*, p. 402, n. 85. I am grateful to Dr Nicholas Karn for providing me with his new edition and translation.

[220] 'corpus beati Danielis Banchorensis episcopi': *Opera*, vi, p. 124; *Journey and Description*, pp. 184 and 224.

[221] *AWR*, pp. 322–3. As the letter is only preserved in his *De Invectionibus* it has been suggested that it may have been doctored by Gerald to emphasise the brothers' submission to St Davids: *ibid.*, p. 323. Further commentary in Pryce, 'Owain Gwynedd (*d*. 1170)', *ODNB*, and Lloyd, *History of Wales*, ii, pp. 483–4. If the letter is in anyway spurious, it does not detract from the fact that Gerald himself recorded the church of Bangor as being the church of St Daniel/Deiniol (in 1191 and again by 1216).

[222] *Acta* **66** and **67**.

[223] *RC*, p. 134 and p. 255; *CChR, 1257–1300*, p. 279; Willis, *Survey*, pp. 190–1; Haddan and Stubbs, i, pp. 580–1.

[224] *Actum* **88**.

[225] Salisbury Cathedral Archives, Indulgences BS/5/52.

Iniunctio

Unlike at St Davids, injunctions/mandates are rare in the corpus of Bangor *acta*, indeed *mandamus* was never used, neither was *iniungimus*.[226] *Precipimus* was used once by Gwion, when ordering the parishioners of Nefyn to pay the canons of Haughmond tithes (**11**);[227] and four times by Alan, but all in the same *actum* in favour of Haughmond (**14**), when confirming the charters of Gwion and Meurig in respect of confirmations and grants of the church of Nefyn, and the church of Trefeglwys, and the abbey's right to the tithes at the former.[228] The wording in Alan's *actum* (e.g. *auctoritate qua fungimur districte precipimus quatinus* and *precipimus auctoritate apostolica et nostra quatinus*) is similar, but not identical, to wording in English episcopal mandates and in those for St Davids.[229]

Corroboratio

Meurig in his confirmation of Hywel ab Ieuaf's grant to Haughmond, 1143 x 1151, stated: *Et ideo hanc donationem quantum ad episcopalem auctoritatem pertinent presenti scripto confirmamus* (**5**).[230] The use of a corroboration became more common during the second half of the twelfth century, and as J. Barrow noted, the opening words of the *corroboratio* were often a monosyllable followed by a disyllable, then there was a wish that the transaction should be preserved, followed by one or two 'strengthening' verbs.[231] Thus Gwion's grant, gift and confirmation of Trefeglwys church to Haughmond, 1177 x 1191, read: *Quod quare futuris temporibus ratum et firmum permanere volumus scripti et sigilli nostri testimonio communimus et confirmamus* (**9**).[232] His grant, gift and confirmation of St Mary's church, Nefyn (**8**) to the same house had: *Et ut hec nostra donatio rata et inconcussa permaneat eis sigilli nostri munimine corroboravimus.*[233] The use of a corroboration clause which mentioned the bishop's seal, as Gwion's charters do, was, according to Cheney, 'exceptional' in the first sixty years of the twelfth century.[234] It is not surprising, therefore, that Meurig's charter did not mention his seal. At the end of the century, Alan in his confirmation of the gift and sale made by Cadwaladr ap Hywel, in favour of Strata Marcella (**15**), went further than his predecessors in explaining the evils that the *corrobatio* was meant to address: *Sed quoniam ad malum presens etas prona est et ingeniosa et id calumpniose temptat infringere unde sibi lucrum conatur extorquere hanc donationem et venditionem sigilli nostri impressione confirmamus.*[235] Interestingly, Llywelyn ab Iorwerth, in 1209, used similar wording in his grant to the same house: *Sed quia presens etas prona est ad malum unde si possit*

---

[226] Cf. *St Davids Episcopal Acta*, p. 197. In England, surviving mandates are comparatively rare, given the number of total *acta* recorded, at for example, Hereford: *EEA, VII, Hereford, 1079–1234*, p. xcvi, and Lincoln: *EEA, I, Lincoln, 1067–1185*, p. 255.

[227] *Actum* **11**.

[228] *Actum* **14**.

[229] See for example, Hereford: *EEA, VII, Hereford, 1079–1234*, p. xcvi, and *St Davids Episcopal Acta*, pp. 65 and 88.

[230] *Actum* **5**.

[231] Hereford: *EEA, VII, Hereford, 1079–1234*, p. xcvii.

[232] *Actum* **9**.

[233] *Actum* **8**.

[234] Cheney, *English Bishops' Chanceries*, p. 75.

[235] *Actum* **15**.

extorquere lucrum, … sigilli mei impressione … corroboravi;[236] perhaps suggesting that Alan's confirmation and Llywelyn's grant were products of Strata Marcella, or perhaps that Llywelyn had borrowed from Alan's charter.[237]

It was not until the second quarter of the thirteenth century that the formula *in cuius rei testimonium* was used, with Cadwgan being the first to use it (**30**): *In cuius rei testimonium hiis litteris patentibus sigillum nostrum apponi fecimus* (*c.*1225–1235/6).[238] Interestingly, Llywelyn ab Iorwerth first used *In cuius rei testimonium* in 1223.[239] As regards Cadwgan's thirteenth-century successors, the formula is found in three of Richard's *acta*, and fourteen of Anian's.[240]

On seven occasions, mostly grants/confirmations, both witness lists and sealing clauses were included in the same *actum* by the bishops.[241]

Sanctio

Sanctions, in the form of threats of anathema, occur throughout the twelfth century. Meurig included one in his confirmation of the grant by Hywel ab Ieuaf in favour of Haughmond (**5**).[242] Gwion included a sanction of anathema when he ordered the parishioners of Nefyn to pay tithes to the canons of Haughmond (**11**); he included one in his confirmation of the grant made by Hywel ab Ieuaf to the same house (**10**), and a further one in his grant in favour of St Werburgh's Abbey, Chester (which had had goods stolen), the latter *actum* adding a threat of interdict (**12**).[243] At the end of the century, Alan included a sanction in his confirmation in favour of Strata Marcella (**15**).[244] The sentence threatened was always one of anathema (*anathematis*); in the case of St Werburgh's (**12**), Gwion used the verb *anathematizo/anathematizare*.[245] It was not until 1283, when Anian invoked the threat of a sentence of excommunication (*excommunicationis sentenciam*) in six bonds taken from members of the communities of Gwynedd to keep the peace, that sanctions re-appeared in the *acta* of the bishops of Bangor.[246]

Date

The first *actum* that is precisely datable is Robert's indulgence in respect of Kingsthorpe Hospital, Northampton (**19**).[247] The date of 25 May 1201 is given by way of reference to the recently deceased Hugh of Avalon, bishop of Lincoln, in

---

[236] *AWR*, pp. 385–6, no. 231.

[237] Cf. *AWR*, pp. 64–5, and n. 502.

[238] *Actum* **30**, and 'In huius rei testimonium hiis litteris nostris patentibus sigillum nostrum apposuimus' in *c.*1236 (*Actum* **34**). The note in *AWR* at p. 65, n. 504, that Cadwgan's *acta* did not contain the formula can now be revised.

[239] *AWR*, p. 65, and n. 503.

[240] Richard: *Acta* **45**, **52** and **53**. Anian: *Acta* **58**, **60**, **66**, **67**, **73**, **74**, **75**, **76**, **77**, **78**, **79**, **80**, **82** and **88**.

[241] *Acta* **8**, **9**, **15**, **18**, **25**, **45** and **92**.

[242] *Actum* **5**.

[243] *Acta* **10**, **11** and **12**.

[244] *Actum* **15**.

[245] A frequently cited canon from Gratian's *Decretum* defined anathema as 'damnation of eternal death': Hill, 'Excommunication and Politics in Thirteenth-Century England', p. 47, quoting C.11 q.3. c.41.

[246] *Acta* **73**, **74**, **75**, **76**, **77** and **78**.

[247] *Actum* **19**.

whose diocese Northampton lay: *anno primo post obitum felicis memorie Hugonis quondam Lincol(niensis) episcopi octavo kalendas Iunii'*.

English episcopal *acta* rarely bore a date until the last decade of the twelfth century.[248] Dates were rare too in the episcopal *acta* of St Davids before the time of Bishop Anselm (1231–1247), becoming more common under Bishop Thomas (1248–1255).[249] At Bangor, dates become increasingly common from about the same time, namely during the episcopate of Richard (1237–1267). Thus, Richard's first indulgence in favour of St Paul's (**40**) was *Datum London' apud sanctum Paulum die sancte Lucie virginis, pontificatus nostri anno quarto* (13 December 1240).[250] Six years later, his letter to Henry III was *Actum apud Wyndesor vicesimo die Aprilis anno regni regis eiusdem tricesimo* (**43**).[251] His confirmation in favour of Haughmond (**45**) was *Dat' apud Haghmon' anno gratie millesimo ccxIvii kal' Januarii.*[252] So Richard, in three *acta* during a seven year period, used his own pontifical year, the regnal year, and the year of grace to date his documents. The place was given in all three. Reference to *anno domini* and the nearest significant feast day was used to date one of the arbitration awards (**53**) in the disputes between Richard and Llywelyn ap Gruffudd: *apud Rydyraru anno domini mo cco lxo primo die iovis proxima post festum assumptionis Beate Marie* (18 August 1261).[253] Anian used the year of grace too (**58** and **92**).[254] On one occasion (**80**), he used a feast day and the regnal year.[255] However, he preferred *anno domini*; sometimes by reference to the Roman calendar,[256] on one occasion in conjunction with the regnal year,[257] but mostly in conjunction with a specified feast day.[258] In all these *acta*, a place-name was given, often preceded by *Dat'/Datum apud*.

[248]   Cheney, *English Bishops' Chanceries*, p. 81.

[249]   See for example *St Davids Episcopal Acta*, pp. 25–6 and 50–1.

[250]   *Actum* **40**. Evidence from Salisbury points to the date of consecration (rather than of election, royal/papal assent, grant of temporalities, or installation) as the start of the pontifical year. *EEA, IX, Winchester, 1205–1238*, p. lxxiv, and n. 13. See also *EEA, XIII, Worcester, 1218–1268*, p. li. The first use of the pontifical year to date an episcopal *actum* at St Davids was by Bishop Anselm within the first year of his consecration, 9 February 1231 x 8 February 1232: *St Davids Episcopal Acta*, p. 26 and p. 127, no. 108. His successor, Thomas Wallensis, used his pontifical year to date three of his *acta*: *ibid.*, p. 26, and pp. 130–3, nos. 114, 116, and 117. Some bishops never used their pontifical year for dating purposes, see, for example, *EEA, VII, Hereford, 1079–1234*, p. xcix.

[251]   April 1246: *Actum* **43**.

[252]   January 1247/8: *Actum* **45**.

[253]   *Actum* **53**.

[254]   *Acta* **58** and **92**.

[255]   *Actum* **80**.

[256]   *Acta* **62**, **66**, **67** and **102**.

[257]   *Actum* **71**. Here the date was given as 'incipiente an(no) do(mi)ni mcclxxxiii et a(nno) r(egni) reg(is) Edw(ardi) fil(ii) reg(is) Hen(rici) xi'; at the beginning of the year ('incipiente anno domini'), perhaps meaning the feast of the Annunciation, Lady Day, 25 March, 1283. For the feast of the Annunciation as the beginning of the year: Cheney, *Handbook of Dates*, p. 5.

[258]   *Acta* **60**, **65**, **73**, **74**, **75**, **76**, **77**, **78**, **79**, **82** and **88**.

Eschatocol

The most common eschatocol was a witness list which was usually introduced by *Hiis testibus* (**1**, **5**, **10**, **14**, **18**, **25**, and **45**).[259] On one occasion *Teste* was used (**9**), and *Testes igitur* on another (**15**).[260] Witness lists were always placed at the end of the relevant document except in Bishop Anian's joint testimony of a miracle (**92**) where the list preceded the sealing clause, and Bishop Alan's confirmation in favour of the abbey of Strata Marcella (**15**) where the witnesses were listed before the sealing clause and a *sanctio*; interestingly, a grant by Gruffudd ap Llywelyn (d. 1244) to the same house placed the witness list before a warranty clause.[261] *Inter alia*, witness lists provide (i) some of the earliest information about the possible make-up of the episcopal household,[262] (ii) an indication of possible internal divisions within the *familia*,[263] and (iii) the names of those who were likely to have been companions of the bishops whilst in exile.[264] However, witness lists in cartulary copies were often shortened to record only the first, more eminent individuals.[265]

Farewells were restricted to letters and indulgences and were never used in conjunction with a witness list.[266] The simplest form of farewell, or valediction, was *Valete*.[267] Cadwgan used *Valeat universitas vestra semper in domino* at the end of his sealed letter patent granting an indulgence in favour of St Ethelbert's Alms-House, Hereford (**30**), and *Valeat universitas vestra* in his notification concerning services rendered by his nephew (**35**).[268] More personal forms were used for addressing superiors or secular dignitaries, so for example Robert when writing to the archbishop of Canterbury, Hubert Walter (**17**), used *Valeat in domino paternitas vestra*.[269] Anian ended two of his letters to the chancellor, Robert Burnell (who was also bishop of Bath and Wells) with *Valeat et vigeat vestra humilitas devota semper in domino*, and *Valeat et vigeat vestra paternitas per tempora multa*, respectively (**64** and **70**).[270]

---

[259] *Acta* **1**, **5**, **10**, **14**, **18**, **25** and **45**. Only one Bangor *actum* with a witness list is dated: *Actum* **45**.

[260] *Actum* **9** and *Actum* **15** respectively.

[261] *AWR*, pp. 450–1, no. 283, see also *ibid.*, p. 66.

[262] See for example *Acta* **8**, **9**, **10**, **14** and **25**. Cf. Brooke, 'English Episcopal *Acta* of the Twelfth and Thirteenth Centuries', p. 46.

[263] See the section entitled '*Clas* and *Familia*', and McGuinness, 'The Medieval Bishops of Bangor, 1092–1283: Intrusion, Exile and Diplomacy' (forthcoming).

[264] For example, see *Actum* **15**, a confirmation by Bishop Alan, the former prior of the Hospital of Jerusalem in England, in which the first-named witness was 'Laurentius hospitalarius'. For Alan's intrusion into, and subsequent exile from, Bangor see *De Invectionibus*, p. 95; *Autobiography*, p. 213; and McGuinness, 'The Medieval Bishops of Bangor, 1092–1283: Intrusion, Exile and Diplomacy' (forthcoming).

[265] See *Acta* **5**, **8**, **9**, **10**, **14**, **25** and **45**. Cf. Hoskin, 'Authors of Bureaucracy', p. 75.

[266] On three occasions dates were given: *Actum* **19** (albeit the date is the date Robert dedicated the chapel for which he granted an indulgence), *Actum* **62**, and *Actum* **102**.

[267] *Acta* **11**, **19** and **26**.

[268] *Actum* **30** and *Actum* **35** respectively.

[269] *Actum* **17**.

[270] *Acta* **64** and **70**.

Conclusion

In conclusion, the bishops of Bangor appear to have been little disadvantaged by their see's apparent remoteness on the western periphery of Latin Christendom. The internal and external features of their *acta* suggest that they kept up with current trends and that their scribes and households were every bit as capable as their contemporaries in far larger and wealthier dioceses. This should perhaps come as no surprise, after all, the bishops themselves were often well travelled, and well connected. David had been master at the cathedral school of Würzburg; the reforming Meurig spent a great deal of time with Archbishop Theobald; Gwion had the learned, cosmopolitan and influential Alexander Llywelyn as his archdeacon; Alan had been prior of the Hospital of Jerusalem in England; the versatile Master Robert, before taking up residence in his see, had stayed and travelled with Richard I and his court, and then King John and his; Cadwgan who had been abbot of Whitland, the mother-house of all the Cistercian houses in *Pura Wallia*, lost no time in writing a confessional formulary for his diocesan clergy to assist them with one of the onerous canons issued at the Fourth Lateran Council; Master Richard, former archdeacon of Bangor, returned to Gwynedd after long periods spent at St Albans in the company of Matthew Paris and others; and Master Anian, another former archdeacon, who attended the Second Council of Lyon, could, after securing a London residence for himself from the king of England, describe himself as Edward I's chaplain in Wales, and call the chancellor of England his friend.

Plate VI Professions of Obedience to Canterbury.

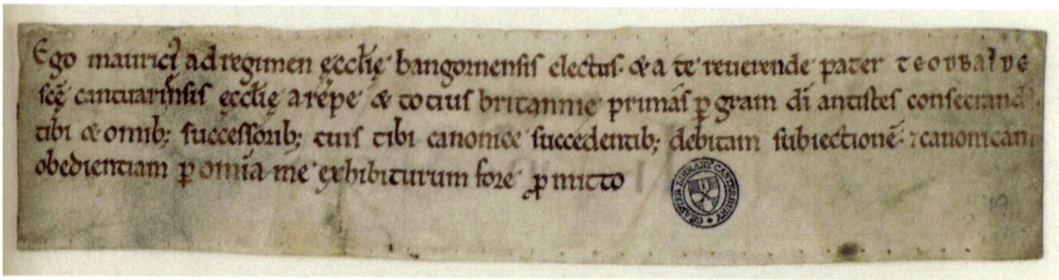

Plate VI (i) *Actum* **3** – Meurig's profession of obedience to Archbishop Theobald of Bec. [*c.*31 January 1140]. Canterbury Cathedral Archives, CCA-DCc-ChAnt/C/115/19. Reproduced with permission from the Chapter of Canterbury Cathedral.

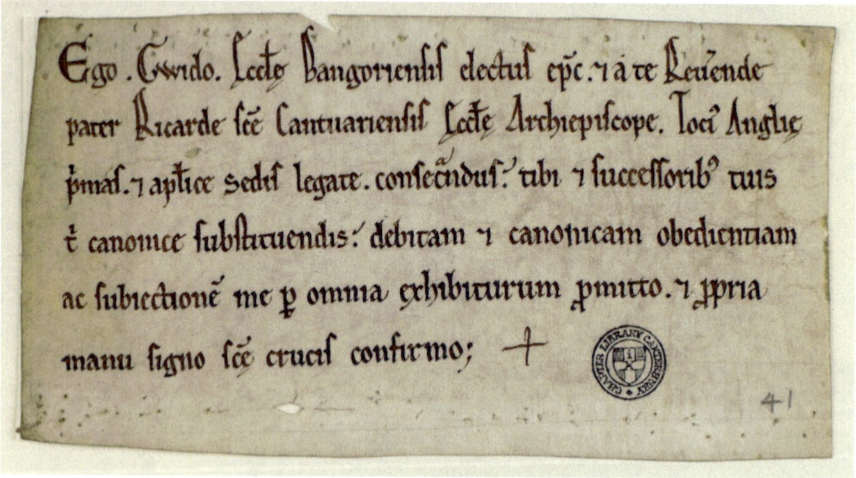

Plate VI (ii) *Actum* **7** – Gwion's profession of obedience to Archbishop Richard of Dover. 22 May 1177. Canterbury Cathedral Archives, CCA-DCc-ChAnt/C/115/41. Reproduced with permission from the Chapter of Canterbury Cathedral.

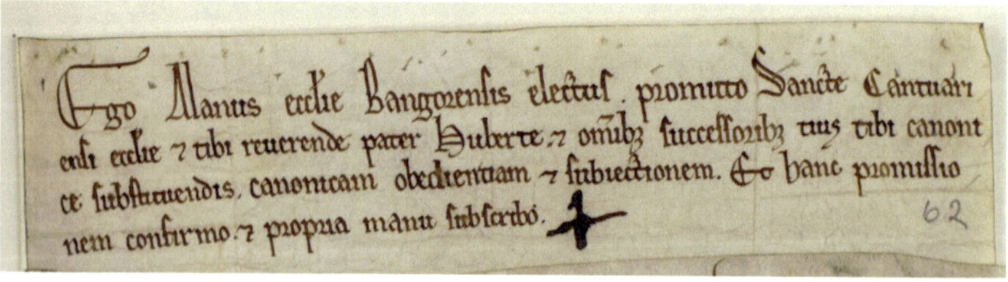

Plate VI (iii) *Actum* **13** – Alan's profession of obedience to Archbishop Hubert Walter. 16 April 1195. Canterbury Cathedral Archives, CCA-DCc-ChAnt/C/115/62. Reproduced with permission from the Chapter of Canterbury Cathedral.

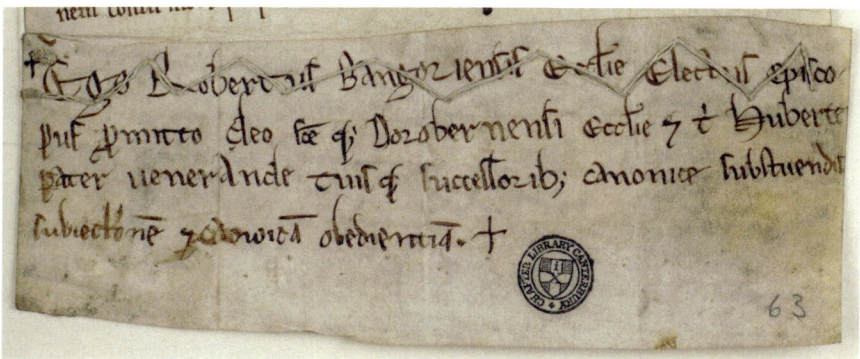

Plate VI (iv) *Actum* **16** – Robert's profession of obedience to Archbishop Hubert Walter. [16 March 1197]. Canterbury Cathedral Archives, CCA-DCc-ChAnt/C/115/63. Reproduced with permission from the Chapter of Canterbury Cathedral.

Plate VI (v) *Actum* **24** – Cadwgan's profession of obedience to Archbishop Stephen Langton. [21 June 1215]. Canterbury Cathedral Archives, CCA-DCc-ChAnt/C/115/146. Reproduced with permission from the Chapter of Canterbury Cathedral.

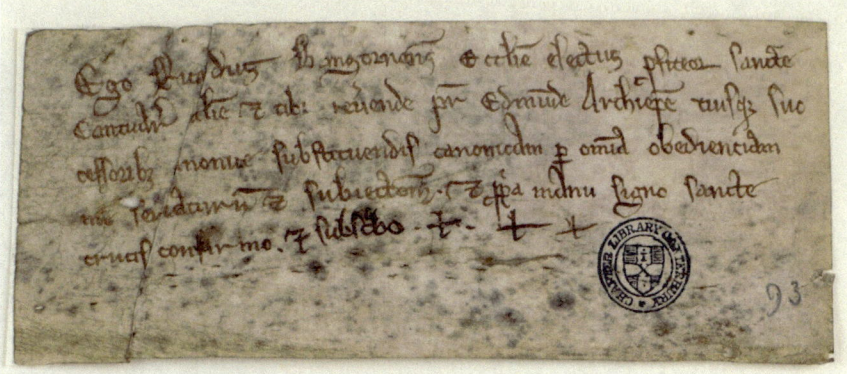

Plate VI (vi) *Actum* **36** – Richard/Rhirid's profession of obedience to Archbishop Edmund of Abingdon. [1237]. Canterbury Cathedral Archives, CCA-DCc-ChAnt/C/115/93. Reproduced with permission from the Chapter of Canterbury Cathedral.

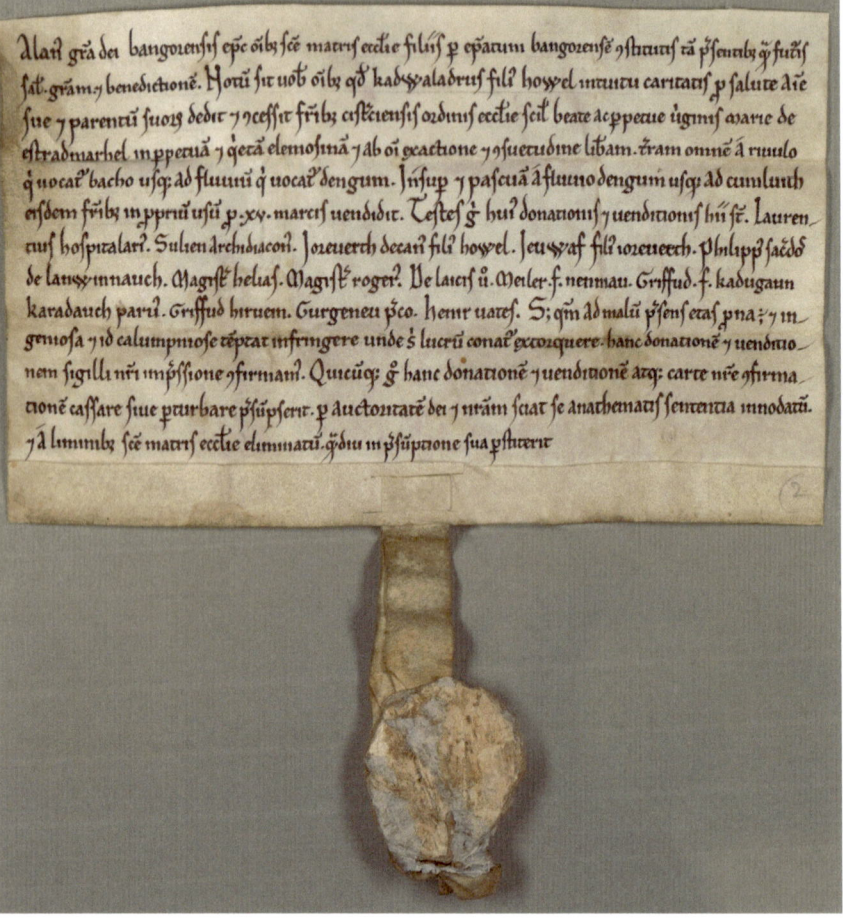

Ego anianus Bangorenensis ecclie electus et are reuerende pater Bonefaci gre cantuariensis ecclie Archiepe et tocī anglie Primas consecrandus antistes tibi et cantuariensi ecclie et successorib; tuis canonice substituendis debitam et canonicam obedientiam et subiectione me p omnia exhibiturū profiteor et promitto scdm decreta romanoy pontificū tuoyeq; et cantuar ecclie Iurium aduture ero ad defendendū et retinendū saluo ordine meo. Sic me deus adiuuet. Et predicta omnia ppria manu subscribendo confirmo. ✠

136

Plate VI (vii) *Actum* **56** – Anian's profession of obedience to Archbishop Boniface of Savoy. 1267 [after 12 December]. Canterbury Cathedral Archives, CCA-DCc/ChAnt/C/115/136. Reproduced with permission from the Chapter of Canterbury Cathedral.

Plate VII *Actum* **15** – Alan's confirmation of a gift and sale made by Cadwaladr ap Hywel of Arwystli in favour of Strata Marcella Abbey. [16 April 1195 x 19 May 1196]. Aberystwyth, NLW, Wynnstay Estate Records – Ystrad Marchell charter GT16. By permission of Llyfrgell Genedlaethol Cymru/The National Library of Wales.

Plate VIII *Actum* **19** – Robert's indulgence at his dedication of a chapel in Kingsthorpe Hospital, Northampton. 25 May 1201. From the British Library Collection. BL Additional Charter No. 22381.

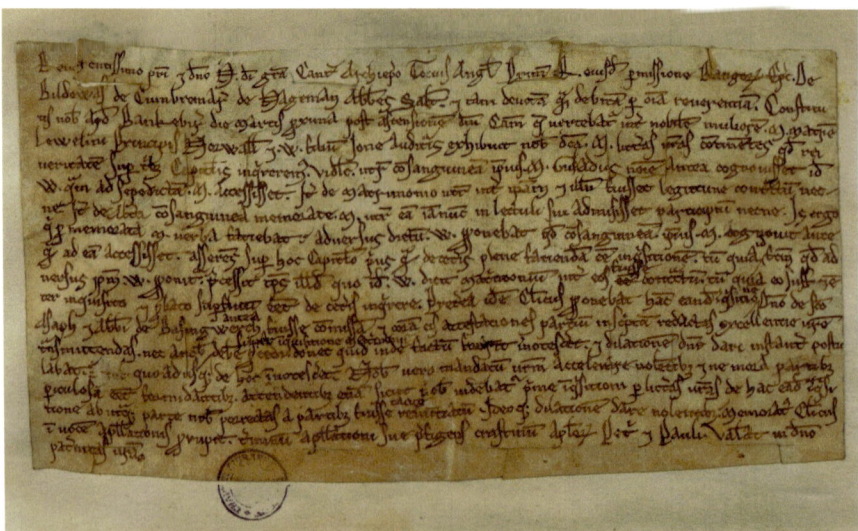

Plate IX *Actum* **17** – Report from Robert, and the abbots of Buildwas, Comb-
ermere, and Haughmond, to Archbishop Hubert Walter, in the matrimonial
cause between the noblewoman M(arared), mother of Llywelyn prince of north
Wales, and W., son of Ione. [16 March 1197 x 13 July 1205]. Canterbury Cathedral
Archives, CCA-DCc-ChChLet/II/251. Reproduced with permission from the
Chapter of Canterbury Cathedral.

Plate X *Actum* **30** – Sealed letters patent of Cadwgan granting an indulgence
in favour of St Ethelbert's Alms-House, Hereford. [*c*.1225 x 1235/1 March 1236].
Hereford Cathedral Archive 1514. By permission of Hereford Cathedral.

Plate XI (i) *Actum* **34** – Sealed letters patent of Cadwgan – profession to Stephen of Worcester, abbot of Dore. [*c.*1236]. The National Archives, ref. E 326/11297.

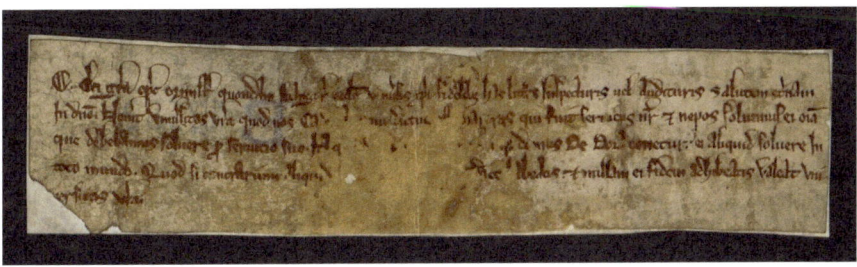

Plate XI (ii) *Actum* **35** – Notification by Cadwgan to Abbey Dore concerning services rendered by his nephew. [*c.*1236]. The National Archives, ref. E 326/12582.

Plate XII *Actum* **40** – Richard's first indulgence in favour of St Paul's. St Paul's, London, 13 December [1240]. The London Archives, St Paul's Cathedral MS 25124/1. Copyright The Chapter of St Paul's Cathedral/The London Archives.

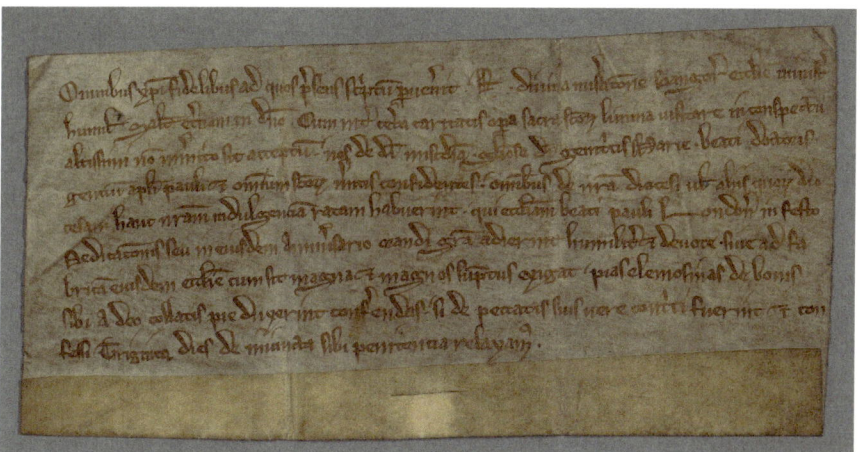

Plate XIII *Actum* **41** – Richard's second indulgence in favour of St Paul's. [13 January 1241 x before 8 November 1267, probably 13 January 1241 x -3 November 1246]. The London Archives, St Paul's Cathedral MS 25124/13. Copyright The Chapter of St Paul's Cathedral/The London Archives.

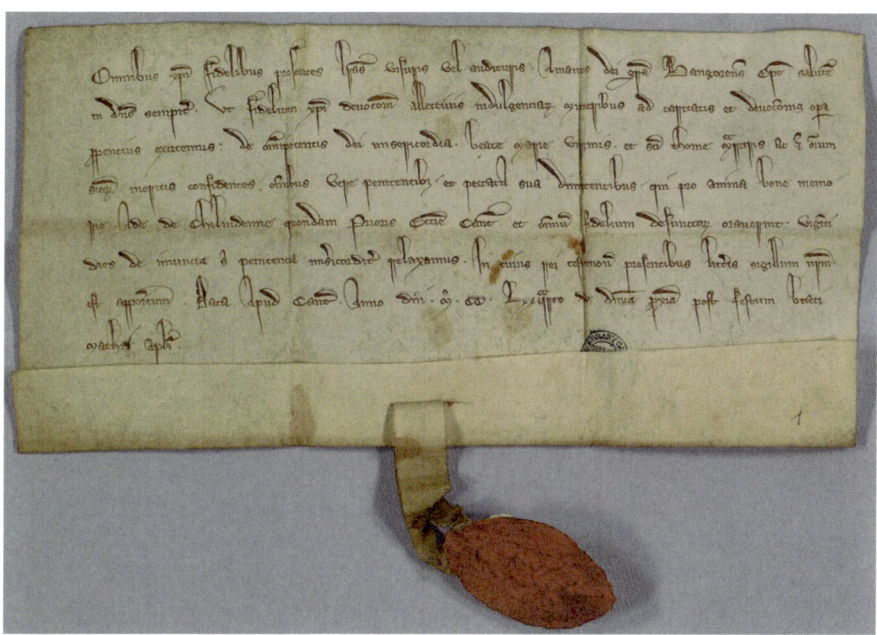

Plate XIV *Actum* **60** – Anian's grant of an indulgence in favour of Canterbury Cathedral Priory. Canterbury, 23 September 1274. Canterbury Cathedral Archives, CCA-DCc-ChAnt/C/167. Reproduced with permission from the Chapter of Canterbury Cathedral.

Plate XV *Actum* **82** – Anian's confirmation and indulgence in favour of Beddgelert Priory. Maes-y-llan, 1 April 1286. The National Archives, ref. C 270/29/5.

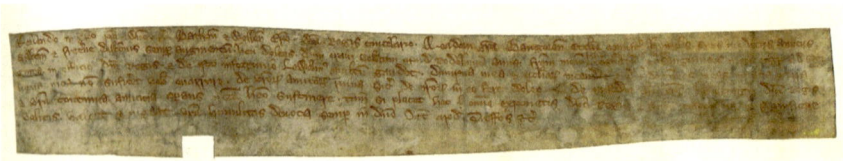

Plate XVI (i) *Actum* **64** – Anian's letter to Robert Burnell from Treffos. [after *c.*9
November 1277]. The National Archives, ref. SC 1/22/101.

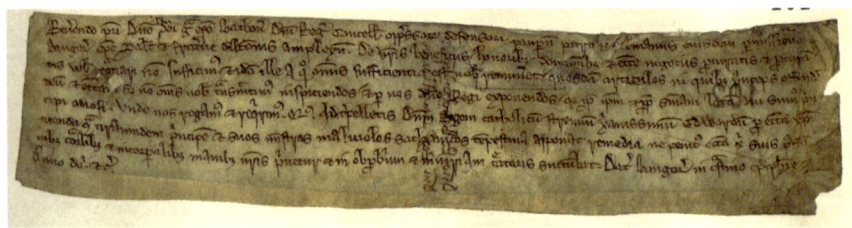

Plate XVI (ii) *Actum* **65** – Anian's letter to Robert Burnell from Bangor. 7 January [possibly 1278, 1279 or 1280]. The National Archives, ref. SC 1/22/102.

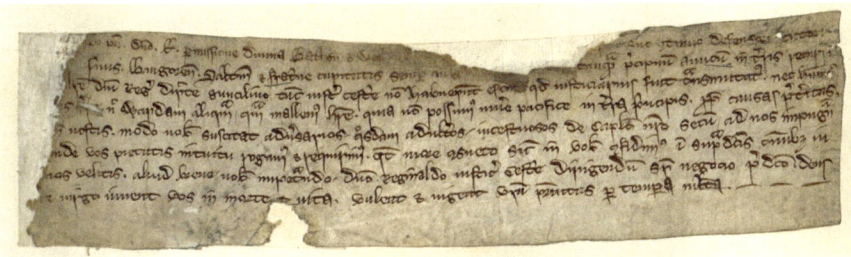

Plate XVI (iii)   *Actum* **70** – Anian's third letter to Robert Burnell. [14 November 1281 x 1282]. The National Archives, ref. SC 1/22/103.

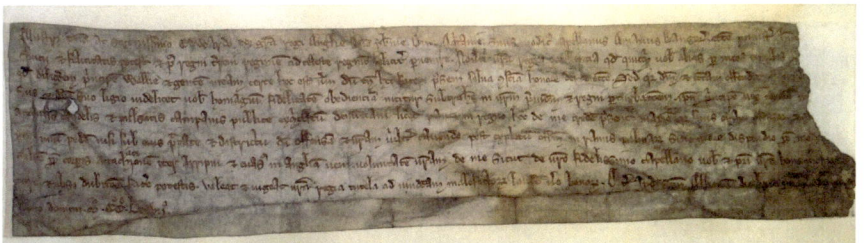

Plate XVII (i)   *Actum* **62** – Anian's letter to King Edward I. St Albans, 1277 [probably 29 March or 5 April]. The National Archives, ref. SC 1/15/6.

Plate XVII (ii)   *Actum* 72 – Anian's letter to John de Kirkby. [*c.*18 April 1283]. The National Archives, ref. SC/1/9/8.

Plate XVIII *Actum* **88** – Anian's indulgence in favour of Salisbury Cathedral. London, 16 November 1295. Salisbury Cathedral Archives, Indulgences, BS/5/37. Reproduced by kind permission of Salisbury Cathedral.

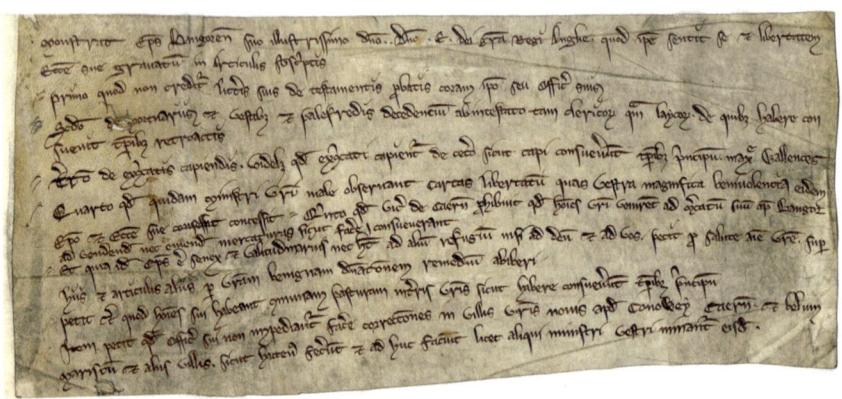

Plate XIX *Actum* **89** – Anian's petition to King Edward I. [*c.*1295 x 1305/6, possibly 1298]. The National Archives, ref. SC 8/276/13767.

EDITORIAL METHOD

The editorial method used for the edition of the *acta* is essentially that followed by the editors of the volumes in the *EEA* series.[1] Episcopates are set out in chronological order. However, the *acta* are given *in extenso*, whether previously published or not. Since no twelfth-century *acta* bear dates, non-profession *acta* are listed alphabetically, according to the name of the beneficiary or recipient, up to and including the episcopate of Alan of St Cross. As *acta* which bear dates, or which are more easily dateable, become increasingly common in the thirteenth century, the *acta* of Bishops Robert, Cadwgan, Richard and Anian are listed chronologically.[2] Where there is evidence of an *actum* but the *actum* no longer exists and there are no copies, an asterisk is placed before the number (for example *Actum* ***61**).

After the summary or caption in English, the place, if known, where the *actum* was given is noted. Place-names which are identifiable are spelled in their modern form. The place-name is followed by the date of the *actum*. If the date is not known, limiting dates are given, the same being separated by a multiplication sign and enclosed in square brackets, for example [16 October 1277 x 17 October 1291]. The list of manuscript sources then follows, designated by sigla: A for originals, B, C, D etc. for copies, listed in chronological order. B serves as the basis for the edition of texts for which no originals survive. Where the original survives, brief descriptions are given of its dimensions (greatest width and greatest depth in millimetres), its medieval endorsements, if any seal is attached, and the sealing arrangements, if any. In the case of copies, rubrics and marginalia are given, as is the approximate date of the manuscript and any pagination.[3] Details of previous editions, and calendars, if any, follow the list of manuscripts.

The spelling of original manuscripts has been retained, save that 'u' is used as a vowel and 'v' as a consonant. Christ is spelt *Cristus*. Abbreviated Christian names are extended (as indicated by round brackets) where the name is clear. However, if Christian names are indicated by initials only they are not extended. Vernacular words, other than proper nouns, are italicised. The same rules apply to copies, but in addition 'c' has been changed to 't' according to the practice of classical Latin, e.g. *confirmatio, donatio*. Modern usage has been applied to capital letters throughout. Conjectural readings are placed within square brackets. Dots indicate words or letters that are not recoverable due to the parchment being faded, damaged or torn away. Modern punctuation has been applied in the case of both originals and

---

[1]   See, for example, *EEA, VII, Hereford, 1079–1234*, pp. cxiv–cxvii. Thank you to Professor Philippa Hoskin for providing me with the 'Directive for Editors', produced by the British Academy Committee on Episcopal Acta. I have also consulted *AWR*, pp. 142–3.

[2]   J. Barrow employed a similar editorial method in *St Davids Episcopal Acta*, p. 31.

[3]   Dates of manuscripts are expressed according to established conventions (see *AWR*, p. xvii): thus s. xiii in., s. xiii med. and s. xiii ex. for the early, mid- and late thirteenth century respectively, and s. xiii/xiv for the end of the thirteenth or beginning of the fourteenth century.

copies, and the ampersand, and Tironian *nota* for 'and', have been expanded to '*et*'. Textual notes, if any, immediately follow the transcription.

Modern dating practice is followed, i.e. starting the year on 1 January. If an *actum* does not bear a date, detailed reasons for the limiting dates proposed are given in the notes which follow the transcription (and any textual notes). Guidance on the location of place-names is also given.

BANGOR EPISCOPAL ACTA
1092–1306

HERVEY

1. Alfric, reeve of Fen Ditton

Notification that Hervey, by the grace of God, bishop, has, with the counsel and concession of the whole convent of Ely, granted and given to Alfric, his reeve of Fen Ditton, and to Robert his heir, and to all their heirs, three virgas *of land in Fen Ditton formerly held by three* rustici, *Hunning, Wlnoth and Edwin Cacabred, nine acres of waste land, and three houses, for the rent of one mark of silver every year for the bishop, and three* summas *of flour each year for the monks, one on the feast of St Etheldreda (23 June) and two on the other feast of the same virgin (Feast of the Translation of St Etheldreda, 17 October). Witnesses: the clerics Gocelin, Walter, Nicholas, Turold, William; the knights Richard, Berald, Harsculf, William, Walter, Jordan, Alan; and Henry, Robert, Sihtric, Ordmer, William, Richard, Gosfrid, Simon, and many others.*

[16 June 1107 x October 1109; possibly mid-January x October 1109]

B = CUL MS EDR G3/28 (Ely 'Liber M', general cartulary of the cathedral priory) *c.*1300, pp. 145b–146a (classmark B I. 5. appears next to the entry). Rubric: Carta episcopi de tribus virgis terre in Dittun' pro quibus monachi recipiunt tres summas farine

C = Bodleian MS Laud miscellaneous 647 (*Liber Eliensis* with substantial additions), fos. 78vb–79ra (formerly 4v–5r). s. xiv in.

D = CUL MS Additional 2948 (transcript from B by James Bentham), fo. 171r. s. xviii med.

E = BL MS Additional 5809 (transcript from B by William Cole), fo. 15v. s. xviii med.

F = BL MS Additional 5847 (transcript from B by William Cole), fo. 32r (formerly p. 57) (abbreviated). s. xviii med.

Printed in Miller, *The Abbey and Bishopric of Ely*, p. 284, appendix, no. vii.

Printed in *EEA, XXXI, Ely, 1109–1197*, pp. 1–2.

Transcribed from B.[1]

Herveus dei gratia episcopus cum toto conventu fratrum Elyens(is) ecclesie omnibus fidelibus eiusdem ecclesie salutem. Notum sit cunctis presentibus et futuris me concessisse et dedisse per consilium et concessum totius conventus Alvrico preposito meo de Dittun'[a] et Rob(er)to heredi suo et cunctis heredibus suis post eum tres virgas terre in eadem villa quas ante eum habuerunt tres rustici, scilicet Hunningus, Wlnothus,[b] AEdwinus[c] Cacabred,[d] et ix acras terre desolates ad supplementum terre sue et illas tres mansiones que ad predictas virgas pertinent. [p. 146a] Et pro illis tribus[e] virgis dabit unoquoque anno in meam firmam unam marcam argenti pro omni servitio et pro omni consuetudine. Monachis vero dabit

---

[1]   Following *EEA, XXXI, Ely, 1109–1197*, p. 1, only readings of B and C are noted.

ipse Alricus et omnes heredes sui post*ʲ* eum eandem terram habentes*ᵍ* unoquoque
anno tres*ᵉ* summas de farina, unam in festivitate sancte Etheldrede,*ʰ* que est in
vigilia sancti Ioh(ann)is Baptiste, et duas in alia festivitate euisdem virginis que
est post festivitatem sancti Michaelis. Hiis testibus: Gocelino, Walt(er)o,*ⁱ* Nich(ola)
o, Turoldo, Will(elm)o, clericis; Ricardo, Beraldo, Harsculfo, Will(elm)o, Walt(er)
o, Iordano, Alano, militibus; Henrico, Roberto, Sihtrico, Ordmero, Will(elm)o,
Ricardo, Gosfrido, Symone, et alii quamplures [*sic*].

> *ᵃ*Dittone, *C.* *ᵇ*Ulnothus, *C.* *ᶜ*Edwinus, *C.* *ᵈ*Kakebred, *C.* *ᵉ*iii, *C.*ʲ(fo. 79ra), *C.* *ᵍ*tenentes,
> *C.* *ʰ*AEdheldrede virginis, *C.* *ⁱ*C adds et aliis and omits all other witnesses.

It is likely that at the time of this notification, Hervey was administrator of Ely
Abbey as well as bishop of Bangor. After the death of Abbot Richard on 16 June
1107, Hervey, at the direction of the king, was made administrator of the abbey.[2]
Richard had wanted to turn the abbacy into a bishopric.[3] Hervey's appointment
allowed him to continue the abbot's scheme and see it through to fruition. The
king sent Hervey to Rome to obtain papal approval.[4] Hervey took with him letters
from Henry,[5] and Anselm.[6] His mission was a success, and after impressing Paschal
II, he returned with papal letters, dated 21 November 1108, approving the scheme
outlined above and authorising his translation to a vacant see.[7] The foundation
of the new see was discussed at a royal council held at Nottingham castle on the
Feast of the Translation of St Etheldreda (the patron saint of the abbey of Ely), 17
October 1109, and approved.[8] Hervey was enthroned as the new bishopric's first
bishop, in the same month.[9]

If indeed given while he was administrator of Ely Abbey, and before he became
bishop of Ely, this is Hervey's sole surviving *actum* when he was bishop of Bangor.
In it he is styled '*Herveus dei gratia episcopus*', and whilst there is no mention of a see,
he is unequivocally bishop of Ely in all his later *acta*.[10] It is clear, from the wording
of the notification, that both administrator and convent considered themselves to

---

[2] *Liber Eliensis*, p. 297; *EEA, XXXI, Ely, 1109–1197*, p. lxxi; Owen, 'Hervey (*d.* 1131)', *ODNB*; *Heads of Religious Houses*, i, p. 45.
[3] *Liber Eliensis*, pp. 270–2 and 283; Karn, 'The Twelfth Century', p. 3.
[4] *Liber Eliensis*, p. 298. *EEA, XXXI, Ely, 1109–1197*, p. liii. *Liber Eliensis, Blake*, p. 246.
[5] *Liber Eliensis*, p. 298. *EEA, XXXI, Ely, 1109–1197*, p. liii. *Liber Eliensis, Blake*, p. 246.
[6] *Eadmer's History*, pp. 209–10; *Eadmeri Historia Novorum*, pp. 195–6. *EEA, XXXI, Ely, 1109–1197*, p. liii.
[7] *St. Anselm Letters*, iii, pp. 245–51; *Liber Eliensis*, pp. 298–302. Willis, *Survey*, pp. 184–5 (Appendix, Number II); Haddan and Stubbs, i, pp. 303–6; *EEA, XXXI, Ely, 1109–1197*, p. liii; *Liber Eliensis, Blake*, pp. 246–9.
[8] This was taken to be the date of establishment of the see and was confirmed in a charter of Henry I: *Liber Eliensis*, pp. 302–3. *EEA, XXXI, Ely, 1109–1197*, p. liii.
[9] *Monasticon*, i, p. 482. *Fasti Welsh Cathedrals*, p. 1. The *Winchcombe Annals* record for the year 1109: 'Rex Anglorum Henricus Heliensem abbatiam ad episcopalem mutavit sedem, et Herveum Bancornensem episcopum eidem ecclesie prefecit.': *Winchcombe Annals*, p. 123.
[10] *EEA, XXXI, Ely, 1109–1197*, p. 2. He may have stopped referring to himself as bishop of Bangor as early as 1106, for in that year he was a witness to a charter of John of Tours, bishop of Bath, and was described merely as 'episcopus' with no reference to Bangor: *EEA, X, Bath and Wells, 1061–1205*, p. 3.

be in joint control of the lands the subject of the disposal, whereas in later *acta* of Hervey, as bishop of Ely, it is clear he considered himself to be the sole possessor of the lands pertaining to the church of Ely.[11] As Nicholas Karn has averred, the notification may have been made after Hervey had returned from Rome (the earliest date for arrival back in England, given the journey time, being mid-January 1109) because it is clear that he had some proprietorial right in the land concerned.[12] That right may have been seen as emanating from his royally appointed position as administrator, greatly reinforced by the letters from Paschal II of November 1108.

[11] *EEA, XXXI, Ely, 1109–1197*, p. 2.
[12] *EEA, XXXI, Ely, 1109–1197*, p. 2.

DAVID THE SCOT

2. Profession of obedience

I David, by the grace of God, bishop-elect of Bangor, promise canonical subjection and obedience to the holy church of Canterbury, and to you father Ralph (d'Escures, archbishop of Canterbury) and all your successors canonically introduced.

Westminster, 4 April 1120

B = BL Cotton MS Cleopatra E i (fos. 17r–38r consist of a collection of copies of episcopal professions), fo. 32r. s. xii in. Rubric: Professio David Pangornensis episcopi

C = Canterbury Cathedral Archives, Dean and Chapter, CCA-DCc-ChAnt/C/117 (roll with copies of professions), no. 28. s. xii in.

D = Canterbury Cathedral Archives, Dean and Chapter, Register A (The Prior's Register), fo. 250v. s. xiv med.

Calendared in *Episc. Acts Welsh Dioceses Unpublished*, B30.

Printed in *Canterbury Professions*, p. 38, no. 67.

Printed in Haddan and Stubbs, i, p. 314.

Transcribed from B.

Ego[a] David, electus dei gratia Pangorensis episcopus, promitto canonicam subiectionem et [b]obedientiam sancte Cantuariensi ecclesie[b] et tibi, pater Radulfe, et omnibus successoribus tuis canonice introductis.

[a]large, decorative E written in green ink, B. [b-b]written obędientiam sanctę Cantuariensi ęcclesię, B.

This is the first known profession of canonical obedience given by a bishop-elect of Bangor to an archbishop of Canterbury. Urban, who was consecrated as bishop of Llandaff in 1107, had been the first bishop-elect of a Welsh see to profess obedience to Canterbury.[13] When Bernard was consecrated to St Davids in 1115 he too had professed obedience to Canterbury.[14]

The date of David's profession is confirmed by the Canterbury monk and historian Eadmer.[15]

---

[13] Davies, *Age of Conquest*, p. 179; *Canterbury Professions*, no. 59; *Fasti Welsh Cathedrals*, p. 13.
[14] *Canterbury Professions*, no. 64; *Fasti Welsh Cathedrals*, p. 46.
[15] *Eadmeri Historia Novorum*, p. 260.

Under archbishops Anselm (1093–1109), Ralph d'Escures (1114–1122), and William de Corbeil (1123–1136), the standard form of profession included '*totius Britannie primas*', or '*Britanniarum primas*', however, neither of these styles were used in David's profession. The only other occasion on which these words were omitted, during the tenures of the three archbishops, was for the profession of Seffrid (I) of Chichester, the half-brother of Ralph d'Escures, who was consecrated in 1125 in the presence of the papal legate, Giovanni da Crema.[16]

---

[16] *EEA, XXVIII, Canterbury, 1070–1136*, p. lxxii. Marritt, 'Seffrid (I) [nicknamed Pelochin] (*d.* 1150)', *ODNB*.

MEURIG

3. Profession of obedience

I Maurice, elect to the governance of the church of Bangor, to be consecrated a priest by you, reverend father Theobald, archbishop of the holy church of Canterbury, and through the grace of God, primate of the whole of Britain, promise that I will show due canonical subjection and obedience in all things, to you and to all your successors canonically succeeding you.

[*c.*31 January 1140]

A = Canterbury Cathedral Archives, Dean and Chapter, CCA-DCc-ChAnt/C/115/19. 228 x 50 mm. Stitching holes at head and foot. Sewn to 115/20. Endorsed with 'THEOD'' in red lettering.[17]

B = BL Cotton MS Cleopatra E i (fos. 17r–38r consist of a collection of copies of episcopal professions), fo. 36r. s. xii med.

C = Canterbury Cathedral Archives, Dean and Chapter, CCA-DCc-ChAnt/C/117 (roll with copies of professions), no. 41. s. xii med.

D = Canterbury Cathedral Archives, Dean and Chapter, Register A (The Prior's Register), fo. 250v. s. xiv med.

Calendared in *Episc. Acts Welsh Dioceses Unpublished*, B42.

Calendared in *Canterbury Professions*, p. 42, no. 83.

Printed in Haddan and Stubbs, i, pp. 345–6.

Transcribed from A.

Ego Maurici(us), ad regimen ecclesie Bangornensis[a] electus, et a te, reverende pater Teodbalde[b], sancte Cantuariensis ecclesie [c]archiepiscope[c] et totius Britannie[d] primas, per gratiam Dei, antistes consecrandus, tibi et omnibus successoribus tuis tibi canonice succedentibus debitam subiectionem et canonicam obedientiam [e]per omnia[e] me exibiturum fore promitto.

[a]Pangornensis, *C, D.* [b]Teobalde, *C.* [b]Theobalde, *B, D.* [c-c]omitted, *D.* [d]Britannie on erasure, *A.* [e-e]omitted, *C.*

---

[17]   Image of A at Plate VI (i). Canterbury Cathedral Archives' online record: https://archives.canterbury-cathedral.org/CalmView/Record.aspx?src=CalmView.Catalog&id=CCA-DCc-ChAnt%2fC%2f115%2f19&pos=5, accessed 29 April 2024.

Uhtred of Llandaff's profession is, *mutatis mutandis*, the same as that given by Meurig. Patrick, elect of Limerick, was also consecrated in the same year and his profession is in like form.[18]

*4. Haughmond Abbey

Confirmation of a gift by Cadwaladr ap Gruffudd ap Cynan and his sons, Maredudd, Einion and Cadwallon, of Nefyn church and all the land which is between the two streams between which the church is situated, and all the Cerniog land with all its appurtenances and easements.

[1140 x 12 August 1161]

Mention only in a *confirmatio*, 16 April 1195 x 19 May 1196, of Alan, bishop of Bangor (**14**) which confirmed the charters of Meurig and Gwion in favour of Haughmond Abbey. Included was Meurig's confirmation of Cadwaladr's gift of the church at Nefyn,[19] which charter Meurig attested (along with his three brothers).[20] Meurig's confirmation could have been made at any time during his episcopate, but perhaps was made at the same time as Cadwaladr's gift.[21]

Nefyn is in Llŷn. Cerniog lay to the east of Mynydd Nefyn.[22]

See also *Actum* **8** and the note to *Actum* **5** below.

5. Haughmond Abbey

Confirmation of a gift of lands made by Hywel (ab Ieuaf), lord of Arwystli, to the church of St Michael, Trefeglwys, and the canons of Haughmond, of all the land which is called Bryn Bedwyn from the ditch of the cemetery to Gleiniant, all the land of Tregymer from the cross to Gleiniant, and all the land of Cilceirenydd with the adjacent wood, namely from (?) Nantheilyn (Nantelin) *to the river which is called Cerist. Witnesses: Cadell (ap Gruffudd) king of south Wales, Iorwerth* (Jervord) *the priest, etc.*

[1143 x 1151]

---

[18]   *Canterbury Professions*, p. 42.
[19]   'ex dono Cathwaladri et filiorum eius Mareduth et Eimonn et Cathwadlan': *Actum* **14**. The wording which described the land gifted is very similar to the wording used in Cadwaladr's own charter, however, Cadwaladr's gift does not mention his sons, other than to say that it was given 'pro salute anime mee et omnium antecessorum et heredum meorum': *AWR*, pp. 329–31, no. 197; *Cartulary of Haughmond Abbey*, p. 159, no. 784. The reference to Cadwaladr's sons might help date Meurig's non-extant confirmation more precisely.
[20]   'Hiis testibus: Mauric(i)o episcopo, David et Reso et Moyse fratribus eius, Aliz de Clara uxore mea etc.': *AWR*, p. 329, no. 197.
[21]   U. Rees suggested a date range for Cadwaladr's gift of 1141 x 1143: *Cartulary of Haughmond Abbey*, p. 159. H. Pryce suggests a date range of 1140 x 1152 or 1157 x -12 August 1161: *AWR*, p. 329. However, see n. 19 above re mention of Cadwaladr's sons in Meurig's confirmation/ Alan's confirmation (*Actum* **14**).
[22]   *AWR*, p. 330.

B = Shrewsbury, Shropshire Archives, MS 6001/6869 (Haughmond Cartulary), fo. 215. s. xv ex. Rubric: Confirmatio episcopi Manricii predictorum

Calendared in *Episc. Acts Welsh Dioceses Unpublished*, B47.

Printed in part in *Charters of Trefeglwys, Arch. Camb.*, 330–3.[23]

Printed (minus sealing clause) in *Cartulary of Haughmond Abbey*, pp. 222–3, no. 1219.

Transcribed from B.

Universis Cristi fidelibus presens scriptum inspecturis Mairici(us)[a] dei gratia Bangor' episcopus salutem in domino. Ad universorum volumus pervenire noticiam quando Hoelus, dominus de Arewistil, donavit ecclesie de Treveglus et canonicis de Haghmon' totam terram que vocatur Brenbedwin a fossa cimiterii usque ad Gleinant et totam terram de Trefkemere a cruce usque a Gleinant et totam terram de Gilgremit cum nemore adiacente videlicet a Nantelin usque ad amnem qui vocatur Kerist tunc ibidem presentes fuimus. Et ideo hanc donationem quantum ad episcopalem auctoritatem pertinent presenti scripto confirmamus. Nos autem hanc donationem observantibus benedictionem dei et nostram conferimus contradicentes autem anathematis vinculo innodamus. Hiis testibus Gatel rege Sudwallie, Jervord presbitero, etc.

[a]Meurig's name is written as Mairici(us), not Maurici(us), *B*.

Based on the fact that the first witness was Cadell ap Gruffudd, king of Deheubarth, the date range convincingly proposed by Una Rees is 1143 x 1151.[24]

Hywel ab Ieuaf's gift, which was witnessed by Meurig and his brother Rhys, is printed in *AWR*.[25] Iorwerth, the priest, also witnessed Hywel's gift.[26]

The lands referred to all lie in the vicinity of Trefeglwys (in Arwystli).[27] *Nantelin* may be Nantheilyn.[28]

---

[23]   'Jervord presbitero' is omitted, but 'Res fr[atr]e n[ost]ro &c' is added after 'Catel rege Sudwalliae' in the witness list: *Charters of Trefeglwys, Arch. Camb*, 331. *Cartulary of Haughmond Abbey*, p. 222, no. 1219, n. 1 makes the same point.

[24]   Rees explains that the confirmation was probably given after Cadell ap Gruffudd succeeded to Deheubarth (in 1143) but before 1151 when, according to *Brut y Tywysogyon (Brut, Hergest*, pp. 130–1, and *Brut, Pen20 Tr*, p. 57) he was seriously wounded: *Cartulary of Haughmond Abbey*, pp. 222–3, no. 1219, n. 1. Thereafter, Rees argues, it seems that he retired from public life: *ibid*. Certainly Cadell went on pilgrimage to Rome, possibly in 1153, possibly in 1156: *Brut, Hergest*, pp. 132–3, and p. 291; *Brut, Pen20 Tr*, pp. 58 and 178; *AC*, p. 46. See also *AWR*, p. 145, note to no. 1, and note to no. 2, and Pryce, 'Church of Trefeglwys', 41.

[25]   'Hiis testibus: domino Mauricio episcopo, Reso fratre eius, Iorvert presbitero etc.': *AWR*, p. 145, no. 2. See also *Cartulary of Haughmond Abbey*, pp. 221–2, no. 1214, and the Biography of Meurig.

[26]   *AWR*, p. 145, no. 2; *Cartulary of Haughmond Abbey*, pp. 221–2, no. 1214.

[27]   Pryce, 'Church of Trefeglwys', 34–7 (with map).

[28]   *AWR*, p. 145.

Arwystli formed a detached portion of the diocese of Bangor.[29] As to the place where the confirmation was given, and witnessed, it is perhaps more likely that Meurig travelled to Arwystli (perhaps on a visitation of the rural deanery) or to Haughmond, than Cadell ap Gruffudd travelled to Gwynedd Uwch Conwy. Indeed, Meurig is known to have spent periods in exile from Bangor, and he might have found refuge, for a time, in Arwystli.[30]

Meurig's confirmations in favour of Haughmond are referred to in a *confirmatio* (**14**) of Alan, bishop of Bangor, in the last decade of the twelfth century.[31] Alan confirmed the charters of bishops Meurig and Gwion in favour of the abbey. In the thirteenth century, first Bishop Richard, and then Bishop Anian, confirmed the charters of their predecessors concerning the churches of Nefyn and Trefeglwys (**45** and **58**).[32] A little later, the dean and chapter of Bangor confirmed the charters of six bishops, including Meurig, relating to the same churches.[33]

*6. Reading Abbey

Grant of indulgence for 15 days, for those going to Reading Abbey, at any time of the year.
[1140 x 12 August 1161]

Mention in BL MS Harley 1708 (Chartulary of Reading Abbey) which contains a list of archiepiscopal and episcopal grants of indulgences in favour of Reading Abbey.[34] Calendared in *Reading Abbey Cartularies*, i, p. 177.[35]

Under the heading '*Per totum annum*', the list records '*Mauritius menevens[is] xv.d*',[36] but the reference to St Davids is surely a scribal error as there were no bishops of St Davids with that name.

'At any time of the year' appears to mean at feasts (other than those for St Philip and St James the Great) and anniversaries throughout the year, rather than the whole year.[37] The feast days for St Philip and St James the Great were 1 May and 25 July respectively.[38]

---

[29] A. D. Carr made the suggestion that the claim to Arwystli, by Gwynedd, originated from the rule of Gwynedd by Hywel ab Ieuaf's great-grandfather, Trahaearn ap Caradog, from 1075 to 1081: Carr, 'A Debatable Land', 44. See also the section of the Introduction entitled 'Gwynedd Uwch Conwy, Dyffryn Clwyd and Arwystli'.

[30] See the section of the Introduction entitled 'Meurig', and McGuinness, 'The Medieval Bishops of Bangor, 1092–1283: Intrusion, Exile and Diplomacy' (forthcoming).

[31] *Actum* **14**.

[32] *Actum* **45** and *Actum* **58**.

[33] *Cartulary of Haughmond Abbey*, p. 162, no. 799.

[34] Compiled *c*.1258 x 1259: *Reading Abbey Cartularies*, i, pp. 174–9.

[35] Cf. Bodleian, Tanner MS 342, fo. 272b. Also calendared in *Episc. Acts Welsh Dioceses Unpublished*, B46.

[36] 'Chartulary of Reading Abbey' BL Harley MS 1708, fo. 187.

[37] *Reading Abbey Cartularies*, i, p. 174, n. 4.

[38] *ibid*.

GWION

7. Profession of obedience

I Gwion, bishop-elect of the church of Bangor, to be consecrated by you, reverend father Richard (of Dover), archbishop of the holy church of Canterbury, primate of the whole of England, and legate of the apostolic see, promise that I will show due canonical obedience and subjection in all things to you and to your successors canonically substituted, and by (my) own hand, I confirm with the sign of the holy cross. +

Amesbury, 22 May 1177

A = Canterbury Cathedral Archives, Dean and Chapter, CCA-DCc-ChAnt/C/115/41. 165 x 85 mm. Stitching holes at head and foot.[39]

B = Canterbury Cathedral Archives, Dean and Chapter, Register A (The Prior's Register), fo. 250v. s. xiv med.

Calendared in *Episc. Acts Welsh Dioceses Unpublished*, B71.

Printed in *Canterbury Professions*, p. 53, no. 113.

Transcribed from A.

Ego Gwido[a], ecclesie Bangoriensis electus episcopus et a te, reverende pater Ricarde, sancte Cantauriensis ecclesie archiepiscope, tocius Anglie primas, et apostolice sedis legate, consecrandus, tibi et successoribus tuis tibi canonice substituendis debitam et canonicam obedientiam ac subiectionem me per omnia exhibiturum promitto, et propria manu signo sancte crucis confirmo. +

[a]Guydo, B.

Signed with cross. In the first half of the twelfth century, it seems that bishops were not required to confirm their profession with an autograph cross. However, the custom was revived in 1148.[40]

8. Haughmond Abbey

Grant, gift and confirmation of St Mary's Church, Nefyn, with all its appurtenances and tithes in pure and perpetual alms, to the abbot and convent of Haughmond, and of the land between the two streams around the church, and the tithes of Nefyn mill, and the land which is called (?) Boduan (Bothenav) which Troitbrummete at some time held, and all the tithes, both from the sea and the land. Sealing clause. In the presence of the bishop's brother, Adam Rhirid, Philip the bishop's son, etc.

[22 May 1177 x 1191]

---

[39]   Image at Plate VI (ii). Canterbury Cathedral Archives' online record: https://archives.canterbury-cathedral.org/CalmView/Record.aspx?src=CalmView.Catalog&id=CCA-DCc-ChAnt%2fC%2f115%2f41&pos=8, accessed 24 February 2024.

[40]   *EEA, XXXIII, Worcester, 1062–1185*, p. 32.

B = Shrewsbury, Shropshire Archives, MS 6001/6869 (Haughmond Cartulary), fos. 149v–150r. s. xv ex. Folio heading: Nevyn. Rubric: Confirmatio episcopi pro ecclesia ibidem

Printed (minus sealing clause) in *Cartulary of Haughmond Abbey*, p. 161, no. 791.

Transcribed from B.

Guido dei gratia Bangorensis episcopus omnibus sancte matris ecclesie filiis tam clericis quam laicis salutem et dei benedictionem. Noverit universitas vestra nos concessisse et dedisse ex concensu et assensu dominorum fundi ecclesiam beate Marie cum omnibus pertinentiis decimacionibus obvencionibus suis abbati et conventui de Haghmon' in puram et perpetuam elemosinam et nominatim terram inter duos rivulos circa ecclesiam et decimacionem molendini eiusdem ville et terram que vocatur Bothenav quam Troitbrummete aliquando tenuit et omnem decimacionem tam de mari quam de terra ab omnibus ibi manentibus sine aliqua contradictione predictis canonicis confirmamus. Et ut hec nostra donatio rata et inconcussa permaneat eis sigilli nostri munimine corroboravimus. Siquis vero cartam nostram violare attempserit ma勒diccionem compo [fo. 150] tentis dei et <nostram>[a] noverit se incursurum. Coram hiis fratre episcopi, Adam Ririt, Philippo filio episcopi, etc.

[a]superscript above et noverit, *B*.

Cadwaladr ap Gruffudd ap Cynan had granted to Haughmond (1140 x 1152 or 1157 x -12 August 1161), *inter alia*, the church of Nefyn (in Llŷn) and all the land where the church is situated between two small streams.[41] Bishop Meurig confirmed (**4**) a gift to Haughmond by Cadwaladr (and his sons) of Nefyn church and, *inter alia*, the land between the two streams. The same was mentioned in a *confirmatio*, 16 April 1195 x 19 May 1196, of Alan, bishop of Bangor (**14**). See also the note to *Actum* **5**.

Dafydd ab Owain Gwynedd granted to Haughmond (May 1177 x September 1187) a parcel of *Bodenan* land ('*de terra Bodenan*') in the township of Nefyn, which '*Troit de Brumm*'' had.[42] Gwion's charter has *Bothenav* and the (previous) owner as *Troitbrummete*. Bishop Alan's confirmation (**14**) of the charters of Meurig and Gwion, in favour of Haughmond, in the last decade of the twelfth century, has *Bodenav* and *Troithbremeth*.[43]

Huw Pryce has stated that *Bothenav/Bodenan* is probably the bond township of Boduan, near Plas Boduan (SH 327381), south-east of Nefyn, in the commote of Dinllaen in Llŷn.[44]

In the thirteenth century, first Bishop Richard, and then Bishop Anian, confirmed the gifts of their predecessors concerning the church of Nefyn (**45** and **58**).[45]

[41] *AWR*, pp. 329–31, no. 197.
[42] *AWR*, pp. 331–2, no. 198.
[43] *Actum* **14**.
[44] *AWR*, p. 332.
[45] *Actum* **45** and *Actum* **58**.

For Gwion's brother(s) and son see the sections of the Introduction entitled 'Gwion' and '*Clas* and *Familia*'.

9. Haughmond Abbey

Gwion has granted and given, and by his present charter confirmed, the church of Trefeglwys to Haughmond, to be possessed by perpetual right, with all its appurtenances, free and released from all episcopal and earthly customs. Sealing clause. Witnessed by Philip the bishop's brother, etc.

[22 May 1177 x 1191]

B = Shrewsbury, Shropshire Archives, MS 6001/6869 (Haughmond Cartulary), fo. 214v. s. xv ex. Marginal heading: Treffegles. Rubric: Donatio ecclesie ibidem

Printed in *Cartulary of Haughmond Abbey*, p. 221, no. 1212.

Transcribed from B.

Wido dei gratia Bangorensis ecclesie humilis minister omnibus fidelibus perpetuam in domino salutem. Ne quid a nobis intuitu pietatis et honestatis puplice et solempniter gestum est aliquot temporis tractu in ambiguitatem et contencionem venire possit ad omnium notitiam pervenire volumus nos concessisse et dedisse, atque presenti carta confirmasse, ecclesie Hamonensi ecclesiam de Treffegles perpetuo iure possidendam cum omnibus pertinentiis suis liberam et solutam ab omnibus episcopalibus et terrenis consuetudinibus. Quod quare futuris temporibus ratum et firmum permanere volumus scripti et sigilli nostri testimonio communimus et confirmamus. Teste Philippo fratre episcopi, etc.

The marginal heading is '*Treffegles*', and it is noteworthy that this is the first of the Trefeglwys charters to appear in the Haughmond Cartulary, suggesting that the canons considered Gwion's charter to be the title deed to the church.[46]

In the thirteenth century, first Bishop Richard, and then Bishop Anian, confirmed the gifts of their predecessors concerning the church of Trefeglwys (**45** and **58**).[47]

For a discussion of Gwion's brother(s) see the Introduction.[48]

10. Haughmond Abbey

Confirmation of a gift of lands made by Hywel (ab Ieuaf), lord of Arwystli, to the church of St Michael, Trefeglwys, and the canons of Haughmond; of all the land which is called Bryn Bedwyn from the ditch of the cemetery to Gleiniant, the land of Tregymer from the cross to Gleiniant, and all the land of Cilceirenydd with the adjacent wood, namely from (?) Nantheilyn (Nantelin) *to the river which is called Cerist. Witnesses: Philip the bishop's brother, etc.*

[22 May 1177 x 1191]

B = Shrewsbury, Shropshire Archives, MS 6001/6869 (Haughmond Cartulary), fos. 215r–215v. s. xv ex. Rubric: Alia confirmatio Widonis episcopi

[46]   Pryce, 'Church of Trefeglwys', 42.
[47]   *Actum* **45** and *Actum* **58**.
[48]   The sections entitled 'Gwion' and '*Clas* and *Familia*'.

Calendared in *Cartulary of Haughmond Abbey*, p. 223, no. 1220.

Transcribed from B.

Wido dei gratia Bangorensis episcopus omnibus Cristi presens scriptum inspecturis salutem in domino. Noverit universitas vestra nos concessisse et quantum ad episcopalem auctoritatem pertinent confirmasse donationem [fo. 215v] quam Hoelus, dominus de Arewistill, fecit ecclesie sancti Mich(ael)is de Trevegles et canonicis de Haghmonde de tota terra que vocatur Brenbedwin a fossa cimiterii usque ad Gleinant et de terra de Trefkemere a cruce usque ad Gleinant et de tota terra de Gilgremit cum nemore adiacente videlicet a Nantelin usque ad amnem qui vocatur Kerist sicut carta eiusdem Hoeli testatur. Nos autem hanc donationem inperpetuum observantibus benedictionem dei omnipotentis et nostram conferimus et eos qui illam adnichillare vel iniuriere [*sic*] attemptaverint sub anathematis vinculo nihil ad emendationem venerint episcopali auctoritate ponimus. His testibus Philippo fratre episcopi, etc.

Hywel ab Ieuaf's gift is printed in *AWR*.[49] It was witnessed by one of Gwion's predecessors, Meurig, who also confirmed (**5**) the gift.[50] Gwion's confirmations in favour of Haughmond are referred to in a *confirmatio* (**14**) of Alan, bishop of Bangor.[51] See also the note to *Actum* **5**.

The lands referred to all lie in the vicinity of Trefeglwys.[52] *Nantelin* may be Nantheilyn.[53]

For a discussion of Gwion's brother(s) see the Introduction.[54]

11. Parishioners of Nefyn

Gwion orders the parishioners of Nefyn to pay the canons of Haughmond tithes of all sea fishing and tithes of the produce of the land. He warns and exhorts them in the Lord and by the apostolic authority of the archbishop of Canterbury. Valediction.
     [22 May 1177–16 February 1184 x 17/18 December 1185–19 November 1190]

B = Shrewsbury, Shropshire Archives, MS 6001/6869 (Haughmond Cartulary), fo. 150r. s. xv ex. Rubric: Confirmatio decimarum ibidem per episcopum

Printed in *Cartulary of Haughmond Abbey*, p. 161, no. 792.

Transcribed from B.

Guido dei gratia Bangorensis episcopus omnibus parochianis de Nevin salutem et benedictionem. Cum universis dei fidelibus de iure teneamur obnoxii super eorum tamen commoditate deligenciores existere debemus quos habitu religionis vidimus insignatos et animum cum habitu credimus concordare. Inde est quod

[49] *AWR*, p. 145, no. 2.
[50] *Actum* **5**.
[51] *Actum* **14**.
[52] Pryce, 'Church of Trefeglwys', 34–7 (with map).
[53] *AWR*, p. 145.
[54] The sections entitled 'Gwion' and '*Clas* and *Familia*'.

universitatem vestram rogamus, monemus, et exhortamur in domino atque auctoritate apostolica Cantuariensis archiepiscopi sustulti super Cristianitatem vestram vobis precipimus quatinus dilectis filiis nostris canonicis de Haghmon' tam de omni piscatura maris quam de frugibus terre plenarie persolvatis decimas. Quod si non feceritis sciatis vos anathematis vinculo auctoritate apostolica Cantuariensi et nostra esse innodatos. Inhibemus itaque ne detentores predictarum decimarum ausu temerario ad piscandum maris intrare presumpserint nam si marinis fluctibus submersi vel alio aliquo modo periclitati fuerint corpora eorum in cimiterio non sepelientur nec inter Cristianos deputabuntur. Valete.

Gwion, along with one of his brothers, Madog, was a witness to Dafydd ab Owain Gwynedd's order that the parishioners of Nefyn pay to the abbot and canons of Haughmond Abbey the tithes of all sea fishing and fruits of the earth.[55] Dafydd stated that the bishop of Bangor, by his own 'charter', confirms and orders the parishioners to pay the said tithes.[56]

Save for the reference to the apostolic authority of the archbishop of Canterbury (either Richard of Dover or Baldwin of Forde could have been the relevant archbishop – the former was created papal legate before Gwion's consecration and died on 16 February 1184,[57] whilst the latter was appointed papal legate on 17 or 18 December 1185 and died on 19 November 1190),[58] Gwion's order cannot be dated more precisely than at some time during his episcopate. However, as it seems probable that *Actum* **11** is the 'charter' to which Dafydd referred, Gwion's order would have been made shortly before, or on the same occasion as, Dafydd's order.[59]

12. St Werburgh's Abbey, Chester

Gwion has granted, and by his charter confirmed, that if goods stolen from the lands or men of the church of St Werburgh are found in the parishes of his diocese, and the detainers do not restore them to the messengers of St Werburgh, at the instance of the clergy of the said diocese, they shall be excommunicated and their church shall be placed under interdict until everything shall have been restored.

[22 May 1177 x 1191]

B = BL MS Harley 1965 (Cartulary or Register of St Werburgh's Abbey, Chester), fo. 25r. s. xiii/xiv. Rubric: De restitutione bonorum ecclesie in diocesi Bangorensi

Calendared in *Episc. Acts Welsh Dioceses Unpublished*, B76.

Printed in *Cartulary of St. Werburgh's Abbey, Chester*, ii, p. 278, no. 478.

Transcribed from B.

---

[55]   *Cartulary of Haughmond Abbey*, p. 159, no. 785, and *AWR*, pp. 332–3, no. 199.
[56]   *ibid.*
[57]   Richard of Dover was appointed legate on 7 April 1174 by Pope Alexander III: Duggan, 'Richard [Richard of Dover] (d. 1184)', *ODNB*; Barlow, *Feudal Kingdom*, p. 341.
[58]   Baldwin was appointed legate by Pope Urban III: Holdsworth, 'Baldwin [Baldwin of Forde] (c.1125–1190)', *ODNB*.
[59]   Perhaps an indication of a more precise date can be gleaned from Dafydd styling himself 'David rex Norwallie' (*Cartulary of Haughmond Abbey*, p. 159, no. 785, and *AWR*, pp. 332–3, no. 199) as opposed to 'David rex filius Owini' in the 'Bodanen' grant (see note to *Actum* **8**, *Cartulary of Haughmond Abbey*, p. 160, no. 786, and *AWR*, pp. 331–2, no. 198). In his two other, later, known *acta* he used 'David filius Owini princeps Norwallie' (*AWR*, p. 333, no. 200) and 'David filius Owini' (*ibid.*, p. 334, no. 201).

Wido Bangorens(is) episcopus concessit, et carta sua confirmavit, quod si quando bona ecclesie sancte Werburge furto ablata a terris vel ab hominibus suis in parochiis sue diocesis inveniantur nec ad instanciam clericorum dicte diocesis eorum detentores nunciis dicte ecclesie ea non restituerint, anathematizentur, et ecclesia cuius ipsi parochiani fuerint interdicatur donec omnia fuerint restituta.

A similar concession was obtained by the abbey from Bishop Reiner of St Asaph (1186–1224/5).[60] The abbey had lands in Tegeingl, as well as on Anglesey, and there is evidence that St Werburgh's suffered losses in the second half of the twelfth century.[61]

[60]   *Cartulary of St. Werburgh's Abbey, Chester*, i, pp. 126–7, and ii, p. 278; *Fasti Welsh Cathedrals*, p. 34.
[61]   Lloyd, *History of Wales*, ii, p. 456, n. 238; Kettle, 'Houses of Benedictine Monks: The Abbey of Chester', in *VCH Cheshire*, iii, pp. 132–45; *Monasticon*, ii, pp. 385–6; *CChR, 1257–1300*, p. 316; *Cartulary of St. Werburgh's Abbey, Chester*, i, pp. 30, 45, 101, 108, 127, 212, and 215.

ALAN OF ST CROSS

13. Profession of obedience

I Alan, elect of the church of Bangor, promise to the holy church of Canterbury and to you,
reverend father Hubert (Walter, archbishop of Canterbury), and all your successors canonically
substituted, canonical obedience and subjection. And I confirm this promise and sign by (my) own
hand. +

16 April 1195

A = Canterbury Cathedral Archives, Dean and Chapter, CCA-DCc-
ChAnt/C/115/62. 160 x 38 mm. Stitching holes at head, stitched to 115/63 at
foot.[62]

B = Canterbury Cathedral Archives, Dean and Chapter, Register A (The Prior's
Register), fo. 250v. s. xiv med.

Calendared in *Episc. Acts Welsh Dioceses Unpublished*, B86.

Printed in *Canterbury Professions*, p. 58, no. 134.

Transcribed from A.

Ego Alanus, ecclesie Bangorensis*ᵃ* electus, promitto sancte Cantuariensi ecclesie et
tibi, reverende pater Huberte, et omnibus successoribus tuis tibi canonice substituendis canonicam obedientiam et subiectionem. Et hanc promissionem confirmo
et propria manu subscribo. +

*ᵃ*Bangoriensis, *B.*

Signed with cross. See note to *Actum* **7** (Gwion's profession to Canterbury).

14. Haughmond Abbey

Confirmation of the charters of bishops Meurig and Gwion, specifically the gift by Hywel (ab
Ieuaf), king of Arwystli, of the church of Trefeglwys with all its appurtenances; the gift by
Cadwaladr (ap Gruffudd ap Cynan), and his sons, Maredudd, Einion and Cadwallon, of Nefyn
church with all its appurtenances, and all the land which is between the two streams between which
the church is situated, and all the Cerniog land with all its appurtenances and easements; the gift
by Dafydd (ab Owain Gwynedd) king of north Wales of that land which Troithbremeth *had*
of the (?) Boduan (Bodenav) *land in the township of Nefyn; the gift by Gwion, of good memory,*

---

[62]   Image at Plate VI (iii). Canterbury Cathedral Archives' online record: https://
archives.canterbury-cathedral.org/CalmView/Record.aspx?src=CalmView.
Catalog&id=CCA-DCc-ChAnt%2fC%2f115%2f62&pos=1, accessed 24 February
2024.

our predecessor, of the tithes of the mill of Edern and a third part of the tithes of the lordship of Nefyn with another third part of the same tithes which is owed to the church of Nefyn. Alan orders the parishioners of Nefyn to pay the canons of Haughmond tithes of all sea fishing and tithes of the produce of the land and all other things. He also grants that the canons may appoint and remove the chaplains of their churches in his diocese. Witnesses: Archdeacon Abraham ap Gruffudd, Gervase the archdeacon of Bangor, Archdeacon Philip son of the bishop, and Cynddelw the archdeacon of Llŷn, etc.

[16 April 1195 x 19 May 1196]

B = Shrewsbury, Shropshire Archives, MS 6001/6869 (Haughmond Cartulary), fos. 150r–150v. s. xv ex. Rubric: Confirmatio donationum ibidem. Followed by, in a later hand: 'et de capellanis constituendis vel a[m]movendis'.

Printed in *Cartulary of Haughmond Abbey*, p. 161, no. 794.

Transcribed from B.

Alanus dei gratia Bangor' episcopus omnibus sancte ecclesie filiis et fidelibus salutem in salutis auctore. Cum sit opus pietatis locis religiosis providere et eadem in libertatibus sibi misericorditer indultis conservare nos ex pastoralis sollicitudinis officio nobis divinitus collato possessiones et iura ecclesie sancti Johannis evange-liste de Haghmon' in nostra diocese fidelium devocione collata in nostra protec-tione suscipimus et predecessorum nostrorum Mauricii et Widonis donationes et confirmationes super hiis ratas habentes eadem predicte ecclesie presenti scripto confirmamus. Specialiter autem hec duximus annotanda ex dono Hoel, regis Arwistili, ecclesiam de Treveglos cum omnibus pertinentiis suis, ex dono Cath-waladri et filiorum eius Mareduth et Eimonn et Cathwadlan ecclesiam de Nevyn' cum omnibus pertinentiis suis et totam terram que est inter duos rivulos inter quos ecclesia sita et totam terram Cremioch cum omnibus pertinentiis et eisiamentis suis, ex dono David, regis Norwallie, illam terram quam Troithbremeth habuit de terra Bodenav in villa de Nevyn', ex dono bone memorie Widonis predecessoris nostri decimacionem de molendino de Edern et terciam partem decimacionum dominii de Nevyn cum alia tercia parte earundem decimacionum que debetur ecclesie de Nevyn'. Concedimus preterea ut in omnibus ecclesiis suis in nostra diocesi constitutis capellanos constituant vel amoveant dum eis de eisdem ecclesiis necessaria provideant. Precipimus etiam omnibus clericis de Lcin et sub intermi-nacione anathematis prohibemus ne quis decimas aut aliquam obvencionem [fo. 150v.] parochianorum canonicorum de Nevin ausu temerario presumat accipere. Preterea precipimus auctoritate apostolica et nostra quatinus de omnibus molend-inis pratis et piscariis infra parochias suas constitutis et de omnibus rebus que decimari debent canonicis de Haghmon' decime plenarie persolvantur. Omnibus autem parochianis de Nevyn piscantibus auctoritate qua fungimur districte precip-imus quatinus dilectis filiis nostris canonicis de Haghmon' tam de omni piscatura maris quam de frugibus terre et omnibus aliis rebus plenarie decimas persolvant. Prohibemus etiam ne sepedicte ecclesie possessionibus officiales nostri gravamen aliquod vel molestiam nobis inconsultis inferre presumant. Siquis autem contra huius concessionis et confirmacionis nostre tenorem venire presumpserit indigna-cionem dei omnipotentis et nostram se noverit incursurum. Hiis testibus Abraham

<filio>[a] Griffini archidiacono, Gervasio archidiacono de Bangor', Philippo filio episcopi archidiacono, Candelano archidiacono de Lein, etc.

> [a]superscript with an arrow pointing to where the word is to be inserted between Abraham and Griffini, *B.*

As regards the gift by Hywel ab Ieuaf (d. 1185) of the church of Trefeglwys, with all its appurtenances, see *AWR*, pp. 144–7, nos. 1, 2, and 3, and *Acta* **5** and **10**, and cf. *Actum* **9**.

As regards the gift by Cadwaladr ap Gruffudd ap Cynan (d. 1172) of Nefyn church, and all the land where the church is situated between two streams, and all the Cerniog (*Cremioch*) land with all its appurtenances and easements; see *AWR*, pp. 329–31, no. 197, and *Actum* **4**, and the note to the same.

As regards Dafydd ab Owain Gwynedd (d. -27 May 1203), Gwion, and the land which *Troithbremeth* had of the *Bodenav* land in the township of Nefyn, see note to *Actum* **8**.

Edern mill could be Nefyn mill, the tithes of which Gwion granted and confirmed to Haughmond (*Actum* **8**). Gruffudd ap Cynan ab Owain (d. 1200) also confirmed the grant of tithes of the mill of Edern to St Mary's church, Nefyn and the canons of Haughmond.[63]

The reference to a third part of the tithes of the lordship of Nefyn with another third part of the same tithes which is owed to the church of Nefyn could be a reference to *Actum* **8** (see also *Actum* **11**) or another charter of Gwion's, one which is not recorded in the Haughmond Cartulary.

The witnesses, as recorded in the abbey's cartulary, were all archdeacons; Archdeacon Abraham ap Gruffudd, Iorwerth ('Gervase') the archdeacon of Bangor, Archdeacon Philip son of the bishop, and Cynddelw the archdeacon of Llŷn. This is the only mention of an archdeacon of Bangor by the name of Iorwerth ('Gervase'); however, he might have been the same 'Gervase' who was the brother of Gwion.[64] Cynddelw occurs once more, together with his brother John, 1194 x 1200, again in connection with Haughmond.[65] It is unclear which archdeaconries Abraham, and Philip, represented; possibly Anglesey and Meirionnydd.[66] Philip may have been the son of Alan, but it is much more likely, given the previously-existing institution of the *clas* at Bangor from which the *familia* was drawn, that he was the son of Gwion; if so, he had already been a witness to one charter in favour of Haughmond (**8**).[67] There is one other possibility, and that is that Philip was the son of Arthur de Chargan.

---

[63] *AWR*, pp. 339–40, no. 207.
[64] Gervasio fratre episcopi: *Cartulary of Haughmond Abbey*, p. 160, no. 786, and *AWR*, p. 331. See the section entitled 'Gwion' in the Introduction.
[65] *Cartulary of Haughmond Abbey*, p. 160, no. 787; *Fasti Welsh Cathedrals*, p. 7.
[66] *Fasti Welsh Cathedrals*, p. 8. Discussed in Pryce, 'Esgobaeth Bangor', p. 47.
[67] See *Actum* **8**, and the section entitled 'Gwion' in the Introduction.

In the thirteenth century, first Bishop Richard, and then Bishop Anian, confirmed the gifts of their predecessors concerning the churches of Nefyn and Trefeglwys (**45** and **58**).[68]

15. Strata Marcella Abbey

Confirmation of a gift and sale made by Cadwaladr ap Hywel (of Arwystli), being a gift, in perpetual alms, free of all custom and exaction, of all the land from the stream called Bacho to the river called Dengwm, to the Cistercian brothers of Strata Marcella, for the salvation of the souls of himself and his parents, and furthermore the sale for 15 marks to the same brothers of pasture for their own use from the river Dengwm to Cwm Llwyd. Witnesses to the gift and sale: Lawrence the hospitaller, Archdeacon Sulien, Dean Iorwerth ap Hywel, Ieuaf ab Iorwerth, Philip the priest of Llanwnnog, Master Helias, Master Roger, and the laymen Meilyr ap Nennau, Gruffudd ap Cadwgan, Caradog Bach (parvus), Gruffudd Hiruein, Gwrgenau the rhingyll (preco) and Ynyr the poet (vates). But because the present age is prone and disposed to evil and attempts falsely to break whatever it seeks to wrest gain for itself thereby, we confirm this gift and sale with the impression of our seal. Whoever therefore presumes to annul or to disturb this gift and sale, and the confirmation of our charter, by the authority of God and by ours let him know that he is bound by sentence of anathema and barred from the threshold of the holy mother church as long as he persists in his audacity.

[16 April 1195 x 19 May 1196]

A = Aberystwyth, NLW, Wynnstay Estate Records, Ystrad Marchell Charter GT16. 209 x 130 mm.[69] Early modern endorsements. There are two horizontal slits, for a tag, in the turn-up at the foot of the document. Sealed with an off-white wax seal (fragment), oval in shape; the parchment tag having been passed through the horizontal slits in the turn-up (*sur double queue*). Obverse of seal: *c.*35 mm (wide) x *c.*55 mm (high), depicting a bishop vested, head missing, legend missing. Subsidiary seal on reverse: *c.*27 mm (wide) x *c.*42 mm (high), depicting a bishop vested, head missing, pastoral staff in left hand, right hand raised in blessing, the remaining legend reads: '… GILLVM … BANGORIE' in Roman capitals.[70]

B = NLW MS 1641B, ii, pp. 98–9 (copy of A with omissions, hand of Walter Davies). s. xviii/xix.

Calendared in *Episc. Acts Welsh Dioceses Unpublished*, B87.

Calendared in J. C. Davies, 'Strata Marcella Documents', 167–8, no. 6.

Printed in *Five Strata Marcella Charters*, 50–2, and Plate V (12).

Printed in *Ystrad Marchell Charters*, pp. 158–9, no. 16.

Transcribed from A.

Alan(us) gratia dei Bangorensis episcopus omnibus sancte matris ecclesie filiis per episcopatum Bangorense(m) constitutis, tam presentibus quam futuris, salutem gratiam et benedictionem. Notum sit nobis omnibus quod Kadwaladrus filius

---

[68] *Actum* **45** and *Actum* **58**.
[69] Image at Plate VII.
[70] Image at Plate IV (i). Seal described in *Welsh Episcopal Seals*, 110 (and Plate XVI (I)(2)).

Howel intuiti caritatis pro salute anime sue et parentum suorum dedit et concessit fratribus Cisterciensis ordinis ecclesie scilicet beate ac perpetue virginis Marie de Estradmarhel in perpetuam et quietam elemosinam et ab omni exactione et consuetudine liberam terram omnem ab rivulo qui vocatur Bacho usque ad fluvium que vocatur Dengum. Insuper et pascuam ab fluvio Dengum usque ad Cumluith eisdem fratribus in proprium usum pro xv marcis vendidit. Testes igitur huius donationis et venditionis hii sunt Laurentius hospitalarius, Sulien archidiaconus, Ioreuerth decanus filius Howel, Ieuwaf filius Ioreuerth, Philipp(us) sacerdos de Lanwinnauch, magister Helias, magister Roger(us). De laicis vero Meiler filius Nenniau, Griffud filius Kaduguan, Karadauch parvus, Griffud Hiruein, Gurgeneu *preco*, Henir *vates*. Sed quoniam ad malum presens etas prona est et ingeniosa et id calumpniose temptat infringere unde sibi lucrum conatur extorquere hanc donationem et venditionem sigilli nostri impressione confirmamus. Quicumque ergo hanc donationem et venditionem atque carte nostre confirmationem cassare sive perturbare presumpserit per auctoritatem dei et nostram sciat se anathematis sententia innodatum et ab liminibus sancte matris ecclesie eliminatum quamdiu in presumptione sua perstiterit.

Cwm Llwyd, the stream Bacho, and the river Dengwm were in the township of Esgeiriaeth, in the parish of Trefeglwys, Arwystli.[71] The sale of Cwm Llwyd was also confirmed by Cadwaladr ap Hywel's brothers (Meurig and Hywel) in 1198.[72]

The identity of the first-named witness, *Laurentius hospitalarius*, is interesting. It has been assumed that he was the 'guest-master' of the abbey.[73] However, he is not mentioned in any of the other surviving charters in favour of the abbey, and bearing in mind that Alan was the former prior of the Hospital of Jerusalem in England, Lawrence may well have been a Hospitaller, a knight of the Order of St John of Jerusalem. Certainly, there is evidence of Alan's continued association with the Hospitallers when he was bishop.[74] It is perhaps unlikely that a guest-master would rank first in a hierarchical witness list such as this, containing an archdeacon, and a dean, whereas a knight of the Order of St John of Jerusalem might rank first.[75] Furthermore, Gerald of Wales used the identical term when describing Alan, namely *hospitalarius*.[76]

Sulien the archdeacon, most probably Sulien ap Caradog, the archdeacon based at Meifod, who appears several times in the surviving charters of Strata Marcella,

---

[71] *Ystrad Marchell Charters*, p. 117. *AWR*, p. 148.
[72] *AWR*, p. 148, no. 5, and pp. 149–50, no. 8.
[73] 'Lawrence/Llywarch, guest-master': *Ystrad Marchell Charters*, p. 52.
[74] Bodleian Library, Ashmole MS 833, p. 15; *Early Charters of the Cathedral Church of St. Paul, London*, pp. 225–6 (no. 284); *Cartulaire général de l'ordre des Hospitaliers de Saint-Jean de Jérusalem*, iv, p. 331.
[75] Diana Greenway has noted that in English ecclesiastical charters by the 1180s or 1190s witnesses' names were arranged with careful regard for precedence: Greenway, 'Ecclesiastical Chronology', p. 60. See also Burger, 'Officiales and the Familiae of the Bishops of Lincoln', 41–2, and *EEA, XXXI, Ely, 1109–1197*, p. cxl.
[76] *De Invectionibus*, p. 193.

was the second-named witness.[77] The third witness was one Iorwerth ap Hywel, dean; most probably dean of Arwystli, who also appears in other charters of the same house, and elsewhere.[78] Philip, the priest (*sacerdos*) of Llanwnnog in Arwystli, is also named in other Strata Marcella charters.[79]

The confirmation may have been obtained by the monks of Strata Marcella during a visitation, by Alan, of the rural deanery of Arwystli, a detached portion of the diocese of Bangor; or alternatively when Alan was in exile from Bangor.[80]

Two of the lay witnesses were *Gurgeneu preco* ('Gwrgenau the rhingyll') and *Henir vates* ('Ynyr the poet'). The *preco* or *rhingyll* was the local serjeant.[81] Some years later, Ynyr the poet was also a witness to a notification issued by Maredudd ap Rhobert of Cedewain concerning a dispute heard at Llandinam, Arwystli, Maredudd having been appointed by prince Llywelyn ab Iorwerth to settle the dispute in question.[82]

[77]   *Ystrad Marchell Charters*, p. 50. Also, *Fasti Welsh Cathedrals*, p. 39; Stephenson, *Medieval Powys*, p. 254.
[78]   He appears in five other charters relating to the abbey: *Ystrad Marchell Charters*, p. 49 (including as 'I decanus de Arust(i)li', and 'Geruasio decano de Arwistili': *ibid.*, and see *AWR*, p. 753, no. 548). He is also one of the 'good men' of Arwystli listed in a record of arbitration 1216 x *c.*1226 and referred to therein as 'Ioruerd filius Hewel decanus terre': *AWR*, pp. 158–60, no. 16. He also appears as a witness in a second document connected with the same case (*AWR*, pp. 160–1, no. 17), and possibly as a witness to a charter of Meurig ap Hywel of Arwystli 1185 x *c.*1208 (*AWR*, p. 147, no. 4). See also Stephenson, *Medieval Wales*, p. 43.
[79]   *Ystrad Marchell Charters*, p. 49.
[80]   For the possibility that Alan found refuge in Arwystli see the section of the Introduction entitled 'Alan of St Cross' and McGuinness, 'The Medieval Bishops of Bangor, 1092–1283: Intrusion, Exile and Diplomacy' (forthcoming).
[81]   Charles-Edwards, et al., *Welsh King and His Court*, pp. 573 and 599; *AWR*, p. 862.
[82]   Enir vates/Ynyr the poet: *AWR*, pp. 160–1, no. 17, and pp. 159 and 888.

ROBERT OF SHREWSBURY

16. Profession of obedience

+ *I Robert, bishop-elect of the church of Bangor, promise to God and to the holy church of Canterbury, and to you, venerable father, Hubert (Walter, archbishop of Canterbury), and to your successors canonically substituted, canonical subjection and obedience.* +

[16 March 1197]

A = Canterbury Cathedral Archives, Dean and Chapter, CCA-DCc-ChAnt/C/115/63. 163 x 54/62 mm. Stitched to 115/62 at head, stitching holes at foot.[83]

B = Canterbury Cathedral Archives, Dean and Chapter, Register A (The Prior's Register), fo. 250v. s. xiv med.

Calendared in *Episc. Acts Welsh Dioceses Unpublished*, B97.

Printed in *Canterbury Professions*, p. 58, no. 136.

Transcribed from A.

+ Ego Robertus, Bangoriensis ecclesie electus episcopus, promitto deo sancteque Dorobernensi ecclesie et tibi, Huberte, pater venerande, tuisque successoribus canonice substuendis,*ᵃ* subiectionem et canonicam obedientiam. +

*ᵃ*substituendis, *B.*

Robert's profession is bookended by crosses, perhaps suggesting that the whole profession is autograph. Cf. Cadwgan's profession to Canterbury (**24**, Plate VI (v)) where only the final words, which are in a different hand to the rest of the profession (+ *et propria manu subscribo.* +) are enclosed by crosses.[84] See also the note to *Actum* **7** (Gwion's profession to Canterbury) and the section of the 'Diplomatic Analysis of the *Acta*' entitled 'Autograph'.

17. Hubert Walter, Archbishop of Canterbury

Report from Robert, and the abbots of Buildwas, Combermere, and Haughmond, to Archbishop Hubert Walter, in the matrimonial cause between the noblewoman M(arared), mother of Llywelyn (ab Iorwerth), prince of north Wales, and W., son of Ione. Gwladus, a blood relation of M(arared)'s, with whom W. is alleged to have had a relationship before his marriage to M(arared), is named in the proceedings. The archbishop had appointed Robert and the three

[83]   Image at Plate VI (iv). Canterbury Cathedral Archives' online record: https://archives.canterbury-cathedral.org/CalmView/Record.aspx?src=CalmView.Catalog&id=CCA-DCc-ChAnt%2fC%2f115%2f63&pos=4, accessed 24 February 2024.

[84]   Cf. also with Richard's profession, *Actum* **36**, Plate VI, where the final words (*et subscribo.* + + +) are written in darker ink and seem to be autograph.

abbots at Bankebir' *the Tuesday after Ascension. The clerk who appeared for M(arared) stated that the bishop of St Asaph and the abbot of Basingwerk had already carried out an inquisition into the matter and had reported to the archbishop. Valediction.*

[Tuesday 20 May 1197 x 13 July 1205, possibly Tuesday 8 May 1201 x 13 July 1205]

A = Canterbury Cathedral Archives, Dean and Chapter, CCA-DCc-ChChLet/ II/251. 175 x 91 mm.[85]

Calendared in *Episc. Acts Welsh Dioceses Unpublished*, B127.

Calendared in *Select Cases from the Ecclesiastical Courts*, p. 107.[86]

Printed in *Report on Manuscripts in Various Collections*, i, pp. 240–1, no. 251.

Transcribed from A.

Reverentissimo[a] patri et domino H. dei gratia Cant(uariensi) archiepiscopo tocius Anglie primati, R.[b] eiusdem permissione Bangor'[c] episcopus, de Bildewas, de Cumbremar', de Hageman abbates, salutem et tam devotam quam debitam per omnia reverentiam. Constitutis nobis apud Bankebir' die martis proxima post ascensionem domini causam que vertebatur inter nobilem mulierem M., matrem Lewelini principis Norwallie, et W. filium Ione audituris, exhibuit nobis dicta M. litteras vestras continentes quod rei veritatem super tribus capitulis inquireremus: videlicet, utrum consanguineam ipsius M., Guladus nomine antea cognovisset idem W. quando ad sepedictam M. accessisset. Item, de matrimonio, utrum inter ipsam et illum fuisset legittime contractum, necne. Item, de altera consanguinea memorate M., utrum eam iamnunc in lectuli sui admisisset participium, necne. Is ergo qui pro memorata M. verba faciebat adversus dictum W. proponebat quod consanguineam ipsius M. cognovit antequam ad eam accessisset, asserens super hoc capitulo prius quam de ceteris plene faciendam esse inquisicionem, tum quia id factum quod adversus ipsum W. proponitur precessit tempus quo idem W. dicit matrimonium inter eos <fuisse>[d] contractum, tum quia eo sufficienter inquisito et probato, superfluum esset de ceteris inquirere. Preterea idem clericus propone-bat hanc eandem inquisicionem domino de sancto Asaph et abbati de Basingw-erth <antea>[e] fuisse commissa et coram eis attestaciones partium in scriptum[f] redactas excellentie vestre transmittendas, nec a nobis debere <super inquisicione matrimonii>[g] procedi donec quid inde factum fuerit innotesceret, et dilationem dominos dare instanter postulabat quoad usque de hoc innotesceret. Nobis vero mandatum vestrum accelerare volentibus, et ne mora partibus periculosa esset formidantibus attendentibus, etiam sicut nobis videbatur prime inquisitioni per litteras vestras de hac eadem inquisitione ab utraque parte nobis porrectas a parti-bus fuisse <tacite>[h] remittatum. Ideoque dilationem dare nolentibus, memoratus clericus in vocem appellationis prorupit, terminum appellationi sue prefigens crastinum apostolorum Pet(ri) et Pauli. Valeat in domino paternitas vestra.

[a]tear or cut in parchment passing through the second e, *A*. [b]tear or cut in parchment passing through R, *A*. [c]abbreviation mark for 'rum'. Tear or cut in parchment passing through angor', *A*. [d]in superscript, above double ee, crossed

---

85 Image at Plate IX.
86 Errs in recording the abbot of Cwmhir instead of the abbot of Combermere ('Cumbremar'').

through, 'ᴄᴄ', *A.* ᶠinterlinear above werth, *A.* ᵍthe editors of *Report on Manuscripts in Various Collections* stated that the MS read 'scriptam' but that the correct reading should be 'scripturam'. When the letter at the end of 'script', over which there is a line of contraction, is analysed closely it is very similar to the scribe's 'u' in 'partium' two words before, *A.* ᵍinterlinear above debere procedi donec quid inde, *A.* ʰinterlinear above fuisse remittatum, *A.*

The archbishop appointed Robert and the three abbots on the Tuesday after Ascension; the year is unknown. Ascension is the Thursday following Rogation Sunday (Rogation Sunday being the fifth Sunday after Easter) and normally falls in May.[87] *Prima facie*, the date range for the report is Tuesday 20 May 1197 x 13 July 1205.[88] The year of the *terminus a quo* is provided by the year of the consecration of Robert (consecrated on 16 March 1197), and the *terminus ante quem* is the day Hubert Walter died (13 July 1205).[89] However, it is possible that this date range could be narrowed. Hubert Walter was in Normandy on Tuesday 23 May 1200.[90] As Llywelyn ab Iorwerth is described in the report as prince of north Wales, the *terminus a quo* could be Tuesday 8 May 1201 as Llywelyn is not recorded as being styled *princeps Norwalie* until November 1199,[91] and as we know that the archbishop was in Normandy on 23 May 1200 the earliest date based on the description of Llywelyn as prince of north Wales would be Tuesday 8 May 1201.[92]

Bankebir' could be Banbury, in Oxfordshire, which was recorded in the patent rolls as Banebir' in 1203.[93] The itinerary of Hubert Walter shows that he was in Oxfordshire, at Woodstock, in late April 1204 (being next recorded at Merton in mid-June of that year)[94] and the following year he was in Northampton on 23 May and Woodstock on 25 May, so he could have travelled via Banbury and been there on Tuesday 24 May 1205.[95] If Bankebir' is Banbury then either 1204 or 1205 could be the year that the archbishop appointed Robert and the three abbots.

---

[87]   Cheney, *Handbook of Dates*, pp. 44 and 60.

[88]   Cheney, *Handbook of Dates*, pp. 114–15, table 16.

[89]   *Fasti Monastic Cathedrals*, p. 5.

[90]   *EEA, III, Canterbury, 1193–1205*, p. 313. 1200: Cheney, *Handbook of Dates*, pp. 120–1, table 19.

[91]   Pope Innocent III referred to Llywelyn as 'princeps Norwalie' (24 November 1199) when responding to a petition of Llywelyn's: *Reg. Innocenz' III*, ii, pp. 430–1, no. 224. *AWR*, p. 25.

[92]   Cheney, *Handbook of Dates*, pp. 90–1, table 4.

[93]   Survey of English Place-Names, https://epns.nottingham.ac.uk/browse/Oxfordshire/Banbury/53286e38b47fc40beb000795-Banbury, accessed 12 June 2024.

[94]   *EEA, III, Canterbury, 1193–1205*, p. 314. Thank you to Dr Nigel Tringham for bringing Hubert Walter's Oxfordshire visits to my attention.

[95]   *EEA, III, Canterbury, 1193–1205*, p. 314. 1205: Cheney, *Handbook of Dates*, pp. 122–3, table 20.

Marared or Margaret was the daughter of Madog ap Maredudd (d. 1160) of Pow-ys.[96] Llywelyn's father was Iorwerth Drwyndwn ab Owain who had died *c.*1174.[97] 'W', possibly 'William', may have been Gwilym ap Jonas, nephew of Roger of Powys, and great-great grandson of Rhys Sais.[98] Alternatively, 'W' may have stood for 'Wion'. Gwilym's brother was Gwion ap Jonas who held lands in Shropshire and witnessed two of Llywelyn's charters in favour of Haughmond Abbey, 1205 x 1211.[99] The Jonas family connections with Shropshire together with the fact that all four clerics were connected with the county (albeit Combermere was just across the county border, in Cheshire) perhaps suggests that Marared and her husband were living locally. Who Marared married after the death of Iorwerth Drwyndwn has been the subject of conjecture by scholars.[100] Recently, based on a charter of Gwion ap Jonas ('*Wyon filius Jone*') in favour of Combermere which named his wife as one *domina Margeria*, the daughter of Madog, David Stephenson has sug-gested that Marared may have married Gwion.[101] It does, therefore, seem that the husband of Marared ferch Madog ap Maredudd, named in Robert's joint report to Hubert Walter, was Gwion ap Jonas, not his brother Gwilym. Gwladus, a blood relation of Marared's, with whom W. is alleged to have had a relationship before his marriage to Marared, is named in the proceedings. It is not clear which Gwladus is meant.[102]

The abbot of Buildwas 1197 x 1205 may have been William or 'H.'; the abbot of Combermere 1197 x 1205 may have been Thomas; and the abbot of Haughmond 1197 x 1205 may have been Richard, 'H.' or Ralph.[103]

---

[96] Lloyd, *History of Wales*, ii, p. 587 and n. 62. *AWR*, pp. 24–5. David Stephenson calls her Mared or Margaret: Stephenson, *Medieval Powys*, p. 297.

[97] Lloyd, *History of Wales*, ii, pp. 550 and 587. *AWR*, p. 24. Stephenson, *Medieval Powys*, p. 297, and n. 27. Carr, 'Llywelyn ab Iorwerth, [called Llywelyn Fawr] (*c.*1173–1240)', *ODNB*.

[98] Suppe, 'Roger of Powys', 2.

[99] *AWR*, pp. 414 and 695, and nos. 225 and 226. Eyton, *Antiquities of Shropshire*, ix, 41–3. Interestingly, both Robert and Gwion ap Jonas received monies for their maintenance in the custody of Denbigh castle 1196–1197, and pursuant to the same writ: *Pipe Roll, Richard I, Year 8*, p. 42. Thank you to Dr Nia Wyn Jones for her thoughts concerning the identity of W. in Robert's joint report, and the likelihood that 'W' stood for 'Wion'.

[100] J. E. Lloyd suggested that she may have married into the Corbet family: Lloyd, *History of Wales*, ii, p. 587, n. 62. Cf. *AWR*, p. 391, and Stephenson, *Medieval Powys*, p. 297.

[101] Stephenson dates the charter (pd in *Monasticon*, v, pp. 324–5) to 1175 x *c.*1190: Stephenson, *Medieval Powys*, pp. 295–7. Following Pryce, he points out that the charter may be spurious, but the witness list (which includes 'domina Margeria filia Madoci') may have been incorporated from an authentic document: Stephenson, *Medieval Powys*, pp. 293–4; *AWR*, pp. 696, 698, and 712.

[102] A possible contemporary is Gwladus ferch Ithel, who may have been the wife of Madog ap Gruffudd Maelor (*AWR*, p. 707). A search of the genealogies might reveal other contemporaries. Gwladus ferch Llywarch ap Trahaearn (mother of Iorwerth Drwyndwn) would appear to have been too old, and Gwladus Ddu, Llywelyn ab Iorwerth's daughter by Joan, would not yet have been born.

[103] *Heads of Religious Houses*, i, pp. 129, 131 and 165.

As Hubert Walter became archbishop in 1193, the bishop of St Asaph was almost certainly Reiner (consecrated in 1186, died in 1224/5).[104] The abbot of Basingwerk may have been a certain Robert.[105]

18. Church of SS Peter and Paul, Shrewsbury (Shrewsbury Abbey)

Grant and gift in pure and perpetual alms to the church of SS Peter and Paul, Shrewsbury, and the abbot and monks there, of all messuages which Robert has in Coleham and his grange in the court of the grange [sic]; he will hold that grange, with the court, of them for life or for as long as he pleases, rendering them one pound of cumin at the Feast of St Peter ad Vincula (1 August). Sealing clause. Witnesses: Master Henry, Robert de Heding', William the clerk, and others.

[16 March 1197 x 1212]

B = NLW MS 7851D (Cartularium S. Petri De Salopesberia), fo. 162. s. xiii ex. In margin: Epc Bang' de domibus in Colh'm

C = BL Additional MS 30311 (Chartulary of Shrewsbury Abbey – Halston Library), fo. 134v. s. xviii.

Calendared in *Episc. Acts Welsh Dioceses Unpublished*, B133.

Printed in *Cartulary of Shrewsbury Abbey*, i, p. 160, no. 185.

Transcribed from B.

Omnibus Cristi fidelibus ad quos presens scriptum pervenerit, Rob(er)t(us) permissione divina Bangor'*a* episcopus, salutem in domino. Noverit universitas vestra nos concessisse et dedisse in puram et perpetuam elemosinam deo et ecclesie beatorum Pet(ri)*b* et Pauli apostolorum Salop' et abbati et monachis ibidem deo servientibus omnia mesuagia que habuimus in Coleham et grangiam nostram in curia grangie [*sic*] ita quod nos tenebimus <de>*c* eis grangiam illam cum curia in vita nostra vel quamdiu nobis placuerit reddendo inde annuatim eis unam libram cimini in festo sancti Petri ad vincula et ut hec nostra concessio et donatio rata et inconcussa permaneat eam presenti scripto et sigilli nostri appositione confirmare curavimus. Hiis testibus magistro Henr(ico), Roberto*d* de Heding', Will(elm)o clerico, et aliis.

*a*abbreviation mark for 'rum', *B.* *b*Petri, *C.* *c*interlinear above eis, *B.* *d*Rob(er)to, *C.*

Coleham is a little to the south of Shrewsbury across the river Severn.

Robert had been dean at the college of secular canons at St Mary's, Shrewsbury.[106] He had strong local connections, owned property in Shrewsbury, and his brother,

---

[104] *Fasti Welsh Cathedrals*, p. 34.
[105] *Heads of Religious Houses*, i, p. 126.
[106] Gaydon, 'Colleges of Secular Canons: Shrewsbury', p. 123, and n. 253; Eyton, *Antiquities of Shropshire*, ii, p. 112, n. 14.

Richard, was archdeacon in the town.[107] He appears as a witness to several charters recorded in the cartulary of Shrewsbury Abbey.[108]

The witnesses to Robert's grant and gift all seem to have been local to Shropshire or have had Shropshire connections. Certainly Robert de Heding' (or Hastings) was for a time rector of Oldbury, near Bridgnorth;[109] and William the clerk was a witness to a confirmation in favour of Shrewsbury Abbey made by Bishop Reiner of St Asaph to which Bishop Robert was the first witness.[110] Master Henry may have been Henry of London one of Robert's successors as dean of St Mary's, possibly his immediate successor – he was to become archbishop of Dublin in 1213, but only resigned as dean of St Mary's in 1226.[111]

The rents derived from Robert's grant and gift were amongst certain rents assigned by Hugh, abbot of Shrewsbury, to the monks of the same abbey after Robert's death, 1212 x 1220.[112]

19. Kingsthorpe Hospital, Northampton

Indulgence. Robert dedicated a chapel in a hospital, near Northampton, in honour of the Holy Trinity, in the first year following the death of Hugh (of Avalon), bishop of Lincoln. He granted relaxation of 20 days' enjoined penance for those who were truly penitent and had confessed, who on the anniversary of the dedication conferred some benefit for the sustenance of the said house. Valediction.

25 May 1201

A = BL Additional Charter No. 22381. 150 x 75 mm.[113] On reverse, in later hand: Dedicatio capellae quae est in Hospitale iuxta Norhamton. A black or dark-green seal, now fractured – only two parts of the same remain, namely the mitred head of a figure and part of a torso cloaked in eucharistic vestments. Sealed on a tongue of parchment (*simple queue*) which was cut from the lower left-hand side of the document (the tongue passing through the middle and

---

[107] Local connections and property: Shropshire Archives, MS 322/2/10; Eyton, *Antiquities of Shropshire*, vi, p. 368, viii, pp. 106–7, x, pp. 358–9; Gaydon, 'Colleges of Secular Canons: Shrewsbury', p. 119 and n. 166, p. 121 and n. 196, p. 122 and n. 222; *Pleas before the King and his Justices, 1198–1212*, iii, pp. lxxvii and xciii. For his brother Richard: Eyton, *Antiquities of Shropshire*, ii, p. 133, n. 98. See also the section of the Introduction entitled 'Robert of Shrewsbury'.

[108] *Cartulary of Shrewsbury Abbey*, i, pp. 18–19, no. 16, p. 94, no. 106, p. 269, no. 283, and p. 280, no. 300; ii, pp. 271–2, no. 286, and pp. 316–17, no. 351.

[109] Eyton, *Antiquities of Shropshire*, i, pp. 60 and 136.

[110] 1204 x 1210, confirmation in respect of the church of Oswestry: Eyton, *Antiquities of Shropshire*, x, p. 336.

[111] Dean of St Mary's 1203–1226; archbishop of Dublin 1213–1228: *Rot. Litt. Claus.*, ii, p. 161. Also, Eyton, *Antiquities of Shropshire*, x, p. 150, n. 1; Gaydon, 'Colleges of Secular Canons: Shrewsbury', p. 123, and n. 255.

[112] *Cartulary of Shrewsbury Abbey*, ii, pp. 343–4.

[113] Image at Plate VIII.

reappearing at the bottom of seal). The seal was kept in a red cloth bag which survives. No wrapping-tie.[114]

Calendared in *Episc. Acts Welsh Dioceses Unpublished*, B117.

Transcribed from A.

Omnibus Cristi fidelibus ad quos presens scriptum pervenerit, R. permissione divina Bangor'[a] episcopus, salutem ab auctore salutis. Noverit universitas vestra nos capellam que est in hospitali iuxta Norhamton' anno primo post obitum felicis memorie Hugonis quondam Lincol(niensis) episcopi octavo kalendas Iunii in honore sancte trinitatis[b] dedicasse, attendentes autem domum illam ad hoc pia devotione fundatam ut transeuntibus et egens petentibus subsidium sollicite conferatur, considerantes etiam onus illud absque proborum virorum auxilio non posse sustentari, omnibus qui in anniversario dedicationis die ad sustentationem prefate domus aliquid benefitii contulerint vel transmiserint vere penitentibus et confessis de iniuncta sibi penitentia quantum ad nos pertinet viginti dies relaxamus. Valete.

[a]abbreviation mark for 'rum', *A*. [b]the scribe has emphasised sancte trinitatis by starting both words with a majuscule, *A*.

This is the first Bangor episcopal *actum* for which an accurate date can be assigned. Hugh of Avalon, bishop of Lincoln, died on 16 November 1200.[115]

Robert had been in Lincoln in January 1201.[116]

The hospital of St David and the Holy Trinity was founded in 1200, in Kingsthorpe, by the Cluniac prior and convent of St Andrew's, Northampton.[117] There was a chapel of the Holy Trinity and a chapel of St David. In the body of the house adjoining the chapel of the Holy Trinity there were to be three rows of beds where the poor or travellers who were invalids might lie for the more convenient hearing of mass and prayers, and there were to be six lay brothers to wait on the poor and sick.[118]

20. Pope Innocent III

Certificate by the bishops of London (William), Hereford (Giles), St Asaph (Reiner), Llandaff (Henry), Bangor (Robert) and St Davids (Geoffrey) of the canonical election by the prior and convent of Bath, and the dean and chapter of Wells, of Master Jocelin, canon of Wells, upon the

[114] A black and white image of the seal is printed in *Welsh Episcopal Seals*, Plate XVI (3), and the same is described at *ibid.*, 110. A legend is ascribed by D. H. Williams, but this is taken from a plaster cast, BL Seal LXXXII, 39. No legend remains on the seal attached to BL Additional Charter No. 22381.

[115] *Fasti Lincoln*, p. 2.

[116] On 13 January 1201, in Lincoln, Robert witnessed a charter given by King John: *Rot. Chart.*, 84a–b; *Cartae Antiquae, Rolls 1–10*, p. 79, no. 154; *Rot. Litt. Pat.*, 'Itinerary of King John'.

[117] *Monasticon*, v, pp. 192–3. Serjeantson and Adkins, 'Hospitals: St David & the Holy Trinity, Kingsthorpe', in *VCH Northampton*, ii, p. 154.

[118] Serjeantson and Adkins, 'Hospitals: St David & the Holy Trinity, Kingsthorpe', in *VCH Northampton*, ii, p. 154.

*death of Savaric, bishop of Bath, together with a certificate of King John, in the vacancy of the
church of Canterbury, and petition to confirm the election.*

[23 April x 28 May 1206]

B = Wells, Dean and Chapter Muniments, Liber Albus I (Wells Cathedral Register, vol. I), fo. 54v. s. xiii med. In margin: cciii. Rubric: Testimonium plurium episcoporum de eodem

Calendared in *Calendar of the Manuscripts of the Dean and Chapter of Wells*, i, p. 62, no. cciii.

Calendared in *Episc. Acts Welsh Dioceses*, i, p. 332, no. D390.

Calendared in *St Davids Episcopal Acta*, p. 87, no. 63.

Printed in *EEA, VII, Hereford, 1079–1234*, pp. 201–2, no. 264.

Transcribed from B.

Sanctissimo in Cristo patri I. dei gratia summo pontifici humiles et devoti filii sui W. London', E. Hereford', R. Sancti Asaph, H. Land', R. Bango'ᵃ, G. Menevens(is) episcopi salutem et cum omni devotione ac reverentia debitam domino et patri obedientiam. Noverit sancta paternitas vestra quod cum venerabilis frater noster Savar(icus) bone memorie Bathon(iensis) episcopus concessisset in fata, et tam Bathon(iensis) quam Wellensis ecclesia suo fuisset viduata pastore, prior et conventus Bathon(iensis) et decanus et capitulum Wellens(is), ad quos ius eligendi episcopum pertinere dinoscitur, in unum pariter convenerunt, habitoque prout moris est super electione episcopi diligenti tractatu, pari tandem voto, et unanimi assenu in magistrum Ioscelinu(m), canonicum Wellens(is) ecclesie, virum providum, literatum et honestum, consenserunt, ipsumque invocata spiritus sancti gratia in pastorem et episcopum suum canonice ac sollempniter elegerunt. Cui nimirum electioni illustris rex Anglo(rum) Ioh(ann)es suum adhibuit benignus assensum. Quia vero Cant(uariensis) ecclesia suo noscitur orbata pastore, supplicamus sancte paternitati vestre quatinus nuntios dictarum ecclesiarum benignius admittentes, prenominato electo munus confirmationis conferre dignemini.

ᵃabbreviation mark for 'ruᴉᴉᴉ', *B*.

Following Archbishop Hubert Walter's death (on 13 July 1205), and during the subsequent *sede vacante* at Canterbury, Robert was a party to two certificates concerning the canonical election of Jocelin of Wells, addressed to Pope Innocent III, and the papal legate in England, John of Ferentino, respectively (**20** and **21**). Two further certificates, in the same matter, addressed to the same recipients, were Robert's alone (**22** and **23**).

The other bishops who were party to *Actum* **20** (and also *Actum* **21**) were William de Ste Mère-Église, bishop of London, Giles (Egidius) de Braose, bishop of Hereford, Henry bishop of Llandaff, Reiner bishop of St Asaph, and Geoffrey (Galfridus) of Henlow, bishop of St Davids.[119]

---

[119] *Fasti London*, p. 2; *Fasti Hereford*, p. 4; *Fasti Welsh Cathedrals*, pp. 14, 34 and 47.

Jocelin had been elected following the death of Savaric, bishop of Bath, who had died on 8 August 1205.[120] King John gave his assent to the election, and the certificates petitioned for papal confirmation of the election.[121] Jocelin was consecrated in Reading by William de Ste Mère-Église, bishop of London, on Trinity Sunday, 28 May 1206, and Robert was present.[122]

The episcopal certificates (which added weight to a dossier which had been prepared on Jocelin's behalf) were most probably made with the king's encouragement, and need to be seen in the context of the vacancy at Canterbury and the contest to determine who had the right to elect and approve the next archbishop. The consecration of Jocelin to the see of Bath was a victory for those, notably the king, who might prefer the suffragan bishops, acting as an electoral college, to elect the next archbishop, rather than the monks of Canterbury.[123]

The *terminus a quo*, namely 23 April 1206, is provided by the date of King John's letter of assent to the papal legate, John of Ferentino, recommending Jocelin and seeking papal confirmation.[124] The *terminus ante quem* of 28 May 1206 is the date Jocelin was consecrated as bishop of Bath (and Glastonbury) by William de Ste Mère-Église, bishop of London.[125]

21. Cardinal John of Ferentino

Certificate by the bishops of London (William), Hereford (Giles), St Asaph (Reiner), Llandaff (Henry), Bangor (Robert) and St Davids (Geoffrey) addressed to J(ohn of Ferentino), Cardinal Deacon of Santa Maria in Via Lata, and papal legate, in similar terms to Actum 20 above.

[23 April x 28 May 1206]

B = Wells, Dean and Chapter Muniments, Liber Albus I (Wells Cathedral Register, vol. I), fos. 54v–55. s. xiii med. In margin: ccvi. Rubric: Testimonium de quo prius

Calendared in *Calendar of the Manuscripts of the Dean and Chapter of Wells*, i, p. 62, no. ccvi.

Calendared in *Episc. Acts Welsh Dioceses*, i, p. 332, no. D391.

Calendared in *St Davids Episcopal Acta*, p. 87, no. 64.

Printed in *EEA, VII, Hereford, 1079–1234*, pp. 202–3, no. 265.

Transcribed from B.

---

[120] *Fasti Bath and Wells*, p. 3.
[121] King John's letter of assent, 23 April 1206, to the papal legate, John of Ferentino, recommending Jocelin and seeking papal confirmation: *Calendar of the Manuscripts of the Dean and Chapter of Wells*, i, p. 62. no. ccv; *Fasti Bath and Wells*, p. 3; Cheney, 'Cardinal John of Ferentino', 656.
[122] *Fasti Bath and Wells*, p. 3; *Canterbury Professions*, p. 62.
[123] Vincent, 'Jocelin of Wells', p. 29.
[124] *Calendar of the Manuscripts of the Dean and Chapter of Wells*, i, p. 62, no. ccv; *Fasti Bath and Wells*, p. 3; Cheney, 'Cardinal John of Ferentino', 656.
[125] *Fasti Bath and Wells*, p. 3.

Venerabili patri et domino karissimo I., dei gratia Sancte Marie in Via Lata diacono cardinali, apostolice sedis legato, W. de Lond', E. Hereford', R. Sancti Asaph, H. Land', R. Bango'ᵃ, G. Menevens(is) episcopi salutem, et sincere dilectionis affectum. Noverit paternitas vestra quod cum venerabilis frater noster Savar(icus) bone memorie Bathon(iensis) episcopus in fata concessisset et tam Bathon(iensis) quam Wellens(is) ecclesia suo fuisset viduata pastore, prior et conventus [fo. 55r] Bathon(iensis) et decanus et capitulum Wellens(is), ad quos ius eligendi episcopum pertinere dinoscitur, in unum pariter covenerunt habitoque prout moris est super electione episcopi diligenti tractatu, pari tandem voto et unanimi assenu in magistrum Ioscelinu(m) canonicum Wellens(is) ecclesie virum providum, literatum et honestum, consenserunt, ipsumque invocata spiritus sancti gratia in pastorem et episcopum suum canonice ac sollemniter elegerunt. Cui nimirum electioni illustris rex Anglo(rum) Ioh(ann)es suum adhibuit benignus assensum. Quia vero Cant(uariensis) ecclesia suo noscitur orbata pastore, supplicamus paternitati vestre quatinus nuntios dictarum ecclesiarum benignius admittentes, prenominato electo munus confirmationis conferre dignemini.

ᵃabbreviation mark for 'rum', *B*.

See note to *Actum* **20**.

22. Cardinal John of Ferentino

Certificate by Robert addressed to J(ohn of Ferentino), Cardinal Deacon of Santa Maria in Via Lata, and papal legate, of the canonical election of Master Jocelin, canon of Wells, by the prior and convent of Bath, and the dean and chapter of Wells, on the death of Bishop Savaric, together with the assent of King John, in the vacancy of the church of Canterbury, the fitness of the bishop-elect, and petition to confirm the election.

[23 April x 28 May 1206]

B = Wells, Dean and Chapter Muniments, Liber Albus I (Wells Cathedral Register, vol. I), fo. 55v. s. xiii med. In margin: cc viii. Rubric: Testimonium R. regis [*sic*] Bangorum

Calendared in *Calendar of the Manuscripts of the Dean and Chapter of Wells*, i, p. 63, no. ccviii.

Calendared in *Episc. Acts Welsh Dioceses Unpublished*, B129.

Transcribed from B.

Venerabili patri et domino karissimo I., dei gratia Sancte Marie in Via Lata diacono cardinali, apostolice sedis legato, R. permissione divina Bango'ᵃ episcopus, salutem et sincere dilectionis affectum. Noverit paternitas vestra quod cum venerabilis frater noster Savar(icus) bone memorie Bathon(iensis) episcopus in fata concessisset et tam Bathon(iensis) quam Wellens(is) ecclesia suo fuisset viduata pastore, prior et conventus Bath(oniensis) et decanus et capitulum Wellens(is), ad quos ius eligendi episcopum pertinere dinoscitur, in unum pariter covenerunt habitoque prout moris est super electione episcopi diligenti tractatu, ut a pluribus accepimus, pari tandem voto et unanimi assenu in magistrum Ioscelinu(m) canonicum Wellens(is) ecclesie consenserunt, ipsumque invocata spiritus sancti gratia in pastorem et episcopum suum canonice ac sollemniter elegerunt. Huic etiam electioni ut accepimus illustris rex Anglo(rum) Ioh(ann)es suum adhibuit benignus assensum. Nos autem ipsius electi et mores iam pridem plenius cognoscentes et attendentes ipsum virum providum, literatum et honestum et tante dignitatis ut credimus dignum eiusdem electioni sicut rationabiliter sancta est gratum prebemus assensum paternitati vestre obnixe supplicantes eo quod ecclesia Cant(uariensis) suo viduata sit pastore quatinus nuntios dictarum ecclesiarum benignus admittentes, prenominato electo munus confirmationis conferre dignemini.

> ^aabbreviation mark for 'rum', *B*.

See note to *Actum* **20**.

23. Pope Innocent III

Letter from Robert to Pope I(nnocent III) certifying the canonical election of Master Jocelin, canon of Wells, by the prior and convent of Bath, and the dean and chapter of Wells, following the death of Savaric, bishop of Bath, together with the assent of King John, in the vacancy of the church of Canterbury, the fitness of the bishop-elect, and petition to confirm the election.

[23 April x 28 May 1206]

> B = Wells, Dean and Chapter Muniments, Liber Albus I (Wells Cathedral Register, vol. I), fo. 56v. s. xiii med. In margin: cc xiii. Rubric: Littere R. Bango(rum) episcopi deprecatoris
>
> Calendared in *Calendar of the Manuscripts of the Dean and Chapter of Wells*, i, p. 64, no. ccxiii.
>
> Calendared in *Episc. Acts Welsh Dioceses Unpublished*, B130.
>
> Transcribed from B.

Sanctissimo in Cristo patri I., dei gratia summo pontifici, humilis et devotus filius R. permissione divina Bango'^a episcopus, salutem et cum omni devotione ac reverentia debitam domino et patri obedientiam. Noverit sancta paternitas vestra quod cum venerabilis frater noster Savar(icus) bone memorie Bathon(iensis) episcopus in fata concessisset, et tam Bathon(iensis) quam Wellens(is) ecclesia suo fuisset viduata pastore, prior et conventus Bathon(iensis) et decanus et capitulum Well(ensis), ad quos ius eligendi episcopum pertinere dinoscitur, in unum pariter convenerunt, habitoque prout moris est super electione episcopi diligenti tractatu, ut a pluribus accepimus, pari tandem voto, et unanimi assensu in magistrum Ioscelinu(m), canonicum Wellensis ecclesie, consenserunt, ipsumque invocata spiritus sancti gratia in pastorem et episcopum suum canonice ac sollempniter elegerunt. Huic etiam electioni ut accepimus illustris rex Anglo(rum) Ioh(ann)es suum adhibuit benignus assensum. Ego autem personam ipsius electi et mores iam pridem plenius cognoscens et attendens ipsum virum providum, literatum et honestum et tante dignitatis ut estimo dignum euisdem electioni sicut rationabiliter sancta est, gratum prebeo assensum paternitati vestre obnixe supplicans eo quod ecclesia Cant(uariensis) suo viduata sit pastore quatinus nuntios dictarum ecclesiarum benignus admittentes, prenominato electo munus confirmationis conferre dignemini.

> ^aabbreviation mark for 'rum', *B*.

See note to *Actum* **20**.

CADWGAN OF LLANDYFÁI

24. Profession of obedience

I Cadwgan, humble elect of the church of Bangor, promise to you, venerable father Stephen (Langton, archbishop of Canterbury) and to your successors, and the mother church of Canterbury, due subjection and obedience according to the institutions of the holy fathers, + and I sign by (my) own hand. +

[21 June 1215]

A = Canterbury Cathedral Archives, Dean and Chapter, CCA-DCc-ChAnt/C/115/146. 167 x 35 mm. Stitching holes at head and foot. Damaged and stained.[126]

B = Canterbury Cathedral Archives, Dean and Chapter, Register A (The Prior's Register), fo. 250v. s. xiv med.

Calendared in *Episc. Acts Welsh Dioceses Unpublished*, B145.

Printed in *Canterbury Professions*, p. 64, no. 154.

Transcribed from A.

Ego Caducan(us)^a, humilis ecclesie Bangorensis^b electus, promitto tibi, venerande^c pater Stephane, et successoribus tuis atque matri ecclesie Cantuariensi debitam subiectionem atque obedientiam secundum instituta sanctorum patrum, + et propria manu subscribo. +

^{a}Sa(......) B. ^{b}Bangoriensis B. ^{c}reverende B.

Signed with crosses – see note to *Actum* 7 (Gwion's profession to Canterbury). The signing with crosses, '+ *et propria manu subscribo.* +', is added in another hand (image at Plate VI (v)); which Canterbury Cathedral Archives suggest is 'presumably autograph'.[127] Cf. with Richard's profession, *Actum* **36**, Plate VI (vi), where the final words ('*et subscribo.* + + +') are written in darker ink and would also seem to be autograph.[128] See the section of the 'Diplomatic Analysis of the *Acta*' entitled 'Autograph'.

Canterbury Professions, p. 64, no. 154, adds the endorsement: '*Hec professio facta est apud Oxenefordiam iiii Kalendas Marcii in ecclesia sancte Marie de Oseneia*' ('This profession was made at Oxford, 26 February [1215], in the church of St Mary's Osney') but

---

[126] Image at Plate VI (v). Canterbury Cathedral Archives' online record: https://archives.canterbury-cathedral.org/CalmView/Record.aspx?src=CalmView.Catalog&id=CCA-DCc-ChAnt%2fC%2f115%2f146&pos=1, accessed 24 February 2024.

[127] *ibid.*

[128] Cf. also Robert's profession (*Actum* **16**, Plate VI (iv)) which is bookended by crosses, perhaps suggesting that the whole profession was autograph.

suggests that the 'endorsement is probably incorrectly connected with this profession'. There is, in fact, no endorsement on the reverse of Cadwgan's profession. There is, however, an endorsement on the reverse of the bishop of Rochester's profession, also of 1215, which reads: '*hec professio facta est apud Oxonefordiam viii Kl' Marcii in ecclesia sancte Marie de Oseneia*' (Canterbury Cathedral Archives, CCA-DCc-ChAnt/C/115/81). Perhaps this endorsement has been confused for Cadwgan's. To add to the confusion, the profession of Iorwerth (who was consecrated as bishop of St Davids on the same day and in the same place as Cadwgan was consecrated as bishop of Bangor – 21 June 1215, at Staines church in Middlesex)[129] is recorded as being given on 21 April 1215: *Canterbury Professions*, p. 64, no. 153. J. B. Smith stated that 21 April seems to be given in error for 21 June: Smith, 'Magna Carta', 358, n. 5. However, if we are to assume that both professions were given on the same day and in the same place, one might expect them to be, *mutatis mutandis*, identical. They are not: *inter alia*, Cadwgan's profession, unlike Iorwerth's, is said to be made '*secundum instituta sanctorum patrum*'. Could it be that the professions of Cadwgan and Iorwerth were made on different dates and/or in different places? Or could it be that Bangor and St Davids were treated differently when it came to their subjection to Canterbury?

25. Haughmond Abbey

Notification of the peaceful resolution of a dispute, before the official of Salop and the dean of Newport (Shropshire), concerning the church of Nefyn whereby the abbey agreed to pay the bishop 10s. 10d. annually in recognition of his rights of procuration. Sealing clause. Witnesses: Master Matthew canon of Bangor, Master Richard de Keworth, etc.

[21 June 1215 x 1235/1 March 1236]

B = Shrewsbury, Shropshire Archives, MS 6001/6869 (Haughmond Cartulary), fo. 150r. s. xv ex. Rubric: Compositio de procuratione episcopi pro ecclesia ibidem

Printed (minus sealing clause) in *Cartulary of Haughmond Abbey*, p. 161, no. 793.

Transcribed from B.

Omnibus Christi fidelibus ad quos presens scriptum pervenerit Cadugan(us) permissione divina Bangor' episcopus salutem eternam in domino. Noverit universitas vestra quod cum inter abbatem et conventum de Haghmon' ex una parte et nos ex altera coram officiale Salop' et decano de Novoburgo super procuratione ecclesie de Nevyn' questio auctoritate domini Cantuar(iensis) verteretur lis amicabili [*sic*] sub hac forma conquievit videlicet quod dicti abbas et conventus nobis annuatim persolvent x s. et x d. ratione dicte procurationis. Ita quidem quod nos nichil ab eisdem pretextu procurationis exigere poterimus preter dictos x s. et x d. Et ne hec compositio amicabiliter facta futuris temporibus possit invitari eam sigilli nostri impressione roboramus. Hiis testibus magistro Matheo canonico de Bang(or), magistro Ric(ard)o de Keworth, etc.

---

[129] Consecration of Cadwgan and Iorwerth: *Annals of Southwark and Merton*, 50.

This is the only known reference to Master Matthew, canon of Bangor.[130] He is the first 'canon' of Bangor to be named in the surviving historical record. Master Richard de Keworth may be the '*magistro Ric(ard)o*' who witnessed a charter of Llywelyn ab Iorwerth dated 15 October 1221;[131] or he may be Master Richard de Kagworth who appears as a witness elsewhere in the Haughmond Cartulary.[132]

For the church of Nefyn in Llŷn see *Acta* **4**, **8**, **14**, **45** and **58**.

I take *Novoburg(us)* to be Newport, Shropshire being some 14 miles to the east of Haughmond Abbey. The official of Salop is likely to be the official of the archdeacon of Salop (in the diocese of Lichfield) who appears elsewhere in the Haughmond Cartulary.[133]

26. Church of SS Peter and Paul, Leominster (Leominster Priory)

Indulgence. Relaxation of 13 days' enjoined penance for all those who have confessed and are truly penitent, who confer something of the goods granted to them by God, on the passion of Saints Peter and Paul (29 June) or within the octave of that feast, or on St David's Day (1 March), to the church of SS Peter and Paul, Leominster, where an arm of Saint David, confessor, honourably rests. Valediction.

[21 June 1215 x 1235/1 March 1236, possibly before 27 January 1229]

B = BL Cotton MS Domitian A iii (Leominster Priory Cartulary), fo. 74v. s. xiii med. Rubric: Caducan(us) Bangor(ensis) episcopus

Calendared in *Episc. Acts Welsh Dioceses Unpublished*, B156.

Calendared in *Monasticon*, iv, p. 53, no. 68.

Transcribed from B.

C. dei gratia Bagor' episcopus, omnibus etc. Quoniam, ut ait apostolus, omnes stabimus ante tribunal Cristi, recepturi prout in corpore gessimus, sive bonum sive malum, oportet nos diem messionis extreme misericordie operibus prevenire, ac eternorum intuitu seminare in terris quod reddente domino cum multiplicato fructu recolligere debeamus in celis, firmam spem fiduciamque tenentes quoniam qui parce seminat parce et metet. Cum igitur ad humanitatis industriam pertineat misericordie operibus vacantibus et electos dei venerantibus orationum et beneficiorum spiritualium premia impertiri, nos de misericordia dei confisi omnibus confessis et vere penitentibus qui de bonis sibi a deo collatis ecclesie beatorum apostolorum P. et P. de Lem' in die passionis eorundem apostolorum, sive infra eorum oct', sive in die sancti D. gloriosi confessoris, cuius brachium ibi habetur honorifice repositum aliquid contulerint de iniuncta sibi penitentia xiii dies relaxa-

[130] *Fasti Welsh Cathedrals*, p. 10.
[131] At Caernarfon: *CChR, 1257–1300*, p. 459, and *AWR*, pp. 411–12, no. 250. See also *Fasti Welsh Cathedrals*, p. 11.
[132] *Cartulary of Haughmond Abbey*, p. 79, no. 323, p. 80, no. 358, p. 114, no. 533, p. 157, no. 772, and pp. 206–7, no. 1106; See also Eyton, *Antiquities of Shropshire*, x, pp. 146–7.
[133] See *Cartulary of Haughmond Abbey*, p. 282.

mus, et orationum et beneficiorum que in ecclesia de Bango'ᵃ fiunt quantum in nobis esse participes concedimus. Valete.

　　ᵃabbreviation mark for 'rum', *B*.

After *impertiri*, the colour of the ink changes from black to grey.

Bagor for Bangor is also found in another of Cadwgan's *acta* (**30**).[134]

The text from '*Quoniam*' to '*metet*' inclusive replicates the first sentence of the wording suggested by Canon 62 of the Fourth Lateran Council, save that '*fuerit*' is omitted after '*sive bonum sive malum*', and '*et qui seminat in benedictionibus, de benedictionibus et metet in vitam aeternam*' is omitted at end.[135]

The grant of an indulgence of 21 days to the same house by Bishop Iorwerth of St Davids immediately follows the record of Cadwgan's grant in the priory's cartulary (fos. 74v–75r).[136] If the grants in the cartulary were recorded chronologically then, as Iorwerth died before 27 January 1229, Cadwgan's grant would necessarily be before this date.[137]

There is evidence that the lands, possessions, and indeed the monks themselves of the Benedictine priory of Leominster were subject to Welsh attack, from Maelienydd and elsewhere, during Cadwgan's episcopate, and this may have been his way of helping.[138] Cadwgan's grant may have been issued to coincide with Llywelyn ab Iorwerth's notification to his bailiffs of Maelienydd that he had taken the monks and their possessions under his protection.[139] J. E. Lloyd suggested that Llywelyn's notification was issued in the autumn of 1231, although this is doubted by *AWR*, pp. 394–5, no. 238, on the basis of the style used by Llywelyn, and a *terminus ante quem* of 1230 is suggested.[140]

The presence of a relic of St David at the priory may also have been a factor in Cadwgan's decision to grant an indulgence. As David Stephenson has pointed out, bishops of St Davids were concerned about the safety and well-being of Leominster Priory (which was not in their diocese but in that of Hereford) and postulates that the reason for their concern was the possession by the priory of an arm of

---

[134]　And see the section of the 'Diplomatic Analysis of the *Acta*' entitled 'Intitulatio'.

[135]　As Cadwgan refers to an arm of St David, it is worth noting that Canon 62 was concerned with, *inter alia*, the use of relics. The wording suggested by Canon 62 (*Conciliorum Oecumenicarum Decreta*, pp. 263–4) was later incorporated into Pope Gregory IX's decretal collection: *Liber Extra*, V, 38. 14 (cols. 888–9).

[136]　See *St Davids Episcopal Acta*, pp. 103–4, no. 82.

[137]　Bishop Iorwerth's obit: *Fasti Welsh Cathedrals*, p. 47.

[138]　For a discussion of the attacks on the lands, possessions, and monks of Leominster Priory during the time of Llywelyn ab Iorwerth, see *AWR*, pp. 394–5, no. 238; Lloyd, *History of Wales*, ii, p. 676. See also *St Davids Episcopal Acta*, p. 103, no. 81; *EEA*, *VII, Hereford, 1079–1234*, nos. 269 and 349.

[139]　Notification pd in *AWR*, pp. 394–5, no. 238.

[140]　Lloyd, *History of Wales*, ii, p. 676, n. 117. Cf. *AWR*, pp. 394–5, no. 238, which suggests a date range of 'probably 1215 x 1230; possibly 1218 x 1230'.

St David.[141] Cadwgan is called Cadwgan of Llandyfái in *Brut y Tywysogyon*.[142] Llandyfái (or Lamphey), near Pembroke, was one of the episcopal estates of St Davids.[143] Furthermore, he had been abbot of the Cistercian house of Whitland and before that a monk (and possibly abbot) at Strata Florida, both in the diocese of St Davids.[144]

*27. Reading Abbey

Grant of indulgence for 20 days, for those going to Reading Abbey, on the feasts of both St Philip (1 May) and of St James the Great (25 July).

[21 June 1215 x 1235/1 March 1236]

Mention in BL MS Harley 1708 (Chartulary of Reading Abbey) which contains a list of archiepiscopal and episcopal grants of indulgences in favour of Reading Abbey.[145] Under the heading of '*In festo utriusque apostoli communiter*', the list records '*Caducan[us] Bangorensis*' next to '*xx. d.*'.[146]

Calendared in *Reading Abbey Cartularies*, i, p. 176.

*28. Reading Abbey

Grant of indulgence for 20 days, for those going to Reading Abbey, at any time of the year.

[21 June 1215 x 1235/1 March 1236]

Mention in BL MS Harley 1708 (Chartulary of Reading Abbey) which contains a list of archiepiscopal and episcopal grants of indulgences in favour of Reading Abbey.[147] Under the heading '*Per totum annum*', the list records '*Caducan[us] bangor[ensis]*' next to '*xx. d.*'.[148]

Calendared in *Reading Abbey Cartularies*, i, p. 178.[149]

It appears that '*Per totum annum*' meant at other feasts and anniversaries throughout the year, rather than the whole year.[150]

*29. Strata Florida Abbey

Grant, with consent of his chapter, of the church of Llangurig in Arwystli, which was void due to the resignation of Goronwy, a perpetual vicar being appointed.

[21 June 1215 x 1235/1 March 1236]

---

141 Stephenson, 'St David's arm at Leominster', 209–12.
142 'Chadwgawn Landifei': *Brut, Hergest*, pp. 204–5.
143 *Episc. Acts Welsh Dioceses*, ii, p. 554. *Fasti Welsh Cathedrals*, p. 3, n. 8.
144 See the section of the Introduction entitled 'Cadwgan of Llandyfái'.
145 Compiled *c.*1258 x 1259: *Reading Abbey Cartularies*, i, pp. 174–9.
146 'Chartulary of Reading Abbey' BL Harley MS 1708, fo. 186v.
147 Compiled *c.*1258 x 1259: *Reading Abbey Cartularies*, i, pp. 174–9.
148 'Chartulary of Reading Abbey' BL Harley MS 1708, fo. 187r.
149 Also calendared in *Episc. Acts Welsh Dioceses Unpublished*, B155.
150 *Reading Abbey Cartularies*, i, p. 174, n. 4.

Mention only in the Papal Register of Boniface VIII, Regesta 47, Kalends of March, 1295, at the Lateran (fo. 36d.).

English summary in *Cal. Pap. Reg.*, i, pp. 558–9: 'Confirmation to the Cistercian abbot and convent of St. Mary's, Stratflour, in the diocese of St. Davids, of the grant made to them by C[aducan], sometime bishop of Bangor, with consent of his chapter, of the church of Langyric, in Arvestly, then void by the resignation of Goronue, a perpetual vicar being appointed'.

Cadwgan had been a monk, and possibly abbot, at the Cistercian house of Strata Florida.[151]

Arwystli was a rural deanery of the diocese of Bangor.[152]

The church of Llangurig, in the deanery of Arwystli, was recorded as belonging to the Cistercian Order in the 'Valuation of Norwich', 1254, and as being in the patronage of Strata Florida in the *Taxatio Ecclesiastica* of 1291.[153]

30. St Ethelbert's Alms-House, Hereford

Sealed letters patent granting an indulgence. To all the sons of the holy mother church to whom the present letters shall have come, Cadwgan, by divine permission, bishop of Bangor, greetings in the Lord. Since among works of charity those meritorious things that are granted towards the sustenance of the poor of Christ, by the pious largesse of the faithful, are greatly considered, we have directed you all to be reminded and exhorted in the Lord that you should mercifully bequeath something of the goods granted to you by God with a view to the construction of an alms-house by the dean and chapter of Hereford, situated near to the cemetery of the blessed Ethelbert of Hereford, and for the sustenance of the poor who will be restored in that same house each day. Moreover, trusting in the mercy of God and in the merits of the blessed virgin Mary and all the saints, we relax 15 days of enjoined penance, to all those of our diocese, and also to others whose diocesan bishops shall have ratified this relaxation of ours, who granting their alms to the aforesaid alms-house, have confessed and are truly penitent. Valediction.

[*c*.1225 x 1235/1 March 1236]

A = Hereford Cathedral Archive 1514. 150 x 83/58 mm.[154] Two strips of parchment extend from the lower left-hand side of the document, namely a wrapping-tie below the tongue, and the tongue itself, to which is attached a green-coloured, pointed-oval-shaped, wax seal (with the tongue passing through the middle and reappearing at the bottom of seal). The seal is 41 mm wide at widest point, and 66 mm in height. The obverse side is slightly fractured at the top, the top right-hand side, and also at the base. In relief, on the obverse side, is the figure of a standing, robed bishop, holding, in his left hand, a crosier/pastoral staff (which reaches his eye level in height, and is turned inwards). His right hand is raised, and seems to be rolled up, perhaps with a finger pointing skywards. The remain-

---

[151] See the section of the Introduction entitled 'Cadwgan of Llandyfái'.

[152] See the section of the Introduction entitled 'Gwynedd Uwch Conwy, Dyffryn Clwyd and Arwystli'.

[153] 'Ecclesia de Lankirik que est monachorum Cisterciensis ordinis': *Valuation of Norwich*, p. 191. 'Beneficia abb(at)is de Strata Florida Cycestr' ordinis': *Taxatio Ecclesiastica*, p. 291; https://www.dhi.ac.uk/taxatio/benkey?benkey=BN.ME.AW.01, accessed 20 May 2024.

[154] Image at Plate X.

ing legend around the rim of the seal reads '[I?]: CADVCAN[I? _?]PISCOPI BANGOREN[ ]'.[155] There are fingerprints preserved on the reverse of the wax.

Calendared in *Episc. Acts Welsh Dioceses Unpublished*, B153.

Transcribed from A.

Universis sancte matris ecclesie filiis ad quos presentes littere pervenerint, C. divina permissione Bagoren(sis) episcopus, salutem in domino. Quoniam inter opera caritatis ea valde meritoria reputantur que ad sustentationem pauperum Cristi pia conferuntur largitione fidelium universitatem vestram monendam duximus et hortandam in domino quatinus ad constructionem domus elemosinarie per decanum et capitulum H(er)eford(ensis) iuxta cimiterium beati Ethelb(er)ti H(er)eford(ensis) site et ad sustentationem pauperum in eadem domo reficiendorum singulis diebus de bonis vobis a deo collatis aliquid misericorditer erogetis. Nos autem de dei misericordia et beate virginis Marie et omnium sanctorum meritis confidentes omnibus de nostra diocesi aliis etiam quorum diocesani hanc nostram relaxationem ratam habuerint predicte domui elemosinarie elemosinas suas conferentibus confessis et vere penitentibus xv dies de iniuncta sibi penitencia relaxamus. In cuius rei testimonium hiis litteris patentibus sigullum nostrum apponi fecimus. Valeat universitas vestra semper in domino.

The *terminus a quo* of *c.*1225 is provided by the foundation date of the institution by one of the canons of Hereford, Elias de Bristol, who placed the same under the control of the dean and chapter.[156]

Cadwgan's indulgence was one of a number of indulgences (given by bishops of Welsh as well as English sees, and indeed by the archbishop of Canterbury) which were intended to assist the dean and chapter of Hereford in their charitable endeavours in respect of St Ethelbert's Alms-House. Interestingly, the indulgences fall into two groups: firstly, those based on the arenga prescribed by Canon 62 of the Fourth Lateran Council which was, in the case of St Ethelbert's, propagated by Archbishop Stephen Langton in August 1226,[157] and followed by the bishops of Coventry, Ely, Hereford, Salisbury, and Llandaff;[158] and a second group, into which Cadwgan's letter falls. In fact, the wording of his letter, not just its arenga, is, *mutatis mutandis*, identical to a grant in favour of St Ethelbert's made, *c.*1225 x 29 January 1229, by Iorwerth of St Davids.[159] Furthermore, save for the *inscriptio* (*Universis sancte matris ecclesie filiis* as opposed to *Omnibus Cristi fidelibus*) and the fact that Cadwgan has a sealing clause and a valediction, it is strikingly similar to the grants made on 18 October 1226 at Westminster, by Bishop Walter Mauclerk of Carlisle, and the bishop of London, Eustace de Fauconberg, both '*Datum per manum*

---

[155] Image at Plate I. Recorded in *Welsh Episcopal Seals*, 110.
[156] Barrow, 'The Canons and Citizens of Hereford', 1 and 13. Also, *Hereford Cathedral Charters and Records*, pp. 57–9; and Whitehead, 'St Ethelbert's Hospital, Hereford', p. 599.
[157] See *Acta Stephani Langton*, p. 109, no. 90; Cheney, *English Bishops' Chanceries*, pp. 76–7.
[158] *EEA, XLIII, Coventry and Lichfield, 1215–1256*, pp. 124–5, no. 118; *EEA, XLII, Ely, 1198–1256*, pp. 198–9, no. 222; *EEA, VII, Hereford, 1079–1234*, pp. 275–6, no. 344; *EEA, XXXVI, Salisbury, 1229–1262*, pp. 66–7, no. 50; *Llandaff Episcopal Acta*, pp. 65–6, no. 72.
[159] Hereford Cathedral Archive 1517; *St Davids Episcopal Acta*, p. 102, no. 80.

nostram'.[160] At the Old Temple, on the same day, Bishop Jocelin of Bath and Wells granted his indulgence which, whilst not identical to those of Carlisle and London, is similar enough to those to be considered as part of the same group.[161] The only indulgence that falls into neither group is that of the representative of the bishop of Lincoln, Hugh of Wells, also given at the Old Temple on 18 October 1226, which happens to have been the least generous.[162] The number of days relaxation of enjoined penance granted were: Bangor (15), Bath and Wells (13), Canterbury (13), Carlisle (13), Coventry (15), Ely (15), Hereford (20), Lincoln (10), Llandaff (30), London (13), Salisbury (15), St Davids (15).[163] The grants of Cadwgan and Iorwerth are not in the same hand, but as the wording is identical (and in turn very similar to those for Carlisle and London) this perhaps suggests a precedent/pro forma of Hereford provenance was utilised; one, which if it existed, was available at Westminster on 18 October 1226. If there was a Hereford pro forma at the Old Temple, on the same day, it was slightly different, and, in any event, one which, for whatever reason, was not followed by the representative of the bishop of Lincoln. An interesting question arises as to the two Old Temple grants, as they both refer to a 'hospital' whilst all the other indulgences refer to an alms-house/house for the poor. Could it be that the Hereford canons, if they were present at both Westminster and the Old Temple on the same day in October 1226, had different ideas as to the true nature of the foundation?

Bagor for Bangor is also found in another of Cadwgan's *acta* (**26**).[164]

*31. Pope Honorius III

Petition by Cadwgan, and the bishops of St Davids and St Asaph, requesting that Dafydd ap Llywelyn ab Iorwerth be taken under the pope's protection. The three bishops informed the pope that the magnates of Wales had sworn fealty to Dafydd.

[*c*.March x -29 April 1226]

Mention only in the pope's reply dated at the Lateran, 29 April 1226 (Archivio Segreto Vaticano, Reg. Vat. 13., fo. 122v. no. ccliii).

Transcription of Archivio Segreto Vaticano, Reg. Vat. 13., fo. 122v. no. ccliii:

In margin: .. *Menevensi*, .. *Bangorensi*, *et* .. *de sancto Asaph episcopis ccliii*

Ut sicut dilectus filius nobilis vir Leuwelin(us) princeps Norwalie sua nobis assertione monstravit ipse de mandato karissimi in Cristo filii nostri Hen(rici) illustris regis Anglo-rum a magnatibus Walie David primogenito suo fidelitatis prestari fecerit iuramenta, nos eundem D. quem in alumpnum quasi ecclesie Romane a parentibus nobis oblatum sub speciali apostolice sedis protectione suscepimus in suo iure favorabiliter fovere volentes

---

[160]   *EEA, XXX, Carlisle, 1133–1292*, pp. 69–70, no. 85, and *EEA, XXVI, London, 1189–1228*, p. 188, no. 220.

[161]   See *EEA, XLV, Bath and Wells, 1206–1247*, pp. 81–2, no. 74.

[162]   *Acta of Hugh of Wells, Bishop of Lincoln*, pp. 122–3, no. 257.

[163]   An indulgence was granted by Iorwerth's successor as bishop of St Davids, Anselm, most probably in the spring of 1231. It was also for 15 days, but was much briefer than Iorwerth's and Cadwgan's, or indeed any of the other St Ethelbert's indulgences: *St Davids Episcopal Acta*, pp. 119–20, no. 103.

[164]   See the section of the 'Diplomatic Analysis of the *Acta*' entitled 'Intitulatio'.

fraternitati vestri per apostolicam sedem mandamus quatenus eidem D. super hoc favorem benivolum impendentes ut prestita sibi iuramenta inviolabiliter observentur adhibeatis consilium et auxilium oportunum ita quod regio illa obtata quiete letetur et vos exinde apud deum et homines mereamini commendari. Datum ut supra.

Calendared in *Regesta Honorii Papae III*, ii, p. 418, no. 5907: '<*(Gervasio) Mene- vensi, (Martini) Bangorensi, et (Abrahamo) de sancto Asaph episcopis.*> *Cum Leuwelinus princeps Norwaliae de mandato Hen(rici) regis Anglorum a magnatibus Waliae David primogenito suo fidelitatis praestari fecerit iuramenta, mandat ut eidem David huiusmodo iuramenta observari faciant. Dat. ut supra (Laternai III. Kal. Maii anno decimo)*'.[165]

In 1222, Honorius III had, in response to a petition from Llywelyn ab Iorw- erth, confirmed Dafydd's position as Llywelyn's designated heir (instead of Llywelyn's older, but illegitimate son, Gruffudd).[166]

In the spring of 1226, Cadwgan together with Bishop Iorwerth of St Davids, and Bishop Abraham of St Asaph, informed the pope that the magnates of Wales had sworn fealty to Dafydd, and requested that he be taken under the pope's protection.[167] Llywelyn ab Iorwerth, prince of north Wales, having by the command of King Henry III caused an oath of fealty to be taken by the magnates of Wales to his *primogenitus* Dafydd, Honorius III issued a mandate to the three bishops – they were to give counsel and help so that the oaths so taken might be inviolably observed.[168] The pope had taken Dafydd under his protection as one who had been given to him by his parents as if he were his ward or foster-son (*alumpnus*).[169]

On the same day, Honorius III issued a dispensation (Archivio Segreto Vati- cano, Reg. Vat. 13., fo. 122v. no. cclii) to Joan, the wife of Llywelyn, prince of north Wales, daughter of King John, declaring her legitimate, but without prejudice to the king or the realm of England.[170] The pope did not want Joan's defect of birth to detract from the honour of her husband and her son (Dafydd), and was all the more willing to grant her petition on account of Llywelyn's faith and devotion to the Roman Church.[171]

*32. King Henry III

Request, not necessarily in writing, seeking the king's help in respect of a ship which the bishop of Bangor had caused to be laden with corn in Ireland for the sustenance of the poor in Wales.

[shortly before 4 May 1234]

---

[165] 'Reg. Vat. lib. 10. Epist. 253. fol. 122; MSS. Vall. I. 53: Musaeum Britann. add. MSS. 15352. – <Cum Sicut Dilectus.>' and *Cal. Pap. Reg.*, i, p. 109. Pryce, 'Negotiating Anglo-Welsh Relations', pp. 19 and 22, and ns. 47 and 76.

[166] *AWR*, pp. 414–6, no. 253, and pp. 446–7.

[167] Pryce, 'Negotiating Anglo-Welsh Relations', pp. 19 and 22. Bishops Iorwerth and Abraham: *Fasti Welsh Cathedrals*, pp. 34 and 47.

[168] *Cal. Pap. Reg.*, i, p. 109.

[169] Pryce, 'Negotiating Anglo-Welsh Relations', pp. 19 and 22, and ns. 47 and 76.

[170] *Regesta Honorii Papae III*, ii, pp. 417–18, no. 5906. *Cal. Pap. Reg.*, i, p. 109. *AWR*, p. 446, no. 279.

[171] *AWR*, p. 446, no. 279.

Mention only, in a royal mandate issued on 4 May 1234, whilst Henry III was at Oxford: TNA C 54/45 (Close Rolls, 18 Henry III), m. 24.[172]

CCR, 1231–1234, p. 417:

'*Pro Bagornensi episcopo – Mandatum est Mauricio filio Geroldi, justiciario Hybernie, quod navem quandam quam venerabilis pater Bagornensis episcopus carcari fecit blado in partibus Hibernie ad pauperum sustentationem in partibus suis, libere et sine inpedimento abire permittat ad partes suas Wallie. Teste rege apud Oxoniam, iiij. die Maii. Per ipsum regem*'.[173]

The mandate, which was witnessed by the king, ordered Maurice Fitzgerald the justiciar of Ireland to permit to pass freely and without impediment, a certain ship which the bishop of Bangor had caused to be laden with corn in Ireland for the sustenance of the poor in Wales.[174] The wording of the mandate suggests that Cadwgan had requested the king's help either because the ship was detained in an Irish port, or the bishop feared that it would be. It was not unusual for the English crown to place an embargo on shipping bound for Wales in times of conflict.[175] Llywelyn ab Iorwerth had in October 1233 joined the baronial campaign led by Richard Marshal, earl of Pembroke, against the influence of Peter des Roches, bishop of Winchester, and his nephew Peter de Rivallis at the court of Henry III.[176] The Marshal had begun attacking lands in royal custody in the March of south Wales in the summer of 1233, and the conflict continued in the south of Wales and along the border with England until February 1234.[177] A truce, largely brought about by Edmund Rich (Edmund of Abingdon), the archbishop-elect of Canterbury, was agreed on 6 March 1234 between the king on one side, and Llywelyn and the earl on the other, the truce being ratified on 9 April.[178] Despite the Marshal dying on 16 April, a meeting to determine arbitrators to supervise the truce scheduled for 2 May seems to have taken place with the Welsh.[179] As such, if Cadwgan's request was made shortly before the royal mandate of 4 May, perhaps he was reasonably confident that the king would give the order he did.

*33. Pope Gregory IX

Request, not necessarily in writing, to be allowed to resign his bishopric. Alternatively, a written (or possibly a verbal) resignation which was accepted by the pope.

[c.1235 x -1 March 1236]

---

172 *CCR, 1231–1234*, p. 417.
173 See also *Calendar of Documents Relating to Ireland*, p. 313.
174 *CCR, 1231–1234*, p. 417; *Calendar of Documents Relating to Ireland*, p. 313. Maurice Fitzgerald was justiciar of Ireland from 1232–1245: Smith, 'Fitzgerald, Maurice (c.1194–1257)', *ODNB*.
175 Gruffydd, *Maritime Wales*, pp. 12–13. See also the notes to *Actum* **63**.
176 *AWR*, p. 438.
177 *ibid.*; Lloyd, *History of Wales*, ii, pp. 678–81.
178 *AWR*, pp. 437–9, no. 269; Vincent, *Peter des Roches*, p. 435.
179 Vincent, *Peter des Roches*, p. 442 and n. 56; *AWR*, p. 439.

On the Kalends of March 1236, at Viterbo, the pope issued a mandate (recorded in Archivio Segreto Vaticano, Reg. Vat. 13., fo. 115. no. ccccvi) to the chapter of Bangor, the see being void by resignation, to elect a bishop, applying the goods of the recent bishop, except books and clothes, to the payment of the debts of the church: *Cal. Pap. Reg.*, i, p. 151.

Transcription of Archivio Segreto Vaticano, Reg. Vat. 13., fo. 115. no. ccccvi:

Rubric: capitulo Bangoren(sis)

Cum vestra fraternitas noscat episcopus quondam Bangor(ensis) in manibus nostris spontaneus cesserit oneri officii pastoralis nos cessionem admittentes ipsius mandamus quatenus provideatis vobis de persona idonea per electionem canonicam in pastorem bona dicti episcopi mobilia exceptis libris et indumentis eiusdem convertenda in solutionem debitorum quibus ecclesia vestra gravata dicitur retinentes. Datum Vit(er)bii Kal. Martii anno nono.

Why Cadwgan chose to resign is unclear. However, a bishop could only resign in certain circumstances, and, by the first years of the thirteenth century, only with papal permission.[180] The possible reasons for resigning one's benefice (detailed in a letter of Innocent III, published in the Decretals of Gregory IX shortly before Cadwgan's resignation) included physical debility, awareness that one had committed a crime, grave scandal, and canonical irregularity, as well as maliciousness of the people under one's care, and inadequate education.[181]

34. Abbey Dore

Sealed letters patent of Cadwgan, by the grace of God, bishop, formerly minister of Bangor, that by his free will he has made his profession to Stephen of Worcester, abbot of Dore, renouncing all possessions. Furthermore, he has given and conferred by his good will, for the salvation of his soul, to the monastery of Dore, all whatsoever he owned in books, horses, and everything, entirely, without any claim by anyone, in perpetuity.

[*c*.1236]

A = TNA E 326/11297. 148 x 35 mm.[182] Sealing arrangement: two strips of parchment extend from the lower left-hand side of the document, namely a wrapping tie below the tongue, and the tongue itself, to which is attached a green-coloured, pointed-oval-shaped, wax seal (with the tongue passing through the middle and reappearing at the bottom of seal). The seal is 25 mm wide at widest point, and 39 mm in height. In relief, on the obverse side, is the figure

---

[180] Pennington, *Pope and Bishops*, pp. 101–14, especially 106; Goering and Pryce, 'De Modo Confitendi', 6–7, and ns. 34, 35 and 36. One of Cadwgan's contemporaries, William de Ste Mère-Église, bishop of London, had in 1221 obtained permission from the pope to resign his bishopric. He took the habit of an Augustinian canon at the abbey of St Osyth, Essex, and died there in 1224: Cazel, 'Ste Mère-Église, William de (d. 1224)', *ODNB*. See also *Actum* **55** (Bishop Richard's supplication to Pope Clement IV). For other examples from the thirteenth century, see Moorman, *Church Life in England*, p. 183.

[181] *Liber Extra*, X, 1. 9. 10 (cols. 107–12 at 108). Goering and Pryce, 'De Modo Confitendi', 7, and n. 37. One of the reasons given by Richard, Cadwgan's successor as bishop of Bangor, in his supplication to Pope Clement IV, was the malice of the people (*Actum* **55**).

[182] Image at Plate XI (i).

of a standing, robed bishop, holding, in his left hand, a crosier/pastoral staff (which reaches his eye level in height, and is turned inwards). His right hand is raised, and seems to be rolled up, with a finger pointing skywards. Reading the legend around the rim of the seal is hampered by a light-brownish-wax covering which encloses the reverse of the seal, and partly loops around the obverse side. However, it is still possible to read 'S' SECRETUM CADUCANI EPI'.[183]

Calendared in BL Additional MS 4533, fo. 120v.

Calendared in *Episc. Acts Welsh Dioceses Unpublished*, B152.

Printed in *Formulare Anglicanum*, pp. 302–3.

Printed (with errors) in Willis, *Survey*, pp. 186–7, Appendix, no. iv.

Transcribed from A.

Notum sit omnibus sancte matris ecclesiae filiis presentibus et futuris quod ego, Caducan(us) dei gratia episcopus minister quondam Bangor(e)n(sis), in ultima et libera voluntate mea professionem meam feci domino Steph(an)o de Wigorn(ia) abbati de Dora omni propter deum renuncians proprietati. Dedi insuper et bona voluntate mea contuli pro salute anime mee dicto monasterio de Dora omnia quecunque habui sive in libris sive in equis sive omnino in aliqua alia re sine omni reclamatione aliquorum aliorum in perpetuum. In huius rei testimonium hiis litteris nostris patentibus sigillum nostrum apposuimus.

The seal is not recorded in *Welsh Episcopal Seals*.

For a discussion of why Cadwgan may have chosen to retire to the Cistercian abbey of Dore in Herefordshire see Talbot, 'Cadogan of Bangor', 19; Goering and Pryce, '*De Modo Confitendi*', 7–8, and ns. 41 and 42; and Lloyd, *History of Wales*, ii, p. 689.

35. Abbey Dore

Notification by Cadwgan, by the grace of God, bishop, formerly minister of the church of Bangor, concerning services rendered by his nephew. Valediction.

[*c.*1236]

A = TNA E 326/12582. Previously: PRO Ancient Deeds Court of Augmentation No. B 12582. 165 x 25 mm. Damaged.[184]

Calendared in *Episc. Acts Welsh Dioceses Unpublished*, B159.

Transcribed from A.

C. dei gratia episcopus minister quondam Bangor' ecclesie, universis Cristi fidelibus hiis litteris inspecturis vel audituris, salutem eternam in domino. Noverit universitas vestra quod nos Ca......[a] .....tu. ....a..ras[b] qui fuit servicus noster et nepos solvimus ei omnia que debebamus solvere pro servitio suo. N?...............
........[c] domus de Dora tenetur ei aliquid solvere in toto mundo. Quod si contrarium aliquid ....[d] ....beatis? et nullam ei fidem? adhibeatis. Valeat universitas*e* vestra.

---

[183] Image at Plate III (i).
[184] Image at Plate XI (ii).

*a*parchment damaged; parts of two or more letters visible, *A*. *b*parchment damaged. The length of the words is conjecture, *A*. *c*parchment damaged. Text largely obliterated, *A*. *d*parchment damaged, text obliterated, *A*. *e*the letter v is missing as the corner of the parchment has been torn away, *A*.

C. H. Talbot, writing in 1958, recorded that Cadwgan's nephew's name was 'Cadwaladr',[185] but the name has all but been erased from TNA E 326/12582 as seen in September 2017, with only the letters 'Ca …' being clearly visible.[186] Talbot also recorded that the notification was aimed at making provision for Cadwgan's nephew, 'to whom he owed something for his services'.[187] Talbot had access to the proofs of the projected, but unpublished, third volume of J. C. Davies' *Episcopal Acts and Cognate Documents relating to Welsh Dioceses 1066–1272*.[188] The latter stated that the abbey of Dore was bound to pay the nephew what Cadwgan owed him for his services, and also confirmed that Cadwgan's nephew was called Cadwaladr.[189] And so it does appear that the manuscript has become damaged, or more damaged, since Davies (and Talbot) saw it as not only is the nephew's name largely erased, the summary given by both scholars does not easily tally with the remaining legible parts of the document, which appear to state that Cadwgan had paid his nephew everything he owed him for his services, and was keen that the abbey of Dore should not extend to him any fidelity.

[185] Talbot, 'Cadogan of Bangor', 23, and n. 40.
[186] Image at Plate XI (ii).
[187] Talbot, 'Cadogan of Bangor', 23, and n. 40.
[188] Goering and Pryce, '*De Modo Confitendi*', 6, n. 26.
[189] *Episc. Acts Welsh Dioceses Unpublished*, B159, citing PRO, Ancient Deeds, Court of Augment., No. B 12582.

RICHARD/RHIRID

36. Profession of obedience

I Richard, elect of the church of Bangor, profess that I will maintain canonical obedience and subjection in all things to the holy church of Canterbury and to you, reverend father Edmund (of Abingdon/Edmund Rich), archbishop, and to your successors canonically substituted, and I, by (my) own hand, sign and confirm with the sign of the holy cross. + + +

[1237]

A = Canterbury Cathedral Archives, Dean and Chapter, CCA-DCc-ChAnt/C/115/93. 134 x 53 mm. Stitching holes at head and foot, discolouration.[190]

B = Canterbury Cathedral Archives, Dean and Chapter, Register A (The Prior's Register), fo. 250v. s. xiv med.

Calendared in *Episc. Acts Welsh Dioceses Unpublished*, B164.

Calendared in *Canterbury Professions*, p. 68, no. 173.

Transcribed from A.

Ego Ricardus, Bangornensis*ᵃ* ecclesie electus, profiteor sancte Cantuariensi ecclesie et tibi, reverende pater Edmunde archiepiscope, tuisque successoribus canonice substituendis, canonicam per omnia obedientiam me servaturum et subiectionem, et propria manu signo sancte crucis confirmo et subscribo. + + +

   *ᵃ*Bangoriensis *B.*

The final words ('*et subscribo.* + + +') are written in darker ink and seem to be in a different hand (see Plate VI – note the lack of a loop on either b of *subscribo* and compare with the b in *obedientiam and subiectionem*) suggesting that the final two words and the three crosses were autograph. Cf. Cadwgan's profession to Canterbury (**24**, Plate VI (v)) where the final words, which are, once again, in a different hand to the rest of the profession ('+ *et propria manu subscribo.* +') are enclosed by crosses.[191] See also the note to *Actum* **7** (Gwion's profession to Canterbury), and the section of the 'Diplomatic Analysis of the *Acta*' entitled 'Autograph'.

Canterbury Cathedral Archives, CCA-DCc-ChAnt/C/115/97, being the profession of Richard Wendene, bishop of Rochester, was originally drawn up for a can-

---

[190]   Image at Plate VI (vi). Canterbury Cathedral Archives' online record: https://archives.canterbury-cathedral.org/CalmView/Record.aspx?src=CalmView.Catalog&id=CCA-DCc-ChAnt%2fC%2f115%2f93&pos=3, accessed 24 February 2024.

[191]   Cf. also Robert's profession (**16**) which is bookended by crosses, perhaps suggesting that the whole profession was autograph.

didate from Bangor ('*Roffensis*' having replaced '*Bangornensis*' in the manuscript).[192] Richard Wendene was consecrated on 21 November 1238.[193] CCA-DCc-ChAnt/C/115/97 may have been intended for Richard of Bangor, or possibly Cadwgan.[194]

*37. Reading Abbey

Grant of 10 days indulgence in favour of those going to Reading Abbey throughout the year.
[1237 x 1258/9]

Mention only, in BL MS Harley 1708 (Chartulary of Reading Abbey) which contains a list of archiepiscopal and episcopal grants of indulgences in favour of Reading Abbey.[195] Under the heading '*Per totum annum*', the list records '*Ric[ardus] bangorens[is]*' next to '*x. d.*'[196]

Calendared in *Reading Abbey Cartularies*, i, p. 178.[197]

The other headings are on the feast of St Philip, on the feast of St James, and on the feast of each together, and B. R. Kemp stated that '*Per totum annum*' almost certainly meant other feasts and anniversaries throughout the year, rather than the whole year.[198]

*38. King Henry III

Richard laid a grave complaint before the king concerning the treacherous actions of Dafydd ap Llywelyn in incarcerating his half-brother Gruffudd ap Llywelyn.
1240 [Shortly after Michaelmas, 29 September]

Not necessarily in writing. Mention only, in Cambridge, Corpus Christi College, MS 16 (Matthew Paris, *Chronica Majora*, Part II), s. xiii med., and in Matthew Paris, *Flores Historiarum*, s. xiii med.[199]

Flores Historiarum, ii, p. 236:

'... *Ad quem locum venit Griffinus pacifice in spe pacis optinendae, sub ducatu Ricardi episcopi Bangorensis et aliorum quam plurium virorum venerabilium. At David Griffinum*

---

[192] *Canterbury Professions*, p. 69, and n. 2.
[193] *Fasti Monastic Cathedrals*, p. 76.
[194] It reads as follows: 'Ego Ricardus, Roffensis ecclesie electus, promitto sancte Cantuariensi ecclesie tibique, pater Edmunde, tuisque successoribus canonice substituendis subiectionem et canonicam obedientiam, et propria manu subscribe. + +'. The name Ricardus is preceded by 'frater' which has been cancelled: *Canterbury Professions*, p. 69, and n. 1. The original inclusion of 'frater' could mean it was intended for Cadwgan, or that Canterbury, for some reason, thought that Richard was a regular.
[195] Compiled *c.*1258 x 1259: *Reading Abbey Cartularies*, i, pp. 174–9.
[196] 'Chartulary of Reading Abbey' BL Harley MS 1708, fo. 187r.
[197] Also calendared in *Episc. Acts Welsh Dioceses Unpublished*, B206.
[198] *Reading Abbey Cartularies*, i, p. 174, n. 4.
[199] For an explanation and dating of the *Chronica* and *Flores*: Gransden, *Historical Writing in England*, pp. 357 and 367; Russell Smith, 'Further Manuscripts of Matthew Paris' *Flores Historiarum* and Continuations', 6–7.

in dolo captum custodiae carcerali impudenter mancipavit. Unde praedictus episcopus gravem coram rege Anglorum reposuit querimoniam, ipsum quoque David vincula anathematis innodavit'.

And *Chronica Majora*, iv, pp. 148–9:

'*… Griffinus filius Leolini in carcere fratris sui David tenebatur in arcta custodia vinculis, quem in dolo vocaverat ad pacificum concilium sub ducatu magistri Ricardi Bangorensis episcopi et quorundam aliorum nobilium Walensium, propter quod facinus episcopus ipse recessit a Wallia, ipso David excommunicato. Veniensque ad regem Angliae, super hoc scelere nequiter perpetrato gravem reposuit querimoniam, postulans instantissime, ut rex liberaret injuste a David nepote suo fratrem incarceratum …*'.

According to the *Brut y Tywysogyon* entry for 1239, Dafydd seized his brother Gruffudd breaking faith with him, and imprisoned him.[200] However, Matthew Paris, the monk and historian of St Albans, gave a slightly different account stating that this did not happen until after the death of their father, Llywelyn ab Iorwerth.[201] Llywelyn died on 11 April 1240, whereupon Paris tells us war ensued between the brothers until around Michaelmas 1240 when Dafydd lured Gruffudd to a peace council under the safe conduct of the bishop of Bangor and other great men.[202] Dafydd ordered Gruffudd to be taken, and despite the protests of the bishop and others, to be imprisoned.[203] Richard, incensed, excommunicated Dafydd and fled to England, where he begged Henry III to intervene.[204]

According to Matthew Paris, the bishop laid a grave complaint before the king concerning the treacherous actions of Dafydd; and reminding Henry that Dafydd was the king's nephew urged Henry to have Gruffudd set free lest so villainous a transgression reach the Roman curia to the dishonour of the king.[205] Henry, we are told, advised and ordered Dafydd to release Gruffudd so as to restore his good name and obtain absolution from the sentence of excommunication (which had been imposed by Richard), but Dafydd refused stating that were he to do so Wales would never enjoy peace and security.[206] Richard, according to the St Albans' historian, therefore, laid a second most-grave complaint before the king (see *Actum* **39**).[207]

Richard's complaints are not recorded in any official crown record, and it was quite possibly Richard, himself, who is known not only to have visited St

---

[200] Gruffudd was imprisoned at Cricieth with his son (Owain): *Brut, Hergest*, pp. 235–7; *Brut, Pen20Tr*, p. 105. See also, *Annales Cambriae E-text*, p. 17; 'Cronica de Wallia', 38.

[201] *Chronica Majora*, iv, p. 8, and pp. 47–8. Lloyd, *History of Wales*, ii, p. 694, n. 2.

[202] *Chronica Majora*, iv, p. 8, pp. 47–8, and p. 148. *Matthew Paris's English History*, i, p. 290. Williams, 'Succession', 404.

[203] *Chronica Majora*, iv, p. 8, pp. 47–8, and p. 148. Lloyd, *History of Wales*, ii, p. 694, n. 2.

[204] *Chronica Majora*, iv, pp. 148–9. Williams, 'Succession', 404.

[205] *Chronica Majora*, iv, pp. 148–9; *Flores Historiarum*, ii, p. 236; *Matthew Paris's English History*, i, p. 371.

[206] *Chronica Majora*, iv, pp. 148–9; *Flores Historiarum*, ii, p. 236; *Matthew Paris's English History*, i, p. 371. Williams, 'Succession', 404.

[207] *Flores Historiarum*, ii, p. 239.

Albans but resided there, who was the source of that information recorded in *Chronica Majora* and *Flores Historiarum*.[208]

*39. King Henry III

Richard laid a second most-grave complaint to the king, concerning the betrayal of Dafydd ap Llywelyn in incarcerating his half-brother Gruffudd ap Llywelyn.

[After Michaelmas (29 September) 1240 x August 1241, possibly before *c*.22 June 1241]

Not necessarily in writing. Mention only, in Matthew Paris, *Flores Historiarum*, s. xiii med.[209]

Flores Historiarum, ii, p. 239:

'... *Episcopus autem de Bangor regi super hac proditione, praedicta injuria, iterum querimoniam reponit gravissimam*'.

As mentioned above, Dafydd had seized Gruffudd and imprisoned him and his son at Cricieth (see note to *Actum* **38**).

As with *Actum* **38**, this second complaint is not recorded in any official crown record, and it was quite possibly Richard himself who was the source of the information recorded in *Flores Historiarum* (see the note to *Actum* **38**).

The date of Richard's second complaint to Henry was shortly after his first complaint to the king (**38**) – see note to *Actum* **38**. The *terminus ante quem* may possibly be provided by the date of a letter (22 June 1241) from Hugh de Northwold, bishop of Ely, and Richard Wendene, bishop of Rochester, to the bishops of Bangor, St Asaph, and St Davids, and the archdeacon of Llandaff, which transmitted a copy of Gregory IX's mandate to relax a sentence of suspension by the late archbishop of Canterbury against the prior and convent of Christ Church; the addressees were required to publish the relaxation throughout their respective dioceses.[210] Richard of Bangor was well known to Richard Wendene, and indeed had helped to dedicate Rochester cathedral on 5 November 1240.[211] As such the authors of the letter may have known that by 22 June 1241 Richard was able to publish the relaxation in the three portions of his diocese because he had returned to Wales, or at

---

[208] For a discussion of Richard's visits to, and stays at, St Albans between 1248 and 1257: Williams, 'Succession', 406. Huw Pryce has stated that as Matthew Paris composed the annals in the *Chronica Majora* for the period 1236–1250 between 1245 and early 1251, he could easily have drawn on information supplied by Richard: *AWR*, p. 469, referring to Lloyd, *History of Wales*, ii, p. 744; Vaughan, *Matthew Paris*, pp. 12, 15, 35, and 49–61; Williams, 'Succession', 403–8; and Smith, *Llywelyn*, p. 35, n. 118.

[209] For an explanation and dating of the *Flores*: Gransden, *Historical Writing in England*, pp. 357 and 367; Russell Smith, 'Further Manuscripts of Matthew Paris' *Flores Historiarum* and Continuations', 6–7.

[210] *EEA, XLII, Ely, 1198–1256*, no. 183; Canterbury Cathedral Archives, Sede Vacante Scrapbook, CCA-DCc/SVSB/2/198/1.

[211] *Flores Historiarum*, ii, p. 243.

least was planning to do so.[212] Certainly by *c*.8 x 29 August 1241 at the latest, Richard had returned to Wales, and on his return there had been some sort of reconciliation with Dafydd.[213]

40. St Paul's, London

Indulgence granted on St Lucy's Day (13 December) at St Paul's. Assured of the mercy of God, and the merits of the glorious virgin Mary, the blessed Paul, and all the saints, relaxation of 40 days' enjoined penance for all his parishioners, and all others whose diocesans shall have ratified his indulgence, who have confessed and are truly contrite, and who contribute alms to the St Paul's building fund.

St Paul's, London, St Lucy's Day, 13 December [1240]

A = The London Archives, St Paul's Cathedral MS 25124/1. 186 x 130 mm.[214] Badly damaged green-wax seal, which is vesical/pointed-oval in shape (approximately 33 mm wide and ? mm in height). Sealed on a parchment tag which has been passed through slits in the turn-up at the foot of the document (*sur double queue*). The obverse of the seal depicts a bishop in eucharistic vestments under a canopy, right hand raised in blessing, holding in his left hand a pastoral staff turned inwards. The image on the reverse, created by a subsidiary matrix, is of a figure holding up a large roundel with the Lamb of God facing right, the lamb's head turning back to look at the staff and banner. The human figure could be John the Baptist, but as the figure may be wearing ecclesiastical dress, it could represent Bishop Richard himself.[215] The legends are in Lombardic capitals, but only the word '[]IGILL[ ]' on the obverse is clearly decipherable.[216]

Printed in *Documents Illustrating the History of St Paul's Cathedral*, pp. 1–2, and calendared in Appendix A, 175. (Although incorrectly attributed to Robert of Shrewsbury).

Printed in Armstrong, 'A Misdated St Paul's Fabric Indulgence', 483–7.

Transcribed from A.

Omnibus Cristi fidelibus ad quos presens scriptum pervenerit, R. dei gracia Bangor(e)n(sis) episcopus, salutem in domino. Quoniam, ut ait apostolus, omnes stabimus ante tribunal Ihesu Cristi recepturi prout in corpore gessimus sive bonum fuerit sive malum, oportet nos diem messionis extreme misericordie [operibus]*a* prevenire ac eternorum intuitu seminare in terris quod reddente domino cum multiplicato fructu recolligere debeamus in celis firmam spem fiduciamque tenentes, quoniam qui parce seminat parce et metet et qui seminat in benedictionibus de benedictionibus et metet vitam eternam. Cum igitur inter opera caritatis non

[212] This can only be a supposition, however, because Richard could have instructed his administration to effect publication in the three portions of his diocese if he had not returned.

[213] *AWR*, pp. 465–6, no. 299; *LW*, pp. 153–4, no. 271.

[214] Image at Plate XII.

[215] Thank you to Dr Elizabeth New for her assistance in interpreting the impression created by the subsidiary matrix.

[216] Images at Plate II and Plate IV (ii). See also, Armstrong, 'A Misdated St Paul's Fabric Indulgence', 483–7.

inmerito debeat computari ecclesiarum fabricis pias elemosinarum largiciones misericorditer inpartiri, universitatem vestram rogamus attencius monentes et exortantes in domino quatinus ad fabricam ecclesie sancti Pauli London' de bonis vobis a deo collatis aliqua caritatis subsidia erogetis ut per hec et alia bona que domino inspirante feceritis eterna possitis gaudia promereri. Nos vero de dei misericordia, et gloriose virginis Marie, beati Pauli et omnium sanctorum, meritis confisi omnibus parochianis nostris ac aliis universis quorum diocesani hanc nostram ratam habuerint indulgenciam qui ad fabricam dicte ecclesie suas duxerint elemosinas conferendas, si de peccatis suis vere contriti fuerint et confessi, quadraginta dies de iniuncta sibi penitencia misericorditer relaxamus. Datum London' apud sanctum Paulu(m) die sancte Lucie virginis, pontificatus nostri anno quarto.

   *operibus is missing, see note below, *A*.

The text from '*Quoniam*' to '*vitam eternam*' inclusive replicates the first sentence of the wording suggested by Canon 62 of the Fourth Lateran Council, save that '*operibus*' has been omitted.[217]

The new St Paul's cathedral was not finished until 1327 but attracted many indulgences prior to that, particularly in the mid-thirteenth century.[218] Work had progressed sufficiently for the church to be dedicated on 13 January 1241.[219]

W. Sparrow Simpson identified the author of MS 25124/1, 'R', as Robert of Shrewsbury.[220] However, the identification with Robert is immediately suspect because, as noted, the indulgence employs the '*Quoniam, ut ait apostolus*' arenga suggested by Canon 62 of the Fourth Lateran Council of 1215, three years after Robert died.[221] In fact, L. Armstrong has recently argued that 'R' must stand for 'Richard', and that the fourth year *pontificatus nostri* is 1240.[222]

Furthermore, the document was written by a scribe responsible for three other precisely datable indulgences in the same collection, all of them awarded in London between 1237 and 1241.[223]

---

[217] *Conciliorum Oecumenicarum Decreta*, pp. 263–4. The wording suggested by Canon 62 was later incorporated into Pope Gregory IX's decretal collection: *Liber Extra*, V, 38. 14 (cols. 888–9). Both *Documents Illustrating the History of St Paul's Cathedral*, 1, and n. a, and Armstrong, 'A Misdated St Paul's Fabric Indulgence', 486, and n. 21, note the missing 'operibus'.

[218] Armstrong, 'A Misdated St Paul's Fabric Indulgence', 483, and n. 1 referring to Cragoe, 'Fabric, Tombs and Precincts', pp. 127–42.

[219] *ibid.*

[220] *Documents Illustrating the History of St Paul's Cathedral*, 1–2, and Appendix A, 175. Also: https://deeds.library.utoronto.ca/charters/01520001, accessed 17 February 2024.

[221] For the first use by English bishops of the wording suggested by Canon 62, see Cheney, *English Bishops' Chanceries*, pp. 76–7; *Acta Stephani Langton*, p. 109, no. 90. Also, see the section of the 'Diplomatic Analysis of the *Acta*' entitled 'Arenga'.

[222] Armstrong, 'A Misdated St Paul's Fabric Indulgence', 483–7.

[223] The first, 25124/10, by Christian, bishop of Emly in Ireland (1236 × 1237–1249), is dated 28 October 1237; the second, 25124/12, by Richard Wendene, bishop of Rochester (1238–1250), 25 January 1240; and the third, 25124/15, by Hugh Pattishall, bishop of Coventry and Lichfield (1240–1241), 9 November 1241: Armstrong, 'A Misdated St Paul's

St Lucy's Day is 13 December.[224]

This is the first time a bishop of Bangor dates an *actum* according to his pontifical year.[225]

Licence to elect a new bishop was granted to the canons of Bangor in June 1236, and in July that year royal assent was given to the election of Master Richard, archdeacon of Bangor, with a mandate to Edmund (of Abingdon/Edmund Rich), archbishop of Canterbury, to do his part therein.[226] Richard was consecrated the following year, and professed canonical obedience to Canterbury, Edmund of Abingdon, and his successors.[227]

As Armstrong points out, the date of Richard's consecration in 1237 is unknown, and if he was consecrated between 14 and 31 December 1237, the indulgence should be dated 13 December 1241.[228] However, Archbishop Edmund left England to travel to Rome the week before Christmas in 1237 (*'Hebdomada vero ante Natale …'*)[229] and so the latest date for Richard's consecration is *c.*17 December 1237. In other words, for the indulgence to have been granted on 13 December 1241, Richard's consecration would have to have taken place on one of just three, possibly four, days in 1237, namely the 14, 15, 16, or possibly 17 December. Given this the probability is that he was consecrated before 14 December 1237 – in fact this is supported by the wording of *Actum* **55** which suggests that he was consecrated earlier in the year, before 8 November 1237.[230] Furthermore, the lack of any reference in his grant to the dedication of the church of St Paul's which occurred in January 1241 (cf. Richard's second indulgence in favour of St Paul's, **41**), and the fact that Richard was in England in late September, October and November 1240 and could have stayed to visit St Paul's the following month, suggest that the correct date of this indulgence is 13 December 1240.[231]

The badly damaged green-wax seal is not recorded by D. H. Williams in *Welsh Episcopal Seals*. It is likely that this is Richard's main seal.[232] The image that remains on the obverse differs from that on the detached privy seal (Society of Antiquar-

Fabric Indulgence', 483–7. 'The scribe never identifies himself, but he might have been employed in the household of Roger Niger, bishop of London between 1229 and 1241, or by one of the other ecclesiastical bodies seated in London.': *ibid.*

224 Cheney, *Handbook of Dates*, p. 55.

225 See the section of the 'Diplomatic Analysis of the *Acta*' entitled 'Date'.

226 *CPR, 1232–1247*, pp. 149 and 152.

227 *Actum* **36**. *Canterbury Professions*, p. 68, no. 173. *Fasti Welsh Cathedrals*, p. 4.

228 Armstrong, 'A Misdated St Paul's Fabric Indulgence', n. 18.

229 *Chronica Majora*, iii, p. 470.

230 See notes to *Actum* **55**.

231 Richard in England in 1240: *Chronica Majora*, iv, p. 8, pp. 47–8, and pp. 148–9, *Flores Historiarum*, ii, p. 236, Williams, 'Succession', 404 (shortly after Michaelmas 1240) and *Flores Historiarum*, ii, p. 243 (at Rochester cathedral in November 1240). Richard may not have returned to Wales until August 1241, see the note to *Actum* **39** above.

232 A point made by Armstrong, 'A Misdated St Paul's Fabric Indulgence', 484, at n. 6.

ies, SA. C 7), and the white plaster cast impression (BL Seal LXXXII, 40), both discussed in the section entitled 'Seals' in the 'Diplomatic Analysis of the *Acta*'.

See the note to *Actum* **41** concerning the box catalogued as MS 25124 at The London Archives (formerly held at St Paul's itself, and then the Guildhall Library).

41. St Paul's, London

Indulgence. Trusting in the mercy of God, the merits of the glorious Mary, blessed mother of God, the Apostle Paul, Doctor of the Gentiles, and all the saints, relaxation of 30 days' enjoined penance for all those of Richard's diocese, and others, whose diocesans shall have ratified his indulgence, who have confessed and are truly contrite, who visit the cathedral on the feast of the dedication or on the anniversary of the same, or contribute pious alms from the goods they have been granted by God to the building fund of St Paul's.

[13 January 1241 x before 8 November 1267, possibly before 3 November 1246]

A = The London Archives, St Paul's Cathedral MS 25124/13. 147 x 74 mm.[233] A slit, in the turn-up at the foot of the document, is provided to allow a parchment tag to be passed through for sealing purposes (*sur double queue*), but the tag and seal are missing.

Calendared in *Documents Illustrating the History of St Paul's Cathedral*, Appendix A, 175.

Transcribed from A.

Omnibus Cristi fidelibus ad quos presens scriptum pervenerit, R. divina miseratione Bangor' ecclesie minister humilis, salutem eternam in domino. Cum inter cetera caritatis opera sacra sanctorum limina visitare in conspectu altissimi non immerito sit acceptum nos de dei misericordia, gloriose dei genitricis Marie, beati doctoris gentium apostoli Pauli et omnium sanctorum, meritis confidentes omnibus de nostra diocesi vel aliis quorum diocesani hanc nostram indulgenciam ratam habuerint qui ecclesiam beati Pauli London' in festo dedicationis, seu in eiusdem anniversario, orandi gratia adierint humiliter et devote sive ad fabricam euisdem ecclesie cum sit magna et magnos sumptus exigat pias elemosinas de bonis sibi a deo collatis pie duxerint conferendas si de peccatis suis, vere contriti fuerint et confessi, triginta dies de iniuncta sibi penitentia relaxamus.

St Paul's church was dedicated on 13 January 1241.[234]

Sparrow Simpson attributed 25123/13 to Richard.[235] L. Armstrong has recently commented that if 'the reference is to the dedication itself, the document should be dated to 1241, but there is no reason to exclude any later year of Richard's episcopate. By the same token, the absence of any indication of date might support an earlier attribution, perhaps to Rotoland or Robert of Shrewsbury'.[236]

---

[233] Image at Plate XIII.
[234] Armstrong, 'A Misdated St Paul's Fabric Indulgence', 483, and n. 1, referring to Cragoe, 'Fabric, Tombs and Precincts', pp. 127–42. Cf. Milman, *Annals of S. Paul's Cathedral*, p. 159.
[235] *Documents Illustrating the History of St Paul's Cathedral*, Appendix A, 175.
[236] Armstrong, 'A Misdated St Paul's Fabric Indulgence', n. 19.

I set out here why I think this is an *actum* of Richard's. It is clear that the same scribe was responsible for MS 25124/14, being Robert, the bishop of Salisbury's indulgence to St Paul's, as the handwriting is identical to MS 25124/13. Indeed the wording of the bishop of Salisbury's indulgence is, *mutatis mutandis*, identical to MS 25124/13, save that the former granted an indulgence of twenty days, not thirty days, and preferred '*divina permissione*' to '*divina miseratione*', and '*salutem in domino sempiternam*' to '*salutem eternam in domino*'.[237] Sparrow Simpson assigned MS 25124/14 to 'Robert Bingham', bishop of Salisbury, *c*.1240.[238] Robert de Bingham was bishop of Salisbury from 27 May 1229 to his death in early November (probably 3 November) 1246.[239] It seems unlikely that the scribe would have written an indulgence for Rotoland (sometime before *c*.1204) or for Robert of Shrewsbury (sometime before his death in 1212), and then written an indulgence in exactly the same hand, and in virtually the same terms for Robert de Bingham sometime on or after 13 January 1241. The only other Robert who was a bishop of Salisbury in the thirteenth century was Robert de Wickhampton, who was consecrated in May 1274, seven years or so after Richard's death.[240] On the balance of the evidence, MS 25124/13 appears to be an *actum* of Richard, given on or after 13 January 1241, and possibly before 3 November 1246.

Robert de Bingham's *actum*, MS 25124/14, is not recorded in *EEA, XXXVI, Salisbury, 1229–1262*, and it seems that most of the seventy-seven *acta*, individually parcelled, and contained in the long red box catalogued as MS 25124 at The London Archives (formerly held at St Paul's itself, and then the Guildhall Library) have been overlooked by the *English Episcopal Acta* series, as well as the editions of the *Llandaff Episcopal Acta*, and *St Davids Episcopal Acta*. There is one thirteenth-century *actum* for a bishop of St Davids, MS 25124/6 (Anselm, bearing the date 1233), and two for bishops of Llandaff, namely MS 25124/32 (John de la Warre, bearing the date 1254), and MS 25124/43 (William of Radnor, bearing the date 1264).[241]

The fragment of the seal which survives attached to MS 25124/74 was in 1869 'enclosed in a piece of vellum, folded and sewn' on which was listed the name of

---

[237] Transcription of The London Archives, St Paul's Cathedral MS 25124/14: Omnibus Cristi fidelibus ad quos presens scriptum pervenerit, Rob(er)tus, divina permissione Sa(rum) ecclesie minister humilis, salutem in domino sempiternam. Cum inter cetera caritatis opera sacra sanctorum limina visitare in conspectu altissimi non immerito sit acceptum nos de dei misericordia gloriose dei genitricis Marie beati doctoris gentium apostoli Pauli et omnium sanctorum, meritis confidentes omnibus de nostra diocesi vel aliis quorum diocesani hanc nostram indulgenciam ratam habuerint qui ecclesiam beati Pauli London' in festo dedicationis seu in eiusdem anniversario orandi gratia adierint humiliter et devote sive ad fabricam euisdem ecclesie cum sit magna et magnos sumptus exigat pias elemosinas de bonis sibi a deo collatis pie duxerint conferendas si de peccatis suis vere contriti fuerint et confessi viginti dies de iniuncta sibi penitentia relaxamus.

[238] *Documents Illustrating the History of St Paul's Cathedral*, Appendix A, 175.

[239] Kemp, 'Bingham, Robert (*d*. 1246)', *ODNB. Fasti Salisbury*, p. 4.

[240] *Fasti Salisbury*, p. 5.

[241] The last four indulgences in box MS 25124 are those granted by Robert Braybrooke, bishop of London, all in 1387.

the archbishopric of Canterbury, followed by the names of seven bishoprics, each accompanied by a number of *dies*.[242] The last two in the list were Welsh bishoprics:

Landauen' – xl dies.

Bangoren' – xl dies.[243]

Whether the last entry was a record of *Actum* **40** above, or another Bangor indulgence is not clear.

*42. King Henry III

Charter given to the king, along with a charter from the bishop of St Asaph, in which the bishops agreed to carry out all sentences of excommunication or interdict as commanded by the archbishop of Canterbury, and the bishops of London, Hereford, and Coventry, pursuant to the peace agreement made at Gwerneigron, 29 August 1241, between Dafydd ap Llywelyn and Henry III.

Gwerneigron, 29 August 1241

Mention only, in clause [xvi] of a letter patent, dated 29 August 1241, issued by Dafydd ap Llywelyn. Dafydd stated that he had procured charters from the bishops of Bangor and St Asaph to the king.

'*[xvi] De quibus omnibus et singulis supposui me et heredes meos iurisdictioni archiepiscopi Cant(uariensis) et episcoporum Lond', Hereford' et Coventr' qui pro tempore preerunt, quod omnes vel unus eorum quem dominus rex ad hec elegerit possit nos excommunicare et terram nostram interdicere si aliquid contra predictam attemptaverimus. Et procuravi quod episcopi de Bangor et de Sancto Asaph cartas suas domino regi fecerunt per quas concesserunt quod omnes sentencias tam excommunicationis quam interdicti a predictis archiepiscopo, episcopis vel aliquo eorum ferendas ad mandatum eorum exequentur'.*[244]

Dafydd's letter was copied on the patent roll, TNA C 66/49, Patent Rolls, 25 Henry III, m. 2d (*CPR, 1232–1247*, p. 264) and is printed in *AWR*, pp. 466–70, no. 300, where it is denoted as 'B'. The text preserved in the MS denoted as 'C' (Cambridge, Corpus Christi College, MS 16, fos. 172v–173r. s. xiii med) in *AWR, ibid.*, is the autograph manuscript of Matthew Paris' *Chronica Majora*, and is very closely related to that on the patent roll 'B', save that the St Albans monk and historian copied two further clauses, namely, [xv] and [xvi] omitted in 'B'.[245] Huw Pryce suggests, no doubt correctly, that Paris' source for his text was probably Richard.[246]

---

[242] Milman, *Annals of S. Paul's Cathedral*, Appendix C, p. 521, and *Documents Illustrating the History of St Paul's Cathedral*, Appendix A, 177.

[243] *ibid.*

[244] *AWR*, pp. 466–70, no. 300.

[245] Cambridge, Corpus Christi College, MS 16, contains the text of Matthew Paris' *Chronica Majora* to 1253: Vaughan, *Matthew Paris*, p. 21.

[246] The bishop of Bangor is known not only to have visited St Albans but to have stayed there. For a discussion of Richard's visits to, and stays at, St Albans between 1248 and 1257: Williams, 'Succession', 406. Huw Pryce has stated that as Matthew Paris composed the annals in the *Chronica Majora* for the period 1236–1250 between 1245 and early 1251, he could easily have drawn on information supplied by Richard for his account of events in 1241:

The bishop of St Asaph was Hwyel II.[247] The archbishop of Canterbury was Boniface of Savoy.[248] The bishops of Coventry (and Lichfield), Hereford and London were Hugh of Pattishall, Peter d'Aigueblanche and Roger Niger respectively.[249]

A royal campaign had been launched earlier in the summer of 1241, forcing Dafydd to surrender at Gwerneigron on the banks of the river Elwy near St Asaph.[250]

On 30 August 1241, in the king's tent at Rhuddlan, a revised text of the Gwerneigron agreement was ratified by Henry.[251] On 31 August, also at Rhuddlan, Dafydd issued a notification that he, with the will and consent of the bishops of Bangor (Richard) and St Asaph (Hywell II), and his counsellors, had placed himself under the jurisdiction of the archbishop of Canterbury and the bishops of London, Ely, Hereford, and Coventry and Lichfield, in order that the agreements made at Gwerneigron on 29 August, and renewed at Rhuddlan the following day, might be observed fully for ever by him and his heirs.[252] Richard and Hywel II, at Dafydd's request, promised the king and his heirs on behalf of them and their successors that they would publish, observe and make their subjects observe any sentences issued. The notification of 31 August was sealed by Dafydd, Richard, and Hywel II.[253] On the same day, and once again at Rhuddlan, a further notification was issued by Dafydd that he had undertaken that he, and his heirs, would serve Henry III and his heirs faithfully, and would never be against them. If he, or his heirs, should fail in this, their lands would be forfeit. This notification was also sealed by Dafydd, and, at his request, by the bishops of Bangor and St Asaph.[254]

Both *Brut y Tywysogyon* and Matthew Paris state that the king then summoned Dafydd to a council in London.[255] On *c.*24 October, at Westminster, the peace agreement reached (or rather, imposed on Dafydd) at Rhuddlan, was renewed, with the addition of, *inter alia*, the grant of the castle and lands of Deganwy to the king and his heirs, to cover the cost of the royal expedition to Rhuddlan.[256] Dafydd, with the will and consent of the bishops of St Asaph and Bangor and his counsellors, once again placed himself, together with all his land, under the jurisdiction of the archbishop of Canterbury

---

AWR, p. 469, referring to Lloyd, *History of Wales*, ii, p. 744; Vaughan, *Matthew Paris*, pp. 12, 15, 35, and 49–61; Williams, 'Succession', 403–8; and Smith, *Llywelyn*, p. 35, n. 118.

[247]   *Fasti Welsh Cathedrals*, p. 35.

[248]   *Fasti Monastic Cathedrals*, p. 6.

[249]   Franklin, 'Pattishall [Pateshull], Hugh of (*d.* 1241)', *ODNB*; *Fasti Hereford*, p. 6; *Fasti London*, p. 3.

[250]   Smith, 'Dafydd ap Llywelyn (*c.*1215–1246)', *ODNB*; *AWR*, p. 29.

[251]   *AWR*, pp. 470–2, no. 301, and p. 469.

[252]   The bishop of Ely was Hugh of Northwold: *Fasti Monastic Cathedrals*, p. 46.

[253]   *AWR*, pp. 472–3, no. 302; *LW*, pp. 12–13, no. 6; *CPR, 1232–1247*, p. 264.

[254]   *AWR*, pp. 473–4, no. 303; *LW*, p. 22, no. 22; *CPR, 1232–1247*, p. 264.

[255]   *Brut, Pen20Tr*, pp. 105–6; *Brut, Hergest*, pp. 236–7; *Chronica Majora*, iv. p. 150. Also, *AC*, pp. 83–4. *AWR*, p. 477.

[256]   *AWR*, pp. 474–7, no. 304; *LW*, pp. 10–12, no. 5.

and the bishops of London, Ely, Hereford, and Coventry and Lichfield, with
full power to the aforesaid prelates to enforce, through sentences of excommunication and interdict, the observance of the promises, concessions, and
agreements contained in the document and certain other documents.[257]
Neither Richard nor Hywell II sealed this latest agreement; although, protection without term had been granted at Westminster for Richard a few
days earlier, on 20 October.[258] From the wording of the agreement, and the
grant of protection, it is probable that Richard was present. On 24 October,
again at Westminster, Dafydd issued a notification that should he die without
a legitimate heir, he granted all the land of the principality of north Wales to
the king and his heirs.[259] Richard certainly knew of this notification because
he referred to it in his letter promising fidelity to Henry, at Windsor in April
1246 (see *Actum* **43**).

43. King Henry III

*Letter promising fidelity to Henry III. Richard promised on the word of truth, and swore by
touching relics, that throughout the time he held his bishopric he would serve Henry and his heirs
faithfully, and would, by all means he knew and was able to, procure the honour of Henry's crown.
If he was able to forewarn Henry that his enemies proposed anything against him or his heirs he
would do so as quickly as he could, and he would use the whole of his power to bring those enemies
back to the fealty and service of the king and his heirs. On those things he would perform whatever
manner of security he could as a bishop, and as proof of that security he caused his seal to be
affixed to the letter. Also, he wished it to be made manifest to the king that Dafydd ap Llywelyn, of
his own free will and without compulsion, had appointed Henry his heir of all the lordship which
he, Dafydd, had in Wales, if he died without heir of his body. Also, Richard knew and testified
that Dafydd had bound himself in the same manner to the king, by his charter, that if he should
ever go against the peace made between them at Rhuddlan, and afterwards renewed in London,
that the whole land should lapse to the king and his heirs, and that he, Dafydd, and his heirs should
lose the right which they had in Wales or elsewhere within the kingdom of England for ever.*

Windsor, 20 April 1246

    B = TNA E 36/274 (Miscellaneous Documents, Affairs of Wales, Henry III –
    Edward I, 'Liber A'), *c.*1282–*c.*1292. fos. cccxxxiv^v cccxxxv^r s. xiii ex. In margin:
    Quod episcopus Bangor' fidelis erit regi Anglie et heredibus suis

    Calendared in *Episc. Acts Welsh Dioceses Unpublished*, B177.

    Printed in *LW*, pp. 21–2, no. 21.

    Transcribed from B.

Universis Cristi fidelibus has litteras visuris vel audituris, R. dei gratia episcopus
Bangoren(sis), salutem in domino. Ad universitatis vestre notitiam volumus pervenire quod nos in verbo veritatis promisimus et tactis sacrosanctis iuravimus quod
omni tempore quo episcopatum nostrum habuerimus domino nostro Henrico

---

[257] *AWR*, pp. 474–7, no. 304.
[258] *CPR, 1232–1247*, p. 261.
[259] *AWR*, pp. 477–8, no. 305. *LW*, pp. 22–3, no. 23. For the significance and ramifications
of this see Carpenter, 'Dafydd ap Llywelyn's Submission to King Henry III', 1–12.

regi Angl(ie) illustri et heredibus suis fidelitatem servabimus integram et illesam, et modis omnibus quibus sciverimus et poterimus honorem et indempnitatem corone sue procurabimus, et si forte perpendere poterimus quod inimici sui contra ipsum aut heredes suos aliquid moliantur nos eosdem dominos nostros quamcicius poterimus inde premuniemus et totum posse nostrum apponemus ad reducendum eosdem inimicos ad fidem et servicium eiusdem domini regis et heredum suorum super hiis omnimodam securitatem quam facere decuit episcopum fecimus et in memoriale eiusdem securitatis hiis litteris sigillum nostrum [fo. cccxxxv] apponi fecimus. Ad hec etiam volumus vobis manifestum fieri quod bene scimus quod David filius Leulini quondam principis Norwall(ie) spontanea voluntate sua et non coactus instituit predictum H. regem Angl(ie) illustrem heredem suum de omni dominio quod ipsum D. contingebat in Wall(ia), et hoc si ipse D. decederet sine herede de se genito. Scimus etiam et testificamur quod idem D. eodem modo obligavit se predicto domino regi per cartam suam quod si unquam venerit contra pacem inter eos inhitam apud Ruthela(n) et postea renovatam apud London', quod tota terra sua incurreretur ipsi sui caderent a iure quod habuerunt in Wallia vel alibi infra regnum Angl(ie) in perpetuum. Actum apud Wyndesor' vicesimo die Aprilis anno regni regis eiusdem tricesimo.

The first requirement of the agreement reached at Gwerneigron (pd in *AWR*, pp. 466–70, no. 300) was that Dafydd ap Llywelyn had to hand over his half-brother, Gruffudd, who was then incarcerated in the Tower of London.[260] According to Matthew Paris, Richard went to the king and tried to have Gruffudd set free, but he laboured in vain.[261] Gruffudd died on 1 March 1244 attempting to escape from the Tower, and Dafydd quickly seized the opportunity to form an alliance of Welsh princes against Henry III.[262] On 25 February 1246, Dafydd died suddenly, and it was Gruffudd's second son, Llywelyn, who continued the war that his uncle, Dafydd, had started. Llywelyn was joined by his older brother Owain.[263] Within two months Richard was at Windsor.

The peace agreements referred to are those made between Henry and Dafydd at Rhuddlan in August 1241, and renewed in London in October of the same year (see note to *Actum* **42**).

---

[260] *AWR*, pp. 466–70, no. 300; *CCR, 1237–1242*, p. 328; *CLR, 1240–1245*, p. 70. See also the note to *Actum* **42**.

[261] '… episcopus de Bangor Ricardus veniens ad regem, multum nitebatur liberare Griffinum, filium Leolini, principis Northuualliae, detentum in vinculis in turri Londoniarum; quia in conductu eius venerat ad parlamentum, ubi in dolo ceperat ipsum G[riffinum] frater eius junior David. In quo negotio multum laboravit episcopus R[icardus], sed frustra': *Historia Anglorum*, ii, p. 453. David Carpenter's assertion that it was advantageous for Henry III to persevere with childless Dafydd as sole ruler of Gwynedd, and accept that all the land of the principality of north Wales would pass to the king if Dafydd died without a legitimate heir (Carpenter, 'Dafydd ap Llywelyn's Submission to King Henry III', 7–8) may well explain why Richard's attempts to persuade Henry to release Gruffudd from the Tower proved fruitless.

[262] Smith, 'Dafydd ap Llywelyn (*c.*1215–1246)', *ODNB*; *AWR*, p. 29.

[263] Williams, 'Succession', 410. *AWR*, p. 30.

The relevance of Richard's statement that Dafydd had appointed Henry heir of all the lordship which he, Dafydd, had in Wales if he should die without an heir of his body (a reference to Dafydd's notification of 24 October 1241 – see note to *Actum* **42**), was that Dafydd had done just that, he had died without an heir.

On the same day that Richard promised the king fidelity, letters patent of safe conduct, until Midsummer, were issued for Richard and his men returning to Wales.[264] Llywelyn ap Gruffudd, and his brother Owain, finally submitted to Henry III at Woodstock on 30 April 1247.[265] There is no evidence that Richard had a part to play in their submission, however, it is tempting to view the gilt *cuppa* worth 4*l.*, 'delivered to the bishop of Bangor, of the king's gift, to contain the Eucharist in his principal church' (the gift being recorded on 16 May 1247), as a reward of some sort.[266]

*44. Aberconwy Abbey

Collation and confirmation, with the consent of his chapter, by R., sometime bishop of Bangor, to the abbot and convent of Aberconwy of two parts of the chapel of Cemais (Kemeys) saving to the vicar the third part.

[1246 x before 8 November 1267]

Mention only, in an inspeximus of Edward III, TNA C 53/119 (Charter Rolls, 6 Edward III), m. 21, being an inspeximus and confirmation of certain charters by Edward III, in favour of the abbot and convent of Aberconwy, dated 24 March 1332, at Westminster. s. xiv in. In the margin: Abb[at]e et Conventu de Ab[er]conewey

Calendared in *CChR, 1327–1341*, pp. 267–9.[267]

Transcribed from TNA C 53/119 (Charter Rolls, 6 Edward III), m. 21.

'*Collationem etiam et confirmationem quas R. quondam Bangoren(sis) episcopus, per cartam suam de assensu capituli sui, fecit predictis abbati et conventui de duabus partibus capelle de Kemeys imperpetuum possidendis salva tertia parte vicario*'.

In the inspeximus, the record of Richard's collation and confirmation is preceded by the record of Llywelyn ap Gruffudd's grant of first voidance of the chapels of St Patrick of Cemais, '*capella sancti Patricii de Kenmeys*' (i.e. Llanbadrig in the commote of Talybolion, Anglesey), and St Peplicius of Caernarfon (i.e. Llanbeblig near Caernarfon in the commote of Arfon Is Gwyrfai) to be held as freely as any rector held them in the time of Llywelyn his ancestor (Llywelyn ab Iorwerth): *AWR*, pp. 491–2, no. 319. Llanbadrig church was the church of the *maerdref* of Cemais.[268]

---

[264] April 1246, Windsor: *CPR, 1232–1247*, p. 478. The letters patent also granted safe conduct to the bishop of St Asaph, and his men, returning to Wales, so it is clear that Hywel II of St Asaph was also at court, and perhaps he too had fled to England.

[265] *AWR*, pp. 483–5, no. 312. Lloyd, *History of Wales*, ii, p. 708.

[266] May 1247, Windsor: *CLR, 1245–1251*, p. 123.

[267] Also calendared in *Episc. Acts Welsh Dioceses Unpublished*, B207.

[268] *AWR*, p. 492; Carr, *Medieval Anglesey*, pp. 95 and 215. A 'maerdref' was the townland surrounding the local princely 'llys' (court): Charles-Edwards, et al., *Welsh King and His Court*,

Even though there is no mention of St Patrick in the inspeximus entry for Richard's grant, it appears that Richard's collation and confirmation was in respect of the chapel of St Patrick of Cemais, i.e. Llanbadrig.[269]

As Richard's collation and confirmation followed Llywelyn ap Gruffudd's grant in the inspeximus, the *terminus a quo* for the bishop's grant is likely to be 1246 because Llanbadrig and Llanbeblig appear to have been held by Llywelyn following the division of Gwynedd with his brother Owain in that year.[270]

The *terminus ante quem* is the end of Richard's episcopate.[271]

45. Haughmond Abbey

Letter confirming his predecessors' gifts to the abbot and convent of Haughmond in respect of the churches of Nefyn, and Trefeglwys in Arwystli, with all their appurtenances. Sealing clause. Witnesses: his canons Master David and Madog, etc.

Haughmond, 1 January 1247/8

B = Shrewsbury, Shropshire Archives MS 6001/6869 (Haughmond Cartulary), fo. 150v. s. xv ex. Rubric: <alia>[272] confirmatio dictarum ecclesiarum

Printed (minus sealing clause) in *Cartulary of Haughmond Abbey*, p. 162, no. 795.

Transcribed from B.

Universis Cristi fidelibus has litteras visuris vel audituro, R. dei gratia Bangoren(sis) episcopus, salutem eternam in domino. Noverit universitas vestra nos donationes a predecessoribus nostris factas dominis abbati et conventui de Haghmon' super ecclesiis de Nevyn, et de Treflegees apud Aruystle, cum omnibus pertinentiis suis, ratas et gratas habuisse, et hac presenti carta nostra confirmasse salvo in omnibus iure episcopali. In cuius rei testimonium hiis litteris sigillum nostrum duximus apponendum. Dat' apud Haghmon' anno gratie millesimo ccxlvii, kal' Januarii. Hiis testibus magistro David et Madoco canonicis nostris, etc.

For the church of Nefyn in Llŷn see *Acta* **4**, **8**, **14** and **58**. For the church of Trefeglwys in Arwystli see *Acta* **5**, **9**, **10**, **14** and **58**.

It seems strange that the canons of Haughmond, so keen to have their possessions confirmed by the bishops of Bangor in the twelfth century, took almost ten years

---

pp. 568–9; *AWR*, p. 138; Carr, *Medieval Anglesey*, p. 10; *Geiriadur Prifysgol Cymru*, accessed 24 April 2024.

[269] A collation is the institution to an ecclesiastical benefice when the ordinary is himself the patron (i.e. when presentation and institution are one and the same act): *Oxford Dictionary of the Christian Church*, p. 375.

[270] *AWR*, p. 492, referring to Smith, *Llywelyn*, pp. 66–7. *Brut, Pen20Tr*, p. 107; *Brut, Hergest*, pp. 240–1.

[271] not 1265: cf. Hays, *Abbey of Aberconway*, pp. 116–17, and Carr, *Medieval Anglesey*, p. 215.

[272] Superscript.

after his consecration to obtain Richard's confirmation.[273] Presumably the canons had the opportunity to obtain Richard's confirmation when the bishop witnessed Dafydd ap Llywelyn's grant to the house, 19 October 1238 x 11 April 1240, but seem not to have taken it.[274]

Richard ensured that his confirmation was caveated with '*salvo in omnibus iure epis-copali*'. Cf. Gwion's confirmation in respect of Trefeglwys church to Haughmond: '… *cum omnibus pertinentiis suis liberam et solutam ab omnibus episcopalibus et terrenis con-suetudinibus*' (*Actum* **9**).

Master David (possibly 'Dafydd') and Madog, canons of Bangor, were named as witnesses. Master David is likely to be the future archdeacon of Bangor named as a member of Richard's household in 1259, and recorded a year later with his own household.[275]

*46. King Henry III

Request, not necessarily in writing, for confirmation that the bishop of Bangor and his predecessors were accustomed to have (i) free passage for themselves and their men in the water of Conwy, and (ii) the tithes of the king's demesnes, both of corn and lead and other tithes, everywhere in the king's land of Perfeddwlad.

1250 [Shortly before 22 October]

Mention only, in TNA C 54/63 (Close Rolls, 34 Henry III), m. 2. On 22 October 1250 at Westminster, a mandate, recorded in the close rolls, was issued to Alan de la Zouche.

CCR, 1247–1251, p. 338:

'*Pro episcopo Bangorensi – Mandatum est Alano la Zusch', justiciario Cestrie, quod per sacramentum proborum et legalium hominum diligenter inquirat utrum Bangorensis episcopus et predecessores sui liberum passagium pro se et hominibus suis in aqua de Conewey, et decimas dominicorum nostrorum, tam bladi et aliorum decimalium quam plumby, ubique in terra nostra de Berwehlad habere consueverunt. Et si per inquisitionem illam ei constiterit quod ipsi passagium et decimas illas habere debeant et consueverint, tunc Ricardo Bangorensi episcopo passagium in aqua predicta et decimas illas decetero habere faciat. Teste ut supra'.*

On 22 October 1250 at Westminster, no doubt pursuant to a request from Richard, Henry III ordered Alan de la Zouche (the new justice of Chester and the Four Cantrefs) to diligently enquire, by the oath of upright and lawful men, whether the bishop of Bangor and his predecessors were accus-tomed to have (i) free passage for themselves and their men in the water of Conwy, and (ii) the tithes of the king's demesnes, both of corn and lead and other tithes, everywhere in the king's land of Y Berfeddwlad.[276] On 5 May

---

[273] For example, the canons obtained Alan of St Cross' confirmation very quickly (**14**).

[274] 'Hiis testibus: domino Ririt Bangoren(si) episcopo etc.': *AWR*, pp. 456–7, no. 289.

[275] *CPR, 1258–1266*, p. 57 and p. 83. See also *Actum* **52**, and notes to the same; *AWR*, pp. 529–33, no. 358, and pp. 792–4, no. 601; and *Fasti Welsh Cathedrals*, p. 6. For Madog see *Fasti Welsh Cathedrals*, p. 10.

[276] *CCR, 1247–1251*, p. 338.

1251, a grant for life was made to Richard, bishop of Bangor, of free passage for him and his household by the water of Conwy.[277] It is noteworthy that the grant was only for Richard's lifetime.

The historical record is silent regarding the outcome of the inquisition into the tithes claimed by Richard. Perfeddwlad or Y Berfeddwlad (literally 'The Middle Country'), known in English as the Four Cantrefs, had been ceded to the crown by Llywelyn ap Gruffudd and Owain ap Gruffudd in the Treaty of Woodstock 1247, and perhaps Richard argued that he had been accustomed to receiving such tithes before the treaty, and so should continue to receive them after it.[278]

Certainly, Richard's successor, Anian, stated that the church of Bangor was accustomed to have the tithes of the lead mines in Tegeingl (Englefield in English, one of the cantrefs making up the Four Cantrefs) in the time of Llywelyn ab Iorwerth, Dafydd ap Llywelyn, and Llywelyn ap Gruffudd, as well as in the time of King Henry (III).[279] In 1286, an order was given to Reginald de Grey, as justice of Chester, that Anian was to have a third of the tithes of the king's demesnes and mills of Englefield, and a third of the tithes from the king's lead mine there, which the bishop had claimed, asserting that he and his predecessors had been in seisin thereof in times gone by, as appeared by an inquisition undertaken by the justice.[280]

*47. St Albans Abbey

On the Octave of St Stephen (2 January), in the presence of the bishop of Bangor, John II (John of Hertford), abbot of St Albans, Philip the chief counsellor of Earl Richard (earl of Cornwall), certain nobles of the household of William de Valence (earl of Pembroke), the king's uterine brother, as well as the whole convent of the abbey and innumerable faithful persons, the tomb of St Alban, protomartyr of the English, was discovered in the abbey church. And the bishop of Bangor granted an indulgence of 30 days to all those worshippers present.

St Albans, 2 January 1257

Mention only, in BL Royal MS 14 C VII, fo. 194v. (Matthew Paris, *Chronica Majora*, Part III), s. xiii med.[281]

Chronica Majora, v, pp. 608–9:

'… *Profundius igitur perscrutantes, invenerunt sub terra, sed non profunde, unam tumbam lapideam, satis eleganter compositam … Ubi lux caelestis descendit, et apparuerunt angeli descendentes et ascendentes, et canentes hunc hymnum; "Albanus egregius martir extat gloriosus." In quo etiam mausoleo inventa est quaedam lamina plumbea, in qua secundum antiquorum consuetudinem scriptus est hic titulus; "In hoc mausoleo inventum*

---

[277] At Westminster: *CPR, 1247–1258*, p. 94.
[278] Treaty of Woodstock, 30 April 1247: *AWR*, pp. 483–5, no. 312.
[279] *Actum* **86**.
[280] *CFR, 1272–1307*, p. 232. See note to *Actum* **84**.
[281] BL Royal MS 14 C VII has been digitised: https://www.bl.uk/manuscripts/Viewer.aspx?ref=royal_ms_14_c_vii_f008v, accessed 3 May 2023. BL Royal MS 14 C VII contains the text of Matthew Paris' *Chronica Majora* from 1254 to the end, as well as the whole of his *Historia Anglorum*. It is almost entirely autograph: Vaughan, *Matthew Paris*, p. 21.

est venerabile corpus Sancti Albani prothomartiris Anglorum." Hoc evenit in octavis Sancti Stephani, in praesentia domini episcopi Bangorensis, et domini abbatis Johannis secundi, et domini Philippi de Eia, principalis consiliarii comitis Ricardi, et quorundam nobilium de familia domini Willemi de Valentia, fratris domini regis uterine, et totius conventus, et fidelium innumerabilium, quibus solempniter haec sunt nuntiata. Et concessit episcopus veniam triginta dierum omnibus ipsam inventionem praesentialiter venerantibus. …'.[282]

And mention in BL Cotton MS Nero D I (*Liber Additamentorum*), s. xiii med.[283] Printed in *Chronica Majora*, vi, *Additamenta*, p. 495, n. 1:

'… *praesentibus abbate et conventu et episcopo Bangorensi, a quo collatum est indulgentiae beneficium omnibus locum illum venerater aduentibus triginta dierum, et altare quod ibidem dedicavit idem episcopus, decem dierum*' (See *Actum* **48** below).

Richard (d. 1272), first earl of Cornwall, was King Henry III's brother, and William de Valence (d. 1296), the earl of Pembroke, was Henry III's half-brother.

A week or so earlier, on 26 December 1256, Bishop Richard had been present when the crown of Germany was offered to the earl of Cornwall.[284] It was the bishop of Bangor who reported events to Matthew Paris – the earl of Cornwall was advised by his brother Henry III and others to accept the crown, which he did, turning to the bishops including Richard to make his acceptance speech.[285]

John of Hertford (John II) was the abbot who had welcomed Richard to St Albans in 1248, when, according to Matthew Paris, the impoverished bishop of Bangor came to the abbey so that he and his clerks might stay with the abbot until his bishopric, which had been ruined by war, had been restored.[286]

*48. St Albans Abbey

After the discovery of the body of St Alban, the bishop of Bangor granted an indulgence of 10 days to all those attending the altar, which the bishop had dedicated there.

St Albans, 2 January 1257

Mention only, in BL Cotton MS Nero D I (*Liber Additamentorum*), s. xiii med.

Chronica Majora, vi, *Additamenta*, p. 495, n. 1:

---

[282] English translation: *Matthew Paris's English History*, iii, pp. 213–14. Pryce, 'Esgobaeth Bangor', p. 49.
[283] See Vaughan, *Matthew Paris*, p. 49.
[284] *Chronica Majora*, v, pp. 601–3. Vincent, 'Richard, first earl of Cornwall and king of Germany (1209–1272)', *ODNB*.
[285] '… Et addidit, versa facie ad episcopos, quorum unus Bangorensis Ricardus, qui haec huius paginae scriptori assertive enarravit, extiterat, …': *Chronica Majora*, v, p. 602. *Matthew Paris's English History*, iii, pp. 207–9. Williams, 'Succession', 406.
[286] *Chronica Majora*, v, p. 2.

'… *praesentibus abbate et conventu et episcopo Bangorensi, a quo collatum est indulgentiae beneficium omnibus locum illum veneranter aduentibus triginta dierum, et altare quod ibidem dedicavit idem episcopus, decem dierum*'.

BL Royal MS 14 C VII, fo. 194v. (Matthew Paris, *Chronica Majora*, Part III), s. xiii med. details the discovery of St Alban's tomb in the abbey church, and those present – see *Actum* **47** and notes to the same.

Richard also performed other tasks when at St Albans. In 1254, on Maundy Thursday (9 April), he prepared the chrism in the church of St Albans, and in the same year he dedicated the church of Hexton ('Hacstanestune') near Hitchin, in Hertfordshire, at Abbot John of Hertford's behest.[287]

*49. King Henry III

Prorogation of the truce agreed at Oxford (on 17 June 1258) to last until St Peter ad Vincula (1 August) 1260, from that date to the morrow of St Bartholomew (25 August) 1260. Richard swore on the soul of Llywelyn ap Gruffudd to observe the same, and Imbert Pugeys, steward (of the royal household), swore on the king's soul.

Westminster, 25 July 1260

Mention only, in the patent rolls, TNA C 66/74 (Patent Rolls, 44 Henry III, Part 1), m. 6.

CPR, 1258–1266, p. 83:

'Prorogation made by the king with the bishop of Bangor sent to the king for this by Llewelin son of Griffin, of the truce made in the parliament of Oxford by the counsel of the magnates of the council with Llewelin son of Griffin and his men, and the king and Edward his son and their men, until St Peter's Chains 1260, from that date until the morrow of St Bartholomew; and to the due observance of this truce and prorogation, Imbert Pugeys, the steward, on the king's soul, and the bishop on the soul of Llewelin, have sworn. Mandate to the justice of Chester and the sheriffs of Hereford and Salop to cause this prorogation to be observed'.

For the truce agreed at Oxford on 17 June 1258: *AWR*, pp. 503–4, no. 331; *LW*, pp. 27–8, no. 33; Smith, *Llywelyn*, p. 120.

Richard had returned to Wales by April 1258.[288] In the autumn of 1259, he acted as Llywelyn's envoy and took the prince's peace offer to Henry.[289] Letters patent of safe conduct were issued by the king and his council in favour of Richard and members of his household who were named.[290] This is the earliest record of the members of an episcopal household for Bangor. Richard was back in London in the new year. In the king's absence, on 25 February 1260 at Westminster, mandates to the sheriffs of Gloucester,

---

[287] '… confectum est crisma …': *Chronica Majora*, v, p. 432; also, *Flores Historiarum*, ii, p. 396. Dedication of church of Hexton: *Gesta Abbatum Monasterii Sancti Albani*, i, p. 321.
[288] *AWR*, pp. 501–2, no. 329.
[289] *AWR*, pp. 506–7, no. 338. *CCR, 1259–1261*, pp. 4–5.
[290] October 1259 at Westminster: *CPR, 1258–1266*, p. 57.

Shrewsbury, Stafford, and Hereford were issued, informing them that *venerabilis pater Bangorensis episcopus* on behalf of Llywelyn had recently come to the king to treat with him concerning the disputes between Llywelyn and the king. The 'king' had, by the bishop, fixed a day for Llywelyn a month from Easter (namely 2 May) to send discreet messengers, sufficiently instructed for the purpose, to treat with him. In the hope of peace and for the observance of the truces begun between them, and also lest the labour of the bishop should be in vain (*ne labor episcopi supradicti vacuus habeatur*), with the assent and counsel of Edward, and the magnates of his council, it was granted that the king's lands and those of his son and their men on the one part, and the lands of Llywelyn and his men on the other, should be conserved to the feast of Pentecost next (23 May).[291] Henry returned to England on 23 April 1260.[292] Whilst in France he had heard that Llywelyn was besieging Builth castle.[293] On 17 July, the castle fell to the prince.[294] Llywelyn once again sent Richard to Westminster, and the bishop was there by 22 July.[295] This must have been the most difficult of all Richard's embassies on behalf of the prince. Fourteen years earlier he had sworn fidelity to Henry, promising that throughout the time he held his bishopric he would serve the king faithfully, and forewarn him if his enemies proposed anything against him, and would do all in his power to bring those enemies back to the fealty and service of the king.[296] Henry had heard the news from Builth, and on 22 July, he wrote to Llywelyn to express his astonishment that just at the time Richard had come to him to discuss an extension of the truce, and infractions of the same, Llywelyn should attack Builth, and so be in breach of the truce.[297] In any event, on 25 July, a prorogation of the truce agreed at Oxford was made.

For Imbert Pugeys, steward of the royal household from 1257 see Ray, 'Three Alien Royal Stewards in Thirteenth-Century England', pp. 51–68.

*50. King Henry III

Notification by Richard, bishop of Bangor, that he, on behalf of Llywelyn ap Gruffudd, and the Imbert Pugeys and Robert Walerand, on behalf of the king, have sworn to observe the prorogation referred to in Actum 49 above.

Westminster, 26 July 1260

Mention only, in the patent rolls, TNA C 66/74 (Patent Rolls, 44 Henry III, Part 1), m. 6.

CPR, 1258–1266, p. 83:

In the margin: 'The morrow of St James'.

[291] Witnessed by Hugh Bigod: *CCR, 1259–1261*, pp. 30–1.
[292] Ridgeway, 'Henry III (1207–1272)', *ODNB*.
[293] *ibid*.
[294] *CPR, 1258–1266*, p. 85. Smith, *Llywelyn*, p. 127.
[295] *CCR, 1259–1261*, p. 184.
[296] *Actum* **43**.
[297] *CCR, 1259–1261*, p. 184. Smith, *Llywelyn*, p. 127.

'Notification by the said Richard, bishop of Bangor, that he for the said Llewelyn and the said Imbert and Robert Walerand for the king have sworn to the observance of the said prorogation'.

The feast day of St James the Great is 25 July.[298]

See note to *Actum* **49** for the background to this notification, and for Imbert Pugeys. Robert Walerand, a steward of the royal household, was entrusted by Henry III with many and varied tasks, and for a time held the castles of Carmarthen and Cardigan, and was custodian of the bishopric of St Davids.[299]

On 3 August 1260, Henry III issued mandates to his men to go to the ford at Montgomery by the date agreed with Richard (in the name of Llewelyn) being the Wednesday after the Assumption of the Blessed Mary (so 18 August).[300] At Montgomery, the abbot of Aberconwy joined Richard to represent the prince, and on 22 August 1260 the truce was extended to the feast of the Nativity of St John the Baptist (24 June) 1262.[301] Neither the king or Edward, nor Llywelyn or Dafydd ap Gruffudd, Llywelyn's brother (who was bound to keep the truce) were present. Richard and the abbot attached their seals to the part agreement to be kept by the king, and they also attached the seals of Llywelyn and Dafydd to the same.[302] In other words, Richard and the abbot of Aberconwy had in their possession Llywelyn's and Dafydd's seal matrices.

*51. Llywelyn ap Gruffudd

An exchange of letters patent (possibly in the form of a bipartite indenture) between Richard and Llywelyn ap Gruffudd recording the terms of an arbitration which ordained that fines for sacrilege in churches should be paid to the bishop. Whether individual cases of sacrilege were specified, or any other matters were dealt with, is unclear. However, the parties were obliged to observe the terms inviolably, with a penalty being imposed for non-compliance.

Llandrillo [*c*.26 April 1258 x -29 April 1261, possibly 22 August 1260 x -29 April 1261]

Mention only, in an arbitration award, made by Anian I bishop of St Asaph (1249–1266) and others, dated 29 April 1261 at *Rhydyrarw*: NLW Peniarth MS 231B, pp. 35–9. s. xvii. (*Actum* **52** below).

Calendared in *AWR*, p. 507, no. 339.

Extracts from the arbitration award, dated 29 April 1261 at *Rhydyrarw*, and recorded in NLW Peniarth MS 231B, pp. 35–9 (*Actum* **52**):

---

[298] Cheney, *Handbook of Dates*, p. 53.
[299] Harding, 'Walerand, Robert (*d.* 1273)', *ODNB*.
[300] *CCR, 1259–1261*, p. 89.
[301] *AWR*, pp. 508–12, no. 342. Smith, *Llywelyn*, pp. 129–30. The prior of Wenlock, Simon Passelowe, and Fulk of Orby, justice of Chester represented the king and Edward, with the bishop of Worcester adding his seal to theirs on the part of the document to be kept by Llywelyn: *AWR*, pp. 508–12, no. 342.
[302] *AWR*, pp. 508–12, no. 342.

'*[viii] De hiis qui fregerunt ecclesiam Ban³⁰³gor' et pugnantibus in ecclesia de Rosvyr et apud ecclesiam de Taleboleon respondemus ut continetur in litteris de Llan(n)terillo³⁰⁴ quod talium sicut omnium sacrilegorum tantum emenda pertinet ad episcopum, unde si predicti episcopo non satisfecerunt, plenarie satisfaciant'.*

'*Partes vero supradicte ad ista inviolabiliter servanda teneantur, et ad ea servanda sub obligate sub eadem pena sunt qua in litteris inter ipsas confectis³⁰⁵ apud Llan(n)derillo³⁰⁶ fuerunt³⁰⁷ obligate'.*

The *terminus a quo* for *Actum* **51** is provided by Richard's return to Wales.³⁰⁸ The *terminus ante quem* is provided by the date of the agreement with Llywelyn ap Gruffudd made at *Rhydyrarw* on 29 April 1261 (see *Actum* **52**).

Following Richard's prolonged absence from Bangor between 1248 and 1257/8, Llywelyn may have been keen to seek an accommodation with his bishop and anxious to see an equitable settlement in place.³⁰⁹ Furthermore, as J. B. Smith has said, the bishop's absence may have created a need both for the clarification of, and for stricter adherence to, previously agreed procedures.³¹⁰ The matters were addressed by arbitration and recorded in three agreements: *Acta* **51**, **52** and **53**.³¹¹

The final two arbitration agreements (**52** and **53**) were made in 1261, and it is possible that the first arbitration agreement (**51**) was made shortly before, perhaps after 22 August 1260, the date upon which Richard completed his laborious embassies on behalf of Llywelyn. Richard was busy from the autumn of 1259 acting as the prince's envoy to Henry III and his council, initially carrying Llywelyn's offer of peace to the king, and then arranging a prorogation of the truce agreed at Oxford, followed finally by an extension of that truce agreed on 22 August 1260 (see *Actum* **49** and *Actum* **50**, and notes to the same). Having acted on Llywelyn's behalf, and with a lengthy truce between prince and king in place thanks in no small part to Richard's labours, perhaps the bishop expected a little goodwill from Llywelyn as a

---

³⁰³ The writer inserts 'estius' between 'Ban' and 'gor''. 'estius' is preceded by two parallel oblique strokes //, like the transposition sign used elsewhere in the MS. Haddan and Stubbs, i, p. 490, have 'Llangor', not Bangor, but the first letter is identical to the capital 'B' used by the writer in [vi] for 'archidiaconus Bangor(ensis)'.

³⁰⁴ There is a straight-line contraction mark over the 'n'.

³⁰⁵ Initially the writer had 'confectas', but crossed out the 'a', and added 'i' in superscript.

³⁰⁶ There is a straight-line contraction mark over the 'n'.

³⁰⁷ There are two minims between 'fuer' and 't'. Pryce has 'fuerunt' (*AWR*, p. 517). Haddan and Stubbs, i, p. 491, have 'fuerint'.

³⁰⁸ Richard was back in Wales by 26 April 1258 (at *Ekaedu Vannebedeyr*): *AWR*, pp. 501–2, no. 329. He had been in St Albans in January 1257: see *Actum* **47** and *Actum* **48**. For a discussion of Richard's visits to, and stays at, St Albans between 1248 and 1257: Williams, 'Succession', 406, and notes to *Actum* **42**, *Actum* **47** and *Actum* **48**.

³⁰⁹ David Stephenson certainly thought that might have been the case: *Governance*, p. 171. For Richard's visits to, and stays in, St Albans see previous footnote.

³¹⁰ Smith, *Llywelyn*, p. 209.

³¹¹ Arbitration was not an uncommon method of dispute resolution in medieval Wales: McGuinness, 'Arbitration and Dispute Resolution in Wales during the Age of the Princes *c.*1100–*c.*1283'.

quid pro quo for his many weeks of travel and negotiation, often in difficult circumstances, on the prince's behalf.

The reference to *litteris inter ipsas confectis* suggested to Huw Pryce that letters patent were exchanged by the prince and the bishop recording the terms of the arbitration, quite possibly in the form of a bipartite indenture similar to that recording the later composition between them on 18 August 1261 at *Rhydyrarw* (**53**).[312]

Llandrillo is either Llandrillo-yn-Rhos or Llandrillo-yn-Edeirnion.[313]

52. Llywelyn ap Gruffudd

Agreement between Richard and his chapter on one side, and Llywelyn and his magnates on the other, reached, after hearing the pleas of each party, by the unanimous determination on the Thursday after Easter (1261) of arbitrators namely Anian (I), bishop of St Asaph, [Gwyn] prior of the Dominicans of Bangor, Ieuaf a brother of the same convent, (?)Philip, (?)warden of the friars [(?)minor] of Llan-faes, brother John (?)Rufus of the same convent, Goronwy and Tudur sons of Ednyfed (Fychan), Einion Fychan and Einion ap Caradog, chosen by each side as arbitrators to settle pleas between the parties.

(1) When a cleric has done wrong anywhere, let both his person and his offence be delivered to ecclesiastical jurisdiction. But if he has raped a woman, whereby he has offended both the secular and the ecclesiastical authority, let him make amends there (i.e. in the ecclesiastical court) according to both laws. If he is charged with having found treasure, let him make amends to the lay power in the same place if he is convicted. However, concerning a lay tenement and the transgression of boundaries,[314] let him make amends in the secular court. Concerning Ednyfed ap Hywel who was accused of having found treasure, and concerning the seal of the chapter of Clynnog (Kelly'nn') attached to letters attesting to the manumission of a certain serf, such a case should be heard in the bishop's court. If anything was taken from Ednyfed on account of that treasure, let it be restored to him; and if it is proved that he found that treasure, let him make amends in the court of the bishop, to lord Llywelyn according to the law of the country.[315] Concerning the seal, if on account of the aforesaid use of it he took anything from the canons, he ought to make restitution to them and the case should be heard and decided in the bishop's court and amends made to the injured party. However, if Llywelyn is conscious that on the aforesaid occasions he took something from Ednyfed and the canons, let him make restitution at a time fixed by the bishop of St Asaph.

(2) As regards Llywelyn ap Gruffudd's detaining the goods of shipwrecks while their possessors survive and immediately request the goods, the arbitrators recall that Llywelyn (ab Iorwerth) formerly prince of Wales acted thus, whether justly or unjustly; however, he surrendered such goods,

---

[312] *AWR*, p. 507.

[313] *ibid.*

[314] The wording in the MS is '… et finium transgresione …' and, therefore, the correct translation is 'and the transgression of boundaries', not 'or similar offence' as given in *AWR*, p. 514.

[315] The wording is: '… et si probetur ipsum thesaurum invenisse, in curia episcopi, domino Lewel(ino) satisfaciat secundum legem patrie'. *AWR* errs with '… and if it is proved that he found that treasure, let him make amends in the court of Llywelyn according to the law of the country': *AWR*, p. 514.

not through the compulsion of any prelate but through fear of God, an example they commend to Llywelyn (ap Gruffudd) in good faith. As regards Llywelyn ap Gruffudd's similarly seizing goods cast onto, and treasures found on, the land of the Church, they do not recall that any received such goods apart from Prince Llywelyn (ab Iorwerth) and his successors.

(3) If a lay man of the bishop is charged with having found treasure, let him answer in the secular court, and if proof is lacking against him, in no way let lawful compurgation be denied him.

(4) As regards men of the bishop unfit for war, neither military service nor its commutation should be exacted from those younger than the lawful age of fourteen years; but let older men perform military service or pay the commutation.

(5) If servants of Llywelyn or his bailiffs or those of others seize the draught animals of the bishop's men for their own business without the men's assent, and if, after the men's complaint has been made to Llywelyn's bailiff, satisfaction is not made by severely punishing the robbers as a deterrent to others, Llywelyn should fine his bailiff at least 20s.

(6) Concerning the man allegedly[316] seized in the refuge of the church on the day of its dedication, let trustworthy men from both Llywelyn's side and the bishop's be sent to see the place where he was seized, and if it can be proved in their presence that it is a place of refuge, let (Llywelyn) make full amends; otherwise, let Llywelyn enjoy possession of his prisoner. The names of those assigned to this are: Archdeacon David of Bangor, the dean of Bangor and the archdeacon of Anglesey on behalf of the bishop, and G(oronwy) ab Ednyfed, Einion Fychan and Iorwerth on behalf of Llywelyn; and brother Ieuaf Foel was accepted as a counsellor on the feast of St Trillo (15 June) at Bangor. If one or more of these are absent, let another or others be substituted with the consent of those present.

(7) Concerning those excommunicated by name, if anyone has been excommunicated after receiving canonical warning, the lord is obliged to follow the bishop's mandate and seize him without delay when requested.

(8) Concerning those who have violated the church of Bangor[317] and those fighting in the church of Rhosyr and at the church of Talybolion, the arbitrators reply as set out in the letters of Llandrillo, namely that the fines for these as for all acts of sacrilege belong to the bishop; therefore if they have not made amends to the bishop, let them do so fully.

(9) Concerning the married cleric who knowingly received a publicly banished person, and against whom it may be possible to bring proof, the cleric is obliged to answer in the ecclesiastical court. If he is resident in the prince's land and happens to be fined, all his fine will be given to the prince. If he is resident in the bishop's land, let the fine be divided between the bishop and the prince. If the wife of any man knowingly or willingly receives such a banished person in her husband's absence, let the woman answer in the ecclesiastical court and let the cleric not be punished on account of her deed nor be forced to answer for her unless he wishes.

---

[316] 'ut dicitur'.
[317] Or perhaps, 'Concerning those who broke into the church of Bangor …': 'De hiis qui fregerunt ecclesiam Bangor' …'.

(10) Concerning theft in the houses of certain clerics and men of the bishop, the goods of no one ought to be confiscated other than for theft discovered in the houses where they have their habitation, namely keywannedd, *for such a house is called merely a* halaucty *('polluted house'). The arbitrators have heard this from the elders.*

(11) If the bailiffs of Llywelyn or the bishop fine any persons in their courts, the fine ought to be halved between the bishop and the prince. The prince's bailiff should have with him someone from the bishop's side in whose presence he imposes and halves the fine, and the bishop's bailiff should do similarly in his court.

The aforesaid parties are obliged to observe these terms inviolably, under the same penalty under which they were obliged in the letters drawn up between them at Llandrillo.

The arbitrators attach their seals to these letters patent.

Rhydyrarw, Friday 29 April 1261

B = NLW Peniarth MS 231B (*Llyfr Coch Asaph*), pp. 35–9. s. xvii.[318] Heading: Forma compromissi inter dominum Bangoren' et dominum principem. In margin next to heading: fo. xxii. a

Calendared in *Episc. Acts Welsh Dioceses Unpublished*, B201.

Printed in Haddan and Stubbs, i, pp. 489–91.

Printed in *AWR*, pp. 515–17, no. 345.

Transcribed from B.

Noverint tam presentes quam futuri quod nos Anian(us) episcopus de sancto Assaph', frater [Wyn][a] prior predicatorum Bangor', frater Iewaf eiusdem loci conventus, Ph'[b] naid[c] (?)fratrum[d] (?)<suum>[e] [(?)minorum][f] de Llanvaes[g], frater Joh(ann)es R(?)ufus eiusdem loci conventus, Goron' et Tudur filii Itnevet, Enn' parvus,[h] Enn' filius Keirad', ad diffiniendas querelas motas inter dominum Ri(cardum) Bangorens(em) episcopum et suum capitulum ex una parte[i] et dominum L. filium Griff' et suos magnates ex altera, electi ex utriusque partis consensu arbitrii, anno domini m. cc. lxi° apud Rydyrarw, die iovis proxima post festum pasche, et utriusque partis querelas audientes, eas unanimiter diffinivimus in hunc modum.

[i] In primis, cum clericus forefecerit ubicunque, quatenus[j] personam suam tanquam offensa in foro [p. 36] ecclesiastico rend'at[k]. Sed si mulierem rapuerit, quo regimen et sacerdotium offendit, ibidem satisfaciet secundum utramque legem. Si autem ei imponatur thesaurum invenisse, ibidem dominio laicali satisfaciat si fuerit convictus. De tenemento autem laicali <et>[l] finium[m] transgresione satisfaciat in foro seculari. De Edn' filio Howel, cui imponebatur invenisse thesaurum, et de sigillo capituli de Kelly'nn'[n] apposito litteris testimonialibus manumissionis cuiusd'a[o] servi, nobis videtur quod talis causa in curia episcopi debet ventilari. Et

---

[318] A handwritten note with the manuscript states that 'This Manuscript is in the handwriting of Robert Vaughan of Hengwrt, Esquire, the … antiquary who died in 1667'. There are four manuscripts which are regarded as transcripts of, the now lost, *Llyfr Coch Asaph* – the manuscripts are deposited at the NLW, Aberystwyth – the second of these is Peniarth MS 231B: Jones, 'Llyfr Coch Asaph: A Textual and Historical Study', i, p. xxxv.

si quid occasione illius thesauri predicto Edn' fuerit ablatum, eidem restituatur; et si probetur ipsum thesaurum invenisse, in curia episcopi, domino Lewel(ino) satisfaciat secundum legem patrie. De sigillo autem nobis videtur quod si occasione predicte appo'nis[p] canonicis aliquid abstulit, eisdem restitui debet et causa in curia episcopi ventilari et determinari et cui iniuriatum est satisfieri. Si autem conscientiam habeat dominus L. quod predictis occasionibus predictis Edn' et canonicis aliquid abstulit, restituatur tempore a domino Assavens(i) assignato.

[ii] Quod res de naufragio detinet possessoribus existentibus sanis et res suas instanter petentibus, recolimus dominum L. bone memorie quondam princeps Wall(ie) sic fecisse, sive iuste sive iniuste, tandem nullo prelato compellente sed ductus timore divino talia dimisisse, quod et domino L. bona fide laudamus. Quod res proiectas in [p. 37] terram ecclesie occupat similiter et thesauros inventos in terra ecclesie[q] et c'[r]: non recolimus alium talia recepisse preter solum principem L. et suos successores.

[iii] Si imponitur homini episcopi laico invenisse thesaurum, in curia seculari respondeat, et si desit contra eum probatio, nullo modo ei denegetur legittima purgatio.

[iv] Quod homines episcopi inhabiles ad arma et c'.[s], nobis videtur quod a prius[t] pretaxatis ante legittimationem(?)[u] eta[tem][v], scilicet xiiii annorum, non debet exigi expeditio neque expeditionis redemptio; seniores vero vel in expeditionem eant vel componant.

[v] Si qui servientes domini L. vel suorum ballivorum vel aliorum[w] iumenta hominum episcopi sine ipsorum assensu ad sua negotia facienda rapiunt, nobis videtur, si eorum querimonia ad ballivum domini L. venerit et eis non satisfecerit raptores rigide puniendo ut alii ter<re>antur[x], quod dominus L. debet mulctare ballivum suum in xx solid[os][y] ad minus.

[vi] De capto in die dedicationis in refugio ecclesie, ut dicitur, nobis videtur quod mittantur fide digni [ex parte][z] tam ex[aa] domini Lewelini quam episcopi qui videant locum in quo captus fuit, et si possit probari in ipsorum presentia locum refugii esse, per omnia satisfaciat; sin autem, dominus L. suo incarcerato gaudeat. Nomina autem ad hoc assignatorum sunt hec: dominus D(avi)d[bb] archidiaconus Bangor(ensis) et eiusdem loci decanus et archidiaconus Monie ex parte episcopi, et dominus G. filius Edn' et Enn'[cc] parvus et Ioru(er)th[dd] ex parte Lewelini, et assumpto [p. 38] in conciliarium[ee] fratre Iewaf Voel in festo sancti Terillo apud Bangor. Et <si>[ff] contingerit[gg] [*sic*] aliquem vel aliquos abesse, loco absentis vel absentium alius vel alii cum assensu presentium substituantur.

[vii] De nominatim excommunicatis nobis videtur quod si premissa monitione canonica aliquis fuerit sententia excommunicationis innodatus, quod ad mandatum episcopi tenetur dominus ipsum capere sine dilatione cum ad hec fuerit requisitus.

[viii] De hiis qui fregerunt ecclesiam Ban[hh]gor' et pugnantibus in ecclesia de Rosvyr et apud ecclesiam de Taleboleon respondemus ut continetur in litteris de Llan(n)terillo[ii] quod talium sicut omnium sacrilegorum tantum emenda pertinet ad episcopum, unde si predicti episcopo non satisfecerunt, plenarie satisfaciant.

[ix] De clerico uxorato receptante puplice forbanizarum[jj] scienter et possit contra ipsum probari nobis videtur quod tenetur respondere in foro ecclesiastico. Si vero faciat residentiam in terra principis et contingat ipsum multari, tota multa sua principi dabitur. Si vero residentiam in terra episcopi faciat, mulcta dividatur inter episcopum et principem. Si vero uxor alicuius talem scienter vel volenter in eius

absentia receptaverit, mulier in foro ecclesiastico respondeat et clericus*kk* ratione
sui facti non puniatur nec pro ea nisi velit*ll* respondere cogatur.

[x] De furto in aliquorum clericorum domibus vel hominum episcopi, nobis videtur quod nullius bona debent aufferri*mm* nisi pro furto invento in domibus ubi
fuerit eorum habitatio, id est*nn* [p. 39] *keywanned*[*oo*], quia talis domus ?r<?>*pp* tantum
halaucty. Hoc audivimus a senioribus.

[xi] Si ballivi domini L. seu episcopi in suis curiis aliquos mul<c>tent*qq*, ibi debet
mul<c>ta*rr* dimidiari inter episcopum et principem. Nobis videtur quod bailli-
vus principis debet secum habere aliquem ex parte episcopi in cuius presentia
mulctam faciat et factam dimidiat, et ballivus episcopi in sua curia similiter faciat.
Partes vero supradicte ad ista inviolabiliter servanda teneantur, et ad ea servanda
sub obligate sub eadem pena sunt qua in litteris inter ipsas confectis*ss* apud Llan(n)
derillo*tt* fuerunt*uu* obligate.

In cuius rei testimonium nostra sigilla hiis patentibus litteris fecimus apponi.
Datum Rydyrarw*vv* anno domini m cc lxi° die veneris proxima post pascham.

a'Wyn' is written in the margin with transposition signs (i.e. //) showing that
it should be inserted in the lacuna after 'frater' where indicated by dots in the
MS, *B*. *b*the straight line through the stem of the 'P' suggests 'Per' or 'Por', or
perhaps 'Par'. There is a contraction line running through the top of the following letter, which appears to be a 'h'. *AWR* suggests 'Philip' for his transcribed '…
Ph' …', whereas Haddan and Stubbs have 'presbyter', *B*. *c*dotted underneath.
'gardianus' is postulated by *AWR*, *B*. *d*'fru'' or 'fr' followed by two minims, under-
lined and dotted underneath, *B*. *e*in superscript immediately above 'fru'' (or 'fr'
followed by two minims) *B*. *f*lacuna indicated by gap and dots. [(?)minorum]
is suggested by *AWR*, *B*. *g*'Llan' dotted underneath, *B*. *h*'ap' has been crossed
through, ~~ap~~, after 'Enn' parvus', and before 'Enn' filius Keirad', *B*. *i*'d' followed
by another letter, possibly an 'o', each crossed through with a diagonal line, '~~d o~~',
between 'parte' and 'et dominum'. Both ignored by Haddan and Stubbs. *AWR*
records the 'd' as being struck through, *B*. *j*~~offe~~ inserted after 'quatenus' and
before 'personam'. Ignored by Haddan and Stubbs, *B*. *k*both *AWR*, and Haddan
and Stubbs have 'rendatur'. But the contraction mark immediately follows the
'd' not the 't'. (Whereas the contraction mark for 'imponatur', a little further
on in the text, is placed immediately after the 't', i.e. imponat'. Similarly, the
contraction mark is placed immediately after the 't' in 'imponebatur'), *B*. *l*Superscript, *B*. *m*Haddan and Stubbs have 'similium'. *AWR* has 'finium'. It is doubtful
that the word is 'similium' as no 'l' is discernible. The translation for '… et
finium transgresione …' would, therefore, be 'and transgression of boundaries',
not 'or similar offence' (*AWR*, p. 515), *B*. *n*thought to be Clynnog (i.e. Clynnog
Fawr) by *AWR*, *B*. *o*both *AWR*, and Haddan and Stubbs, have 'cuiusdam'. But
the contraction mark immediately follows the 'd' and is not a straight
line that might indicate a final 'm', *B*. *p*both *AWR*, and Haddan and Stubbs, have
'appositionis', *B*. *q*Above, in superscript, is a letter which has been crossed out
B. *r*'et c':' is omitted by Haddan and Stubbs, but rendered as 'etc.,' by *AWR*, *B*.
*s*Haddan and Stubbs have added '[compelluntur]', after 'ad arma', and in place
of 'et c'.', *B*. *t*there are three minims between 'pr' and 's'. *AWR* has 'quod a prius'
but Haddan and Stubbs have 'quod de prius', *B*. *u*both Haddan and Stubbs, and
AWR, have 'legittimam', but *AWR* questions whether the word should be 'legit-
timationem'. If it is all one word, it is certainly much longer than 'legittimam',
B. *v*'eta'' in the MS. *AWR* has 'etatem'. Haddan and Stubbs have 'aetatem', *B*.
*w*a wave-like pen stroke follows 'aliorum'; it was probably meant to indicate that
there was no word before the next, 'iumenta', which begins on the following

line, *B.* [x]the first 't' is followed by the contraction for 'er', which is then followed, in superscript, by 're' above 'an', *B.* [y]Haddan and Stubbs have 'solidis', *AWR* has 'solidos', *B.* [z]'ex parte', dotted underneath, is written in the margin with transposition signs (i.e. //) showing that those two words should be inserted in the lacuna after 'digni' where indicated by dots, *B.* [aa]immediately following 'ex', and just below the line of text, is an upward pointing arrow indicating an insertion?, *B.* [bb]the name is unclear but *AWR* with 'D(avi)d' must be correct. Haddan and Stubbs have 'Ed.' *B.* [cc]the first letter is unclear, and the writer seems to have made a mistake, or been too heavy-handed in his pen stroke, however, he has written a capital 'E' in the margin to the left, on the same line, and so it appears that the name is 'Enn''. Haddan and Stubbs have 'Enner'. *AWR* has 'Enn'', *B.* [dd]once again the writer has been too heavy-handed in his pen stroke for what appears to be an 'r', and whilst the name is not particularly clear, 'Ioru(er)th' appears as close as anything to what he has written. Haddan and Stubbs have 'Iorwerth'. *AWR* has 'Ioru(e)rth', *B.* [ee]the word is dotted underneath. *AWR* states that the '… second c possibly corrected from an s; ociliarium written in margin to left …'. Haddan and Stubbs have 'conciliarium', *B.* [ff]superscript, *B.* [gg]there are three minims between 'cont and 'gerit'. Haddan and Stubbs have 'contingerit'. *AWR* has 'contigerit', *B.* [hh]the writer inserts 'estius' between 'Ban' and 'gor''. 'estius' is preceded by two parallel oblique strokes //, like the transposition sign used elsewhere in the MS. Haddan and Stubbs have 'Llangor', not Bangor, but the first letter in the MS is identical to the capital 'B' used by the writer in [vi] for 'archidiaconus Bangor(ensis)', *B.* [ii]There is a straight-line contraction mark over the 'n', *B.* [jj]forbanizarum with a dot beneath the 'z', and an 'r' written above it. *AWR* makes the same point but, in the main text, follows Haddan and Stubbs who have 'forbanizatum', *B.* [kk]followed by a wave-like pen stroke probably indicating that there was no word before the next, 'ratione', which starts on the following line, *B.* [ll]the colon sign : immediately follows 'velit' *B.* [mm]there are two letters 'f', not one, *B.* [nn]One dot either side of the letter i. This means 'id est', according to Cappelli, *The Elements of Abbreviation*, p. 22, *B.* [oo]only one 'd' appears in *keywanned*. Both Haddan and Stubbs, and *AWR*, have *dd* (Cf. Rhys, *Lectures on Welsh Philology*, pp. 259–60) *B.* [pp]*AWR* has 'dicitur'. Haddan and Stubbs are unsure and have 'erit(?)'. When compared with the rest of the MS, the first letter does not look like a 'd'. Nor does it look particularly like an 'e'. The first letter is followed by an 'r', which is then followed by an undecipherable mark/letter in superscript *B.* [qq]c inserted in superscript *B.* [rr]c inserted in superscript *B.* [ss]initially the writer had 'confectas', but crossed out the 'a', and added i in superscript *B.* [tt]straight line contraction mark over the 'n', *B.* [uu]there are two minims between 'fuer' and 't'. *AWR* has 'fuerunt'. Haddan and Stubbs have 'fuerint', *B.* [vv]there is a mark, in superscript, above the second 'y', that looks like an undotted i, or a simple vertical pen stroke, *B.*

This was the second arbitration agreement between Richard and Llywelyn ap Gruffudd – for the background to this and the other two arbitration agreements see the note to *Actum* **51**.

The location of *Rhydyrarw*, also the place where *Actum* **53** was made, has not been identified with any certainty. However, it could be Rhyd-y-Garw/Rhyd-y-Carw, in the parish of Trefeglwys, Arwystli.[319]

319 Rhyd-y-Garw, attested in 1699: *List of Historic Place Names Website*: https://historicplacenames.rcahmw.gov.uk/placenames/recordedname/79654891-240f-

Anian I, bishop of St Asaph, was well known to Richard, indeed the bishop of
Bangor had assisted at Anian's consecration in 1249.[320] Llywelyn ap Gruffudd
employed their episcopal clout when he began to cement his ascendancy over the
native princes of Wales; for in April 1258, Richard and Anian sealed 'the earliest
surviving example of a formal agreement between Llywelyn and a prince who
acknowledged his supremacy by doing homage' when Maredudd ap Rhys Gryg
(lord of Ystrad Tywi) did homage to Llywelyn.[321] Then in August 1258, Hywel ap
Rhys Gryg implored the two bishops to affix their seals to a notification that he had
done homage to Llywelyn.[322] In both cases, Richard and Anian agreed to apply
ecclesiastical censure in the event of a breach of faith.[323] In December 1258, they
were jointly engaged by the archbishop of Canterbury, Boniface of Savoy, who
had been charged with coercing Llywelyn ap Gruffudd to observe the peace with
King Henry III.[324]

The Franciscan friary of Llan-faes had been founded by Llywelyn ap Gruffudd's
grandfather, Llywelyn ab Iorwerth, in memory of his wife Joan (d. 1237).[325] The
Dominican friary at Bangor was established by 1251, and there is a strong possibility that Llywelyn ap Gruffudd himself was the founder.[326] Members of both
friaries were again appointed as arbitrators and named in the third and final arbitration agreement between Richard and Llywelyn in August 1261 (**53**). See notes
to *Actum* **53** also.

Goronwy ab Ednyfed Fychan (d. 1268) was Llywelyn's seneschal. He and his
brother Tudur (d. 1278) served the prince as their father Ednyfed Fychan (d. 1246)
had served Llywelyn ab Iorwerth and his son, Dafydd.[327] Einion Fychan, in various capacities, also served Llywelyn ab Iorwerth and Dafydd ap Llywelyn before
Llywelyn ap Gruffudd.[328] Einion ap Caradog, who like Goronwy ab Ednyfed and
Einion Fychan, had been a party to the agreement between Scottish lords and Lly-

---

4817-89d6-da20cd6429bd, accessed 10 June 2024. The later form, Rhyd-y-Carw,
appearing in 1898–1908: https://historicplacenames.rcahmw.gov.uk/placenames/
recordedname/26e1b11c-e59f-45f3-b1ba-45b912c048cf, accessed 10 June 2024. Thank you
to Dr Nia Wyn Jones for bringing this to my attention. Cf. *AWR*, p. 518.

[320] By Walter de Cantilupe, bishop of Worcester: *Annales de Wigornia*, p. 439. *Fasti Welsh
Cathedrals*, p. 35.

[321] The abbots of Aberconwy and Enlli, and the priors of Beddgelert and Ynys Lannog,
also attached their seals – 26 April 1258, at 'Ekaedu Vannebedeyr', which has not been
identified: *AWR*, pp. 501–2, no. 329. Quote from Smith, *Llywelyn*, p. 107.

[322] August 1258, at Caernarfon: *AWR*, p. 225, no. 85.

[323] *AWR*, p. 225, no. 85, and pp. 501–2, no. 329. Smith, 'Llywelyn ap Gruffudd (*d.* 1282)',
ODNB.

[324] December 1258, letters patent of the archbishop, directed to the bishops of Bangor
and St Asaph, concerning the commission made to him to coerce Llywelyn ap Gruffudd to
observe the peace between the king and him: *CCR, 1256–1259*, p. 466.

[325] *Brut, Pen20Tr*, p. 104, *Brut, Hergest*, pp. 234–5. Lloyd, *History of Wales*, ii, p. 686; *AWR*, p.
28.

[326] *CCR, 1247–1251*, p. 401; Burton and Stöber, 'The Dominicans in Wales', pp. 148–9;
Palmer, 'The Friar-Preachers, or Blackfriars of Bangor', 225 and n. 2.

[327] Smith, *Llywelyn*, p. 313.

[328] Stephenson, *Governance*, pp. 210–12.

welyn, 'prince of Wales', and other Welsh lords in 1258, was named by Llywelyn as a possible arbitrator in 1275, this time in a dispute with Bishop Anian II of St Asaph (1268–1293).[329]

David archdeacon of Bangor, mentioned in clause [vi], was one of the members of Richard's household named in the letters of safe conduct issued on 31 October 1259.[330] He was again named in letters of safe conduct issued on 25 July 1260.[331] He was still archdeacon of Bangor on 12 December 1263.[332] It is not known who the dean of Bangor was in 1261. However, the dean in 1254 had been William.[333] It is not known who the archdeacon of Anglesey was in 1261, however, it could have been Anian, Richard's successor, who held that office when he was elected to the bishopric six years later, in 1267.[334]

The churches mentioned in [viii] were both on Anglesey. 'Rhosyr probably referred to the church of St Peter, Newborough, adjacent to the site of the princely court at Rhosyr (SH 419 654) that formed the administrative centre of the commote of Menai. It is unknown which church was meant in the reference to Talybolion, the north-western commote of the island'.[335]

Huw Pryce has commented on the parallels between the provisions in the 29 April 1261 agreement and the rules in the Welsh law-texts regarding treasure-trove, wreck, military service, sacrilege, sanctuary and theft.[336] The use of *halaucty*, 'polluted house', as a term for a house in which stolen goods were discovered, is confined to lawbooks compiled in thirteenth-century Gwynedd.[337] The term was also used in Llywelyn ap Gruffudd's grant of liberties (7 December 1276 x 10 February 1277) to bishop Anian (II), and the dean and chapter, of St Asaph.[338] Pryce also notes that the age of majority in clause [iv] is consistent with the statement in the lawbooks of Gwynedd that a son should be commended to a lord at the age of fourteen, and that the same texts envisage the use of banishment (clause [ix]) as a punishment for theft in certain circumstances.[339]

---

[329] *ibid.*, pp. 209–10. 1275 dispute: *AWR*, pp. 564–6, no. 387. 1258 agreement with Scottish lords: *AWR*, pp. 499–501, no. 328.
[330] *CPR, 1258–1266*, p. 57.
[331] *ibid.*, p. 83.
[332] When Gruffudd ap Gwenwynwyn swore fealty to Llywelyn before Richard, David, and others: *AWR*, pp. 529–33, no. 358, and pp. 792–4, no. 601.
[333] *Valuation of Norwich*, p. 169 and p. 194.
[334] *CPR, 1266–1272*, p. 173.
[335] *AWR*, p. 518.
[336] Pryce, *Native Law*, pp. 191, 198, 220–1, and 229–30.
[337] *AWR*, p. 517; Pryce, *Native Law*, pp. 229–30. 'Keywannedd' meant principal residence: Pryce, *Native Law*, p. 229.
[338] *AWR*, pp. 580–3, no. 397.
[339] Age of majority: *AWR*, p. 517 referring to *Llyfr Iorwerth*, ed. A. R. Wiliam (Cardiff, 1960), §98/5; *Law of Hywel Dda*, p. 131. Banishment: Pryce, *Native Law*, pp. 202, 226, and 227.

Grievances of the lay community with Llywelyn ap Gruffudd regarding military service and wrecks were listed in articles of *gravamina* compiled at a hearing in the presence of Richard's successor, Anian, on 2 August 1283.[340]

The feast day of St Trillo (clause [vi]) is given as 15 June by Baring-Gould and Fisher.[341]

53. Llywelyn ap Gruffudd

Agreement made between Richard, bishop of Bangor, and the chapter of the one part, and Llywelyn ap Gruffudd, of the other, concerning the fixing of boundaries at Tal-y-llyn and between Llanwnda and Botellog, by the arbitration of Anian (I), bishop of St Asaph, brother Adam, prior and brother I[euaf?] lector of the Dominican convent of Bangor, Iorwerth and Trahaearn, friars minor of Llan-faes, and the lords Goronwy and Tudur sons of Ednyfed (Fychan), Einion Fychan and Einion ap Caradog. The settlement of the boundary at Tal-y-llyn made by Llywelyn in the bishop's presence is confirmed, and the fine for moving the boundary shall be in Llywelyn's mercy. Concerning the boundary between Llanwnda and Botellog, it is agreed that this should be fixed on the quinzaine from the feast of St Michael (13 October) by Dafydd Goch ap Cyfnerth, Goronwy ap Gwion (Gviann), Elidir ab Ednyfed, Llywelyn, Heilin (and) Adda ab Ynyr, Cadwgan Fychan (Junior), Madog (and) Llywarch ap Cadwgan, Cyfnerth, Iorwerth Wyddel (and) Iorwerth Goch ap Heilin, Madog Fychan, Maredudd ap Llywelyn (and) Cynwrig Wyddel meeting on the land where the boundary is disputed, under oath and pain of excommunication, who shall adjudicate the boundary between the said townships as they believe it was in the time of Llywelyn (ab Iorwerth) of good memory and the bishop of Bangor and his predecessors. If the said men say that the boundary has been moved to the place alleged, for which the bishop's men were summoned, Llywelyn shall receive a fine both for the moving of the boundary and the contumacy; if they assign the boundary beyond that place but on (the land held by) the bishop, Llywelyn shall receive payment only for the moving of the boundary; if they approve the bishop's boundary, Llywelyn's men shall be fined for their false accusation. If any of the aforesaid fifteen cannot be present for a necessary reason on the said day at the said place, Goronwy ab Ednyfed, Einion Fychan and Einion ap Caradog may arrange for other honest men to be chosen instead of those absent. The part agreement sealed by the bishop and chapter was to remain with Llywelyn, and the part sealed by Llywelyn was to remain with the bishop and his chapter.

Rhydyrarw, 18 August 1261

B = TNA E 36/274 (Miscellaneous Documents, Affairs of Wales, Henry III – Edward I, 'Liber A'), *c*.1282–*c*.1292. fo. ccclxiv[r v]. s. xiii ex. In margin: Conventio facta inter Bangor' episcopum et Lewelinu(m) de terminis assignandis inter quasdam terras per provisionem domini A. Assaven(sis) episcopi

Calendared in *Episc. Acts Welsh Dioceses Unpublished*, B202.

---

[340] The relevant articles being the eighth article and articles XXVIII and XXXII: BL Cotton Vitellius C x, fos. 166–9. Smith, '*Gravamina*', 160, n. 1, 162, 168, and 173–5, and see note to *Actum* **73**.

[341] Baring-Gould and Fisher, *Lives of the British Saints*, iv, p. 264. Although B. Willis gave the date as 14 June: Willis, *Survey*, p. 49. As noted by H. Pryce (*AWR*, p. 518), by the fourteenth century one of the two annual fairs of the bishop of Bangor was held on the four days focused on the feast of St Trillo: *RC*, p. 133. The other annual fair of the bishop was held on the four days focused on the feast of St Luke the Evangelist (18 October): *RC*, p. 133; Willis, *Survey*, p. 49.

Calendared in *Handlist of the Acts of Native Welsh Rulers*, no. 387.

Printed in 'Merionethshire', *Arch. Camb.*, 5th series, 2 (1885), 227–9.

Printed in *LW*, pp. 97–8, no. 192.

Printed in *AWR*, pp. 518–19, no. 346.

Transcribed from B.

Hec est forma compositionis facte apud Rydyraru anno domini m⁰ cc⁰ lx⁰ primo die iovis proxima post festum assumptionis beate Marie inter dominum R. Bang' episcopum et capitulum ex una parte et dominum Lewelinu(m) filium Griffini ex altera super terminis assignandis apud Tallyllynn et inter Lanwndaf et Botelauc per provisionem domini A. Asseven(sis) episcopi, fratris Ade prioris et fratris I. lectoris predicti Bang', Iervas(ii) et T(ra)haern fratrum minorum de Lamaes et dominorum Goron' et Tudry filiorum Edn', Enn' Parvi, Enn' filii Kerradauc, pacis reformatorum inter dictas partes, videlicet quod dominus Bang' ex provisione dictorum virorum ratam habet assignationem termini apud Talyllynn factam a domino L. episcopo et eius presentibus; item quod *ᵃfin dictaᵃ* de dicto termino amoto sit misericordia domini L. et voluntate. De termino autem assignando inter Lamvndaf et Botelauc sic fuit provisum: quod in quindena a festo sancti Mich(ael) is proximo futuri debent convenire David Goch filius Kywnerth, Goron' filius Gviann, Elidyr filius Edn', Lewelin, Heylyn, Adaf filii Ynyr, Kadugaun Iunior, Mad', Lywarch filii Kaduga(n), Kywn(er)th, Ioru(er)th Wydel, Ioru(er)th Coch filii Heylyn, Madauc Bychan, Mared' filius Lewelyn, Kynwric Vydel, super terram ubi est contentio de termino, et tunc ipsi iurati et sub excommunicatione in eorum veredicto assignabunt terminum inter dictas villas secundum quod ipsi viderunt terminum usitatum tempore Lewelini bone memorie et domini Bangor' et suorum accessorum*ᵇ* *[sic]* et credunt esse verum. Si autem dicti viri dixerint terminum usque ad locum ubi dicitur terminus amotus et ad quem homines episcopi fuerunt citati, vindicta tam de termino amoto quam de contumacia erit domino Lewelino; si autem dicti viri assignaverint terminum ultra predictum locum super episcopum, vindicta solum de termino amoto erit domino L.; si dicti viri assignaverint super partem domini L. et approbaverint terminum episcopi, capiat vindictam ab hominibus suis qui ei falsum suggesserunt. Si autem aliqui de predictis quindecim viris dictis die et loco [fo. ccclxiv^v] non poterint interesse et*ᶜ* *[sic]* necessaria causa, tunc per provisionem Goron' filii Edn' et Enn' Parvi et Enn' filii Karad' loco absentium in periculum animarum suarum eligantur <alii>*ᵈ* viri honesti. In cuius rei testimonium parti huius scripti penes dominum L. remanenti sigillum domini episcopi et capituli Bangor' sunt appensa; parti autem remanenti apud dominum episcopum et suum capitulum sigillum domini L. est appensum. Datum anno die et loco supradictis.

ᵃ⁻ᵃLW and *AWR* have findicta, B. *ᵇ*this should presumably be antecessorum, as suggested by *LW* and *AWR*, B. *ᶜ*this should presumably be ex, as suggested by *LW* and *AWR*, B. *ᵈ*superscript with an arrow pointing to where the word is to be inserted between eligantur and viri, *B.*

This was the third and final arbitration agreement between Richard and Llywelyn ap Gruffudd – for the background to this and the first two arbitration agreements see the note to *Actum* **51**.

For the possible location of *Rhydyraru* see the note to *Actum* **52**.

The arbitrators are the same as in *Actum* **52**, made three and half months earlier at the end of April 1261, save that Iorwerth and Trahaearn, friars minor of Llan-faes, have replaced Philip(?) and John (?)Rufus of the same convent, and the prior of the Dominicans at Bangor is named as Adam. According to *Actum* **52**, the prior of the Bangor Dominicans in April was Gwyn (*Wyn*), and so it seems that Adam had succeeded Gwyn by the middle of August 1261.[342] Brother 'I' is possibly Ieuaf, who in April was described as a brother of the Dominican convent of Bangor, although in the August document he is described as 'lector' of that convent.

For Anian I, bishop of St Asaph, as well as Goronwy and Tudur ab Ednyfed Fychan, Einion Fychan and Einion ap Caradog see the note to *Actum* **52** above.

'*Villa*' has been translated as 'township'. Tal-y-llyn may refer to the episcopal township of that name about 3 miles north-east of Aberffraw, on Anglesey.[343] In 1306, when a survey was carried out of the lands held by the bishop of Bangor, the episcopal township of Tal-y-llyn was recorded as having three free tenants, who held one carucate, and nineteen unfree tenants, who held one and half carucates between them.[344]

Llanwnda is located about 3 miles south of Caernarfon.[345] It is also referred to in the survey of the lands held by the bishop of Bangor in 1306.[346] Botellog is associated with Clynnog Fawr, which lies about 9.5 miles south-west of Caernarfon.[347]

Interestingly, when the August 1261 composition was printed in *Archaeologia Cambrensis* the title of the article, and the accompanying notes, show that it was assumed that this was an agreement concerning lands in Meirionnydd; the author stating that it related to certain lands in the neighbourhood of Towyn and Talyllyn; 'Talyllyn is a small village at the southern base of Cader Idris, and Botalog is near the coast, a little south of Towyn; but Lanwndaf is a name I am unable to identify'.[348]

---

[342] However, Huw Pryce has suggested that it is possible that Gwyn was Adam's original Welsh name, or alternatively Robert Vaughan's transcription (*Actum* **52**) could be erroneous – Vaughan seems initially to have been unable to read the name, as 'Wyn' is a marginal addition – in either case, both names could refer to the same individual: *AWR*, pp. 517–18.

[343] Commote: Malltraeth, Anglesey; Tal-y-llyn farm SH 366 734: *AWR*, p. 519.

[344] *RC*, p. 105; Carr, *Medieval Anglesey*, p. 39; Carr, 'Jones Pierce Revisited', p. 137; Carr, 'The Black Death in Anglesey', 40. Also, Jones, *Anglesey Churches*, pp. 70–1.

[345] SH 475 583: *AWR*, p. 519.

[346] *RC*, p. 96; Carr, 'Jones Pierce Revisited', p. 136.

[347] 'Botelok', supposedly a gift by Rhodri ab Idwal to Clynnog, was listed in Edward IV's confirmation charter: *RC*, p. 257. Botelog or Bodellog: 'a hamlet in Clynnog': Evans, 'Three Old Foundations', 106. Botelog: Jones, 'The Collegiate Church of Clynnog Fawr', 254. Sims-Williams, 'Beuno [St Beuno] (*d.* 653/9)', *ODNB*.

[348] 'Merionethshire', *Arch. Camb.*, 5th series, 2 (1885), 227–9.

*54. Llywelyn ap Gruffudd

Interdict placed on Llywelyn's chapel.

1265 [Shortly before 15 May]

Mention only, in an enrolled letter, TNA C 54/82 (Close Rolls, 49 Henry III), m. 6d, from King Henry III to the bishop of Bangor dated 15 May 1265, at Gloucester.

Letter printed in *CCR, 1264–1268*, pp. 117–18:

'*Rex Bangorensi episcopo salutem. Ex parte L. filii Griffini nobis est ostensum quod, cum ipse pro se et hominibus suis vobis caucionem sufficientem frequenter optulerit de parendo mandatis ecclesie in forma juris, si in aliquo contra vos in prejudicium ecclesie libertatis deliquerint, vos caucionem hujusmodi hactenus admittere recusastis, nihilominus pro causis non ad forum ecclesiasticum immo ad curiam laicalem mere pertinentibus, ut de laicalibus feodis, capellam suam interdicto supposuistis. Et quia hoc sustinere nolumus, sicut nec debemus, maxime, cum placita de laicis feodis in regno nostro ad coronam et dignitatem nostram pertineant, vobis mandamus rogantes quod prefatum interdictum sine more dispendio revocetis, vel saltem ponatis in respectum usque ad instans parleamentum nostrum quod habituri sumus apud Westmonasterium, ubi vos una cum ceteris prelatis regni nostri juxta mandatum nostrum intereritis, ut tunc habito tractatu super premissis inde fiat utrique parti quod de jure fuerit faciendum. Teste ut supra*'.

Llywelyn ap Gruffudd had written to Henry complaining that he had frequently offered the bishop a sufficient bond (*cautio*) to obey the mandates of the Church if he had offended against him to the prejudice of ecclesiastical liberty, but that the bishop had refused such a bond even for causes not belonging to the ecclesiastical court (*ad forum ecclesiasticum*) but entirely to the lay court (*ad curiam laicalem*). Instead, Richard had placed an interdict on Llywelyn's chapel. The prince alleged that this was done by the bishop on account of causes such as lay fees that pertain to lay, not ecclesiastical, jurisdiction.[349] Since pleas concerning lay fees in his realm pertained to the crown, Henry, in his letter, ordered Richard to revoke the interdict without delay, or at least put it into respite until the next parliament at Westminster, where the bishop was to be present (with other prelates of the kingdom) and where the matter could be discussed.[350]

In May 1265, Henry III was a prisoner of Simon de Montfort, the king having been captured at the Battle of Lewes the year before, and Llywelyn may have decided that instead of resolving his differences with the bishop of Bangor by arbitration, as he had done in 1261 (see *Acta* **52** and **53**, and *Actum* **51** also), he would get a more sympathetic hearing from de Montfort with whom it appears he was not only collaborating militarily but also negotiating to secure recognition of his supremacy in Wales.[351]

---

[349] *CCR, 1264–1268*, pp. 117–18; *AWR*, p. 533, no. 360.

[350] *CCR, 1264–1268*, pp. 117–18. The next parliament was held at Winchester, on 14 September 1265, though the *Annals of Waverley* state that, because of Llywelyn's attacks into parts of Cheshire, it was continued at Westminster on 13 October: *AWR*, p. 533; *Annales de Wintonia*, p. 102; *Annales de Waverleia*, p. 366; *CPR, 1266–1272*, p. 265.

[351] *Annales Cestrienses*, p. 90. Smith, *Llywelyn*, pp. 164–5 and 167–70. Lloyd, *History of Wales*, ii, p. 735. *AWR*, pp. 333–6, nos. 361 and 362. Stephenson, *Governance*, p. 173.

For the effect and ramifications of an interdict on a specific church or chapel, termed *interdictum particulare*, see the discussion in Peter Clarke's *The Interdict in the Thirteenth Century*.[352]

55. Pope Clement IV

Supplication to Pope Clement IV, via the papal legate Cardinal Ottobuono. Richard felt himself insufficient any longer to undertake the pastoral care of the church of Bangor, the governance of which had been committed to him. He had already been in charge for more than thirty years. Now he desired to resign on account of the afflictions and failings arising from his aged body. The malice of the people oppressed him, for he was disturbed by so many seditions and insolences. He begged, therefore, that he might be relieved of his duties as pastor, and that provision be made for his church.

1267 [before 8 November]

B = NLW Peniarth MS 231B (*Llyfr Coch Asaph*), pp. 31–2. s. xvii.[353] In the margin: 'fol. xvii: a' underneath which is written: Clemens 4. corona 8. Cal Martii a° 1266[354]

C = 'Manuscript in Sir Thomas Sebright's Library, Numb. 102. in 4to'.[355]

Calendared in *Episc. Acts Welsh Dioceses Unpublished*, B208.

C is printed in Willis, *Survey*, pp. 187–8.[356]

B is printed in Haddan and Stubbs, i, pp. 496–7.

Transcribed from B.

Sanctissimo patri et domino C. divina providentia sacrosancte Romane ecclesie summo pontiffici, Ricardus Bangoren(si)s episcopus[a], per[b] [devota][c] oscula beatorum. In desolatione positus[d] et circundatus undique laqueis[e], levo ad pastorem omnium occulos meos, unde mihi auxilium veniat et ervatur a tribulationibus anima mea, expectans ut salvum me faciat a facie tempestatis. Sane, pater sanctissime, consumpsit [cor][f] meum et ebibit labores[g] cure[h] pastoralis officii, in quo licet invitus et insufficiens plusquam triginta annis iam preteritis[i] prefui ecclesie Bangoren(si) quam dum pietas celestis annuit, expositis corporis et anime

---

[352] Clarke, *The Interdict in the Thirteenth Century*, pp. 68–71. Also, *Oxford Dictionary of the Christian Church*, p. 840.

[353] A handwritten note with the manuscript states that 'This Manuscript is in the handwriting of Robert Vaughan of Hengwrt, Esquire, the … antiquary who died in 1667'. There are four manuscripts which are regarded as transcripts of, the now lost, *Llyfr Coch Asaph* – the manuscripts are deposited at the NLW, Aberystwyth – the second of these is Peniarth MS 231B: Jones, 'Llyfr Coch Asaph: A Textual and Historical Study', i, p. xxxv.

[354] Written in a different hand, and more recent. This marginal note is not mentioned by Haddan and Stubbs (or Browne Willis). It could be a reference to Pope Clement IV's coronation, although, if so, it is inaccurate. Clement IV's coronation took place on 15 February (15 kal. Mar.) 1265: Cheney, *Handbook of Dates*, p. 37.

[355] Mentioned only by Willis, *Survey*, p. 187.

[356] Willis notes that he took the wording of the supplication 'Out of a Manuscript in Sir Thomas Sebright's Library, Numb. 102. in 4to': Willis, *Survey*, p. 187. It has been suggested that this was a copy made by Edward Lhuyd (d. 1709) taken from the (original and now lost) Red Book (*Llyfr Coch Asaph*) itself: Haddan and Stubbs, i, p. 497, n. d.

viribus commisso mihi gubernaculo [quam eque]^j ....^{k} tenere novissem studui gubernare. Nunc autem me possident dies afflictionis et deficientibus pre senectute corporis viribus adiacentis quoque infirmitatis debilitas comittatur. Intereuntibus autem inter me que ipsa natura permiserat^l accedit malicia plebis, que tot et tantis seditionum et in [p. 32] solentiarum turbinibus agitatur^m ut etiam potens quisque compescendis^n vix sufficiat sponte corruentibus^o in profundum. Propterea^p iam non pastor sed^q ovis, utinam minus^r morbida vel mutila a summo pastore presidium flagito compatiensque alumpne^s cuius pondus ferre non possum, cui neque [alius]^t debitum prebere solatium [potest]^u, ^{v}sanctitatis apostolice pedibus provolutus, eoque spiritu presens quo adhuc servator meus sinit nostrum habitaculum vegetari$v$, ^{w}clamo, eiulo, vociferor, et pulso^w ad fores patrone vestras, ut sacrum illud coniugium, quo me prefate ecclesie ^{x}fide media copulavi^x, iam conversum in vincula et compedes ergastuli carceralis, solvere dignemini digito quo clementiam vestram providentia divina constituit ^{y}in plenitudine potestatis$y$, et non tam persone quam ecclesie misericorditer providentes, ex predictis tam sufficientibus quam veris causis mihi^z porrigat beata dextra ^{aa}munus <utilis>^{bb} et [iuste]^{cc} cessionis, tam eidem ecclesie de pastore quam michi de brevis vite residue <sustentatione>^{dd} iuxta dispositionem vestre clementissime sanctitatis misericorditer providendo receptionem autem mee cessionis et provisionem de me vite sustentatione ac etiam de provisione ecclesie de pastore, venerabili patri domino O. Sancti Adriani diacono cardinali apostolice sedis legato, supplico pro clementia vestra litteras demandari. Dat'.^{aa}

^{a}*sic* 'episcopo', *B.* ^{b}or 'por', *B.* ^{c}lacuna at this point in the text, *B.* Willis has 'devota' with no mention of a lacuna, *C.* Followed by Haddan and Stubbs, '[devota]', *B.* ^{d}Willis has 'percitus', *C.* ^{e}missing from Willis' transcript, *C.* ^{f}c⁹or me̅u̅ c⁹or, *B.* Haddan and Stubbs suggested 'cor' or 'corpus', *B.* Willis has 'cor', *C.* ^{g}Willis has 'labor', *C.* ^{h}Willis has 'cura', *C.* ^{i}Willis has 'praeteritos', *C.* ^{j}'<?n>ue??'. '?n' is in superscript with an arrow pointing to the place of insertion. '?n' is followed by 'ue??'. Haddan and Stubbs may, following Willis, have interpreted this as '[quam aeque]', *B, C.* Alternatively they conjectured that '[quam aeque]' should fill the lacuna that follows, *B.* ^{k}lacuna, possibly filled with '[quam aeque]' by Haddan and Stubbs, see previous note, *B.* ^{l}Willis has 'promiserat', *C.* ^{m}Willis has '(aestmat)', *C.* ^{n}Willis has 'compescendo', *C.* ^{o}t̅.q̅ precedes corruentibus, *B.* Willis has 'corruentes', *C.* ^{p}Willis has 'Praeterea' *C.* ^{q}Willis has 'si-quidem' *C.* ^{r}Willis does not have 'utinam minus', instead he has 'omnino' *C.* ^{s}Willis has 'compatiens (ut fies) calumpnae', *C.* Haddan and Stubbs have '[alius]', *B.* As does Willis, '(alius)', *C.* ^{t}Haddan and Stubbs have '[potest]', *B.* As does Willis, '(potest)', *C.* ^{v}Willis has 'sanctitatis Apostolice pedibus provolutus (peto), eoque spiritu quoad praesens hoc servator meus sinat nostrum habitaculum vegetari'. *C.* $^{w-w}$Willis has 'Clamo, elevo (vocem), vocifero, et pulso$w$ *C.* $^{x-x}$Willis has 'fide quondam copulari' *C.* $^{y-y}$Willis has 'in plenitudine prefata', *C.* ^{z}Willis has 'vestra', *C.* $^{aa-aa}$Willis ends with '... munus utile, ut non solum de cessione eiusdem Eclesiae, de Pastore verum etiam de me de brevis vitae residuae sustentatione iuxta disponas nostrae, Clementissime, sanctitatis providendo receptionem, aut ex mea cessione de vitae pro mea vita sustentatione ac etiam de provisione Eclesiae de Pastore (cogitantes.) Venerabili Patri Domino, O Sancti *Adriani*, Diacono Cadinali, Apostolicae Sedis Legato, supplico ut Clementiae (vestrae) Literas nostras demandari (velit.) Dat ...', *C.* ^{bb}Superscript above 'munus' *B.* Willis has 'utile', *C.* ^{cc}Haddan and Stubbs conjectured that this abbreviated word (three or four letters with the letter e in superscript) was 'iuste', *B.* ^{dd}Superscript above a word that has been crossed through, *B.*

A bishop could only resign in certain circumstances, and, by the first years of the thirteenth century, only with papal permission. Richard's predecessor, Cadwgan, obtained papal permission to resign.[357] The possible reasons for resigning one's benefice (detailed in a letter of Innocent III, published in the Decretals of Gregory IX) included physical debility, and maliciousness of the people under one's care.[358]

The fact that Richard stated that he had already been in charge of the church of Bangor for more than thirty years (*plusquam triginta annis iam preteritis prefui ecclesie Bangoren(si)*) strongly suggests a date in 1267.[359]

Richard died before 8 November 1267, for on that date, at Winchester, Master Iorwerth ('Gervase'), a canon of Bangor, delivered letters patent from the chapter announcing the death of the bishop of Bangor.[360]

Cardinal Ottobuono was appointed on 4 May 1265, by Clement IV, as papal legate to England where he arrived on 29 October 1265.[361]

Richard's supplication may have been made when Ottobuono was present in the Welsh Marches at the negotiations leading up to, and then at the solemnisation of, the so-called Treaty of Montgomery. The papal legate was in Shrewsbury by 25 August 1267.[362] Agreement was reached on 25 September, and Ottobuono was present in Montgomery (probably at the ford of Rhyd Chwima) at Michaelmas (29 September), when Llywelyn ap Gruffudd ratified the agreement.[363]

---

[357] *Cal. Pap. Reg.*, i, p. 151. See also *Actum* **33**.

[358] *Liber Extra*, X, 1. 9. 10 (cols. 107–12 at 108). Pennington, *Pope and Bishops*, pp. 101–14, especially 106; Goering and Pryce, '*De Modo Confitendi*', 6–7, and ns. 34, 35, 36 and 37.

[359] It is not clear when in 1237 Richard was consecrated – see the section of the Introduction entitled 'Richard/Rhirid', and the note to *Actum* **40** above – however the wording of his supplication suggests he was consecrated earlier in the calendar year than the day and month of his *supplicatio* to the pope. In fact it could be argued that even if the date of his supplication in 1267 was less than thirty years from the date of his consecration in 1237 because he was archdeacon of Bangor in 1236 (royal assent having being given to his election on 3 July that year, after his predecessor, Cadwgan, had resigned the bishopric), he had been in charge of the church of Bangor for more than thirty years in any event. Richard's election: *CPR, 1232–1247*, p. 152.

[360] *CPR, 1266–1277*, p. 165.

[361] Bolton, 'Ottobuono [Ottobuono or Ottobono Fieschi; afterwards Adrian] (*c.*1205–1276)', *ODNB*. Graham, 'Letters of Cardinal Ottoboni', 87–120.

[362] Smith, *Llywelyn*, p. 178, n. 145.

[363] *ibid.*, pp. 177–9. For the text of the Treaty of Montgomery, see *AWR*, pp. 536–42, no. 363.

ANIAN

56. Profession of obedience

I Anian, elect of the church of Bangor, to be consecrated a priest by you, reverend father Boniface (of Savoy) archbishop of the holy church of Canterbury, and primate of the whole of England, profess that I will show due canonical obedience and subjection in all things to you and to the church of Canterbury, and to your successors canonically substituted, and I promise, according to the decretals of the pontiff of the Romans, that I will assist in defending and preserving the rights of yourself and of the church of Canterbury, saving my order. So help me God. And I confirm all the aforesaid by signing by (my) own hand. +

1267 [after 12 December]

A = Canterbury Cathedral Archives, Dean and Chapter, CCA-DCc/ChAnt/C/115/136. 232 x 48 mm. Stitching holes at head and foot.[364] Endorsed: Ista consecratio facta fuit in ecclesia Christi Cantuar' a domino Bonefacio archiepiscopo, anno domino MCCLXVII, astantibus Hugone Elyensi, Willelmo Landauensi episcopis.

B = Canterbury Cathedral Archives, Dean and Chapter, Register A (The Prior's Register), fos. 250v–251r. s. xiv med.

Calendared in *Episc. Acts Welsh Dioceses Unpublished*, B212.

Calendared in *Canterbury Professions*, pp. 78–9, no. 210.

Transcribed from A.

Ego Anianus, Bangornensis ecclesie electus, et a te, reverende pater Bonefaci, sancte Cantuariens(is) ecclesie archiepiscope, et tocius Anglie primas, consecrandus antistes, tibi et Cantuariensi ecclesie et successoribus tuis canonice substituendis, debitam et canonicam obedienciam et subiectionem me per omnia exhibiturum profiteor, et promitto secundum decreta Romanorum pontificium, tuorumque et Cantuariensis ecclesie iurium adiutor ero ad defendendum et retinendum, salvo ordine meo. Sic me deus adiuvet. Et predicta omnia propria manu subscribendo confirmo. +

Signed with a cross – see note to *Actum* 7 (Gwion's profession to Canterbury).

---

[364] Image at Plate VI (vii). Canterbury Cathedral Archives' online record: https://archives.canterbury-cathedral.org/CalmView/Record.aspx?src=CalmView.Catalog&id=CCA-DCc-ChAnt%2fC%2f115%2f136&pos=1, accessed 11 March 2024.

The wording of Anian's profession, first used in 1254 for the profession of John of Climping, elect of Chichester, was used many times during the archiepiscopate of Boniface of Savoy.[365]

On 8 November 1267, at Winchester, Master Iorwerth ('Gervase'), a canon of Bangor, delivered letters patent from his chapter announcing the death of the bishop of Bangor (Richard). Accordingly, he was given licence to elect.[366] On 12 December, signification was given to the archbishop of Canterbury of the royal assent to the election of Master Anian, archdeacon of Anglesey, and a canon of the church of Bangor, to be bishop of that place.[367]

The endorsement to Anian's profession states that he was consecrated at Christ Church, Canterbury by Archbishop Boniface, who was assisted by Hugh de Balsham, bishop of Ely, and William de Braose (Briouze), bishop of Llandaff, '*anno domino MCCLXVII*'. The endorsement is in the same hand as the endorsement to the profession of John II, elect of St Asaph, who was also consecrated at Canterbury in 1267.[368] Hugh de Balsham and William de Braose also assisted at John's consecration.[369]

On 5 January 1268, King Henry III restored, according to 'custom', the temporalities of the bishopric of Bangor to Master Anian, and commanded 'Llewelin son of Griffin, prince of Wales, to let him have seisin thereof so far as pertains to the said Llewelin'.[370]

*57. Bringhurst Church, Leicestershire

Indulgence to all those who should visit the church of Bringhurst (Brenninghurst') *and say there a Paternoster and an Ave for the soul of Sarah Albe of Drayton whose body is buried in the said church.*

[13 December 1267 x 2 August 1293]

Mentioned only, in a *ratificatio* dated 2 August 1293, made at Lyddington by Oliver of Sutton, bishop of Lincoln.[371] The ratification concerned all indulgences granted by the bishops of Hereford, Rochester, Bangor, Dunblane, and St Asaph.[372] Oliver of Sutton was consecrated as bishop of Lincoln on 19 May 1280.[373]

---

[365]   *Canterbury Professions*, pp. 71–2, no. 187 and pp. 72–5 and 78–9.
[366]   *CPR, 1266–1272*, p. 165. Sealed petition from the dean and chapter to Henry III, for licence to elect a pontiff and pastor: TNA, Chancery: Ecclesiastical Petitions, C 84/4/19.
[367]   Clarendon near Salisbury: *CPR, 1266–1272*, p. 173.
[368]   *Canterbury Professions*, pp. 78–9, nos. 209 and 210.
[369]   *ibid.*, p. 78, no. 209.
[370]   Westminster: *CPR, 1266–1272*, p. 178.
[371]   *Rolls and Register of Bishop Oliver Sutton*, iv, p. 101.
[372]   *ibid.*
[373]   *Fasti Lincoln*, p. 3.

It is, of course, possible that the indulgence or indulgences of the bishop(s) of Bangor referred to in Oliver of Sutton's *ratificatio* related to Anian's predecessors, or to Anian and one or more of his predecessors – Richard had been in exile in England notably between 1248 and 1257/8 and Robert of Shrewsbury had been in Lincoln in 1201 – but it seems likely, given the nature of the grant and the date of the ratification, that the reference is to an indulgence granted by Anian.[374] If so, it is possible that the grant was made during one of Anian's periods of exile from Bangor and was perhaps made at nearby Lyddington (now in the county of Rutland) where the bishop of Lincoln had a palace.

Anian's three periods of exile from Bangor were (i) Palm Sunday 1277 to *c.*November 1277, (ii) 1278 to *c.*November 1281, and (iii) *c.*Easter x June/July 1282 to *c.*late December 1282/January 1283.[375] As he was in eastern England in 1279 and 1280, and with Oliver of Sutton himself in Lincoln in October 1280 (see *Acta* **66** and **67**, and the note to *Actum* **69**), the second period, 1278 to *c.*November 1281, is perhaps the most likely.

58. Haughmond Abbey

Letter confirming the gifts and confirmations of his predecessors namely bishops Meurig, Gwion, Alan, Cadwgan, and Richard concerning the churches of Nefyn and Trefeglwys. Sealing clause.
Haughmond, 15 January 1272/3

B = Shrewsbury, Shropshire Archives MS 6001/6869 (Haughmond Cartulary), fo. 150v. s. xv ex. Rubric: alia confirmatio dictarum ecclesiarum

Calendared in *Cartulary of Haughmond Abbey*, p. 162, no. 796.[376]

Transcribed from B.

Omnibus sancte matris ecclesie filiis ad quos presentes littere pervenerint, Anianus dei gratia Bangor' episcopus, salutem in domino sempiternam. Cum sit opus pietatis locis religiosis providere et eadem in libertatibus sibi misericorditer indultis conservare nos ex pastoralis sollicitudinis officio nobis divinitus collato possessiones et iura ecclesie Sancti Joh(ann)is evangeliste de Haghmon' in nostra diocesi fidelium devotione collata in nostra protectione suscipimus et predecessorum nostrorum Mauricii, Guydonis, Alani, Cadugani, Ric(ard)i donationes et confirmationes super ecclesiis de Nevin et Treveglus cum omnibus pertinentiis suis ratas et gratas habentes eadem predicte ecclesie presenti scripto confirmamus, salvo iure nostro et aliorum in omnibus et per omnia. In cuius rei testimonium litteris presentibus sigillum nostrum duximus apponendum. Dat' apud Haghmon', anno gratie millesimo cclxxii, xviii kal' Februarii.

---

[374] Richard, bishop of Bangor in exile: see notes to *Acta* **38**, **39** and **49**. Robert of Shrewsbury, bishop of Bangor in Lincoln: see the note to *Actum* **19**.

[375] See the section of the Introduction entitled 'Anian'.

[376] Rees does not transcribe the *actum* but does say (*Cartulary of Haughmond Abbey*, p. 162, no. 796) that the wording from 'Cum' to 'suscipimus' is identical to that of Alan's confirmacio to Haughmond (see *Actum* **14**).

For the church of Nefyn in Llŷn see *Acta* **4**, **8**, **14** and **45**. For the church of Trefegl-wys in Arwystli see *Acta* **5**, **9**, **10**, **14** and **45**.

This confirmation may well be a product of the beneficiary, as the wording from '*Cum*' to '*predecessorum nostrorum*' is identical to that of Alan's charter to Haughmond (**14**), which confirmed the charters of Meurig and Gwion to the same house – the scribes of Haughmond adding the names of bishops Alan, Cadwgan and Richard to Anian's *actum* of January 1272.[377] Anian, who was at Haughmond when his confirmation was given, ensured that a saving clause was included ('*salvo iure nostro et aliorum in omnibus et per omnia*').[378]

It has been noted in the *English Episcopal Acta* series that arengae often referred to the duties of episcopal office.[379] Here Anian's confirmation repeated Alan's word-ing, *ex pastoralis sollicitudinis officio nobis divinitus*.[380]

Actum **58** was not to be the last charter in favour of the Augustinians of Haugh-mond granted during Anian's episcopate, for Cynddelw ('*Candelau*''), dean of Bangor, together with the chapter of Bangor, were asked by Haughmond (for pre-sumably they only acted on the abbey's request) to confirm the previous charters of bishops of Bangor relating to the churches of Nefyn and Trefeglwys, which they did.[381] As Robert Burnell, bishop of Bath and Wells, witnessed their confirmation, the *terminus a quo* is the date of his consecration as bishop, namely 7 April 1275, and the *terminus ante quem* the date of his death, 25 October 1292.[382] Not only were the charters of bishops Meurig, Gwion, Alan, Cadwgan and Richard listed, but so too that of Anian.[383]

*59. Dafydd and Llywelyn ap Gruffudd

Sealed letter from bishops Anian of Bangor and Anian II of St Asaph, giving their interpretation and explanation of articles in an agreement (of 1269) between Dafydd and Llywelyn which were obscure, and in doubt.

[377] Gwion, in the genitive, is rendered as 'Guydonis' in Anian's confirmation as opposed to 'Widonis' in Alan's confirmation.

[378] His immediate predecessor, Richard, in his confirmation to the same house (*Actum* **45**), had also included a saving clause: 'salvo in omnibus iure episcopali'.

[379] See for example *EEA, VII, Hereford, 1079–1234*, pp. lxxxviii–lxxxix. See also the section of the 'Diplomatic Analysis of the *Acta*' entitled 'Arenga'.

[380] *Actum* **14**.

[381] Shrewsbury, Shropshire Archives, MS 6001/6869 (Haughmond Cartulary), fo. 151. *Cartulary of Haughmond Abbey*, p. 162, no. 799.

[382] *ibid.*; *Fasti Bath and Wells*, p. 6; Harding, 'Burnell, Robert (*d.* 1292)', *ODNB*. For Cynddelw see *Fasti Welsh Cathedrals*, p. 5. U. Rees (relying on '*Le Neve*, i, 110') gave a date range of April 1275 x *c.*1290, stating that Wm. had become dean of Bangor in 1291 (*Cartulary of Haughmond Abbey*, p. 162, no. 799). Browne Willis also stated that William was dean of Bangor in 1291, connecting him to the *Taxatio Ecclesiastica* of that year (Willis, *Survey*, p. 121). An unnamed dean of Bangor is recorded in the *Taxatio* of 1291 but as noted by *Fasti Welsh Cathedrals*, p. 5 and n. 11 any connection with a William is likely to be a confusion with the earlier 1254 taxation which did name a William as dean of Bangor (*Valuation of Norwich*, p. 194).

[383] Shrewsbury, Shropshire Archives, MS 6001/6869 (Haughmond Cartulary), fo. 151. *Cartulary of Haughmond Abbey*, p. 162, no. 799.

1274 [*c.*April x *c.*June]

Mentioned in a letter from Pope Gregory X to Llywelyn ap Gruffudd dated 18 August 1274, at Lyon, in which the pope confirmed his agreement to the interpretation and explanation of the bishops of Bangor and St Asaph. Gregory X's letter is printed in Haddan and Stubbs, i, pp. 501–2, as well as in *Foedera*, i, part ii, p. 515.

Llywelyn had petitioned the pope, June x July 1274, sending the bishops' letter and requesting Gregory X's confirmation of the interpretation and explanation made by the two bishops.[384] The bishops were said to have made a prudent and salutary interpretation and explanation (*interpretationem et declarationem fecerunt providam et salubrem*) concerning the doubt and obscurity in the articles concerned.[385]

The agreement of 1269 made, at *Aberreu*, between Dafydd and Llywelyn, had been sealed by Anian of Bangor and Anian II of St Asaph, and had been made subject to the bishop's joint and several jurisdiction.[386] It included a provision that any trespasses, injuries or grievances that might arise between Llywelyn and Dafydd would be settled by the two bishops acting together with worthy men. It also included a provision allowing the parties to seek papal confirmation of the agreement.[387]

In the summer of 1274, Anian travelled to France and attended the Second General Council of Lyon, called by Gregory X. The Council was held between 7 May and 17 July and met in six sessions.[388] Anian sealed a decree made at the Council on 13 July.[389] The letter from the two Anians, giving their interpretation and explanation of the articles which were in doubt, must have been sent well before 13 July (and possibly before the start of the Council) to give Anian of Bangor time to travel to Lyon.

On 20 December 1274, Llywelyn wrote to the two bishops sending the papal confirmation of their interpretation to be inspected by them.[390] See also the note to *Actum* **61**.

60. Canterbury Cathedral Priory

Indulgence. Trusting in the mercy of omnipotent God and in the merits of the blessed virgin Mary, St Thomas the Martyr and all the saints, relaxation of 20 days' enjoined penance for all those who

---

[384] *AWR*, p. 558, no. 382.
[385] *AWR*, p. 558, no. 382; Haddan and Stubbs, i, pp. 501–2; *Foedera*, i, part ii, p. 515.
[386] *AWR*, pp. 546–7, no. 368.
[387] *ibid.*
[388] *Councils and Synods*, ii, part ii, p. 810. The bishops of St Davids (Richard de Carew) and Llandaff (William de Braose) were present, as were the archbishops of Canterbury and York, and at least six bishops of English sees: *ibid.*, and n. 4.
[389] *Welsh Episcopal Seals*, III (no. 7). Vatican Archive, A. A. Arm. I–XVIII, 2190 (no. 18); *Sigilli Dell' Archivio Vaticano*, i, 76; *Councils and Synods*, ii, part ii, p. 810, n. 4.
[390] *AWR*, pp. 558–9, no. 383.

are truly penitent, and abandoning their sins, pray for the soul of Adam de Chillendenne, of good memory late prior of the church of Canterbury, and all the faithful departed. Sealed.

Canterbury, Sunday 23 September 1274

A = Canterbury Cathedral Archives, Dean and Chapter, CCA-DCc-ChAnt/C/167. 224 x 112 mm.[391] Pointed-oval, red-wax privy seal, 28 mm wide at widest point x 47 mm in height. The obverse of the seal depicts a figure kneeling in prayer beneath an acute arch, above which are the Virgin (crowned) and child. The legend, which is in Lombardic capitals, so far as is decipherable, reads '[]PVAT ...... EPISCOPI BNGOREN'.[392] Sealed on a parchment tag which has been passed through horizontal slits in the turn-up at the foot of the document (*sur double queue*). Endorsed with description in fourteenth-century hand, giving forty rather than twenty days.

Calendared in *Fifth Report of the Royal Commission on Historical Manuscripts*, p. 444.

Transcribed from A.

Omnibus Cristi fidelibus presentes litteras visuris vel audituris, Anianus dei gratia Bangorens(is) episcopus, salutem in domino sempiternam. Ut fidelium Cristi devotionem allectivis indulgenciarum muneribus ad caritatis et devotionis opera propencius excitemus, de omnipotentis dei misericordia, beate Marie virginis, et sancti Thome martiris, ac etiam omnium sanctorum, meritis confidentes, omnibus vere penitentibus et peccata sua dimittentibus, qui pro anima bone memorie Ade de Chilindenne, quondam prioris ecclesie Cant', et omnium fidelium defunctorum oraverint, viginti dies de iniuncta sibi penitentia misericorditer relaxamus. In cuius rei testimonium presentibus litteris sigillum nostrum est appositum. Data apud Cant' anno domini m cc Ixx quarto, die*a* dominica proxima post festum beati Mathei apostoli.

*a*a fold of the parchment runs through this word, but it is fairly clear that the scribe wrote 'de' not 'die', A.

Adam de Chillendenne died on 13 September 1274.[393]

Anian's indulgence was granted on his return from the Second Council of Lyon in the summer of 1274 (see note to *Actum* **59**), and ten days after the death of Prior Adam.

The wording of Anian's grant is very similar to the grant of twenty days indulgence made the same year by the archbishop of Canterbury, Robert Kilwardby, save that the latter refers to the tomb of Adam de Chillendenne.[394]

The seal attached to Anian's indulgence is not recorded in *Welsh Episcopal Seals*.

---

[391] Image at Plate XIV.
[392] Image at Plate III (ii).
[393] *Heads of Religious Houses*, ii, p. 28.
[394] 'tumba': *Fifth Report of the Royal Commission on Historical Manuscripts*, p. 444.

*61. Llywelyn ap Gruffudd, Prince of Wales

Letter(s) from Anian of Bangor and Anian II of St Asaph warning, amongst other things, that Llywelyn should desist from inflicting disturbances and injuries upon Dafydd, his brother, and Gruffudd ap Gwenwynwyn (of southern Powys) and give due satisfaction for these, and furthermore that Llywelyn should observe all the articles of the agreement between him and the aforesaid lords.

1274 [Shortly before 20 December]

Mentioned in a letter patent from Llywelyn ap Gruffudd, prince of Wales, addressed to the two bishops, and dated 20 December 1274 at Llanfair Rhyd Gastell. Llywelyn's letter is printed in *AWR*, pp. 558–9, no. 383.

The agreement between Llywelyn and Dafydd, sealed by the two bishops, was dated 1269 at *Aberreu*.[395] As discussed in the note to *Actum* **59** above, the brothers sought clarification concerning certain articles of the same, which were dubious and obscure in some part. Anian of Bangor and Anian II of St Asaph were asked to interpret and explain the articles in dispute. The bishops set out their interpretation and explanation in a letter (see *Actum* **59**), which Llywelyn sent to Gregory X (June x July 1274) petitioning the pope for his confirmation of the episcopal interpretation and explanation provided.[396] The pope's confirmation, dated 18 August 1274, was sent by Llywelyn to the two bishops with his letter of 20 December 1274.[397] The prince told the two bishops that Dafydd had had the temerity to break the agreement, and asked them to warn his brother to observe the agreement and explanation, and compel him to do so according to the terms (see note to *Actum* **59**) of their execution of the agreement.[398] The bishops' response is not known.

Gruffudd ap Gwenwynwyn (d. 1286), the grandson of Owain Cyfeiliog, who having been dispossessed of his lands in Powys Wenwynwyn (southern Powys) had made an agreement, on 12 December 1263, with Llywelyn.[399] Gruffudd did homage for himself and his heirs, and, touching relics, swore fealty to Llywelyn and his heirs before, amongst others, Richard, Anian of Bangor's predecessor. In return for Gruffudd's homage and fealty, Llywelyn granted and restored to him all his lands and possessions, which he agreed to hold in hereditary right for ever from Llywelyn and his heirs.[400] Llywelyn's letter of 20 December 1274 to the two Anians stated that no agreement existed between him and Gruffudd with regard to settling certain articles or grievances, but, in fact, Gruffudd had withdrawn from Llywelyn's homage and fealty and had abandoned his lands of his own volition 'which is public and notorious to all throughout Wales'.[401] No doubt the notoriety to which

---

[395] *AWR*, pp. 546–7, no. 368.

[396] *ibid.*, p. 558, no. 382.

[397] *ibid.*, pp. 558–9, no. 383. Pope's letter of 18 August 1274: Haddan and Stubbs, i, pp. 501–2; *Foedera*, i, part ii, p. 515.

[398] *AWR*, pp. 558–9, no. 383.

[399] at Ystumanner: *AWR*, pp. 529–33, no. 358, and pp. 792–4, no. 601. *LW*, pp. 77–80, no. 147, and pp. 111–13, no. 204. Tout, revd Carr, 'Gruffudd ap Gwenwynwyn (*d.* 1286)', *ODNB*.

[400] *AWR*, pp. 529–33, no. 358, and pp. 792–4, no. 601. *LW*, pp. 77–80, no. 147, and pp. 111–13, no. 204.

[401] 'quod omnibus per Walliam publicum extitit et notorium': *AWR*, pp. 558–9, no. 383.

Llywelyn was referring was the conspiracy of Gruffudd and his son Owain against the prince of Wales which had recently come to light, together with their trial on 17 April 1274, the confiscation of certain of Gruffudd's lands, as well as the confession (*c.*November 1274) made by Owain to Bishop Anian of Bangor of the full extent of the conspiracy, the subsequent destruction of Gruffudd's castle at Welshpool, and Gruffudd's flight to Shrewsbury.[402]

As Owain ap Gruffudd's confession to Anian of Bangor of the full extent of the conspiracy included that Dafydd had been a party to the plot to kill the prince of Wales, this could explain not only Llywelyn's accusation that his brother had had the temerity to break the (1269) agreement but also the infliction of disturbances and injuries mentioned by Anian I of Bangor and Anian II of St Asaph which presumably Dafydd had complained about.[403] The disturbances and injuries inflicted on Gruffudd, referred to by the two bishops, were presumably Llywelyn's capture and destruction of Gruffudd's castle at Welshpool, the annexation of Gruffudd's lands, and the appointment by the prince of Wales of his own officers to oversee the land taken, all of which was recorded by the Welsh chroniclers.[404]

62. King Edward I

Letter (damaged). Anian informed Edward that it was certainly true that he loved the prince of Wales (Llywelyn ap Gruffudd) and his own people, provided that, he could do so in good conscience and saving the honour of God and the Church. However, because the prince had offended God and the Church in many things and had endeavoured to withdraw his homage from the king, his liege lord, to Edward's prejudice, Anian had publicly excommunicated Llywelyn, candles lit, and bells ringing, although few in the realm could have believed this of him, especially because he was the prince's confessor. Although he could not stir a foot except under the prince's power, he was anxious to avoid offence to God and the king, and therefore, after the celebration of mass on Palm Sunday, he had escaped and come to England for fear of death or at least arrest. He was a most faithful chaplain to the king and the king's father of good memory (Henry III). Valediction.

St Albans, 1277 [a Monday shortly after Palm Sunday,
21 March; possibly 29 March or 5 April]

A = TNA SC 1/15/6. 225 x 52 mm. Damaged.[405]

Calendared in *CAC*, p. 66.

Transcribed from A.

---

[402] Trial and confiscation of lands: *Brut, Pen20Tr*, p. 116; *Brut, Hergest*, pp. 260–1; *LW*, pp. liii–iv, and pp. 98–9, no. 193; *AWR*, pp. 796–8, no. 603, and pp. 798–9, no. 604. Smith, *Llywelyn*, pp. 369–71. Owain's confession: *LW*, p. lv, and pp. 136–8, no. 245. Smith, *Llywelyn*, pp. 369–70 and 372. Welshpool and Shrewsbury: *Brut, Hergest*, pp. 260–1; *Brut, Pen20Tr*, p. 116; *LW*, p. lv.

[403] Owain's confession: *LW*, p. lv, and pp. 136–8, no. 245. Smith, *Llywelyn*, pp. 369–70 and 372.

[404] *Brut, Hergest*, pp. 260–3; *Brut, Pen20Tr*, pp. 116–17. *LW*, p. lv.

[405] Image at Plate XVII (i). Description on TNA website: http://discovery.nationalarchives. gov.uk/details/r/C12207041, accessed 29 April 2024.

Illustri domino ac serenissimo Edwardo dei gratia regi Anglie, domino H(i)b(er)nie, duci Aq(ui)tanie, suus modicus capellanus Anianus Bangor' ecclesie minister hum[ilis]*ᵃ*........*ᵃ* ..... et felicitatis potest et pre*ᵇ* regni terreni regimine ad celeste regnum feliciter pervenire. Noverit vestra regia excellentia quod quicquid vobis alias per meos ......*ᶜ* ....*ᵃ* quod diligerem principem Wallie et gentem meam, certe hoc est verum dum tamen hoc facere prebe[a]m salva consciencia honore dei et ecclesie. Sed quia deum et ecclesiam offendit .....*ᶜ* ....*ᵃ* suis et domino*ᵈ* suo ligio videlicet vobis homagium fidelitatem obedientiam nititur subtrahere in vestram prejudicium et regni perturbationem ipsum principem .... tenorem .....*ᵃ* accensis candelis*ᵉ* et pulsatis campanis publice excommunicatum denuntiavi, licet pauci in regno hoc de me credere present maxime quia suus eram confessor et ....*ᵃ* ....*ᶜ* unum pedem nisi sub eius potestate et districtu dei offensam et vestram viriliter cavendo post expletum officium in ramis palmarum sine ....e dispendio propter mor[tem]*ᶠ* .....*ᵃ* saltem propter corporis attachiationem iter arripui et evasus in Anglia(m) veni voluntatem vestram de me sicut de vestro fidelissimo capellano vobis et patri vestro bone memorie ...*ᵃ* [cu]re et absque dubitatione facere potestis. Valeat et vigeat vestra regia tutela ad vindictam malefactorum laudem [ver]o bonorum. Dat' apud Sanctum Albanum die lune proxima post Ma...*ᵍ* .....*ʰ* anno domini mᵒ.ccᵒ.lxxviiᵒ.

> *ᵃ*edge of parchment torn away, *A.* *ᵇ*the letter 'p' has a curled 'ꝯ' above it suggesting 'pre', *A.* *ᶜ*faded and consequently difficult to read, *A.* *ᵈ*hole and tear in parchment, *A.* *ᵉ*hole in parchment above the letter 'n', *A.* *ᶠ*text not legible, *A.* *ᵍ*not completely legible, but the first letter appears to be a majuscule 'M' and the second is a superscript 'a', *A.* *ʰ*text not legible before edge of parchment torn away, *A.*

As J. G. Edwards noted, the date of the letter is not completely legible, however, it was written not long after Palm Sunday, which in 1277 fell on 21 March.[406] It was written on a Monday at St Albans, and given the time it would have taken Anian to reach the Benedictine abbey in Hertfordshire, 29 March was the first Monday on which he could feasibly have written the letter. The following Monday was 5 April, the date which has been assigned to the *actum* by TNA.[407]

J. G. Edwards' English summary of Anian's letter begins: 'Those who are jealous of the bishop have told the king that the bishop loves the prince of Wales and his own people ...': *CAC*, p. 66. Unfortunately, the letter is badly damaged (Plate XVII (i)) and on inspection in 2020, I could identify no reference to jealousy in the undamaged/legible parts of the manuscript. The wording recorded by Edwards in 1935 suggests that Anian was concerned that unflattering reports had reached the king, and as such he wished to set the record straight and tell his side of the story. This rings true, for the bishop of Bangor had waited more than five weeks to excommunicate the prince of Wales after Archbishop Robert Kilwardby had called, on 10 February 1277, for the bishops of the province of Canterbury to

[406] *CAC*, p. 66.
[407] http://discovery.nationalarchives.gov.uk/details/r/C12207041, accessed 30 May 2024.

excommunicate the prince.[408] Furthermore, in January of the same year, Anian had acted as Llywelyn's envoy, delivering the prince's ultimately unsuccessful proposals for peace to the king.[409]

It is noteworthy that Anian used not only *minister humilis*, but also *suus modicus* (*capellanus*), in his very deferential *intitulatio*.[410] Furthermore, before the valediction, he described himself as a most faithful chaplain to the king. This could be linked to the deferential tone he wished to take, and therefore may be explicable primarily as a rhetorical device.[411] However, if not, then it is unclear when he became chaplain to Edward. If it was a recent appointment, it could suggest that the king was not just recruiting the secular lords of Wales to his cause against Llywelyn ap Gruffudd, and his impending invasion of Gwynedd.[412] Anian described himself as Edward's chaplain once again in 1287/8, this time 'chaplain in Wales' (**86**), and by this time, after Edward had defeated Llywelyn ap Gruffudd, it is quite believable that Anian was the king's chaplain in Wales.[413]

In his letter of 1277, Anian also described himself as a most faithful chaplain to the king's father of good memory (Henry III). This is the first and last mention of him holding such a position – it too may have been a mere rhetorical device, or he may indeed have been chaplain to Edward I's father (presumably in Wales).

Bells ringing and candles lit (and extinguished) was a common way of publicly announcing an excommunication – the overt nature of the act being all important.[414] Palm Sunday, when everyone would be gathered for the traditional annual procession, would have been the perfect occasion.

*63. Robert Burnell, Bishop of Bath and Wells, Chancellor

Request, not necessarily in writing, to have a ship restored to him.
[16 October 1277 x 11 February 1278/6 January 1279 x May 1279/19 June 1279 x 13 May 1286/10 August 1289 x 17 October 1291]

> TNA SC 1/23/172: Peter de la Mare, constable of Bristol, wrote to Robert Burnell, bishop of Bath and Wells, and chancellor, restoring a ship to the bishop of Bangor.[415]

---

[408] Archbishop Kilwardby's call for Llywelyn to be excommunicated: *Councils and Synods*, ii, pp. 820–2; *AWR*, p. 583; Smith, *Llywelyn*, p. 412.

[409] He was accompanied by Master Gervase, the prince's vice-chancellor: *AWR*, pp. 586–7, no. 400; *CAC*, p. 87. Smith, *Llywelyn*, p. 409. Master Gervase can probably be identified as Iorwerth, a canon of Bangor: *AWR*, p. 587; Stephenson, *Governance*, pp. 36–7, and 224.

[410] For further discussion, see the section entitled 'Intitulatio' in the 'Diplomatic Analysis of the *Acta*'.

[411] *ibid*.

[412] Defections to Edward included Rhys ap Maredudd of Deheubarth and Gruffudd ap Maredudd of Ceredigion who were, on the same day as Anian excommunicated Llywelyn and fled to England, to swear fealty to the king: Smith, *Llywelyn*, p. 420.

[413] See *Actum* **86**.

[414] Hill, 'Excommunication and Politics in Thirteenth-Century England', pp. 65–6.

[415] Summary on TNA website: http://discovery.nationalarchives.gov.uk/details/r/C12216561, accessed 2 March 2024.

Peter de la Mare, former 'underconstable', was given custody of Bristol castle on 16 October 1277; he died in post on 17 October 1291.[416] Robert Burnell was both chancellor and bishop throughout this fourteen-year period.[417] The restoration of the ship to Anian was no doubt pursuant to a request by the bishop of Bangor himself.

Save for the times when Robert Burnell was away in France and/or Gascony, on the business of Edward I, in 1278/9, 1279 and 1286–1289, the request may have been made at any time during de la Mare's tenure as constable of Bristol castle.[418] It is possible that it was brought about as a result of one of the two Welsh wars of 1277 and 1282–1283. In the lead up to the war of 1277, Llywelyn ap Gruffudd was declared a rebel and disturber of the peace at a council of prelates and magnates in November 1276.[419] As such, an embargo 'by land and sea' was placed on victuals, horses, arms and other things that might have been useful to the rebels.[420] Similarly, in the war of 1282–1283 stringent measures were put in place to prevent supplies, including those carried by sea, from reaching those Welsh who had risen against the English.[421] One of the casualties of the measures put in place during either war may have been the bishop of Bangor's ship.

64. Robert Burnell, Bishop of Bath and Wells, Chancellor

Letter concerning his losses in the war. Whilst he had been with the chancellor at Rhuddlan, he had lost his brother, his sister's son, his cousin, and kinsmen to the number of sixty, in the king's service, and Llywelyn greatly rejoiced at his misfortune. His tongue was not sufficient to describe his losses, and the burnings of churches, in the war. He expressed his hope in the liberality of the king and in the chancellor's continued friendship. He asked Robert to explain all these things to the king and inform Anian of the king's reply. Valediction.

Treffos [after *c*.9 November 1277]

A = TNA SC 1/22/101. 247 x 39 mm. Faded and illegible in parts.[422]

---

[416]   *CFR, 1272–1307*, p. 82; *Accounts of the Constables of Bristol Castle*, p. 28, n. 2, p. 82 and p. 90, ns. 109, 110, 111 and 112.

[417]   Robert Burnell became chancellor immediately after Edward I's coronation on 21 September 1274. He was consecrated as bishop of Bath and Wells on 7 April 1275. He remained in both posts until his death on 25 October 1292: Harding, 'Burnell, Robert (*d.* 1292)', *ODNB*; *Fasti Bath and Wells*, p. 5.

[418]   Burnell in France or Gascony or both: left Dover on 11 February 1278, returning to England by 6 January 1279 at the latest, as on that date he witnessed royal charters at Windsor (Huscroft, 'The political career and personal life of Robert Burnell', p. 86 and n. 42, and pp. 89–90 and n. 58. Also, Powicke, *The Thirteenth Century*, p. 288; Prestwich, *Edward I*, p. 304); May–19 June 1279 (Huscroft, 'The political career and personal life of Robert Burnell', p. 90 and n. 63; *Itinerary of King Edward I*, i, pp. 95–6); and 13 May 1286–10 August 1289 (Huscroft, 'The political career and personal life of Robert Burnell', p. 100 and n. 115, p. 104 and n. 130; Prestwich, *Edward I*, p. 323; Harding, 'Burnell, Robert (*d.* 1292)', *ODNB*). Also, Prestwich, *Edward I*, pp. 301, 305, and 311; Powicke, *The Thirteenth Century*, p. 286.

[419]   *CCR, 1272–1279*, pp. 359–61; Smith, *Llywelyn*, p. 406.

[420]   *CCR, 1272–1279*, p. 361; Gruffydd, *Maritime Wales*, p. 16.

[421]   See for example: *CVCR*, pp. 235–6 and 241. Also, Smith, *Llywelyn*, p. 512.

[422]   Image at Plate XVI (i).

Calendared in *CAC*, p. 112.

Transcribed from A.

Reverendo in Cristo patri domino R. Bathon(ensis) et Wellen(sis) episcopo, domini regis cancelario, A. eadem gratia Bangoren(sis) ecclesie minister humilis suus …*ᵃ* *ᵇ*[de]cus amicus salutem et fraterne dilectionis semper augmentum. Heu dolens, dum eram vobiscum apud Rodoland amisi fratrem meum <filium>*ᶜ* <sororis mee>*ᶜ* cognatum consanguineos meos usque ad sexaginta in officio domini regis, et de isto infortunio Lewelin(us) multum gaudet. Dampna mea et ecclesiarum incendia*ᵈ* et [depredationes]*ᵇ* [in]*ᵇ* ….. …..*ᵃ* [gu]erra lingua mea non suficeret vobis enarrare de vestrorum amicorum ruina sicut de nostrorum in eo fere doleo de …….*ᵃ* [misericordia] …. ………*ᵃ* domini regis et vestra continua amicicia sperans [necesse]*ᵇ* habeo sustinere tamen, si placet, hec ..*ᶜ* omnia exponatis domino regi …. …. ….*ᵃ* significare velitis. Valeat et vigeat vestra humilitas devota semper in domino. Dat' apud Treffos etc.

> *ᵃ*parchment faded and illegible, A. *ᵇ*parchment faded, A. *ᶜ*superscript, A. *ᵈ*tear in parchment running through the 'dia' of 'incendia' to 'et', A. *ᶜ*possibly 'l' with a dot underneath indicating it should be deleted, A.

Robert Burnell became chancellor immediately after Edward I's coronation on 21 September 1274, and was consecrated as bishop of Bath and Wells on 7 April 1275.[423]

An extent made in 1306/7 of the lands of the bishop of Bangor recorded that the bishop had a manor at Treffos (in Dindaethwy on Anglesey).[424]

J. G. Edwards suggested, rather persuasively, that the reference to the war in Anian's letter, and the fact that Llywelyn was spoken of as still alive, seemed to point to Edward I's first Welsh war of 1277.[425] The king was at Chester by 15 July that year, and the main English army moved from there, via 'the camp near Basingwerk' (*c*.21 July) and Flint (25 July) to Rhuddlan, which it reached by late August.[426] It then moved on to the river Conwy at Deganwy, Edward withdrawing from there back to Rhuddlan on 12 September to await events. He was there for some time, and possibly continuously until 20 November.[427] The patent rolls show that his chancellor, Robert Burnell, was kept very busy, moving between Chester, the camp near Basingwerk, Rhuddlan and Shrewsbury, although during September

---

[423] He remained in both posts until his death on 25 October 1292: Harding, 'Burnell, Robert (*d.* 1292)', *ODNB*; *Fasti Bath and Wells*, p. 5.

[424] *RC*, p. 93 and p. 100; Carr, 'Jones Pierce Revisited', p. 135; Carr, *Medieval Anglesey*, pp. 99, 132 and 269. See also the section of the Introduction entitled 'Extent of 1306/7 – Manors, Lands and Tenants of the Bishop of Bangor'.

[425] *CAC*, p. 112.

[426] Prestwich, *Edward I*, pp. 179–80; Smith, *Llywelyn*, p. 427 and n. 137; Morris, *Welsh Wars*, pp. 127–8 and p. 131.

[427] Prestwich, *Edward I*, p. 180 and n. 37; Smith, *Llywelyn*, p. 437, n. 175. Cf. Morris, *Welsh Wars*, p. 136.

Robert seems to have spent most of his time in Chester.[428] He is recorded as being at Rhuddlan on 1 October, and is mentioned in entries made at Rhuddlan on 4 and 5 October.[429] He was at Shrewsbury on 9 October, Chester on 12 October, and Shrewsbury again on 15, 18, 20, 28 and 29 October.[430] On the balance of the evidence, the most likely time when Anian would have been with Robert at Rhuddlan was the first week of October 1277.[431]

Bishop Anian of Bangor was not the only Welsh bishop to complain about church property being damaged in the war, for his namesake Anian (II), bishop of St Asaph, complained to Archbishop Kilwardby that English forces had desecrated churches and churchyards, damaged church property and had burnt an episcopal manor.[432]

Having excommunicated Llywelyn and fled to England on Palm Sunday 1277, claiming that he feared death or at least arrest (**62**), Anian may have only felt confident in returning to Gwynedd Uwch Conwy (Gwynedd to the west of the river Conwy) once Llywelyn had submitted to the king.[433] The prince, by way of the Treaty of Aberconwy, did this on 9 November 1277, and on the following day, Llywelyn crossed the Conwy and made his way to Rhuddlan to swear fealty to Edward (the treaty specifying that Robert Burnell was one of those who were to accompany Llywelyn to the king).[434] It is, therefore, likely that Anian's letter to Burnell, from his manor at Treffos, was written after *c.*9 November.[435]

The grant of a wardship, on 18 January 1278, to the value of £20 yearly may have been the result of Anian's letter to Burnell.[436] At Westminster on that day, a notification was made that the king had granted to the bishop of Bangor the wardship of the manor of Fernham (Oxfordshire) which had belonged to Gilbert de Berneval, tenant in chief (and which had passed into the king's hands by reason of his death) until Gilbert's heir should come of age.[437] Burnell certainly knew of the

---

[428]   *CPR, 1272–1281*, pp. 227–34. Also, *CFR, 1272–1307*, p. 86 and *CCR, 1272–1279*, p. 432.

[429]   *CPR, 1272–1281*, pp. 230–1.

[430]   1302 *ibid.*, pp. 231–4.

[431]   1303 One other possible date is 16 October, as the editor of the patent roll (*CPR, 1272–1281*, p. 232) has transcribed the record of a writ issued at Rhuddlan on that date as being issued 'By the hand [of the chancellor]', although Robert had been at Shrewsbury the day before and was there again on 18 October: *CPR, 1272–1281*, pp. 231–2.

[432]   Smith, *Llywelyn*, p. 428 and n. 143, Haddan and Stubbs, i, pp. 522–3.

[433]   See *Actum* **62**.

[434]   Treaty of Aberconwy: *AWR*, pp. 589–94, no. 402; *LW*, pp. 118–22, no. 211, and p. 157, no. 279. Discussion in Smith, *Llywelyn*, pp. 437–44.

[435]   However, as a substantial English force, commanded by John de Vescy and Otto de Grandison, had sailed to Anglesey in the summer to occupy the island and gather the harvest, and a force was still there in October under William de Hameldon (Prestwich, *Edward I*, p. 180 and n. 34; Smith, *Llywelyn*, p. 428 and n. 141; Morris, *Welsh Wars*, pp. 135–6) it is possible that Anian may have felt it safe to visit his manor at Treffos, in the south-east corner of the island, some time before *c.*9 November.

[436]   *CVCR*, pp. 163–4. A point made by J. G. Edwards, *CAC*, p. 112.

[437]   If the manor exceeded the value of £20 yearly, the excess was to remain with the king, but if it did not reach that value, the king wished Ralph de Sandwich ('Sandwyco') to

manor for, on 21 November 1277, he had sent orders to the king's steward concerning the same, including the order to keep the moiety falling to the heir safe.[438] The chancellor may have decided to recommend to the king that Anian be granted the wardship of the manor in light of the bishop of Bangor's losses.

For assertions of *amicitia*, friendship, by medieval clergymen see the work of Julian Haseldine.[439]

65. Robert Burnell, Bishop of Bath (and Wells), Chancellor

Letter to Robert Burnell, bishop of Bath (and Wells), Chancellor, defender of the oppressed, protector of the poor, concerning Llywelyn ap Gruffudd's offences against the Church. He cannot sufficiently thank Robert for the benefits, honours, and gifts which he has conferred on the Church. He sends for his inspection certain articles in which the prince has offended God and the Church and prays that they may be explained to the king, so that he may assign remedies, as the Church of Christ should be defended against the tyrannical prince and his malevolent and satanic ministers.

Bangor, 7 January [possibly 1278, 1279 or 1280]

A = TNA SC 1/22/102. 217 x 48 mm.[440]

Calendared in *CAC*, pp. 112–13.

Transcribed from A.

Reverendo patri domino <R.>*a*, dei gratia episcopo Bathon(ensis), domini regis cancellario, oppressorum defensori pauperum patro[n]o*b*, Anianus, eiusdem permissione Bangor' episcopus, salutem et fraterne dilectionis amplexum. De vestris beneficiis, honoribus, donationibus et ecclesie negotiis procuratis et procurandis vobis [gra]tiari*c* non sufficimus, et ideo ille a quo omnis sufficientia est vobis renunciaret quosdam articulos in quibus princeps offendit deum et ecclesiam*d* sed non omnes vobis transmittimus inspiciendos et per vos, domino regi exponendos, quia propter ipsum et propter summam latam ….*e* sumus principi odiosi. Unde nos rogamus et requirimus [quaten]us …pelletis dominum regem catholicum strenuum christianissimum Edwardu(m) pro ecclesia Cristi tuenda contra tirannidem principem et suos ministros malivolos sathanicos tempestiva apponat remedia ne penitus ecclesia Cristi suis personibus corporalibus et incorporalibus manibus nostris privetur et in obprobrium et iniuriam creatoris succumbat. Dat' Bangor' in crastino epiphanie anno domini etc.

*a*superscript, *A*. *b*parchment damaged, and there could be further letters after patrono, *A*. *c*parchment damaged, *A*. *d*hole in parchment, *A*. *e*faded, three minims can be seen, possibly with a letter preceding them, *A*.

---

provide the bishop with what was lacking from other wardships in his bailiwick as soon as the opportunity presented itself: *CVCR*, pp. 163–4.

[438] *CFR, 1272–1307*, p. 88.

[439] Haseldine, 'Friendship and Rivalry'; Haseldine, 'Understanding the Language of Amicitia'; Haseldine, *Friendship in Medieval Europe*. Thank you to Dr Nicholas Karn for bringing the works of J. Haseldine to my attention and for discussing 'amicitia' with me.

[440] Image at Plate XVI (ii). TNA online description: https://discovery.nationalarchives.gov.uk/details/r/C12216268, accessed 29 April 2024.

The articles have not survived.

Anian's letter is dated 7 January ('*in crastino epiphanie*') but no year is given.

J. G. Edwards considered that the likeliest year was 1278, although he conceded that the letter might belong to 1279, or 1280, because 'it was not until July 1280 that a settlement of the dispute between Llywelyn and the Bishop of Bangor came into sight'.[441] In the summer of 1280, Archbishop Pecham visited Wales in the hope that an amicable arrangement could be reached between Anian and Llywelyn.[442] After his return, the archbishop was able to write to Llywelyn to say that he rejoiced that a composition with the bishop of Bangor was imminent.[443]

One reason for thinking that Anian's letter was written in January 1278 was that King Edward I did write to Llywelyn later that same year concerning the affairs of the bishop of Bangor.[444] In response, Llywelyn complained that Edward sought to diminish the prince's liberties in what he had written to him concerning the bishop.[445] The king's reply, dated 14 July 1278, stated that he did not wish to diminish Llywelyn's liberties in any way or to detract from his rights but rather Edward wished that he might foment peace and concord between the prince and the bishop, as befitted Llywelyn's honour. The king had been anxious that the bishop should not have any just matter of complaint on any point which might injure the bishop's liberties or the rights of his church, for which reason the king requested Llywelyn to conduct himself, as befits a prince, courteously and modestly concerning the spiritual rights and temporalities of the bishop.[446] Edward ended by saying that he would not believe the 'sinister reports' of Llywelyn[447] – this may be a reference to Anian's accusation that the prince was tyrannical and his ministers were malevolent and satanic.

As Anian's letter of 7 January to the king's chancellor refers to the benefits, honours and gifts conferred on the Church, the years 1279 or 1280 are also possible for on 18 January 1278 Anian was granted a wardship to the value of £20 yearly, a notification being made that the king had granted the bishop of Bangor the wardship of the manor of Fernham (see note to *Actum* **64** above). Furthermore, on 18 November 1278, Edward confirmed the rights, liberties, possessions, and customs of the see of Bangor.[448]

---

[441] *CAC*, pp. 112–13.

[442] *Welsh Assize Roll*, p. 64.

[443] July 1280: *Registrum Epistolarum Peckham*, i, pp. 125–6. Although, David Stephenson points out that whilst it has been assumed that the settlement had already been reached, such an interpretation is not supported by the text: Stephenson, *Governance*, p. 180, n. 64.

[444] *CVCR*, pp. 174–5; *Foedera*, i, part ii, pp. 559–60; *AWR*, p. 599; *Welsh Assize Roll*, pp. 47–8.

[445] *AWR*, p. 599, no. 409.

[446] *Foedera*, i, part ii, pp. 559–60; *CVCR*, pp. 174–5; *Welsh Assize Roll*, pp. 47–8.

[447] *CVCR*, pp. 174–5.

[448] At Rhuddlan: *RC*, p. 254 and p. 255; Willis, *Survey*, pp. 212–13; Haddan and Stubbs, i, p. 526. The grant was in similar terms to a grant made to the bishop of St Asaph in 1276: Haddan and Stubbs, i, p. 509–10.

66. Clare Friary, Suffolk

Indulgence. Trusting in the mercy of omnipotent God, and in the merits of the glorious virgin, his mother, of the apostles, Peter and Paul, of the blessed Deiniol, bishop and confessor, and of all the saints, the grant of 20 days' relaxation of enjoined penance for all those parishioners of the diocese of Bangor, and others, whose diocesan bishops shall have ratified the indulgence, and who have confessed and are truly contrite, and who visit the Augustinian friars of Clare out of devotion, on pilgrimage, to pray or to hear preaching and who walk around the cemetery, or who give from their goods pious alms for the construction or repair of the house or for any commendatory office for the dead, and who pray for the souls of all the faithful departed resting there or elsewhere, and for the soul of Anian himself, who dedicated the cemetery, on the anniversary of the dedication or on any day throughout the year. Sealing clause.

Clare, 24 April 1279

B = BL MS Harley 4835 (Cartulary of Clare), fo. 52v. s. xiv ex.[449] 'GO' in margin.[450]

C = Prifysgol Bangor University Archives and Special Collections, Bangor Pontifical, fo. 166. s. xv.[451]

D = Prifysgol Bangor University Archives and Special Collections, Bangor Pontifical, fo. 165v. s. xviiii. (Transcription of C by Alfred Stowe of Wadham College, Oxford).

Printed in *English Austin Friars*, ii, p. 36.

Translated in *Cartulary of the Augustinian Friars of Clare*, p. 95.

Transcribed from B.

Omnibus Cristi fidelibus has litteras visuris vel audituris Avianus, permissione divina Ba(n)gore(ns)is ecclesie minister humilis, salutem in domino sempiternam. Nos de dei omnipotentis misericordia et gloriose virginis matris eius, beatorum Pet(ri) et Pauli apostolorum, beati Daniel(is) episcopi et confessoris, omniumque sanctorum meritis confidentes, omnibus parochianis nostris et aliis, quorum diocesani hanc nostram indulgentiam ratam habuerint, de pecatis suis vere contritis et confessis, qui cimiterium*ᵃ* fratrum ordinis sancti Aug(ustin)i Clar(e) peregrinationis, devotionis seu orationis vel predicationis causa devote circu[i]erint*ᵇ* vel de bonis suis ad constructionem, reparationem seu commendationem quamcumque*ᶜ* domus dictorum*ᵈ* fratrum pias elemosinas contulerint ac pro animabus omnium fidelium defunctorum ibidem ac ubique quiescentium ac pro anima Aviani, episcopi Bang(ore)n(sis)*ᵉ*, dicti cimiterii*ᶠ* dedicatoris die dedicationis eius*ᵍ* annuatim et per totum annum viginti dies de iniuncta sibi penitentia misericorditer relaxamus.

---

[449] Davis, *Medieval Cartularies of Great Britain and Ireland*, p. 53, no. 261; *Cartulary of the Augustinian Friars of Clare*, p. 22.

[450] The record of Anian's indulgence marked 'GO' appears below the record of his indulgence 'GN' on fo. 52 of the cartulary. The record of the indulgences in the Bangor Pontifical follows the same order.

[451] Image available on DIAMM website, https://www.diamm.ac.uk/sources/3785/#/images, accessed 6 June 2024. The text on a flyleaf, fo. 166, has been dated to the fifteenth century: Harper, 'The Bangor Pontifical', 76.

In cuius rei testimonium sigillum nostrum hiis litteris fecimus apponi. Dat'*ʰ* aput Clar' viii kal' Maii, anno domini milesimo cc° lxxix°.*ⁱ*

> *ᵃ*conventum, *D.* *ᵇ*convenierint, *D.* *ᶜ*quamcunque, *D.* *ᵈ*predictorum, *D.* *ᵉ*Bangoren(sis), *C.* *ᶠ*conventiculi, *D.* *ᵍ*eiusdem, *C, D.* *ʰ*Datum, *D.* *ⁱ*apud Clar' viii xx Maii anno domini millesimo ducentesimo septuagesimo nono, *C, D.*

William Middleton, bishop of Norwich, had issued a licence in 1278 for the consecration of a cemetery at Clare by any Catholic bishop who might act on his behalf.[452] Clare was the foremost house of the order of Austin Friars in England – founded by Richard de Clare, sixth earl of Gloucester and fifth earl of Hertford (d. 1262).[453]

The inclusion of St Deiniol ('Daniel') in a Bangor episcopal *actum* is unusual and interesting. The only other occasions Deiniol is referred to in the *acta* of the bishops of Bangor during the period 1092–1306 are in *acta* of Anian himself (**67** and **88** below, both indulgences).[454] C. Harper-Bill noted that of those bishops who granted indulgences to Clare, saints that were 'dear to them or associated with their dioceses' were included in the saints in whom they expressed confidence.[455]

As well as being recorded in the fourteenth-century cartulary of the Augustinian friary of Clare (MS Harley 4835) Anian's indulgence in favour of the house, together with a second indulgence, *Actum* **67** below, is recorded in a fifteenth-century hand on a flyleaf to the Bangor Pontifical.[456] The Bangor Pontifical, which is a complete liturgical manuscript, states that *Iste liber est pontificalis domini Aniani Bangor' ep[iscop]i* ('this book is the pontifical of Lord Anian, bishop of Bangor'),[457] and thus Anian may have been the original owner of the book.[458] It is noteworthy that there is a fifteenth-century connection between Suffolk and Bangor, for the dean of the college of secular priests at Stoke by Clare (near the Augustinian friary) from 1470 to 1493 was Richard Ednam, the bishop of Bangor, later owner of the book who

---

[452] Licence issued at Chippenham, 20 February 1278: *English Austin Friars*, ii, pp. 33–4; *Cartulary of the Augustinian Friars of Clare*, p. 19 and p. 93.

[453] Harper, 'The Bangor Pontifical', 76; *English Austin Friars*, i, p. 260; *Cartulary of the Augustinian Friars of Clare*, p. 3.

[454] See the section of the Introduction entitled 'References to St Deiniol'.

[455] *Cartulary of the Augustinian Friars of Clare*, p. 19.

[456] Prifysgol Bangor University Archives and Special Collections, Bangor Pontifical, fo. 166.

[457] *ibid.*, fo. 164v. Image available on DIAMM website: https://www.diamm.ac.uk/sources/3785/#/images, accessed 6 June 2024.

[458] However, this entry may equally relate to Anian II of Bangor (1309–1328) and there has been scholarly debate as to which Anian was the first owner. J. E. Lloyd followed Browne Willis who assumed that the book was the work of Anian I (Lloyd, *History of Wales*, ii, p. 745; Willis, *Survey*, p. 69). H. Pryce has said it is uncertain whether the Pontifical first belonged to Anian I or to his namesake: Pryce, 'Anian [Einion] (*d.* 1305x7)', *ODNB*. However, based on an examination of the illumination which appears in the book (fo. 8v.) a date of 1310 x 1320 has been proposed which would make Anian II the first owner (Harper, 'The Bangor Pontifical', 74), although it has also been mooted that the manuscript could be a fourteenth-century copy of a pontifical made for Anian I (Harper, 'The Bangor Pontifical', 85).

gave the Pontifical to Bangor cathedral in 1485.[459] It is also interesting to note that an East-Anglian provenance has been assigned to the Pontifical.[460]

67. Clare Friary, Suffolk

Indulgence. Trusting in the mercy of omnipotent God, and in the merits of the glorious virgin, his mother, of the apostles, Peter and Paul, of the blessed Deiniol, bishop and confessor, and of all the saints, the grant of 10 days' relaxation of enjoined penance for all those parishioners of the diocese of Bangor, and others, whose diocesan bishops shall have ratified the indulgence, and who have confessed and are truly contrite, and who visit the house of the Augustinian friars of Clare, and there pray for the soul of Richard of Chrishall, whose body is entombed in front of the friars' chapterhouse, and for the souls of all the faithful departed, piously saying the Lord's Prayer and the Angelic Salutation. Sealing clause.

Clare, 25 April 1279

B = BL MS Harley 4835 (Cartulary of Clare), fo. 52v. s. xiv ex.[461] 'GN' in margin.[462]

C = Prifysgol Bangor University Archives and Special Collections, Bangor Pontifical, fo. 166. s. xv.[463]

D = Prifysgol Bangor University Archives and Special Collections, Bangor Pontifical, fo. 165v. s. xviiii. (Transcription of C by Alfred Stowe of Wadham College, Oxford).

Printed in *English Austin Friars*, ii, p. 36.

Translated in *Cartulary of the Augustinian Friars of Clare*, pp. 94–5.

Transcribed from B.

Omnibus Cristi fidelibus has litteras visuris vel audituris Avianus, permissione divina Bangoren(sis) ecclesie minister humilis, salutem in domino sempiternam. Cum*a* sit sancta et salubris cogitatio preces fundere*b* pro defunctis ⟨ut a peccatorum nexibus mereantur*d* absolvi*c*, nos de dei omnipotentis misericordia et gloriose virginis matris eius, beatorum Pet(ri) et Pauli apostolorum, beati Daniel(is) episcopi et confessoris, omniumque sanctorum meritis confidentes, omnibus parochianis nostris et aliis, quorum diocesani hanc nostram indulgentiam ratam habuerint, de pecatis*f* suis vere contritis et confessis, qui ad domum fratrum*g* de Clar' ordinis

---

[459] Richard Ednam was bishop of Bangor from 1465 to 1496: Harper, 'The Bangor Pontifical', 76. Prifysgol Bangor University Archives and Special Collections, Bangor Pontifical, fo. 164v. records Bishop Richard's ownership of the book and his gift of the same to Bangor cathedral.

[460] Harper, 'The Bangor Pontifical', 65–99.

[461] Davis, *Medieval Cartularies of Great Britain and Ireland*, p. 53, no. 261; *Cartulary of the Augustinian Friars of Clare*, p. 22.

[462] The record of Anian's indulgence marked 'GN' appears above the record of his indulgence 'GO' on fo. 52 of the cartulary. The record of the indulgences in the Bangor Pontifical follows the same order.

[463] Image available on DIAMM website, https://www.diamm.ac.uk/sources/3785/#/images, accessed 6 June 2024. The text on a flyleaf, fo. 166, has been dated to the fifteenth century: Harper, 'The Bangor Pontifical', 76.

sancti Aug(ustin)i devote accesserint ac ibidem pro anima Ricardi de[h] Cristeshale, cuius corpus ante capitulum dictorum fratrum intumulatur, ac pro animabus omnium fidelium defunctorum orationem dominicam cum salutione angelica[i] pia mente[j] dixerint, x[k] dies de iniuncta sibi[l] penitentia misericorditer relaxamus. In cuius rei testimonium sigillum nostrum hiis litteris fecimus apponi. Dat'[m] Clar' vii kal' Maii, anno domini m° cc° lxxix°.[n]

> [a]word lost in a fold of the parchment, *C.* '[Quum]' is conjectured by, *D.* [b]'preces fundere' omitted, *C, D.* [c]exorare added after 'defunctis' and before 'ut', *C, D.* [d]meant but the word is affected by a fold in the parchment, *C.* mereant, *D.* [e]word lost in a fold of the parchment, *C.* '[solutionem]' conjectured by, *D.* [f]peccatis, *D.* [g]fratrum omitted, *C, D.* [h]de omitted, *C, D.* [i]angelica omitted, 'beate Marie' in its place, *C, D.* [j]pie mente or pre mente, *C.* praemeritae, *D.* [k]decem, *C, D.* [l]eis, *C, D.* [m]Datum, *D.* [n]apud Clar' vii xx Maii anno domini millesimo ducentesimo septuagesimo nono, *C, D.*

See notes to *Actum* **66** above.

The manor of Chrishall or Chishall was located in Utlesford Hundred, Essex.[464]

*68. John Pecham, Archbishop of Canterbury

Complaint, not necessarily in writing, that Llywelyn ap Gruffudd had usurped ecclesiastical property and disregarded the Church's right to dispose of the moveable goods of people who had died intestate.

1279 [Before 20 October, probably after 29 July]

Alluded to in a letter from Archbishop John Pecham to Llywelyn ap Gruffudd dated 20 October 1279, at Lambeth – the letter is recorded in *Registrum Epistolarum Peckham*, i, pp. 77–8.[465] The distribution of such goods, said the archbishop, 'pertained to the administration of the ordinary according to canonical rules'.[466]

As J. B. Smith and Huw Pryce both noted, the archbishop viewed Llywelyn's confiscation of the goods of intestates in the diocese of Bangor as a serious violation of the liberties of the Church.[467] Pecham asserted the exclusive jurisdiction of the Church in testamentary matters. The said goods were the bishop's responsibility; it was he who would supervise their distribution.[468] In fact, as Huw Pryce made clear, the real conflict between bishop and prince, no doubt, concerned the seignorial right to moveables of intestate tenants.

---

[464] *English Austin Friars*, ii, p. 36, n. 35, and Morant, *History and Antiquities of the County of Essex*, ii, p. 606.

[465] Pryce, *Native Law*, pp. 113–14 and pp. 117–18; Smith, *Llywelyn*, pp. 211 and 258–9; Smith, 'Gravamina', 165, and n. 6.

[466] 'quorum dispositionem non est dubium ad loci ordinarium secundum canonicas sanctiones pertinere': Smith, 'Gravamina', 165, and n. 6; Smith, *Llywelyn*, pp. 258–9, and n. 323. *Registrum Epistolarum Peckham*, i, pp. 77–8.

[467] Smith, *Llywelyn*, p. 211; Pryce, *Native Law*, pp. 113–14 and pp. 117–18; *Registrum Epistolarum Peckham*, i, pp. 77–8.

[468] Smith, 'Gravamina', 165, and n. 6; *Registrum Epistolarum Peckham*, i, pp. 77–8.

Under Welsh law the bishop was entitled to the moveables of intestate episcopal tenants.[469]

Anian had attended a council of the province of Canterbury called by Pecham, which was held in the chapterhouse of Reading Abbey, 29 July to 1 August 1279.[470] It was perhaps at Reading, or later by letter, that Anian complained to the archbishop about Llywelyn's actions in respect of the chattels of those who died intestate. At about the time of Pecham's letter to Llywelyn, Edward I ordered ten librates of land in the Marches of Wales to be assigned, *de gratia nostra speciali*, to Anian.[471] The two matters might be unrelated, but the timing is interesting.

*69. King Edward I

Request, not necessarily in writing, for timber.
                    1280 [Before 26 October, possibly on or shortly after 6 October]

On the 26 October 1280, at Westminster, an order to Geoffrey de Picheford, constable of Windsor castle, was made to cause A. bishop of Bangor to have six oaks fit for timber in the forest of Windsor, by the king's gift (TNA C 54 (Close Rolls), C 54/97 (8 Edward I), m. 2).[472]

Earlier the same month (6 October), Anian had been present at the translation of the body of St Hugh of Avalon within Lincoln Cathedral. The translation was carried out in the presence of, amongst others, Edward I, Queen Eleanor, and Edmund, the king's brother.[473] On the same day, Anian was present at the consecration, by Archbishop John Pecham, of Thomas Bek as bishop of St Davids, once again in the presence of the king.[474] The bishop of Bangor may have taken the opportunity of being with the royal party to request timber.

The oaks gifted by the king may have been destined for Bangor Cathedral or an episcopal palace in north Wales, however, given that the trees were in Windsor it is logical to assume they were destined for Anian's new property in Shoe Lane, Holborn, granted to the bishop in July 1280.[475]

---

[469] Pryce, *Native Law*, p. 117. See also Smith, 'Gravamina', 165, n. 6.
[470] *Council and Synods*, ii, part ii, pp. 828–9.
[471] On 17 and 26 October 1279, at Westminster: *CPR, 1278–1279*, p. 12. See BL Add MS 15664 (fo. 5. 7 Edw. I) for the bounds of the land assigned.
[472] 1344 *CCR, 1279–1288*, p. 35.
[473] *Opera*, vii, pp. 219–21 (*Vita S. Remigii et Vita S. Hugonis* – Appendix F). Perry, *Life of St. Hugh*, p. 329, n. 1. Also, *Annales Oseneia*, pp. 285–6, *Annales Dunstaplia*, p. 283, and *Chronicle Abbatie de Parco Lude*, ed. E. Venables (1891), pp. 18–19.
[474] 1346 Oliver of Sutton, bishop of Lincoln was present, as were the bishops of Llandaff (William de Braose) and St Asaph (Anian II): *Opera*, vii, p. 220. *Councils and Synods*, ii, part ii, p. 871, and n. 3. *Fasti Welsh Cathedrals*, p. 49.
[475] July 1280. The grant of land and buildings in Shoe Lane, in the parish of St Andrew, Holborn, was to Anian and his successors in perpetuity: Willis, *Survey*, pp. 68 and 189; Pryce, 'Anian [Einion] (d. 1305x7)', *ODNB*. A further grant of land in Shoe Lane was made on 10 November 1281: Willis, *Survey*, p. 189.

70. Robert Burnell, Bishop of Bath and Wells (and Chancellor)

Letter (badly damaged). He is not able to live peacefully in the land of the prince (Llywelyn ap Gruffudd) on account of past causes. His adversaries, certain incestuous adulterers of his chapter, were being encouraged to impugn him. Letters of the lord king (Edward I) were directed to Guncelin (de Badlesmere), then justice of Chester. Robert may wish that another writ is directed to Lord Reginald (de Grey, current) justice of Chester regarding the aforesaid business. Valediction.

[14 November 1281 x 11 December 1282]

A = TNA SC 1/22/103. 182 x 48 mm. Damaged.[476]

Transcribed from A.

[Reverendo in Crist]o*ᵃ* patri domino R. permissione divina Bathon(ensis) et Wel[lensis]*ᵇ* [episcopo]*ᶜ* …………………………..*ᶜ* sue continuo defensori tutori ………*ᵃ* suus Bangoren(sis) salutem et fraterne caritatis semper aug[mentum] ………………*ᶜ* tanquam precipimus amicum in terris recurri ..*ᵃ* litere domini regis directe Guncilino tunc justiciario Cestrie non habuerunt ef..*ᵈ* quod justici-arius fuit transmutatus nec ……. …s*ᵃ* …..*ᵉ* nec wardam aliquam quam mallemus habere quia non possumus vivere pacifice in terra principis propter causas preter-itas ….*ᵃ* nostis modo nobis suscitat adversarios quosdam adulteros incestuosos de capitulo nostro secum ad nos impugna[ndos] [u]nde*ᵃ* vos pietatis intuitu rogamus et requirimus quatenus more consueto sicut inde vobis confidimus in supradictis omnibus in ..s*ᵃ* velitis*ᶠ* aliud breve nobis impetrando domino Reginaldo, justiciario Cestrie, dirigendum super negotio predicto. Deus …*ᵃ* virgo iuvent vos in morte et*ᵍ* vita. Valeat et vigeat vestra paternitas per tempora multa.*ʰ*

> *ᵃ*left-hand side of parchment missing, *A.* *ᵇ*text faded and illegible, *A.* *ᶜ*section of top of parchment missing/damaged, *A.* *ᵈ*parchment damaged/text obscured, *A.* *ᵉ*hole/tear in parchment, *A.* *ᶠ*dot after velitis, *A.* *ᵍ*parchment damaged, *A.* *ʰ*followed by three straight lines to the end of the line, seeming to indicate that there were no more words, and that was the end of the letter, *A.*

The undamaged parts of the *intitulatio* in this extant letter do not state Anian's name, not even by way of an initial. Instead, the formula '*suus Bangoren(sis)*' is used. The same formula is used again in Anian's letter to John de Kirkby (**72**) *c.*18 April 1283.[477]

Reginald de Grey was reappointed justice of Chester on 14 November 1281.[478] Guncelin de Badlesmere had been the justice from 16 October 1274 to 14 Novem-ber 1281.[479]

It seems probable that the letter was written during 1282, and certainly before Lly-welyn's death on 11 December. Anian had returned to his diocese by 7 November

---

[476] Image at Plate XVI (iii).

[477] *Actum* **72** and see the section of the Introduction entitled 'Intitulatio' in the 'Diplomatic Analysis of the *Acta*'.

[478] *CAC*, p. 79; *AWR*, p. 556. Reginald de Grey had previously been justice of Chester between 1270 and 1274: *ibid.*

[479] *CAC*, p. 79; *AWR*, p. 650.

1281,[480] a week before de Grey's reappointment as justice of Chester. There may have been a short détente between bishop and prince during the autumn and winter of 1281/2, with matters deteriorating the following spring/summer. Llywelyn's brother, Dafydd, attacked Hawarden castle on Palm Sunday (22 March) 1282 but as J. B. Smith suggested, the prince of Wales may not have committed himself to the conflict for some weeks, and possibly not before his wife Eleanor de Montfort died giving birth to their daughter, Gwenllian, on 19 June that year.[481] Anian was present at a council of the province of Canterbury, called by Archbishop John Pecham on 1 April 1282, and held at the Old Temple in London on 19–25 April.[482] If his letter to the chancellor was connected with the war of 1282, and he was in Wales when he wrote it, it is possible that it was written either on or after Palm Sunday (22 March), and before Anian left to attend Pecham's council, or after the bishop returned to his diocese from London (if he did return) and sometime after Llywelyn joined the armed struggle. If it was after he returned from the council, and J. B. Smith's theory that the prince did not join the war until after Gwenllian's death is correct, Anian's letter might not have been written until late June or early July. That might account for the record in the close rolls for 17 July 1282, that, at Rhuddlan, the bishop of Bangor was granted letters of protection under the royal privy seal until Michaelmas.[483] On 28 July, again at Rhuddlan, he and Robert Burnell witnessed a grant by Edward I to a loyal Welsh lord – the other witnesses included some of the king's foremost military commanders; the Earl Marshal Roger Bigod, John de Warenne, Otto de Grandison and Henry de Lacy, earl of Lincoln.[484]

It is stated in The National Archives' online description of Anian's letter that he was requesting 'safe refuge in Cheshire', which many well be true but it is difficult to confirm this from the legible portions of the manuscript.[485]

---

[480]   At Ystumgwern (south of Harlech in Dyffryn Ardudwy) on that day he affixed his seal to a pledge made by the abbot and convent of the Cistercian house of Cymer of all their land in Cyfeiliog to Llywelyn ap Gruffudd for twelve years: *LW*, p. xvii, and pp. 45–6, no. 69. Master Gervase, 'clericus' to the prince, was one of the witnesses. Another witness was Dafydd ab Einion – possibly the same man to whom Edward I had referred when he wrote to Anian on 4 January 1278 enlisting the bishop's help concerning a dispute over corn on Anglesey: Haddan and Stubbs, i, pp. 524–5.

[481]   Smith, 'Llywelyn ap Gruffudd (d. 1282)', *ODNB*.

[482]   The bishop of St Asaph was also present. The archbishop had called the council on 1 April to meet on the third Sunday after Easter (i.e. 19 April): *Councils and Synods*, ii, part ii, p. 921, n. 3., and p. 934. The bishop of Bangor was certainly in London on 23 April, when the archbishop and his suffragans (including the bishop of Bangor) announced to the pope the formal release of Amaury de Montfort: *Foedera*, i, part ii, p. 605. *Councils and Synods*, ii, part ii, p. 921.

[483]   *CCR, 1279–1288*, p. 173.

[484]   Edward's grant was to Rhys ap Maredudd of Deheubarth: *LW*, pp. 165–6, no. 290. Rhys was the only member of the dynasty of Deheubarth to support Edward in 1282: *AWR*, p. 237.

[485]   http://discovery.nationalarchives.gov.uk/details/r/C12216269, accessed 29 April 2024.

Anian described his adversaries as certain incestuous adulterers of his own chapter. His slur of 'incestuous' is interesting. Anian's immediate predecessor Richard, and indeed Gwion in the twelfth century – both of whom were similarly appointed from the local diocese – had sons who witnessed their *acta* and appear to have been members of the clerical elite at Bangor.[486] Furthermore, it seems, for a time at least, certain benefices, notably the position of archdeacon of Bangor, were seen as hereditary and passed from father to son – see the section of the Introduction entitled '*Clas* and *Familia*'.

*71. Abbey of Stanlaw ('Locus Benedictus de Stanlaw', later Whalley)

Indulgence. Assured of the mercy of omnipotent God, and the merits of the glorious virgin Mary, and all the saints, relaxation of 30 days' enjoined penance for those of his diocese, and others whose diocesans shall have ratified his indulgence, who go to the monastery and utter devoted prayers to the Almighty for the souls of the founders, the constable(s) of Chester and earls of Lincoln, whose bodies are buried in the same place, or give alms for the emendation of the danger to the monastery, or should the danger of the sea touching the house be hastened, for the removal from that place, the brothers seeking habitation at a safer place, and for the transfer of the bones of the patrons and nobles to a place of quiet.

Aberconwy, 1283 [possibly 25 March]

Printed in Whitaker, *A History of the Original Parish of Whalley*, pp. 113–14.[487]

Printed from Whitaker. Extensions in brackets are mine.

Univ(ersis), etc. Nos Œnianus*a* mis(eratione) div(ina) Bangorensis eccl(esie) episcopus notum fieri volumus per praesentes, quod, de dei omnipotentis misericordia et gloriose virginis Marie, omniumq(ue) sanctorum meritis confisi, omnibus nobis jure diocesano subjectis et aliis quorum diocesani hanc nostram indulgentiam ratam habuerint, vel penitentibus qui ad mon(asteriu)m Loci Benedicti de Stanlaw, ord. Cist. Covent. et Litcf. dioc. accesserint et ib(ide)m pro animabus constabular' Cestr. et comitum Lincoln fundatorum d(ict)e domus, et quorum corpora ib(ide)m sepulture traduntur, devotas preces fuderint altissimo, vel qui ad emendationem periculosi accessus ad dictum mon(asteriu)m de bonis sibi a deo collatis aliquam eleemosynam fecerint, vel si contingat propter periculum maris fugiendum dictum mon(asteriu)m ab eo loco amoveri, et fratres in loco tutiori sibi habitaculum quaerere, et ossa patronorum suorum p(re)dictorum at aliorum nobilium ib(ide)m humatorum inde ad locum quieti religiosorum competentiorem transferre – qui ad ista procuranda d(i)ctis fr(atribus) condigna caritatis subsidia fecerint, xxx dies de injungenda eis secundum antiquos canones poenitentia relaxamus. Dat. apud

---

[486] Anian did not have a son, at least not one who is recorded in any of his *acta* or in any other source.

[487] Available online via Google Books: https://books.google.co.uk/books/about/An_History_of_the_Original_Parish_of_Wha.html?id=EO1EAQAAMAAJ&redir_esc=y, accessed 4 May 2024. Writing in 1818, T. D. Whitaker stated that his transcription was taken 'From the original at Whalley Abbey': Whitaker, *A History of the Original Parish of Whalley*, p. 114, n. *.

Aberconwey in Snawdon', incipiente an(no) do(mi)ni mcclxxxiii et a(nno) r(egni) reg(is) Edw(ardi) fil(ii) reg(is) Hen(rici) xi.

> *a*Whitaker has written Œ (an O and E together), instead of the usual A, and he repeats it in his notes.

Anian's indulgence was given *incipiente anno domini* – at the beginning of the year, perhaps meaning the feast of the Annunciation, Lady Day, 25 March.[488]

Prima facie, it seems a little unusual that an indulgence in favour of a house founded in the twelfth century, which had never sought an indulgence from a bishop of Bangor before, should be granted in the penultimate decade of the thirteenth century, and in *Pura Wallia*. However, the date and place of the grant must be a clue. It may have been Henry de Lacy, fifth earl of Lincoln (d. 1311), who asked Anian to provide an indulgence in favour of the Cistercian abbey which his family had founded. Henry was in constant royal service, proving himself to be one of Edward's most reliable, faithful, and trusted servants and friends.[489] Anian is known to have been in the company of de Lacy and the king in July 1282.[490] In April 1283, at Aberconwy, a number of grants were made by the crown to the bishop.[491] The earl's forbears (both constables of Chester, and earls of Lincoln) lay buried at Stanlaw. Anian's grant stipulated that prayers were to be said '*pro animabus constabular' Cestr. et comitum Lincoln fundatorum d(ict)e domus …*'. Those interred at Stanlaw included Roger de Lacy, constable of Chester, who died there on 1 October 1211, and his son John de Lacy, third earl of Lincoln, who died on 22 July 1240.[492] Roger's father, John, constable of Chester, founded the abbey and in his foundation charter of 1178 he expressed a wish that the place should be re-named 'Benedictus Locus'.[493] According to Anian's grant of 1283, the sea was posing a danger to the brothers and the tombs alike at Stanlaw, and so it comes as no surprise that Henry de Lacy, fifth earl of Lincoln, ensured that the abbey was transferred to drier ground at Whalley in Lancashire, stipulating that it was to be called 'Locus Benedictus de Whalley'.[494]

---

[488] For the feast of the Annunciation, 25 March, as the beginning of the year: Cheney, *Handbook of Dates*, p. 5.

[489] Hamilton, 'Lacy, Henry de, fifth earl of Lincoln (1249–1311)', *ODNB*.

[490] July 1282, Rhuddlan: *LW*, pp. 165–6, no. 290.

[491] Grants made to Anian in April 1283: 15 April: *CCR, 1279–1288*, p. 205; 17 April: *CPR, 1281–1292*, p. 61; 18 April: *CAC*, pp. 43–4.

[492] Kingsford, revd Dalton, 'Lacy, Roger de (*d.* 1211)', *ODNB*. John de Lacy was buried near his father in the choir of the abbey, his bones being moved to Whalley when the monks transferred there in the 1290s: Vincent, 'Lacy, John de, third earl of Lincoln (*c.*1192–1240)', *ODNB*.

[493] *Coucher Book of Whalley Abbey*, i, pp. 1–5. 'Houses of Cistercian monks: The abbey of Whalley', ii, p. 131 and n. 1; Suppe, 'John (*d.* 1190)', *ODNB*.

[494] Keele University Library Special Collections and Archives, M72/46/11. *Coucher Book of Whalley Abbey*, i, pp. 189–93. Kingsford, revd Dalton, 'Lacy, Roger de (*d.* 1211)', *ODNB*; 'Houses of Cistercian monks: The abbey of Whalley', ii, pp. 131–9.

72. John de Kirkby, Counsellor of the King

Letter. He is greatly indebted to the king's counsellor, and because, by divine aid and Kirkby's help, the bishop's business in England has been straightened out and arranged, he prays that Kirkby instruct the clerks and barons of the exchequer at Shrewsbury, about the close of Easter, not to detain the money which the bishop ought to have from his wardships in Devon and Dorset, but that they might permit Anian's attorneys to receive the said money in the bishop's name and keep it for his use. [Valediction]. Additionally, as his clerks and nephews are perishing … for lack of money, he is compelled to ask Kirkby for letters of safe-conduct for their messenger, who is taking a little of the money to them, especially because all their parents have long returned to the king's peace.

[About 18 April 1283]

A = TNA SC 1/9/8. 203 x 55 mm.[495]

Calendared in *CAC*, p. 41.

Transcribed from A.

Viro venerabili et dilecto domino Joh(ann)i de Crykyby domini regis consiliario non minimo deo et hominibus fidelissimo suus Bangoren(sis) minimus salutem in salutis auctore. Quid vobis pro meritis reddere debeamus penitus ignoramus g..[a] ad remuneratorem omnium bonorum recursum habentes vobis grates quas p[o]ssumus non quas debemus persolvimus. Et quia fere per adiutorium divinum et vestrum, nostrum negotium in Anglia[b] est instructum et ordinatum vestri gratia attamen vos rogamus et requirimus quatinus clericos et barones scacarii domini nostri regis apud Salops' existentes circa clausum pascha moneatis et instruatis quod ipsi non detineant nec impediant pecuniam quam debemus[c] habere de gardis <nostris>[d] apud Devonam et Docest(ri)am sed permittant quod nostri attornati accipiant dictam pecuniam nomine nostro et custodiant ad nostrum opus et utilitatem et usum tamen super hoc factum quod de nobis uter devotis in futuro nos devotiores <vobis> efficiamur. Valeat vestra prosperitas per tempora multa. Ad hec si placet quia clerici nostri et nepotes pereunt pro… et orl.a….. ..a….[e] propter defectum pecunie vos rogare cogimur pro litteris de conductu eorum nuntio aliquantulum de pecunia eisdem pertinentem[e] maxime parentes eorum omnes ad pacem domini nostri regis iam diu sunt conversi.

[a]this appears to be an abbreviation, 'g' followed by a contraction mark, *A*. [b]hole in parchment, partially obscuring the second 'a', *A*. [c]text faded and difficult to read, *A*. [d]contracted and interlinear above the space between 'gardis' and 'apud', *A*.

John de Kirkby, a member of the royal council, who was to become bishop of Ely in 1286, was in 1283 vice-chancellor in all but name. When the chancellor, Robert Burnell, was absent, it was Kirkby who always had custody of the great seal.[496]

---

[495] Image at Plate XVII (ii). TNA online description: https://discovery.nationalarchives.gov.uk/details/r/C12298333, accessed 29 April 2024.

[496] Prestwich, *Edward I*, pp. 234–5; Prestwich, 'Kirby, John (d. 1290)', *ODNB*; *Fasti Monastic Cathedrals*, p. 46.

J. G. Edwards averred that the date of Anian's letter was about 18 April 1283, noting that the references to people coming to the king's peace, and the presence of the exchequer at Shrewsbury show that a war was in progress in Wales; and furthermore that the wardships referred to were doubtless those granted (at Aberconwy) the same month.[497] In 1283, the close of Easter fell on 25 April.[498]

After having been granted the wardship of the manor of Fernham in Oxfordshire in 1278 (see the note to *Actum* **64** above), further grants were made to Anian on 15, 17 and 18 April 1283 at Aberconwy.[499] A grant, on account of the losses suffered by the bishop of Bangor in the war (of 1282–1283), was made of land in England to the yearly value of fifty librates, during the minority of heirs, out of the first wardships that should happen; John de Kirkby was instructed to consider how provision for the same could best be made.[500] An order was also issued to the sheriff of Devon to deliver to the bishop of Bangor 40*l*. 4*s*. 0*d*. of yearly rent in the manor of Alphington ('*Alfington*'), which had belonged to John de Nevill, tenant-in-chief, and which was in the king's hands by reason of the minority of his son and heir. The bishop was to have the same until the heir came of age, and the rent was expressed to be in part satisfaction of the 50*l*. of yearly rent that the king had granted to him from wardships.[501] Another mandate was issued to John de Kirkby 'to order the treasurer and barons of the exchequer to grant the issues of the manor of *Alfinton* for the Easter term last past freely to the bishop of Bangor. The same order to be made concerning the manor of *Cormolyn* as [lacuna]'.[502]

The *intitulatio* in this extant letter does not state Anian's name, not even by way of an initial. Instead, the formula '*suus Bangoren(sis)*' is used, the same formula as Anian used in one of his letters to Robert Burnell (**70**), but with the addition of '*minimus*'.[503]

73. Community of the Cantref of Arfon

Bond to maintain the peace, in the sum of £2,000, of lord Anian, bishop of Bangor, and six of the more upright, noble, and trustworthy members of the communitas *of the cantref of Arfon* (Aruen').

Lamerwylle, 9 July 1283

---

[497] *CAC*, p. 41. Grants to Anian at Aberconwy made between 15 and 18 April 1283: *CAC*, pp. 43–4; *CCR, 1279–1288*, p. 205; *CPR, 1281–1292*, p. 61.
[498] *CAC*, p. 41.
[499] *CAC*, pp. 43–4; *CCR, 1279–1288*, p. 205; *CPR, 1281–1292*, p. 61.
[500] and 18 April 1283: *CPR, 1281–1292*, p. 61; *CAC*, p. 44.
[501] April: *CCR, 1279–1288*, p. 205. See also *CAC*, p. 44. Alphington lies about two miles south of the centre of Exeter.
[502] April: *CAC*, pp. 43–4. 'Cormolyn' could be Corfe Mullen in Dorset: cf. 'Corf Mulyn': *Notes and Queries for Somerset and Dorset*, xvi, p. 116. On 15 April, at Aberconwy, Edward I had ordered an extent of the manor of 'Cormolyn' (which had been held by the late Henry Erdington) to be made: *ibid*.
[503] See *Actum* **70** and the section of the Introduction entitled 'Intitulatio' in 'Diplomatic Analysis of the *Acta*'.

B = TNA E 36/274 (Miscellaneous Documents, Affairs of Wales, Henry III – Edward I, 'Liber A'), *c.*1282–*c.*1292. fo. cccciiii^r–cccciiii^v. s. xiii ex. In margin: Littera Aniani episcopi et sex proborum hominum de Aruen' de duobus milibus librarum nomine interesse domino regi solvendarum a communitate hominum de Aruen' pro pace habenda de consensu communitatis predicte.

Printed in *LW*, pp. 151–2, no. 267.

Transcribed from B.

Anno domini milesimo ducentesimo octuagesimo tercio die sancti Cirelli apud Lam(er)wylle congregata communitate hominum de Aruen' coram domino Aniano, miseratione divina Bangorr' episcopo, ex consensu unanimi communitatis predicte et expresso ut pax firma fidelis et stabilis domini regis regnique sui servetur in posterum et secura, sex de probioribus, nobilioribus, et fidedignioribus quorum nomina sigillorum ipsorum appositio representat, per quos pax predicta securius potest servari, de cantredo predicto se heredesque suos pro dicta pace fideliter obseruanda dicto domino regi suisque heredibus ad duo milia librarum nomine interesse domino regi vel suis heredibus solvendarum obligant per presentes, si aliquis vel aliqui guerram moverit vel moverint, vel guerre causam consilio auxsilio vel consensu dederint machinati fuerint vel quoquomodo procuraverint, seu in pacem predictam committentes receperint, vel ignotos aut notos pacis predicte suspectos exhibuerint, bannitos domini regis vel fugitivos a quocumque loco admiserint seu alimenta prestiterint, vel per suos clam vel palam ministraverint ullo modo, in quam pecuniam tenentur ipso facto potestate regia vel censura ecclesiastica exigendam. Ad hec communitas predicta de plano et voluntate expressa consentit quod si quicquam contra formam predictam procuratum fuerit per quoscumque seu attemptatum [fo. cccciiii^v] quod extunc ecclesiastico subiaceant interdicto. Et nichilominus prefatus episcopus Bangorrens(is) in omnes personas contra formam predictam aliquid attemptantes excommunicationis sentenciam profert in hiis scriptis per se vel successores suos seu ministros quoscumque extunc sine difficultate aliqua exequendam. Et renunciat communitas predicta et singuli de eadem in hac parte omni absolutionis beneficio necnon et quolibet iuris remedio quousque domino regi vel suis successoribus in premissis satisfactum fuerit competenter, salva etiam regia in omnibus potestate omnes et singulos quotiens deliquerint secundum qualitatem et quantitatem ac delicti exigentiam puniendi. In cuius rei testimonium predictus dominus Anianus et sex de cantredo predicto de voluntate expressa totius communitatis dicti cantredi ex deliberato consilio presenti scripto signa sua apposuerunt.

On 9 July 1283, bonds were taken by Anian from the more upright, noble, and trustworthy members (*de probioribus, nobilioribus, et fidedignioribus*) of the *communitates* of Arfon, Arllechwedd, Llŷn, Dunoding, Meirionnydd, and Penllyn who bound themselves in the sum of £2,000, under threat of sentence of excommunication, to ensure that the peace was maintained.[504] All six areas were described as *cantrefi*

---

[504] *Acta* **73**–**8**. J. G. Edwards assigned 9 July as the date for each of the six bonds: *LW*, pp. 151–2, 154–7, and nos. 267, 272–7. For Cyrillus/Kyrillos, the bishop and martyr of Gortyna in Crete, see Efthymios Rizos, Cult of Saints, E06913: http://csla.history.ox.ac.uk/record.php?recid=E06913, accessed 10 June 2024.

save Penllyn.[505] The number of trustworthy men differed. For Arfon, Llŷn, Meirionnydd, and Penllyn there were six men. For Arllechwedd eight, and Dunoding
ten.

As Llinos Beverley Smith has noted, similar bonds were taken from men of Rhos
and Rhufoniog by officers of the earl of Lincoln, Henry de Lacy, on 26 July 1283,
and also from the community of Tegeingl (Englefield) by Roger de Meuland, the
bishop of Coventry and Lichfield, and Gruffudd, the archdeacon of St Asaph, on
25 September the same year.[506]

Lamerwill / Lam(er)wylle / Lamerwille, the variations of the place-name given in *Acta*
73–8, could be Llanerfyl (SJ 03400 09700) in the commote of Caereinion, southern Powys (and in the diocese of St Asaph).[507]

On 2 August '*post mortem Lewelini principis Wallie*', an assembly of bailiffs and representatives from each commote of Gwynedd was held in the presence of Anian
– the result was the compilation of a list of *gravamina* against the rule of Llywelyn,
presented by the 'community of Wales' to the king in the presence of the bishop
of Bangor.[508] The assembly was held at Nancall, a grange of Aberconwy Abbey
in Eifionydd.[509] The prince was criticised, *inter alia*, for matters relating to military
service of tenants, shipwreck, and intestacy of tenants, as well as the right to make
a will; all matters that figured in the disputes that had arisen between the bishops
of Bangor and St Asaph and Llywelyn.[510]

74. Community of the Cantref of Arllechwedd

*Bond to maintain the peace, in the sum of £2,000, of lord Anian, bishop of Bangor, and eight
of the more upright, noble, and trustworthy members of the* communitas *of the cantref of
Arllechwedd* (Arthegweth).

Lamerwill, 9 July 1283

B = TNA E 36/274 (Miscellaneous Documents, Affairs of Wales, Henry III –
Edward I, 'Liber A'), *c*.1282–*c*.1292. fo. ccccvi[r]. s. xiii ex. In margin: Littera Aniani
episcopi Burdeg' [*sic*] et octo proborum hominum de cantredo de Arthegweth

---

[505] *Acta* **73–8**.
[506] Smith, '*Gravamina*', 160, and n. 1; Jones, 'Welsh Bonds for Keeping the Peace', 142–4;
LW, p. 154, no. 272. Roger de Meuland is named as the bishop of 'Chester and Lichfield' in
the bond of 25 September: *LW*, p. 154, no. 272.
[507] J. G. Edwards indexed the place-name for the six bonds under 'Llanerfyl': *LW*, p. 220.
See also *List of Historic Place Names Website*: https://historicplacenames.rcahmw.
gov.uk/placenames/recordedname/7e6f92fb-39f8-4dc4-87cc-d999c7d25fa9,
accessed 7 June 2024.
[508] The document ends with a list of the prince's policies which found favour with the
community. The text is recorded in a late sixteenth- or early seventeenth-century transcript
of a thirteenth-century record (BL Cotton Vitellius C x, fos. 166–9). It has been transcribed,
and considered in detail, by L. B. Smith in '*Gravamina*', 158–76. The assembly met on the
morrow of the feast of St Peter in Chains (2 August). The year has not been recorded but
1283 is Smith's persuasive conclusion: *ibid.*, 160.
[509] Smith, '*Gravamina*', 160, n. 1, and 173.
[510] *ibid.*, 162–3 and 168–9, and see *Actum* **52** and *Actum* **68**.

de duobus milibus librarum nomine interesse regi solvendarum a communitate hominum predictorum pro pace habenda.[511]

Printed in *LW*, pp. 155–6, no. 275.

Transcribed from B.

Anno domini m° cc° octuagesimo tercio die sancti Cerelli apud Lam(er)will congregata communitate hominum de cantredo de Arthegweth coram domino Aniano, miseratione divina Bangoren(si) episcopo, ex consensu unanimi communitatis predicte et expresso ut pax firma fidelis et stabilis domini regis regnique sui servetur in posterum et secura, octo de probioribus, nobilioribus, et fidedignioribus quorum nomina sigillorum ipsorum appositio representat, per quos pax predicta securius potest servari, de cantredo predicto se heredesque suos pro dicta pace fideliter observanda dicto domino regi suisque heredibus ad duo milia librarum nomine interesse domino regi vel suis heredibus soluendarum obligant per presentes, si aliquis uel aliqui guerram moverit vel moverint, vel guerre causam consilio auxsilio vel consensu dederint machinati fuerint vel quoquomodo procuraverint, seu in pacem predictam committentes receperint, vel ignotos aut notos pacis predicte suspectos exhibuerint, bannitos domini regis vel fugitivos a quocumque loco admiserint seu alimenta prestiterint, vel per suos clam vel palam ministraverint ullo modo, in quam pecuniam tenentur ipso facto potestate regia vel censura ecclesiastica exigendam. Ad hec communitas predicta de plano et voluntate expressa consentit quod si quicquam contra formam predictam procuratum fuerit per quoscumque seu attemptatum quod extunc ecclesiastico subiaceant interdicto. Et nichilominus prefatus episcopus Banorens(is) [*sic*] in omnes personas contra formam predictam aliquid attemptantes excommunicacionis sentenciam profert in hiis scriptis per se vel successores suos seu ministros quoscumque extunc sine difficultate aliqua exequendam. Et renunciat communitas predicta et singuli de eadem in hac parte omni absolutionis beneficio necnon et quolibet iuris remedio quousque domino regi vel suis successoribus in premissis satisfactum fuerit competenter, salva etiam regia in omnibus potestate omnes et singulos quociens deliquerint secundum qualitatem et quantitatem ac delicti exigentiam puniendi. In cuius rei testimonium predictus dominus Anian(us) et octo predicti de communitate predicta de voluntate expressa tocius communitatis ex deliberato consilio presenti scripto signa sua apposuerunt.

See note to *Actum* **73** above.

75. Community of the Cantref of Dunoding

Bond to maintain the peace, in the sum of £2,000, of lord Anian, bishop of Bangor, and ten of the more upright, noble, and trustworthy members of the communitas *of the cantref of Dunoding* (Dinnedin) *which has two commotes namely Eifionydd* (Euyonith) *and Ardudwy* (Hardidew).

Lamerwill, 9 July 1283

---

[511] The scribe has mistakenly recorded 'Burdeg' (presumably Burdigalensis, i.e. Bourdeaux) instead of 'Bang''. See the marginal notes to *Acta* **75** and **77**, and *LW*, p. 155, ns. 3 and 4.

B = TNA E 36/274 (Miscellaneous Documents, Affairs of Wales, Henry III – Edward I, 'Liber A'), *c*.1282–*c*.1292. fos. ccccv^v–ccccvi^r. s. xiii ex. In margin: [Littera] domini Aniani Burd [*sic*] episcopi et [x proborum] hominum de [cantredo] de Dinnedin [de duobus] milibus librarum [nominee int]eresse a communitate [predictorum] regi solvendis pro pa[ce haben]da.[512]

Printed in *LW*, p. 155, no. 274.

Transcribed from B.

Anno domini m^o ducentesimo octuagesimo tercio die sancti Cirilli apud Lam(er) will congregata communitate hominum de cantredo de Dinnedin qui habet duas commotas videlicet Euyonith et Hardidew coram domino Aniano, miseratione divina Bango' ^{a} episcopo, ex consensu unanimi communitatis predicte et expresso ut pax firma fidelis et stabilis domini regis regnique sui servetur in posterum et secura, decem de probioribus, nobilioribus, et fidedignioribus quorum nomina sigillorum ipsorum appositio representat, per quos pax predicta securius potest servari, de cantredo predicto se heredesque suos pro dicta pace fideliter observanda dicto domino regi suisque heredibus ad duo milia librarum nomine interesse domino regi vel suis heredibus solvendarum obligant per presentes, si aliquis uel aliqui guerram moverit vel moverint, vel guerre causam consilio auxsilio vel consensu dederint machinati fuerint vel quoquomodo procuraverint, seu in pacem predictam committentes receperint, vel ignotos aut notos pacis predicte suspectos exhibuerint, bannitos domini regis vel fugitivos a quocumque loco admiserint seu alimenta prestiterint, vel per suos clam vel palam ministraverint ullo modo, in quam pecuniam tenentur ipso facto potestate regia vel censura ecclesiastica exigendam. Ad hec communitas predicta de plano et voluntate expressa consentit quod si quicquam contra formam predictam procuratum fuerit per quoscumque seu attemptatum quod extunc ecclesiastico subiaceant interdicto. Et nichilominus prefatus episcopus Bango(rum)^b in omnes personas contra formam predictam aliquid attemptantes excommunicacionis sentenciam profert in hiis scriptis per se vel successores suos seu ministros quoscumque extunc sine difficultate aliqua exequendam. Et renunciat communitas predicta et singuli de eadem in hac parte omni absolucionis beneficio necnon et quolibet iuris remedio quousque domino regi vel suis successoribus in premissis satisfactum fuerit competenter, salva etiam regia in omnibus potestate omnes et singulos quotiens deliquerint secundum qualitatem et quantitatem ac delicti exigentiam puniendi. In cuius rei testimonium [fo. ccccvi^r] predictus dominus Anianus et decem predicti de communitate predicta de voluntate expressa totius communitatis ex deliberato consilio presenti scripto signa sua apposuerunt.

^{a}abbreviation mark for 'rum', *B*.

See note to *Actum* **73** above.

The description of Dunoding as a cantref with two commotes, Eifionydd and Ardudwy, is interesting. It is generally accepted that, in the thirteenth century,

---

[512] The start of each line in the marginal note on fo. ccccv^v is obscured by the way the page has been bound to the spine. The scribe has mistakenly recorded 'Burd' (presumably Burdigalensis, i.e. Bourdeaux) instead of 'Bang''. See the marginal notes to *Acta* **74** and **77**, and *LW*, p. 155, n. 3.

whilst Eifionydd was a commote, Ardudwy was a cantref in its own right (see *AWR*, p. 21). There is clearly some ambiguity, and attention has been drawn to the passage in the medieval Welsh tale the Fourth Branch of the Mabinogi which in referring to the cantref of Dunoding clarifies that it 'is now called Eifionydd and Ardudwy'; a remark, which as J. Beverley Smith has pointed out, is difficult to attribute to any particular period.[513] If '*Dinnedin*' is Dunoding, and it is difficult to see what else it could be, then according to those gathered at *Lamerwill* in July 1283 Dunoding was a cantref, and Eifionydd and Ardudwy were its constituent commotes.

76. Community of the Cantref of Llŷn

Bond to maintain the peace, in the sum of £2,000, of lord Anian, bishop of Bangor, and six of the more upright, noble, and trustworthy members of the communitas *of the cantref of Llŷn* (Thlen).

Lamerwill, 9 July 1283

B = TNA E 36/274 (Miscellaneous Documents, Affairs of Wales, Henry III – Edward I, 'Liber A'), *c.*1282–*c.*1292. fo. ccccv^r–ccccv^v. s. xiii ex. In margin: Littera Aniani episcopi et sex proborum hominum de cantredo de Thlen de duobus milibus librarum nomine interesse domino regi solvendarum a communitate hominum de cantredo de Thlen pro pace habenda de consensu communitatis predicte.

Printed in *LW*, pp. 154–5, no. 273.

Transcribed from B.

Anno domini m^o ducentesimo octuagesimo tercio die sancti Cirilli apud Lamerwill congregata communitate hominum de cantredo de Thlen coram domino Aniano, miseratione divina Bangorensi episcopo, ex consensu unanimi communitatis predicte et expresso ut pax firma fidelis et stabilis domini regis regnique sui servetur in posterum et secura, [sex]^a de probioribus, nobilioribus, et fidedignioribus quorum nomina sigillorum ipsorum appositio representat per quos pax predicta securius potest servari, de communitate predicta se heredesque suos pro dicta pace fideliter observanda dicto domino regi suisque heredibus ad dua milia [fo. ccccv^v] librarum nomine interesse domino regi vel suis heredibus soluendarum obligant per presentes, si aliquis uel aliqui guerram mouerit vel mouerint, vel guerre causam consilio auxsilio vel consensu dederint machinati fuerint vel quoquomodo procuraverint, seu in pacem predictam committentes receperint, vel ignotos aut notos pacis predicte suspectos exhibuerint, bannitos domini regis vel fugitivos a quocumque loco admiserint seu alimenta prestiterint, vel per suos clam vel palam ministraverint ullo modo, in quam pecuniam tenentur ipso facto potestate regia vel censura ecclesiastica exigendam. Ad hec communitas predicta de plano et voluntate expressa consentit quod si quicquam contra formam predictam procuratum fuerit per quoscumque seu attemptatum quod extunc ecclesiastico subiaceant interdicto. Et nichilominus prefatus episcopus Bangor' in omnes personas contra formam predictam aliquid attemptantes excommunicationis sentenciam profert in hiis scriptis per se vel successores suos seu ministros quoscumque extunc sine difficultate aliqua exequendam. Et renunciat communitas predicta et singuli de

---

[513] Smith, *Llywelyn*, p. 194. *Mabinogion*, p. 59. See also Davies, *Wales in the Early Middle Ages*, p. 101.

eadem in hac parte omni absolutionis beneficio necnon et quolibet iuris remedio quousque domino regi vel suis successoribus in premissis satisfactum fuerit competenter, salva etiam regia in omnibus potestate omnes et singulos quotiens deliquerint secundum qualitatem et quantitatem ac delicti exigentiam puniendi. In cuius rei testimonium predictus dominus Anian(us) et sex predicti de communitate predicta de voluntate expressa totius communitatis ex deliberato consilio presenti scripto signa sua apposuerunt.

> *a*There is an erasure in the MS here, but as noted by J. G. Edwards the last sentence confirms that 'sex' is the number missing: *LW*, p. 155, n. 1, B.

See note to *Actum* **73** above.

77. Community of the Cantref of Meirionnydd

Bond to maintain the peace, in the sum of £2,000, of lord Anian, bishop of Bangor, and six of the more upright, noble, and trustworthy members of the communitas *of the cantref of Meirionnydd* (Meronnyth).

Lamerwill, 9 July 1283

> B = TNA E 36/274 (Miscellaneous Documents, Affairs of Wales, Henry III – Edward I, 'Liber A'), *c*.1282–*c*.1292. fo. ccccvi^r–ccccvi^v. s. xiii ex. In margin: Littera domini Aniani Burdig' [*sic*] episcopi et sex proborum hominum de cantredo de Meronnyth de duobus milibus librarum nominee interesse regi solvendarum pro pace habenda a communitate hominum predictorum.[514]
>
> Printed in *LW*, p. 156, no. 276.
>
> Transcribed from B.

Anno domini m⁰ ducentesimo octuagesimo tercio die sancti Crilli*a* apud Lamerwill congregata communitate hominum de cantredo de Meronnyth coram domino Aniano, miseratione divina Bangorr' episcopo, ex consensu unanimi communitatis predicte et expresso ut pax firma fidelis et stabilis domini regis regnique sui servetur in posterum et secura, sex de probioribus, nobilioribus, et fidedignioribus quorum nomina sigillorum suorum appositio representat per quos pax predicta securius potest servari, de communitate predicta se heredesque suos pro dicta pace fideliter observanda [fo. ccccvi^v] dicto domino regi suisque heredibus ad duo milia librarum nomine interesse domino regi vel suis heredibus solvendarum obligant per presentes, si aliquis uel aliqui guerram moverit vel moverint, vel guerre causam consilio auxsilio vel consensu dederint machinati fuerint vel quoquomodo procuraverint, seu in pacem predictam committentes receperint, vel ignotos aut notos pacis predicte suspectos exhibuerint, bannitos domini regis vel fugitivos a quocumque loco admiserint seu alimenta prestiterint, vel per suos clam vel palam ministraverint ullo modo, in quam pecuniam tenentur ipso facto potestate regia vel censura ecclesiastica exigendam. Ad hec communitas predicta de plano et voluntate expressa consentit quod si quicquam contra formam predictam procura-

---

[514] The scribe has mistakenly recorded 'Burdig'' (presumably Burdigalensis, i.e. Bourdeaux) instead of 'Bang''. See the marginal notes to *Acta* **74** and **75**, and *LW*, p. 155, n. 3 and p. 156, n. 1.

tum fuerit per quoscumque seu attemptatum quod extunc ecclesiastico subiaceant interdicto. Et nichilominus prefatus episcopus Bangorr' in omnes personas contra formam predictam aliquid attemptantes excommunicationis sentenciam profert in hiis scriptis per se vel successores suos seu ministros quoscumque extunc sine difficultate aliqua exequendam. Et renunciat communitas predicta et singuli de eadem in hac parte omni absolutionis beneficio necnon et quolibet iuris remedio quousque domino regi vel suis successoribus in premissis satisfactum fuerit competenter, salva etiam regia in omnibus potestate omnes et singulos quociens deliquerint secundum qualitatem et quantitatem ac delicti exigentiam puniendi. In cuius rei testimonium predictus dominus Anianus et sex predicti de communitate predicta de voluntate expressa totius communitatis ex deliberato consilio presenti scripto signa sua apposuerunt.

ªLW has 'C[i]rilli', *B.*

See note to *Actum* **73** above.

78. Community of Penllyn

Bond to maintain the peace, in the sum of £2,000, of lord Anian, bishop of Bangor, and six of the more upright, noble, and trustworthy members of the communitas *of Penllyn* (Penthelyn).
Lamerwille, 9 July 1283

B = TNA E 36/274 (Miscellaneous Documents, Affairs of Wales, Henry III – Edward I, 'Liber A'), *c.*1282–*c.*1292. fos. ccccviᵛ–ccccviiʳ. s. xiii ex. In margin: [Littera] domini Aniani episcopi et sex proborum [homin]um de Penthelyn [de duobus] milibus marcarum [nomine] interesse regi solven[darum] pro pace habenda [a communita]te predictorum.[515]

Printed in *LW*, pp. 156–7, no. 277.

Transcribed from B.

Anno domini milesimo ducentesimo octogesimo tercio die sancti Cerilli apud Lamerwille congregata communitate hominum de Penthelyn coram domino Aniano, miseratione divina Bangorensi episcopo, ex consensu unanimi communitatis predicte et expresso ut pax firma fidelis et stabilis domini regis regnique sui servetur in posterum et secura, sex de probioribus, nobilioribus, et fidedignioribus quorum nomina sigillorum ipsorum appositio representat, per quos pax predicta securius potest servari, de communitate predicta se heredesque suos pro dicta pace fideliter observanda dicto domino regi suisque heredibus ad duo milia librarum nomine interesse domino regi vel suis heredibus solvendarum obligant per presentes, si aliquis uel aliqui guerram moverit vel moverint, vel guerre causam consilio auxsilio vel consensu dederint machinati fuerint vel quoquomodo procuraverint, seu in pacem predictam committentes receperint, vel ignotos aut notos pacis predicte suspectos exhibuerint, bannitos domini regis vel fugitivos a quocumque loco admiserint seu alimenta prestiterint, vel per suos clam vel palam ministraverint ullo modo, in quam pecuniam tenentur ipso facto potestate regia vel censura eccle-

---

[515] The start of each line in the marginal note on fo. ccccviᵛ is obscured by the way the page has been bound to the spine.

siastica exigendam. Ad hec communitas predicta de plano et voluntate expressa consentit quod si quicquam contra formam predictam procuratum fuerit per quoscumque seu attemptatum quod extunc ecclesiastico subiaceant interdicto. Et nichilominus prefatus episcopus Bangor' in omnes personas contra formam predictam aliquid attemptantes excommunicationis sentenciam profert in hiis scriptis per se vel successores suos seu ministros quoscumque extunc sine difficultate aliqua exequendam. Et renunciat communitas predicta et singuli de eadem in hac parte omni absolutionis beneficio necnon et quolibet iuris remedio quousque domino regi vel suis successoribus in premissis satisfactum fuerit competenter, salva etiam regia in omnibus potestate omnes et singulos quociens deliquerint secundum qualitatem et quantitatem ac delicti exigentiam puniendi. [fo. ccccvii^r] In cuius rei testimonium predictus dominus Anianus et sex predicti de communitate predicta de voluntate expressa totius communitatis ex deliberato consilio presenti scripto signa sua apposuerunt.

See note to *Actum* **73** above.

79. Appointment of Attorneys and Proctors

Letter concerning the appointment of Matthew, archdeacon of Anglesey, and Elias, the bishop's chaplain, to be attorneys and proctors to receive compensation on his behalf (from the commissioners appointed, by Archbishop John Pecham, to inquire into ecclesiastical damages). Sealing clause.
Llanfaglan (*Bamvagan*), 27 October 1284

B = TNA E 36/274 (Miscellaneous Documents, Affairs of Wales, Henry III – Edward I, 'Liber A'), *c*.1282–*c*.1292. fo. ccclxi^v. s. xiii ex. In margin: [Littera B]ang' episcopi per quam [constituit] attornatos ad re[cipiendum p]eccuniam concessam [a rege Ang]lie [pro dampni]s datis ecclesiis suis.[516]

Printed in *LW*, p. 89, no. 175.

Transcribed from B.

Omnibus Christi fidelibus presentes litteras visuris vel audituris Anianus, permissione divina Bang' episcopus, salutem eternam in domino. Noveritis nos constituisse, fecisse et ordinasse discretos viros, Matheu(m) archdiaconum de Angligeya et Eliam capellanum nostrum, nostros attornatos et procuratores coniunctim et divisim ad nostra negocia tractanda et exequenda, et specialiter et expresse coram venerabilibus viris priore et gardiano de Lamayes et Rothlan et magistro clerico domini regis et canonico Bangoren(si), ad recipiendum et computandum peccuniam a domino rege nobis concessam et dandam Cestrie, et ad dandum litteram quietancie de summa peccunie nobis debita, et ad alia facienda circa hoc que nos si presentes essemus faceremus [et] facere deberemus, ratum et gratum habiturum quicquid ipsi seu unus eorum nomine nostro duxerit faciendum. In cuius rei testimonium sigillum nostrum hiis litteris fecimus apponi. Dat' apud Bamvagan in vigilia Symonis et Iude apostolorum, anno domini m° cc° lxxx quarto.

---

[516] The start of each line in the marginal note on fo. ccclxi^v is obscured by the way the page has been bound to the spine.

On 25 June 1284, in Bangor, the archbishop of Canterbury, John Pecham, had appointed commissioners to make a visitation of the dioceses of St Asaph and Bangor to inquire into ecclesiastical damages.[517] They were the prior of the friars preachers of Rhuddlan (Nicholas de Rademere), the warden of the friars minor of Llan-faes (Robert de Chester), and Master Ralph de Broughton, king's clerk.[518] The archdeacon of Anglesey, '*Matheus*', was Madog ap Cynwrig, who may have been Anian's brother.[519]

'*Bamvagan*' is a variant of head-name 'Llanfaglan', being Llanfaglan, Gwynedd (SH 47000 60000) lying to the south-west of Caernarfon.[520]
The feast day of the apostles St Simon and St Jude is 28 October.[521]

80. Letter acknowledging receipt of compensation

Letter acknowledging receipt of £250, by the hand of the inquisitors, the prior of Rhuddlan (Nicholas de Rademere), Robert (de Chester) warden of Llan-faes, and Ralph de Broughton, by way of compensation for ecclesiastical damages in the last war. Sealing clause.

Chester, 3 November 1284

B = TNA E 36/274 (Miscellaneous Documents, Affairs of Wales, Henry III – Edward I, 'Liber A'), *c*.1282–*c*.1292. fo. ccclxi[v]. s. xiii ex. In margin: [Item] de eodem.[522]

Printed (without dating clause) in *Foedera*, i, part ii, p. 648.

Printed (without dating clause) in Haddan and Stubbs, i, p. 581.

Printed in *LW*, p. 90, no. 179.

Transcribed from B.

Universis quorum interest, Anian(us) permissione divina Bang' episcopus, salutem eternam in domino. Noveritis nos recepisse ducentas libras et quinquaginta libras per manus prioris de Rothelan, Roberti gardiani de Lamas, et domini Radulfi de Brocton', inquisitorum dampnorum ex parte illustris Edwardi regis Angl(ie) et suorum ecclesiis Wallie et personis ecclesiasticis illatorum, et hoc pro dampnis nobis illatis in ultima gwerra[a]. In cuius rei testimonium sigillum nostrum presentibus duximus apponendum. Dat' Cestrie in crastino animarum anno regni regis Ed(wardi) xii.

[a] *Foedera* has 'guerra', as does Haddan and Stubbs.

---

[517] *LW*, p. xix, and p. 71, no. 127. *Foedera*, i, part ii, p. 644.
[518] *LW*, pp. xix and 219, and p. 71, no. 127. Raban, 'Edward I's Other Inquiries', p. 55.
[519] See the section of the Introduction entitled 'Anian', as well as *Actum* **85**; and the note to *Actum* **81**; Stephenson, *Governance*, p. 237; *Fasti Welsh Cathedrals*, p. 7; Smith, *Llywelyn*, p. 554 and n. 154; *CVCR*, pp. 35 and 284; *CPR, 1343–1345*, p. 228; *RC*, p. 206.
[520] *List of Historic Place Names Website*: https://historicplacenames.rcahmw.gov.uk/placenames?q=bamvagan, accessed 7 June 2024.
[521] Cheney, *Handbook of Dates*, p. 61.
[522] This is under the general heading: [De de]naris solutis pro [dampnis fac]tis ecclesiis in [Wallia]: fo. ccclxi[v] of TNA E 36/274 ('Liber A'). See also *LW*, p. 89, no. 176.

On the same day, at Chester, the dean of Bangor and Elias the chaplain acknowledged receipt of 30 shillings, the seal of the archdeacon of Anglesey (Madog ap Cynwrig) being affixed to the same.[523] Furthermore, also on the same day, and in the same place, the archdeacon of Bangor acknowledged receipt of £10;[524] and Gregory, canon of Bangor, acknowledged receipt of £3 and 10 shillings.[525] The following day, 4 November, in Chester Abbey, the dean and chapter of Bangor acknowledged receipt of £60 sterling, as compensation for damage to the church of Bangor in the last war.[526]

The prior of the friars preachers of Rhuddlan (Nicholas de Rademere), the brother warden of the friars minor of Llan-faes (Robert de Chester), and the clerk, Master Ralph de Broughton had been appointed on 25 June 1284 at Bangor by Archbishop John Pecham (see note to *Actum* **79** above).

All Souls' Day is 2 November.[527]

*81. Abbot and Convent of Aberconwy Abbey

Grant, possibly jointly with the offeiriad teulu, *at the king's request, to the abbot and convent of Aberconwy of the tithes of the king's demesnes at* Kauruwylys *and Penmynydd* (Peynmeynyd), *which Edward I had granted to the bishop and* offeiriad teulu.

1284 [On, or shortly before, 5 November]

Mention only. Likely to have been in writing.

Mentioned in TNA C77 (Chancery: Welsh Rolls) 12 Edward I, m. 1. Calendared in *CVCR*, p. 292.

On 5 November 1284, at Castell y Bere, a notification was enrolled that the king had granted to Anian, bishop of Bangor, and to the *offeiriad teulu* ('*Effeyriat Teulu*') of Wales, the townships of Tref Ieuan ab Iddon and Bodychen, which were extended at 50 shillings yearly. This was in recompense for the tithes of the king's demesnes at '*Kauruwylys*' and Penmynydd ('*Peynmeynyd*'), also extended at 50 shillings yearly, which they had granted, at the king's request, to the abbot and convent of Aberconwy, whose monastery the king had caused to be re-founded at Maenan, and to whom he had granted the said demesnes.[528] Penmynydd was in the commote of Dindaethwy, Anglesey.[529] '*Kauruwylys*' is unidentified. The townships of Tref Ieuan ab Iddon

---

[523] 'In cuius rei testimonium sigillum archidiaconi de Angleseya huic apposuimus.': *LW*, p. xxi and p. 68, no. 119. The dean of Bangor is likely to have been Cynddelw: see the notes to *Actum* **58** and *Actum* **85**, and *Fasti Welsh Cathedrals*, p. 5.

[524] *LW*, p. xxiii and p. 134, no. 236. The archdeacon of Bangor may also have been named Cynddelw: see the note to *Actum* **85**, and *Fasti Welsh Cathedrals*, p. 6.

[525] *LW*, p. xxi and p. 66, no. 110. For Gregory ('Grigorius'), see *Fasti Welsh Cathedrals*, pp. 9–10.

[526] *LW*, p. xxiv and p. 90, no. 180.

[527] Cheney, *Handbook of Dates*, p. 43.

[528] *CVCR*, p. 292. A proviso was added that Anian and his successors should satisfy the offeiriad teulu and his successors for the portion of the said tithes due to the offeiriad teulu: *ibid*. See also *Actum* **83**.

[529] Carr, *Medieval Anglesey*, 2nd edn, p. 273 (map).

and Bodychen were in the commote of Llifon, Anglesey.[530] The king had appointed the archdeacon of Anglesey (Madog ap Cynwrig) *offeiriad teulu* earlier that year.[531] *Offeiriad teulu* translates as 'the household priest'.[532]

82. Beddgelert Priory

Confirmation and Indulgence. The bishop had seen various charters of the princes in favour of the prior and convent of the Valley of the Blessed Mary of Snowdonia; one had been granted by Llywelyn ab Iorwerth (Lewelinus magnus), *three by Llywelyn ap Gruffudd, one by* dominus Owenus, *and two by* dominus David. *The bishop had also seen confirmatory papal bulls concerning the lands granted. The priory was the senior religious house of all of Wales, save for Bardsey, the Island of Saints, and for those in need who were crossing from England and west Wales to north Wales, and from Ireland and north Wales going into England, it was better for hospitality. The house had been damaged in a fire and as such Anian granted 40 days' relaxation of enjoined penance to all those who had confessed and were truly contrite, and who contributed pious alms or favours from the goods granted to them by God. Sealing clause.*

Maes-y-llan, 1 April 1286

A = TNA C 270/29/5. 213 x 110 mm. Turn-up at the foot of the document with horizontal slits for sealing purposes (*sur double queue*). Parchment sealing tag and seal missing.[533]

Printed (with omissions) in *Prynne*, iii, p. 1280.[534]

Printed (with omissions) in *Foedera*, i, part ii, p. 664.

Printed (with omissions) in *Monasticon*, vi, part i, p. 200.

Printed (with omissions) in Haddan and Stubbs, i, pp. 584–5.

Translated in Jones, 'Arvona Mediaeva II: Beddgelert Priory'.

Transcribed from A.

Universis Cristi fidelibus has litteras visuris vel audituris, Anian(us) permissione divina Bangor' ecclesie minister humilis, salutem eternam in domino. Noveritis nos vidisse cartas varias diversorum principum priori et conventui de valle beate Marie de Snaudonia videlicet cartam Lewelini magni super totam terram Kyndew …nt..*ᵃ* de Pennant*ᵇ* et cartam Lewelini filii Grifini super*ᶜ* omnes terras filiorum Ithael de Penard et cartam *ᵈ*Lewelini filii Grifini super*ᶜ* totam terram hominum

---

[530] *ibid.*, p. 276 (map). As calendared, three townships are named as having been granted by Edward to the bishop and offeiriad teulu; '*Trefyevan, Abydon, and Bodychen*' (*CVCR*, p. 292), however A. D. Carr has rendered these names as just two townships: 'Tref Ieuan ab Iddon and Bodychen': Carr, *Medieval Anglesey*, 2nd edn, p. 213.

[531] April 1284: *CVCR*, p. 284; Pryce, 'Offeiriad Teulu', p. 91.

[532] For the office and role of the offeiriad teulu see Pryce, 'Offeiriad Teulu', pp. 82–93.

[533] Image at Plate XV.

[534] 'The Monastery of the Vale of St. Mary in Snowdon in Wales being burnt with fire, the Bishop of Bangor made this Certificate of its antiquity, Charters of endowments by Welsh Princes confirmed by Popes Bulls, and former hospitality; and granted 40 dayes indulgence of the penance enjoyned to all who should contribute towards the rebuilding thereof.': Early English Books Online: https://quod.lib.umich.edu/e/eebo/A70867.0001.001 (p. 1280), accessed 4 February 2024.

de Trehan aput*ᶜ* Kenynbeind et Lecheitaur, et cartam domini Oweni super*ᶜ* totam villam quae vocatur Tref Ybeyrd apud Kynind Meney, et cartam domini Lewelini filii G(ri)fini super*ᶠ* totam terram illam et locum de Beckellert, et cartam domini David super*ᶠ* totam terram *ᵍ*Adoer apud Epennant, et cartam domini David super totam terram Tegwaret *vab* Gueyr de Pennant,*ᵍ* et cartam domini David super*ᶜ* totam terram quam habuerit Jorberd *vab yr efeyntt* et F[r]eraul*ʰ* apud Epennant. Et super*ᶜ* dictis terris vidimus literas papales confirmatorias bullatas non cancellatas, non abollitas, nec in aliqua parte*ⁱ* viciatas. Ad hec sciant universi, quod dicta domus beate Marie, senior domus religiosa est de tota Walia, excepta insula sanctorum Bardigeia, et melioris hospitalitatis et communioris indigentibus et transeuntibus Anglicis et Walensibus de A(n)glia et Westi*ʲ* Walia transeuntibus ad Norwaliam, et de Ybernia et Norwalia euntibus ad Agliam [*sic*]. Sec [*sic*] in dapnum*ᵏ* non modicum et defectum communem omnium, dicta domus incendio casuali penitus est*ˡ* destructa, licet hospitalitatis tempore maximam pateretur ruinam, per tamen regem pium catholicum liberalem, dei gratia dominum Edwardum ad plenum fuisset restaurata.*ᵐ ⁿ*Et quia pium est oppressis et afflictis subvenire, nos, de dei misericordia et de intercessione eiusdem genetricis, et omnium sanctorum suffragiis*ᵒ* confidentes, omnibus benefactoribus dicte domus undicunque subvenientibus, qui de bonis a deo collatis pias elemosinas vel favores contulerunt, xl. dies de iniuncta sibi penitentia misericorditer relaxamus, dum sint vere contriti*ᵖ* et confessi. In cuius rei testimonium sigillum nostrum huic carte duximus apponendum. Dat' apud Maes yllan, in octabis anunciationis beate Marie, anno domini mᵒ ccᵒ lxxxᵒ sexto.

ᵃPrynne, *Foedera*, *Monasticon*, and Haddan and Stubbs all have 'Kyndewewic'. There is no second 'e' evident. Furthermore, there appears to be not one but two words. The same is written 'Kindeluluyt' in Edward I's letter of 10 May 1286 (*Monasticon*, vi, part i, p. 200). In *AWR*, at p. 347, no. 217, this is said to be (the land of) Cynddelw Llwyd (of Pennant). *ᵇFoedera* has 'Rennaut'. *ᶜ*the abbreviation here, 's' followed by the letter 'r' with a contraction line above it, is nothing like the abbreviation 'sup' which precedes 'totam terram Kyndew …nt.. de Pennant'. It is still possible though to construe it as 'super' (Cappelli, *The Elements of Abbreviation*, p. 8) and it does make sense – see the notes below for a possible explanation for the use of different abbreviations. *Monasticon* and Haddan and Stubbs both have 'super', *A*. *ᵈ*text erased before 'Lewelini', leaving a lacuna, *A*. *ᵉ*this is clearly 'aput'. *Foedera*, *Monasticon*, and Haddan and Stubbs, all have 'apud', *A*. *ᶠ*the scribe has reverted to the first abbreviation he used for 'super' namely: 'sup', *A*. *ᵍ⁻ᵍ*omitted by *Foedera*, *Monasticon*, and Haddan and Stubbs. *ʰ*the scribe's pen has blotted ink at the second letter, which, as a consequence, is difficult to decipher (*Prynne*, *Monasticon*, and Haddan and Stubbs, all have 'r' for the second letter), *A*. *ⁱ*'**p**' is followed by a letter which is difficult to read, because the ink is very heavy at this point, followed by 'e'. (Prynne has 'parie'; *Monasticon*, and Haddan and Stubbs, have 'parte'), *A*. *ʲ*a letter follows 't', and it looks like an 'i' (it is ignored by *Prynne*, *Monasticon*, and Haddan and Stubbs), *A*. *ᵏ*the scribe presumably meant to write 'dampnum' but missed out the first 'm'. (*Prynne*, *Monasticon*, and Haddan and Stubbs, all have 'damnum'), *A*. *ˡ*omitted by *Prynne*, *Monasticon*, and Haddan and Stubbs. *ᵐ*Haddan and Stubbs have 'restorata'. *Prynne*, and *Monasticon*, have 'restaurata'. *ⁿ*erased script preceding 'Et', *A*. *ᵒ*omitted by Haddan and Stubbs. *ᵖPrynne*, *Monasticon*, and Haddan and Stubbs, all have 'convicti', which is incorrect, not least because there is no 'v'/'u'.

Anian listed the charters he had seen, commencing with a grant by '*Lewelinus magnus*' (Llywelyn ab Iorwerth/Llywelyn Fawr, d. 1240). There followed three charters granted by Llywelyn ap Gruffudd (d. 1282), one by *dominus Owenus*, and two by *dominus David*. It is likely that '*cartam domini Oweni*' referred to a charter granted by Owain ap Gruffudd (d. *c.*1282), Llywelyn ap Gruffudd's older brother, rather than one granted by Owain Gwynedd (d. 1170).[535] Furthermore, it is likely that those two charters referred to individually as '*cartam domini David*' were charters granted by Dafydd ap Gruffudd (d. 1283), Llywelyn ap Gruffudd's younger brother, as opposed to Dafydd ab Owain (d. 1203) or Dafydd ap Llywelyn (d. 1246).[536]

The lands granted were: all the land of Cynddelw Llwyd[537] of Pennant (a township in the commote of Eifionydd); all the lands of the sons of Ithel of Pennardd (in the cantref of Arfon); all the land of the men of Trefan at Cenin fynydd and Llecheiddior (in Eifionydd); the township of Tre'r-beirdd in the commote of Menai (Anglesey); all that land [of Tre'r-beirdd?] and the site of Beddgelert; all the land of *Adoer* in Pennant (Eifionydd); all the land of Tegwared ap Gwair of Pennant (Eifionydd); and all the land which Iorwerth son of the priest and *F[r]eraul* had in Pennant (Eifionydd).[538]

Edward I referred to Anian's letter on 10 May 1286, at Canterbury, and recited the charters Anian had said he had seen.[539] According to the king, Anian had sent his letter patent to Edward, and the same may have been delivered by Madog, prior of Beddgelert, and Hugh, a canon of the same house, who were mentioned by Edward.[540]

Anian was gushing in his praise for the priory; not only was it the senior religious house of all of Wales, save for Bardsey (Ynys Enlli), the Island of Saints, for those in need who were crossing from England and west Wales to north Wales, and from Ireland and north Wales going into England, it was better for hospitality. This seems an odd thing to say, and it could be the product of the beneficiary; however, Anian may have been merely giving practical encouragement to his parishioners, and others, to visit the house, to add to the spiritual enticements of his indulgence. The priory had suffered damage by fire in the war of 1282–1283 and had been awarded 50 pounds sterling as compensation on 2 November 1284.[541] Any sug-

---

[535] See *AWR*, pp. 482–3, and Stephenson, *Governance*, p. 156, and ii. 94.

[536] See *AWR*, pp. 633–4.

[537] Cynddelw Llwyd ('Kindeluluyt') is referred to in a letter of Edward I, 10 May 1286, reciting the charters listed by Anian: TNA C 53/74, m. 1; *Monasticon*, vi, part i, p. 200; *AWR*, pp. 633–4.

[538] *AWR*, p. 347, no. 217, pp. 482–3, no. 311, p. 496, nos. 324 and 325, pp. 545–6, no. 367, and pp. 633–4, nos. 437, 438 and 439, and Gresham, *Eifionydd*, 4–6, 64, and 201. 'Adoer' has not been identified: *AWR*, p. 633. 'F[r]eraul' appears as 'Steyraul' in Edward I's letter dated 10 May 1286 reciting the charters listed by Anian: *AWR*, p. 634, no. 439. 'yr efeyntt' ('yr efeyrat' in Edward's letter: *AWR*, p. 634, no. 439), i.e. 'yr effeiriad'/'yr offeiriad', is Welsh for 'the priest': *AWR*, p. 634; *Geiriadur Prifysgol Cymru*, accessed 29 April 2024.

[539] TNA C 53/74, m. 1; *Monasticon*, vi, part i, p. 200; *AWR*, pp. 633–4.

[540] '… venerabilis pater Anianus Bangorensis episcopus, misit nobis literas suas patentes, per quas testabatur, se vidisse cartas diversorum principum …': *Monasticon*, vi, part i, p. 200.

[541] The prior acknowledged receipt of the same: *LW*, p. 61, no. 91.

gestion that the *actum* might be spurious must be caveated by the fact that Edward referred to it in his charter of 10 May 1286, and specifically stated that Anian had sent the letter to the king.[542]

If we accept that the wording of the charter of Llywelyn ap Gruffudd *super totam terram hominum de Trehan aput Kenynbeind et Lecheitaur* was faithfully copied in Anian's *actum*, the use of '*aput*' as opposed to '*apud*' is interesting. '*aput*' was also used by Llywelyn in a grant of 1243, to which Bishop Richard was the first witness.[543] J. C. Davies highlighted the prince's use of 't' as opposed to 'd' in the 1243 charter, but without further comment.[544] It could be that this was the habit of a particular clerk in the service of Llywelyn ap Gruffudd. The use, in Anian's *actum*, of two different abbreviations for '*super*' is also interesting, and perhaps suggests that the writer was copying the descriptions of land in the various charters particularly faithfully.

Anian prefaced his grant of an indulgence with the arenga *Et quia pium est oppressis et afflictis subvenire* … ('And because it is pious to help the oppressed and the afflicted …') which is the first use of those words as an arenga by a bishop of Bangor.

A search of the place-name Maes-y-llan reveals that there are many possible locations both in the diocese of Bangor, and elsewhere in Wales, where Anian's *actum* may have been given. In the diocese the place-name Maes-y-llan is recorded in Anglesey, Arllechwedd, Dyffryn Clwyd, Llŷn, and Meirionnydd.[545]

The date given is '*in octabis annunciationis beate Marie*'. Haddan and Stubbs recorded this as 2 April, whereas Huw Pryce records it as 1 April.[546] The difference, it seems, can be accounted for by the differing interpretation, or rather, calculation, of *octaba, -e*: 'the eighth day inclusive/eight days inclusive'.[547]

*83. Consent to transfer of Aberconwy Abbey to Maenan

Mention only in a letter of Pope Honorius IV to Edward I, confirming the kings' foundation and endowment of a Cistercian monastery on royal land in the diocese of St Asaph, and the transfer of the abbot and convent of Aberconwy to that place.

[*c.*1284 x before 24 April 1286]

Consent not necessarily in writing, although likely to have been so.

Mentioned in a letter from the pope to Edward I dated 8 Kal. Mai. (24 April) 1286, at Perugia: Honorius IV, *Regesta*, vol. xliii, fo. 6d. Calendared in *Cal. Pap. Reg.*, i, p. 480.

---

[542] TNA C 53/74, m. 1; *Monasticon*, vi, part i, p. 200; *AWR*, pp. 633–4.

[543] *AWR*, pp. 491–2, no. 318.

[544] Davies, 'A Grant by Llewelyn Ap Gruffydd', 158.

[545] *List of Historic Place Names Website*: https://historicplacenames.rcahmw.gov.uk/placenames?q=Maes-y-llan, accessed 7 June 2024.

[546] Haddan and Stubbs, i, p. 584. *AWR*, pp. 482–3, 633–4.

[547] Gooder, *Latin for Local History*, p. 149.

The land concerned was at Maenan, north of Llanrwst, on the east bank of the river Conwy, and therefore in the diocese of St Asaph. The bishop of St Asaph (Anian II) gave his assent to the foundation and endowment, and the bishop of Bangor gave his consent.[548]

Edward's desire to move the abbot and convent was a consequence of the construction of his new castle and walled town at Conwy, where the abbey was situated. Archbishop Pecham had objected (on 14 June 1284) to Edward's proposal of re-founding the abbey at Maenan and suggested that it be moved to a new location within the diocese of Bangor instead.[549]

See also the note to *Actum* **81**.

*84. The Crown

Claim, not necessarily in writing, asserting that he and his predecessors had been in seisin of a third of the tithes of the king's demesnes and mills of Englefield [Tegeingl in Welsh] *and a third of the tithes from the king's lead mine there in times gone by.*

1286 [Shortly before 16 December]

Mention only. On 16 December 1286, at Westminster, an order was given, to Reginald de Grey, justice of Chester, that A(nian), bishop of Bangor, was to have, until further order, a third of the tithes of the king's demesnes and mills of Englefield, and a third of the tithes from the king's lead mine there, which the bishop had claimed, asserting that he and his predecessors had been in seisin thereof in times gone by, as appeared by an inquisition undertaken by the justice; in accordance with the king's grant to the bishop and his successors that they should enjoy the same rights, liberties, possessions, and customs long held as he and his predecessors had enjoyed.[550]

Reginald de Grey had been reappointed justice of Chester on 14 November 1281.[551]

Englefield, called Tegeingl in Welsh, was one of the cantrefs making up the Four Cantrefs (Perfeddwald).

Anian's predecessor, Richard, had claimed that he and his predecessors were accustomed to have the tithes of the king's demesnes, both of corn and of all other things, including lead everywhere in the king's land of Perfeddwlad (**46**).[552]

Edward I had confirmed the rights, liberties, possessions, and customs of the see of Bangor, in 1278.[553]

---

[548] *Cal. Pap. Reg.*, i, p. 480.

[549] *Registrum Epistolarum Peckham*, ii, pp. 726–7.

[550] *CFR, 1272–1307*, p. 232.

[551] *CAC*, p. 79; *AWR*, p. 556.

[552] See *Actum* **46**.

[553] November 1278, at Rhuddlan: *RC*, p. 254 and p. 255; Willis, *Survey*, pp. 212–13; Haddan and Stubbs, i, p. 526. See also the note to *Actum* **65**.

It seems that Reginald de Grey did not comply with the order to allow Anian to have the tithes from the lead mining to which he was entitled, as the bishop soon had cause to write to Edmund, earl of Cornwall, asking for justice to be done in respect of the same (**86**).[554] Edward I was in Gascony from 13 May 1286 to 12 August 1289, and during that period Edmund served as regent.[555]

*85. Commission to investigate a matrimonial case

The bishop authorised and commissioned the dean and archdeacon of Bangor, and the archdeacon of Anglesey, to investigate a matrimonial case involving Tudur Fychan and Madroun, _the wife of Dafydd._

[Before 15 February 1287]

Not necessarily in writing. Mention only, in a letter dated 15 February 1287 written by the archbishop of Canterbury, John Pecham, to Master K, dean of Bangor, Master K, the archdeacon of Bangor, Master M, archdeacon of Anglesey (at South Malling: _Registrum Epistolarum Peckham_, iii, pp. 940–1). By _auctoritate et ex commissione_ of the bishop of Bangor, the three senior Bangor clerics had petitioned the archbishop for his advice in a case involving the nobleman (_nobilis vir_) Tudur Fychan, and a woman (_mulier_) by the name of 'Madroun', the wife of a certain David/Dafydd. The archbishop, by his letter, replied to their _petitio_ with his advice.[556]

The dean of Bangor is likely to have been Cynddelw, and the archdeacon of Bangor may also have been named Cynddelw.[557] The archdeacon of Anglesey was Madog ap Cynwrig.[558]

Tudur Fychan had been granted the vill of Nantmawr, in the commote of Twrcelyn, Anglesey, in August 1284, and according to the extent of the lands of the bishopric of Bangor undertaken in the autumn of 1306, he owed the bishop of Bangor 5 shillings per annum for the same.[559]

---

[554] See _Actum_ **86**.

[555] Gough, _Itinerary_, ii, pp. 21–60; and Vincent, 'Edmund of Almain', _ODNB_.

[556] _Registrum Epistolarum Peckham_, iii, pp. 940–1.

[557] Dean Cynddelw granted a charter in favour of Haughmond Abbey during Anian's episcopate: 'Candelau decanus Bangorensis': Shrewsbury, Shropshire Archives, MS 6001/6869 (Haughmond Cartulary), fo. 151. _Cartulary of Haughmond Abbey_, p. 162, no. 799. See also the note to _Actum_ **58** and _Fasti Welsh Cathedrals_, p. 5. 'K' (possibly 'K[yndelw]') the archdeacon of Bangor appeared in the documentary record on 3 November 1284: _LW_, p. 82, no. 153; _Fasti Welsh Cathedrals_, p. 6.

[558] See the section of the Introduction entitled 'Anian'; as well as _Actum_ **79**; the note to _Actum_ **81**; Stephenson, _Governance_, p. 237; _Fasti Welsh Cathedrals_, p. 7; Smith, _Llywelyn_, p. 554 and n. 154; _CVCR_, p. 35 and p. 284; _CPR, 1343–1345_, p. 228; _RC_, p. 206.

[559] _CVCR_, p. 288; _RC_, p. 109; Stephenson, _Governance_, pp. 235 and 236. See also the section of the Introduction entitled 'Extent of 1306/7 – Manors, Lands and Tenants of the Bishop of Bangor'.

*86. Edmund, Earl of Cornwall

In the king's absence, Anian, the king's chaplain in Wales, asks Edmund, the earl of Cornwall, for justice to be done in respect of the tithes of the lead mines in Tegeingl, which had been proved to be due to him, and which had been detained by Reginald de Grey. The king had written often to de Grey. The church of Bangor was accustomed to have the tithes in the time of Llywelyn ab Iorwerth (Lewellinus magnus), *Dafydd his son (Dafydd ap Llywelyn), Llywelyn ap Gruffudd, as well as King Henry (III); notwithstanding that the abbot of Vale Royal received some part in time of war. Valediction.*

[20 November 1287 x 19 November 1288]

Apparently lost. Mentioned only in *Prynne*, iii, p. 1294, a footnote to the same recording '*Bundela Brevium de Privato sigillo, An. 16 E. 1. in Turri London*'.[560]

Printed from *Prynne*.

Excellenti viro ac nobili domino Edmundo comiti Cornubiae, locum domini regis in Anglia tenenti, Amanus permissione divina Bangorensi [*sic*] ecclesiae minister humilis, domini regis capellanus in Wallia, salutem etc. Licet dominus rex saepe et saepius scripsit domino R. de Grey, quod faceret nobis habere decimas plumbifodiarum de Thegeygl, quod facere minime curavit, licet coram eo inquisitio apud Rocolan fuisset per duodecim homines majores juratos de Thegeygl, et pro jure nostro deposuissent ad plenum. Et idem dominus R. de Grey subtraxit nobis justitiae complementum. Quare recursum habuimus ad dominum regem propter defectum justitiae, qui vobis scripsit pro nobis et jure nostro; quare vos rogamus et requirimus, sicut zelator veritatis estis et justitiae defensor, quatinus manum vestram auxiliatricem et adjutricem pro nobis porrigere dignemini; ita quod ecclesia Bangoren(sis) non cedat a jure suo, quominus possit gaudere decimis plumbifodiarum de Thegeygl, sicut consuevit temporibus retroactis Lewellini magni, et David filii eius, et Lewellini filii Griffini, et domini Henrici regis, et aliorum regum et principum Wallie, non obstante quod abbas de Valle Regali recepit aliquam partem tempore guerrae, quam adhuc tenet. Valeat, etc.

'An. 16 E. 1.': Edward I's sixteenth regnal year was 20 November 1287 to 19 November 1288.[561]

The *inscriptio* includes the words '*locum domini regis in Anglia tenenti*': Edward was in Gascony from 13 May 1286 to 12 August 1289, during which period Edmund served as regent.[562]

---

[560] Available online via Early English Books Online: https://quod.lib.umich.edu/e/eebo/A70867.0001.001 (p. 1294 and n. 2.147), accessed 4 February 2024.

[561] Cheney, *Handbook of Dates*, p. 20.

[562] Gough, *Itinerary*, ii, pp. 21–60; and Vincent, 'Edmund of Almain', *ODNB*. If the note in *Prynne* is incorrect, there are two other possible date ranges, firstly when Edmund acted as Edward's lieutenant in the government of England, April 1282 x December 1284, whilst Edward campaigned in Wales (Vincent, 'Edmund of Almain', *ODNB*), and secondly, 23 August 1297 x 13 March 1298, when Edward was in Flanders, and Gascony (Gough, *Itinerary*, ii, pp. 156–63. Edmund was in Gascony for part of 1297: Vincent, 'Edmund of Almain', *ODNB*).

Tegeingl, called Englefield in English, was one of the cantrefs making up the Four Cantrefs (Perfeddwald).

In 1286, an order was given to Reginald de Grey, the justice of Chester, that the bishop of Bangor was to have a third of the tithes of the king's demesnes and mills of Englefield (Tegeingl) and a third of the tithes from the king's lead mine there.[563] See *Actum* **84** above and the notes to the same. Reginald de Grey had been reappointed justice of Chester in 1281 and been granted Dyffryn Clwyd (later the barony of Ruthin), one of the Four Cantrefs in 1282.[564]

For a discussion of when Anian may have become chaplain to Edward I see the notes to *Actum* **62** above.

*87. Constitutions

Constitutions issued at a synod of all the clergy of the diocese of Bangor.
Llanfair Garth Branan, Bangor, 21 July 1291

Mention only in Prifysgol Bangor University Archives and Special Collections, Bangor Pontifical, fo. 166. s. xv.[565] A nineteenth-century transcription of the same, by Alfred Stowe of Wadham College, Oxford, is on fo. 165v.

Printed in Willis, *Survey*, p. 199. Printed in Haddan and Stubbs, i, p. 597. Transcribed from the Bangor Pontifical, fo. 166:

'*Constitutiones domini Aniani episcopi Bangorensis in sinodo sua celebrata in ecclesia sancte[566] Marie de Garthbranan apud Bangoriam,[567] in crastino sancte Margarete virginis, anno domini millesimo ducentesimo nonagesimo primo, sub continuatione et prorogatione dierum tunc sequentium, toto clero diocesis Bangorensis ad hoc convocato*'.

Folio 166 is a flyleaf. The actual constitutions issued are not recorded and, so far as is known, have not survived. However, a strip of parchment has been pasted to the foot of the flyleaf, immediately below the record of the synod and (whilst this may be unconnected to the constitutions promulgated at the synod) the wording on the strip is recorded here for the sake of completeness. The text is upside down due to the way the strip has been attached to the flyleaf:

---

[563] December 1286, at Westminster: *CFR, 1272–1307*, p. 232.
[564] Reappointed justice of Chester: *CAC*, p. 79; *AWR*, p. 556. Granted Dyffryn Clwyd: Powicke, *The Thirteenth Century*, p. 424; Prestwich, *Edward I*, p. 204.
[565] Image available on DIAMM website, https://www.diamm.ac.uk/sources/3785/#/images, accessed 6 June 2024. The text on the flyleaf, fo. 166., has been dated to the fifteenth century: Harper, 'The Bangor Pontifical', 76.
[566] Both Willis, *Survey*, p. 199, and Haddan and Stubbs, i, p. 597, read the three-letter contraction as 'beatae'; however, I think the word is 'sancte' ('ste') because the first letter is the same as the first letter of 'sub'. Alfred Stowe's transcription has 'sanctae' (Bangor Pontifical, fo. 165v.).
[567] There is some discolouration of the parchment which makes it difficult to be certain about the letters that follow the 'r' of 'Bangor'. Both Willis, *Survey*, p. 199, and Haddan and Stubbs, i, p. 597, have 'Bangoriam'.

'……………[568] *ecclesie vel cimiterii ac cynllaw officium*'

Cynllaw is a variant of *canllaw*.[569] *Canllaw* meant a litigant's advocate, or a proctor/mediator.[570]

The synod was held on 21 July ('*in crastino sancte Margarete virginis*') 1291. Llanfair (St Mary's) Garth Branan or Brenan is thought to have stood north of Bangor Cathedral, across the now-culverted river, Afon Adda, and to the south of the present Main Arts building of Bangor University, on the slope to the north-east of the modern Pontio building.[571] According to Browne Willis, it was 'the parochial church of Bangor Town'.[572]

The record of the synod on folio 166 of the Bangor Pontifical immediately follows the record, on the same flyleaf, of two indulgences granted by Anian in 1279 in favour of the Augustinian friary of Clare in Suffolk (*Actum* **66** and *Actum* **67**). See notes to *Actum* **66**.

88. Salisbury Cathedral

Indulgence. Trusting in the mercy of omnipotent God, and in the merits of the blessed virgin Mary, his mother, of the blessed apostles, Peter and Paul, of the blessed Deiniol, bishop and confessor, our patron, and of all the saints, the grant of 40 days' relaxation of enjoined penance for all those parishioners of the diocese of Bangor, and others whose diocesan bishops shall have ratified our indulgence, who have confessed and are truly penitent, and who piously say the Lord's Prayer and the Ave Maria for the soul of William de la Corner, recently bishop of Salisbury, who lies buried in the cathedral church of Salisbury, and for the souls of all the faithful departed. Sealing clause.

London, 16 November 1295

A = Salisbury Cathedral Archives, Indulgences, BS/5/37. 184 x 99 mm. Cut away at foot of parchment to form a wrapping-tie and tongue (no seal survives).[573] Endorsed on reverse: 'Bangorensis xl dies Anianus Indulgentia 1295', and in a modern hand: '16 Nov 1295'.

Transcribed from A.

Omnibus Cristi fidelibus presentes litteras inspecturis vel audituris, Anianus permissione divina Bangoren(sis) episcopus, salutem in domino sempiternam.[a] Obsequium deo gratum totiens impendere rationabiliter opinamur quotiens mentes fidelium ad [pieta]tis[b] et sancte devotionis opera propencius excitamus. Nos igitur de dei omnipotentis misericordia, et beate Marie virginis matris eius, beatorum Petri et Pauli apostolorum, beati Danielis episcopi et confessoris patroni nostri, et

---

[568]   A word or words of some fourteen or so letters.
[569]   Thank you to Professor Paul Russell for discussing this with me. Cf. *cynghellor/canghellor*.
[570]   See *Law of Hywel Dda*, pp. 322–3; *Geiriadur Prifysgol Cymru*, accessed 2 June 2024.
[571]   Grid Reference SH5802272275: Coflein website: https://coflein.gov.uk/en/site/43677/details/llanfair-garth-brenan-site-of-medieval-church, accessed 10 June 2024.
[572]   Willis, *Survey*, p. 69, and p. 46. Similarly, Haddan and Stubbs, i, p. 597, n. a, stated that it was the parish church of Bangor at the time.
[573]   Image at Plate XVIII.

omnium sanctorum, meritis et precibus confidentes, omnibus parochianis nostris ac aliis quorum diocesani sunt nostram indulgentiam ratam habuerint de peccatis suis vere contritis et confessis, qui pro anima Will(elm)i de la Cornere nuper episcopi Sarum, cuius corpus^c in ecclesia cathedrali Sarum iacet humatum, ac pro animabus omnium fidelium defunctorum, orationem dominicam cum salutatione virginis gloriose pia mente dixerint, quadragincta [*sic*] dies de iniuncta sibi penitentia misericorditer relaxamus. In cuius rei testimonium sigillum nostrum presentibus duximus apponendum. Datum London' in festo sancti Edmundi archiepiscopi domini millesimo ducentesimo nonagesimo quinto.

> ^{a}small hole in parchment between the 'i' and 't' of sempiternam, *A*. ^{b}ink faded, *A*.
> ^{c}small hole in parchment immediately after the 's' of 'corpus', *A*.

Anian was in London because he had been summoned to attend a parliament at Westminster fixed for 13 November 1295 which was, in the end, prorogued until 27 November.[574]

In the archives at Salisbury Cathedral are a number of similar indulgences granted in 1294 by the bishop of Exeter, Thomas Bitton (BS/5/28), Llywelyn, bishop of St Asaph (BS/5/29), the archbishop of York, John le Romeyn (BS/5/31) and the bishop of Norwich, Ralph de Walpole (BS/5/34).

William de la Corner, bishop of Salisbury, died in 1291.[575] He died abroad, and his body was returned to Salisbury and buried in the cathedral on or before 4 November 1291.[576] On a visit to Salisbury in May 2019, it became apparent that there was no tomb assigned to William de la Corner. There is, indeed, some doubt as to where in the cathedral he was buried.[577]

Anian's reference to St Daniel (Deiniol) is only the third time such a reference is made in an *actum* of a twelfth- or thirteenth-century bishop of Bangor. The other two *acta* which include a reference to St Daniel are Anian's also, both in 1279, and both indulgences (in favour of Clare Friary): *Acta* **66** and **67**. Daniel is described as bishop and confessor in all three, but Anian's grant in favour of Salisbury adds 'our patron' ('*patroni nostri*') or perhaps, 'our protector'. Anian II of Bangor was also to refer to St Daniel in one of his early grants, another indulgence in favour of Salisbury in 1310 (Salisbury Cathedral Archives, Indulgences BS/5/52).

---

[574] *Parliamentary Writs and Writs of Military Summons*, i, p. 443.

[575] Probably on 10 October: *Fasti Salisbury*, p. 7; Kemp, 'Corner, William de la (*d.* 1291)', *ODNB*.

[576] Kemp, 'Corner, William de la (*d.* 1291)', *ODNB*.

[577] There appear to be two schools of thought. Firstly, in the middle of the nave towards the east end ('in navi ecclesiae inter altare matutinum et Spiritus Sancti') according to A. R. Malden, 'The burial places of the bishops of Salisbury', 345–6. Secondly, in the middle of the quire 'nearly under the eagle' according to C. Ross, *Canons of Salisbury*. (Seth Ward and Canon Rich-Jones are quoted by Malden as stating the bishop was buried 'in medio chori': 'The burial places of the bishops of Salisbury', 346.) There is a miniature episcopal effigy now near the west end of the nave, under its north arcade, but originally further east, which could be his memorial: Kemp, 'Corner, William de la (*d.* 1291)', *ODNB*.

89. King Edward I

Petition. The bishop shows to his most illustrious lord E(dward), by the grace of God, king of England, that he acquaints himself and the liberty of his church, burdened in the underwritten articles:

first, that he does not believe in his letter concerning wills proved before him or his officers;

second, concerning mortuaries, vestments and horses (palfreys) of both clerics and laymen dying intestate which he was, in times past, accustomed to have;

third, concerning excommunicates to be captured, viz., that excommunicates be taken henceforth as they were accustomed to be taken in the times of the princes, especially the Welsh;

fourth, that certain of the king's ministers do not observe the charters of liberties which the king has conceded to the bishop and his church;

fifth that the sheriff of Caernarfon prohibited the king's men coming to the bishop's market at Bangor to buy and sell merchandise as they were accustomed.

And because the bishop is old and indifferent in health, he has no other refuge except God and the king, and he, for the safety of the king's soul, seeks by the king's benign gift, a remedy concerning these and other articles.

He also seeks that his men shall have common pasture in the king's lands as they did in the time of the princes.

He also seeks that his officials shall not be impeded in making corrections in the king's new towns at Conwy, Caernarfon and Beaumaris and other towns, as they have done up until now, and still do, even though certain of the king's ministers make threats to so impede his men.

[*c.*1295 x 1305/6, possibly 1298]

A = TNA SC 8/276/13767. 213 × 88 mm.[578]

Printed in *Prynne*, iii, p. 811.[579]

Printed in Willis, *Survey*, pp. 210–11.

Translated in *CAP*, pp. 464–5.

Transcribed from A.

Monstrat episcopus Bangoren(sis) suo illustrissimo domino, domino E. dei gratia regi Anglie quod ipse sentit se et libertatem ecclesie sue gravatum in articulis subscriptis:

primo, quod non creditur literris suis de testamentis probatis coram ipso seu officiariis[a] suis;

secundo, de mortuariis[b] et vestibus et palefredis decedentium ab intestato tam clericorum quam laicorum, de quibus habere consuevit temporibus retroactis;

---

[578] Image at Plate XIX. Many thanks to Dr Euryn Roberts for kindly providing me with an initial photograph of the petition to work on. Image also available on TNA website: http://discovery.nationalarchives.gov.uk/details/r/C9517714, accessed 29 October 2023.

[579] Early English Books Online: https://quod.lib.umich.edu/e/eebo/A70867.0001.001 (p. 811 and n. 36.172), accessed 4 February 2024.

tertio, de excommunicatis capiendis, videlicet quod excommunicati capientur de cetero sicut capi consueverunt temporibus principum, maxime Wallences*c*;

quarto, quod quidam ministri vestri male observant cartas libertatum quas vestra magnifica benevolentia eidem episcopo et ecclesie sue concessit*d*;

quinto, quod vicecomes de Caern' prohibuit quod homines vestri venirent ad mercatum suum apud Bangor, ad vendendum nec emendum mercaturas sicut facere consueverant.*e*

Et quia idem episcopus est senex et valetudinarius, nec habet ad aliud*f* refugium nisi ad deum et ad vos, petit pro salute anime vestre super hiis et articulis aliis per vestram benignam donationem*g* remedium [adhiberi]*h*.

Petit etiam, quod homines sui habeant communam pasturam in terris vestris sicut habere consueverunt temporibus principum.

Item petit, quod officiales*i* sui non impediantur facere correctiones in villis vestris novis apud Conowey, Caern' et Belum Mariscu(m) et aliis villis, sicut hactenus fecerunt, et adhuc faciunt*j*; licet aliqui ministri vestri minantur eisdem.

> *a*the scribe wrote 'offic''. Willis extended this to 'officiariis', *A*. *b*there is a hole in the parchment partly obscuring the 'm', *A*. *c*Willis has 'Wallensium' but the word is clearly 'Wallences', *A*. *d*the scribe has written 'consessit', and has crossed it out, 'consessit', before correcting himself with 'concessit', *A*. *e*Willis has 'consueverint' but the word is clearly 'consueverant', *A*. *f*the scribe has written 'aliu''. Willis must be correct in completing this as 'aliud', *A*. *g*Willis has 'dominationem' but it is more likely that 'dnatonem' with contraction marks over 'dna' and, separately, over 'ton', means the word is 'donationem', and indeed *CAP* translated the word as 'gift', *A*. *h*the scribe wrote 'abiberi'. Willis has 'adhiberi'. *CAP* is unsure and suggested a translation of 'to be [provided](?)', *A*. *i*the scribe wrote 'offic''. Willis has 'officiales'. Gooder, *Latin for Local History*, p. 149, defined 'officialis, -is', as an officer or official of a bishop or archdeacon. Also, Cheney, *English Bishops' Chanceries*, p. 20. Cf. *DMLBS*, *A*. *j*Willis has 'facient'.

W. Rees assigned a date range of *c*.1289 x 1305 for Anian's petition.[580] However, the bishop's complaint refers to Edward's new town at Beaumaris ('*Belum Mariscum*'). It was the rebellion of Madog ap Llywelyn in 1294–1295 that prompted Edward's new castle at Beaumaris, followed by the establishment of a borough, the relocation of the market at Llan-faes to the new town, and the grant of a charter.[581] So we can narrow the date range to *c*.1295 x 1305/6. Anian also stated that he was old and indifferent in health ('*senex et valetudinarius*') so one would assume his petition to Edward was written closer to the end of his episcopate, i.e. closer to 1305/6. However, W. Prynne stated that he found this 'memorable remonstrance and petition' in 'the White Tower': *Bundela Brovium [sic] & Petitionum in Turre London, de annis*

---

[580] *CAP*, p. 464.
[581] Carr, *Medieval Anglesey*, p. 234 (23 November 1295, Edward ordered the market relocated from Llan-faes to Beaumaris), p. 237, and n. 32 (November 1294, decision to build a castle), and p. 238 (charter of 15 September 1296). Prestwich, *Edward I*, p. 208.

26 & 27 E 1,[582] and Browne Willis assigned the year 1298,[583] a date accepted by J. E. Lloyd.[584]

As regards the second article, the rights to the goods and chattels of intestates had been a cause of dispute between Anian and Llywelyn ap Gruffudd. Archbishop John Pecham wrote to Llywelyn, on 20 October 1279, about the prince's confiscation of the goods of intestates in the diocese of Bangor (see *Actum* **68**). Pecham asserted the exclusive jurisdiction of the Church in testamentary matters – the goods were the bishop's responsibility; it was he who would supervise their distribution.[585] According to Welsh law, the bishop was entitled to the moveables of intestate episcopal tenants.[586] The matter was still in contention, however, in 1305, when Anian petitioned that he should not be impeded from having the goods and chattels of his men dying intestate, just as he was always accustomed to have (**98**).[587]

As regards the third article, one of the items in an arbitration award between Anian's predecessor, Richard, and Llywelyn ap Gruffudd, concerned those who, after having received canonical warning, had been excommunicated by name – the lord was obliged, when requested, to follow the bishop's mandate and seize the excommunicate without delay (see *Actum* **52**, clause [7]).

The fourth article was no doubt referring to Edward I's confirmation of the rights, liberties, possessions, and customs of the see of Bangor, in 1278.[588]

At about the point where the scribe misspelled 'concessit' (spelling it 'consessit' and crossing it out) he seems to have realised that he is running out of space. Up until '*episcopo et ecclesie sue*' he has spread the text out, beginning each new article on a new line, but from this point onwards the text is much more compact. He does not start the fifth article on a new line, rather he continues on the same line after finishing the fourth article.[589]

*90. King Edward I

An application to the crown for licence to alienate land, namely an acre of land, to the prior and friars preachers of Bangor.

[Shortly before 1 April 1300]

[582] Early English Books Online: https://quod.lib.umich.edu/e/eebo/A70867.0001.001 (p. 811 and n. 36.172), accessed 4 February 2024.
[583] Willis, *Survey*, pp. 72, and 210–11.
[584] *YBC*, https://biography.wales/article/s-ANIA-N00-1306, accessed 4 February 2024.
[585] *Registrum Epistolarum Peckham*, i, pp. 77–8. The distribution of such goods 'pertained to the administration of the ordinary according to canonical rules': Smith, '*Gravamina*', 165, and n. 6. Also, Pryce, *Native Law*, pp. 113–14 and pp. 117–18; Smith, *Llywelyn*, p. 211.
[586] Pryce, *Native Law*, p. 117. For 'marwdy' see *Law of Hywel Dda*, p. 237, and Pryce, *Native Law*, pp. 113–18.
[587] See *Actum* **98**.
[588] November 1278, at Rhuddlan: *RC*, p. 254 and p. 255; Willis, *Survey*, pp. 212–13; Haddan and Stubbs, i, p. 526. See also the notes to *Acta* **65** and **84**.
[589] See image at Plate XIX.

The application resulted in Edward issuing a mandate to John de Havering to carry out an *inquisitio ad quod damnum*. Edward's mandate, dated 1 April 1300 at Westminster, is extant: TNA C 143/31/1:[590]

'Edwardus dei gratia rex Angl', dominus Hyb(er)n', et dux A(c)q(ui)tan', dilecto et fideli suo John' de Havering justiciario suo, et Ioh(anni) Will', salutem. Mandamus vobis quod per sacramentum proborum et legalium hominum de ballia vestra per quos rei veritas melius sciri poterit diligenter inq[uiras] ....[591] ad dampnum vel prejudicium nostrum aut aliorum si concedamus venerabili patri Aniano Bangoren(si)[592] episcopo quod nostri unam acram terre cum pertinentiis in Bangor que est de episcopatu suo ...... dare possit et assignare dilecto nobis in Cristo priori et fratribus ordinis predicatorum de Bangor habend' et tenend' eisdem priori et fratribus successoribus suis imperpetuum necne ... si .....[593] ad dampnum vel prejudicium nostrum aut aliorum tunc ad quod dampnum et quod prejudicium nostrum et ad quod dampnum et quod prejudicium aliorum et [qu]orum et qualiter et quomodo et de quo vel quibus terra illa teneatur et per quod [servitium] [et] qu[antum] valeat per annum in omnibus exitibus et terra illa sit de episcopatu predicto necne, et inquisitionem inde distincte et aperte factam nobis sigillo vestro et sigillis eorum per quos facta fuerit sine dilatione, mittatis et hoc breve. Teste me ipso, apud Westmonasterium, primo die April' anno regni nostri vicesimo octavo'.[594]

The Friars Preachers, or Black Friars, were established in Bangor by 1251.[595]

John de Havering was justiciar of north Wales from 1295 to 1301.[596]

See also the notes to *Actum* **91** below.

*91. Bangor Friary

Gift or assignment of an acre of land in Bangor belonging to the bishopric, valued at 4 pence a year, with appurtenances, to the prior and friars preachers there.

[After 23 February 1301]

The proposed gift or assignment ('*dare ... aut assignare*') was the subject of an *inquisitio ad quod damnum* of 9 May 1300, which is printed in Willis, *Survey*, pp. 211–12.[597]

[590] Link to TNA summary: http://discovery.nationalarchives.gov.uk/details/r/C7569250, accessed 4 May 2024.

[591] Writing faded.

[592] The word is faded but the 'B', 'ng', and 'en' can be made out.

[593] Writing faded.

[594] Cf. Hall, *Formula Book*, ii, p. 89, no. 50: https://archive.org/details/aformulabookengoosciegoog/page/n101, accessed 4 May 2024.

[595] *CCR, 1247–1251*, p. 401; Burton and Stöber, 'The Dominicans in Wales', pp. 148–9; Palmer, 'The Friar-Preachers, or Blackfriars of Bangor', 225 and n. 2.

[596] Davies, *Age of Conquest*, pp. 336 and 519.

[597] 'Inquisitio capta per breve domini regis, coram Johanne de Havering, apud Conwey, nono die Maii, anno regni regis Edwardi 28. Si sit ad dampnum domini regis aut aliorum, si rex concedat venerabili patri A. Bangor episcopo quod ipse unam acram terre cum pertinentiis in Bangor dare possit aut assignare priori et fratribus ordinis predicatorum de Bangor; habend' eisdem priori et fratribus et successoribus suis imperpetuum, necnon et si sit ad dampnum vel prejudicium domini regis, aut aliorum et quorum et qualiter et

The king had instructed, the justiciar of north Wales, John de Havering to carry out the inquisition on 1 April 1300.[598]

The inquisition found that the land belonged to the bishopric (*predicta acra terrae est dominia terra episcopatus Bangor in Bangor*) and that it would not be prejudicial to the king if the bishop granted the said land to the prior and brothers, save that the crown would lose 4*d.* a year when the land was in the king's hands during a vacancy (*in manu domini regis per vacationem sedis Bangor*).[599]

On 23 February 1301, a 'licence for the alienation in mortmain by Anian, bishop of Bangor, to the prior and friars preachers of Bangor of an acre of land there' was granted.[600]

What might have been the reason for Anian's gift/assignment? In 1284, the then prior of the friary, Adam, received 100*l.* as part of the compensation paid to ecclesiastics for damage caused during the second Welsh war of 1282–1283.[601] In 1293, the crown ordered the justice of Snowdon to cause the friars preachers to have thirty oaks fit for timber from the forest of Snowdon, by the king's gift, to rebuild their church in Bangor, which had been burnt.[602] It has been mooted that the friary may have suffered again during

---

quomodo et de quo vel quibus terra illa teneatur, et per quod servitium et quantum valet per annum, et si sit de episcopatu predicto necne …. Per Keri Seys, Howel Goch, Lewerch ap Adam, Rees ap Jor, Griffith Vachan, Bledyn ap Llewelyn, Llywelyn Voit, Eden ap Griffith, Griffith ap Kenworth, et Eynon ap Jor, juratores: qui dicunt super sacramenta sua quod predicta acra terrae est dominia terra episcopatus Bangor in Bangor, et quod non est ad prejudicium nec dampnum domini regis aut aliorum, si dictus episcopus terram illam cum pertinentiis concedat predictis priori et fratribus, habendum ut premissum est, nisi tantum ad dampnum domini regis quatuor denariorum per annum, cum terra episcopatus predicti, sit in manu domini regis per vacationem sedis Bangor; et dicunt quod terra illa valet per annum 4 denarios in omnibus exitibus, et quod dictus episcopus terram illam tenet de domino rege eo modo quo tenet aliam terram episcopatus predicti. In cuius rei testimonium huic inquisitioni predicti juratores sigilla sua apposuerunt'.

[598]   TNA C 143/31/1. See *Actum* **90**. An *inquisitio ad quod damnum* was an inquisition carried out as a result of, *inter alia*, an application to the crown for licence to alienate land. 'The sheriff, escheator or other local official was ordered to inquire whether such a grant or licence would be prejudicial to the interests of the Crown or others. In the case of the alienation of land, the inquiry had to discover the tenure, service and yearly value of the land alienated, what lands would be left to the alienator and the effect on his financial status and position. In many cases, such inquisitions were endorsed with the Crown's final order and were used as warrants for the issue of letters patent.': TNA website: https://discovery. nationalarchives.gov.uk/browse/r/h/C3701, accessed 4 May 2024.

[599]   Willis, *Survey*, pp. 211–12; Palmer, 'The Friar-Preachers, or Blackfriars of Bangor', 226 and n. 9.

[600]   Edward I, m. 25: *CPR, 1292–1301*, p. 576. Five hundred masses were to be celebrated for the king, the queen, and their children. The usual services being reserved to the capital lords of the fief: *ibid.*; Inquis. p. mort. 28 Edw 1., no. 49; Palmer, 'The Friar-Preachers, or Blackfriars of Bangor', 226 and n. 9.

[601]   November 1284: *LW*, p. 76, no. 143. This is unlikely to be the Prior Adam referred to in 1261 in *Actum* **53**, as Llywelyn ap Gruffudd ab Ednyfed Fychan was prior at Bangor in 1283, and had been for some time: TNA, E101/351/9; Smith, *Llywelyn*, p. 191 and n. 21; see also *ibid.*, pp. 430–1; and Smith, 'Welsh Dominicans and the Crisis of 1277', 353–4.

[602]   *CCR, 1288–1296*, p. 278.

the rising of Madog ap Llywelyn in 1294–1295, and that when reconstruction was completed, Anian's gift may have sealed the rebuilding.[603]

92. Testimony of a Miracle. Roger of Conwy

Sealed testimony of the miraculous resuscitation of an infant, Roger (aged 2 years and 3 months) the son of Dyonisia and a certain servant at Conwy castle whose name was Gervase. The boy had fallen some twenty-eight feet from a bridge at the castle into a rock-cut ditch and had lain overnight. On the following day, when the coroners of the town came to look into this misfortune they found the boy dead. Afterwards, a certain John Siward, burgess of Conwy, came to the dead body and bent a penny, making the sign of the cross on the forehead and above the chest of the boy, vowing to God and the holy Thomas de Cantilupe of good memory, formerly bishop of Hereford, that if God resuscitated the boy through the merits of the blessed Thomas, the same infant would visit the threshold of Thomas. As if in the twinkling of an eye, the boy revived and was immediately restored to his mother, and sucked her breasts and was happy and without bodily injury. The people and the clerics of the church, after hearing and seeing the miracle, singing Te Deum took the body to the church, where Lord Anian, bishop of Bangor and Brother Dafydd, the abbot of Maenan of the Cistercian order were celebrating divine mass for the soul of John of St John of good memory on the day of his anniversary. Witnesses of the miracle were John de Havering, William de Sutton, and William de Cicon, knights, members of the council and household of the Lord Edward, son of the king of England and prince of Wales, Thomas de Cambridge, Hugh de Leominster and Thomas de Asthall, clerics of the council and household of the same prince, Simon, the vicar of Conwy, Richard de Newcastle, Roger de Bridgnorth, and Thomas de Denbigh priests of the church of Conwy and besides this more than two hundred men and women saw the boy dead and then restored to life. The seals of the lord bishop and the abbot, together with the seals of the aforesaid knights, clerics and priests were appended.

Conwy, 7 September 1303

B = Oxford, Exeter College MS 158, fos. 38v–39r. s. xiv in. Heading: Item sequitur miraculus[a] excellentius[b] probatum et sigillis[c] multorum magnatum et testimonio communitum quod sequitur sub isto tenore verborum.

C = Vatican City, BAV MS Vat. Lat. 4015, fos. 188v–189r. s. xiv in.[604] Prefaced by: Patentes litteras ad probationem miraculi antedicti sigillatas ut prima facie comparebat sigillis in pendenti in pressis in cera rubea dominorum Aniani, quondam episcopi Bangorens(is), David abbatis de Abberconewey, Joh(ann)is de Haveryng' militis, Will(elm)i de Sutton, Cicons, Esthale, Hugonis de Leominstre, et aliorum quorum nomina non poterant bene legi in sigillis predictis.

D = Vatican City, BAV MS Vat. Lat. 4015, fos. 306r–307r. s. xiv in.[605] Heading: as B.

Printed in Bass, 'Communities of Remembrance', 260–4.

Transcribed from B.

---

[603] See Burton and Stöber, 'The Dominicans in Wales', p. 150 and n. 60.
[604] Images available on Vatican website: https://digi.vatlib.it/view/MSS_Vat.lat.4015, accessed 2 May 2024.
[605] Images available online: *ibid.*

Pateat universis sancte matris ecclesie filiis quod sexto die Septembris anno ab incarnatione domini m° ccc° tercio contigit[d] apud castrum de Conewey in Wall'[e] quod quidam [f-]infans duorum annorum et trium mensium[-f] cui nomen Rogerus filius cuiusdam servientis castri cui nomen Gervasius[g] et nomen matris euisdem pueri Dyonisia[h]. Idem puer cecidit nocturno tempore[i] in prima hora noctis de ponte eiusdem castri usque ad profundem fossati excisi in rupe forti et durissima[j] nudus cecidit et nudus iacuit in fossato super ripem[k] usque in crastinum circa mediam horam prime. Et est altitudo ab primo fossati usque ad pontem xxviii pedum. Cum vero coronatores eiusdem ville venissent ut inquirerent de illo infortunio die sequenti inve[fo. 39r]nerunt puerum mortuum. Postmodum quidam[l] Ioh(anne)s Syward burgensis de Coneweye venit ad corpus mortuum et cepit unum denarium de bursa sua et de eodem denario fecit signum crucis in fronte et super pectus pueri vovens deo et beato Thome de Cantulupo[m], bone memorie quondam episcopo Hereforden(si)[n], quod si deus per merita[o] ipsius beati Thome resuscitaret puerum quod[p] idem infans visitaret limina eiusdem beati Thome episcopi. Hoc facto quasi in ictu oculi puer revixit benedictus altissimus. Statim puer fuit restitutus[q] matri sue et mater ostendit ei ubera et statim puer suggebat mammas matris sue. Et post pusillum fuit puer hilaris et gaudens absque aliqua lesione corporis sui. Populus vero et clerici ecclesie currentes audientes et videntes istud mirabile[r] ceperunt corpus et duxerunt[s] ad ecclesiam cantantes te deum laudamus presentibus venerabilibus patribus domino[t] Aniano, Bangoren(si)[u] episcopo, et fratre David, abbate de Maynan ord[in]is Cisternen(sis)[v], qui tunc fuerunt[w] in eadem ecclesiam divina celebrantes[x] pro anima bone memorie domini Ioh(ann)is de Sancto Ioh(anne) die anniversarii sui. Huius miraculi sunt testes domini Ioh(anne)s de Averinge[y], Will(elmu)s de Sutton'[z], et Will(elmu)s de Cintons[aa] milites qui sunt de consilio et familia [bb-]illustris domini Edwardi filii regis Anglie et principis Wallie[-bb],[cc] domini Thom(as) de Cantebrigg'[dd], Hugo de Leoministr'[ee], et Thomas de Esthalle[ff] clerici de consilio[gg] et familia de eiusdem principis, domini Symon, vicarius de Conewey[hh], Ricard(us) de Novo Castro, Roger(us) de Bruges[ii], et Thom(as) de Dindey[jj] sacerdotes deservientes ecclesie memorate in eadem villa commorantes, et preter hec plus quam ducenti viri et mulieres qui predictum puerum viderunt mortuum et postea resuscitatum. Et ad perpetuam huius miraculi memoriam sigillum venerabilis patris domini episcopi predicti et sigillum eiusdem abbatis una cum sigillis militum clericorum et sacerdotum predictorum huic scripto sunt appensia. Dat'[kk] apud Conewey[ll], vii° die Septembris, anno gratie[mm] supradicto.

[a]miraculum, *D.* [b]excellenter, *D.* [c]singulis, *D.* [d]contingit, *C.* [e]Wallia, *C, D.* [f-f]infans etatis duorum annorum et trium mensium, *C.* [g]Gervacsius, *C,* Gervasi(us), *D.* [h]Dionisya, *C.* [i]tempore nocturno, *C.* [j]durissimo, *C.* [k]rupem, *C, D.* [l]the scribe has written 'quidem' but has added a superscript 'a' immediately over the 'e' as a correction, *C.* [m]Cantelupo, *C.* [n]Hereford', *C.* [o]per merita is written in the left-hand margin, replacing 'mortuo' which is crossed through in the main text, *C.* [p]puerum quibidem quod, quibidem crossed through, *C.* [q]restitutus fuit, *C.* [r]mirabile is followed by a word that could be 'miraculare' but which is crossed through, *C.* [s]adduxerunt, *D.* [t]dominis, *D.* [u]Bangorens', *C.* [v]Cisterniens' *C,* Cistercien', *D.* [w]fuerunt is written in the right-hand margin, replacing 'erant' which is crossed through in the main text, *C.* [x]divina officia celebrantes, *C.* [y]Haverigg', *C.* [z]'Surton'' is written in the left-hand margin, replacing 'Stonweye' which is crossed through in the main text, *C.* [aa]Cicon, *C.* [bb-bb]'illustris domini Edwardi

filii Regis Anglie et principis Wallie' is written in the right-hand margin, *C.* *ᶜᶜ*eiusdem principis domini Symon vicarius de Coneweye, Ricard(us) de Novo Castro, Rog(eru)s de Buges et Thomas Dynbeyent. From 'domini' to 'Dynbeyent' is crossed through, *C.* *ᵈᵈ*Thomas de Cantebugia *C*, Thome de Cantebregge, *D.* *ᵉᵉ*Hug' de Leominstre, *C*, Hugo de Leomenistre, *D.* *ᶠᶠ*Thomas de Estalle, *C*, Thom(as) de Easthalle, *D.* *ᵍᵍ*clerici qui sunt de consilio, *C.* *ʰʰ*Conewye, *C*, *D.* *ⁱⁱ*Brugges, *C.* *ʲʲ*Dynbey *C*, Dynby *D.* *ᵏᵏ*Data, *C.* *ˡˡ*Coneweye, *C*, Conewy, *D.* *ᵐᵐ*domini, *D.*

On 6 September 1303, Anian was celebrating a memorial mass at Conwy church for the knight, royal servant, and diplomat John of St John.[606] Whilst the service was in progress, an infant, Roger, two years and three months old (the son of Dionysia and her husband, Gervase, a cook serving the constable of the castle) was brought to the church.[607] Dafydd, the abbot of the Cistercian house of Maenan (the church of Conwy being the former church of the order in Aberconwy) was present with Anian celebrating mass.[608]

John of St John was one of Thomas de Cantilupe's nephews.[609] He had died on 6 September 1302.[610] So the mass was being celebrated on the anniversary of his death.

Of the others present, William de Sutton, justiciar of north Wales, John de Havering (the former justiciar), and William de Cicon, constable and mayor, described as members of the council and household of the Lord Edward, son of the king of England and prince of Wales, were the most prominent.[611] Also present were Thomas de Cambridge, Hugh de Leominster and Thomas de Asthall (clerics of the council and household of the prince of Wales), and four priests of the church of Conwy, namely Simon (of Watford), the vicar of Conwy, Richard de Newcastle, Roger de Bridgnorth, and Thomas de Denbigh.[612]

---

[606] For John of St John see Bass, 'Communities of Remembrance', 249 and n. 48, and 263, n. 81; Vale, 'St John, Sir John de (*d.* 1302)', *ODNB*.

[607] The story is told in detail in two recent articles: Ridyard and Ashbee, 'The Resuscitation of Roger of Conwy', and Bass, 'Communities of Remembrance'. I am extremely grateful to Dr Ian Bass for bringing both these articles and the miracle story to my attention.

[608] Anian had consented to the transfer of the Cistercians from Aberconwy to Maenan: see *Actum* **83**. Abbot Dafydd, or David, is first recorded in October 1284 (*LW*, p. 47, no. 71, and p. 95, no. 187). 7 September 1303 is the last time he appears in the historical record, for Tudor became the new abbot later the same year: *Heads of Religious Houses*, ii, p. 275.

[609] Bass, 'Communities of Remembrance', 263, n. 81.

[610] Vale, 'St John, Sir John de (*d.* 1302)', *ODNB*; Bass, 'Communities of Remembrance', 263, n. 81.

[611] See Ridyard and Ashbee, 'The Resuscitation of Roger of Conwy', p. 64. William de Cicon had been constable at Rhuddlan castle before becoming constable of Conwy castle: Bass, 'Communities of Remembrance', 264, n. 84; Prestwich, *Edward I*, p. 209.

[612] See Ridyard and Ashbee, 'The Resuscitation of Roger of Conwy', p. 64. Hugh de Leominster would have been known to Anian in an ecclesiastical capacity as he had been presented to the church of Caernarfon in 1285 (*CPR, 1281–1292*, p. 190). He had been clerk of works at Caernarfon and Harlech 1283–1284, becoming chamberlain of Caernarfon in 1300: Bass, 'Communities of Remembrance', 264, n. 87.

The following day, 7 September, those men along with Anian and Dafydd committed their testimony of events to writing, attaching their seals to the same.

The miracle of Roger of Conwy was investigated by canonisation commissioners
between July and November 1307 in London and Hereford.[613] The deed of 7 September 1303 was recorded in a catalogue of Cantilupe miracles kept at his shrine
in Hereford (now Oxford, Exeter College MS 158).[614] A copy was also written into
the dossier of the miracle inquiry on the last day of the inquiry – BAV, MS Vat.
Lat. 4015.[615] The earlier record is, therefore, Oxford, Exeter College MS 158.[616]

After the inquiry, the papal commissioner Ralph Baldock, bishop of London
(1306–1313), took Roger in. He was entrusted to Thomas de Leighton, canon of St
Paul's, for his education. In 1311, Bishop Baldock wrote to the abbot of St Osyth in
Essex asking him to provide £4 annually to support Roger, to be paid to Thomas.[617]

*93. Edward of Caernarfon, Prince of Wales

Petition regarding the bishop's entitlement to amercements.
                    1305 [Shortly before, or during, 28 February x late April]

Mention only, in Crown's response to petition. London, BL Harley MS 696
(Record of Caernarvon), fo. 129 b. s. xv ex.[618] *RC*, p. 216.

Transcribed from Harley MS 696.

In the left-hand margin: *Episcopi Bang'*

'*Ad petitionem episcopi Bangorensis quod possit habere amerciamenta hominum suorum
in quibuscumque curis fuerint amerciati non obstante quod iidem tenentes episcopi terras
teneant de domino principe:*

*Responsum est quod amerciamenta tenentium episcopi contingencia ratione ten' de feodo
principis debent ad opus principis levari amerciamenta tamen contigencia ratione ten' de
feodo episcopi debent ad opus episcopi levari'.*

This *actum*, and *Acta* **94** to **101** inclusive, are mention only, as they are known
only from the responses to Anian's petitions, rather than being the original
petitions or copies of the same.

Parliament had been summoned for the first Sunday in Lent (28 February
1305), by which time Edward I had arrived at Westminster, whilst his son,
the prince, stayed south of the river Thames in Kennington. Numerous petitions concerning English, Scottish, Irish and Gascon matters were presented

---

[613] The depositions are recorded in BAV, MS Vat. Lat. 4015, fos. 188r–203v: Bass,
'Communities of Remembrance', 262, n. 74.

[614] The miracles being recorded in chronological order from 1287 onwards: *ibid.*, 238, n. 2.

[615] Image available on Vatican website: https://digi.vatlib.it/view/MSS_Vat.lat.4015,
accessed 2 May 2024.

[616] Thank you to Dr Ian Bass for this information.

[617] Bass, 'Communities of Remembrance', 262, n. 74.

[618] *RC*, p. iii; Smith, 'Crown and Community', 168.

to the king (or the king in council). Simultaneously, petitions from the men of north Wales were 'exhibited to the lord prince and his council'. The prince left Kennington in late April.[619]

*94. Edward of Caernarfon, Prince of Wales

Petition concerning villeins who hold lands of the prince and the bishop.
1305 [Shortly before, or during, 28 February x late April]

Mention only, in Crown's response to petition. London, BL Harley MS 696 (Record of Caernarvon), fo. 129 b. s. xv ex.[620] *RC*, p. 216.

Transcribed from Harley MS 696.

'*Ad petitionem eiusdem episcopi quod villani qui hereditarie terras tenent de domino principe et episcopo morari possint pro voluntate sua in terra alterius dominorum sine calumpnia:*

Responsum est quod villani domini principis alibi quam super terram principis morari non debet'.

See notes to *Actum* **93**.

*95. Edward of Caernarfon, Prince of Wales

Petition regarding entitlement to a moiety of the amobr (ammobragium) *of episcopal tenants settled on the prince's land in accordance with the convention between Llywelyn, prince of Wales, and Anian.*
1305 [Shortly before, or during, 28 February x late April]

Mention only, in Crown's response to petition. London, BL Harley MS 696 (Record of Caernarvon), fo. 129 b. s. xv ex.[621] *RC*, p. 216.

Transcribed from Harley MS 696.

'*Ad petitionem eiusdem episcopi quod si filia alicuius tenentis episcopi moram faciat in terra principis et ibi deliquerit per quod ammobragium solvere debeat vel e converso quod dominus princeps habeat medietatem illius ammobragii et episcopus aliam secundum conventionem habitam inter Leweli(num) quondam principem Wall(ie) et dictum episcopum de ammobragiis levandis:*

Responsum est quod ostendat conventionem illam et fiat ei super hoc quod fuit rationis: et justiciarius informet se de his ammobragiis et habita plena informatione permittat episcopum uti et gaudere inde sicut rationabiliter sine interruptione hucusque usus fuit et gavisus'.

See notes to *Actum* **93**.

Amobr was a payment due under Welsh law to a woman's lord in respect of a sexual relationship, both marital and extra-marital, that continued to be

---

[619] Johnstone, *Edward of Carnarvon*, pp. 96–7; Sayles, *Functions of the Medieval Parliament*, pp. 265–6; Prestwich, *Edward I*, p. 227; *CAP*, p. 465.
[620] *RC*, p. iii; Smith, 'Crown and Community', 168.
[621] *ibid.*

levied after the Edwardian conquest.[622] In Harley MS 696 it is recorded as *ammobragium*. In a petition of Emma of Bromfield to the king, 11 December 1282 x 1283, as *ambroges*.[623] H. Ellis defined it as a marriage fee for a daughter (but also a fine for fornication and adultery), stating that it was very often 10 shillings; Tony Carr stated 10 shillings was the fine for a free tenant, it was 6 shillings 8 pence for an unfree tenant.[624]

In 1290, Edward I had granted the office or bailiwick of *amobragium*, 'which the Welsh call "*amobret*"', in Anglesey, to one William Daniel.[625]

The bishop of Bangor received both *amobr* and *ebediw* from his tenants according to an extent of 1332.[626]

*96. Edward of Caernarfon, Prince of Wales

Petition concerning the bishop's villeins of Meilyr (Meilure). *They should not be compelled to fish for the bailiffs, nor to procure a horse for the rhaglaw* (raglot) *of the prince of the manor of Penrhos.*

1305 [Shortly before, or during, 28 February x late April]

Mention only, in Crown's response to petition. London, BL Harley MS 696 (Record of Caernarvon), fo. 129 b. s. xv ex.[627] *RC*, p. 216.

Transcribed from Harley MS 696.

'*Ad petitionem eiusdem episcopi quod villani sui de Meilure non compellantur ad piscandum ballivis neque ad procurandum equum ragl(oto) principis de manerio de Penros:*

Responsum est quod testatum est placitum pendet inde coram justiciario indiscussum quia placitum illud adpresens est incognitum et obscurum, ideo justiciarius teneat placitum illud et faciat ei quod fuerit rationis'.

See notes to *Actum* **93**.

Ragl' (written in the MS with a majuscule R) is the *rhaglaw*, who, by the thirteenth century, had become the Welsh princes' main local representative,[628]

---

[622]   *AWR*, p. 723.

[623]   *ibid.*, pp. 722–3, no. 520. See also Charles-Edwards, et al., *Welsh King and His Court*, p. 561; *Law of Hywel Dda*, p. 311; *Welsh Law of Women*, p. 190; and *Geiriadur Prifysgol Cymru*, accessed 10 November 2023.

[624]   *RC*, p. xvi; Carr, *Medieval Anglesey*, p. xv. It had been set at a low rate of 12*d.* in the arbitration award reached in 1252 between the Augustinian house on Enlli (Bardsey), and the secular canons of Aberdaron and men of the *abadaeth*, to which Anian's predecessor, Richard, had appended his seal: *RC*, p. 252; *AWR*, pp. 634–8, no. 440. For an explanation of the term *abadaeth* see Pryce, *Native Law*, pp. 186 and 244.

[625]   October at Abergavenny ('Bergeveny'): BL Add MS 15664 (fo. 7. 18 Edw. I.).

[626]   Pryce, *Native Law*, p. 200, and n. 77. *Ebediw* was a fee for succession to land, due at death, comparable to the Anglo-Saxon heriot: *AWR*, pp. 637 and 895.

[627]   *RC*, p. iii; Smith, 'Crown and Community', 168.

[628]   Stephenson, *Governance*, pp. 41–4, and Jones, 'Llys and Maerdref', p. 304.

and the chief resident officer of a commote,[629] having replaced the *maer* and *cynghellor*.[630] In Harley MS 696 the noun is expanded as *raglot*.[631]

It is not clear where *Meilyr* (*Meilure*) is.[632] However, *Penros* could be the manor of Penrhos on Anglesey (the administrative centre of the commote of Twrcelyn in the cantref of Cemais).[633] A township of *Moelur'*, in the commote of Twrcelyn, is recorded in the extent of the bishop's lands in 1306/7, and it includes land held *in villenagio*.[634] Although not described as a manor, Penrhos half way between Llanbedrog and Pwllheli, on the southern coast of the Llŷn Peninsula, is another possibility.[635] Of the twelve men sworn to carry out the 1306/7 extent in Llŷn, which included the township of *Penros*, two were called *Meilir*.[636]

*97. Edward of Caernarfon, Prince of Wales

Petition concerning the non-impediment of the bishop's seneschals to hold pleas in the bishop's court.

1305 [Shortly before, or during, 28 February x late April]

Mention only, in Crown's response to petition. London, BL Harley MS 696 (Record of Caernarvon), fo. 129 b. s. xv ex.[637] *RC*, p. 216.

Transcribed from Harley MS 696.

'*Ad petitionem eiusdem episcopi quod sen(escalli) sui non impediantur tenere placita in curia ipsius episcopi de excedent' xl. s. sine brevi quia numquam fuerunt inde impediti:*

Responsum est quod statutum est per dominum regem in Statutis de Rothelan quod omnia placita excedencia summa xl. s. placitentur per brevia et non sine brevibus nec princ' aliter utitur in terra sua'.[638]

See notes to *Actum* **93**.

---

[629] Charles-Edwards, et al., *Welsh King and His Court*, p. 572, and *Geiriadur Prifysgol Cymru*, accessed 10 March 2024.

[630] Stephenson, *Governance*, p. 41, and Jones, 'Llys and Maerdref', p. 304.

[631] See for example: *RC*, p. 136, line 27.

[632] An alternative spelling of 'Melure' is also recorded: *RC*, p. 216, n. 7.

[633] Smith, '1284 Extent of Anglesey Revisited', 90–2.

[634] *RC*, pp. 108–9. See also the section of the Introduction entitled 'Extent of 1306/7 – Manors, Lands and Tenants of the Bishop of Bangor'.

[635] *List of Historic Place Names Website*: https://historicplacenames.rcahmw.gov.uk/placenames/recordedname/598e666e-e898-449c-9307-a9be4e39d115, accessed 4 May 2024.

[636] At Edern: 'Meilir Goch' and 'Iorwerth ap Meilir': *RC*, pp. 97–8.

[637] *RC*, p. iii; Smith, 'Crown and Community', 168.

[638] Breve, -is (writ), neuter, 3rd declension: *DMLBS*, via https://logeion.uchicago.edu/breve, accessed 23 March 2024. Also, Gooder, *Latin for Local History*, p. 125, referring to Kennedy, *The Shorter Latin Primer*, p. 16, no. 31.

*98. Edward of Caernarfon, Prince of Wales

Petition that the bishop should not be impeded from having the goods and chattels of his men dying intestate, just as he was always accustomed to have.

1305 [Shortly before, or during, 28 February x late April]

Mention only, in Crown's response to petition. London, BL Harley MS 696 (Record of Caernarvon), fo. 131 b. s. xv ex.[639] *RC*, p. 220.

Transcribed from Harley MS 696.

'*Ad petitionem episcopi Bangor*' *quod non impediatur per justiciarium habere bona et catalla hominum suorum ab intestato decedencia sicut semper habere consuevit:*

Responsum est quod consuetudo patrie talis est quod dominus princeps habere debet catalla quorumcumque decendencium ab intestato quam dominus non intendit mutaro [sic] nisi dominus episcopus habeat super hoc exemptionem pro tenentibus suis per aliquod factum speciale quod si habeat ostendat et fiat ei quod iustum fuerit.

'*mutaro*' should presumably be '*mutare*'.

See notes to *Actum* **93**.

Rights to the goods and chattels of intestates had been a cause of dispute between Anian and Llywelyn ap Gruffudd. Archbishop Pecham wrote to Llywelyn, on 20 October 1279, about the Welsh prince's confiscation of the goods of intestates in the diocese of Bangor (see *Actum* **68**). Pecham asserted the exclusive jurisdiction of the Church in testamentary matters. The goods were the bishop's responsibility; it was he who would supervise their distribution.[640]

According to Welsh law the bishop was entitled to the moveables of intestate episcopal tenants.[641]

Anian had had cause to petition Edward I, possibly in 1298, concerning, *inter alia*, mortuaries, vestments and horses (palfreys) of both clerics and laymen dying intestate which he said he was, in times past, accustomed to have (**89**).[642]

*99. Edward of Caernarfon, Prince of Wales

Petition regarding a claim to amercements.

1305 [Shortly before, or during, 28 February x late April]

---

[639]   *RC*, p. iii; Smith, 'Crown and Community', 168.

[640]   *Registrum Epistolarum Peckham*, i, pp. 77–8. The distribution of such goods 'pertained to the administration of the ordinary according to canonical rules': Smith, '*Gravamina*', 165, and n. 6. Also, Pryce, *Native Law*, pp. 113–14 and pp. 117–18; Smith, *Llywelyn*, p. 211.

[641]   Pryce, *Native Law*, p. 117. For 'marwdy' see *Law of Hywel Dda*, p. 237, and Pryce, *Native Law*, pp. 113–18.

[642]   See *Actum* **89**.

Mention only, in Crown's response to petition. London, BL Harley MS 696 (Record of Caernarvon), fo. 131 b. s. xv ex.[643] *RC*, p. 220.

Transcribed from Harley MS 696.

'*Ad petitionem eiusdem episcopi quod possit habere amerciamenta hominum suorum in quibuscumque curia amerciati fuerint non obstante quod terras teneant de domino principe*:'

See notes to *Actum* **93**.

This petition is similar to Anian's petition regarding amercements (*Actum* **93**). Indeed, this petition and the next recorded petition of Anian in Harley MS 696 (*Actum* **100**) were both treated as duplicates of earlier petitions, by Edward's officials.

The official response to *Actum* **99** is recorded as a joint response after the record of Anian's next petition, see *Actum* **100** below.

*100. Edward of Caernarfon, Prince of Wales

Petition regarding the non-impediment of the bishop's seneschals to hold pleas in the bishop's court.
                    1305 [Shortly before, or during, 28 February x late April]

Mention only, in Crown's response to petition. London, BL Harley MS 696 (Record of Caernarvon), fos. 131b–132. s. xv ex.[644] *RC*, p. 220.

Transcribed from Harley MS 696.

'*Et ad petitionem eiusdem episcopi quod senescalli sui non impediantur tenere placita in curia euisdem episcopi sine brevi de cancellario principis de placitis [fo. 132] que excedunt summa. xl s.:*

Responsum est quod alibi ad consimiles petitiones. Responsum est sufficientus ut patet ibidem'.

See notes to *Actum* **93**.

Edward's officials realised that Anian had lodged a similar petition already (see *Actum* **97**).

*101. Edward of Caernarfon, Prince of Wales

Petition regarding entitlement to the chattels of the fugitive Madog ap Madog, the bishop's tenant in the vill of Stroganan, whose chattels had been seized by the rhaglaw of Nanconwy.
                    1305 [Shortly before, or during, 28 February x late April]

Mention only, in Crown's response to petition. London, BL Harley MS 696 (Record of Caernarvon), fo. 132. s. xv ex.[645] *RC*, p. 220.

Transcribed from Harley MS 696.

---

[643] *RC*, p. iii; Smith, 'Crown and Community', 168.
[644] *ibid.*
[645] *ibid.*

'*Ad petitionem eiusdem episcopi quod possit habere catalla Mad(oci) filii Madoci fugitivi tenentis sui in villa de Stroganan que quid' catalla nunc arestantur in manu rag(l)o(ti) Nancon*':

Responsum est quod sequatur coram justiciario et fiat ei justicia'.

See notes to *Actum* **93**.

The commote of Nanconwy (*Nancon*) was in the cantref of Arllechwedd.[646] I have not been able to identify *Stroganan*. However, it could possibly be the vill of *Stratgemio/Stradgennon* – which, although in the diocese of St Asaph, was according to the *Taxatio Ecclesiastica* of 1291, half owned by the bishop of Bangor and half owned by the canons of Bangor.[647]

For *rhaglaw* (*raglot*), see note to *Actum* **96** above.

102. Pope Clement V

Letter petitioning the pope for a canonisation inquiry to be set in motion in respect of Thomas de Cantilupe, former bishop of Hereford. Valediction.

Bangor, 15 September 1305

B = Vatican City, BAV MS Vat. Lat. 4015, fos. 264v–265r. s. xiv in.[648]

Transcribed from B.

Sanctissimo patri ac domino reverentissimo dei gratia sacrosancte universalis ecclesie summo pontifici, Anianus eiusdem permissione Bangoren(sis) ecclesie minister humilis, cum devotis subiectione et reverentia pedum oscula beatorum. Cum pro felicis recordationis domino Thoma de Cantilupo quondam Herefordien(si) episcopo, cuius ossa in Herefordien(si) ecclesia requiescunt, dominus multipliciter operare miracula sic dignatus prout de hoc per regnum Angl' testatur fama publica et solennis, id vestre scitatis excellentie duxi presentibus intimandum ut ad canonizationis sue petitionem exaudiendam. Conferat si placet hoc meum testimonium *a*quatenus illud valere decreverit vestra paternitas reverenda sane prefatus *b*episcopus ex nobili ortus progenie a primo sue inventutis evo moribus [fo. 265r] se nobilem reddere non cessavit unde vite sue scitatem [*sic*] probare videntur miracula supertacta. Valeat semper vestre paternitatis reverentia in domino Jh(es) u Cristo*c*. Dat' Bang', xvii kl Octob', anno domini m° ccc° quinto.

*a*sue petione*2* before quatenus, B. *b*exi before episcopus, B. *c*Xpisto, B.

Anian was one of a number of churchmen and nobles who petitioned the pope for a canonisation inquiry to be set in motion in respect of Thomas de Cantilupe

---

[646] *AWR*, p. 494.
[647] *Taxatio Ecclesiastica*, p. 290. For alternate spelling: Jones, 'Llyfr Coch Asaph: A Textual and Historical Study', i, p. 189.
[648] Image available on Vatican website: https://digi.vatlib.it/view/MSS_Vat.lat.4015, accessed 2 May 2024. I am very grateful to Dr Ian Bass for bringing this *actum* to my attention.

(d. 1282).[649] Two years earlier, on 7 September 1303, Anian had been a party to a sealed testimony concerning the infant, Roger of Conwy, who had been miraculously resuscitated after the name of the former bishop of Hereford had been invoked (**92**).[650]

---

[649] Ridyard and Ashbee, 'The Resuscitation of Roger of Conwy', p. 65, and n. 22.
[650] See *Actum* **92**.

APPENDIX: ITINERARIES OF THE BISHOPS OF

BANGOR, 1092–1306

The most important sources are given.
Further details are provided in the Introduction.

HERVEY

1092

Date unknown	**York/Canterbury/London?**
	Hervey was consecrated as bishop of Bangor, by Thomas I, archbishop of York, during the *sede vacante* at Canterbury. (*Hugh the Chanter*, pp. 12–13).

1093

Date unknown	**Chester?**
	Hervey witnessed, and affixed his seal to, a charter of Hugh, earl of Chester, granting to the abbey of St Werburgh, Chester, *inter alia*, land in Anglesey. (*Monasticon*, ii, pp. 385–6).
25 December Christmas	**Gloucester**
	Hervey attended William Rufus' Christmas court, at Gloucester, where he witnessed a notification by the king. Other witnesses included Anselm, archbishop of Canterbury, Thomas, archbishop of York, eleven bishops of English sees, as well as the abbots of Glastonbury and Westminster. (*Regesta Willelmi Conquestoris et Willelmi Rufi*, p. 88, no. 338; Karn, 'The Foundation Narrative', pp. 402–3).
*c.*1097 and dates unknown thereafter	**Aston Somerville, Gloucestershire/Worcestershire Border**
	A gift to Hervey of '*Estona*', identified as the manor of Aston Somerville, was confirmed by William Rufus, probably in 1097. The property had previously been owned by one Hascoit, or Harscuid, Musard (another Breton). (*Liber Eliensis*, p. 245 and p. 336, n. 121).

1100

15 July	**Gloucester Abbey**
	Present at the consecration and dedication of the church which Abbot Serlo had built in the town. The bishops of Hereford, Rochester, and Worcester were also present. (*John of Worcester*, iii, pp. 92–3).

1101 x 1102

Date unknown | **Monmouth**
Hervey dedicated the church of St Mary's, assisted by a chaplain of Henry I, Bernard, later bishop of St Davids. Hervey also witnessed a charter by William, son of Baderon, confirming he had given land, on the banks of the Monnow, called the Wice, to St Florent, Saumur at the time of the dedication of St Mary's. Bernard was a witness to the grant also, and undertook the breaking of a knife, and the placing of the same on the altar.
(*Calendar of Documents Preserved in France*, i, pp. 408–9).

1102

29 September
Michaelmas | **Westminster**
Henry I was at Westminster with all the chief men of his kingdom, both clerical and secular, and 'a great council', pertaining to ecclesiastical rules, was held by Archbishop Anselm. Hervey was present, along with the archbishop of York, eight bishops of English sees, as well as two of Henry's clerks who had just been invested by the king (with the bishoprics of Hereford and Salisbury, respectively) and the bishop-elect of Winchester.
(*Eadmer's History*, p. 149; *John of Worcester*, iii, pp. 102–3).

1100 x 1105

Date unknown | **York (possibly Évreux)**
Hervey witnessed, together with chaplain Bernard, the future bishop of St Davids, a grant by Queen Matilda of a church (Laughton-en-le-Morthen) as a prebend, to St Peter's, York.
(*Regesta Henrici Primi*, p. 38; *Hugh the Chanter*, p. 25, n. 4).

1105

February | **Romsey**
Hervey was with Henry I, at Romsey, where he witnessed a charter, along with bishops Ranulf of Durham, John of Bath, Robert of Lincoln, Roger bishop-elect of Salisbury, Waldric the chancellor, and others granting land to St Mary's, Abingdon.
(*Regesta Henrici Primi*, p. 40).

1106

July x 23
September | **Bath?**
Hervey was named as the first witness to a charter of John of Tours, bishop of Bath, in favour of St Peter's, Bath. Herlewin, the abbot of Glastonbury was a co-witness, together with three archdeacons, and others.
(*EEA, X, Bath and Wells, 1061–1205*, p. 3; *Cartularies of St. Peter's Priory Bath*, pp. 53–4).

*c.*June **1107**– October **1109**	**Ely Abbey** Sometime after the death of Richard, the abbot of Ely, in June 1107, Hervey, at the direction of Henry I, was made administrator of Ely Abbey. (*Liber Eliensis*, p. 297).

1107

August	**London** Hervey attended the Council of London. The king and queen also attended. He witnessed, together with both archbishops, seven bishops of English sees, various abbots, earls, and others, a charter given by Henry in favour of the churches of St Albans and St Mary of Binham. (*Regesta Henrici Primi*, pp. 68–9).

1108

21 November	**Rome** Henry I sent Hervey to Rome. He took with him letters from the king and Archbishop Anselm. His mission was a success, and he returned with bulls and letters, dated 21 November 1108, authorising his translation to a vacant see, and approving the scheme to make Ely a bishopric. (*St. Anselm Letters*, iii, pp. 245–51; *Liber Eliensis*, pp. 298–302).

1109

27 June	**St Paul's, London** Hervey attended the consecration of the new archbishop of York, Thomas II. Also present were the bishop of London, and five other bishops of English sees. (*Radulfi de Diceto*, i, p. 238).

In October 1109, Hervey was enthroned as the first bishop of Ely. His appearances in the historical record, thereafter, are in that capacity.

DAVID THE SCOT

Prior to 1110	**Würzburg** David was a master at the Cathedral School of Würzburg. (*Ekkehardi Chronicon*, p. 243; *Annales Hirsaugensis*, i, p. 349).

1110/11

Winter	**Germany/Alps/Rome** David, who had already been appointed as chaplain to the Emperor Henry V was enlisted by Henry as his chronicler, and literary apologist, on the emperor's expedition to Rome. (*Ekkehardi Chronicon*, p. 243; *Orderic Vitalis*, v, pp. 198–9).

IIII

Spring   **Rome**
With Henry V when the emperor took Pope Paschal II from
Rome and browbeat him, during the continuing 'Investiture
Controversy'. Probably at the emperor's crowning on 13
April IIII.
(*Orderic Vitalis*, v, pp. 198–9; *William of Malmesbury, Gesta Regum
Anglorum*, i, pp. 764–5).

1120

Late March/   **London/Lambeth**
Early April   According to Eadmer, David came to the archbishop of
Canterbury, Ralph d'Escures, as bishop-elect of Bangor. He
brought with him a letter from Gruffudd ap Cynan, and the
clergy and people of Wales. The archbishop is said to have
kept David honourably for several days, while he instructed
him in some matters of divine learning.
(*Eadmeri Historia Novorum*, pp. 259–60; *AWR*, p. 321, no. 191).

Sunday 4 April   **Westminster Abbey**
David was consecrated as bishop of Bangor by Archbishop
Ralph d'Escures, who was assisted by bishops Roger of
Salisbury, Richard of London, and Robert of Lincoln, all
leading royal servants, and also by Bishop Urban of Llandaff.
David professed his canonical obedience to Canterbury.
(*John of Worcester*, iii, pp. 146–7; *Eadmeri Historia Novorum*, p.
259; *Actum* **2**).

7 May   **Gwynedd/Ynys Enlli?**
According to *The Book of Llan Dâv*, David gave his assent
to the translation of the relics of St Dubricius (St Dyfrig)
from Ynys Enlli (Bardsey Island) to Bishop Urban's Llandaff.
The first part of the translation took place on 7 May 1120.
Gruffudd ap Cynan is recorded as giving his assent also, and
as being present on Bardsey.
(*Book of Llan Dâv*, p. 5., and pp. 84–5).

1121

7 January   **Westminster**
David witnessed a notification by Henry I, confirming the
grant to the new bishop of Hereford, Richard de Capella,
of certain privileges. The archbishop of Canterbury was the
first named witness, followed by ten bishops of English sees
and the three bishops of Welsh sees; Bernard of St Davids,
Urban of Llandaff, and David.
(Hereford Cathedral Archive, MS no. 1820).

Furthermore, the *signa* of the archbishop, and various bishops, including David, were appended to a charter of Henry
I in favour of St Peter's Abbey, Shrewsbury; doubt has, however, been cast on the authenticity of this charter.
(*Regesta Henrici Primi*, p. 154; *Cartulary of Shrewsbury Abbey*, i,
p. 35).

2 October	**Lambeth**
	David was at the consecration of the Irish clerk, Gregory, as bishop of Dublin, by Archbishop Ralph d'Escures. Eadmer stated that the bishops of Lincoln (Robert), and Salisbury (Roger) were present; John of Worcester adds the bishops of London (Richard) and Norwich (Everard).
	(*Eadmeri Historia Novorum*, p. 298; *John of Worcester*, iii, pp. 150–1).

1125

12 April	**Lambeth**
	Present at the consecration, by Archbishop William de Corbeil, of Seffrid (Seffrid Pelochin or Siegfried) as bishop of Chichester. The cardinal-priest and papal legate Giovanni da Crema, as well as the archbishop of York, Thurstan, were present, together with bishops Everard of Norwich and Richard of Hereford, and John the bishop-elect of Rochester. All three bishops of Welsh sees were present, Bernard, Urban and David.
	(*John of Worcester*, iii, pp. 158–9).

17 May Whit Sunday	**Canterbury Cathedral**
	Present at the ordination of Simon as bishop of Worcester, and John as bishop of Rochester, by the archbishop of Canterbury. The bishops of Hereford (Richard), Bath (Godfrey) and Chichester (Seffrid) were also present.
	(*John of Worcester*, iii, pp. 158–9).

24 May	**Worcester Cathedral**
	Present at the enthronement of Simon as bishop of Worcester, and later Simon's consecration of Benedict, as abbot of Tewkesbury. David is said to have escorted the new bishop in the consecration procession, together with the bishops of Hereford and Bath (who, it seems, had also made the journey from Canterbury). The abbots of Pershore, Gloucester, and Winchcombe, and the priors of Evesham and Malvern were also part of the procession.
	(*John of Worcester*, iii, pp. 160–1).

September	**Westminster**
	Present at Giovanni da Crema's legatine council together with both archbishops, nineteen other bishops, and some forty abbots.
	(Barlow, *The English Church*, p. 143).

1127

May	**Westminster**
	Present at the council summoned by Archbishop William de Corbeil, now papal legate. The three bishops of Welsh sees, David, Bernard, and Urban were all present. Hervey, formerly bishop of Bangor, now of Ely, was present also, as were at least nine other bishops of English sees.
	(*John of Worcester*, iii, pp. 168–9; *Councils and Synods*, i, part ii, p. 745).

1137

Date unknown   **Gwynedd**
Present at Gruffudd ap Cynan's deathbed. Famous and wise men, from the whole of Gruffudd's realm, are said to have been present. The first person to be named was David, the second, David's archdeacon Simeon. Gruffudd was buried in David's church at Bangor 'with a gleaming monument erected to the left of the high altar'.
(*Vita Griffini*, pp. 88–91; *Historia Gruffud vab Kenan*, p. 32).

1138 onwards   **Würzburg?**
Although not certain, David may have returned to Würzburg to become a monk at the *Schottenkloster* of St James, where his kinsman Macarius had recently become the first abbot.
(*Annales Hirsaugensis*, i, p. 349 and p. 403).

MEURIG

1139

3 December   **Worcester Castle**
As bishop-elect of Bangor, Meurig was presented to King Stephen by Robert, bishop of Hereford, and Seffrid, bishop of Chichester who attested his canonical election and fitness for office. The king confirmed the election, but when urged by the two bishops to do homage to the king, Meurig refused. He was finally persuaded and gave fealty. Archdeacon Simeon also seems to have been present.
(*John of Worcester*, iii, pp. 278–9).

1140

31 January   **Worcester Cathedral?**
Meurig, and Uhtred bishop-elect of Llandaff, were consecrated by the archbishop of Canterbury, Theobald of Bec, on or shortly after 31 January 1140. The bishops of Hereford and Exeter assisted.
(*John of Worcester*, iii, pp. 284–5).

1140 x 1142

Date unknown   **Northampton**
Meurig witnessed a notification by the bishop of Lincoln, Alexander, at a synod called by the latter.
(*Cartulary of Cirencester Abbey*, p. 566; *EEA, I, Lincoln, 1067–1185*, p. 15, no. 20).

1141 x 1151

Date unknown   **Haughmond Abbey, Shropshire/Trefeglwys, Arwystli?**
Meurig stated, in his confirmation of the same, that he was
present at the donation by Hywel ab Ieuaf, lord of Arwystli,
of three parcels of land to the church of Trefeglwys and the
canons of Haughmond.
(*Actum* **5**).

1148

14 March   **Canterbury Cathedral**
Meurig assisted Archbishop Theobald at the consecration of
Walter, as bishop of Rochester, and Nicholas, as bishop of
Llandaff. Nigel, bishop of Ely, and Robert, bishop of Exeter
also assisted.
(*Canterbury Professions*, p. 44).

*c.***1148 x 1157**

Date unknown   **Canterbury/Lambeth?**
Archbishop Theobald wrote to the pope on Meurig's behalf
complaining that Owain Gwynedd had despoiled the bishop
of his possessions, and then driven him from his see ('*ab
episcopatu*'); the bishop now being 'an exile in our house'.
(*Letters of John of Salisbury*, pp. 135–6).

ARTHUR DE CHARGAN

1165

October?   **Dublin?**
The evidence suggests that Arthur, as bishop-elect, was
consecrated bishop of Bangor in Dublin.
(*Becket Correspondence*, i, pp. 240–3, no. 61; see 'Vacancy and
Arthur de Chargan').

GWION

1177

13–16 March   **London?**
The 'bishop of Bangor' is recorded as being (i) present at the
council, called by Henry II, on 13 March, and (ii) a witness
to an award in a dispute between the king of Castile, and the
king of Navarre, on 16 March, at the same venue. Gwion,
if indeed present in London, would have been there in his
capacity as bishop-elect only.
(*Gesta Regis Henrici Secundi*, i, pp. 144–5 and 154; *Roger de Hoveden*, ii, p. 131).

22 May   **Amesbury Abbey, Wiltshire**
Shortly after he had met the Lord Rhys, Dafydd ab Owain
Gwynedd, and certain other Welsh princes at Oxford,
Henry II visited Amesbury Abbey, where, on 22 May, he
was met by Richard, archbishop of Canterbury, bishops
Bartholomew of Exeter, John of Norwich, Reginald of Bath,
Adam of St Asaph, and Gwion bishop-elect of Bangor.
The archbishop, Richard of Dover, instituted twenty-four
nuns from Fontevraud, in the presence of the said bishops
(and presumably Gwion himself). Gwion was consecrated
as bishop of Bangor by the archbishop the same day, after
having made his profession of canonical obedience to
Richard and his successors.
(*Gesta Regis Henrici Secundi*, i, pp. 165–6; *Actum* **7**).

1188

Sunday 10 April   **Bangor**
In the evening, Gwion entertained Baldwin of Forde, the
archbishop of Canterbury, and his travelling companion,
Gerald of Wales, who were travelling around Wales
preaching the cross in order to recruit troops for the Third
Crusade.
(*Opera*, vi, p. 125; *Journey and Description*, pp. 35 and 185).

Monday 11 April **Bangor Cathedral and Anglesey**
In the morning, Archbishop Baldwin said mass before the
high altar in Bangor Cathedral. Gwion stood to the right of
the altar and was 'hard pressed' by the archbishop to take the
cross, which he finally did causing 'great concern' amongst
the congregation.
(*Opera*, vi, pp. 125–6; *Journey and Description*, pp. 35–6 and 185).

The travelling party crossed by boat to Anglesey (and one
must assume that Gwion was with them). They were greeted
by Rhodri ab Owain Gwynedd. Confession was heard, and
then Baldwin gave a sermon, as did Alexander, archdeacon
of Bangor (who also acted as interpreter), and Seisyll, the
abbot of Strata Florida. Many, but not all, who attended
were persuaded to take the cross.
(*Opera*, vi, p. 126; *Journey and Description*, p. 185).
On returning to Bangor, the archbishop and Gerald were
shown the tombs of Owain Gwynedd, and his brother
Cadwaladr, 'who were buried in a double vault in the
cathedral by the high altar'. Gwion was ordered, presumably
by Baldwin, to watch for an opportunity to remove Owain's
body from the cathedral as soon as possible (as he had died
excommunicated).
(*Opera*, vi, p. 133; *Journey and Description*, p. 192).

1189

3 September   **Westminster Abbey**
Gwion was present at the coronation of King Richard I. The coronation procession and service were described in great detail by the chroniclers. The bishops of St Davids and St Asaph were also present, together with the archbishops of Canterbury, Rouen, Dublin, and Treves (Trier), bishops of English sees (Durham, Lincoln, Chester, Hereford, Worcester, Exeter, Bath, Norwich, Chichester, and Rochester), the bishops of the Irish sees of Ferns and Aghadoe, as well as 'nearly all the abbots, priors, earls and barons of England'.
(*Roger de Hoveden*, iii, p. 8; *Annals of Roger de Hoveden*, ii, pp. 116–17).

ALAN OF ST CROSS

Before   **Hospital of St Cross, near Winchester**
c.Autumn **1190**   Alan was a brother at St Cross.
(Round, 'Garnier de Nablous', 384–5 and 389; *Early Charters of the Cathedral Church of St. Paul, London*, pp. 224–5, no. 283).

1185

10 April   **Dover**
Alan was witness to a charter transferring the hospital of St Cross to the bishop of Winchester. Also present were Henry II, the patriarch Heraclius, Garnier, (grand) prior of the Hospital of Jerusalem in England, and Roger de Moulins, Master of the Order of St John.
(Round, 'Garnier de Nablous', 384–5; *EEA, VIII, Winchester, 1070–1204*, pp. 146–8).

c.Autumn   **Clerkenwell, London**
1190–April   Alan was (grand) prior of the Hospital of Jerusalem in
1195   England.
(*EEA, X, Bath and Wells, 1061–1205*, pp. 107–8, no. 145; see the section entitled 'Alan of St Cross').

1195

16 April   **Canterbury Cathedral/London?**
Alan was consecrated as bishop of Bangor by Hubert Walter, archbishop of Canterbury.
(*Annales de Wigornia*, p. 388; *Flores Historiarum*, ii, p. 113).

16 April x 29   *Timbei* castle (**?Denbigh castle**)
September   At Michaelmas 1195, it was recorded that 100 shillings had been paid, by the king's writ, to the bishop of Bangor *ad warnisturam castelli de Timbei*. He had also received 12 pounds for the wages of twelve mounted sergeants.
(*Pipe Roll, Richard I, Year 7*, p. 244).

16 April x 31   *Senegeia[m]*
December   Alan was a witness to a confirmation by Gilbert de Vere, of
                the Hospital of Jerusalem in England, to Adam de Worcester
                clerk, of a messuage outside Worcester.
                (Bodleian Library, Ashmole MS 833, p. 15).

ROBERT OF SHREWSBURY

*c.***1186**   **St Mary's, Shrewsbury**
*–c.*March **1197**   Robert was dean of the college of secular canons.
(and possibly   (*Cartulary of Shrewsbury Abbey*, ii, pp. 271–2, no. 286, pp. 316–17,
to *c.***1200)**   no. 351).

1189–1191   **Shrewsbury**
                Recorded as being a royal clerk and a royal justice.
                (*Pleas before the King and his Justices, 1198–1212*, iii, pp. lxxvii and
                xciii).

1192
6 July   **Gloucester**
                Sat as one of five itinerant royal justices.
                (*Historia et Cartularium Monasterii Sancti Petri Gloucestriæ*, ii, pp.
                7–8).

*c.***1194–***c.***1195**   **Carreghofa Castle and Shrewsbury Mint**
                Robert was keeper (*custos*) of the silver mine at Carreghofa
                castle, Powys, and warden of Shrewsbury mint.
                (Eyton, *Antiquities of Shropshire*, x, pp. 358–9).

Before *c.*16   **Wolverhampton**
March **1197**   Robert held the prebend of Wolverhampton.
                (*Petri Blesensis Bathoniensis Archiadiaconi Opera*, ii, pp. 74–6;
                Patrologia Latina, ccvii, cols. 434–6).

Tuesday after   Bankebir' **(?Banbury)**
Ascension   Appointed by Archbishop Hubert Walter, along with the
20 May **1197** x   abbots of Buildwas, Combermere, and Haughmond, to
24 May **1205**   investigate a matrimonial case between Marared ferch
(but not 23 May   Madog ap Maredudd (mother of Llywelyn ab Iorwerth) and
1200)   W. son of Ione, possibly Gwion ap Jonas.
                (*Actum* **17**).

Before 29 Sep-   **Denbigh Castle**
tember **1197**   Robert was paid ten marks for the maintenance of himself in
                the custody of Denbigh castle.
                (*Pipe Roll, Richard I, Year 8*, p. 42).

1197
31 October   **Merton Priory, Surrey**
                Robert dedicated the altar of the Holy Cross at the priory.
                (Brett, 'The annals of Bermondsey, Southwark, and Merton',
                p. 304).

1198

Date unknown | **Burton (Upon Trent), Staffordshire?**
Burton had escheated to the king, and Robert held it for him.
(*Book of Fees*, ii, appendix, p. 1323 and p. 1331).

18 September | **Château Gaillard, Normandy**
Robert was at the newly constructed castle with King Richard I, Archbishop Hubert Walter, the bishop of Durham, the archdeacons of Canterbury and Wells, and Count John, Richard's brother, the future king. Robert witnessed the renewal of a charter by Richard I.
(*Cartae Antiquae, Rolls 11–20*, pp. 44–8).

20 and 30 October | **Lyons-la-Forêt, Normandy**
Robert witnessed at least two renewals of charters by Richard I. Archbishop Hubert Walter and Count John were with Robert on 30 October.
(*CChR, 1226–1257*, i, pp. 323–4; *CChR, 1341–1417*, v, pp. 194–5).

30 November | **Lyons-la-Forêt, Normandy**
Robert witnessed the resealing of a charter. Archbishop Hubert Walter, Thomas of Heydon (the vice-chancellor), Count John, Hugh de Gournai and Thomas de S. Valerie were also present.
(*Calendar of Documents Preserved in France*, p. 91).

1199

After 25 August | **Rome**
At the Roman curia, on the business of King John's nephew, King Otto (IV), in the company of William, bishop of Angers, and Stephen Ridel.
(*Rot. Chart.*, 31a).

1200

11 April | **Worcester**
Robert was a witness to a charter of grant and confirmation by King John to the abbot and monks of Strata Marcella, of all the gifts given to them by Owain Cyfeiliog, and his son Gwenwynwyn. Other witnesses included Hubert Walter, Geoffrey fitz Peter (the justiciar), William Marshal, the earl of Pembroke, William fitz Alan, Hugh Bardolf, William Brewer, Robert Corbett and John Lestrange. John de Gray, archdeacon of Gloucester, and Simon, archdeacon of Wells, were also present.
(*Ystrad Marchell Charters*, pp. 167–8, no. 25; *Rot. Chart.*, 44b).

9 November | **Feckenham, Worcestershire**
With the king. The bishop of Coventry, as well as the justiciar Geoffrey fitz Peter, and Simon, archdeacon of Wells, were also present.
(*Rot. Chart.*, 80a; *Rot. Litt. Pat.*, 'Itinerary of King John').

11 and 13 November	**Bridgnorth, Shropshire**
	With the king. The bishop of Coventry, as well as the justiciar Geoffrey fitz Peter, and Simon, archdeacon of Wells, were also present.
	(*Rot. Chart.*, 80a; Eyton, *Antiquities of Shropshire*, i, p. 265).

15 November	**Haywood, Staffordshire**
	With the king. The bishop of Coventry, as well as the justiciar Geoffrey fitz Peter, and Simon, archdeacon of Wells, were also present.
	(*Rot. Chart.*, 80a; *Rot. Litt. Pat.*, 'Itinerary of King John').

1201

13 January	**Lincoln**
	With the king. Robert was witness to a charter given by John. Hubert Walter, Geoffrey fitz Peter, William Brewer, William de Briouze, and Ranulf (III) earl of Chester, were the other witnesses. Simon of Wells also present. Also, by that date a decision had been taken to extend a truce with Llywelyn ab Iorwerth.
	(*Rot. Chart.*, 84a–b and 100b; *Cartae Antiquae, Rolls 1–10*, p. 79, no. 154).

25 May	**Kingsthorpe, Northampton**
	Robert dedicated a chapel at Kingsthorpe Hospital, near Northampton, and also granted an indulgence.
	(*Actum* **19**).

11 July	**English/Welsh Border?**
	Llywelyn ab Iorwerth swore fealty to the king before Robert, Reiner, bishop of St Asaph, Geoffrey fitz Peter, and many barons. Hubert Walter sealed the agreement.
	(*AWR*, pp. 371–4, no. 221).

26 x 31 December	**Shrewsbury**
	Robert made a complaint to the justiciar, Geoffrey fitz Peter, about Gerald of Wales, in front of the local barons.
	(*Opera*, iii, p. 200; *Autobiography*, p. 225).

1206

28 May Trinity Sunday	**Reading Abbey**
	Robert was present at the consecration of Jocelin of Wells, as bishop of Bath, by Bishop William of London. Also present were John of Ferentino, the papal legate, and the bishops of Salisbury, Norwich, Ely, Exeter, Worcester, Chichester, and Chester, as well as Llandaff (Henry) and St Asaph (Reiner).
	(*Canterbury Professions*, p. 62).

1211

Late July x early   **Bangor Cathedral**
August   King John's Brabançons seized Robert, who was standing in
                    front of the altar at Bangor cathedral, dressed in his episcopal
                    vestments. He was imprisoned and later ransomed for 200
                    falcons.
                    (*Brut, Hergest*, pp. 190–1; *Brut, Pen20 Tr*, p. 85; Jones, '*O Oes
                    Gwrtheyrn*: A Medieval Welsh Chronicle', pp. 169, 215, 221
                    and 227; *Annales Cambriae C-text*, p. 45).

1212

Date unknown   **Shrewsbury**
                    In accordance with his wishes, on his death Robert was bur-
                    ied in Shrewsbury.
                    (*Annales de Waverleia*, p. 273).

CADWGAN OF LLANDYFÁI

1202 x 1203?   **Strata Florida Abbey**
or 1212/13?   Monk.
                    (*Opera*, iv, pp. 153–5; *Autobiography*, pp. 250–1).

1203? x   **Strata Florida Abbey**
1212/13?   Abbot?
                    (*Opera*, iv, pp. 153–5 and 162–3).

From   **Whitland Abbey**
1203? or   Abbot.
1212/13–1215   (*Opera*, iv, pp. 162–3 and 166–7).

1215

21 June   **Staines**
                    Cadwgan was consecrated as bishop of Bangor, in the
                    church at Staines by the archbishop of Canterbury, Stephen
                    Langton. Iorwerth was consecrated as bishop of St Davids
                    the same day.
                    (*Annals of Southwark and Merton*, 50; *Brut, Hergest*, p. 204).

1216

Date unknown   **Aberdyfi, Meirionnydd?**
                    All 'the learned men of Gwynedd' were summoned by
                    Llywelyn ab Iorwerth to Aberdyfi where he apportioned
                    Deheubarth amongst the descendants of the Lord Rhys. It is
                    possible Cadwgan was present.
                    (*Brut, Hergest*, pp. 206–7; *Brut, Pen20 Tr*, p. 92).

Date unknown   **Powys?**
                    According to *Brut y Tywysogyon*, Llywelyn ab Iorwerth
                    sent bishops, abbots, and other men of great authority to
                    Gwenwynwyn ab Owain Cyfeiliog, who had sided with
                    King John. Cadwgan may have been among those sent by
                    Llywelyn.
                    (*Brut, Pen20 Tr*, p. 92; *Brut, Hergest*, pp. 206–9).

12 November   **Bristol**
Present at the court of the young Henry III, along with
Bishop Reiner of St Asaph, Bishop Henry of Llandaff, and
Bishop Iorwerth of St Davids, when a revised version of
Magna Carta was issued.
(Archives Nationales, MS J655 Angleterre sans date no. 11).

1218

8 June   **Worcester Cathedral**
Present at the consecration of the cathedral, along with
Henry III, seven bishops of English sees, Reiner of St Asaph,
Henry of Llandaff, and Iorwerth of St Davids, and many
abbots, priors, earls, barons and other nobles. (*Annales de
Wigornia*, p. 409).

1219

21 September   **Temple, London**
Cadwgan was the first witness to a letter from Ragnvald
(Rǫgnvaldr Guðrøðarson) King of the Isles, to Pope Honorius
III. The letter, which was said to be at the exhortation of the
papal legate Pandulf, acknowledged the king's gift of the Isle
of Man to the pope, the same to be held by Ragnvald and
his heirs as a fief of the papal see. Other witnesses included
Master M., official of Man, and Holanus, steward of the king
of Man, as well as members of Pandulf's household.
(*Cal. Pap. Reg.*, i, pp. 69–70; *Le Liber Censuum de l'Eglise Romaine*,
i, 260b–261a).

1223

*c.*4 November x   **Carmarthen?**
*c.*6 December   Following the peace agreed at Montgomery in October 1223,
Cadwgan was one of the six representatives appointed on
behalf of Llywelyn ab Iorwerth to diligently inquire into
which lands Llywelyn's adherents, Maelgwn ap Rhys, Rhys
Gryg, and Owain ap Gruffudd, were seized as of fee, the day
Llywelyn took Kinnerley castle. The abbot of Talley, Ednyfed
Fychan, Einion ap Gwalchmai, Iorwerth ab Ednyfed,
and Bleddyn ap Meurig were also appointed on behalf of
Llywelyn. Six royal representatives were appointed, including
the abbot of St Dogmaels, and the prior of Cardigan and
all twelve were required to report to the king's bailiff of
Carmarthen.
(*Pat. Rolls, 1216–1225*, pp. 413 and 481).

*c.***1236–1241**   **Abbey Dore, Herefordshire**
Cadwgan retired to the Cistercian house of Dore,
Herefordshire, in *c.*1236. He died, and was buried, there
in 1241. (*Cal. Pap. Reg.*, i, p. 151; *Acta* **34** and **35**; *Annales de
Theokesberia*, p. 122; *Brut, Hergest*, pp. 234–5).

RICHARD/RHIRID

1237   **Canterbury/Westminster?**
Professed canonical obedience to Canterbury, the archbishop, Edmund of Abingdon, and his successors. Consecrated by Archbishop Edmund.
(*Actum* **36**; *CPR, 1232–1247*, p. 152).

1240

Shortly after   **Westminster?**
Michaelmas?   Richard laid two grave complaints before the king concerning the actions of Dafydd ap Llywelyn.
(*Acta* **38** and **39**; *Flores Historiarum*, ii, pp. 236 and 239; *Chronica Majora*, iv, pp. 148–9).

5 November   **Rochester Cathedral**
Richard dedicated the cathedral together with the bishop of Rochester, Richard Wendene. (*Flores Historiarum*, ii, p. 243).

13 December   **St Paul's, London**
Richard granted an indulgence to those contributing towards the construction of the soon-to-be dedicated church. (*Actum* **40**).

1241

13 January   **St Paul's, London?**
Richard may have been present when the cathedral was dedicated on 13 January 1241. He granted an indulgence that refers to the day of dedication. (*Actum* **41**).

29 August   **Gwerneigron, near St Asaph**
Issued a charter in favour of Henry III.
(*Actum* **42**).

30–31 August   **Rhuddlan**
Sealed two notifications, in favour of Henry III, made by Dafydd ap Llywelyn.
(*AWR*, pp. 472–3, no. 302, and 473–4, no. 303; *LW*, pp. 12–13, no. 6, and p. 22, no. 22; *CPR, 1232–1247*, p. 264).

20–*c.*24 October **Westminster**
Protection without term granted, at Westminster, for Richard on 20 October. Seems probable that he was present with Dafydd ap Llywelyn (who had been summoned by Henry III) when the agreements reached at Gwerneigron and Rhuddlan were renewed at Westminster, *c.*24 October.
(*CPR, 1232–1247*, p. 261; *AWR*, pp. 474–7, no. 304; *LW*, pp. 10–12, no. 5).

1243

27 September   **Llannerch, Dyffryn Clwyd**
Richard was the first witness to Llywelyn ap Gruffudd's grant to Einion ap Maredudd of Dyffryn Clwyd. Richard's son, Philip, was the second-named witness.
(*AWR*, p. 491, no. 318).

1246

20 April   **Windsor**
                Richard promised fidelity to Henry III. (*Actum* **43**).

1247/8

1 January   **Haughmond Abbey, Shropshire**
                Richard confirmed his predecessors' gifts to the abbot and
                convent in respect of the churches of Nefyn and Trefeglwys.
                (*Actum* **45**).

1248

Date unknown   **St Albans Abbey**
                Matthew Paris recorded that Richard came to the abbey so
                that he might stay with the abbot until his bishopric, which
                had been ruined by war, had been restored to some degree.
                (*Chronica Majora*, v, p. 2)

1249

Date unknown   **Worcester Cathedral?**
                Richard was present when the bishop of Worcester (Walter de
                Cantilupe) consecrated the bishop of St Asaph (Anian I). Rich-
                ard and the bishop of Meath assisted. (*Annales de Wigornia*, p. 439).

1252

27 March   **Westminster**
                Simple protection for the bishop of Bangor was granted
                so long as he and his men were in the king's peace. (*CPR,
                1247–1258*, p. 133).

11 July   **Aberdaron, Cymydmaen**
                Present at an arbitration award in a dispute between the
                abbot and convent of the Augustinian house on Ynys Enlli
                (Bardsey), and the secular canons of Aberdaron and men
                of the *abadaeth*. Award before Dafydd ap Gruffudd. Lady
                Senana also present. (*AWR*, pp. 634–8, no. 440; *RC*, p. 252).

Date unknown   **St Albans**
                Matthew Paris recorded that Richard came to St Albans and
                reported on the submission of the Welsh (just as Alan de la
                Zouche, justice of Chester and the Four Cantrefs, did on 18
                May the same year). (*Chronica Majora*, v, p. 288).

1254

9 April   **St Albans Abbey**
Maundy   Matthew Paris recorded that Richard made the chrism in the
Thursday   church of St Albans. (*Chronica Majora*, v, p. 432; *Flores Histori-
                arum*, ii, p. 396).

Date unknown   **Hexton, Hertfordshire**
                Richard dedicated the church at 'Hacstanestune' (Hexton).
                (*Gesta Abbatum Monasterii Sancti Albani*, i, p. 321).

1255

24 August   **Strata Florida Abbey**
                The great bell was raised and consecrated by the bishop of
                Bangor. (*Brut, Pen20 Tr*, p. 110; *Brut, Hergest*, pp. 246–7).

1256

26 December **London**
Richard was present when the crown of Germany was offered to Henry III's brother Richard, earl of Cornwall, by the archbishop of Cologne.
(*Chronica Majora*, v, pp. 601–3).

1257

2 January **St Albans Abbey**
Following the discovery of the body of St Alban, Richard dedicated a new altar and granted indulgences.
(*Acta* **47** and **48**; *Chronica Majora*, v, pp. 608–9; *Chronica Majora*, vi, *Additamenta*, p. 495, n. 1).

1258

26 April *Ekaedu Vannebedeyr* (unidentified)
Richard sealed an agreement made between Llywelyn ap Gruffudd and Maredudd ap Rhys Gryg confirming the latter's homage to the former. The bishop of St Asaph (Anian I), the abbots of Aberconwy, and Enlli (Bardsey), and the priors of Beddgelert, and Ynys Lannog (Priestholm) also attached their seals.
(*AWR*, pp. 501–2, no. 329).

11 August **Caernarfon**
Richard sealed a notification that Hywel ap Rhys Gryg had done homage to Llywelyn ap Gruffudd. Anian I, bishop of St Asaph added his seal also.
(*AWR*, p. 225, no. 85).

*c.*26 April **1258** **Llandrillo-yn-Rhos or Llandrillo-yn-Edeirnion**
x 29 April **1261** Agreement, reached by arbitration, and made between Richard and Llywelyn ap Gruffudd.
(*Actum* **51**).

1259

31 October **Westminster**
Letters patent of safe conduct were issued in favour of Richard and members of his household. Richard swore before the king's council to abide by the terms imposed. The members of Richard's household were named as Master David, archdeacon of Bangor, Guy the chaplain, David the clerk, Adam Hen, David Foel, Adam the chaplain, and Iorwerth ('Gervase') of Llanfair.
(*CPR, 1258–1266*, p. 57).

1 November **Westminster**
Henry III responded to Llywelyn ap Gruffudd's offer of peace terms, which Richard had delivered. The king's response appears to have been entrusted to Richard.
(*CCR, 1259–1261*, pp. 4–5; *AWR*, pp. 506–7, no. 338).

1260

25 February   **Westminster**
Mandates issued to sheriffs of various counties near Wales, informing them that Richard had recently come to the king, on behalf of Llywelyn ap Gruffudd, to treat. Witnessed by Hugh Bigod, justiciar of England.
(*CCR, 1259–1261*, pp. 30–1).

22–26 July   **Westminster**
Llywelyn ap Gruffudd once again sent Richard to Westminster, and the bishop was there by 22 July, when Henry III wrote to the prince expressing his astonishment that he should send Richard at the very time Llywelyn had captured Builth castle. On 25 July, Richard agreed to a prorogation of the truce agreed at the parliament of Oxford. On 26 July, Richard, on behalf of Llywelyn, swore to observe the prorogation made the day before. Letters of safe conduct were issued to take effect from 26 July (until 4 August) for Richard, and Master David, archdeacon of Bangor, with their households.
(*CCR, 1259–1261*, p. 184; *Acta* **49** and **50**; *CPR, 1258–1266*, p. 83).

*c.*18–22 August   **Montgomery**
On 22 August, Richard and the abbot of Aberconwy, representing Llywelyn, agreed to an extension of the truce agreed with Henry III. They attached their seals to the part agreement to be kept by the king, and they also attached the seals of Llywelyn and Dafydd ap Gruffudd to the same. In other words, Richard and the abbot had in their possession Llywelyn's and Dafydd's seal matrices.
(*AWR*, pp. 508–12, no. 342).

1261

29 April   *Rhydyrarw* (possibly Rhyd-y-Garw/Rhyd-y-Carw, Trefeglwys, Arwystli)
Agreement, reached by arbitration, and made between Richard, and his chapter on one side, and Llywelyn and his magnates on the other.
(*Actum* **52**).

8–13 May   **Lambeth**
Richard was present at the council held by the archbishop of Canterbury, Boniface of Savoy.
(*Councils and Synods*, ii, part i, 1205–1265, pp. 668–9; Canterbury Cathedral Archives, CCA-DCc/ChAnt/L/138A).

18 August   *Rhydyrarw* (possibly Rhyd-y-Garw/Rhyd-y-Carw, Trefeglwys, Arwystli)
Agreement, reached by arbitration, and made between Richard, and his chapter on one side, and Llywelyn on the other.
(*Actum* **53**).

6 December	**Coleshill, Tegeingl**

Richard affixed his seal to another agreement between Llywelyn ap Gruffudd and Maredudd ap Rhys Gryg.

(*AWR*, pp. 519–21, no. 347; *LW*, pp. 104–5, no. 199).

1263

12 December   **Ystumanner, Meirionnydd**

An agreement made between Llywelyn, 'Prince of Wales', and Gruffudd ap Gwenwynwyn, whereby Gruffudd did homage for himself and his heirs, and, touching relics, swore fealty to Llywelyn and his heirs before Richard, the abbots of Aberconwy and Strata Marcella, Brother Ieuaf of the order of Preachers, Master David, archdeacon of Bangor, Addaf, dean of Ardudwy, David, son of William, official of Dyffryn Clwyd, and others.

(*AWR*, pp. 529–33, no. 358, and pp. 792–4, no. 601).

1265

14 September   **Winchester**

Richard may have been present at the parliament held on this day; Henry III certainly expected him to be there.

(*CCR, 1264–1268*, pp. 117–18; *Annales de Wintonia*, p. 102; *Annales de Waverleia*, p. 366; *CPR, 1266–1272*, p. 265; *AWR*, p. 533, no. 360).

13 October   **Westminster**

The parliament commenced at Winchester was continued at Westminster. Richard may have been present.

(*CCR, 1264–1268*, pp. 117–18; *Annales de Wintonia*, p. 102; *Annales de Waverleia*, p. 366; *CPR, 1266–1272*, p. 265; *AWR*, p. 533, no. 360).

ANIAN

1267

12 x 31   **Canterbury Cathedral**
December
Anian professed canonical obedience and subjection to Boniface of Savoy, archbishop of Canterbury, and his successors. Consecrated by Boniface, who was assisted by Hugh de Balsham, bishop of Ely, and William de Braose, bishop of Llandaff.

(*Actum* **56**).

1268

27 September   **Pontymynaich, near Gwenddwr, Cantref Selyf**

Anian was named as one of Llywelyn ap Gruffudd's arbitrators with a view to settling various disputes between the prince and Gilbert de Clare, earl of Gloucester and Hertford. The three other arbitrators for Llywelyn were Goronwy ab Ednyfed, Tudur ab Ednyfed and Dafydd ab Einion. All the arbitrators swore that they would faithfully settle the matters according to justice.

(*AWR*, pp. 543–5, no. 366).

1269

10 January–2
February

Eadbryn (unidentified), **Brycheiniog**
The arbitrators appointed at Pontymynaich, including Anian,
were to begin their office on Wednesday 10 January, and were
to deliberate day by day until agreement was reached. In the
event, no settlement was agreed by 2 February.
(*AWR*, pp. 543–5, no. 366).

11 March

Caernarfon
Anian gave his consent to an exchange of land in Gwynedd
Uwch Conwy between Llywelyn ap Gruffudd and the prior
and convent of Beddgelert.
(*AWR*, pp. 545–6, no. 367).

Date unknown

Aberreu (unidentified)
Anian and Anian II, bishop of St Asaph, sealed a letter patent
confirming a peace agreement between Llywelyn, Prince of
Wales, Lord of Snowdon, and his brother, Dafydd.
(*AWR*, pp. 546–7, no. 368).

1272

12 April

Caernarfon
Anian attached his seal to a gift and quitclaim made by Rhodri
ap Gruffudd to Llywelyn ap Gruffudd of all his hereditary
right and claim to lands and possessions in north Wales or
elsewhere in the principality of Wales. Anian II, bishop of St
Asaph, and the abbots of Aberconwy, Basingwerk, and Enlli
(Bardsey), together with the archdeacons of Bangor and St
Asaph, added their seals. The witnesses included Tudur ab
Ednyfed, steward of Wales.
(*AWR*, pp. 657–8, no. 458).

1272/3

15 January

Haughmond Abbey, Shropshire
Anian confirmed certain of his predecessors' gifts and confir-
mations in favour of the Augustinians at Haughmond.
(*Actum* **58**).

1273

3 September

Llanfair Rhyd Gastell?
Llywelyn ap Gruffudd, when writing to Reginald de Grey
(justice of Chester), stated that the bishop 'had come by
chance to the said place', probably Llanfair Rhyd Gastell,
a grange of Aberconwy Abbey, lying between Ysbyty Ifan
and Gwytherin. Llywelyn was there with his brother, Dafydd,
when Anian arrived.
(*AWR*, pp. 555–6, no. 378).

1274

18 April   **Dolforwyn Castle, Cedewain?**
Anian may have been present when Gruffudd ap
Gwenwynwyn, and his son Owain (following their trial for
plotting against Llywelyn ap Gruffudd) issued letters patent
in favour of Prince Llywelyn.
(*Brut, Pen20 Tr*, p. 116; *Brut, Hergest*, pp. 260–1; *AWR*, pp. 796–8,
no. 603, and pp. 798–9, no. 604).

13 July   **Lyon**
Anian attended the Second General Council of Lyon, called
by Pope Gregory X. The Council was held between 7 May
and 17 July and met in six sessions. Anian's green-wax seal
survives, attached to a decree made at the council on 13 July.
(*Councils and Synods*, ii, part ii, p. 810, and n. 4; *Welsh Episcopal
Seals*, 111, no. 7).

23 September   **Canterbury**
On his return from Lyon, Anian granted an indulgence for
those praying for the soul of Adam de Chillendenne, late
prior of the Cathedral Priory.
(*Actum* **60**).

c.late Sep-   **Bangor**
tember x 29   Owain ap Gruffudd ap Gwenwynwyn confessed the full
November   extent of the conspiracy against Llywelyn ap Gruffudd before
Anian, and certain members of the Bangor chapter.
(*LW*, p. lv, and pp. 136–8, no. 245; *Brut, Hergest*, p. 260; *Brut,
Pen20 Tr*, p. 116).

1277

22 January   **Aberalwen, Edeirnion?**
Llywelyn ap Gruffudd wrote to Edward I from Aberalwen
(a township belonging to Corwen, Edeirnion) and asked
the king to grant safe conduct to his messengers, stating
that he was sending Anian, bishop of Bangor, and Master
Gervase, his clerk and vice-chancellor. He asked the king to
believe what these messengers were to inform him about the
prince's proposals for peace. Anian may have been present in
Aberalwen.
(*AWR*, pp. 586–7, no. 400).

21 March   **Bangor Cathedral?**
Palm Sunday   Obeying instructions from the archbishop of Canterbury,
Robert Kilwardby, Anian excommunicated Llywelyn
ap Gruffudd, candles lit, and bells ringing, and after the
celebration of mass, fled to England.
(*Actum* **62**).

Monday 29   **St Albans**
March or 5   Anian wrote to Edward I.
April   (*Actum* **62**).

*c.*September? x *c.*October?	**Rhuddlan** Anian was with Robert Burnell, bishop of Bath and Wells, and chancellor, at the English camp at Rhuddlan. (*Actum* **64**; *CPR, 1272–1281*, pp. 227–34).
After *c.*9 November x *c.*December	**Treffos, Anglesey** Anian wrote to Robert Burnell, bishop of Bath and Wells, and chancellor, from Treffos (in Dindaethwy on Anglesey) where the bishop had a manor. (*Actum* **64**; *RC*, p. 100).

1278

7 January	**Bangor** Anian wrote to Robert Burnell, sending for the chancellor's inspection, articles specifying Llywelyn ap Gruffudd's alleged offences against God and the Church, praying that they might be explained to the king. The letter is dated 7 January, and whilst no year is given, the year is likely to be 1278. (*Actum* **65**).
*c.*14 January x 30 January	**London?** Anian is likely to have attended the council of the province of Canterbury called by Archbishop Robert Kilwardby. (*Councils and Synods*, ii, part ii, p. 825).
1 February	**London** Anian was with the archbishop of Canterbury, Robert Kilwardby, certain bishops of English sees, as well as the bishops of the three other Welsh dioceses. (*Concilia*, ii, p. 31; *Register of Godfrey Giffard*, ii, pp. 94–5).
18 November	**Rhuddlan?** Edward I confirmed the liberties, privileges and customs of the see of Bangor. Anian may have been present. (*RC*, p. 254 and p. 255; Willis, *Survey*, pp. 212–13; Haddan and Stubbs, i, p. 526).
Unknown dates **1278** x July **1280**	**Devon and Cornwall** Prynne records that the bishop of Exeter, Walter of Bronescombe (d. 22 July 1280) by command of the archbishop of Canterbury, procured the bishop of Bangor to go into his diocese, and excommunicate clerks and others who had complained to the justices about Bronescombe, or given evidence against him, and to do so in every parish church. Many people from both Devon and Cornwall were summoned to appear before the bishop of Bangor, he travelling from one county to the other. (*Prynne*, iii, p. 209).

1279

24 and 25 April	**Clare Friary, Suffolk** Anian dedicated the cemetery at the Augustinian friary and granted two indulgences. (*Acta* **66** and **67**).

29 July to 1 August	**Reading Abbey**
	Anian attended a council of the province of Canterbury, called by the new archbishop, John Pecham, held in the chapterhouse of Reading Abbey. An extant letter of protection (dated 31 July at the council) to the chancellor, masters and scholars of the University of Oxford was prepared to carry the seals of the archbishop and twelve suffragans, including the bishop of Bangor.
	(*Council and Synods*, ii, part ii, pp. 828–9; Oxford, University Archives, I. 2.).
17 and 26 October	**Westminster?**
	Anian may have been present when Edward I granted ten librates of land in the Marches of Wales to the bishop, his successors, and his church.
	(BL Add MS 15664 (fo. 5. 7 Edw. I); *CPR, 1278–1279*, p. 12).

1280

15 July	**London?**
	Anian may have been present when, at husting, the bishop was granted land and buildings in Shoe Lane, Holborn.
	(Willis, *Survey*, pp. 68 and 189).
6 October	**Lincoln Cathedral**
	Anian was with Archbishop Pecham, and Edward I, for the translation of the body of St Hugh of Avalon. Thomas Bek was consecrated by Pecham as bishop of St Davids on the same day.
	(*Opera*, vii, pp. 219–21, *Vita S. Remigii et Vita S. Hugonis* – Appendix F; Perry, *The Life of St. Hugh*, p. 329, n. 1; *Annales Oseneia*, pp. 285–6; *Annales Dunstaplia*, p. 283).
29 August x late **1281**	**Hereford/Diocese of Hereford?**
	On 29 August 1280, Thomas de Cantilupe, bishop of Hereford, asked for Anian's assistance during his absence in dedicating or reconciling churches and cemeteries. Cantilupe returned to his see in late 1281.
	(*Register of Thomas De Cantilupe*, p. 253).

1281

7 November	**Ystumgwern, Ardudwy**
	At Ystumgwern, south of Harlech, in Dyffryn Ardudwy, Anian attached his seal to a pledge made by the abbot and convent of the Cistercian house of Cymer of all their land in Cyfeiliog to Llywelyn ap Gruffudd for 12 years.
	(*LW*, p. xvii, and pp. 45–6, no. 69).

1282

19–25 April   **London**
Council of the province of Canterbury, called by Archbishop
Pecham on 1 April. On 23 April, the archbishop and his
suffragans, including Anian, announced to the pope the
formal release of Amaury de Montfort. Anian II, the bishop
of St Asaph was also present.
(*Councils and Synods*, ii, part ii, p. 921, n. 3, and p. 934; *Foedera*,
i, part ii, p. 605).

17 July   **Rhuddlan**
Anian granted letters of protection, under the privy seal,
until Michaelmas.
(*CCR, 1279–1288*, p. 173).

28 July   **Rhuddlan**
Anian was a witness to Edward I's grant to Rhys ap Maredudd
of Deheubarth of commotes in Ceredigion and Cantref
Mawr. The other witnesses included Robert Burnell, Roger
Bigod, earl marshal of England, Henry de Lacy, fifth earl of
Lincoln, and Otto de Grandison.
(*LW*, pp. 165–6, no. 290).

1283

25 March?   **Aberconwy**
Anian granted an indulgence in favour of the Cistercian
abbey of Stanlaw, in Cheshire (later Whalley) perhaps at the
behest of Henry de Lacy, fifth earl of Lincoln.
(*Actum* **71**).

15–18 April   **Aberconwy**
Various royal grants were made to Anian to compensate him
for the losses suffered in the second Welsh war.
(*CPR, 1281–1292*, p. 61; *CCR, 1279–1288*, p. 205; *CAC*, pp.
43–4).

9 July   **Llanerfyl?**
Bonds to keep the peace were taken by Anian from upright
and trustworthy members of the *communitates* of Arfon,
Arllechwedd, Llŷn, Dunoding, Meirionnydd, and Penllyn.
(*Acta* **73–8**).

2 August   **Nancall, Eifionydd**
An assembly, in the presence of Anian, and bailiffs and
representatives from each commote of Gwynedd, was held
at Nancall, a grange belonging to Aberconwy Abbey in
Eifionydd. The result was the compilation of a list of *gravamina*
against the rule of Llywelyn ap Gruffudd.
(BL Cotton Vitellius C x, fos. 166–9; Smith, 'Gravamina',
158–76).

1284

*c.*25–*c.*28 June   **Bangor Cathedral**
Visitation by Archbishop John Pecham.
(*Registrum Epistolarum Peckham*, ii, pp. 727–36 and 737–43;
Annales Cambriae C-text, p. 56).

21 October   **Caernarfon?**
Anian may have been present when a grant was made to him,
his successors, and the cathedral church, of the return of the
king's writs within all lands of the bishopric of Bangor, so
that no royal official should enter those lands to perform any
office, and furthermore, that the bishops and their household ('*familiares*') were to be quit of toll throughout the king's
dominion, both on land and sea, so far as their goods were
concerned.
(*RC*, p. 134 and p. 255; *CChR, 1257–1300*, p. 279).

27 October   **Llanfaglan, Arfon**
Anian appointed his chaplain Elias, and Matthew (Madog
ap Cynwrig), archdeacon of Anglesey, to be attorneys and
proctors to receive compensation on his behalf from the
commissioners appointed by Archbishop John Pecham to
inquire into ecclesiastical damages.
(*Actum* **79**).

3 November   **Chester**
Letter issued by Anian acknowledging receipt of £250 by way
of compensation for ecclesiastical damages in the last war.
(*Actum* **80**).

5 November   **Castell y Bere?**
Anian may have been present when the king granted to him
and the *offeiriad teulu* of Wales, the townships of Tref Ieuan ab
Iddon and Bodychen, on Anglesey, in recompense for tithes
granted, at the king's request, to the abbot and convent of
Aberconwy (re-founded at Maenan). A proviso stated that
Anian and his successors were to satisfy the *offeiriad teulu,* and
his successors, for the portion due of the said tithes.
(*CVCR*, p. 292; *Actum* **81**).

1285

10 May   **Westminster?**
Edward I granted licence to Anian to make a will. Anian may
have been present.
(BL Add MS 15664 (fo. 6. 13 Edw. I.); *Foedera*, i, part ii, p. 654;
Haddan and Stubbs, i, p. 584; *CPR, 1281–1292*, p. 161).

1286

1 April   **Maes-y-llan**
Anian attested that he had seen various charters of the
princes in favour of the Augustinian priory of Beddgelert.
He also granted an indulgence in favour of the same house.
(*Actum* **82**).

1291

21 July   **Llanfair Garth Branan, Bangor**
               Diocesan synod held at the church of Llanfair (St Mary's)
               Garth Branan, at which Anian issued constitutions.
               (*Actum* **87**).

1295

16 November   **London**
               Anian granted an indulgence for those who said the Lord's
               Prayer and the Ave Maria for the soul of William de la
               Corner, bishop of Salisbury, 'whose body lies buried in the
               cathedral church of Salisbury'. Anian had been summoned
               to attend a parliament fixed for 13 November at Westminster
               (which was prorogued until 27 November).
               (*Actum* **88**; *Parliamentary Writs and Writs of Military Summons*, i,
               p. 443).

1301

28 April   **Conwy**
               Anian swore fealty to Edward of Caernarfon.
               (*CPR, 1343–1345*, p. 231).

1303

6–7 September **Conwy Church**
               On 6 September, Anian was celebrating a memorial mass at
               Conwy church to remember the knight, royal servant, and
               diplomat John of St John. Whilst the service was in progress,
               an infant called Roger was brought to the church. Roger had
               fallen from a bridge at Conwy castle, had been pronounced
               dead, but had then been resuscitated; Thomas de Cantilupe
               being invoked. On 7 September, Anian and others recorded
               their testimony of the miraculous resuscitation of the boy.
               (*Actum* **92**).

1305

*c.*February x **Kennington?**
late April   Nine petitions from Anian were presented to Edward of
               Caernarfon, Prince of Wales. The bishop may have been
               present.
               (*Acta* **93–101**).

15 September   **Bangor**
               Letter issued by Anian petitioning Pope Clement V for a can-
               onisation inquiry to be set in motion in respect of Thomas de
               Cantilupe, the former bishop of Hereford.
               (*Actum* **102**).

INDEX OF PERSONS AND PLACES

Numbers in italic type refer to pages of the Introduction as well as the Itineraries of the Bishops in the Appendix, numbers in roman type to individual *acta*. The letter W following a number in roman type indicates a witness. The letter n and a full stop following a number in roman type indicates the notes to an *actum* (e.g. 3n.). As far as possible, place-names are given in their modern forms, as well as the original spellings found in the *acta*. Relevant pre-1974 counties are given, in parentheses, for Welsh and English place-names. Further guidance on certain Welsh place-names is provided in the notes to individual *acta*.

INDEX OF SUBJECTS

Numbers in italic type refer to pages of the Introduction as well as the Itineraries of the Bishops in the Appendix, numbers in roman type to individual *acta*. The letter n and a full stop following a number in roman type indicates the notes to an *actum* (e.g. 3n.).

DRAGON RIVER

Stanley Johnson

Frederick Muller
London Sydney Auckland Johannesburg

© Cadena 1989

First published in Great Britain by Frederick Muller
an imprint of Century Hutchinson Ltd, Brookmount House,
62–65 Chandos Place, London WC2N 4NW

Century Hutchinson Group (Australia) Pty Ltd
89–91 Albion Street, Surry Hills, NSW 2010

Century Hutchinson Group (NZ) Ltd
PO Box 40–086, 32–34 View Road, Glenfield, Auckland 10

Century Hutchinson Group (SA) Pty Ltd
PO Box 337, Bergvlei 2012, South Africa

British Library Cataloguing in Publication Data
Johnson, Stanley, *1940–*
   Dragon river.
   I. Title
   823′.914

   ISBN 0–09–173526–2

Phototypeset by Input Typesetting Ltd, London
Printed and bound by Courier International Ltd

Book One

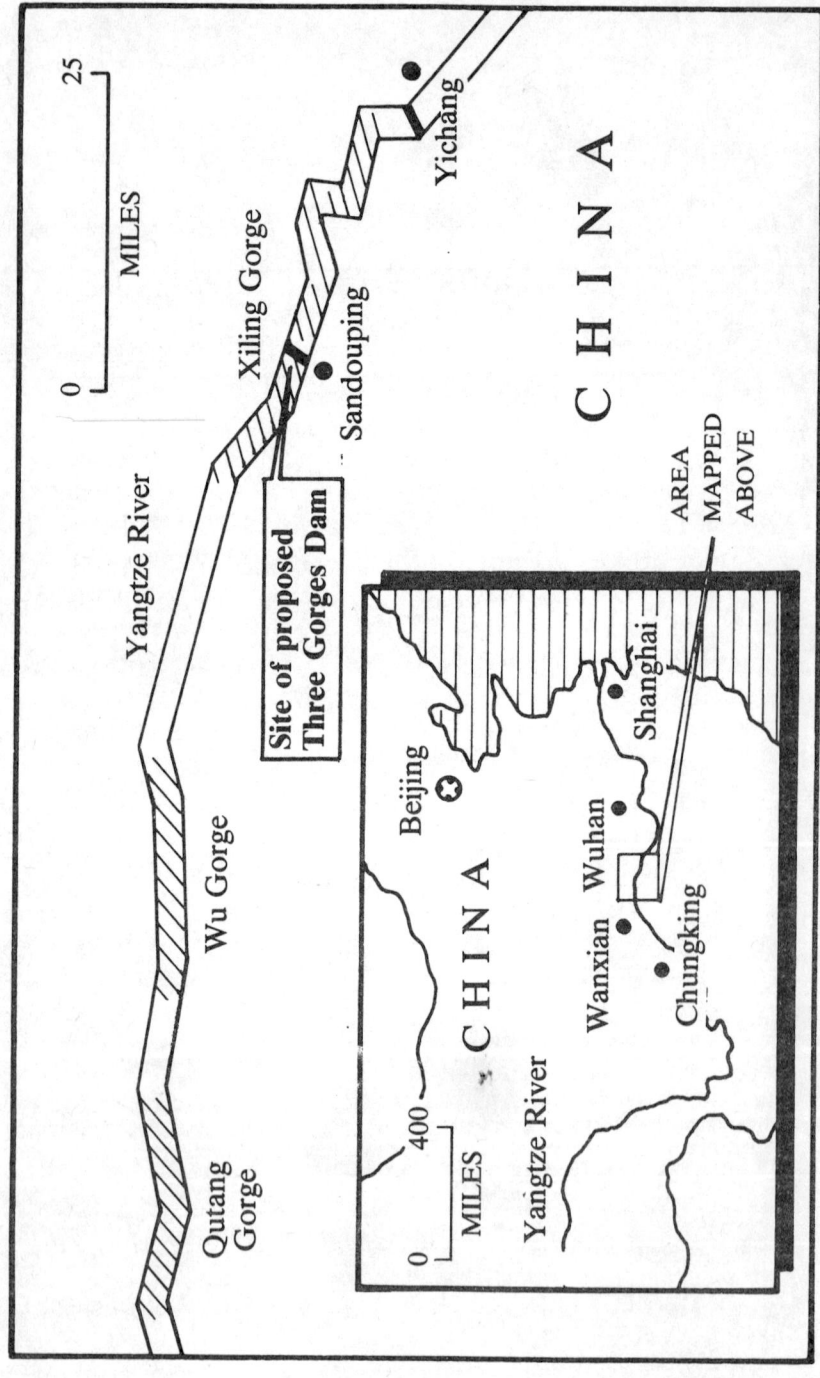